# THE INDIAN FINANCIAL SYSTEM AND FINANCIAL MARKET OPERATION

***New Pace. New Momentum.***

**VASANT DESAI**
DIRECTOR,
VISVESVARAYA INSTITUTE OF
SOCIO-ECONOMIC RESEARCH (VISER),
MUMBAI.



**SECOND UPDATED EDITION : 2012**

Himalaya Publishing House

MUMBAI • NEW DELHI • NAGPUR • BENGALURU • HYDERABAD • CHENNAI • PUNE • LUCKNOW • AHMEDABAD • ERNAKULAM • BHUBANESWAR • INDORE • KOLKATA • GUWAHATI

| | | |
|---|---|---|
| **FIRST EDITION** | : | **2005** |
| **REPRINT** | : | **2007** |
| **REPRINT** | : | **2009** |
| **SECOND UPDATED EDITION** | : | **2012** |

---

**Published by** : Mrs. Meena Pandey for **Himalaya Publishing House Pvt. Ltd.**,
"Ramdoot", Dr. Bhalerao Marg, Girgaon, **Mumbai - 400 004.**
Phone: 022-23860170/23863863, Fax: 022-23877178
**E-mail: himpub@vsnl.com; Website: www.himpub.com**

**Branch Offices** :

**New Delhi** : "Pooja Apartments", 4-B, Murari Lal Street, Ansari Road, Darya Ganj, New Delhi - 110 002. Phone: 011-23270392, 23278631; Fax: 011-23256286

**Nagpur** : Kundanlal Chandak Industrial Estate, Ghat Road, Nagpur - 440 018. Phone: 0712-2738731, 3296733; Telefax: 0712-2721215

**Bengaluru** : No. 16/1 (Old 12/1), 1st Floor, Next to Hotel Highlands, Madhava Nagar, Race Course Road, Bengaluru - 560 001. Phone: 080-32919385; Telefax: 080-22286611

**Hyderabad** : No. 3-4-184, Lingampally, Besides Raghavendra Swamy Matham, Kachiguda, Hyderabad - 500 027. Phone: 040-27560041, 27550139; Mobile: 09390905282

**Chennai** : No. 8/2, Modley 2nd Street, Ground Floor, T. Nagar, Chennai - 600 017. Phone: 044-28144004/28144005; Mobile: 09345345051

**Pune** : First Floor, "Laksha" Apartment, No. 527, Mehunpura, Shaniwarpeth (Near Prabhat Theatre), Pune - 411 030. Phone: 020-24496323/24496333; Mobile: 09370579333

**Lucknow** : Jai Baba Bhavan, Church Road, Near Manas Complex and Dr. Awasthi Clinic, Aliganj, Lucknow - 226 024 (U.P.). Phone: 0522-2339329, 4068914; Mobile: 09307501550

**Ahmedabad** : 114, "SHAIL", 1st Floor, Opp. Madhu Sudan House, C.G. Road, Navrang Pura, Ahmedabad - 380 009. Phone: 079-26560126; Mobile: 09377088847

**Ernakulam** : 39/104 A, Lakshmi Apartment, Karikkamuri Cross Rd., Ernakulam, Cochin - 622011, Kerala. Phone: 0484-2378012, 2378016; Mobile: 09344199799

**Bhubaneswar** : 5 Station Square, Bhubaneswar - 751 001 (Odisha). Phone: 0674-2532129, Mobile: 09861046007

**Indore** : Kesardeep Avenue Extension, 73, Narayan Bagh, Flat No. 302, IIIrd Floor, Near Humpty Dumpty School, Indore - 452 007 (M.P.). Mobile: 09301386468

**Kolkata** : 108/4, Beliaghata Main Road, Near ID Hospital, Opp. SBI Bank, Kolkata - 700 010, Phone: 033-32449649, Mobile: 09910440956

**Guwahati** : House No. 15, Behind Pragjyotish College, Near Sharma Printing Press, P.O. Bharalumukh, Guwahati - 781009, (Assam). Mobile: 09883055590, 09883055536

**DTP by** : Athurva Graphics, Mumbai - 400 002.

**Printed at** : Geetanjali Press Pvt. Ltd., Kundanlal Chandak Industrial Estate, Ghat Road, Nagpur - 440 018. On behalf of HPH.

# PREFACE

The financial system in India comprising of financial institutions, financial markets, instruments and services is characterised by two major segments – a growing organised sector and a traditional informal sector. The key to maintaining high growth with reasonable price stability lies in rapid capacity additions through investments, productivity improvements, removal of infrastructural bottlenecks ameliorating the skill shortages and improving the effectiveness of government intervention in critical areas for more inclusive growth.

*The Financial System* is a subject that is assuming greater importance and is bound to be one of the key topics of discussion during the next two/three decades. This is, as it should be, to consider what sorts of financial institutions will be best suited to the economic environment in the forthcoming millennium.

I have immense pleasure in placing into the hands of my esteemed readers — students, teachers, research scholars, financial managers and policymakers — this edition of *Indian Financial System and Financial Market Operation.*

A financial system provides services that are essential in a modern economy. The use of a stable, widely accepted medium of exchange reduces the costs of transactions. It facilitates trade and, therefore, specialization in production. Financial assets with attractive yield, liquidity, and risk characteristics encourage saving in financial form. By evaluating alternative investments and monitoring the activities of borrowers, financial intermediaries increase the efficiency of resource use. Access to a variety of financial instruments enables economic agents to pool, price, and exchange risk. Trade, the efficient use of resources, saving, and risk taking are the cornerstones of a growing economy.

In the past, governments' efforts to promote economic development by controlling interest rates, directing credit to priority sectors, and securing inexpensive funding for their own activities have undermined financial development. In recent years financial systems came under further stress; when, as a result of the economic shocks of the 1980s, many borrowers were unable to service their loans. In more than twenty-five developing countries, governments have been forced to assist troubled intermediaries. The restructuring of insolvent intermediaries provides governments with an opportunity to rethink and reshape their financial systems.

Conditions that support the development of a more robust and balanced financial structure will improve the ability of domestic financial systems to contribute to growth. By restoring macroeconomic stability, building better legal, accounting, and regulatory systems, specifying rules for fuller disclosure of information, and levying taxes that do not fall excessively on finance, governments can lay the foundations for smoothly functioning financial systems.

The financial system consists of many institutions, instruments, and markets. Financial institutions range from *paan* (betel) shops and moneylenders to banks, pension funds, insurance companies, brokerage houses, investment trusts, and stock exchanges. Financial instruments range from the common — coins, currency notes, and cheques; mortgages, corporate bills, bonds, and stocks — to the more exotic — futures and swaps of high finance. Markets for these instruments may be organised formally (as in stock or bond exchanges with centralised trading floors) or informally (as in over-the-counter or curb markets).

The whole text has been discussed in seventeen comprehensive chapters grouped into two parts. Care is taken to cover all aspects of the syllabus to facilitate students and teachers to benefit and enrich their knowledge.

# ACKNOWLEDGEMENTS

My debt to those who have helped me in one way or the other is worth appreciating. While I take this opportunity to thank all of them — they are too numerous to mention individually in a brief preface — I would like to acknowledge my deep sense of gratitude to Mr. K.N. Pandey, Mr. Niraj and Anuj Pandey for their cooperation at all stages.

I take this opportunity to express my sincere appreciation and gratitude to Ms. Pratibha Chaudhari for reading the book carefully and suggesting changes to make it more crisp, lucid and informative. If the book spontaneously arouses the attention of the students, entrepreneurs, faculty members of entrepreneurial studies, policymakers and researchers, the credit naturally goes to her for her studied help in presenting a new look and newer format.

No words can adequately express my debt of gratitude to my late father, Shri. Ranganath Balawant Mutalik Desai and my late mother Smt. Laxmidevi, for generating in me a perennial interest in higher studies.

I am particularly indebted to my wife, Mandaramala, whose patience, support, encouragement, understanding and love helped this effort to fruition.

I acknowledge the secretarial assistance rendered by varied people.

The Himalaya Publishing House, which is in the forefront of publications, enthusiastically came forward to undertake the publication of this book. I wholeheartedly thank them.

Finally, I thank all those who directly or indirectly helped me in bringing out this unique study on time.

*Mumbai,* **VASANT DESAI**

# CONTENTS

# COST-BENEFIT ANALYSIS OF FINANCIAL SECTOR OPENNESS: THEORY AND EVIDENCE

The benefits of opening up of the economy are varied. Financial openness permits domestic firms to finance investment projects with rates of return greater than the cost of borrowing, and makes higher yielding assets accessible to savers. As long as the marginal return on investments is at least equal to the cost of capital, net resource inflows can supplement the domestic saving, a binding constraint to higher growth in developing countries. Openness also provides to the residents the gains of greater portfolio diversification. This would increase levels of physical capital per worker. The potential benefits are particularly large for certain types of capital inflows like FDI. By facilitating the transfer of managerial and technological know-how, and by improving the skills composition of the labour force. FDI may have significant positive long-run effects on growth. World capital markets play a counter-cyclical role as a country can borrow from abroad in bad times and lend at good times. Opening up would thus permit an improved inter-temporal allocation of consumption. This counter-cyclical role is justified if shocks are temporary in nature. By increasing the rewards of good policies and the penalties for bad policies, financial openness may induce countries to follow more disciplined macro-policies and reduce the frequency of policy mistakes. To the extent that greater policy discipline translates into greater macro-stability, it may also facilitate higher rates of growth.

On the impact on banks, it has been observed that opening of the economy, among others, results in more competition and greater banking efficiency and stability. It enables the banks to reap economies of scale and scope. It helps in diversification of risks. Foreign bank penetration improves the quality and availability of domestic financial services by increasing competition and enabling the application of more sophisticated banking techniques and technology. The risk management capabilities are upgraded. It serves to stimulate the development of the domestic bank supervisory and legal framework. It enhances a country's access to international capital, either directly or through their parent banks. It contributes to the stability of the domestic financial system, if, for example, during turbulent times depositors shift their funds to foreign institutions that are perceived to be stronger than local banks, instead of transferring their asset abroad. Empirical evidences in Asia support the view that presence of foreign financial intermediaries leads to decline in cost of financial intermediation and improvement in quality of financial services.

The capital flows can be harmful also. The ability to monitor the financial system gets eroded with increasing capital flows. Large capital inflows can lead to rapid monetary expansion, inflationary pressures, and real exchange rate appreciation. Under a fixed exchange rate regime loss in competitiveness and external imbalances may eventually lead to currency crisis. Many countries can borrow in world capital markets in good times, whereas in unfavourable times, they face credit constraints. Procyclicality, particularly of short-term flows, as well as herding, contagion and volatility of capital flows expose the economy to greater instability. The capital inflows may finance low quality investments, such as speculation in the real estate sector, which would have limited impact on growth and may increase instability. Low-productivity investments in the non-tradable sector may reduce overtime the economy's capacity to export and lead to growing external imbalances.

Entry of foreign banks may lead to relatively greater flow of resources to large firms while the flow of resources to small firms may be rationed. This would have adverse impact on output and employment. The foreign banks may enjoy regulatory advantages and the possibility of domestic savings fleeing the economy also increases. Mergers, resulting from increased competitiveness, may create banks that are too big to fail and lead to greater moral hazard. Opening up of the economy and greater competition also impel domestic banks and firms to take on greater foreign exchange risks and riskier projects than domestic financial liberalisation. By calling loans and drying up credit lines, foreign banks may aggregate a shock. They can also propagate the crisis by calling loans elsewhere.

Based on cross-country experience in 1980s and 1990s, it has been observed that instability of banking systems distinguishes economic crises from ordinary recessions. Some of the suspected reasons for banking crises were found to be lending booms, exchange rate regime, destabilising external factors, rapid financial liberalisation, inadequate prudential supervision and weakness in the legal and institutional framework. Robust causes of banking crises have been found to be rapid domestic credit growth, large bank liabilities relative to the reserves, and deposit rate control. There is little evidence of any particular relationship between the exchange rate regime and banking crises. The relationship that weak institutional environment causes greater risks of financial liberalisation was empirically found to be weak. The relationship between deposit insurance and crisis risks in emerging markets was also not well established (Eichengreen and Arteta, 2002).

On implications for global stability, it has been argued that financial events, such as devaluation or defaults, trigger adverse chain reactions in other countries in the presence of "the unholy trinity": (*i*) these events follow a large surge in capital flows: (*ii*) they come as a surprise; and (*iii*) they involve a leveraged common creditor. Similar events, however, have little international repercussions when they are widely anticipated or take place at a time when capital flows are already subsidised (Kaminsky *et al.*, 2003).

## INITIATIVES IN BANKING TECHNOLOGY

Technology is the new buzzword in the Indian Banking and Financial Sector. Every Bank is moving on to the technology bandwagon in a big way to offer innovative services and catch the imagination of the customers. Banking is going modern and catalyzing this process is the Institute for Development and Research in Banking Technology (IDRBT), an Institute of the Reserve Bank of India.

The only Institute in the country exclusively focused on Banking Technology, IDRBT has in a very short span played a key role in putting the Indian Banking and Financial Sector on the Technotrack. Be it creating Technology Infrastructure and Products, engaging in quality Research and Development or moulding the talent to lead the technology challenge for the Sector, this Institute at Hyderabad is the fulcrum of Banking Technology in the country. It's this blend of Technology, Research and Education that makes IDRBT a unique institution. Each domain reinforces the other, making IDRBT the torchbearer of Banking Technology.

The latest offering from the Institute is the National Financial Switch (NFS), which will enable mutual sharing of ATM resources among banks. Expected to go live shortly, the NFS will facilitate switch-to-switch connectivity and act as an e-commerce facilitator, thereby opening up a range of possibilities for banks, corporates, government and the citizens.

The Indian Financial NETwork (INFINET) — the nationwide communication backbone for the Industry is another major service towards making the sector technology-enabled. Various inter-bank and intra-bank applications ranging from Simple Messaging, MIS, EFT, ECS, Electronic Debit, Online Processing and Trading in Government Securities (PDO-NDS), Centralised Funds querying for Banks and Financial Institutions, Anywhere/Anytime Banking, and Inter-Branch Reconciliation are being implemented using the INFINET.

The Institute also plays a key role in ushering in the digital economy in the country through its Certifying Authority (CA) Services. With the Digital Certificates issued by IDRBT, Banks and FIs are now building-in full-fledged Security including Digital Signatures and Data Encryption in their electronic communications, transactions and applications.

The Institute's Structured Financial Messaging System (SFMS) answers the demand for a secure and common messaging system that would serve as the basic platform for intra-bank and inter-bank applications, apart from enabling free flow of financial messages across the industry. The Mail Messaging System (MMS) is another industry-level initiative that facilitates easy and secure communication within and among banks and FIs.

In order to ensure that technology is absorbed at the fastest possible pace, IDRBT instituted the Banking Technology Awards to act as catalysts by recognizing and rewarding the efforts of banks in this direction. The Awards are given away in the following categories: Best Branch Award for Techno-Savvy and Customer-Friendly Branch, Best Bank Award for Delivery Channels, Best Bank Award for Business Computerization and Best Bank Award for Back Office Applications.

## RESEARCH FOR RESULTS

Research and Development activities of the institute are aimed at providing state-of-the-art services and products for the success of Banking Technology in the country. While addressing the immediate concerns of the Banking Sector, the Research at the Institute is focused towards anticipating the future needs and requirements of the sector and developing technologies to address them. The Institute's current focal Research areas include:

1 Financial Networks and Applications 1 Electronic Payments and Settlement Systems 1 Security Technologies for the Financial Sector 1 Financial Information Systems and Business Intelligence

A galaxy of focused Research Projects, which include long-term basic, developmental, application-oriented and industry-oriented research projects, form the crust of the Institute's Research activities.

**Sector Specific Academics**

With the Indian Banking and Financial Sector moving on to adopting technology in a big way, the need of the hour is trained manpower to lead these technology initiatives and make a success of them. Responding to this huge demand for qualified techno-manpower, the Institute started a range of academic programmes, specifically designed to meet the requirements of the Sector.

The M.Tech. course in Information Technology with specialisation in Banking Technology and Information Security is offered in collaboration with the University of Hyderabad. The programme, referred to by Dr. Y.V. Reddy as the 'first-of-its-kind in India and perhaps in the world' is a multidisciplinary programme that merges the new and emerging Information Technologies with the domain expertise in the evolving field of Banking and Financial Services.

## CORPORATE GOVERNANCE

Any business is an organisational coalition of shareholders, managers, employees, marketeers and most importantly, customers. Each has as many different objectives as common goals. Expansion of business benefits each of these coalition partners with different motives. Growth ensures higher profits, sustains market share, discourages competitors and increases availability. Marketing is looked upon as an effort to sell products and services in such manner and volume that it creates and adds to shareholders' value. The prime objective most often than not is to make 'profits' for the stakeholders. Stakeholder.... Who? Market dynamics are defining the customer as the main stakeholder of business.

In order to woo and attract customers, marketeers and organizations flash innovative and trendy terminology and strategies — 'Customer Satisfaction', 'Grievance Redressal', 'Customer Needs', 'Corporate Governance', 'Corporate Social Responsibility', etc. But most of these serve mainly as publicity and promotion tools rather than forming a part of the corporate culture. Tough competition in the market is forcing an opinion that profitability of a business depends on its ability to find, grow and keep the most profitable customers. Strict business sense stresses the need to acquire only profitable customers and retain them, enhance the value of existing customers and maximize customer profitability. Though this school of thought is not wrong, but it often becomes the cause of restricting the above stated strategies to the stage of being mere words.

As mentioned earlier, shareholders, managers, employees, marketeers and customers, are all partners in the business. Each has the instinct to extract the maximum gain out of the business activity. A consensus with these different groups is essential for collective prosperity. Each one thinking about self and focusing only about own progress may prove to be counterproductive in the long-run. Ignoring the long-term perspective of market dynamism can potentially bring disastrous days for any business. Let's acknowledge this fact.

## DURING THE YEAR MAY YOU HAVE

- Enough happiness to keep you sweet.
- Enough trials to keep you strong.
- Enough sorrow to keep you human.
- Enough hope to keep you happy.
- Enough failure to keep you humble.
- Enough success to keep you eager.
- Enough friends to give you comfort.
- Enough wealth to meet your needs.
- Enough enthusiasm to make you look forward to tomorrow.
- Enough determination to make each day better than the day before.

# PART I

## WINDOWS TO FINANCE

# THE INDIAN FINANCIAL SYSTEM

## FINANCIAL SYSTEM

The financial system consists of many institutions, instruments, and markets. Financial institutions range from pawnshops and moneylenders to banks, pension funds, insurance companies, brokerage houses, investment trusts and stock exchanges. Financial instruments range from the common — coins, currency notes, and cheques; mortgages, corporate bills, bonds, and stocks — to the more exotic — futures and swaps of high finance. Markets for these instruments may be organized formally (as in stock or bond exchanges with centralized trading floors) or informally (as in over-the-counter or curb markets). The financial system provides services that are essential in a modern economy. It is a core factor of development and growth. The primary role of any financial system is to act as a conduit for the transfer of financial resources from net savers to borrowers, i.e., from those who spend less than they earn to those who earn less than what they spend.

The economic development of a country depends, *inter alia,* on its financial structure. In the long-run, the larger the proportion of financial assets to real assets, the greater the scope for economic growth. Investment is a precondition of economic growth. This apart, to sustain growth, continued investment in the growth process is essential. Since finance is an important input in the growth process, it has a crucial role to play in the economy. The more efficient composition of real wealth is obtained by the promotion of financial assets which provide incentives to savers to hold a large part of their wealth in financial form. The increasing rate of saving is correlated with the increase in the proportion of savings held in the form of financial assets relative to tangible assets.

The major function of financial institutions, whether short-term or long-term, is to provide the maximum financial convenience to the public. This may be done in three ways:

(*i*) Promoting the overall savings of the economy by deepening and widening the financial structure;

(*ii*) Distributing the existing savings in a more efficient manner so that those in greater need, from the social and economic point of view, get priority in allotment;

(*iii*) Creating credit and deposit money and facilitating the transactions of trade, production and distribution in furtherance of the economy.

## THE MOVEMENT OF MONEY DOWN THE AGES

**3000 BCE:** Banking originates in Mesopotamia in the form of storage of valuables at temples and palaces.

**1200 BCE:** Cowrie shells were used as money in China. This form of money existed in some parts of Africa till the middle of the 20th century.

**687 BCE:** Crude coins were developed in Lydia. Lydians are credited to have been the first people to coin money on open retail outlets.

**600 BCE:** Round, base metal coins were invented in China. Silver and copper punch-marked coins of this period have been found all over India.

**550 BCE:** Lydians made gold and silver coins. This is the world's first bimetallic coinage.

**406 BCE:** Athens issued bronze coins with silver coating. This led to large-scale hoarding and the ultimate disappearance of these coins from circulation.

**394 BCE:** Pasion, a slave, becomes the wealthiest and most famous Greek banker and gains his freedom and Athenian citizenship in the process.

**350 BCE:** Greek lending comes of age with normal loans charged 10% and risky business like shipping charged between 20% and 30%.

**118 BCE:** Leather money issued in China. Around the same time, Indo-Greek rulers issued gold coins in India for the first time. India, prior to this, had traditionally used silver for money and gold for jewellery.

**14 BCE:** Augustus Caesar reformed the Roman monetary and taxation systems by issuing new, almost pure gold and silver coins.

**300-400:** Gold coins were issued by the Gupta dynasty depicting Indian themes.

**765:** King Heaberth of Kent produces the first English pennies.

**770:** After the conquest of Kent by Offa, king of Mercia, production of the silver penny increases enormously and replaces the older, more crudely designed sceat as the main English coin, except in Northumbria.

**806:** Reign of Emperor Hien Tsung and the development of paper money. In China, a severe shortage of copper for making coins caused the emperor to issue paper money notes.

**1156:** The first noted foreign exchange contract signed. Two brothers borrow 115 Genoese pounds and agreed to reimburse the bank's agents in Constantinople the sum of 460 bezants one month after their arrival in that city. In the following century, the use of such contracts grew rapidly particularly when profits from the time differences are seen as not infringing canon laws against usury.

**1300** : Indian Sultan Muhammed bin Tughlaq tried to make his coinage reflect the gold/silver price ratio prevailing in the free market. Then, inspired by Chinese paper currency he attempted to create a fiduciary system of coinage between 1329-1332.

**1401** : Bank of Barcelona founded.

**1403** : Charging interest on loans is ruled as legal in Florence, Italy.

**1455** : China abandon the use of paper money.

**1545** : Henry VIII legalised interest charges on loans and acted as a central bank governor by setting a 10% upper limit.

**1619** : Tobacco was used as a currency in Virginia. Around this time, Mughal emperor Jehangir issued zodiac series of gold coins.

**1659** : First British cheque was issued.

**1694** : Bank of England was formed.

**1821** : The gold standard was introduced in Britain.

**1835** : East India Co. was authorised to issue the Indian rupee which was accepted as legal tender.

**1862** : The first coinage under the crown was introduced.

**1900** : US Gold Standard Act came into being.

**1906** : The Indian Coinage Act was passed.

**1914** : Bank of England withdraws gold from circulation.

**1935-37** : The gold standard was abandoned.

**1940** : The Enaternery silver coins were issued.

**1944** : The agreement, reached at Bretton Woods in New Hampshire, USA, envisages a system of convertible currencies, fixed exchange rates and free trade. IMF and World Bank was established.

**1950** : India introduces its own coinage on August 15.

**1959** : The first credit card (Diners) transaction.

**1971** : US moves off the gold standard, leads to a free float of the dollar.

**1971** : The Bretton Woods monetary system was abandoned.

**1979** : European Currency Union was established with a virtual currency ECU.

**1985** : ATMS started operating in the US.

**1990-99** : Banking operations are computerised and internet banking and e-commerce came into being.

**1999** : Eleven European countries merge their currencies into the EURO.

**2000** : Money goes digital, banks become URLs.

**2001** : Money goes global.

**2002** : Internet Banking gains popularity.

**2003** : Spread of Universal banking.

**2004** : New innovative products and practices were operational.

**2005** : Rise in global financial imbalances remain a major risk.

**2006** : More countries join EURO. 15 countries have adopted EURO currently.

**2007** : Conditions in the sub-prime mortgage market sector in the US have deteriorated significantly.

**2008** : The global financial system went into severe stress after the Lehman Brothers Holdings Inc. collapsed and a meltdown was barely avoided through very aggressive policy responses by policymakers around the world. The entire global economy contracted resulting in a severe recession. This severe global recession transgressed into a stag-deflation, a deadly combination of economic stagnation/recession and deflation. In the advanced economies, with aggregate demand falling below aggregate supply, slack in markets led to deflationary pressures as companies' pricing power got restrained.

: The RBI took a major policy initiative to provide rupee liquidity, ensuring comfortable dollar liquidity and maintaining conducive environment for the continued flow of credit to productive sectors.

**Actual / potential Release of Primary Liquidity – since mid-September 2008**

| Measures / Facility | Amount |
|---|---|
| CRR Reduction | 1,60,000 |
| MSS Securities | 1,55,544 |
| Open Market Operations (Purchases) | 80,080 |
| Term Repo Facility | 60,000 |
| Increase in Export Credit Refinance | 26,576 |
| Special Refinance Facility of SCBs (Non-RRBs) | 38,500 |
| Refinance Facility for SIDBI/NHB/EXIM Bank | 16,000 |
| Liquidity Facility for NBFCs through SPV | 25,000 |
| **Total** | **5,61,700** |

* CRR was reduced by 400 basis points during 2008-09 to 5.0% of NDTL by January 17, 2009.

* The repo rate under Liquidity Adjustment Facility (LAF) reduced by 425 points to 4.75% from July, 2008 by April, 2009. The reverse repo rate reduced by 275 basis points for 6.0% in November, 2008 to 3.25% by April, 2009.

SLR was reduced by one point to 24.

**2009** : Consolidation process of the financial system streamlined.

: Spread of financial inclusion while ensuring continued financial stability.

**2010** : Developing economies are showing signs of economic revival.

## THE FELDSTEIN-HORIOKA PUZZLE

Testing the Feldstein-Horioka (FH) hypothesis involves finding correlation between savings and investment as an indicator to measure the degree of capital mobility. The long-term relationship between savings and investment provides a reflection of the future sustainability of the current account deficit. Empirical estimates show that in Argentina, Chile, Honduras, Venezuela, Guatemala, Peru, Algeria, China, Indonesia, Thailand and Turkey, high saving-investment correlations were associated with a stationary current account (Schneider, 1999). On the other hand, a low saving-investment correlation and current account non-stationarity were observed in Mexico, India, South Korea, Brazil, Egypt, Uganda, Madagascar, Cote de Ivory, Mauritania, Haiti and Trinidad and Tobago. A low saving-investment correlation with a non-stationary current account indicates a greater degree of capital mobility.

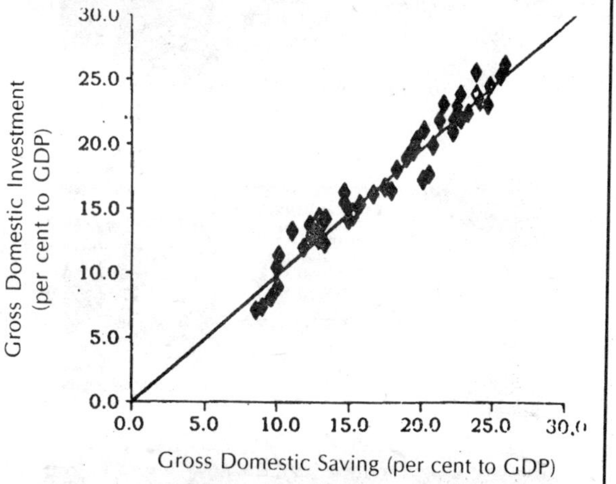


**Relationship between Domestic Saving and Investment Rate in India (1951 to 2002)**

Several studies found that inclusion of developing countries in the cross-section analysis reduced the strength of saving-investment correlation (Dooley *et al.*, 1986; Summers, 1988). Developing countries recorded lower saving-investment coefficients as compared with the industrialised countries (Wong, 1990; Montiel, 1993; Schneider, 1999). It is further estimated that the long-run current account deficit of a developing country is expected to be 0.22 per cent higher than the average if its long-run savings rate is one per cent higher than the average (Ventura, 2002).

In the Indian context, studies have provided conflicting results, i.e., very high saving-investment correlation coefficients indicating capital immobility on the one hand, and a low saving-investment correlation in 1970-97 as also a non-stationary current account, on the other. Unit root tests for the current account balances for India for the period 1950-51 to 2001-02 indicate that the current account deficits are stationary. Stationarity of the current account is further reinforced by high correlation ($r = 0.82$) between savings and investment. In the recent period, this co-movement has further strengthened. The long-run current account deficit is estimated to be higher by 0.16 per cent in response to one per cent change in long-run saving rate. This implies that changes in domestic savings induce a more or less equivalent change in investment. The coordinates of savings and investment for the period 1950-51 to 2001-02 also reveal that these two variables have moved in close tandem during the entire period (Chart). Thus, the lower current account deficits during the 1990s are perhaps a reflection of high correlation between changes in saving and investment rates.

*Source :* Currency & Finance Report.

**INDIAN CURRENCY NOTES**

CHAPTER 1

# THE FINANCIAL SYSTEM: AN OVERVIEW

## INTRODUCTION

A well functioning financial system is a *sine qua non* for the pursuit of economic growth with stability. The core of a well developed financial system is to facilitate smooth and efficient allocation of resources from savers to the ultimate users. An efficient financial system is a key to socio-economic development. According to Levine (1997), financial services affect economic growth through five main channels, *viz.*, saving mobilisation, resource allocation, risk management, management monitoring and trade facilitation. Each of the five main channels contributes to both capital accumulation and the process of technological innovation.

For years, the Indian financial system was caught in the vise of narrow, inflexible regulations that made it tough to manoeuvre. In a market where everyone was equally handicapped, individual institutions had little chance or reason to excel. Interest rates were regulated for both deposits and lending. Real change started when RBI governor R. N. Malhotra kicked off a gradual deregulation in 1988. Suddenly, things have changed. In a rare burst of innovation, the RBI has taken some major policy initiatives to liberalise the over-regulated financial markets. Short-term interest rates on call money, bill rediscounting, and even cash credit have been freed. New instruments for short-term trading like commercial paper and certificates of deposit have been introduced without any restrictions on the interest rates or the number of participants.

The economic scene in the post-independence period has seen a sea change; the end result being that the economy has made enormous progress in diverse fields. There has been a quantitative expansion as well as diversification of economic activities. The experiences of the 1980s have led to the conclusion that to obtain all the benefits of greater reliance on voluntary, market-based decision-making, India needs efficient financial systems.

The financial system is possibly the most important institutional and functional vehicle for economic transformation. Finance is a bridge between the present and the future and whether it be the mobilisation of savings or their efficient, effective and equitable allocation for investment, it is the success with which the financial system performs its functions that sets the pace for the achievement of broader national objectives.

## FINANCIAL SYSTEM

The financial system of a country is like the circulatory system of a human body, controls the health of the economy and growth of business and society, through the circulation of money. A healthy economy needs an efficient financial system.

The financial system consists of many institutions, instruments, and markets. Financial institutions range from pawnshops and moneylenders to banks, pension funds, insurance companies, brokerage houses, investment trusts and stock exchanges. Financial instruments range from the common — coins, currency notes and cheques; mortgages, corporate bills, bonds and stocks — to the more exotic — futures and swaps of high finance. Markets for these instruments may be organized formally (as in stock or bond exchanges with centralized trading floors) or informally (as in over-the-counter or curb markets). The financial system provides services that are essential in a modern economy. It is a core factor of development and growth. The primary role of any financial system is to act as a conduit for the transfer of financial resources from net savers to borrowers, i.e., from those who spend less than they earn to those who earn less than what they spend.

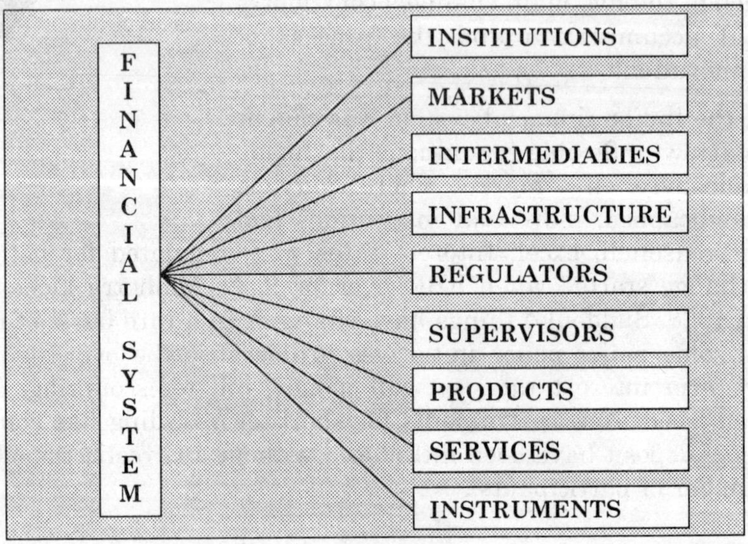


**Fig. 1**

The economic development of a country depends, *inter alia,* on its financial structure. In the long-run, the larger the proportion of financial assets to real assets, the greater the scope for economic growth. Investment is a precondition of economic growth. This apart, to sustain growth, continued investment in the growth process is essential. Since finance is an important input in the growth process, it has a crucial role to play in the economy. The more efficient composition of real wealth is obtained by the promotion of financial assets which provide incentives to savers to hold a large part of their wealth in financial form. The increasing rate of saving is correlated with the increase in the proportion of savings held in the form of financial assets relative to tangible assets.

The major function of financial institutions, whether short-term or long-term, is to provide the maximum financial convenience to the public. This may be done in three ways:

(*i*) Promoting the overall savings of the economy by deepening and widening the financial structure;

(*ii*) Distributing the existing savings in a more efficient manner so that those in greater need, from the social and economic point of view, get priority in allotment;

(*iii*) Creating credit and deposit money and facilitating the transactions of trade, production and distribution in furtherance of the economy.

*North Block: Government needs to address many issues*

## WHY DOES FINANCE MATTER? BOX : 1

Financial systems provide payment services. They mobilize savings and allocate credit and they limit price, pool, and trade the risks resulting from these activities. These diverse services are used in varying combinations by households, businesses, and governments and are rendered through an array of instruments (currency, checks credit cards, bonds and stocks) and institutions (banks, credit unions, insurance companies, pawnbrokers, and stockbrokers). A financial system's contribution to the economy depends upon the quantity and quality of its services and the efficiency with which it provides them.

Financial services make it cheaper and less risky to trade goods and services and to borrow and lend. Without them an economy would be confined to self-sufficiency or barter, which would inhibit the specialization in production upon which modern economies depend. Separating the timing of consumption from production would be possible only by first storing goods. The size of producing units would be limited by the producers' own capacity to save. Incomes would be lower, and complex industrial economies would not exist.

Finance is the key to investment and hence to growth. Providing saved resources to others with more productive uses for them raises the income of saver and borrower alike. Without an efficient financial system, however, lending can be both costly and risky. Self-financed investment is 'one way to overcome these difficulties, but profitable investment opportunities may exceed the resources of the individual enterprise'. Investment by the public sector is another answer; in this case additional savings are mobilized through the tax system. But excessive centralization brings its own difficulties, especially in gathering the information needed to make sound investments. Efficiency therefore requires a balance among internally generated resources, centrally organized saving and investment, and market-based financial arrangements.

Market-based arrangements are voluntary. As such, they are driven by the desire for profit, tempered by concerns about risk. Competition ensures that transaction costs are held down, that risk is allocated to those most willing to bear it, and that investment is undertaken by those with the most promising opportunities.

Such arrangements may take many forms but tend to mirror an economy's complexity and political orientation. Informal finance, such as loans within families and between friends or from pawnbrokers and moneylenders is still important in many countries. But as economies grow, these arrangements need to be augmented by the services that only formal institutions — commercial banks, collective investment institutions, and capital market — can apply. For example, by transforming the size and maturity of financial assets, formal institutions can mediate between the many small depositors who prefer liquid assets and the few large borrowers who need long-term loans to finance investment. They can provide other useful services too: insurance, hedging (using options and futures contracts), and so on. In a diversified market-based system, governments retain a key role as prudential regulators, because experience has shown that financial markets — essential though they are, can be prone to instability and vulnerable to fraud.

**Finance and Growth**

Malthus predicted that growing populations and fixed amounts of land and other natural resources would ultimately stifle economic growth. But natural resource endowments have declined in importance in most high-income countries.

The biggest difference between rich and poor is the efficiency with which they have used their resources. The financial system's contribution to growth lies precisely in its ability to increase efficiency.

**Finance and Trade**

The financial system makes its biggest contribution to growth by providing a medium of exchange. In a barter economy, trade requires a "mutual coincidence of wants". It is therefore limited by the costly search for trading partners. Specialization is discouraged in economies with no medium of exchange, so their productivity is low. Money facilitates specialization by reducing trading costs and linking different markets. The adoption of a standard unit of account serves the same goal.

**Finance and Saving**

Saving determines the rate at which productive capacity, and hence income, can grow. On average, the more rapidly growing developing countries have had higher saving rates than the slower growing countries. These rates are influenced by many factors. In analyzing them it is useful to distinguish between the flow of "saving" and the stock of "savings". Saving will always refer to the flow of real resources that are not consumed in the period under study and that are therefore available for investment. "Savings" will refer to the stock of accumulated saving, or wealth. An increase in the stock of financial assets will be called "financial deepening".

Many factors affect the saving rate, the rate of income growth, the age composition of the population and attitudes toward thrift. The services provided by government, such as social security, can affect saving as can taxes and government deficits. Macroeconomic and political stability affect expectations and thus affect saving. Whether financial variables affect the saving rate is still an open question.

**Finance and Investment**

The financial system intermediates only part of a country's total investment, because firms and households finance much of their investment directly out of their own saving. Only when investment exceeds saving it is necessary to borrow, just as when saving exceeds investment it is necessary to lend. The financial system's task is to move excess savings into investment, thereby creating credit to facilitate economic development. Finance and corporate sector industrialisation is *sine qua non* for economic progress. More importantly, *"Finance is the life blood of industry"*. The corporate sector depends on the financial system for risk, capital, equity, debt, working capital and so on.

All in all, the influence of governments on the financial system is greater than it is visible. Finance does matter in socio-economic development. It is one of the key input.

## SUSTAINABLE DEVELOPMENT

Development involves not merely economic change but also social and institutional changes. In many developing and underdeveloped countries, it calls for new sets of values and new concepts of society and government. As a continuous process, it calls for structural adjustments, innovations as well as new institutions to fulfil the aspirations of the people as well as national objectives.

For more than four decades, there has been growing awareness of the development process associated with certain aspects of economic growth. Challenges of persistent poverty, degradation of natural resources are leading to radically new ways of assessing economic development. The direction of global thinking is towards sustainable development.

The Brundtland Commission defined sustainable development as:

*"... a process of change in which the exploitation of resources, the direction of investments, the orientation of technological development and institutional change are all in harmony and enhance both current and future potential to meet human needs and aspirations."*

The concept of economic development is itself complex, including not only simply growth in total monetary production but also additional concerns for equity, the quality of life and less tangible human aspirations for education, security and aesthetic values.

## FINANCING DEVELOPMENT

The economic development depends upon a multiplicity of factors. Amongst these varied factors, the rate of capital formation is one of the most important determinants of the rate of growth of an economy. It is one of the key inputs of development.

The economic development of a country depends, *inter alia*, on its financial structure. In the long-run, the larger the proportion of the financial assets to real assets, the greater will be the scope for economic growth. Investment is a precondition of economic growth. To sustain growth, continued investment in the growth process is necessary. Since finance is an important input in the growth process, it plays a crucial role in the economy. A more efficient composition of real wealth is obtained by the promotion of financial assets which provide incentives to savers to hold a large part of their wealth in the financial form. An increasing rate of savings correlates with the increase in the proportion of savings held in the form of financial assets — relative to tangible assets.

A major function of financial institutions, whether short or long-term, is to provide the maximum financial convenience to the public. This can be done in three ways:

(*i*) Promotion of the overall savings in the economy by an authentic widening of the financial structure;

(*ii*) Purveying the existing savings in a more efficient manner so that those in greater need, from the social and economic points of view, get priority in allotment; and

(*iii*) Monetary financial institutions assist by creating credit and deposit money and facilitating transactions in trade, production and distribution in the economy.

The financial sector plays a major role in the mobilisation and allocation of financial savings in the economy and in facilitating funds flow among the various sub-sectors. Financial institutions, instruments and the financial markets together act to transfer financial resources from net savers to net borrowers. The resultant gains to the real sector of the economy depend on the efficiency of the financial sector to perform the function of financial intermediation.

## IN PERSPECTIVE

The process of socio-economic change is an intrinsic part of human civilization. Man has been striving endlessly to discover the secrets of nature and thereby benefit immensely in creating a peaceful, rich life for himself and his fellow-beings. Man has benefited by agricultural, industrial and information activities. According to J. K.

Galbraith, there are three types of economic development that are currently in vogue. These are symbolic modernisation, maximised economic growth and selective growth. Economic growth is the *sine qua non* of change and better living standards. Over the years, a middle-of-the-road social democratic thinking is becoming consolidated.

## THE PRIMARY OBJECTIVE OF DEVELOPMENT

The primary objective of developing countries like India is to achieve rapid, balanced and sustained rate of economic growth. Hence, efforts are directed towards the creation of conditions in which a fast development of productive resources can take place. This inevitably necessitates the transformation of social and economic structures which will not restrain the potential productive forces and inhibit the development of resources. The state has, therefore, to devise efficient and effective strategies, at once political, economic, social, technological and cultural, so as to ensure a desirable co-ordination of all sectors of the economy and assure deliberate and requisite interest and involvement of the people. This is largely secured by adopting politically, the technique of planning and economically, the tool of management. Countries on an individual basis in the underdeveloped world are progressively and intensively resorting to centralised state management of the economy and to a restructured and neo-cultured society.

Economic development, if conceived without appropriate social changes, soon becomes stultified and stagnated. Social change cannot be achieved, if political, technological and cultural aspects are not combined and woven strategically into the fabric of economic planning. Comprehensive national planning is increasingly becoming an instrument of socio-economic transformation in developing countries. Planning delineates strategies.

## LAWS OF DYNAMICS OF DEVELOPMENT

*(i) 'Economic development is organically related to the impulse of change, reflecting the developmental urge of the society for self-reliance and willingness to observe rigorous discipline.'*

This is a social law. This explains why there is no economic development in a particular society — regional, national or continental. The impulse to change must lead to action aimed at becoming self-reliant as quickly as possible. Self-reliance demands observance of a rigorous discipline. An urge for development, efforts towards self-reliance and a sense of discipline are the three important elements in the social law of dynamics of economic development.

*(ii) 'Economic development is quickened with the degree of appropriate and intimate relationship established between and/or among competing claims, of various apparently conflicting objectives.'*

## CONSTRUCTING INDICES OF FINANCIAL DEVELOPMENT — BOX : 2

**Comprehensive index:** The development of this index closely followed work done by Gelbard and Leite (1999) for sub-Saharan Africa. We began by scoring each of the dimensions of financial development. Whenever possible, quantitative data, appropriately rescaled, were used to score a country. These data included the ratio of commercial bank assets to total central bank and commercial bank assets and the ratio of broad money to GDP. In cases where qualitative data were used, a 0-1-2 scoring mechanism was adopted. All scores were rescaled so that they fell in the 0 to 2 range, with higher scores corresponding to higher levels of financial development. Next, weights were assigned to each of the 36 variables used in the construction of this index. To ensure robustness, the index was calculated using assigned weights, equal weights among the six themes, and equal weights among each of the components within the six themes. We found that the grouping of countries into high, medium, and low financial development categories was robust to the different weighting schemes, although the relative ranking of countries within each grouping changed slightly.

**Alternative index:** This index is related to the one developed by Beim and Calomiris (2001) and is based on quantitative data only. To construct the index, we selected four variables commonly used in the literature. The four variables were ratio of broad money to GDP; ratio of the assets of deposit-money banks to the total assets of the central bank and deposit-money banks; reserve ratio; and ratio of credit to private sector by deposit-money banks to GDP. These variables measure the size of the financial sector, the importance and relative ease with which commercial banks provide funds, and the extent to which funds are provided to the private as opposed to the public sector. We then aggregated these variables using a statistical technique called Principal Components Analysis. Aggregating not only captures different aspects of financial development in a single measure but also reduces biases or errors that may plague a particular data series. Furthermore, in keeping with the standard practice of averaging the variables in either 5-year panels or 10-year panels to smooth out business cycle fluctuations and focus on trends, we averaged the data in 10-year panels to obtain observations for the 1960s, 1970s, 1980s and 1990s.

This is a political law. With growing consciousness of the market economy, undeveloped and underdeveloped sectors clamour for and claim priority in development plans. Fixing of sectoral priorities and deciding the rate of progress at a given time are political decisions. The conflicting claims are to be resolved by the political leadership of the country by weaving them into supplementary and complementary relationships so as to minimise, if not entirely neutralise, their dissipating influence. The economic statesmanship of a national political leadership is displayed in harmonising the conflicting claims for economic development sectorwise, sectionwise and regionwise.

*(iii) 'Economic development depends upon the ability to restructure the economy with the identification of and the insistence on the economies of scale and the operational choices of technologies, resolving to the highest degree possible, the seeming or real conflict of capital versus labour.'*

This is a technological law. Economy must be restructured, if it is to be balanced and self-sustained. There are economies of scale which should determine the status of economy. The relationship between large and small-scale industrial sectors should progressively settle down on this technological basis. Technologies change constantly in the modern scientific age and consequently, even the economies of scale undergo corresponding changes. This readjustment in the large and small-scale industries should be painlessly brought about. So also, the capital-intensive and labour-intensive operations ought to be carefully sorted out, categorised and communicated to the entrepreneurs and managers for compliance. For instance, capital-intensive techniques should give way to labour-intensive techniques in economies where labour is abundant; but this may not apply rigidly to all spheres of the economy.

*(iv) 'Economic development takes place in proportion to the administrative calibre and motivation and in the direction of the comprehensive infrastructural facilities — social, educational, fiscal, financial, technical, distributional, medical, logistical and others.'*

This is an administrative law. That is to say, developmental plans founded due to administrative inadequacies and procedures. Demands of development planning outstrip the administrative capabilities — not so much in terms of talent but in terms of skills. For economic development, the administration needs to know and be in tune with developmental processes, techniques and will. The administration must be fully involved and committed to development. It must be motivated so as to feel that it has the highest stake in the participation and in execution of programmes of development. Furthermore, the administration should not forget that economic development holds essence in a potential market. It tends to move in the direction of and relishes to thrive in the location, where comprehensive infrastructure exists or is shortly expected to exist. Again, economic infrastructure and fiscal/financial benefits are not enough. Man brings about development. Economic developmental facilities, without doubt, need to be provided. But many more amenities expected by the modern man are also required to be created. This naturally leads to identification of potential growth centres, which when furnished with a comprehensive infrastructure, would radiate industrial and productive activities in the ever-widening circles, round the potential epicentre.

*(v) 'Economic development originates and fosters in relation to the strength and health of the local entrepreneurship and depends on the rate of its generation and equally to the intensity of its sense of social responsibility, its innovation quotient and its index of management capabilities.'*

This is an entrepreneurial law. It is the entrepreneur who powers the process of economic development. The strength of an economy is in one way the strength of the entrepreneur class in the society. Mere mercantile entrepreneurship has different attributes and thrives in an entirely different atmosphere. It has to be cultured systematically in the underdeveloped regions and sub-regions. The higher the birth rate of genuine industrial and innovative entrepreneurship, faster is the rate of economic growth. Entrepreneurship must also acquire new managemental skills. Entrepreneurial density, innovative propensity and management capability in the society in a particular period determine the character and future of economic development.

*(vi) 'Economic development is decisively dependent on the state of the balance of trade.'*

This is a commercial law. Adverse balance of trade position restricts the development process, particularly in underdeveloped countries importing machinery, raw materials, know-how and even experts. Favourable balance of trade provides considerable latitude in the choice of imports and in the source of imports. International trade brings economic strength and techno-economic self-reliance. Again, mere exports outgrowing imports is not necessarily a sign of commercial strength. Composition of imports and exports is of great importance in this context. Commodities and unprocessed minerals may earn a fairly good amount of foreign exchange for the country; but the share of manufactured goods in the total exports of the country will indicate the degree of industrial progress and strength achieved by that country. While attempting to balance exports with imports, effort should be made to constantly expand the contribution of the manufacturing sector to national exports.

*(vii) 'Economic development is directly related to the rate of national savings and of national investment in conformity with national priorities and real needs, based on social justice, economic stability and national security.'*

This is a financial law. The countries and communities in which the rate of savings is high and where savings are institutionalised and thus made available for investment in productive activities according to the national priorities, are strategically advancing faster.

Economic stability leads to increased savings. Stability cannot be ensured without growth. In fact, growth and stability can be said to be synonymous terms. National investment must also ensure national security. This is possible if ample investible funds would be available at reasonable rates of interest for desirable productive purposes. It is, therefore, necessary to ensure an adequate rate of savings and institutional investments for productive activities. Mobilisation of public savings is possible when adequate incentives are provided.

The techniques of planning may have to be based on these laws of dynamics of economic development. Their ignorance or non-compliance is likely to retard and restrict the process and pace of economic development, which all the developing communities and countries cherish. Development is essentially a matter of social and economic management. In India, perhaps, the emphasis was and still is largely on the economic aspect rather than on the social. If social motivation is taken care of, economic development will begin to take care of itself. Perhaps, our planners need this advice. But will they heed to it?

## Trends in Economic Development

There are seven major trends affecting the direction of economic development:

- Technology as a resource
- Competition in domestic and international markets
- The role of invention
- Government as stimulator
- Entrepreneurial and Intrapreneurial development
- Innovative capital formation
- Collaborative relationships.

Technology is more than a thing, a gadget, or even a process. It is a self-generating resource that is not consumed in the process of use. Consequently, it is an important form of economic wealth.

Competition is forcing a reassessment of our individual and collective responses to the marketplace. Fierce domestic and international competition for scientific, technological, and economic preeminence is forcing communities and regions to leverage all their resources — human, technological and financial — to compete effectively for vibrant and diversified economies.

The countries are experiencing an unprecedented burst of invention. Myriad technological advances are occurring with incredible speed and frequency. The ability to commercialize these inventions will have direct and immediate economic consequences.

The governments are trying to find positive non-interventional approaches to encouraging entrepreneurship and technological diversification. They seek to create jobs, provide benefits to the small business sector, and push technology for maximum benefits. The creation of an environment that promotes entrepreneurial activity has become a more important focal point in the government's policy on development.

People with raw energy and a proclivity for risk-taking built and sustained the countries. They are continuing to build it today — in new ways and, with new approaches. These entrepreneurs and intrapreneurs are breaking tradition and providing a dynamic source of creative and innovative enterprises. In simple words, they are giving a boost to their local economies.

Innovative capital formation is providing the catalyst for the entrepreneurial process. Mechanisms for providing seed capital and venture capital as well as an expanding venture capital industry are helping to chalk out new ventures. If the entrepreneurial process is to succeed, it is essential to continue to support and expand the formation of capital and its strategic utilization in new business development.

Finally, creative collaborative relationships are being formed between business, government, and the academicia on a large-scale. These ties are forging new opportunities for commercialization, thus accelerating the technology transfer process.

## THE ROLE OF THE FINANCIAL SYSTEM

The financial sector plays a crucial role in the functioning of the economy because it allows a more efficient transfer of resources from savers to investors as well as facilitates the use of funds by households, businesses, traders and governments. In fact, an efficient financial sector spurs economic growth.

Conditions that support the development of a more robust and balanced financial structure will improve the ability of domestic financial systems to contribute to their growth. By restoring macroeconomic stability, building better legal, accounting, and regulatory systems, specifying rules for fuller disclosure of information, and levying taxes that do not fall excessively on finance, governments can lay the foundations for smoothly functioning financial systems. This study reviews the lessons of experience of the key financial sectors and tries to identify the measures that will enable domestic financial systems to provide the services needed in the next decade.

**FOREIGN EQUITY INVESTMENT** **BOX : 3**

Economic policies that promote sustainable growth are also likely to attract equity investment. Investor surveys show that growth and stability of the host economy are key factors in determining the attractiveness of a foreign investment. In part, this is because equity investment is relatively illiquid and sometimes requires a lengthy development phase before earning positive returns. When the foreign investment produces for the host market, as in Brazil and Korea, the investor's concern with the long-term macroeconomic environment is reinforced.

Industrial and trade policies also strongly influence foreign investment. Outward-oriented strategies supported by tax, foreign exchange, and other policies usually attract more foreign equity investment, especially to the export processing sectors. Transparent and consistent investment policies are important. Singapore, for example, treats foreign investments on essentially the same terms as domestic investments. It has attracted large flows, which, along with domestic investment, have contributed to rapid growth.

Mauritius shows that policies to provide incentives for foreign investment can work, provided the macroeconomic environment is stable. To attract foreign investment and diversify from its traditional reliance on raw sugar, it adopted an Export Processing Zone programme in 1970. Mauritius successfully expanded the share of manufactures from almost nothing to 24 per cent of total exports by 1977. But growth slowed in the late 1970s and early 1980s, partly because of failures in macroeconomic policy (currency overvaluation, fiscal overexpansion, and a tax policy that discouraged domestic saving). Foreign investment plummeted. The country adopted a structural adjustment programme in the early 1980s that called for better credit allocation, an expansion of term finance for the private sector, and investment policies aimed at further export diversification. Growth and foreign investment have revived.

## FINANCIAL INCLUSION

Financial inclusion refers to deliver of banking services at an affordable cost to the vast sections of disadvantaged and low-income groups who tend to be excluded from the formal banking channel. Despite widespread expansion of the banking sector during the last three decades, a substantial proportion of the households especially in rural areas, is at present outside the coverage of the formal banking system. The Reserve Bank's broad approach to financial inclusion aims at 'connecting people' with the banking system and not just credit dispensation: giving people access to the payments system: and portraying financial inclusion as a viable business model and opportunity. Efforts towards 'financial inclusion' include sensitising the banks to the banking and financial needs of the common person and ensuring access to basic banking facilities. In consonance with the above approach, the Reserve Bank has undertaken a number of measures in recent years for attracting the financially excluded population into the formal financial system.

Introduction of 'zero balance' or 'no frills' accounts has enabled the common person to open bank account. However, providing banking facilities closer to the customer, especially in remote and unbanked areas, while keeping transaction costs low, remains a challenge. This has to be done with affordable infrastructure and low operational costs with the use of appropriate technology. Pursuant to the announcement banks were urged to scale up their financial inclusion efforts by utilising appropriate technology, while ensuring that the solutions developed are: (i) highly secure; (ii) amenable to audit; and (iii) follow widely accepted open standards to allow interoperability among the different systems adopted by different banks. Banks have initiated pilot projects utilising smart cards/mobile technology to increase their outreach. Biometric methods for uniquely identifying customers are also being increasingly adopted.

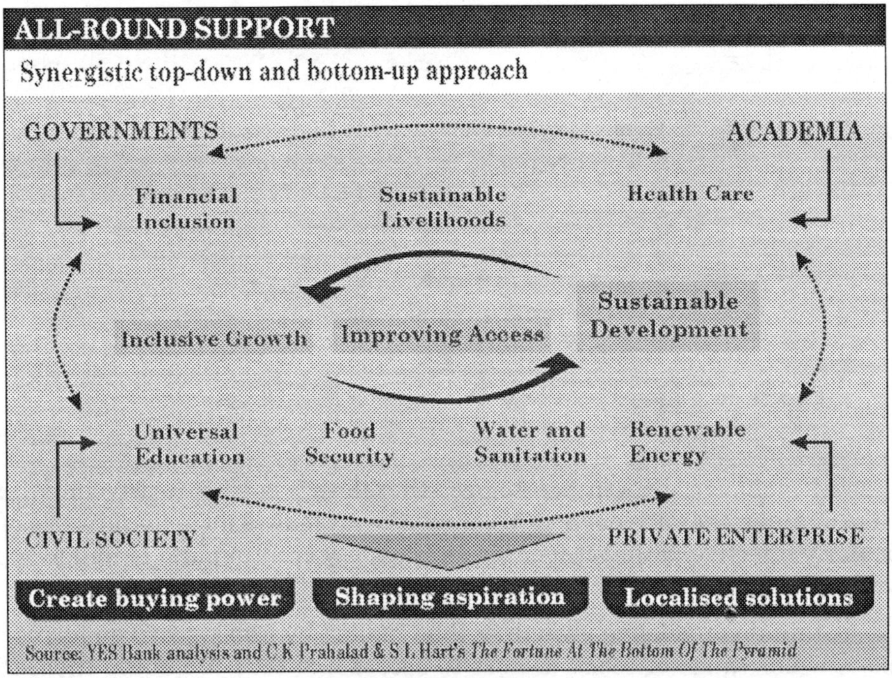


The linkages between macroeconomic performance and financial stability are schematically presented in Chart 1. These shocks can emanate from the real or the financial sector. Such shocks affect the banks' balance sheets through the conventional channels of credit and market risk. They also affect balance sheets through the financial markets and asset prices. Both effects may amplify the first round balance sheet impact, in particular the liquidity and network effects. Taken together, all of these channels then translate into a final impact on balance sheets, as reflected in aggregate loss distribution. A stable and resilient financial system is therefore vital for achieving sustained growth with low inflation as it can withstand fluctuations resulting from dynamic changes in economic conditions, as well as sudden and substantial increases in uncertainty.

The resilience of the financial system can be tested by subjecting the system to stress scenarios. Since the early 1990s, stress tests at the level of individual institutions have been widely applied by internationally active banks. In addition to applying such stress tests to the portfolios of individual institutions at the microlevel, stress-testing is assuming an increasingly important role in the macro-prudential analysis as well.

**Chart 1: Macroeconomic Shocks and Financial Stability**

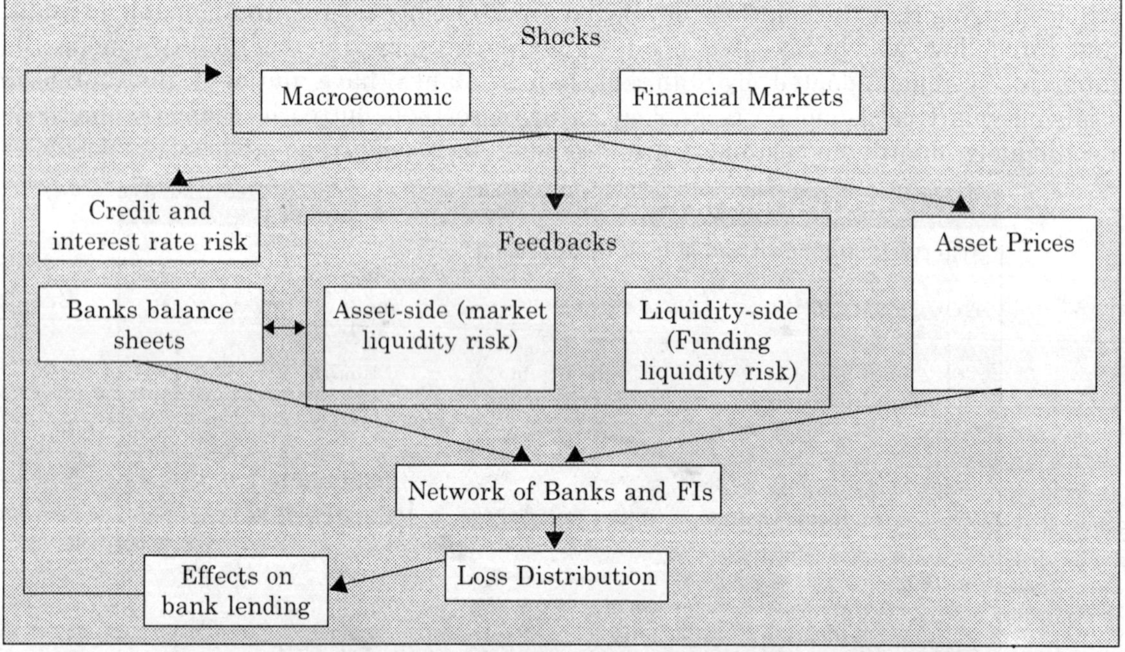


Successful inclusive growth strategies, therefore, seek to rectify imbalances in a business-like manner; they are not acts of charity. What makes inclusive growth sustainable and particularly effective is that it focuses on 'capacity creation and skill development for productive employment rather than on direct income redistribution'.

While sustainable inclusive growth will be fuelled by market-driven forces of growth that enable a wider range of social sectors to access markets and equip them to be more productive, the government plays a key role in broadening access to economic opportunities and build resilience of the most-vulnerable against economic shocks.

In sum, actualising the inclusive growth vision requires coordinated efforts to synergise the initiatives of the government, private sector, community-based organisations and civil society both from top-down and bottom-up perspectives. And, private enterprise is poised to stand front and centre of India's development story, partnering key stakeholders to build collaborative frameworks for sustainable development.

## FINANCIAL STABILITY: CONCEPT AND MEASUREMENT

The challenge of monetary policy is to strike an optimal balance between preserving financial stability, maintaining price stability, anchoring inflation expectations, and sustaining the growth momentum. The relative emphasis between these objectives has varied from time-to-time, depending on the underlying macroeconomic conditions. The global financial crisis has underlined the importance of preserving financial stability and this has made the task for the conduct of monetary policy even more complex and challenging than before.

## What is Financial Stability?

Financial stability, as a concept, is widely known. However, there is no unanimous agreement on a working definition of this concept. Some define financial stability in terms of what it is not, *i.e.*, the absence of financial instability. Others take a macro-prudential view and specify financial stability in terms of limitation of risks of significant real output losses in the presence of episodes of system-wide financial distress. Financial stability is a situation in which the financial system is capable of satisfactorily performing its three key functions simultaneously. First, the financial system is efficiently and smoothly facilitating the inter-temporal allocation of resources from savers to investors and the allocation of economic resources in general. Second, forward-looking financial risks are assessed and priced reasonably accurately and are relatively well-managed. Third, the financial system is in such a condition that it can comfortably, if not smoothly, absorb financial and real economic surprises and shocks. If any one or more of these key functions are not being satisfactorily performed. It is likely that the financial system is moving in the direction of becoming less stable, and at some point might exhibit instability. For example, inefficiencies in the allocation of capital or shortcomings in the pricing of risk can, by laying the foundations for imbalances and vulnerabilities, compromise future financial system stability.

Since financial stability poses a severe threat to important macroeconomic objectives there is a greater need for it. Financial stability as the prevalence of a financial system, which is able to ensure in a lasting way an efficient allocation of savings to investment opportunities, maintenance of a level of confidence in the financial system amongst all the participants and stakeholders and absence of excessive volatility that unduly and adversely affect real economic activity, well developed precautionary measures help in maintaining financial stability of the economy. These include development of a set of standards and codes, prudential regulation, early warning signals, supervision of financial intermediaries, compliance with international standards as regards capital adequacy norms, asset classification procedures and methods, income recognition principles, market valuations of assets and recovery mechanisms regular auditing and enforcement of rules and regulations.

The importance of financial stability emanates from four major trends in the financial systems which have become evident in recent years. There are: (i) an imbalance of growth between the financial sector and the real economy; (ii) a change in the mode of financial operations are to financial deepening (credit/debit cards); (iii) emergence of a globally integrated financial system; and (iv) an evolution of sophisticated financial instruments and attendant tasks. Consequently, the sources of crises have multiplied, necessitating the coordination of a number of authorities both within and outside country.

## FINANCIAL MARKET INTEGRATION

Integration of financial markets is a process of unifying markets and enabling convergence of risk adjusted returns on the assets of similar maturity across the markets. The process of integration is facilitated by an unimpeded access of participants to various market segments. Financial markets all over the world have witnessed growing integration within as well as across boundaries spurred by deregulation, globalisation and advance in information technology integrated financial markets assume vital importance for the following reasons;

Integrated markets serve as a conduit for authorities to transmit important price signals. Efficient and integrated financial markets constitute an important vehicle for promoting domestic savings, investment and economic growth.

Fosters the necessary condition for a country's financial sector to emerge as international or as regional financial centre.

By enhancing competition and efficiency of intermediaries in their operations and allocation of resources contribute to financial stability.

Lead to innovations and cost-effective intermediation improves access to financial services for members of the public institutions and companies.

Induce market distribution and information efficiency, and

Promotes the adoption of modern technology and payment systems to achieve cost-effective financial intermediation services.

The increased importance of financial stability is related to four major trends in the financial system. First, the financial system has expanded at a significantly faster pace than the real economy. Second, this process of financial deepening has been accompanied by a changing composition of the financial system, with an increasing share of non-monetary assets. Third, as a result of increasing cross-industry and cross-border integration, financial systems have become interwoven, both nationally and internationally. Fourth, the financial system has become much more complex in terms of the intricacies of financial instruments and diversity of activities. As a result, the sources of crises have also become manifold, necessitating the coordination of a number of authorities, both within and outside the country.

**Chart: A Framework for Maintaining Financial System Stability**

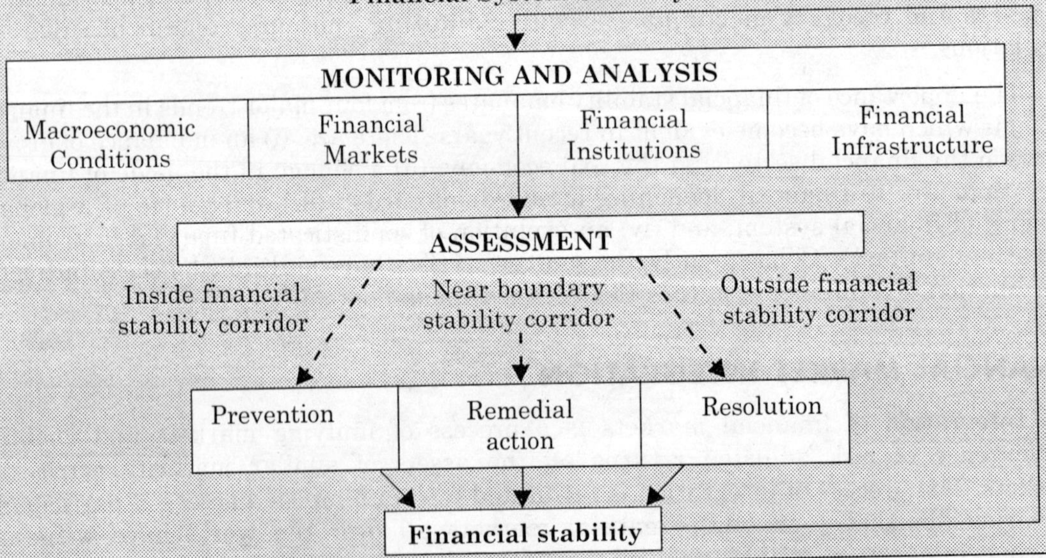


In the prevention mode, existing policies are maintained and updated for structural changes in order to prevent future imbalances. Surveillance of financial markets, institutions and infrastructure constitutes an important element of preventive policy. The situation changes if the financial system is close to, or at the boundary of, the range of stability.

Looking forward, the shift to a larger, more integrated, leveraged, complex and market-based financial system will continue to change the nature of financial risks. In this respect, the financial stability framework needs to be viewed as a flexible tool that can be used to interpret changes and translate these into policy implications. A major challenge, therefore, remains in developing a deeper understanding of how the different dimensions of financial stability interact with each other and with the real economy, and how these interactions are influenced by policy actions.

**Table: Policy Instruments for Financial Stability**

| | Prevention | Remedial Action | Resolution |
|---|---|---|---|
| | Implementing existing policies to safeguard financial stability | Implementing pre-emptive measures to reduce emerging risks to financial stability | Reactive policy interventions aimed at restoring financial stability |
| Market disciplining mechanisms | Maintain, Update | Strengthen | Discretionary measures |
| Self-regulation | Maintain, Update | Strengthen | Discretionary measures |
| Financial safety nets | Maintain, Update | Strengthen | LOLR, deposit insurance |
| Surveillance | Maintain, Update | Intensify | Further intensify |
| Supervision/regulation | Maintain, Update | Intensify | Discretionary measures |
| Official communication | Existing policies | Moral suasion | Restore confidence |
| Macroeconomic policies | Maintain, Update | Reduce imbalances | Discretionary measures |
| Legal system | Maintain, Update | Strengthen | Discretionary measures |

LOLR – Lender of last resort

## FINANCIAL GLOBALIZATION

The financial globalization is a key determinant for growth and stability. The more developed a country's financial sector the greater the growth benefits of capital inflows and the lower the country's vulnerability to crises.

- It has a positive effect on macroeconomic stability.
- Institutional quality plays an important role in determining financial integration.
- Sound fiscal and monetary policies increase the growth benefits of capital account liberalization and help avert crises in country's open capital accounts.
- Trade integration improves the cost-benefit trade-off associated with financial integration.
- Financial globalization brings in innovative products, practices in operation.
- New technology will bring in greater growth benefits.

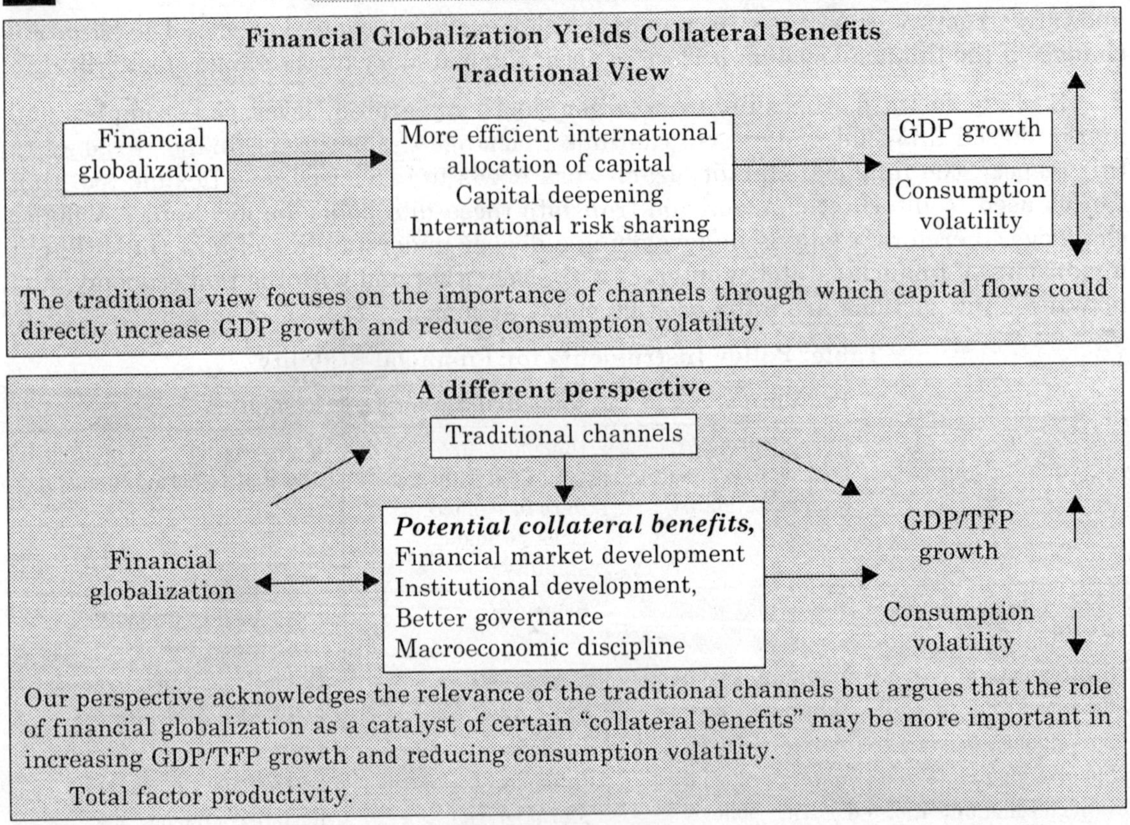


*Source:* **Finance & Development** March 2007

**Fig. 2**

## REGULATION AND SUPERVISION

Regulation and supervision of the financial system has received renewed focus in recent years in the context of the phenomenal expansion of the financial sector, technology-enabled innovations in financial products and deepening of global integration. The strategic importance of the banks in the financial system makes it imperative for the central bank — historically, the lender of the last resort and the supervisor of the banking system to pursue financial stability as an important macroeconomic objective, although, in India, there are separate institutions (viz., the SEBI the PERDA and the IRDA) to oversee the functioning of individual segments of the financial system. A number of initiatives have been taken by the Reserve Bank in reorienting the supervisory and regulatory framework and aligning it with the international best practices, while providing sufficient flexibility to the financial institutions to respond to the growing competition and the regulatory and supervisoy process in India at the current juncture is at an exciting phase and is progressing towards further, maturity aiming to impart greater strength and stability to the financial system. Therefore, the legitimate question to be posed at this juncture is 'from here to where'? It would be useful to identify the factors that may affect the functioning of the Indian banking system in the short, medium and long-term. Accordingly, the regulatory focus and the supervisory processes would need to be altered in some areas and fine-tuned in some other areas in the light of the challenges identified.

Financial systems worldwide are still evolving and the Indian financial system is not an exception. Rapid growth of computer and telecommunication technology would continue to transform the Indian financial sector. Financial innovations have been the driving force behind the blurring of distinctions among what were, traditionally, very distinct forms of financial firms. In recognition of the new market realities and progression towards universal banking, appropriate legal and regulatory changes would need to follow. The deregulation and liberalization process is like to get further expedited. Regulatory response in India has already been focused on promoting a financial system, which is based on market principles. The economic rationale for banking sector consolidation in India is unquestionable at the present juncture. The character of the ownership is undergoing change always from a predominantly government ownership. The regulatory response, against this backdrop, could play a role of facilitator while leaving the major forces to decide the extent and content of the consolidation process.

The process regulation and supervision in India has to be sharpened and diversified to ensure financial stability and maintain confidence in the financial system by enhancing the soundness and efficiency.

**Chart 2: Regulatory Structure of the Indian Financial System – Institutions and Markets**

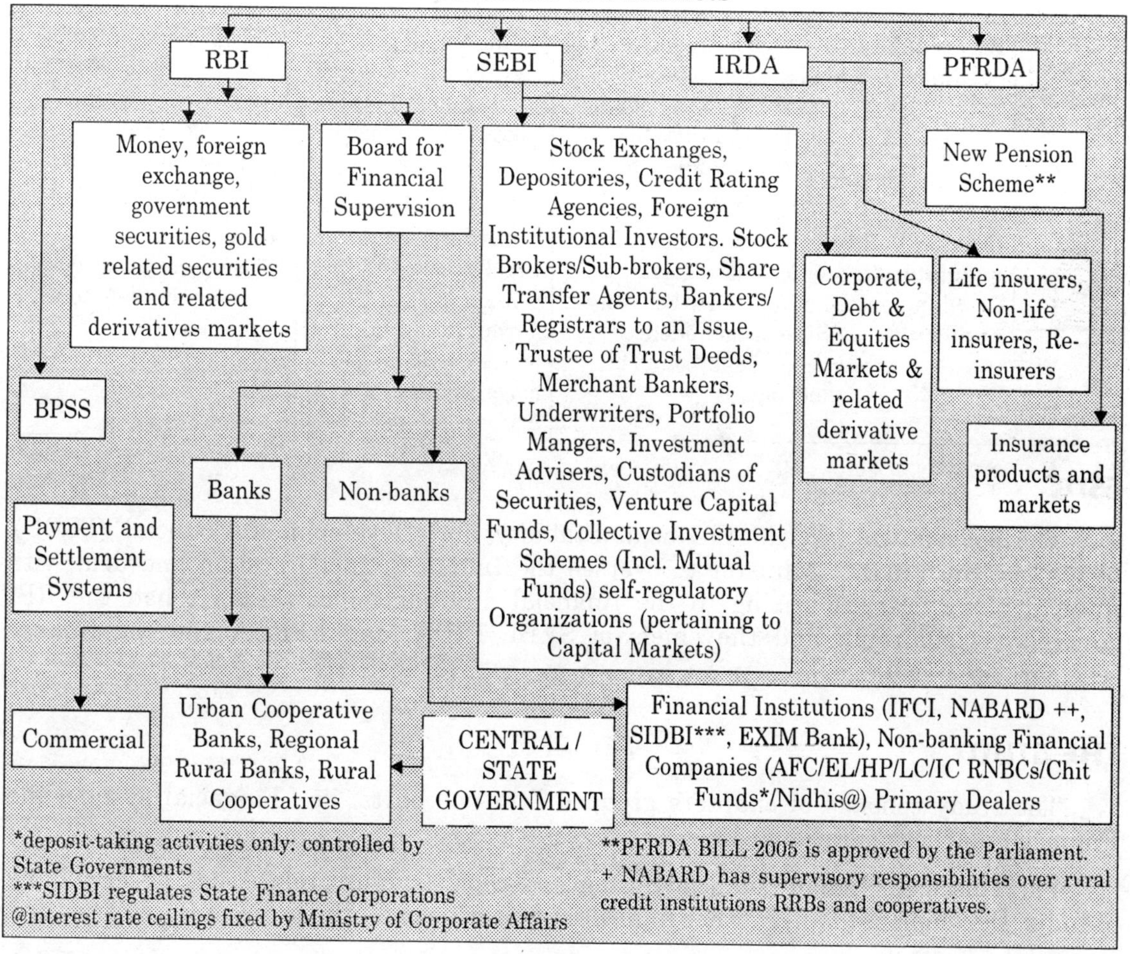


*deposit-taking activities only: controlled by State Governments
***SIDBI regulates State Finance Corporations
@interest rate ceilings fixed by Ministry of Corporate Affairs

**PFRDA BILL 2005 is approved by the Parliament.
+ NABARD has supervisory responsibilities over rural credit institutions RRBs and cooperatives.

## FINANCIAL REGULATORS

| Regulator | Core Area | What's In It For You | Punitive Powers |
|---|---|---|---|
|  **Competition Commission of India** | To prohibit anti-competitive agreements and abuse of dominant position by enterprises. | CCI is empowered to take action against companies forming cartels to keep prices high. | Competition Appellate Tribunal, a quasi-judicial body, is empowered to impose punitive measures. |
|  **Securities & Exchange Board of India** | To protect the interests of investors in securities and to promote the development of, and to regulate the securities market. | SEBI takes steps to protect investors from frauds. It has banned many brokers from trading. | It can investigate and pass orders against persons found to be guilty of manipulating markets. |
|  **Insurance Regulatory & Development Authority** | To regulate, promote and ensure orderly growth of the insurance business and reinsurance business. | The regulator takes steps to protect the interests of the insured at the hands of insurers. | It can issue warnings and penalties on insurers and it can withdraw, suspend or cancel the registration of insurers. |
| **Reserve Bank of India** | It is the government's banker; the bankers' banker and the banking regulator. It also plays a key role in inflation management. | As the banking regulator, it's the first court of appeal for an aggrieved customer. | All banks need a licence from the RBI to carry-out their business within India, and it can be cancelled on violation of certain conditions. |
|  **Pension Fund Regulatory & Development Authority** | Regulator for the pension sector and regulates the flagship. New Pension System that offers pension solution to all individuals. | It has designed the world's cheapest pension product. Going forward, pension products will be a major savings instrument. | It can only alter any clause, it may consider necessary in the interest of the subscribers. |

## FSDC

The government set up Financial Stability and Development Councial (FSDC), headed by the Finance Minister to oversee the Indian financial system and deal with inter-regulatory issues arising in the financial and capital markets. It had the RBI governor as chairman and the chiefs of SEBI, IRDA, and PFRDA and the finance secretary as members.

## THE STUDY

The study consists of chapters grouped into two parts, i.e., Financial system and Financial market operations.

Part I discusses Indian Financial System's concept, structure, role, issues, Reserve Bank of India, Development banks, other financial institutions and the Interest Rate Structure.

Part II discusses Financial sector operations and reforms in a lucid manner.

The financial system is in the process of liberalisation. A search is underway for policies as well as reforms that will strengthen the financial sector, so that it can make its full contribution to the efficient use of resources, while keeping its tendency towards instability and volatility in check. Part III and Part IV examine varied facets of the financial system in sixteen chapters.

As we enter the new millennium, we see the global economy undergoing a transition from the 'old' to the 'new' fostered by rapid advances in information technology and telecommunications, and the emergence of the internet as a mainstream medium for conducting business. Consequently, traditional businesses are being forced to innovate and rethink the way they conduct business. With the volume of online business transactions increasing at an exponential rate, the momentum of this transition is only getting stronger and traditional players are being forced to realign organizational structures to meet the changing needs of the new economy.

While the internet revolution has far-reaching implications for all businesses, its most dramatic impact has been on the services sector and in particular the financial services and banking industry. Internet banking or e-banking has emerged as a mainstream service delivery channel, which is providing customers unmatched convenience in terms of a location-and-time-independent service offering. E-banking presents lower transactions costs for banks, unrivalled opportunities for customization and encourages a greater degree of interactivity. At the pace and degree of technological innovation being witnessed today, customers are able to or will soon be able to carry-out all their banking through electronic devices like personal computers, palmtops, laptops, mobile phones and other handheld devices. Once this trend gains acceptance, banks with large physical branch networks will gradually lose their competitive edge.

Though the leadership status of the Indian software industry has come to be acknowledged the world over, the internet has not impacted the Indian economy to the same extent as in the West. However, this situation is expected to be remedied shortly with the growing popularity of cybercafes and the emergence of set-top boxes, both of which are expected to provide internet access at affordable rates. Further, an enabling regulator framework for e-commerce is expected shortly, with the passing of cyber-laws by Parliament. As a result, India has an opportunity to make the transition towards a knowledge-based society, which in turn promises an overall improvement in the quality of life. There is every evidence that this improvement will take place across a broad spectrum of the society including the semi-urban and rural areas. The globalization of the economy has pushed competition in the Indian financial sector to unprecedented heights.

## STRENGTHENING OF FINANCIAL INSTITUTIONS

The Indian financial system is a complex netwrok of institutions having a variety of functions and governed by different regulations. Besides commercial banks, which are the predominant intermediaries of the financial system, there are cooperative banks, development finance institutions, non-banking financial companies, insurance companies, provident funds and mutual funds. The Reserve Bank exercises its supervisory role over the banking system encompassing commercial and cooperative banks (UCBs) by virtue of powers provided under the Banking Regulation Act, 1949 and the Reserve Bank of India Act, 1934. The Reserve Bank also regulates select all-India financial institutions under the Reserve Bank of India Act, 1934. Consequent upon amendments to the RBI Act in 1997, a comprehensive regulatory framework in respect of NBFCs was also introduced. In respect of state and district central cooperative banks, and regional rural banks, while the Reserve Bank is the regulator, the supervision is vested with the National Bank for Agriculture and Rural Development (NABARD). Insurance companies and mutual funds are regulated by the Insurance Regulatory and Development Authority (IRDA) and the Securities and Exchange Board of India (SEBI), respectively.

(i) Broadly, the financial system comprises banking insurance, development finance, universal banking, specialised financial agencies, mutual funds, venture capital funds, stock market leasing and hire purchase, chit funds, nidhis, saving agencies, post office, factoring, housing finance, non-banking finance companies, financial consultancy, credit rate finance and other related sectors. Thus, the financial system is the backbone of the economy.

(ii) The financial system, like any other system, is to be controlled by a well defined and designed mechanism that should ensure smooth functioning, flexible operative methods and an efficient human resource pool to handle the system. The last is the most critical because the quality of the system does not ensure better results unless the human factor is capable, efficient and honest.

Finance is managing money — how to get and use it to achieve the best possible returns. It implies earning revenues by raising financial resources through various methods, planning its use, designing methods of paying back the borrowed money and interest on it, and above all, ensuring good profits on all business operations.

Technical skill is the ability to use the appropriate financial tools and techniques, procedures and systems, methods and practices. Human skill is the ability to work with other individuals and groups. You must demonstrate the ability to work, and later lead, a group of people called "a team". Conceptual skill is the mental ability to coordinate and integrate all of the organisation's interests and activities.

## CONCLUSION

In the post-liberalisation era, the finance sector is witnessing a complete metamorphosis. Deregulation measures have included the freeing up of direct controls over ownership, liberalizing interest rates and credit allocation, deregulating foreign exchange transaction controls, freeing up the entry of new firms, and expanding and broadening the base of the banking system, both for nationals and international business ventures. At the same time, non-banking financial institutions, securities markets and money markets have developed to mobilize and allocate savings. Experience suggests that financial liberalisation needs to be undertaken alongside macroeconomic reforms.

❖❖❖

CHAPTER 2

# THE INDIAN FINANCIAL SYSTEM

## INTRODUCTION

The forces of change unleashed in the Indian economy over the last decade have transformed the opening environment across the entire spectrum of businesses. This coincided with rapid developments in technology that created both an opportunity and a challenge for businesses worldwide — the opportunity to innovate in product offerings to customers and improve operating efficiency, and the challenge of keeping pace with change and gaining first-mover advantage. These two developments catalysed significant shifts in the structure of the Indian economy, perhaps the most visible and farreaching of which was the increased share of the services sector in the economy.

The liberalisation of the financial sector, which formed a key part of the overall liberalisation process, blurred the distinction between various financial intermediaries and promoted greater efficiency and competitiveness in the financial markets. The structure of the financial markets itself began to change — with the growth of the debt capital markets and the entry of new market participants like mutual funds, disintermediation gradually set in. This started the process of evolution of the financial intermediary into a provider of services in addition to an originator of credit.

The word *'system'* stands for a set of bodily organs like composition or concurring in function, a scheme of classification and a method of organisation.

Finance holds the key to all human activities. Finance is the study of money — its nature, creation, behaviour, regulation and administration. So, all those activities dealing in finance are organised in a system known as the financial system or financial sector.

## THE CONCEPT

The term *financial system* is a set of interrelated activities/services working together to achieve some predetermined purpose or goal. It includes different markets, the institutions, instruments, services and mechanisms which influence the generation of savings, investment capital formation and growth.

*Van Horne* defined the financial system as *the purpose of financial markets to allocate savings efficiently in an economy to ultimate* users *either for investment in real assets or for consumption*. Christy has opined that the objective of the financial system is to *"supply funds to various sectors and activities of the economy in ways that promote the fullest possible utilisation of resources without the destabilising consequence of price level changes or unnecessary interference with individual desires"*.

According to Robinson, the primary function of the system is *"to provide a link between savings* and *investment for the creation of new wealth and to permit portfolio adjustment in the composition of the existing wealth"*.

From the above definitions, it may be said that the primary function of the financial system is the mobilisation of savings, their distribution for industrial investment and stimulating capital formation to accelerate the process of economic growth.

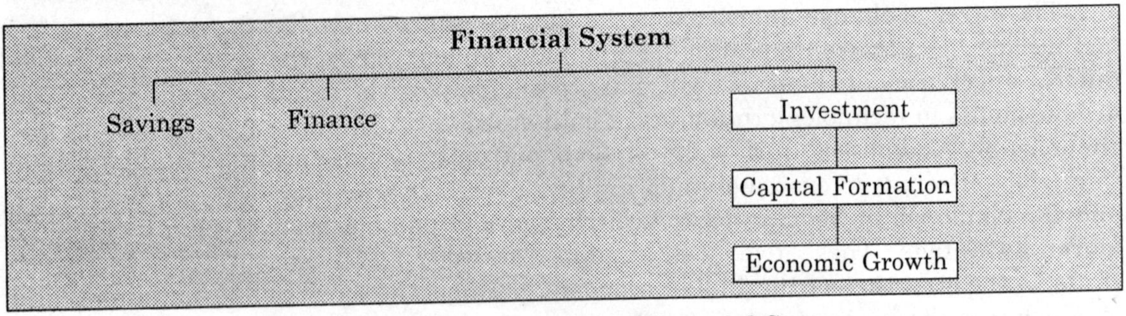


**Fig. 1 The Objectives of the Financial System**

The process of savings, finance and investment involves financial institutions, markets, instruments and services. Above all, supervision control and regulation are equally significant. Thus, financial management is an integral part of the financial system. On the basis of the empirical evidence, Goldsmith said that "... a case for the hypothesis that the separation of the functions of savings and investment which is made possible by the introduction of financial instruments as well as enlargement of the range of financial assets which follows from the creation of financial institutions increase the efficiency of investments and raise the ratio of capital formation to national production and financial activities and through these two channels increase the rate of growth...."

Thus, the interrelationship between varied segments of the economy are illustrated below:

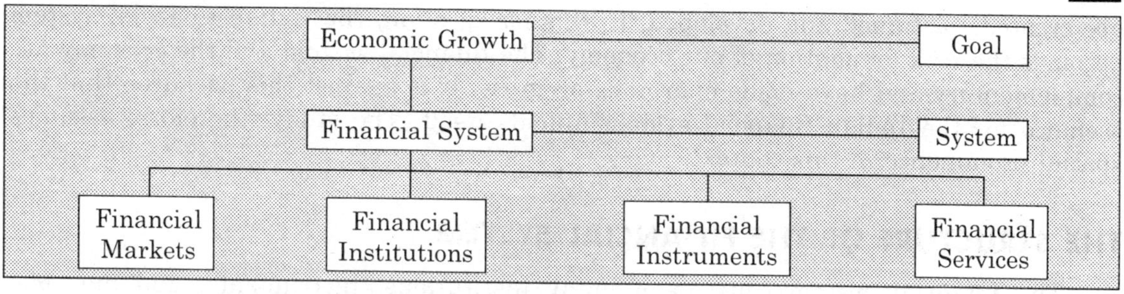


**Fig. 2 Interrelationship in the Financial System**

A financial system provides services that are essential in a modern economy. The use of a stable, widely accepted medium of exchange reduces the costs of transactions. It facilitates trade and, therefore, specialization in production. Financial assets with attractive yield, liquidity and risk characteristics encourage saving in financial form. By evaluating alternative investments and monitoring the activities of borrowers, financial intermediaries increase the efficiency of resource use. Access to a variety of financial instruments enables an economic agent to pool, price and exchange risks in the markets. Trade, the efficient use of resources, saving and risk taking are the cornerstones of a growing economy. In fact, the country could make this feasible with the active support of the financial system. The financial system has been identified as the most catalysing agent for growth of the economy, making it one of the key inputs of development.

**CURRENCY, BANKING, AND DEBT CRISES** **BOX : 1**

A foreign exchange or *currency* crisis occurs when a speculative attack on a country's currency results in a devaluation or sharp depreciation or forces the central bank to defend the currency by selling large amounts of reserves or by significantly raising interest rates. Some analysts distinguish between "old-style" or "slow motion" currency crises, and "new-style" crises. The former climax after a period of overspending and real appreciation that weaken the current account, often in a context of extensive capital controls, and end in devaluation. In the latter, investors have concerns about the creditworthiness of the balance sheet of a significant part of the economy (public or private), which, in an environment of more liberated and integrated capital and financial markets, can lead very rapidly to exert pressure on the exchange rate.

A *banking* crisis occurs when actual or potential bank runs, or failures, induce banks to suspend the internal convertibility of their liabilities or force the government to intervene to prevent this by providing banks with large-scale financial support. Banking crises tend to last longer than currency crises and have more severe effects on economic activity. Banking crises were relatively rare in the 1950s and 1960s because of capital and financial controls but have become increasingly common since the 1970s, often in tandem with currency crises.

A *debt* crisis occurs either when a borrower defaults or when lenders believe default is likely and therefore withhold new loans and try to liquidate existing ones. Debt crises can be associated with either commercial (private) or sovereign (public) debt. A perceived risk that the public sector will cease to honour its repayment obligations is likely to lead to a sharp drop in private capital inflows and a foreign exchange crisis.

The Indian financial system has established a strong link between savings and investments by creating a unique mechanism through which varied economic activities are created, sustained and developed. In this background, the Indian financial system becomes the rock foundation of our economy. The financial system and the economy are complementary and have made enormous progress. It is against this backdrop that the scenario for the Indian financial system unfolds itself. The study, therefore, assumes special prominence in this context.

## THE STRUCTURE OF THE FINANCIAL SYSTEM

The financial system consists of many institutions, instruments, and markets. Financial institutions range from pawnshops and moneylenders to banks, pension funds, insurance companies, brokerage houses, investment trusts, and stock exchanges. Financial instruments range from the common — coins, currency notes, and cheques; mortgages, corporate bills, bonds, and stocks to the more exotic — futures and swaps of high finance. Markets for these instruments may be organized formally (as in stock or bond exchanges with centralized trading floors) or informally (as in over-the-counter or curb markets). For analytical purposes, the system can be divided into users of financial services and providers.

## USERS OF FINANCIAL SERVICES

Financial institutions sell their services to households, businesses and government.

The household sector includes small mainly unregulated firms and individuals. Their main financial needs are for payment of services, saving and small credit. They seek convenience, liquidity and security.

Businesses have more complicated financial needs. It needs short-term credit to finance inventories and long-term funds to finance capital expansion.

All governments use payment services. In most developing countries, governments, like businesses, are net borrowers, and they use the financial system as a source of funding for current and capital spending. In industrial countries, government deficits are financed mainly by selling securities to the public. In developing countries they are usually financed by borrowing from banks. Governments have also used the financial system to serve development or other goals.

## PROVIDERS OF FINANCIAL SERVICES

Different financial institutions provide services that are both complementary to and competitive with each other. Deposit institutions offer payment and liquid deposit facilities, and contractual savings institutions provide illiquid savings opportunities that cater to the longer-term needs of customers. Collective investment institutions offer small investors the benefits of professional management and low-cost risk diversification, encouraging them to diversify their savings into marketable securities. On the lending side, commercial banks have traditionally provided working capital and trade finance, but longer-term lending is gaining with the spread of universal banking. Factoring companies provide long-term investment finance.

Money and capital markets provide investment instruments appropriate for contractual savings and collective investment institutions, whose services to the saving public are thereby improved. The efficient functioning of financial markets also depends on institutions that lend and borrow little on their own account: investment banks, securities brokers, and credit rating agencies. Commercial banks also improve the working of financial markets by providing credit and payment facilities to market participants.

Different financial institutions and markets compete for a limited pool of savings by offering different instruments. Money and capital markets increase competition between suppliers. Money markets give merchant banks, or commercial banks with limited branch networks, greater access to funds. Because such banks specialize in lending to larger corporations, the corporate loan market may be highly competitive, even though few large domestic banks may continue to dominate the retail deposit market.

Money markets also provide large corporations and non-bank financial institutions with efficient short-term instruments for investing their liquid funds and thus compete directly with commercial banks' traditional deposit facilities. They also enable large corporation to issue short-term securities in the form of commercial paper and thus further reduce the market power that large banks may have in the domestic banking sector. Finally, capital markets enable contractual savings and collective investment institutions to play a more active role in the financial system.

The complementary and competitive interaction of financial institutions has policy implications. To promote an efficient financial system there must be competition, but the system must also offer an array of services. Rather than restrict the growth and diversification of the main banking groups, governments in the greater competition by encouraging money and capital markets, specialized credit institutions (such as leasing and factoring companies), and contractual savings and collective investment institutions. Economies too small to support such specialized institutions can spur competition by allowing economic agents to buy.

## FINANCIAL SYSTEMS IN DEVELOPING COUNTRIES

The evolution of financial systems in developing countries reflected their diverse political and economic histories. Latin America and the Mediterranean countries, politically independent since at least the first quarter of the nineteenth century, suffered frequent bouts of financial instability. These prevented the emergence of mature financial systems. In contrast, developing countries in Africa and Asia, under colonial rule until the end of World War II, enjoyed relative financial stability — but their financial systems suffered from colonial neglect and stagnation.

The financial systems of most developing countries were heavily oriented toward agricultural exports, other primary production and foreign trade. In Africa and Asia, financial systems catered principally to expatriate communities. Financial services for the indigenous population were limited. Foreign banks confined their operations to port towns and other centres of commerce where the expatriate communities were gathered. The domestic population, especially in Asia, hoarded precious metals and jewellery.

Hoarding was insurance against financial emergencies caused by war, crop failure, natural disaster and personal crop failure — but it was saving denied to productive investment.

Sound banking promoted financial stability in Africa and Asia. Currency boards regulated the money supply and maintained reserves that were invested in London and Paris. The financial systems of most African countries, however, were underdeveloped until independence. They comprised a few foreign colonial banks, post office savings banks, co-operative societies, and moneylenders. Nigeria was the only African country with indigenous commercial banks before the late 1940s.

Financial development was more advanced in Asia. As in Africa, foreign banks confined their operations largely to the financing of foreign trade, but they also helped to finance internal trade. Most Asian countries also had a fairly well-developed indigenous banking system, with commercial banks, co-operative credit societies, informal bankers and moneylenders. India, in particular, had a sophisticated indigenous banking structure. It had evolved over several centuries, developing the use of commercial bills known as *hundi* for financing non-local trade and relying on an elaborate system of personal relations to finance local, mostly small-scale activities.

Foreign banks operated in pre1949 China, mostly in treaty ports, and some indigenous banks *(shansi)* remitted funds across regions and financed local trade. Foreign banks promoted foreign direct investment in rail/road construction, mining and manufacturing. They also made massive loans to the Chinese government and in the process gained control of its customs and salt revenues. Modern Chinese banks came into being in the 1930s. They had close links with the government and the ruling families and were able to seize the initiative from foreign banks and emerge as the dominant group. After 1949, China built a mono-banking system typical of centrally planned economies.

Indigenous bankers and moneylenders were able to meet the borrowing needs of local traders and farmers by maintaining close personal contact with them and acquiring intimate knowledge of their operations. Their services were accessible but expensive. Informal financial institutions such as rotating savings and credit associations (ROSCAs), also emerged in most countries (see Chapter 7). Indigenous bankers and informal financial institutions, however, could not mobilize the resources required for industrialization.

## THE EVOLUTION OF THE FINANCIAL SYSTEM IN INDIA

The evolution of the financial system has been interlinked with the growth of the macroeconomics. The financial system has travelled up and down from the barter system in pre-industrial economies to universal banking. The evolution of the financial system is greatly influenced by the spread of urban society, and above all the advent of large-scale industrialisation in the second half of the nineteenth century, altered the role that finance had to play. Financial development accelerated with the expansion of the railways and, especially, with the revolutionalisation of the information technology.

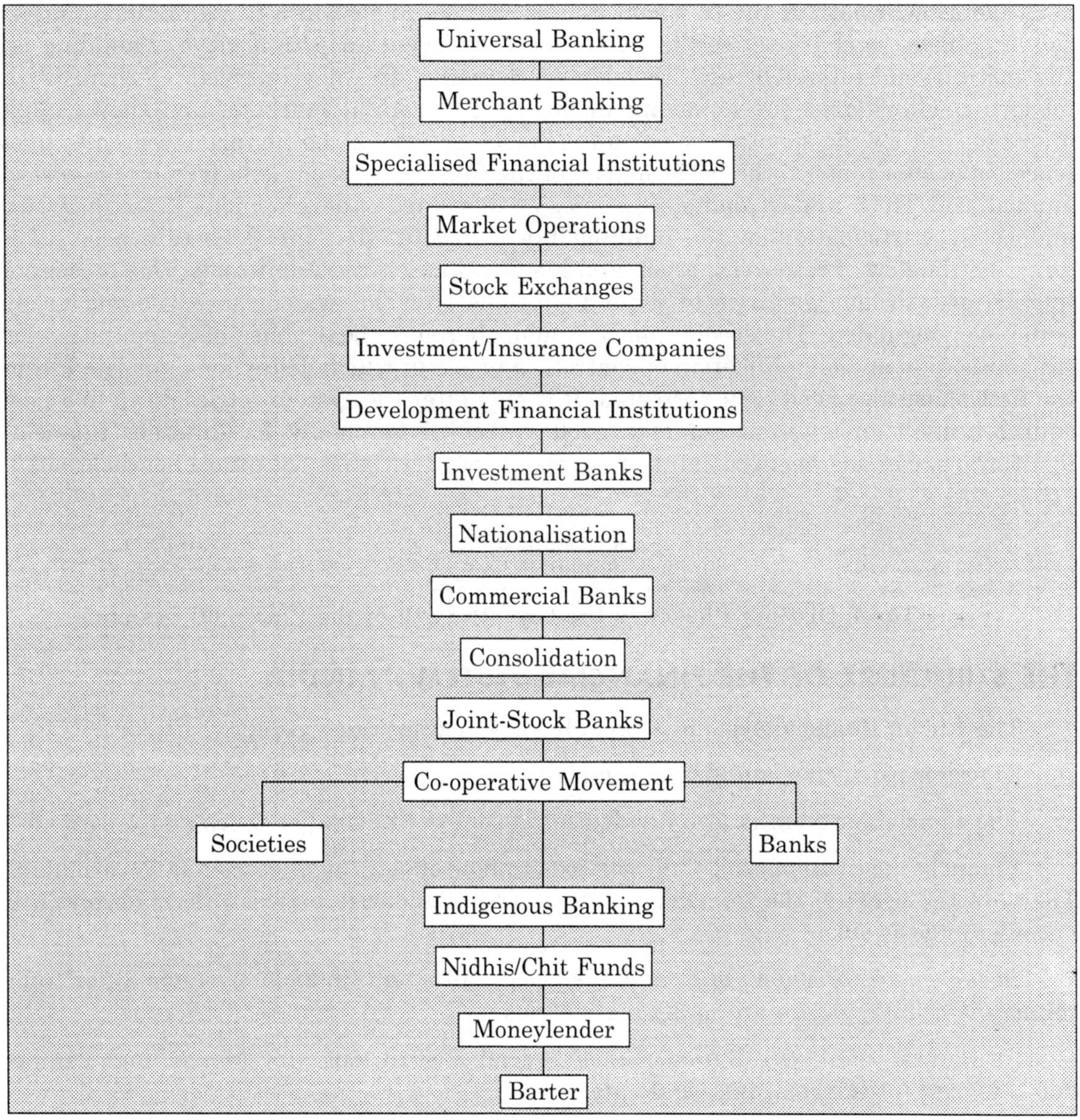


**Fig. 3 The Evolution of the Indian Financial System**

In India, the evolution of the financial systems reflected its political, social and economic needs and aspirations.

Government has played a large role in the creation and broad basing of the financial system and financial deepening in the country. The government has exerted its influence over the flow of credit, interest rates, credit control and direction. It is also a big borrower as well as regulator of the financial system.

A bulk contributor of the Indian financial system is in the public sector, even though cooperative and private sectors are there to compete with other institutions.

The growth path of the financial system can be divided into three distinct phases: the first phase is characterised by active state intervention with a view to building up the institutional infrastructure. Developing countries are in a hurry to catch up with modern banking, and developments in money and capital markets; and they cannot afford to wait for the spontaneous or autonomous growth of the financial system to take place. In such a context, the performance of the financial system is judged by the test of 'immediacy'. Thus, in developing economies at this stage of development, state initiative and active participation in the building up of institutional infrastructure as also in directing the flow of resources, becomes a historical necessity. Admittedly, this process of hurried growth may give rise to some distortions; and the system may also end up by being over-regulated. The second phase would, therefore, be a phase of deregulation, or rationalisation and simplification of controls, a phase in which distortions inherited from the first phase also need to be corrected. It is only after the system settles down to a new equilibrium in an environment of a good degree of autonomy for different financial institutions, can one begin to think in terms of the third phase of total liberalisation.

| | | |
|---|---|---|
| Active State Intervention | Deregulation Rationalisation Simplification | Total Liberalisation |

**Fig. 4 Three Distinct Phases in the Growth Path of the Financial System.**

## THE STRUCTURE OF THE FINANCIAL SYSTEM IN INDIA

The Indian financial system is broadly classified into two groups:

(*i*) organised sector, and (*ii*) unorganised sector.

The financial system is also divided into users of financial services and providers.

Financial institutions sell their services to households, businesses and government. They are the users of the financial services. The boundaries between these sectors are not always clear-cut.

*In the case of providers of financial services,* although financial systems differ from country-to-country, there are many similarities.

(*i*) Central bank (*ii*) Banks (*iii*) Financial institutions (*iv*) Money and capital markets, and (*v*) Informal financial enterprises.

## ORGANISED INDIAN FINANCIAL SYSTEM

The organised financial system comprises of an impressive network of banks, other financial and investment institutions and a range of financial instruments, which together function in fairly developed capital and money markets. Short-term funds are mainly provided by the commercial and cooperative banking structure. Nine-tenth of such banking business is managed by twenty-eight leading banks which are in the public sector. In addition to commercial banks, there is the network of co-operative banks and land development banks at state, district and block levels. With around two-thirds share in the total assets in the financial system, banks play an important role. Of late, Indian banks have also diversified into areas such as merchant banking, mutual funds, leasing and factoring.

The Indian financial system comprises a wide network of financial institutions, financial markets and financial infrastructure. The financial institutions in India mainly consist of commercial banks (including regional rural banks - RRBs), urban co-operative banks, rural co-operative banks, (which, in turn, comprise short-term co-operative credit structure (state co-operative banks and district central co-operative banks) and long-term credit structure (state co-operative agriculture and rural development banks and primary co-operative agriculture and rural development banks, non-banking financial institutions insurance companies, and mutual funds.

The organised financial system comprises the following sub-systems:

(1) Banking system

(2) Co-operative system

(3) Development banking system

 (*i*) Public sector

 (*ii*) Private sector

(4) Money markets, and

(5) Financial companies/institutions.

Over the years, the structure of financial institutions in India has developed and become broad-based. The system has developed in three areas — state, co-operative and private. Rural and urban areas are well served by the co-operative sector as well as by corporate bodies with national status. There are more than 9,200 institutions channellising credit into the various areas of the economy. A broad structure of the financial system in India has been presented in the chart.

## UNORGANISED FINANCIAL SYSTEM

On the other hand, the unorganised financial system comprises relatively less controlled moneylenders, indigenous bankers, lending pawn brokers, landlords, traders, etc. This part of the financial system is not directly amenable to control by the Reserve Bank of India (RBI). There are a host of financial companies, investment companies, chit funds, etc., which are also not regulated by the RBI or the government in a systematic manner.

However, they are also governed by rules and regulations and are, therefore within the orbit of the monetary authorities.

## RURAL FINANCIAL SYSTEM

Rural financial system has been evolved over a period of time from the year 1904, when the first Primary Agricultural Credit Society was organized, by accepting and implementing important recommendations of expert committees appointed by the Government of India/RBI from time-to-time. During the pre-reform period, more

**Chart 1 : Structure of Financial Institutions in India**

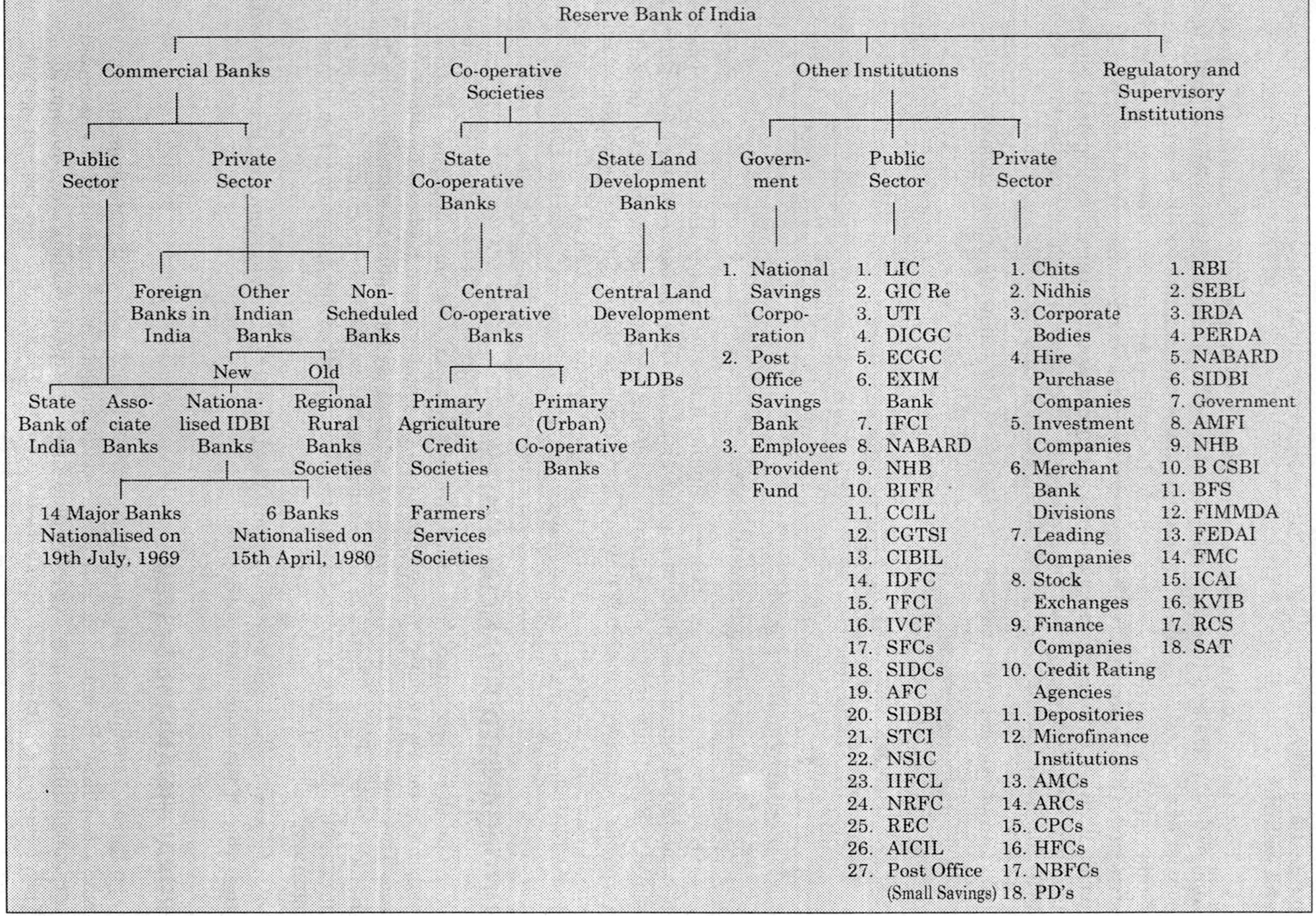

**Table 1**

**The Institutional Structure of Selected Financial Systems**

| Country | *Assets as a percentage of total gross assets of the financial system* | | | | | | *As a percentage of GNP* | |
|---|---|---|---|---|---|---|---|---|
| | *Central banks* | *Deposit banks* | *Specialized lending institutions* | *Contractual savings institutions* | *Collective investment institutions* | *Long-term debt securities and equities*[a] | *Net financial assets* | *Total external debt* |
| *Developed markets* | | | | | | | | |
| Australia | 5 | 31 | 14 | 17 | 1 | 33 | — | — |
| Canada | 1 | 33 | 2 | 26 | 8 | 30 | 165 | — |
| France | 6 | 56 | 10 | 7 | 5 | 16 | 109 | — |
| Fed. Re. of Germany, | 4 | 41 | 14 | 9 | 2 | 30 | 158 | — |
| Japan | 2 | 45 | 9 | 6 | 7 | 30 | 300 | — |
| Sweden | 4 | 27 | 18 | 16 | 1 | 35 | — | — |
| United Kingdom | 1 | 35 | 1 | 26 | 3 | 34 | 188 | — |
| United States | 2 | 28 | 7 | 19 | 4 | 40 | 210 | — |
| Average | 3 | 37 | 9 | 16 | 4 | 31 | 188 | — |
| *Emerging markets* | | | | | | | | |
| Argentina | 32 | 43 | 11 | 5 | 0 | 10 | — | 80 |
| Brazil | 27 | 32 | 12 | 2 | 4 | 23 | 59 | 50 |
| Chile | 14 | 44 | 1 | 11 | 1 | 28 | 75 | 145 |
| India | 10 | 47 | 6 | 12 | 1 | 24 | 65 | 19 |
| Rep. of Korea, | 9 | 53 | 14 | 4 | 10 | 10 | 56 | 57 |
| Malaysia | 7 | 34 | 12 | 13 | 3 | 32 | 247 | 52 |
| Nigeria | 23 | 46 | 2 | 3 | 7 | 19 | 49 | 26 |
| Pakistan | 21 | 65 | 1 | 2 | 1 | 11 | 45 | 39 |
| Philippines | 30 | 38 | 14 | 3 | 3 | 14 | 38 | 82 |
| Portugal | 20 | 72 | 1 | 2 | 1 | 4 | 124 | 85 |
| Thailand | 16 | 55 | 12 | 1 | 0 | 17 | 89 | 47 |
| Turkey | 33 | 54 | 4 | 6 | 0 | 3 | 27 | 50 |
| Venezuela | 20 | 46 | 25 | 1 | 0 | 8 | 65 | 74 |
| Average | 20 | 48 | 9 | 5 | 2 | 16 | 79 | 62 |

*Note:* Total financial system assets are the assets of all the institutions shown in this table plus the stock of outstanding securities and equities. To eliminate double-counting caused by the assets of one institution being the liabilities of another, net financial assets have been approximated by the sum of total liquid liabilities (IFS, line 551) plus securities and equities. To deflate these stocks by the flow of GNP, five-quarter arithmetic averages are constructed from year-end data for 1984 and 1985, assuming constant exponential growth during the year.

a. The sum of government bonds, corporate bonds, and corporate equity.

*Source:* IMF: International Financial Statistics, and World Bank data.

**Table 2 : Structure of Indian Financial Institutions**

(As at end-March 2008)

| Institution | Number of Institutions | Total assets (₹ crore) | Per cent |
|---|---|---|---|
| 1 | 2 | 3 | 4 |
| **Financial Sector ( I + II)** | **3,815** | **74,75,310** | **100.0** |
| **The Banking Sector (I + II)** | **3,062** | **50,00,821** | **66.9** |
| **I. Commercial banks** | **173** | **44,50,681** | **59.5** |
| Scheduled commercial banks | 169 | 44,50,027 | 59.5 |
| Public sector banks | 28 | 30,22,237 | 40.4 |
| State Bank group | 8 | 10,11,169 | 13.5 |
| Nationalised banks | 19 | 18,80,374 | 25.2 |
| Private sector banks | 23 | 9,40,150 | 12.6 |
| Old private banks | 15 | 1,94,555 | 2.6 |
| New private banks | 8 | 7,45,595 | 10.0 |
| Foreign banks | 28 | 3,64,099 | 4.9 |
| Regional Rural Banks | 91 | 1,23,541 | 1.7 |
| Non-scheduled commerical banks (Local area banks) | 4 | 654 | 0.01 |
| **II. Cooperative banks** | **2,889** | **5,50,140** | **7.4** |
| (a) Urban co-operative banks | 1,770 | 1,79,421 | 2.4 |
| Scheduled | 53 | 79,318 | 1.1 |
| Non-scheduled | 1,717 | 1,00,103 | 1.3 |
| (b) Rural co-operative banks | 1,119 | 3,70,719 | 5.0 |
| Short-term structure | 402 | 3,24,609 | 4.3 |
| State co-operative banks (STCBs)* | 31 | 85,756 | 1.1 |
| District central co-operative banks (DCCBs)* | 371 | 1,58,894 | 2.1 |
| Primary Agriculture Credit Societies (PACS) @ | .. | 79,959 | 1.1 |
| Long-term structure | 717 | 46,110 | 0.6 |
| SCARDBs | 20 | 24,336 | 0.3 |
| PCARDBs | 697 | 21,774 | 0.3 |
| **III. The Broader Financial Sector** | **753** | **24,74,489** | **33.1** |
| **III. 1 Development Finance Institutions**** | **4** | **1,77,765** | **2.4** |
| **III. 2 State Financial Corporations#** | **18** | **12,841** | **0.2** |
| **III. 3 Insurance Institutions** | **37** | **10,39,704** | **13.9** |
| Life insurance | 1 | 7,98,685 | 12.1 |
| Public | 1 | 7,98,685 | 10.7 |
| Private | 17 | 1,08,595 | 1.5 |
| Non-life insurance | 19 | 1,32,424 | 1.8 |
| GIC (re-inurer) | 1 | 36,013 | 0.5 |
| Public | 4 | 79,208 | 1.1 |
| Private | 12 | 12,237 | 0.2 |
| Others & % | 2 | 49,666 | 0.07 |
| **III. 4 Other Institutions***** | **1** | **25,744** | **0.3** |
| **III. 5 Non-banking Financial Companies ##** | **565** | **6,79,927** | **9.1** |
| NBFC (Deposit-taking) | 335 | 70,292 | 0.9 |
| NBFCs (non-deposit-taking) | 176 | 4,08,705 | 5.5 |
| RNBC | 2 | 24,452 | 0.3 |
| Primary Dealers | 9 | 10,882 | 0.1 |
| Housing Finance Companies | 43 | 1,65,596 | 2.2 |

| | | | |
|---|---|---|---|
| **III. 6 Mutual Funds** | **101** | **5,38,508** | **7.2** |
| Bank-sponsored | 2 | 81,229 | 1.1 |
| Institution-sponsored | 2 | 14,337 | 0.2 |
| Private | 97 | 4,42,942 | 5.9 |
| Indian | 27 | 1,66,104 | 2.2 |
| Foreign | 7 | 31,168 | 0.4 |
| Joint ventures (predominantly Indian) | 33 | 1,65,790 | 2.2 |
| Joint ventures (predominantly foreign) | 30 | 79,880 | 1.1 |

* : Data for rural co-operative banks pertain to end March 2007.
@ : 97.224 Primary Agricultural Credit Societies (PACS) with loans outstanding of ₹ 58,600 crore at end March 2007
** : Comprising NABARD, NHB, SIDBI and EXIM Bank.
*** : Pertains to DICGC (Deposit insurance fund)
# : Total assets pertain to end March 2007.
## : Pertains to reporting NBFCs
**Source:** RBI, SEBI, IRDA and Association of Mutual Funds of India (AMFI) documents

particularly, after the advent of the scientific and technological revolution in the sphere of agriculture, the Government of India and the RBI have evolved several new concepts, innovations and novel approaches, which the Rural Financial Institutions (RFIs) have responded very favourably by implementing them. These are asunder:

- Adoption of multi-agency approach comprising (*a*) short-term and long-term co-operative credit structure (*b*) nationalization of 20 commercial banks in two phases in 1969 and 1980, besides State Bank of India and its seven Associates, and (*c*) establishment of 196 Regional Rural Banks from the year 1975, thereby strengthening the supply side of credit to meet the emerging demand for credit of various sectors of rural economy/poor households.

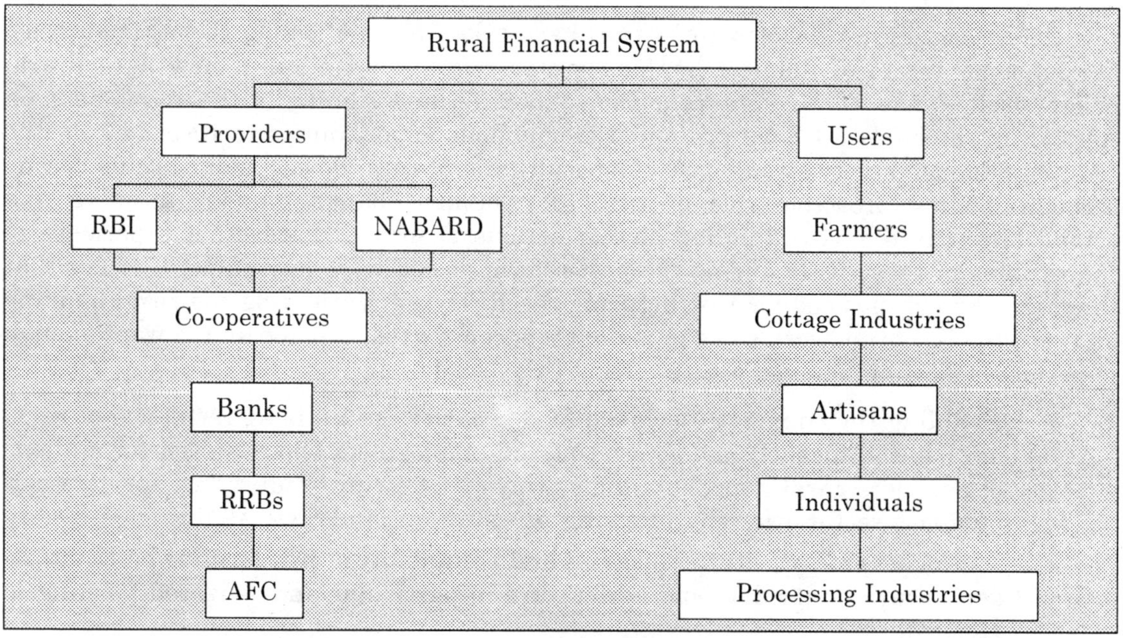


**Fig. 5**

- Established Agricultural Refinance Corporation (1966)/Agricultural Refinance & Development Corporation (1978) which has now been reconstituted as National Bank for Agriculture and Rural Development (National Bank) from the year 1982 to play promotional, development, supervision, co-ordination and institutional building role, augment the resource base of RFI through provision of finance and refinance to primary lending institutions on reasonably liberal terms and several other functions connected with the process of accelerating the pace for agriculture and rural development.
- Introduction of the Lead Bank Scheme in 1972 to provide banking facilities throughout the length and breadth of the country, mobilize financial resources and deploy credit through formulating district credit plans/annual action plans, co-ordinating with developmental agencies and monitoring the performance of RFIs at the level of block, district and state on a quarterly basis for harnessing the productive resources for economic development through provision of credit in each of the districts of the country.
- Adopting of the Service Area Approach (1989) to refine the credit planning exercise at village level, and improving the quality and productivity of lending at the level of individual branch of the RFIs.
- The Rural Infrastructural Development Fund (1995) created at the level of National Bank through mobilizing the shortfall in the deployment of 40% of net bank credit to priority sectors by commercial banks, to provide adequate and qualitative infrastructure for enhancing productivity of capital and labour invested in agriculture.

## RESTRUCTURING NEEDED

Recent significant developments that have taken place affecting the RFIs such as, the implementation of financial/banking sector reforms, adoption of new agricultural policy, draft of the Tenth Five Year Plan (2002-07) and signing of the Agreement on Agriculture under WTO have presented tremendous opportunities to RFIs to help the country establish a very strong base of agriculture and rural development in this decade through playing proactive role of rural development banks, taking initiative and establishing effective co-ordination among various agencies. However, if experience of the working of these RFIs during the post-reform period were any guide, it is felt that there is most urgent need for restructuring the RFIs and reorienting the rural banking and credit policy framework so as to make them committed, capable and vibrant enough to perform following herculean task during this decade.

- Enabling the country to achieve food security, minimizing incidence of rural poverty significantly and generating self-employment opportunities for millions of assetless rural household under tiny/cottage/rural industries, services and business sectors thereby reducing pressure on land/farm sector.
- Improving productivity, productions and profitability of crop farming/horticulture/ sericulture under dry land agriculture in particular and irrigated farming in general.

- Provision of adequate credit to support post-harvest management requirements, *viz.*, agro-processing, storage/preservation, transport, packaging and marketing farm commodities in domestic and international markets.
- Supporting rural and social infrastructure for a sustainable integrated rural development which has suffered quite considerably in the past several years.
- RFIs have to build-up their capacity to manage cost, risk and non-performing assets prudentially while performing the above tasks.

## THE BANKING SYSTEM

The structure of the banking system is determined by two basic factors — economic and legal. The development of the economy and the spread of banking habit calls for increasing banking services. The demand for these banking services affects the banks' structure and organisation. National objectives and aspirations result in government regulations, which have a profound influence on the banking structure. These regulations are basically of two types. First, regulations which result in the formation of new banks to meet the specific needs of a group of economic activities. Secondly, legislation that affects the structure by means of nationalisation, mergers or liquidation.

**Table 3 : Progress of Commercial Banking in India**

| | *June 1969* | *March 2000* | *March 2010* |
|---|---|---|---|
| Public Sector Banks | 22 | 27 | 27 |
| Regional Rural Banks | — | 196 | 88 |
| Foreign Banks | 14 | 44 | 30 |
| Other Scheduled Commercial Banks | 37 | 29 | 26 |
| Total | 73 | 296 | 171 |

The Reserve Bank of India, as the central bank of the country, is at the head of this group. Commercial banks themselves may be divided into two groups, the scheduled and the non-scheduled, the former banks being akin to member banks in the Federal Reserve System of the USA. Their names are included in the Second Schedule of the Reserve Bank of India Act, and they are entitled to borrowing facilities from the Reserve Bank. On their part, they are required to maintain a certain minimum balance in their accounts with the Reserve Bank of India, and do certain other things prescribed by law. They come within the direct influence of the various credit control measures of the Reserve Bank; and the effects of these measures diffuse through the length and breadth of the economy.

**INDIGENOUS BANKING IN INDIA** **BOX : 2**

At independence, India had an indigenous banking system with a centuries-old tradition. This system had developed the *hundi*, a financial instrument still in use that is similar to the commercial bills of Western Europe. *Hundis* were used to finance local trade as well as trade between port towns and inland centres of production. They were often discounted by banks, especially if they were endorsed by indigenous bankers.

Indigenous bankers combined banking with other activities, much as the goldsmiths, merchants, and shippers of eighteenth and nineteenth-century Europe had done. They usually belonged to certain castes or communities, such as the Multanis, Marwaris and Chettiars, and they differed in the extent to which they relied on their own resources, rather than deposits and other funds for their lending. Indigenous bankers often endorsed *hundis* issued by traders and sometimes provided personal guarantees for loans from commercial banks. Such bankers were collectively known as Shroffs, a term that probably originally referred to money changers but overtime came to refer to the more sophisticated and influential indigenous bankers. The main moneylenders were the Sowkars (who lent to farmers from their own resources or funds borrowed from the Chettiars and other indigenous bankers) and the Pathans (who lent mainly to poor people and often resorted to intimidation to ensure repayment).

Indigenous banking was based on an elaborate and extensive network of personal relations that overcame the problems of dealing with a large number of customers. Brokers were used for making introductions and vouching for the creditworthiness of individual borrowers but did not offer personal guarantees. Some brokers specialized in introducing indigenous bankers to commercial banks, while others brought together traders and indigenous bankers.

The commercial banking system may be distinguished into:

## A. Public Sector Banks

| | |
|---|---|
| (*i*) State Bank of India<br>(*ii*) Associate Banks | State Bank Group |
| (*iii*) 14 Nationalised Banks (1969)<br>(*iv*) 6 Nationalised Banks (1980) | Nationalised Banks |
| (*v*) Regional Rural Banks | Mainly sponsored by Public Sector Banks |

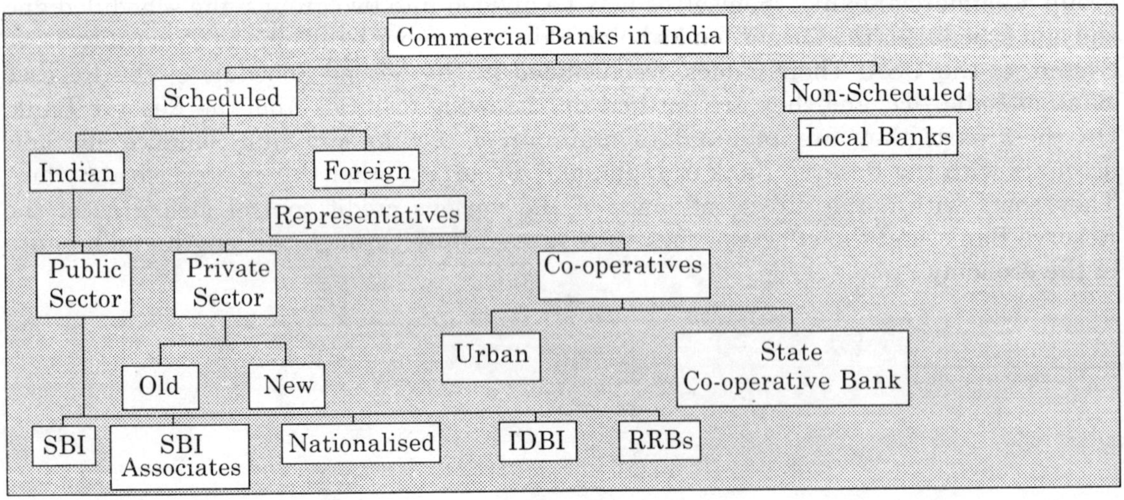


**Fig. 6**

## B. Private Sector Banks

(*i*) Other private banks;

(*ii*) New sophisticated Private Banks;

(*iii*) Co-operative Banks included in the second schedule;

(*iv*) Foreign Banks in India, representative offices; and

(*v*) Non-scheduled Banks (Local Banks)

The banks in the last group are prominent names in the country's foreign trade, of which they once held almost a monopoly, the Indian banks confining themselves to domestic business. In the post-World War II period, major Indian banks have achieved a notable growth, and now occupy an important place in the country's foreign trade. Until the Reserve Bank of India (RBI) came into existence, and for a considerable time afterwards, the State Bank of India (then known as the Imperial Bank of India) used to be a source of financial accommodation to the rest of the banking system, thus performing a part of the functions of the central bank, though not the main central banking function, *viz.*, discretionary control of the credit mechanism. However, with the progress of development plans, and with the growth of demand for bank finance by various sectors of the economy, the quasi-central banking functions of the State Bank of India (SBI) gradually disappeared. On the other hand, the nationalised sector, headed by the State Bank of India, has been given special responsibilities in connection with the development of banking in unbanked areas, and provision of finance to the small-scale industries sector and the co-operative industries sector. In terms of organisation, size and methods of operations, these compare quite favourably with similar institutions in the more developed countries.

The Reserve Bank of India and the commercial banks form the organised money market in India, the core of which is the inter-bank call money market. The rate of interest in this section of the market is the most sensitive indicator of the day-to-day developments in the money market. The market has a host of ancillary institutions, such as call-loan brokers, general finance brokers, stockbrokers, and so on. The unorganised sector of the money market consists largely of indigenous bankers. In the course of time, deposit banking, which was introduced in the thirties of the last century, has come to acquire a position of overwhelming importance in the monetary system of the country. The indigenous bankers have correspondingly lost their importance.

## CO-OPERATIVE SECTOR

The co-operative banking sector has been developed in the country to supplant the village moneylender, the predominant source of rural finance, as the terms on which he made finance available have generally been usurious and detrimental to the development of Indian agriculture. Although the sector receives concessional finance from the Reserve Bank, it is governed by the State legislation. From the point of view of the money market, it may be said to lie between the organised and the unorganised markets.

A very significant feature of the Indian money market (organised and unorganised) is the strong seasonality which derives from the seasonal crop pattern, as a result of which substantial amounts of funds are required during the busy season, lasting approximately between November-April,

(*a*) To finance the movement of crops from the producing to consuming centres within the country; and

(*b*) To finance exports based on agricultural commodities. This leads to an expansion of bank credit.

During the next six months, May-October, the funds return to the banking system and bank credit contracts. Although as a result of the process of industrial development and other factors, this pattern is modified somewhat, the seasonality still persists to a marked degree. As will be seen later, it has an important bearing on the Bank's credit control policy.

The co-operative banking structure comprises urban and rural co-operative banks. While urban co-operative banks (UCBs) have a single tier structure, rural co-operative credit institutions comprise two distinct structures: the short-term and the long-term. The short-term structure, comprises Primary Agricultural Credit Societies (PACs) at the village level, District Central Co-operative Banks (DCCBs) at the intermediate level and State Co-operative Banks (StCBs) at the apex level.

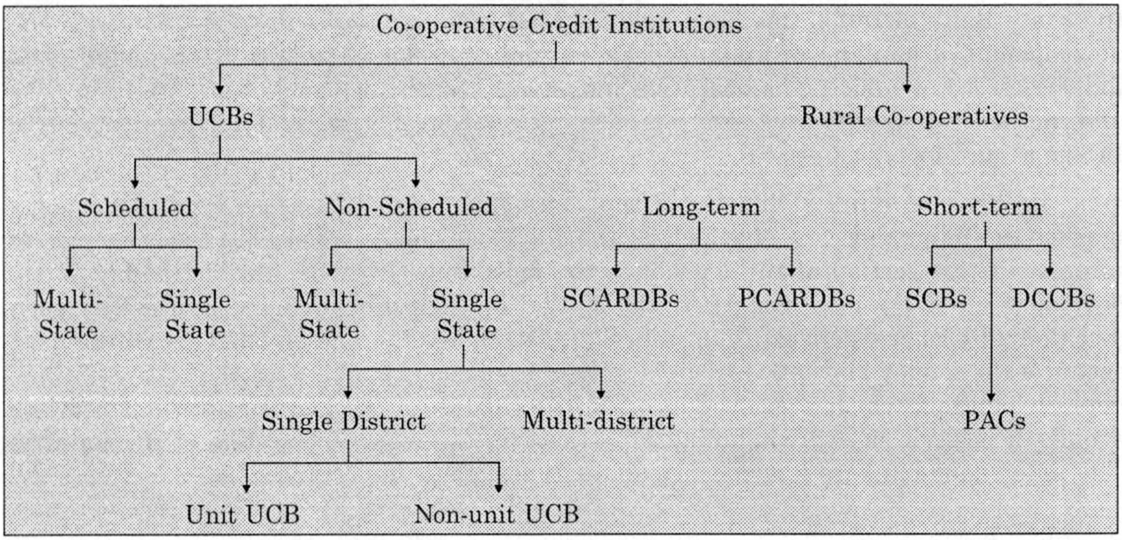


**Fig. 7 : Structure of Co-operative Banking Sector**

*Source:* RBI

The co-operative banking structure in India is also divided into four component parts:

## Primary Co-operative Credit Societies

The primary co-operative credit society is an association of borrowers and non-borrowers residing in a particular locality. The funds of the society are derived from the share capital and deposits of members and loans from Central Co-operative Banks.

The borrowing power of the members as well as of the society is fixed. The loans are given to members for the purchase of cattle, fodder, fertilisers, pesticides, implements, etc.

## Central Co-operative Banks

These are the federations of primary credit societies in a district, and are of two types — those having a membership of primary societies only and those having a membership of societies as well as individuals. The funds of the bank consist of share capital, deposits, loans and overdrafts from State Co-operative Banks and joint stocks. These banks finance member societies within the limits of the borrowing capacity of societies. They also conduct all the business of a joint-stock bank.

## State Co-operative Banks

The State Co-operative Banks is a federation of central co-operative banks and acts as a watchdog of the co-operative banking structure in the state. Its funds are obtained from share capital, deposits, loans and overdrafts from the Reserve Bank of India. The State co-operative banks lend money to central co-operative banks and primary societies and not directly to farmers.

## Land Development Banks

The Land Development Banks, which are organised in three tiers, namely, State, Central and Primary level, meet the long-term credit requirements of farmers for developmental purposes, *viz.,* purchase of equipment like pump sets, tractors and other machineries, reclamation of land, fencing, digging up new wells and repairs of old wells, etc. Land Development Banks are co-operative institutions and they grant loans on the security of mortgage of immovable property of the farmers. These banks have a two-tier organisational structure — at the state level, there are Central Land Development Banks and at the district or taluka level, there are Primary Land Development Banks. In some states like Gujarat, Jammu & Kashmir and UP, the structure is unitary, i.e., there are Apex Land Development Banks which operate directly through their own branches at the district level.

The financial resources of the Central Land Development Banks are raised by floating debentures in the market. Such debentures carry the guarantee of the State Government and are subscribed by the Central and State Governments, Commercial Banks, Life Insurance Corporation and other Land Development Banks as a measure of mutual support. Land Development Banks also avail of the refinancing facilities provided by the National Bank for Agriculture and Rural Development (NABARD) in respect of the term loans granted by them for the schemes of agricultural development. They also secure short-term accommodation from the State Governments, Commercial Banks and the State Co-operative Banks.

**MICROFINANCE INSTITUTIONS** **BOX : 3**

Microfinance institutions (MFI) are of utmost importance for financial inclusion, as these institutions connect with the people constituting the lowest state of the society. It is obvious that when MFI targest customers with no recorded credit history, it increases the risk for its business as well. It is due to this inherent risk and lack of awareness that it was extremely difficult for MFI to raise money.

**Mukesh Gandhi,**
Director,
Finance MAS Financial

There was a time when donor agencies and a handful of private individuals were the only two sources of funding for MFI. A lot has changed since then. Today, a number of funds also invest in such institutions. The potential in this business is huge as more than 50% of Indians still does not have bank account. This made various professional investors and fund managers consider investments in MFI.

It was an uphill task though, as market have not reached a consensus with regard to valuation of investments in MFIs. This is because such investments are not traded and there is no market for the same. In the absence of a market, such investments are valued on the basis of their networks and the potential they have in a lifetime.

A wayside tea stall owner in Gujarat wears a big smile. His loan of ₹ 20,000 has been sanctioned within 48 hours, without which he would have been literally on the streets. He is not alone. There are several others including a ladies garment store owner, a bakery owner, snack shop owner and vendors who are happy for a similar reason.

Individual lending of microfinance is gaining speed and in the process changing many lives, that too within two days. Microfinance institutions such as MAS Financial Services and Bandhan target a group of people just above 'the poorest-of-the-poor' and help them graduate upwards while maintaining a high repayment rate of 98-99 per cent.

Through individual lending, MAS has mobilised banking culture among people in Gujarat and has also expanded its network to Maharashtra and Rajasthan spread over 60 branches. Bandhan has a significant presence in the North-East besides West Bengal, Bihar and is slowly expanding to Delhi and Mumbai.

## Development Banks

Another important feature of the structure and organisation of Indian banking system is the establishment of many financial corporations, which provide finance to those sectors of the economy to which commercial banks do not provide finance.

It becomes difficult for commercial banks to participate in the financing of long-term requirements of the industry. Mixed banking also has certain disadvantages. Although mixed banking has been successful in Germany and some other countries, it cannot be relied upon in a developing country like India, where banking habits are still in a nascent stage. At best, our bigger banks can resort to term lending in a limited way. Therefore, certain special institutions are necessary to handle the problem of long-term financing of industries. Broadly speaking, such institutions are known as "Development Banks".

Medium-and long-term finance is provided mainly by a few large development banks with all-India status, and state level institutions in the various states. For each category of term financing activity, an apex all-India development bank has been promoted — Industrial Development Bank of India, National Bank for Agriculture and Rural Development, Export-Import Bank of India, National Housing Bank, etc. Besides these development banks, All-India investment institutions such as Unit Trust of India, Life Insurance Corporation, General Insurance Corporation also play a major role in channelling financing savings to the industrial and other sectors. There are besides, institutions exclusively supporting tourism, small-scale industry, etc. In recent years, a number of public sector mutual funds set up by banks and financial institutions have been added to the institutional framework. Para-banking activities, mainly in the area of hire-purchase and leasing are undertaken by newly set up large number of private sector non-banking financial companies.

## FINANCIAL MARKETS

Financial markets in India have seen considerable development since financial sector reforms were initiated in the 1990s. Given the imperatives of the prevailing context, the initial nudge had to be provided through specific policy instruments and actions, but over a period of time these markets have acquired a dynamic of their own. The process of transition in respect of all financial market segments has been largely disruption-free, accommodating the unique features of the existing system while trying to align with the best international practices.

Assessed purely in terms of outcomes, the movement towards achieving the intended objectives of improving the allocative efficiency of resources, ensuring financial stability and maintaining confidence in the financial system by enhancing its soundness and efficiency has been undoubtedly positive. The current situation provides an ideal vantage point for undertaking a review of the process and preparing a guide for future direction.

Indian financial markets can be broadly categorised into the money market, foreign exchange market, government securities market, equity market, corporate bond market and credit market. While equity, government securities, foreign exchange and money markets along with their corresponding derivative segments have developed into reasonably deep and liquid markets, credit derivative markets are yet to take-off in any significant manner. As regards corporate bonds, while primary issuances have been significant, though concentrated in terms of issuers to public sector financial institutions, these have largely been on a private placement basis and the secondary market has not developed commensurately. The Reserve Bank's Report on Currency and Finance 2005-06, delineates the approaches for making financial markets in India more developed, efficient and integrated in light of the experience gained so far and keeping in view international best practices while recognising the country context.

The capital market has evidenced tremendous growth in the last decade in terms of resource mobilisation, listing and market capitalisation. Activities in a network of twenty-four stock exchanges listing over six thousand companies, are being regulated by the special purpose institution — Securities & Exchange Board of India (SEBI). The development of short-term money market has, however, lagged behind that of other sub-sectors of the market. It comprises five segments — the call money market, inter-bank term deposit market, bills rediscounting market, treasury bills market and the inter-corporate funds market.

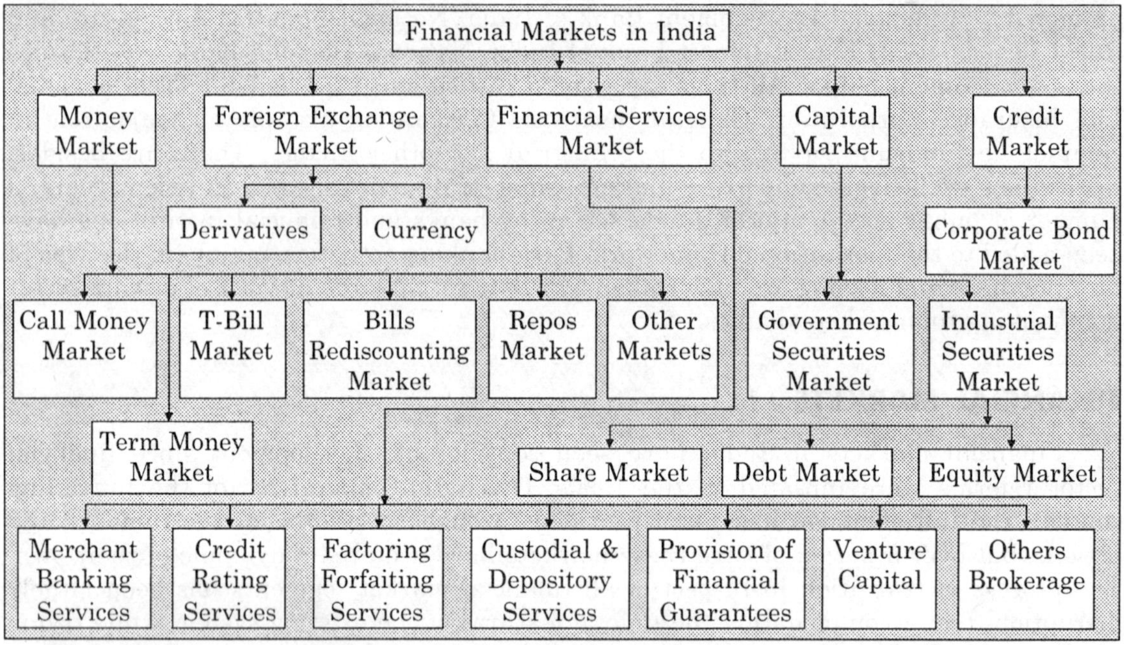


**Fig. 8**

The Discount & Finance House of India Ltd., (DFHI) is the leader of the money market, namely, of money overnight to a fortnight in the case of inter-bank market, money for a few days to a few months in the case of treasury bills, commercial bills, commercial paper, etc. Since 1992, DFHI has been permitted to operate in the government securities also. SEBI was empowered in 1992 to regulate legally all intermediaries and operations in the stock and capital markets. Stock brokers, dealers and a host of other intermediaries, controlled and regulated by the RBI and SEBI are part of the organised financial system in India. The RBI is the leader in the money market and SEBI is the regulator in the capital market in the organised system.

Mutual funds, both in the public and private sectors, play a key role in mobilising savings and in the market operations.

The interrelations and relevant submarkets are visually shown in the chart below:

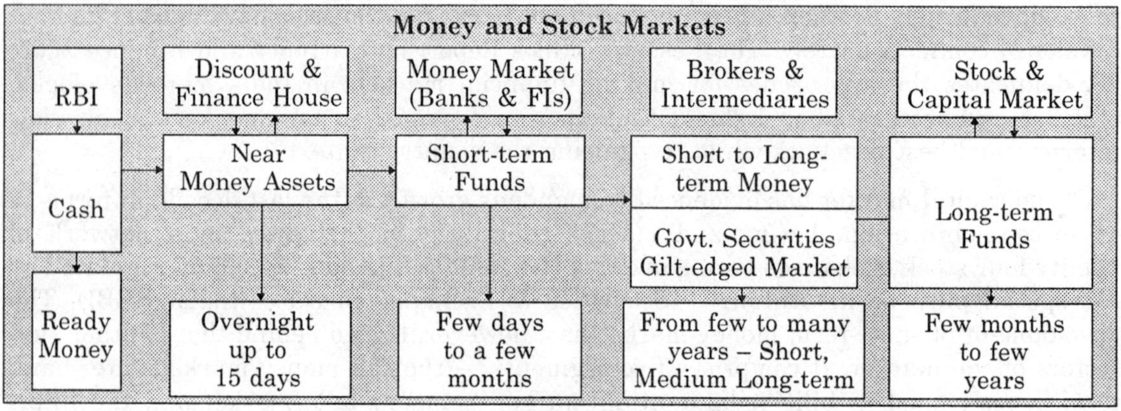


**Fig. 9**

## DEVELOPMENT OF FINANCIAL MARKET

The importance of developing appropriate financial institutions and financial markets in promoting economic growth can be hardly overemphasized. Central banks in emerging markets have made conscious efforts towards developing efficient markets and institutions in recent years, especially after some weaknesses in the system were revealed during several financial crises that occurred in the 1990s in different parts of the world. There is a growing recognition among central bankers around the world that a well-functioning financial market enables efficient use of market-based instruments of monetary policy by improving interest rate signal in the economy. Apart from enhancing the efficiency of monetary policy, deep and well functioning financial markets promote mobilization of domestic savings and improve the allocative efficiency of financial intermediation, and foster the necessary conditions to emerge as an international of a regional financial centre (Turner and t'dack 1996). Strong domestic financial markets also act as a buffer against external disturbances and help in observing shocks to the domestic banking system during crises. Further, they provide incentives for development of hedging instruments, and lower macroeconomic volatility and financial instability. Efficient financial markets also have several indirect benefits such as rapid accumulation of physical and human capital, more stable investment financing, and faster technological progress.

Financial market development is a complex and time-consuming process. There are no short cuts for developing well-functioning markets with depth and liquidity (Tarapore, 2000). Some of the preconditions for financial market reforms are macroeconomic stability sound and efficient financial institutions and structure, prudential regulation and supervision, strong creditor rights, and contract enforcement. Measures to improve market infrastructure must be implemented at an early stage of reform alongside appropriate legal framework. These conditions facilitate growth of financial transactions including inter-bank transactions and active liquidity management. At the same time, there are at least three major macroeconomic features which can inhibit reform of domestic financial markets. First, large government deficits can crowd out financing of the private sector thereby inhibiting the growth of corporate debt markets. Second, high and variable inflation rates and unrealistic exchange rates also stifle the financial markets by raising uncertainties about the risks and returns to financial activity. Third financial repression policies such as high inflation taxation, high required reserve ratios, subsidized or directed credit programmes, credit rationing, and ceilings on deposit and loan interest rates also hinder financial market development.

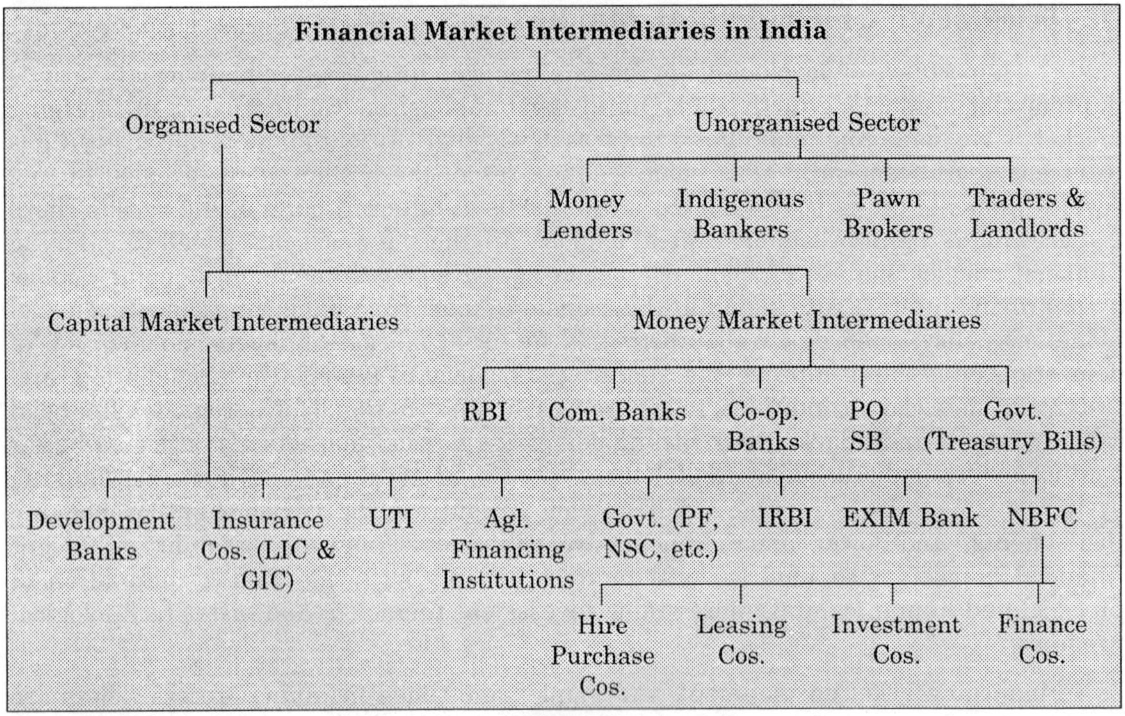


**Fig. 10**

## FINANCIAL COMPANIES

These investment and finance companies, housing finance, chit funds, etc., also mobilise and channel savings into investment. They are only partly controlled by the Reserve Bank in respect of resource mobilisation through deposits. For the rest of their activities, they are controlled and regulated like any other company by the Registrar of Companies, under the Companies Act. Similarly, moneylenders and indigenous bankers are licenced under the state laws and regulated by the state agencies. But there is hardly any system of regulation on them worth the name.

While the capital market is a wider term encompassing all long-term borrowings and lendings, issue of long-term securities, and all unsecuritised debts of long-term nature, the new issue market in particular relates to the new issues of marketable securities by existing or new companies. These two together fall into the organised financial system.

### A. Apex Financial Institutions

(1) Reserve Bank of India — Apex Central Bank

(2) National Bank for Agriculture and Rural Development — Agriculture

(3) Industrial Development Bank of India — Industry

(4) Small Industries Development Bank of India — Small Sector

(5) Export-Import Bank of India — Foreign Trade

(6) Khadi and Village Industries Commission — Khadi and Village Industries

(7) National Housing Bank — Housing

(8) Securities and Exchange Board of India — Capital Market, Mutual Funds, Merchant Banks and Other Institutions.

(9) The Insurance Regulatory and Development Authority (IRDA)

(10) The Pension Fund Regulatory and Development Authority (PFRDA) – Pension

(11) Post Office — Small savings.

(12) Securities Appellate Tribunal (SAT) – Arbitration Authority.

## B. Agriculture

(1) Agriculture Finance Consultants

## C. Capital Markets

(1) Discount and Finance House of India Ltd., (DHFI)

(2) Investor Services of India

(3) National Stock Exchange of India (NSE)

(4) OTC Exchange of India (OTCEI)

(5) Stock Exchanges (Regional)

(6) Stock Holding Corporation of India (SHCl)

(7) National Depository Corporation of India Ltd., (NDCIL)

(8) Indian Securities Depository Nominee Company Ltd., (ISDNCL)

(9) Investor Services of India Ltd., (ISI)

(10) Central Depository Company (CDC)

(11) Securities Trading Corporation of India Ltd., (STCI)

(12) National Securities Depository Ltd., (NSD)

(13) MCX' Exchange (MCX'SX)

(14) United Stock Exchange (USE)

(15) Bombay Stock Exchange (BSE)

(16) Primary Dealers (PDs)

## D. Commercial Banks

(1) Public Sector:

   (*i*) State Bank of India

   (*ii*) Associate Banks

   (*iii*) 14 Nationalised Banks (1969)

   (*iv*) 6 Nationalised Banks (1980)

   (*v*) Regional Rural Banks

(2) Private Sector:

(*i*) Foreign Banks in India

(*ii*) Private Sector Banks

(*iii*) New Private Banks

(*iv*) Non-scheduled Banks (Local Banks)

(*v*) Scheduled Co-operative Banks

## E. Consultancy

(1) Technical Consultancy Organisations

(2) Merchant Banks

(3) Financial Companies

(4) Non-financial Companies

## F. Co-operative Sectors

(1) State Co-operative Banks

(2) Central Co-operative Banks

(3) Primary Agriculture Credit Societies

(4) Urban Co-operative Banks

(5) Land Development Banks

(6) Primary Agricultural Development Banks

(7) Primary Land Development Banks

(8) State Land Development Banks

## G. Credit Rating Agencies

(1) Credit Analysis and Research Ltd., (CARE)

(2) Credit Rating Information Services of India Ltd., (CRISIL)

(3) Investment Information and Credit Rating Agency of India Ltd., (ICRA)

(4) Duff & Phelps Credit Rating India Pvt. Ltd., (DCR India)

(5) Credit Information Burea of India Ltd., (CIBIL)

## H. Housing

(1) Housing Development Finance Corporation

(2) LIC Housing Finance

(3) GIC Housing Finance

(4) SBI Housing Finance

(5) Housing Finance Companies set up by Banks

(6) Other Housing Finance Companies

(7) Housing and Urban Development Corporation
(8) National Housing Bank

## I. Industrial

(1) ICICI Bank
(2) Industrial Finance Corporation of India (IFCI)
(3) Infrastructure Leasing & Financial Services
(4) Industrial Investment Bank of India
(5) Khadi & Village Industries Commission
(6) National Small Industries Corporation
(7) Risk Capital and Technology Finance Corporation
(8) Infrastructure Finance Development Company (IFDC)
(9) State Financial Corporations
(10) Specialised Financial Institutions
(11) State Industrial Development Corporations
(12) State Small Industries Development Corporations
(13) Technology Development and Information Company of India
(14) Tourism Finance Corporation of India
(15) Venture Capital Institutions
(16) Lease & Hire Purchasing Companies
(17) Factoring Companies
(18) North Eastern Development Finance Corporation Limited

## J. Insurance & Credit Guarantee

(1) Deposit Insurance and Credit Guarantee Corporation (DICGC)
(2) Export Credit Guarantee Corporation of India (ECGC)
(3) Agricultural Insurance Corporation of India Ltd., (AICIL)

## K. Investment

(1) General Insurance Corporation of India (GIC)
(2) Life Insurance Corporation of India (LIC)
(3) Unit Trust of India (UTI)
(4) Merchant Banks
(5) Mutual Funds
(6) Asset Management Companies
(7) Investment Companies
(8) Insurance Companies ( 21 life and 20 non-life in the private sector)

## L. Others

(*i*) Government

(1) National Savings Corporation

(2) Post Office Savings Banks

(3) Employees Provident Fund

(4) Public Provident Fund

(*ii*) Private Sector

(1) Chit Funds

(2) *Nidhis*

(3) Hire Purchase Companies

(4) Indigenous Bankers

(5) Moneylenders

(6) Microfinance Institutions

## FINANCIAL INTERMEDIARIES

Financial intermediaries are the institutions which collect savings from others, issuing in return claims against themselves, and use the funds thus acquired to purchase ownership or debt claims, such as: banks, financial institutions, investment institutions and financial intermediaries. They are interposed between ultimate borrowers and lenders to acquire the primary securities of borrowers and provide other securities for the portfolios of lenders. Their outstanding feature is that they issue to savers claims whose characteristics are quite different from those that they buy and hold. They do not merely intermediate, but in the process they also create higher degree of safety and liquidity. Their basic function is to satisfy simultaneously the portfolio preferences of lenders and borrowers.

The increasing differentiation of financial assets tends to promote the development of financial structure. New types of financial assets are created to suit the needs of different spending units and a variegated structure of financial intermediaries emerges out in a rapidly developing economy. Markets for goods and markets for securities are simultaneously the media through which spending units seek optimal adjustment between income and spending, net worth and wealth.

Financial intermediaries play a very important role in the saving-investment process by raising the level of saving and investment and allocating more efficiently scarce savings among most productive investments. Commercial banks, which are one of the oldest financial intermediaries, often fall short of the diversified requirements of ultimate savers and investors. This creates a favourable climate for the emergence and growth of NFI. The new specialised types of financial assets are created to suit the demand structure and an array of new types of financial intermediaries are established to meet the demand for increasing specialisation.

A satisfactory classification of financial intermediaries will vary from place-to-place and time-to-time. Generally, they are grouped under five different categories as follows:

(1) The banking system (Central Bank, Commercial Banks, Co-operative Banks, Savings Banks, etc.)

(2) Other depository organisations (mutual funds, savings and loan associations, credit unions, etc.)

(3) Insurance organisations (Life Insurance, General Insurance, Postal Insurance, Pension Funds, Provident Funds, etc.)

(4) Development Banks, and

(5) Other financial intermediaries (investment and finance companies, stock exchanges and other related intermediaries.)

Function of the financial system is the sum total of functions of varied financial intermediaries. The functions of the financial system extend from creation of money to proper management. It touches all aspects of the economy.

Let us recapulate the functions of key financial intermediaries to have a broad view of the functions of the financial system.

## ROLE OF THE GOVERNMENT

In the Indian context, the government initiated the process of remodelling the financial system to ensure that resources were allocated in accordance with their development strategies. Towards this end, the government nationalised banks, created new financial institutions, directed other financial institutions to channelise their resources to the sectors that are to be at the forefront of industrial development. The government also set up specialised supervisory as well as refinance apex institutions to foster the development of agriculture, industry, small-scale sector, exports, rural industries, housing, leasing, merchant banks and mutual funds. The government also borrowed heavily, both from the domestic financial system and abroad, to finance budget deficits and the needs of the state-owned undertakings in the core sectors. This apart, the government directly participates in mobilising resources through its agencies like post office and provident funds and/or pension funds. Through the post office, it also operates small savings, supplemented by the National Savings Organisation. In addition, post office offers savings bank and insurance schemes and services.

## IDENTIFY INSTITUTIONAL PROBLEMS

The first step is recognizing when institutional inadequacies are to blame for problems in developing countries. This means asking which institution is missing or not working properly. Here, we define institutions as rules (informal customs as well as laws) that govern behaviour, the mechanisms (often organizations or reputations) that enforce these rules, and the organizations (for example, clubs and banks) that affect peoples' incentives and support market transactions.

We have learned that attention needs to be focussed, first, on the *functions* that institutions need to perform, and, second, on a particular institutional *design* or *structure*. Institutions that support market transactions perform three functions, smoothing information asymmetrics (that is, ensuring that all market participants have access to reliable information), defining and enforcing property rights and contracts, and regulating competition.

By focussing on needed functions, governments can figure out whether the problems they face are caused by institutional failures and, if so, what kind. An Eastern European country found that its small and medium-sized firms were unable to obtain financing, even though it had created special banks to provide financing to these type of firms. The special banks proved to be risk averse and did not want to lend to smaller enterprises. What the country really needed was not specialized banks but an institution that decreased lenders perception of risk or reassured them that they would be able to recover their loans — for example, a court that enforced small claims.

Once it is decided what type of institution is needed, the next step is getting the right design and building consensus for reform. For some reforms, the demand is already there, for others, various groups might need to be convinced, and for still others, there is neither opposition nor support. But one thing is certain: institutional change never occurs in a vacuum. It alters the impact of existing laws, so identifying the groups or individuals the new institutions with affect, is critical. At least in the short-term, there are likely to be losers as well as winners. It is also important for policymakers to be aware of the incentives the new institutions will create — that is, the rewards and penalties for not complying with new rules and regulations — which will be heavily influenced by the kinds of institutions that exist already.

## EMERGING FINANCIAL SYSTEM

In the years to come that is the dawn of the 21st century, there is no doubt that the Indian financial system will grow in size and complexity. Different segments of the market will become closely linked and it will become difficult to influence or act on only one segment without affecting others. The major link connecting the various segments will be the interest rate as is the case in many of the industrially advanced countries now. In order to influence the entire system, the monetary authorities will have to act on interest rates. There will be increasing specialisation; simultaneously there can emerge financial conglomerates dealing in different financial products and services. The existence of healthy and sound financial institutions should be able to put pressure on investors and other borrowers, to use resources in an efficient and productive manner in order to repay the existing obligations and qualify for new finances.

Banks will begin to function increasingly under competitive pressures. These pressures may emanate from within the banking system as well as from non-banking institutions. With the increasing participation of private shareholders even in public sector banks, there will be greater accountability to shareholders, including the government. Competitive pressures can also result in some degree of consolidation.

Another area which will become important relates to regulatory harmonisation among various regulators, both domestic and international, of the financial markets including capital markets. Regulators will have to increase efforts towards converging their policies and procedures and have a greater element of information share.

The role of financial supervision in a system that is rapidly emerging as market based is an important one. The current supervisory approach emphasises follow-ups and compliance by the financial intermediaries with banking policy and credit allocative directives and foreign exchange regulations.

In the changing circumstances, bank supervisors will have to focus on issues which ensure the safety and soundness of the system, depositor protection and reduction of systematic risk. These are issues which will have important monetary policy implications. Ensuring compliance with prudential norms will be a major task. The supervisory system has a two-fold task: it must be responsive to changes that are occurring in the financial markets and it must simultaneously instil confidence in the integrity and soundness of the markets and the participants in the market.

## CONCLUSION

The Indian financial system is broad-based, yet inadequate and less efficient. Efficient financial systems will help India to grow, partly by mobilising additional financial resources and partly by allocating these resources to the best uses. As economies develop, so must the financial systems that serve them. The next chapter illustrates the central role of finance in development by reviewing the macroeconomic dimensions of the financial system, *viz.*, institutions, instruments and markets.

Further, different segments of the market will become closely linked making it difficult to influence or act on only one segment without affecting others. The major link connecting the various segments will be the interest rate as is the case in many of the industrially advanced countries now. In order to influence the entire financial system, the monetary authorities will have to act on interest rates. There will be increasing specialisation; simultaneously, there can emerge financial conglomerates dealing in different financial products and services. The existence of healthy and sound financial institutions should be able to put pressure on investors and other borrowers, to use resources in an efficient and productive manner in order to repay the existing obligations and qualify for new finances for major projects.

Most industrial countries have encouraged the development of government bond markets, so that they can finance their public sector deficits in a non-inflationary way, and have established or revived their money markets, so that monetary and credit control can be achieved through open market operations. All this marks a considerable shift in the balance of power from governments to financial markets. In addition, equity markets have been reformed to allow commercial banks to play an active part as market makers and securities houses, and new markets with less demanding listing requirements have been created for smaller companies. Governments have used fiscal incentives to stimulate venture capital and personal investments in mutual funds and equities. Financial futures and traded options markets have been established to allow hedging against the greater volatility in exchange rates, interest rates, and equity prices that followed the move to floating exchange rates and the use of indirect methods to control money and credit.

**Chart - 2 : Schematic Presentation of Function of the Financial System**

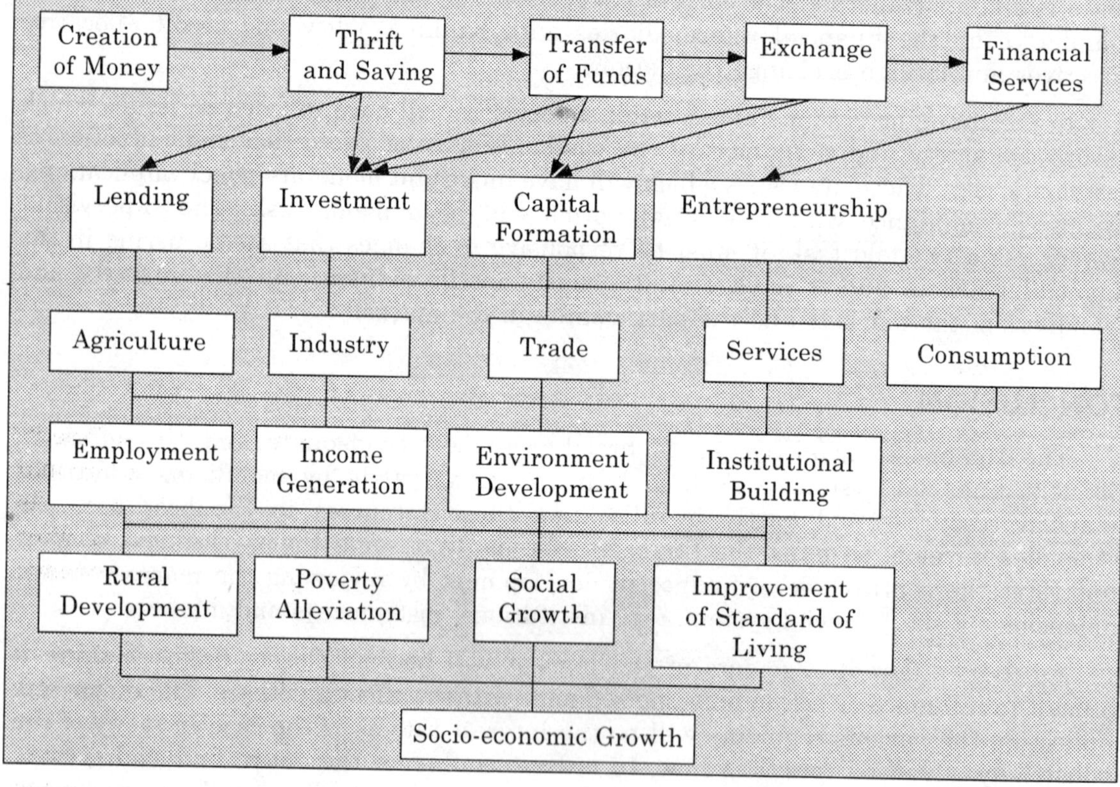


Recent years have also witnessed a major expansion in international transactions fuelled by the accumulation of insurance and pension reserves and the liberalization and modernization of stock exchanges. As in the nineteenth century, however, this expansion of capital flows has exerted a destabilizing influence on markets, because foreign investors tend to repatriate their funds in troubled times.

Effective competition in banking, especially for corporate business, has increased with the opening of domestic markets and the creation of specialized non-bank financial intermediaries. But retail banking has also become more competitive, because commercial banks are turning toward the household sector and offering new credit, deposit and payment instruments.

Deregulation has eliminated many of the man-made barriers to global finance, and technology has lowered the barriers imposed by nature. Advances in computing, information processing, and telecommunications have boosted the volume of business by reducing transaction costs, expanding the scope of trading and creating information systems that enable institutions to control their risk more efficiently.

Deregulation, technology and other common trends have caused a growing convergence of national financial systems. Universal banks and specialized institutions as well as institutional investors and securities markets all now play important part in the financial systems of most high-income countries. Nowhere is this convergence more evident than in Japan, which has successfully expanded the non-banking segments of its financial system to the point that it now has the largest securities houses and stock market in the world, as well as the largest commercial banks, postal savings bank, and housing finance institutions.

The trend of convergence has been reinforced by the vast accumulation of financial assets by both households and corporations in most high-income countries. This under scores the growing importance of the financial sector as a service industry and its shift from the mobilization and reallocation of existing resources.

## ANNEXURE : A

### LIST OF STATE FINANCIAL CORPORATIONS (SFCs)

| *Sr. No.* | *Name of the SFC* | *State of Operation* |
|---|---|---|
| 1. | Andhra Pradesh State Financial Corporation (APSFC) | Andhra Pradesh |
| 2. | Assam Financial Corporation (AFC) | Assam |
| 3. | Bihar State Financial Corporation (BSFC) | Bihar |
| 4. | Delhi Financial Corporation (DFC) | Delhi |
| 5. | Gujarat State Financial Corporation (GSFC) | Gujarat |
| 6. | Haryana Financial Corporation (HFC) | Haryana |
| 7. | Himachal Pradesh Financial Corporation (HPFC) | Himachal Pradesh |
| 8. | Jammu & Kashmir State Financial Corporation (JKSFC) | Jammu |
| 9. | Karnataka State Financial Corporation (KSFC) | Karnataka |
| 10. | Kerala Financial Corporation (KFC) | Kerala |
| 11. | Maharashtra State Financial Corporation (MSFC) | Maharashtra |
| 12. | Madhya Pradesh Financial Corporation (MPFC) | Madhya Pradesh |
| 13. | Orissa State Financial Corporation (OSFC) | Orissa |
| 14. | Punjab Financial Corporation (PFC) | Punjab |
| 15. | Rajasthan Financial Corporation (RFC) | Rajasthan |
| 16. | The Tamil Nadu Industrial Investment Corporation Ltd., (TIIC) | Tamil Nadu |
| 17. | Uttar Pradesh Financial Corporation (UPFC) | Uttar Pradesh |
| 18. | West Bengal Financial Corporation (WBFC) | West Bengal |

## ANNEXURE : B

### LIST OF STATE INDUSTRIAL DEVELOPMENT CORPORATION (SIDCs)

| Sr. No. | Name of the SIDC | State of Operation |
|---|---|---|
| 1. | Assam Industrial Development Corporation Ltd., (AIDC) | Assam |
| 2. | The Andaman & Nicobar Islands Integrated Development Corporation Ltd., (ANIIDCO) | Andaman & Nicobar |
| 3. | Andhra Pradesh Industrial Development Corporation Ltd., (APIDC) | Andhra Pradesh |
| 4. | Arunachal Pradesh Industrial Development & Financial Corporation Ltd., | Arunachal Pradesh |
| 5. | Bihar State Credit and Investment Corporation Ltd., (BSCIC) | Bihar |
| 6. | EDC Ltd., | Goa |
| 7. | Gujarat Industrial Investment Corporation Ltd., (GIIC) | Gujarat |
| 8. | Haryana State Industrial Development Corporation Ltd., (HSIDC) | Haryana |
| 9. | The Himachal Pradesh State Industrial Development Corporation Ltd., (HPSIDC) | Himachal Pradesh |
| 10. | Industrial Promotion and Investment Corporation of Orissa Ltd., (IPICOL) Orissa | |
| 11. | The Jammu and Kashmir State Industrial Development Corporation Ltd., (J&K SIDCO) | Srinagar, Jammu |
| 12. | Karnataka State Industrial Investment & Development Corporation Ltd., (KSIIDC) | Karnataka |
| 13. | Kerala State Industrial Development Corporation Ltd., (KSIDC) | Kerala |
| 14. | Manipur Industrial Development Corporation Ltd., (MANIDCO) | Manipur |
| 15. | Meghalaya Industrial Development Corporation Ltd., (MIDC) | Meghalaya |
| 16. | Nagaland Industrial Development Corporation Ltd., (NIDC) | Nagaland |
| 17. | Omnibus Industrial Development Corporation of Daman & Diu and Dadra & Nagar Haveli Ltd., (OIDC) | Daman |
| 18. | Madhya Pradesh State Industrial Development Corporation Ltd., (MPSIDC) | Madhya Pradesh |
| 19. | Pondicherry Industrial Promotion Development and Investment Corporation Ltd., (PIPDIC) | Pondicherry |
| 20. | The Pradeshiya Industrial and Investment Corporation of UP Ltd., (PICUP) | Uttar Pradesh |
| 21. | Punjab State Industrial Development Corporation Ltd., (PSIDC) | Punjab |
| 22. | Rajasthan State Industrial Development & Investment Corporation Ltd., (RIICO) | Rajasthan |
| 23. | SICOM Ltd., | Maharashtra |
| 24. | Sikkim Industrial Development & Investment Corporation Ltd., (SIDICO) | Sikkim |
| 25. | State Industries Promotion Corporation of Tamil Nadu Ltd., (SIPCOT) | Tamil Nadu |
| 26. | Tripura Industrial Development Corporation Ltd., (TIDC) | Tripura |
| 27. | West Bengal Industrial Development Corporation Ltd., (WBIDC) | West Bengal |
| 28. | Zoram Industrial Development Corporation Ltd., (ZIDCO) | Mizoram |

## ANNEXURE: C

### LIST OF TECHNICAL CONSULTANCY ORGANISATIONS

| Sr. No. | Name of the TCO Establishment | Year of Operation | State/Union Territory Financial Institution | Lead Sponsoring |
|---|---|---|---|---|
| 1. | APITCO Ltd., | 1976 | Andhra Pradesh | IDBI |
| 2. | Bihar Industrial & Technical Consultancy Organisation Ltd., (BITCO) | 1974 | Bihar | IDBI |
| 3. | Gujarat Industrial & Technical Consultancy Organisation Ltd., (GITCO) | 1978 | Gujarat | CICI |
| 4. | Haryana-Delhi Industrial Consultants Ltd., (HARDICON) | 1985 | Haryana and Delhi | IFCI |
| 5. | Himachal Consultancy Organisation Ltd., (HIMCON) | 1977 | Himachal Pradesh | IFCI |
| 6. | Industrial & Technical Consultancy Organisation of Tamil Nadu Ltd., (ITCOT) | 1979 | Tamil Nadu | ICICI |
| 7. | Jammu & Kashmir Industrial & Technical Consultancy Organisation Ltd., (J&K ITCO) | 1977 | Jammu & Kashmir | IDBI |
| 8. | KITCO Ltd., | 1972 | Kerala | IDBI |
| 9. | Madhya Pradesh Consultancy Organisation Ltd., (MPCON) | 1979 | Madhya Pradesh | IFCI |
| 10. | MITCO Consultancy Services Ltd., (MITCON) | 1982 | Maharashtra, Goa, Daman & Diu | ICICI |
| 11. | North-Eastern Industrial Consultants Ltd., (NECON) | 1987 | North-Eastern Region | IDBI |
| 12. | North-Eastern Industrial & Technical Consultancy Organisation Ltd., (NEITCO) | 1973 | Nagaland, Manipur, Tripura and Mizoram | IDBI |
| 13. | North India Technical Consultancy (NITCON) Organisation Ltd., | 1984 | Punjab and Chandigarh | IFCI |
| 14. | Orissa Industrial & Technical Consultancy Organisation Ltd., (ORITCO) | 1976 | Orissa | IDBI |
| 15. | Rajasthan Consultancy Organisation Ltd., (RAJCON) | 1978 | Rajasthan | IFCI |
| 16. | UP Industrial Consultants Ltd., (UPICO) | 1974 | Uttar Pradesh | IDBI |
| 17. | West Bengal Consultancy Organisation Ltd., (WEBCON) | 1979 | West Bengal, Sikkim, Andaman and Nicobar Islands | IDBI |
| 18. | Technical Consultancy Service Organisation of Karnataka (TECSOK) | 1977 | Karnataka | Sponsored by Govt. of Karnataka |

CHAPTER 3

# THE RESERVE BANK OF INDIA

## INTRODUCTION

While financial institutions and financial markets are two generic mechanisms for transferring resources from the surplus sectors to deficit sectors, their relative significance varies from country-to-country. In the context of the underdeveloped capital market in India, financial intermediaries or institutions have traditionally played a predominant role in meeting the fund requirements of various sectors in the form of credit and investment. The major institutional purveyors of credit in India are banks (commercial banks and co-operative banks), BFIs and NBFCs. Traditionally, banks and NBFCs predominantly extended short-term credit and DFIs mainly provided medium and long-term loans. Insurance companies and mutual funds provided medium to long-term loans. Insurance companies and mutual funds provided medium-to long-term funds mainly in the form of investments. This distinction has got somewhat blurred in recent years. While financial intermediaries play an important role in the growth process by encouraging saving and investment and by improving the allocative efficiency of resources, this role is performed well only when financial intermediaries are sound, stable and efficient.

In the last century, across the world, central banks have played an increasingly important role in macroeconomic policymaking and have continually reoriented their policies to cope with new challenges thrust upon them. To strengthen the monetary policy transmission channels, central banks have also played a vital role in the development of financial markets and the related institutions, especially after the South-East Asian crisis of 1997. The central banks of developing countries have matured immensely in terms of policymaking and have leap-frogged by adopting the best practices in the payment systems and banking technology. Indeed many central banks have taken over a whole range of functions, becoming multi-tasking institutions that conduct monetary policy, regulate and supervise the banking system, perform a crucial role in the payment and settlement system, and seek to maintain financial stability in the economy. Interestingly, central banking was initially practised with a large number of informal norms, conventions and self-imposed codes of conduct. These were later formalised and institutionalised into laws that form the basis of modern central banks in recent years.

## THE RBI LOGO

The selection of the Bank's common seal to be used as the emblem of the Bank on currency notes, cheques, and publications, was an issue that had to be taken up at an early stage of the Bank's formation.

The Government's general ideas on the seal were as follows:

(1) The seal should emphasize the governmental status of the Bank, but not too closely.

(2) It should have something Indian in the design.

(3) It should be simple, artistic, and heraldically correct.

(4) The design should be such that it could be used without substantial alternation for letterheads, etc.

For this purpose, various seals, medals, and coins were examined. The East India Company's double mohur, with the motif of the lion and palm tree, was found most suitable; however, it was decided to replace the lion by the tiger, the latter being regarded as more characteristic of India.

To meet the immediate requirements in connection with the stamping of the Bank's share certificates, the work was entrusted to a Madras firm. The Board, at its meeting on February 23, 1935, approved the design of the seal but desired improvement in the animal's appearance. Unfortunately, it was not possible to make any major changes at that stage. Deputy Governor Sir James Taylor took keen interest in getting fresh sketches prepared by the Government of India Mint and the Security Printing Press, Nasik. As a basis for good design, he arranged for a photograph to be taken of the statue of the tiger on the entrance gate at Belvedere, the residence of the Governor of Bengal (now the

National Library, Kolkata). The early sketches were a bit disappointing, leading Sir James, writing in September 1938, to remark:

> ......'s tree is all right but his tiger looks too like some species of dog, and I am afraid that a design of a dog and a tree would arouse derision among the irreverent. ......'s tiger is distinctly good but the tree has spoiled it. The stem is too long and the branches too spidery, but I should have thought that by putting a firm line under the feet of his tiger and making his tree stronger and lower we could get quite a good result from his design.

The Security Printing Press, Nasik, prepared another set of proofs. However, it was eventually decided not to make any change in the existing seal of the Bank, and the new sketches came to be used as an emblem for the Bank's currency nots, letterheads, cheques, and publications.

**Source:** RBI History, Vol. 1

*The seal of the Bank was based on the design of the double mohur of 1935 which in turn was based on prototypes provided by Flaxman at the Calcutta Mint. In the Bank's seal the lion was replaced by the Bengal Tiger. Seen above are the gold mohur of the East India Company, the Bank's seal appearing on early banknotes, and on a contemporary note.*

The functions of central banks have evolved with their respective financial systems and successfully transited from direct to indirect instruments of monetary policy. But, most importantly, since the early 1990s, the objectives of monetary policy have become increasingly focused and more precisely defined, consistent with the central banks' goals of price and financial stability.

In recent years, the emphasis on regulation and supervision of financial system has been intensified as central banks are increasingly focusing their attention on financial stability. Commercial banks, generally the most prominent part of the financial system, are subjected to more intense regulation as compared to the non-financial firms, as banks are much more leveraged than other firms due to their capacity to garner public deposits. In view of rapid globalisation, integration of financial markets and free movement of capital, bank regulation is increasingly becoming risk-centric. The adoption of Basel norms by many central banks, especially Basel II, has not only brought regulation and risk management in focus but also helped in universalising uniform standards across the banks in different countries.

Central banks have served as a reservoir of expertise that is generally drawn upon by governments and institutions, both domestic and international. In this context, economic research has played a critical role in defining the functional responsibilities of any central bank. Central banks have occupied the centre-stage of the financial system in any economy despite a continuous change in their functions and are expected to continue to make a significant contribution in policymaking and financial stability.

## APEX FINANCIAL INSTITUTION

The Reserve Bank of India (RBI) is the apex financial institution of the country's financial system entrusted with the task of control, supervision, promotion, development and planning. RBI is the queen bee of the Indian financial system which influences the commercial banks' management in more than one way. The RBI influences the management of commercial banks through its various policies, directions and regulations. Its role in bank management is quite unique. In fact, the RBI performs the four basic functions of management, *viz.,* planning, organising, directing and controlling in laying a strong foundation for the functioning of commercial banks.

As India's central bank, RBI came into existence on 1st April, 1935 (under the Reserve Bank of India Act, 1934), as the culmination of a long series of efforts to set up an institution of this kind in the country following the recommendation of the Hilton Young Commission that the dichotomy of functions and the division of responsibility for control of currency and credit should be terminated. One of the major tasks that the Reserve Bank chose to undertake since the late thirties was the building up of a sound and adequate banking and credit structure on modern lines.

## ORIGIN OF THE RBI

Strategic efforts were made to establish a central bank in our country. The earliest attempt may be traced back to 1773, when Warren Hastings, the Governor of Bengal (later Governor-General), felt the need for a central bank in the country and recommended that a "General Bank in Bengal and Bihar" be founded. The Report of the Chamberlin Commission in 1913 also raised the issue of the founding of a central bank in the country. As a supplement to this report, Professor J.M. Keynes chalked out the first comprehensive plan for an Indian central bank. Keynes' plan, however, did not come into effect, owing to the outbreak of the First World War.

In 1921, the Imperial Bank of India was set up by the amalgamation of the three Presidency Banks, which performed a few central banking functions, though primarily it remained as a commercial bank. Specifically, the Imperial Bank served as a banker to the government and in some capacity as the bankers' bank till the establishment of the Reserve Bank of India in 1935.

The question of starting a central bank in the country again received serious attention with the publication of a *White Paper* on Indian Constitutional reforms. It insisted that the British make the transfer of responsibility from the Central Government to Indian hands provided a Reserve Bank, free from political influences, is founded and it operates successfully. Eventually, a fresh bill to this effect was introduced in the

Indian Legislative Assembly on September 8, 1933. The bill was passed and received the assent of the Governor-General on March 6, 1934 and became the Reserve Bank of India Act, 1934. In accordance with the Act, the Reserve Bank of India was constituted and it commenced operations from April 1, 1935.

Smith was the first Governor. The first meeting of Sir Osborne the Board of Directors was held on January 14, 1935. The Bank was set up as a shareholders' institution. Its objectives, laid out in the preamble to the RBI Act, were to

- Regulate the issue of banknotes
- Maintain reserves with a view to securing monetary stability
- Operate the credit and currency system of the country to its advantage.

The Bank began its operations by taking over from the government the functions performed by the Controller of the Currency, and from the Imperial Bank of India the management of government accounts and public debt. The existing Currency Offices at Calcutta, Bombay, Madras, Rangoon, Karachi, Lahore, and Cawnpore (Kanpur) became branches of the Issue Department. Offices of the Banking Department were established in Calcutta, Bombay, Madras, Delhi, and Rangoon. The first Central Office of the Bank was at 8, Council House Street, Calcutta in the building that had earlier housed the Alliance Bank of Simla.

## FROM PRIVATE OWNERSHIP TO STATE OWNERSHIP

Originally, the Reserve Bank was constituted as a shareholders' bank, based on the model of leading foreign central banks of those days. The bank's fully-paid share capital was 5 crore dividend into shares of 100 each. Of this, 4,97,80,000 were subscribed by the private shareholders and 2,20,000 were subscribed by the Central Government for disposal of 2,200 shares at par to the Directors of Bank (including members of the Local Boards) seeking the minimum share qualification. The share capital of the bank has remained unchanged until today.

However, realising the need for a close integration of the monetary and credit policies of the Bank and the macroeconomic policies of the government, the notion of state ownership of the Bank was raised and justified from time to time. After Independence, the Government of India took the decision to nationalise the Reserve Bank. The Reserve Bank (Transfer to Public Ownership) Act, 1948 was passed and the government took over the Reserve Bank of India from private shareholders by paying adequate compensation to them. On January 1, 1949, the Reserve Bank started functioning as a state-owned central banking institution.

## OBJECTIVES OF CENTRAL BANK

The objectives of the Central Bank are broadly:

(1) To maintain the internal value of the nation's currency;
(2) To preserve the external value of the currency;
(3) To secure reasonable price stability; and

(4) To promote economic growth with rising levels of employment, output and real income.

These objectives are common to all countries, developed or developing. More relevant to the developing countries are those of economic growth and price stability which means that the Central Bank should strive to achieve economic growth with reasonable price stability.

## OBJECTIVES OF THE RESERVE BANK OF INDIA

The preamble to the Reserve Bank of India Act, 1934 spells out the objectives of the Reserve Bank as: *"to regulate the issue of Banknotes and the keeping of reserves with a view to securing monetary stability in India and generally to operate the currency and credit system of the country to its advantage".*

Prior to the establishment of the Reserve Bank, the Indian financial system was totally inadequate on account of the inherent weakness of the dual control of currency by the Central Government and of credit by the Imperial Bank of India. The Hilton-Young Commission, therefore, recommended that the dichotomy of functions and division of responsibility for control of currency and credit and the divergent policies in this respect must be ended by setting up of a central bank — called the Reserve Bank of India — which would regulate the financial policy and develop banking facilities throughout the country. Hence, the Bank was established with this primary object in view.

Another objective of the Reserve Bank has been to remain free from political influence and be in successful operation for maintaining financial stability and credit.

The fundamental object of the Reserve Bank of India is to discharge purely central banking functions in the Indian money market, i.e., to act as the note-issuing authority, bankers' bank and banker to government, and to promote the growth of the economy within the framework of the general economic policy of the government, consistent with the need of maintenance of price stability.

A significant object of the Reserve Bank of India has also been to assist the planned process of development of the Indian economy. Besides the traditional central banking functions, with the launching of the five-year plans in the country, the Reserve Bank of India has been moving ahead in performing a host of developmental and promotional functions, which are normally beyond the purview of a traditional Central Bank.

As has been stated by the First Five-Year Plan document, "central banking in a planned economy can hardly be confined to the regulation of the overall supply of credit or to a somewhat negative regulation of the flow of bank credit. It would have to take on a direct and active role, firstly, in creating or helping to create the machinery needed for financing developmental activities all over the country and secondly, ensuring that the finance available flows in the directions intended".

The Reserve Bank of India, as such, aims at the promotion of monetisation and monetary integration of the economy, filling in the "credit gaps" and gaps in the financial infrastructure, catering to the financial needs of the economy with appropriate sectoral allocation, as well as supporting the planners in the efficient and productive deployment of investible funds with a view to attain the macroeconomic goals of maximisation of growth with stability and social justice.

## MISSION OF RBI

The mission statement of the Reserve Bank is to foster price stability coupled with productivity-led economic growth consistent with employment objectives while ensuring the integrity, efficiency of the financial and payment systems.

### The Organisational Values

The values underlining the mission statement include:

(1) Public interest
   (i) accountability
   (ii) responsiveness
(2) Integrity endorsing professional ethics and standards in operations and dealings
(3) Excellence
(4) Fostering motivation
(5) Independence of views, and
(6) Responsiveness and dynamism.

## VISION FOR FUTURE

The vision statement states, "The Bank (RBI) aims to be a leading central bank with credible, transparent, proactive and contemporaneous policies and seeks to be a catalyst for the emergence of a globally competitive financial system that helps deliver a high quality of life to the people of the country.

The mission statement and the organisational values are long-term principles, whereas, the vision for future, strategic objectives and the guidelines are subject to regular reviews in response to internal and external transformation affecting the Reserve Bank.

## FUNCTIONS OF A CENTRAL BANK

Central bank functions have evolved overtime, especially after the economies encountered difficult periods or crises. These functions vary in nature and with the stage of economic development of the country where the central bank is situated, the nature of mandate for it and the degree of operational independence it enjoys. The functions of a central bank can be broadly categorised into monetary policy functions, banker to the banks, banker to the government and developmental functions. The functions of note issuance, maintenance of internal and external value of currency evolved as the key objectives of monetary policy. The task of promotion of growth was subsequently added to it. This set of functions became the core monetary policy functions. With the development of the financial sector, subsequently, lender-of-the-last resort function grew to encompass the role of a regulator and supervisor. It has assumed wider objective of financial stability in recent years and includes allied activities pertaining to adoption of technology in banking. Many central banks were established predominantly to finance the activities of their governments. This function has been reviewed and many central banks have ceased to finance their governments in recent years. Central banks have assumed many new functions that focus on development of markets, institutions and communication policies.

The Reserve Bank of India performs all the typical functions of a good central bank. In addition, it carries out a variety of developmental and promotional functions attuned to the course of economic planning in the country:

**(A) Monetary Functions**

(1) Issue and management of currency
(2) Maintaining internal value of currency
(3) Maintenance of the external value of currency
(4) Anchoring economic agents
(5) Conduct of monetary policy
(6) Monetary regulation and management
(7) Price stability
(8) Regulation of interest rates
(8) Promotion of growth
(10) Banker to the government
(11) Banker to banks
(12) Supervisor and regulator of the banking system
(13) Financial sector regulation and supervision
(14) Ensuring financial stability
(15) Exchange management and control
(16) Credit control
(17) Liquidity management
(18) Regulating and controlling financial sector

**(B) Payment System Functions**

The Reserve Bank continued to play a major role in developing a fast, efficient and secure payment and settlement system based on the technological development.

(1) National Electronic Funds Transfer (NEFT)
(2) Real Time Gross Setlement (RTGS)
(3) Electronic Clearing Services (ECS)
(4) MICR Cheque Processing
(5) Cheque Transcation System (CTS)
(6) National Electronic Clearing Services (NECS)
(7) Systemically Important Payment System (SIPS)

(8) Mobile Payments

(9) Electronic Fund Transfer (ECT)

(10) Automated Teller Machines (ATM)

**(C) Development Functions**

(1) Fostering the financial sector

(2) Developing and nurturing financial markets

(3) Policy-oriented research

(4) Institution building

(5) Dissemination of information

(6) Co-ordination and co-operation

(7) Financial inclusion

(8) Miscellaneous developmental and promotional functions and activities.

## REGULATION AND SUPERVISION

The primary purpose of banking regulation in India by the RBI has been to ensure financial stability and maintain confidence in the financial system by enhancing its soundness and efficiency. The regulation and supervisions functions are:

(*i*) Ensuring financial stability

(*ii*) Implementation of Basel Norms

(*iii*) Regulation of financial conglomerates

(*iv*) Electronic banking in India

(*v*) Promotion of internet and mobile banking

(*vi*) Ensuring e-security

(*vii*) Control of banks, financial market segments, financial institutions and non-banking finance companies

(*viii*) Risk management.

The sound financial position and strength of the banking system reflects the effectiveness of the Reserve Bank's regulatory and supervisory approaches. Over the years, India has started adopting international best practices and implementing standards and codes to ensure that the Indian financial system functions on sound lines.

The changing role of financial regulation and supervision of the Reserve Bank is one of less accent on 'micro regulation' but more focus on 'prudential supervision'; less emphasis on 'regulatory intervention' but more thrust on creating an environment in which the banks think freely and innovate, less reliance on 'rules' but more importance to 'principles'; and less weightage to 'monitoring the banks' day-to-day activities' but more attention to 'risk assessment and risk containment'. In future, the regulatory and supervisory role would not only be 'friendly' and 'frank', but also 'prompt' and 'firm'. The Reserve Bank's new role recognises the differences among various segments of the Indian banking system and accommodates appropriate flexibility in the regulatory treatment. The changing face of regulation and supervision would accord importance to intensified use of technology in supervisory processes and substantially enhancing the skills and capacities of the supervisors. The regulatory and supervisory role of the Reserve Bank in future would guide and facilitate the metamorphosis of the domestic banks into strong and globally acknowledged players, while fully meeting the socio-economic objectives, and would continue to maintain stable and orderly conditions in the financial system.

## ROLE OF THE RESERVE BANK OF INDIA

This concept of dual responsibility is crucial to an understanding of the role of the Reserve Bank in the context of planned development. About the time India launched her First Five-Year Plan in 1951, the Reserve Bank began to operate on a new concept of its promotional role, which implied the development of monetary and banking institutions in a planned manner. This new concept was very different from the accepted functions of a central bank. Further this role was frequently in conflict with its traditional restrictive role of controlling the inflation that was generated in the economy as a result of deficit financing which resulted on account of the fiscal policy. However, the Reserve Bank's promotional role was so essential that it had to be pursued with enthusiasm in the larger interest of the country. Simultaneously, with the acceptance by the Indian government of the concept of development planning, the monetary authorities were obliged to keep inflationary pressures under effective control. Ostensibly, therefore, the success of the monetary measures depended not only upon the ingenuity with which the policy was formulated but also upon the development of financial institutions within the

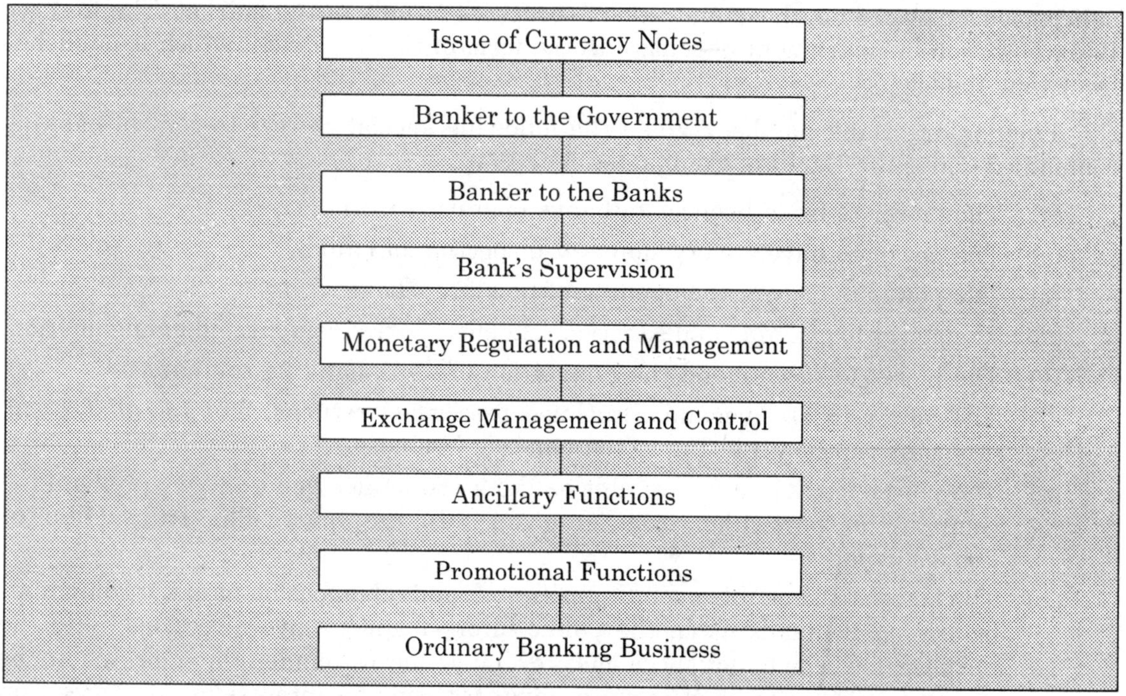


**Fig. 1 Functions of The Reserve Bank of India**

framework of which the authorities had to function. The conclusion, therefore, is inescapable that, beginning with the First Plan, it was essential for the Reserve Bank to deviate from the norm; and together with its normal central banking functions of credit regulation, the bank also devoted its energies to the development of credit institutions and modifying and normalising banking practices attune to development.

## PROMOTIONAL ROLE

A striking feature of the Reserve Bank of India Act was that it made agricultural credit the Bank's special responsibility. This reflected the realisation that the country's central bank should make special efforts to develop, under its direction and guidance, a system of institutional credit for a major sector of the economy, namely, agriculture, which then accounted for more than 50 per cent of the national income. However, major advances in agricultural finance materialised only after India's independence. Over the years, the Reserve Bank has helped to evolve a suitable institutional infrastructure for providing credit in rural areas.

Another important function of the Bank is the regulation of banking. All the scheduled banks are required to keep with the Reserve Bank a consolidated 3 per cent of their total deposits, and the Reserve Bank has power to increase this percentage up to 15. These banks must have capital and reserves of not less than ₹ 5 lakh. The accumulation of these balances with the Reserve Bank places it in a position to use them freely in emergencies to support the scheduled banks themselves in times of need as the lender of last resort. To a certain extent, it is also possible for the Reserve Bank to influence the credit policy of scheduled banks by means of an open market operations policy, that is, by the purchase and sale of securities or bills in the market. The Reserve Bank has another instrument of control in the form of the bank rate, which it publishes from time-to-time.

Further, the Bank has been given the following special powers to control banking companies under the Banking Companies Act, 1949:

(*a*) The power to issue licences to banks operating in India.

(*b*) The power to have supervision and inspection of banks.

(*c*) The power to control the opening of new branches.

(*d*) The power to examine and sanction schemes of arrangement and amalgamation.

(*e*) The power to recommend the liquidation of weak banking companies.

(*f*) The power to receive and scrutinise prescribed returns, and to call for any other information relating to the banking business.

(*g*) The power to caution or prohibit banking companies generally or any banking company in particular from entering into any particular transaction or transactions.

(*h*) The power to control the lending policy of, and advances by banking companies or any particular bank in the public interest and to give directions as to the purpose for which advances may or may not be made, the margins to be maintained in respect of secured advances and the interest to be charged on advances.

The various aspects of the supervisory/regulatory functions exercised by the Reserve Bank may be briefly mentioned asunder:

**(1) Licensing of Banks:** There is a statutory provision that a company starting banking business in India has first to obtain a licence from the Reserve Bank. If the Reserve Bank is dissatisfied on account of the defective features of the proposed company, it can refuse to grant the licence. The Bank is also empowered to cancel the licence of a bank when it will cease to carry on banking business in India.

**(2) Approval of Capital, Reserves and Liquid Assets of Banks:** The Reserve Bank examines whether the minimum requirements of capital reserve and liquid assets are fulfilled by the banks and approves them.

**(3) Branch Licensing Policy:** The Reserve Bank exercises its control over expansion of branches by the banks through its branch licensing policy.

In September 1978, the RBI formulated a comprehensive branch licensing policy with a view to accelerate the pace of expansion of bank offices in the rural areas. This was meant to correct regional imbalances of the banking coverage in the country.

**(4) Inspection of Banks:** The Reserve Bank is empowered to conduct inspection of banks. The inspection may relate to various aspects such as the banks' organisational structure, branch expansion, mobilisation of deposits, investments, credit portfolio management, credit appraisal, profit planning, manpower planning as well as assessment of the performance of banks in developmental areas such as deployment of credit to the priority sectors, etc. The Bank may conduct *ad hoc* investigation whenever there are complaints about major irregularities or frauds by certain banks.

The inspections are basically meant to improve the working of the banks and safeguard the interests of depositors and thereby develop a sound banking system in the country.

**(5) Control Over Management:** The Reserve Bank also looks into the management side of the banks. The appointment, reappointment or termination of appointment of the chairman and chief executive officer of private sector banks is to be approved by the Reserve Bank. The Bank's approval is also required for the remuneration, perquisites and post-retirement benefits given by a bank to its chairman and chief executive officer.

The boards of the public sector banks are to be constituted by the Central Government in consultation with the Reserve Bank.

**(6) Control Over Methods:** The Reserve Bank exercises strict control over the methods of operation of the banks to ensure that no improper investment and injudicious advances are made by them.

**(7) Audit:** Banks are required to get their Balance Sheets and Profit and Loss Accounts duly audited by the auditors approved by the Reserve Bank. In the case of the State Bank of India (SBI), the auditors are appointed by the Reserve Bank.

**(8) Credit Information Service:** The Reserve Bank is empowered to collect information about credit facilities granted by individual banks and supply the relevant information in a consolidated manner to the banks and other financial institutions seeking such information.

**(9) Control Over Amalgamation and Liquidation:** The banks have to obtain the sanction of the Reserve Bank for any voluntary amalgamation. The Reserve Bank in consultation with the Central Government can also suggest compulsory reconstruction or amalgamation of banks. It also supervises banks in liquidation. The liquidators have to submit to the Reserve Bank returns showing their positions. The Reserve Bank keeps a watch on the progress of liquidation proceedings and the expenses of liquidation.

**(10) Deposit Insurance:** To protect the interest of depositors, banks are required to insure their deposits with the Deposit Insurance Corporation. The Reserve Bank of India has promoted such a Corporation in 1962, which has been renamed in 1978 as the Deposit Insurance and Credit Guarantee Corporation.

**(11) Training and Banking Education:** The RBI has played an active role in making institutional arrangement for providing training and banking education to the bank personnel, with a view to improve their efficiency.

## CONTROL OF CREDIT BY THE RESERVE BANK

It has been provided in the preamble to the Reserve Bank of India Act that one of the functions of the Bank is to control currency and credit. The control that a central bank is able to exercise on the monetary system largely depends upon the control that it is able to exercise on the constituents of the purchasing power. In all countries, including India, token coins and currency notes form the bulk of the purchasing power, the latter being more important than the former. In countries where banking has developed, the deposit currency also plays an important role in the creation of credit and purchasing power.

Under Section 40 of the Reserve Bank of India Act, it is obligatory for the Bank to maintain the external value of the rupee.

The Reserve Bank of India is the custodian of the country's foreign exchange reserves. It has authority to enter into foreign exchange transactions both on its own and on behalf of the government. It is obligatory for the Bank to sell and buy currencies of all the member countries of the International Monetary Fund to ensure smooth and orderly exchange arrangements and to promote a stable system of exchange rates.

The Reserve Bank of India has resorted to the technique of exchange control to allocate its limited foreign exchange resources according to a scheme of priorities.

In India, exchange control was introduced under the Defence of India Rules in September 1939. It was, however, statutorily laid down by the Foreign Exchange Regulation Act (FERA) of 1947.

This has been again stipulated by the FERA, in 1973.

**Table 1: Impact of the Evolution of Select Functions of the Reserve Bank on the Reserve Bank's Balance Sheet in Various Phases: A Stylised Evolution Matrix.**

| *Phases* | *Note Issuance* | *Banker to Government* | *Banker to Banks* | *Exchange Rate and Foreign Exchange Management* | *Developmental Role* |
|---|---|---|---|---|---|
| *1* | *2* | *3* | *4* | *5* | *6* |
| Formative Years (1935-1949) | Remains the sole currency issuer and the function remains broadly the same through different phases | Driven by event-based shocks like war. | – | Accumulation of foreign exchange reserves. | – |
| Foundation Phase (1950-1967) | | Automatic monetisation initiated – expansionary effects on the balance sheet. | Increasing reserve requirements. Sector specific refinance – expansionary effect on the balance sheet. | Balance sheet driven by net domestic assets. Deterioration in balance of payments. | Introduced balance sheet support to development finance institutions |
| Phase of Social Control (1968-1990) | | Heavy automatic monetisation – heavy credit to the government. | | | Very strong and consequent large transfers to LTO funds. |
| Phase of Financial Liberalisation (1991 onwards) | | Credit to government shrinking with stoppage of *ad hoc* treasury bills, increasing sterilisation and introduction of MSS. | Reduction in reserve requirements–bankers' deposits coming down. | Balance sheet driven by net foreign assets. Huge stock of foreign exchange reserves. Reserve accumulation non-debt creating in nature. | Change of role towards developing institutions and markets–but transfer to LTO funds became nominal. |

In case of exchange rate fluctuations, the Reserve Bank revalues the foreign currency on the asset side and parks the gains/losses in its Currency and Gold Revaluation Account on the liability side.

FERA was amended in 1973. FERA 1973 was replaced by the market-friendly Foreign Exchange Management Act (FEMA), 1999. More importantly, the FEMA diluted the rigorous enforcement provisions. In fact, the FEMA provided a *dejure status* to the shift in the external sector policies.

## ISSUER OF CURRENCY

The Bank has the monopoly of note issue in India. This is on the basis of the RBI Act, 1934. The Bank ensures an adequate supply of good quality genuine notes and coins and it mops up notes and coins unfit for circulation. The Reserve Bank advises government on note design and the security features of notes, which are enhanced from time-to-time to deter counterfeiting. Coinage is the prerogative of the Central Government and is governed by the Indian Coinage Act, 1906. Coins are issued and withdrawn through the Reserve Bank.

The Department of Currency Management in Mumbai, in co-operation with the Issue Departments in the Bank's regional offices, oversees the production and manages the distribution of currency. Currency chests at more than 4,000 bank branches – typically commercial banks – contain adequate quantities of notes and coins so that currency is accessible to the public in a parts of the country.

Four printing presses print notes, at Dewas in Madhya Pradesh, Nasik in Maharashtra, Mysore in Karnataka, and Salboni in West Bengal. The presses in Madhya Pradesh and Maharashtra are owned by the Security Printing and Minting Corporation of India (SPMCIL), a wholly-owned company of the Government of India. The presses in Karnataka and West Bengal are set up by the Bharatiya Reserve Bank Note Mudran Private Limited (BRBNMPL), a wholly-owned subsidiary of Reserve Bank.

Coins are minted by the Government of India. The RBI is the agent of the government for the distribution, issue, and handling of coins. Four mints are in operation: Mumbai, Noida, Kolkata, and Hyderabad.

The Bank's focus is to ensure availability of clean notes and to strngthen the security features of banknotes. Given the volumes involved and costs incured in the printing, transport, storage, and removal of unfit/soiled notes, the RBI is evaluating ways to extend the life of banknotes – particularly in the lower denominations.

## CONTROL OF CURRENCY

The Reserve Bank of India has been given the monopoly of note issue to enable it to exercise control over the volume of bank notes. Ordinarily, the expansion or contraction of currency is effected under Section 33(i) by increasing or decreasing the assets of the Issue Department, which are kept in the form of rupee coins, including rupee notes, gold coin and bullion, rupee securities, including treasury bills and foreign securities. An expansion in currency can be effected by increasing any of these forms of assets and issuing notes of equal value from the Issue Department. A contraction in currency can be similarly effected by withdrawing notes from circulation and reducing any of the assets held by the Reserve Bank. Ordinarily, when it wants to expand currency, the bank increases the assets of the Issue Department by transferring rupee or foreign securities or both from the Banking Department to the Issue Department or by cancelling *ad hoc* treasury bills held in the Issue Department. Sometimes, currency is expanded or contracted as a result of a revaluation of securities held in the Issue Department.

The Reserve Bank is authorised to transact the following ordinary banking business:

(*a*) Acceptance of money on deposits without interest from the Central and State Governments, banks, local bodies and any other person.

(*b*) The purchase, sale and rediscount of bills of exchange and promissory notes drawn and payable in India and arising out of *bonafide* transactions, bearing two or more signatures, one of which must be that of a scheduled bank, and maturing within 90 days from the date of purchase or rediscount.

(*c*) The purchase, sale and rediscount of bills, drawn and payable in India for financing agricultural operations or marketing of crops, and maturing within 15 months from the date of purchase or rediscount.

(*d*) The purchase, sale and rediscount of bills issued or drawn for holding or trading in securities of the Central or State Governments and maturing within 90 days.

(*e*) The making of loans and advances to states, local bodies, scheduled banks and State co-operative banks.

(*f*) The making of ways and means advances to Central and State Governments.

(*g*) The purchase and sale of securities of the Central and State Governments.

(*h*) The issue of demand drafts made payable at its own offices or agencies and making, issuing and circulating bank post bills.

(*i*) The borrowing of money from a scheduled bank in India or from central banks in other countries.

(*j*) The opening of an account, or making of an agency agreement, with central banks in other countries and acting as their agent and investing funds in their shares.

(*k*) The purchase and sale of gold and bullion.

(*l*) RBI also plays an important role in the maintenance of exchange value of the rupee and acts as an agent of the government in respect of India's membership of International Monetary Fund.

(*m*) All such functions as may be incidental to or consequential upon the exercise of its powers or the discharge of its duties under the Act.

## MONEY AND CAPITAL MARKETS

The Indian money market is less insulated from the money markets abroad due to the prevailing liberalisation in India and the absence of many controls on inflow and outflow of funds. The core of the Indian money market is the inter-bank call money market where the lenders and borrowers are mostly the banks. The UTI and the LIC also enter this market. The funds dealt with are the overnight money and funds up to seven days. There is no true secondary market for bills, either commercial or government, nor is there any acceptance business in India. Most of the bills are not genuine trade bills. Treasury bills are sold on tap by the RBI on behalf of the government and the main buyers are commercial banks.

In the long-term section of the organised sector, namely, the capital market, there are a number of institutions such as stock market where the old securities are dealt with, new issues market where new capital is raised, bullion exchange where gold and silver bullion are purchased and sold. The gilt-edged market has a special characteristic in that it includes both short-term and long-term. This market is also narrow and the main holders are commercial banks and other financial institutions. There are a number of specialised financial institutions in the capital market. Some of these institutions are Industrial Finance Corporation, Industrial Credit and Investment Corporation, Provident Funds, Pension Funds, State Financial Corporations, State Insurance Corporation, etc.

## RBI AND THE FINANCIAL SYSTEM

The Reserve Bank is the centre-piece of the financial system and the apex institution in the money market. It is concerned with the efficient and smooth functioning of the financial system. The Reserve Bank has to keep a watch on the developments both of daily, and seasonal nature, in the financial system. It provides liquidity with a view to facilitating the smooth functioning of the system and controlling it. The flow of liquidity is controlled through money supply change, reserve requirements of banks, open market purchases/sales of government securities, etc. The cost and availability of credit is also regulated by suitable monetary policy. The Reserve Bank can influence the operations in the financial system through not only the liquidity flow, but also through regulation of banking system, of bank loans, bank holdings of liquid assets, interest rates, public deposits with banks and non-bank, etc. In brief, the RBI has three types of functions in relation to the financial system — (*a*) Financial, (*b*) Regulatory, and (*c*) Developmental.

In India, the money market and the capital market are not properly developed. The link between these two segments as also between the organised and unorganised sectors, is poor. The RBI has in the past attempted to link unorganised and organised sectors in a systematic way, but even now the dichotomy between these two sectors persists. There is inadequate integration, cohesion and specialisation among the components in the financial system. The savings and banking habits are underdeveloped with the result that the operation of the monetary policy becomes less effective, throwing greater burden on the Reserve Bank.

## RBI AS THE LEADER

The preamble to the Reserve Bank of India Act says that the main function of the Bank is to regulate the issues of banknotes and keeping of reserves with a view to securing monetary stability in India and generally to operate the currency and credit system of the country to its advantage. Thus, it is not only a banker to the government, but also a banker to the commercial banks, co-operative banks and other financial institutions, in which capacity the Reserve Bank grants accommodation and keeps the reserves of these institutions.

The Bank has also an important role to play statutorily on the maintenance of the external value of the rupee in view of the close interdependence of international trade and national economic well-being. The Bank has been entrusted with the custody of the country's international reserves and also represents the government at the IMF and operates exchange control and other restrictions on foreign payments and receipts.

It would thus appear that the Reserve Bank's functions can be set out in terms of the various contact points it has with the economy: (*i*) Government finance, (*ii*) Finance to banking sector and thus to the private sector of the economy, (*iii*) Finance to foreign sector, and (*iv*) finance to non-banking financial sector. The Reserve Bank as the apex institution in the financial system is the source of all currency and credit in the economy by virtue of its being the creator of currency and also the custodian of the reserves of the commercial and co-operative banks.

The operations of the RBI influence the economy and are influenced by the economy in the sense that it is environment and the context which shape the policies of the Bank and the policies of the Bank have in turn their impact on the economy. The interactions between the RBI and the economy can be set out in terms of the changes in its assets and liabilities. The liabilities of the RBI give rise to changes in reserve money which produce a multiplier effect on the actual changes in money supply. The assets of the RBI explain the factors influencing the changes in liabilities and thus of reserve money.

The Reserve Bank's main activities in relation to these sectors can be classified under a finance function and a regulatory function. There is also a third function, *viz.*, a development function with reference to the financial system. As a regulator of the financial system, the Reserve Bank would need a well-developed and well-organised financial system in which its actions could percolate from one segment to the other easily and quickly with the result that its control could become effective. It would thus be in the interest of the Reserve Bank's control that it should help develop an integrated and cohesive functional system, mature in all respects, *viz.,* in respect of the institutional structure, the instruments traded and the interest rates in the economy. It should also ensure that credit gaps, both geographical and functional, are duly filled up. These credit gaps may be in the short-term or the long-term credit-end. The Reserve Bank has not only a stake in the short-term money market but also long-term money market; its actions percolate to the long-end in view of the various direct controls that it operates.

| *Sectors of the Economy Influencing* | *Liabilities Side* | *Assets Side* | *Sectors of the Economy Influencing* |
|---|---|---|---|
| Govt. Sector | Deposits of Government | Loans and advances to government | Govt. sector |
| Private and business sector | Deposits of banks | Loans and advances to financial sector | Bank and non-banking financial sector |
| Private and foreign sector | Other deposits | Investments | Govt. sector |
| All sectors (Households in particular) | Other liabilities (notes in circulation) | (a) In Govt. securities<br>(b) In private assets<br>(c) In foreign assets<br>Other assets | Private sector<br>Foreign sector<br>All sectors |

The process of liberalisation of the economy added several new dimensions to the responsibilities of the Reserve Bank in the backdrop of financial sector reforms, the monetary policy framework was adjusted and conventional central banking functions were revamped in consonance with global trends, technological developments and domestic expediency. The first phase of reforms focused on deregulation of the banking industry, strengthening of the institutional framework in banking, non-banking financial companies and financial institutions through prudential norms, and improvements in payment and settlement systems. The second phase of reforms emphasised the adoption of prudential norms in the financial system, in a gradual manner with an objective to converge to the international standards.

A number of innovative measures were undertaken by the Reserve Bank in the earlier years of reforms to overhaul the financial system. The important measures were deregulation of interest rates, rationalisation and lowering of reserve ratios, elimination of automatic monetisation of the fiscal deficit, activation of the Bank Rate and introduction of indirect instruments of monetary policy, especially the Liquidity Adjustment Facility, to modulate daily liquidity. Although there is no formal targeting of overnight interest rates, the LAF has enabled the Reserve Bank to de-emphasise targeting of bank reserves and to focus increasingly on maintaining an interest rate corridor. The introduction of measures has been gradual and has generally been done after wide consultations with market participants, policymakers, international experts and academicians through various technical committees and subgroups.

In the context of the monetary policy framework, there has been greater activism in liquidity management and an enhanced focus on the short-end of the market in the deregulated framework with the role of market forces becoming critical, there has been increasing evidence of changes in the underlying transmission mechanism of monetary policy, i.e., interest rates and the exchange rate gaining importance *vis-a-vis* quantity variables in India. With the liberalisation of the external sector, the monetary targeting framework came under stress owing to increasing capital inflows. These developments solicited review of the monetary policy framework and in accordance with this, the Reserve Bank switched to a more broad-based "multiple indicators approach" in 1998 in monetary policy formulation.

## RBI AND BANKS

As regards its regulatory role, the Reserve Bank controls and regulates the activities of the commercial banks in terms of the Banking Regulations Act, 1949. These regulatory provisions were extended to co-operative banks in 1966 in terms of the Banking Laws (application to Co-operative Societies) Act, 1965. To protect the interests of the depositors, the Bank had set up the Deposit Insurance Corporation in 1962 to insure are the deposits of the public and infuse confidence in the banking system. The bank had acquired powers to effect compulsory amalgamation of banks with a view to weed out the weak and sick units and to control the management and other aspects of operations of banks including loans, advances, investments, etc.

In respect of its promotional role, let us take the commercial and co-operative banks or short-term financial institutions, which are also part of the organised financial system. To bring about a wider diffusion of the benefits of banks, they were exhorted to open branches in rural and underdeveloped regions and to lend to neglected, weaker and underprivileged sections of the population. The scheme of social control of banks and the subsequent nationalisation of the 19 major banks were aimed at these promotional objectives. The lead bank scheme of allotting each of the districts to one or more of the banks for the purpose of development of these regions is yet another example of the promotional role of banks. Mention may also be made here of the promotional aspects of encouragement and concessional refinance from the RBI for priority sector lending by banks as well as the credit authorization scheme which requires prior sanction for lending to bigger industrial houses, which has since been withdrawn.

## BANKER TO THE GOVERNMENT

Before the formation of the Reserve Bank, the Imperial Bank performed many of the functions as banker to the government. As the banker to the Central Government and the State Governments, the Reserve Bank provides a range of banking services for these governments such as:

- Acceptance of money on government account
- Payment/withdrawal of funds
- Collection and transfer of funds through different means.

During the plan era, the Reserve Bank's role in plan financing evolved in the form of deficit financing.

## BANKER AND DEBT MANAGER TO GOVERNMENT

The Reserve Bank acts as banker to the Central Government, i.e., the Bank maintains the government's accounts, receives money (e.g., for the payment of taxes) on its behalf, makes payments, provides exchange facilities, as well as provides ways and means advances to the government. While it is obligatory on the Bank to act as banker to the Central Government, it also acts as banker to State Governments with whom it signs agreements. The Bank also performs merchant banking functions on behalf of Central and State Governments and floats public debt on their behalf.

At the end of each day, the Bank consolidates the government's transactions to determine the net final position. If the balance in the government's account shows a negative position, the Bank extends a short-term, interest-bearing advance, called a ways and means advance (WMA), the limit or amount for which is set at the beginning of each financial year in April.

The Reserve Bank's Department of government and bank accounts oversees the government's banking-related activities. This department encompasses:

## INSTITUTION BUILDING

A major task thrust upon the Reserve Bank was to put in place the necessary institutional mechanism to complement the planning efforts. In the process, it developed adequate necessary financial infrastructure. As a mother-of-institutions, the Reserve Bank played a crucial role in the development of the financial sector in India. In the reform era, focus has been on developing and nurturing the financial markets and consolidation of the financial system.

## REGULATION AND SUPERVISION

The regulatory and supervisory role of the Reserve Bank gained prominence after independence but has been in focus since nationalisation of commercial banks in 1969. At present, the complex financial system in India, mainly consisting of commercial banks, co-operative banks, financial institutions and non-banking financial companies, is regulated and supervised by different authorities. The Reserve Bank regulates and supervises major part of the financial system covering commercial banks, co-operative banks, some financial institutions and deposit taking non-banking finance companies. In the initial years, the regulation of banking system was geared towards meeting the demands of a developing economy and a number of measures undertaken to strengthen the banking system were successful. Then, the regulatory and supervisory functions of the Reserve Bank focused primarily on ensuring soundness of banking operations and protection of small depositors through measures of compulsory mergers and liquidations, and introduction of deposit insurance scheme. Reserve Bank's new era of regulation began with the 'Social Control' of banking which took the shape of nationalisation directed lending to priority sector and administered interest rate regime. The need for social control over banks, was felt in the context of the major lacuna that banking services were not available in many rural and urban areas, as well as in many preferred sectors, notwithstanding the considerable progress made in both functional and geographic coverage of the banking system since 1951. In terms of outcome, nationalisation succeeded in spreading the network of banks in rural areas and mobilising private savings. However, the savings so mobilised were mainly used for supporting government borrowings through *hitherto* neglected genuine credit needs in the rural areas were also met to a certain extent. The Reserve Bank supported nationalisation of the banks to ensure compliance with social control norms. This called for significant changes in the institutional arrangements and more stringent regulation and supervision of the banking system.

## A NEW MILLENNIUM AND A NEW MOMENTUM

The first decade of the new millennium witnessed a consolidation of the reform measures. The economy made a decisive break from the 'Hindu rate of growth' and moved onto a higher growth trajectory – clocking a growth rate of over 9% in 2007; this brought in a new momentum, both economic and psychological.

Capital flows altered the scarcity mindset and the challenge was to meet the problems of plenty; the forex inflows had to be sterilized, resulting in the market stabilization scheme. Interest rates were deregulated further. The enactment of the Fiscal Responsibility and Budget Management Act was the defining event in the area of monetary policy. It imposed limits on the fiscal and revenue deficits of the Central Government and prohibited the Reserve Bank from participating in primary issuances of Government securities.

Another area of focus was the payments system where legislations were enacted, the Real Time Gross Settlement (RTGS) systems put in place and Structured Financial Messaging Solution (SFMS) and cheque truncation introduced. The Government Securities Act replaced the Public Debt Act of 1944, a new settlements mechanism was introduced for the G-secs market, data dissemination provided for better price discovery, and G-secs with options were introduced for the first time.

Concerns related to urban co-operative banks were addressed in the wake of a series of urban bank failures, and the period witnessed a number of bank mergers. The regulatory response led the Bank to set up a number of state-level Task Forces on Urban Co-operative Banks (TAFCUBs) to sign memoranda of understanding with State Governments to strengthen urban banks.

The regulatory thrust revolved around the decision to implement Basel II guidelines and the system of prompt corrective action was put in place with auto-corrective measures to enhance response time. The Know Your Customer (KYC) guidelines and the Anti Money Laundering Act impacted on the public at large and opening bank accounts involved more documentation. To mitigate the effects of liberalization and the move to efficiency, the Bank worked towards the inclusion of those who had no access to financial services.

The focus of the Reserve Bank shifted to customer-service with the beefing up of the Banking Ombudsman Scheme and the setting up of the Customer-Services Department and of a Banking Codes and Standards Board to put into effect minimum standards of fair practices. The Right to Information (RTI) Act was a landmark event that introduced greater transparency in the Bank's operations. The new millennium saw the Bank open new offices in states of Chhattisgarh, Uttarakhand, Jharkhand, Himachal Pradesh, and Sikkim. And the era of development banks ended as the ICICI and the IDBI both merged with their subsidiaries and converted themselves into universal banks.

The Bank's monetary policy response to mitigate the effects of the global financial crisis marked the high point of this period. The world over, in moves reflecting the triumph of expediency over doctrine, orthodox thought sacred cows were thrown overboard as the sheer momentum of events mired the earlier intellectual consensus in turbidity. The events, in some ways, vindicated the RBI's contrarian stance on monetary issues. In its 75th year, the Bank seeks to carry forward its legacy in a post-crisis world with the 'humility of central bankers' and not the 'arrogance of central banking'.

## CONCLUSION

The RBI was formed based on a report in 1914, which included a memorandum by John Maynard Keynes, one of its members, proposing that the three Presidency Banks, Bank of Bombay, Calcutta and Madras – which had been printing currency since 1861 – be merged into one Central Bank. This enactment came through in March 1934. The RBI was first established as a shareholders' bank, and, subsequently, nationalised in 1949 (separating the State Bank of India from it).

Since then, the Central Bank has seen two wars, the swift and unexpected move of nationalising 14 commercial banks in 1969, and a transfer of gold in 1991 to coffers in London. Yet, some of today's premier development and market institutuions like the National Bank for Agriculture and Rural Development, IDBI Bank and the Unit Trust of India had their beginnings as specialised departments and divisions within the RBI. With 26 departments, 26 regional and field offices across the country, four subsidiaries and a staff of over 20,000 employees, the Central Bank is a large and complex organisation.

It may be pointed out that Special Credit Management is not competitive with but complementary to quantitative credit management. Credit management to be effective must be comprehensive and must include both quantitative and qualitative credit measures. The problem of credit management cannot be tackled through a fragmented approach. An effective credit management requires a well-coordinated and comprehensive approach. The essence of the comprehensive approach lies not only in the integration of quantitative and selective credit management weapons but also hinges on an effective co-ordination and simultaneous and timely use of the three main techniques — monetary measures, fiscal measures, and measures of economic policy — for direct regulation, management and physical flow of funds to socially desirable and economically viable purposes or projects.

In addition, the Reserve Bank, like many other central banks in emerging market economies, has had to increasingly contend with maintaining financial stability. Besides, the Reserve Bank's role as manager of public debt also implies that the internal debt management function gets inextricably mixed with the monetary management function. In view of the limited number of instruments, the Reserve bank has to prioritise its objectives given the circumstances. This constrains the degree of flexibility available to monetary policy in a complex macroeconomic environment. As the economy becomes increasingly open and global, the role of the Reserve Bank of India will undergo further change and will need to equip itself for coping with those emerging challenges on a continuous basis.

The initiatives of the Reserve Bank have strengthened the financial sector in India, enabling into adapt to the emerging environment and this is reinforced in the change in perception of the world community towards India as an upcoming economic power house.

While successfully facing the challenges of globalisation, the RBI has earned international credibility in terms of efficiency and transparency in its operations. Notwithstanding the changing challenges, the RBI has managed to evolve constructively on a continuous basis to cope with demands for stable macroeconomic management and financial stability, while meeting the objectives of economic growth and development.

- RBI has seen 22 governors down to the present chief, Duvvuri Subbarao.
- The terms of the governors have varied in length from eight years to just 20 days.

|  |  |  |  |  |  |
|---|---|---|---|---|---|
| **Osborne A Smith** 1935-1937 | **C. D. Deshmukh** 1943-1949 | **L. K. Jha** 1967-1970 | **M. Narasimham** May 1977-Nov.1977 | **I. G. Patel** (1977-1982) | **S. Venkitaramanan** (1990-1992) |
| **"We are now in a position to tackle the agricultural problem and we hope... to show that the Reserve Bank will prove of benefit to the ryot."** | **"While partition has resulted in a contraction of RBI's area of action, its constitution is likely to undergo a change on account of nationalisation."** | **"(Making) priority products less profitable through price controls while leaving less essential products free (encourages) investment in non-essentials."** | **"We have had an attitudinal change on the part of bankers, and the system shedding its elitist image to become more truly an operation for the masses."** | **"Nationalisation of banks (has made) term deposits... a major instrument for mobilising the savings of a vast section of society."** | **"In spite of a legal ban on import of gold into India.... about 150 tonnes of gold came into India in 1991, compared to 25 tonnes smuggled in 1981."** |

## GOVERNORS OF THE RESERVE BANK OF INDIA
## January 1, 1935 to March 31, 2011

**Sir Osborne Smith**
(January 1, 1935–
June 30, 1937)

**Sir James Braid Taylor**
(July 1, 1937–
February 17, 1943)

**C. D. Deshmukh**
(August 11, 1943–
June 30, 1949)

**Sir Benegal Rama Rau**
(July 1, 1949–
January 14, 1957)

**K. G. Ambegaokar**
(January 14, 1957–
February 28, 1957)

**H.V.R. Lengar**
(March 1, 1957–
February 28, 1962)

**P.C. Bhattacharyya**
(March 1, 1962–
June 30, 1967)

**L.K. Jha**
(July 1, 1967–
May 3, 1970)

**B. N. Adarkar**
(May 4, 1970–June 15, 1970)

**S. Jagannathan**
(June 16, 1970–May 19, 1975)

**N.C. Sen Gupta**
(May 19, 1975–August 19, 1975)

**K.R. Puri**
(August 20, 1975–
May 2, 1977)

**M. Narasimham**
(May 2, 1977–
November 30, 1977)

**Dr I. G. Patel**
(December 1, 1977–
September 15, 1982)

**Dr. Manmohan Singh**
(September 16, 1982–
January 14, 1985)

**A. Ghosh**
(January 15, 1985–
February 4, 1985)

**R. N. Malhotra**
(February 4, 1985–
December 22, 1990)

**S. Venkitaramanan**
(December 22, 1990–
December 21, 1992)

**Dr. C. Rangarajan**
(December 22, 1992–
November 21, 1997)

**Dr. Bimal Jalan**
(November 22, 1997–
September 6, 2003)

Dr. Y. Venugopal Reddy
(September 6, 2003–
September 5, 2008)

Dr. D. Subbarao
(September 6, 2008 to date)

## ANNEXURE 1

### ASSESSMENT OF REFORMS: FINANCIAL INSTITUTIONS

In line with the deregulation and liberalisation policies of the 1990s, financial sector reforms were undertaken in the early phase of reforms. The basic objectives of the reforms were to enhance stability and efficiency of the financial system. It was felt that directed allocation of resources during the pro-reform period, although in accordance with the Plan priorities, was not conducive to allocative efficiency, and the higher rate of growth of financial saving was not matched by a proportionate increase in the rate of growth. The recurrence of domestic banking crises in developed and developing economies alike during the 1980s, and the financial crises in a host of countries in the 1990s underscored the necessity of financial stability for sustained growth. It was recognised that a vibrant, resilient and competitive financial sector is vital for sustaining the reform process in the real sectors of the economy.

The most significant achievement of the financial sector reforms has been the marked improvement in the financial health of the commercial banking sector, in terms of asset quality, capital adequacy and profitability. Despite these improvements, the commercial banking sector continues to face several challenges. First, a major concern for the banking system has been the high cost and low productivity as reflected in relatively high spreads and cost of intermediation. An important challenge for the banking sector, therefore, remains in transforming itself to a more efficient, productive and competitive set up.

Second, although the capitalisation level of almost all banks operating in India is above the prescribed minimum levels, banks may face difficulties to maintain their capital levels in coming years. The capital requirement of banks is likely to increase with pick up in credit demand and the implementation of the New Capital Accord sometime in 2006, which has accorded greater emphasis on risk-sensitivity in credit allocation. Banks would need to consider these factors while estimating their capital requirements. Given depressed capital market conditions and banks' limited ability to generate sufficient funds internally, maintaining the capital position in line with the prescribed norms would be a major challenge.

Third, commercial banks continue to face the problem of overhang of NPAs attributable, *inter alia* to systemic factors such as weak debt recovery mechanism, non-realisability of collateral and poor credit appraisal techniques. Policy measures have yielded mixed results. The recent enactment of the Securitisation and Reconstruction of Financial Assets and

Enforcement of Security Interest Act, 2002 has increased the momentum for the recovery of NPAs. However, banks need to intensify their efforts to recover their overdues and prevent generation of fresh NPAs.

Fourth, in a regulated regime, risks were essentially compartmentalised with various categories of market and credit risks being managed separately. Increasingly, risk is viewed as multi-dimensional. To enable banks to cope with risks, the Reserve Bank has been engaged in preparing banks for pro-active risk management. Banks would need to establish technical systems and management processes necessary not only to identify risks associated with their activities, but also to effectively measure, monitor and control them.

Fifth, it is important that financial institutions possess means and measures of corporate governance. The quality of corporate governance would become critical as competition intensifies ownership is diversified and banks strive to retain their client base. Banks would be required to further improve their internal management systems in terms of housekeeping, audit practices, asset-liability management and systems management to attain international best practice levels.

Sixth, a sound and well-diversified banking system envisages development of a banking sector with a diverse array of well-capitalised and healthy banks. As the dynamics of reforms gathers momentum, the coming years are likely to witness consolidation in the banking sector. Such consolidation will be driven by market forces in an enabling environment, which brings together willing institutions. A related issue is that of ownership of banks. Public sector banks (PSBs) continue to dominate the Indian banking sector and progressively the ownership needs to be diversified to make them more amenable to market discipline and reduce the possibility of regulatory forebearance.

Finally, bank lending tends to be pro-cyclical while the level of NPAs tends to behave in a counter-cyclical fashion. Consequently, in a downturn, as this condition of borrowers deteriorates, they tend to be downgraded by banks with the consequence that extra provisioning has to be set aside, potential exacerbating the capital shortage. Such behaviour of the part of banks tends to accentuate cyclical fluctuations. In these circumstances, dynamic or forward-looking provisioning by banks may be useful for circumventing such outcome.

With the phased withdrawal of government from direct intervention in the financial sector and gradual divestment of government ownership in major financial institutions, the importance of deposit insurance arrangements has increased in the context of attainment of financial stability. Introduction of risk based deposit insurance premium, separation of deposit insurance arrangements for co-operative and commercial banks and introduction of co-insurance among others, would help foster greater systems stability as also provide a safety net for depositors.

In co-operative banks, the impact of reforms appears to be limited, if assessed in terms of stability and efficiency parameters. One of the reasons for this appears to be delay in the initiation of reforms and the slow paced reform in the sector. Duality of control has also posed concern over the sharing of responsibilities among the regulatory and supervisory authorities. The current duality of control over co-operative banks by the Reserve Bank and the respective State Governments is impeding effective supervision of such entities, which needs to be resolved.

In the changed operating environment, development finance institutions (DFIs), which have traditionally been among the main sources of long-term finance for the corporate sector in India, are finding it increasingly difficult to maintain their viability. In view of this, the future role of these DFIs needs to be addressed urgently as the alternative source of long-term funds has not developed. As some DFIs convert themselves into banks or NBFCs, an important source of long-term funds would dry up. Thus, there is a concern regarding the vacuum which would be created by the withdrawal of DFIs from the scene. Although banks have entered the domain of term-lending there are limits on the extent to which commercial basis may be able to fill this vacuum. The shift from fixed to flexible interest rate regime, development of instruments for hedging interest rate risk, and effectiveness of timely resolution of NPA-related problems would influence the flow of funds from banks long-term financing requirements. Banks alone, however, may not be able to compensate the decline in long-term funds by DFIs to the corporate sector. To fill the gap, the development of a private corporate debt market is of crucial importance. The development of a benchmark in the fixed securities market and development of secondary market for corporate debt would also stimulate banks' investment in corporate securities.

In the case of mutual funds, while reforms have been successful in creating a competitive environment, the growth of mutual funds slowed down sharply partly due to depressed market conditions and partly due to the problems faced by the Unit Trust of India. Reforms in the insurance sector, which are of recent origin, have also been successful in enhancing competition even as the impact of increased competition on the insurance penetration is yet to be felt.

❖❖❖

CHAPTER 4

# MONETARY POLICY AND CREDIT CONTROL

## INTRODUCTION

The conduct of the monetary policy has been changing in response to the process of financial liberalisation. The increasing volume of cross-border trade in goods and services along with that of financial flows have enhanced interdependence in monetary formulation across countries. Sharp swings in capital flows and volatile exchange rate movements have emerged as key concerns in monetary management in emerging market economies. Accordingly, the Reserve Bank of India is paying a greater attention to financial stability consideration in their overall design of monetary policy formulation. Financial innovations have also induced significant transformation in the operating procedures of monetary management, more so in the background of the global crisis in 2007-08. The monetary policy of the RBI is influenced by the process of financial reforms, liberalisation and globalisation. Further more, the reorientation towards a market based economy to foster greater efficiency and growth, growth of the financial market during the last two decades had far-reaching effects on the monetary management, as well as monetary policy framework.

The Reserve Bank of India is mainly constituted as an apex authority for monetary management. Its primary function is to formulate and administer monetary policy. Monetary policy refers to "the use of instruments within the control of the central bank to influence the level of the aggregate demand for goods and services by regulation of the money supply and credit".

The Reserve Bank seeks to control and regulate the flow of credit in the economy such that it can sustain the tempo of development and promote the maintenance of internal price stability. It uses quantitative controlling weapons such as bank rate policy, open market operations and the reserve ratio requirement. Since 1956, it has increasingly relied on and resorted to selective credit controls for accelerating the rate of growth and for checking inflationary spurts.

In the post-independence era, with the enactment of the Banking Regulation Act, 1949, the Reserve Bank of India was invested with overriding powers to control the banking system and thus it emerged as a conscientious guardian and watchdog of the monetary structure of Indian economy. With the lapse of time, the scope of monetary policy in the country has been considerably widened to make adequate adjustments in the money credit structure in view of the changing needs of the developing economy envisaged under the Five-Year Plans.

## OBJECTIVES OF ECONOMIC POLICIES

Governments in the post-World War II era have proclaimed the objectives of their economic policies in wide humanitarian terms — the maintenance of full employment, well-rounded economic progress, and so on; and towards this end, they have also been easily adapting existing tools and fashioning new ones both in the national as well as the international sphere. These acts of the government have resulted in setting up central banks which non-existed before nationalizing the existing ones, in placing additional responsibilities on them, in conferring, amending and extending it, and setting up several ancillary institutions to serve the ends of national and international economic policies in the monetary and banking spheres.

While the goals of a country's economic policy provide the general setting for the functioning of a central bank, the precise nature of its relationship with the banking system depends on the matrix of economic and environmental conditions in which it has to work and the type of responsibilities that are placed upon it. As regards the latter, while the exact wording differs as between the statute of one central bank and that of another, the maintenance of monetary stability through the regulation of the country's currency and credit system is the basic responsibility of all central banks. Some statutes spell out monetary stability into internal and external stability. But those that do not, imply this all the same. Again, in some statutes, the broad overall objectives of economic policy, such as sound economic development or the maintenance of full employment, are also specifically incorporated. However, even where this has not been done, central banks have to keep such objectives consciously before them all the time. This widening of the scope of the responsibility of central banks, whether explicit or implicit, has made their task much more difficult than it was in the past. The maintenance of monetary stability is now not an objective to be pursued for its own sake but only for the contribution that it can make to the attainment of the overall objectives. Too much of the former stifles the progress towards the latter, while a too rapid pursuit of the latter endangers the former and becomes the process of self-defeating, for it hinders the progress towards the attainment of these wider objectives. Central banks have, therefore, to strike a balance between the two and evolve a policy that ensures the maximum progress in an atmosphere of stability. In addition, many central banks are entrusted with mechanisms to cater to the needs of certain vital sectors of the economy of administering banking legislation with a view to protecting the interests of depositors and of administering exchange control.

## CENTRAL BANK AND THE BANKING SYSTEM

The main relationship between the central bank and the banking system is the one that arises as a result of the former's basic responsibility. "The essence of central banking", Prof. Sayers observed, "is discretionary control of the monetary system". The discretion is to be exercised in the light of the objective the central bank happens to be pursuing. In the absence of a central bank, a country's monetary system suffers from certain rigidities. Discretionary control of the central bank, which means control adjusted to the needs of the situation, removes these. To enable them to make these adjustments, a central bank —

(*i*) Is given the monopoly of note issue;

(*ii*) Is required to hold the country's principal reserves of international liquidity;

(*iii*) Works as the bankers' bank;

(*iv*) Works as the government's bank not only by handling the inflows and outflows of its funds but also by handling its debt operations; and

(*v*) Is armed with a host of 'weapons'. Thus, on the one hand, central banks are the ultimate source of liquidity in a country while, on the other, they possess a number of devices to control and direct its flow in the desired channels. Apart from the discharge of their basic function through the use of these powers, central banks are advisors to the governments on monetary and banking matters and maintain a liaison between governments and banking and financial institutions by appropriate solutions to them; and through these actions, they facilitate the attainment of their basic objective.

The Government of India, like many other growing nations, has been, and continues to be, anxious to embark on accelerated development plans in order to reach the stage of "drive to maturity" within the shortest possible time. As might be expected, the internal resources of the country have perpetually fallen short of the financial requirements of the government-sponsored Five-Year Plans. Consequently, the government has had to resort to the well-known method of deficit financing, through the creation of central bank credit. This method of financing is inflationary in character. Consequently, to keep the inflation within "safe limits", the Reserve Bank has been called upon to play the role of a "controller of inflation". Thus, with slight modifications, Senator Douglas' analogy has become applicable to the Reserve Bank. The task of trying to check inflation while extending credit, according to Douglas, "will be just as futile as when...(one fills) the glass of water and keep(s) pouring it in, and... (tries) to mop up the overflow water with a pocket handkerchief".

To analyse the issue, two fundamental factors that characterize the role of the Reserve Bank in the economic development of India may be mentioned. First, India has an economy of planned development, and the central banking policy has to fit itself within the framework of development plans. Second, the size and structure of the Five-Year Plans are primarily decided upon not on the basis of the available financial resources but on the basis of the determination of the authorities to formulate plans of large dimensions. Once the size of a Five-Year Plan is determined, given limited financial resources, the government has to resort to deficit financing for the reasons

**MONETARY POLICY** **BOX : 1**

Governments intervene in finance partly to control the supply of money and credit. When the budget deficit is larger, governments often cover it by creating money. Excessive creation of money to cover budget deficits is the most common cause of inflation. When the fiscal deficit is not a consideration, the objective of monetary and credit policy is usually to maintain stable price.

Governments have various tools to control the monetary aggregates. Perhaps the most common technique in developing countries is for the central bank to specify credit ceilings for each commercial bank. Such ceilings have been criticized because they discourage competitions and the mobilization of deposits.

Another approach is for the central bank to fix the amount of deposit liabilities that can be created by the banking sector by imposing reserve requirements and controlling the quantity of reserves available to banks. But if refinancing is used to channel credit to preferred sectors, it cannot easily be used for monetary control as well. Other countries use the movement of government deposits between commercial banks and the central bank to control the level of reserves. In countries with more developed financial systems, central banks adjust bank reserves, and hence the money supply, through the purchase or sale of government securities. These transactions are called open market operations. When the central bank buys a security it pays with a cheque drawn on itself, thereby increasing its liabilities. Open market operations cannot be used in a system without an established government bill market. Monetary control with open market operations leaves the allocation of credit to market forces.

The degree of integration with world financial and capital markets also affects the execution of monetary policy. An open and fully integrated economy that chooses to maintain fixed exchange rates would have to maintain the money supply at the level demanded at the "World" price level and interest rate. Any other quantity of money would result in changes in the foreign exchange reserves of the central bank. The central bank's purchase or sale of foreign exchange would replace open market operations as the tool for determining bank reserves and, hence, the money supply.

A fixed exchange rate constrains the central bank's ability to create money and is thus a potential source of monetary discipline. A market-determined exchange rate restores a measure of domestic monetary independence. With either fixed or floating exchange rates, central banks will need to set reserve requirements at levels comparable to those in other countries if banking business is not to be driven abroad. Non-interest-earning reserve requirements are a tax on banks and as such will affect their competitiveness.

mentioned above. This is more than likely to create an inflationary situation, and the Bank has necessarily to function within the conditions created by the effort to implement the plan.

The primary responsibility of the monetary authorities of an underdeveloped country like India is to reduce the pressure of monetary demand without at the same time hampering production, so as to help maintain the predetermined pace of development. It has been reiterated on numerous occasions by the Reserve Bank that its aim is to "keep inflationary pressures at bay while the production forces are gathering momentum". It follows that an attempt to provide adequate finances for production on the one hand, and to control the inflation generated through deficit financing on the other, make the task of the Bank all the more difficult. Nevertheless, the nature of the problem of economic development of India, at least in the initial stages, was such that aiming at one of the above objectives at the cost of the other would only be self-defeating. Consequently, the monetary policy of necessity has to assume this dual responsibility.

## ROLE OF THE RESERVE BANK OF INDIA

This concept of dual responsibility is crucial to our understanding of the role of the Reserve Bank. About the time India launched her First Five-Year Plan, the Reserve Bank began to operate on a new concept of its promotional role, which implied the development of monetary and banking institutions in a planned economy. That concept was very different from the accepted functions of a central bank. Further, that role was frequently in conflict with its traditional restrictive role of controlling the conflict inflation that was generated in the economy as a result of deficit financing. However, the Reserve Bank's promotional role was so essential that it had to be pursued with enthusiasm. Simultaneously, with the acceptance by the Indian government of the concept of development planning, the monetary authorities were obliged to keep inflationary pressures under effective control. Ostensibly, therefore, the success of the monetary measures depended not only upon the ingenuity with which the policy was formulated but also upon the development of financial institutions within the framework of which the authorities had to function. The conclusion therefore, is inescapable that, beginning with the First Plan, it was essential for the Reserve Bank to deviate from the norm; and together with its normal central banking functions of credit regulation, the Bank also devoted its energies to the development of credit institutions and practices.

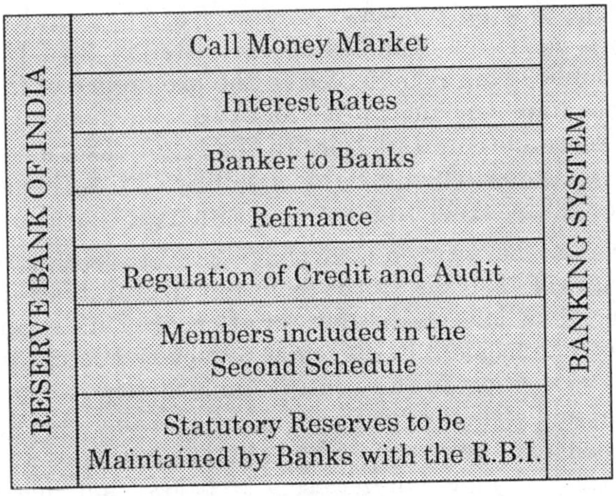


**Fig. 1 The Relation of the Reserve Bank with the Banking System**

While the Reserve Bank's new concept of central banking was a happy one, as mentioned above, it often created a conflict between its promotional role and its restrictive role, which was often a thorny problem for it. The development of credit institutions and the advances by the Bank of productive credit through these institutions generated inflationary pressures in the economy. Such a situation only made the restrictive role of the Bank more imperative which was to control the inflation generated by accelerated deficit financing. This situation duly emphasized the conflict in the development phase of a developing nation which often arises between the short-run and long-run objectives of the monetary policy. The conflict could not be resolved by the

**INFLATION TARGETING AS A MONETARY POLICY RULE** **BOX : 2**

With the money demand function becoming increasingly unstable in a number of advanced economies, the monetary policy framework began to shift away from a monetary targeting regime towards using short-term interest rates as an intermediate target of monetary policy. The framework underwent a further significant transformation as central banks, starting with New Zealand in 1989, began to target the final objective of monetary aggregate or an interest rate as an intermediate target. During the 1990s, a number of emerging economies also adopted inflation targeting (IT), especially as a device to stress their commitment to lowering the inflation rate. At present, 18 countries follow IT (IMF, 2003). Fulfledged IT is based on five pillars (an institutional commitment to price stability, absence of other nominal anchors, absence of fiscal dominance, policy instrument independence, and policy transparency and credibility) although some countries adopted IT without satisfying all of them (Mishkin and Schmidt-Hebbel, 2001). For instance, Chile and Israel adopted IT even as they had another nominal target (exchange rate) while the Bank of England adopted IT before attaining instrument independence.

Most of the central banks which have adopted IT have chosen an inflation target in the vicinity of two per cent. Almost all central banks are known to follow a 'flexible' rather than 'strict' IT, i.e., deviations of output from the potential are also taken into account. This is clearly reflected in the fact that the horizon over which deviations from the inflation target are tolerated is usually close to eight quarters. Too short a horizon and a very narrow range of the inflation target can induce undesirable output fluctuations. Alternatively, to overcome the deviations on account of supply shocks, a number of IT central banks have put escape clauses or focus on core measures of inflation, the latter in turn leading the problems of understanding by the public. This is indicated in the preference of the emerging market IT central banks for the headline consumer price index (CPI) although the industrial countries appear to have a preference for core inflation. In the latter case, a few countries (Australia and New Zealand ) have also switched towards headline CPI, with their statistical agencies redefining the headline CPI by excluding, *inter alia* interest charges.

IT does not purport to be an iron-clad policy rule; rather, it represents constrained discretion. The advantages of IT, *vis-a-vis* the monetary aggregate or exchange rate-anchored framework, with its focus on low and stable inflation, are: its support to macroeconomic stability and growth; an enhancement in the transparency and accountability of the monetary as well as fiscal policies; a scope to the central bank for short-run stabilisation; and, an impetus for institutional and structural reforms in the economy. Available evidence suggests that IT matters as it enabled the former high-inflation countries to achieve low inflation coupled with low volatility though not necessarily below that achieved by some non-IT industrial economies. Sceptics have, however, pointed out that the 1990s did not face severe adverse shock and as such, IT remains an untested framework. Moreover, many countries succeeded in reducing their inflation rates without a change in the monetary policy framework (Friedman and Knuter, 1996). The evidence, thus, does no support the superiority of IT over that of the US Federal Reserve Policy or that of the monetary targeting regime of the Bundesbank (before the formation of the European Central Bank) and the Swiss National Bank (until recently). This is attributed to the fact that the monetary targeting banks like the Bundesbank had also an inflation objective in mind and were quite willing to miss their monetary targets as and when they conflicted with their inflation objectives.

sacrifice of one function in favour of the other. For, if through undue caution, the Bank withheld legitimate credit for agricultural and industrial production, these areas might never develop. In the ultimate analysis, therefore, the Bank could not help but endeavour to ensure a reconciliation between the two equally important aspects of its role: its promotional role of developing new institutions and helping certain sectors of the economy in acquiring the requisite credit, and its restrictive role as the controller of credit expansion in the economy.

A central bank necessarily functions within the limitations set by the current economy philosophy of a country. If the dominant problem in a country like India is one of planned development, and the efforts of the whole country are directed towards the mobilization of national resources with a view to optimising the rate of development, then there is a need for a new perspective on central bank objectives, namely, the necessity for augmenting credit facilities and giving a purposive direction to credit. The development of this new perspective is likely to compel the central bank to reformulate the monetary policy in a way which would encourage the flow of credit into desired directions without necessarily bringing about a contraction in the total quantum of credit.

In India, the monetary policy framework underwent a significant transformation to emerge as the chief instrument of macroeconomic stabilization as well as a vehicle for the subsequent structural freeform in the financial system. The objective is to create a competitive environment in the financial sector while ensuring price stability and growth.

## RULES FOR MONETARY POLICY

Much of recent research has sought to use economic analysis to determine the consequences of alternative rules for the conduct of monetary policy, and to formulate rules that will be desirable from the standpoint of individual welfare. Interest in the study of monetary rules has increased over the past decade, for reasons having to do with progress in central banking and progress in macroeconomic theory.

On the one hand, many central banks most notably, but not only, the "inflation targeting" banks have increasingly come to organize their policy deliberations around an attempt to conform to specific targets or objectives, sometimes explicit quantitative targets. Moreover, central banks worldwide have increased the degree to which they discuss their decisions with finical market participants and the general public, and this too has increased the importance that the banks assign to having a clear framework to guide their deliberations.

At the same time, the development of a new generation of quantitative macroeconomic models that can be estimated using macroeconomic time series and have optimizing foundations that allow explicit evaluation of outcomes in terms of individual welfare has allowed modern macroeconomic analysis to be brought to bear on the evaluation of monetary polices, in the context of models with sufficient class to qualitative realism.

## MONETARY POLICY FRAMEWORK

The framework of monetary policy has undergone far-reaching changes all over the world in the 1990s mainly in response to the challenges and opportunities of financial liberalization. With the deregulates of financial markets and globlisation, the process of monetary policy formulation ha acquired a much grater market orientation than ever before, inducing a shift from direct to indirect instruments of monetary control.

The process of globlisation and liberalisation has thus necessitated a widening of the mandate central banks. At the same time, for their policies to be effective, monetary authorities have been required to modify the way in which they conduct monetary policy.

Monetary management is now further complicated by the increasing trade and financial operations. Swings in trade flows and, especially capital flows are quite common and these impart a high degree of volatility in exchange rates. Even in an environment of price stability, ensuring orderly conditions in financial markets and maintenance of systematic financial stability has thus emerged as an important objective to monetary policy. Likewise, financial innovations have also impacted upon the conduct of monetary policies. Thus, the process of monetary policy formulation has become relatively more articulate.

## OBJECTIVES OF THE MONETARY POLICY

Monetary policy refers to the use of instruments under the control of the central bank to regulate the availability, cost, and use of money and credit. The goal: achieving specific economic objectives, such as low and stable inflation, and promoting growth. The relative emphasis among the objectives varies from time-to-time, depending on evolving macroeconomic developments.

The operating framework of the Bank's monetary policy is based on a multiple-indicator approach. This implies that the Bank does not target any one indicator such as price stability alone, but monitors and analyses the movement of a number of indicators such as interest rates, inflation rate, money supply, credit, exchange rate, trade, capital flows, and fiscal position, along with trends in output. The Bank's actions are based on a considered judgement of these indicators as it develops its policy perspectives.

In a developing economy, the monetary policy has often got to be ambivalent. The objectives of the monetary policy may be stated as follows:

(i) To assist in the mobilization of savings in the community and promote capital formation.

(ii) To promote the spread of monetization and monetary integration in the country;

(iii) To provide adequate and timely credit necessary for the fulfilment of the targets of production and trade;

(iv) To extend monetary support to the authorities in the central task of the allocation of resources assisting them in the maintenance of an appropriate structure of relative prices;

(v) To maintain a general price stability and prevent inflationary tendencies from getting out of hand.

(vi) To maintain orderly conditions in the foreign exchange market;

(vii) To enhance the allocative efficiency of the financial markets; and

(viii) To sharpen the operating procedure of monetary policy — introducing transparency.

(ix) To ensure orderly conditions in financial markets and maintenance of systematic financial stability.

(x) To fine tune the financial innovations in the conduct of monetary policy.

(xi) To ensure financial stability in the face of globalisation and financial liberalization.

(xii) To contribute to sustainable economic growth.

(xiii) To reinforce fiscal responsibility.

The importance of the monetary and banking systems in the generation of savings and in their mobilization is obvious. While inflationary financing at the initiative of the government is an accepted method of development, it benefits directly only the public sector. The banking system of the country has, however, a greater responsibility and freedom of operation in the field of financing development plans for the private sector. The monetary and credit policies of the central bank, therefore, will have to take account of the objectives of the monetary policy.

**Table 1 : Objectives of Monetary Policy**

| Central Bank | Objective |
|---|---|
| 1 | 2 |
| **Developed Economies** | |
| Australia | Stability of the currency, maintenance of full employment and economic prosperity and welfare. |
| Canada | Low and stable inflation. |
| ECB | Price stability primary objective. Without prejudice to the objective of price stability, also support the general economic policies with a view to contributing to a high level of employment and sustainable and non-inflationary growth. |
| Japan | Price stability and to ensure the stability of the financial system. |
| New Zealand | Maintaining a stable general level of prices. |
| UK | Monetary stability meaning stable prices and confidence in the currency and financial stability. |
| USA | Maximum employment, stable prices and moderate long-term interest rates. |
| **Emerging Market Economies** | |
| China | Stability of the currency and thereby promote economic growth. |
| **India** | **Price stability and credit availability.** |
| Indonesia | Achieve and maintain currency stability by maintaining monetary stability and by promoting financial system stability. |
| Malaysia | Safeguard the value of the currency, promote monetary stability and a sound financial structure and influence the credit situation to the advantage of the country. |
| Mexico | Price stability. |
| Russia | Stability of currency, development of banking system and efficient settlement system. |
| South Africa | Financial stability. |
| Thailand | Maintain monetary stability. |

***Source:*** Central Bank websites

To sum up, the debate over the objectives that monetary policy can pursue is far from settled. While price stability remains the key objective of monetary policy, global integration is increasingly requiring central banks to focus on financial stability as well. Although the possible multiple goals of price stability, economic growth and financial stability are mutually reinforcing in the long-run, the critical issue in the design of monetary policy is to meet the challenges of the trade-offs in the short-run, which involve conscious policy choices. While there is very little disagreement over the fact that price stability should remain a key objective of monetary policy, reservations persist about adopting it as the sole objective of monetary policy.

## KEY ISSUES IN MONETARY POLICY

It is now widely agreed that monetary policy can contribute to growth and employment by maintaining price stability. Price stability does not mean a zero rate of inflation. For a number of reasons – quality biases in the measurement of — prices, downward wage and price rigidities and the zero bound on nominal interest rates price stability is defined as a low and stable rate of inflation conducive to economic growth. That price stability should be a key objective of monetary policy is reflected in a growing number of central banks, starting with New Zealand in the late 1980s, adopting inflation targeting frameworks. At present, there are more than 20 such central banks in the world who have price stability as the overriding objective of monetary policy. At the same time, a majority of central banks still operate under dual or even multiple mandates for instance, the legislated objectives of the US Federal Reserve are maximum employment, price stability and moderate long-term interest rates. However, even in such cases, it is agreed that central banks can contribute to growth and employment objectives through maintenance of low and stable inflation. Price stability is considered to be a prerequisite for the efficient allocation of resources in the economy and, hence this contributes to growth. There is a near unanimity now that there is no long-run trade-off between growth and inflation, i.e., monetary policy cannot permanently raise output above its potential through inflationary policies. Any attempts to raise output above the economy's potential will be eventually reflected in higher inflation. One reason as to why inflation surged during the 1970s in many economies was the misplaced belief that there existed a long-run trade-off between inflation and output. High inflation has an adverse effect on growth due to a number of factors.

## MONETARY CONTROL

In general, adjustment programmes are designed to achieve a certain growth target in some credit or monetary aggregate. In countries where financial innovations or a shift to a market orientation of the economy are taking place, the target for a particular monetary aggregate may become inappropriate and therefore may have to be revised.

In planned economies, for example, currency targets may be appropriate where use of deposits is strictly limited to plan transactions. Once the economy becomes more market-oriented, the monetary target may have to be changed and the programme modified. Market economies that use direct controls on interest rates and bank-specific credit ceilings to achieve monetary and credit targets may suffer from undesirable effects of such policies on resource allocation. These include low deposit rates and additional loan fees or service charges, disincentives to savings (once the credit targets are reached), and underdevelopment of interbank money markets. For these reasons, it is desirable to switch to indirect monetary control through reserve money management. The fund, through its technical assistance, has assisted Costa Rica, Indonesia, and Mauritius in making this switch, which can take place with or without interest rate liberalization. Where liberalization of interest rates is contemplated, the switch to indirect controls is particularly important to enhance competition in the banking industry.

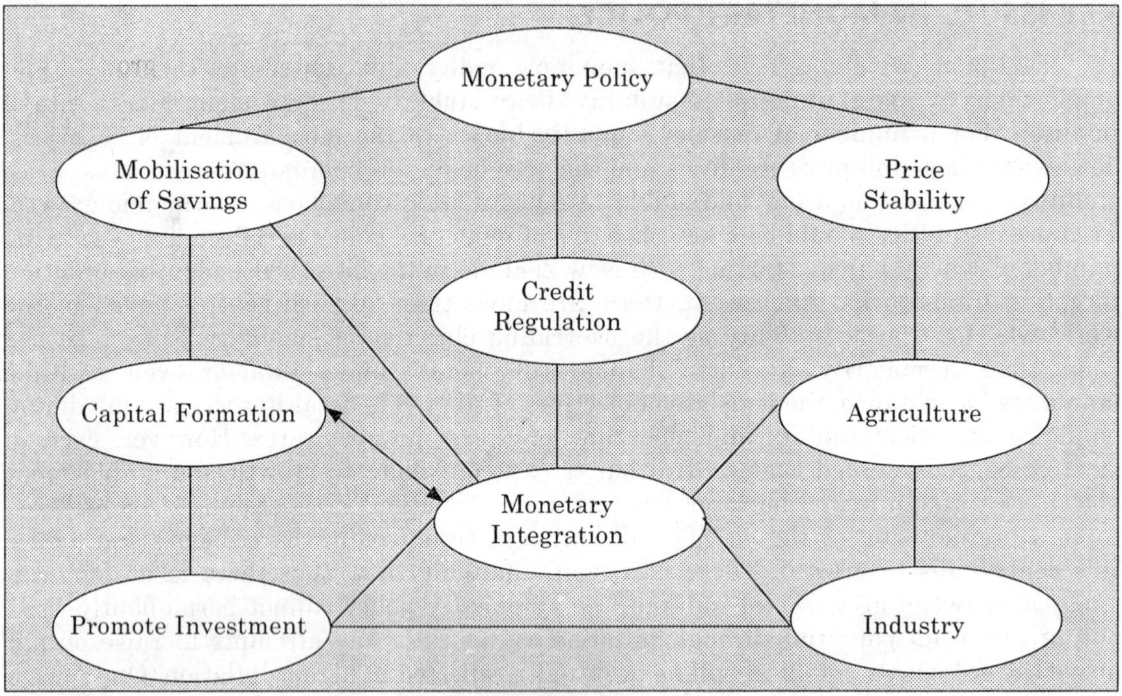


**Fig. 2 : Objectives of the Monetary Policy**

## INSTRUMENTS OF MONETARY POLICY

There are several direct and indirect instruments that are used in the formulation and implementation of monetary policy. Direct instruments involve increasing or decreasing the supply of money in the economy and indirect instruments involve influencing the interest rates (the price of money).

### Direct Instruments

**Cash Reserve Ratio (CRR):** The share of net demand and time liabilities that banks must maintain as cash balance with the Reserve Bank. The RBI requires banks to maintain a certain amount of cash in reserve as a percentage of their deposits to ensure that they have sufficient cash to cover customer withdrawals. By increasing or decreasing this ratio, the RBI can increase or decrease money supply by influencing the banks' ability to lend and hence create money out of the deposits received by them.

**Statutory Liquidity Ratio (SLR):** The share of net demand and time liabilities that banks must maintain in safe and liquid assets, such as government, cash, and gold securities.

**Refinance Facilities:** Sector-specific refinance facilities, (e.g., against lending to export sector) provided to banks. Refinance by the RBI to the banking sector directly augments the quantity of money.

## Indirect Instruments

**Liquidity Adjustment Facility (LAF):** Consists of daily infusion or absorption of liquidity on a repurchase basis, through repo (liquidity injunction) and reverse repo (liquidity absorption) auction operations, using government securities as collateral.

**Open Market Operations (OMO):** Involves the outright sales/purchases of Government securities. The RBI injects money into the economy by buying Government securities from the public/banking system; it withdraws money by selling securities to the public/banking system.

**Market Stabilization Scheme (MSS):** An instrument for monetary management introduced in 2004. Liquidity of a more enduring nature arising from large capital flows is absorbed through sale of short-dated Government securities and Treasury bills. The mobilized cash is held in a separate government account with the RBI.

**Repo/Reverse Repo Rates:** Rates that under the Liquidity Adjustment Facility (LAF) determine the corridor for short-term money market interest rates. By influencing these rates, the Bank triggers movement in other segments of the financial market and the real economy.

**Bank Rate:** The rate at which the RBI is ready to buy or rediscount bills of exchange or other commercial papers. It also signals the medium-term stance of monetary policy.

The Reserve Bank's Annual Policy Statement is announced in April. The RBI Governor responds to questions following the release of the *Annual Policy Statement.* There are three quarterly reviews in July, October, and January. A day before the policy review, a detailed background report – Review of Macroeconomic and Monetary Developments – is released.

## A NEW BENCHMARK

- **The Base** Rate system will replace the BPLR system with effect from July 1, 2010. But banks will be allowed to use the BPLR mechanism till December 2010.
- **Base Rate** will be the minimum rate for all loans. Banks are not permitted to resort to any lending below the Base Rate. The formula has been given by the RBI.
- **PLR is** not an independent measure. It's neither the RBI nor the NHB, which sets the benchmark prime lending rate for the home loan market. Nor do they prescribe a standard formula.
- **Under the** base rate regime, both new and old borrowers would be given a similar treatment.
- **Banks are** required to review the Base Rate at least once in a quarter with the approval of the Board or the Asset Liability Management Committees (ALCOs) as per the bank's practice.

- **Base rate** system will be applicable to all new and old loans that come up for renewal. Existing loans based on the BPLR system can run till their maturity.
- **Existing Borrowers** can switch to the new system before expiry of a loan, and they should not be charged any fee for such switchover.
- **Banks are** allowed to choose any benchmark to arrive at the base rate for a specific tenure that may be disclosed transparently. Base rate could, thus, vary from one bank to another.

The tools available to the Reserve Bank for the attainment of its objectives are listed as follows:

(*i*) The Bank Rate and control over the lending rates of banks;
(*ii*) Open market operations;
(*iii*) Variable reserve requirements;
(*iv*) Selective controls; and
(*v*) Moral suasion.

The programmes of economic development have introduced a strong and continuous expansionary trend in bank credit in which two factors cause variations. For a variety of reasons, the use of the two traditional instruments of central bank control, *viz.,* the bank rate and open market operations, has been rather limited in India. Variable reserve requirements, too, have been used only once. On the other hand, selective credit controls and moral suasion have been used fairly widely during recent years.

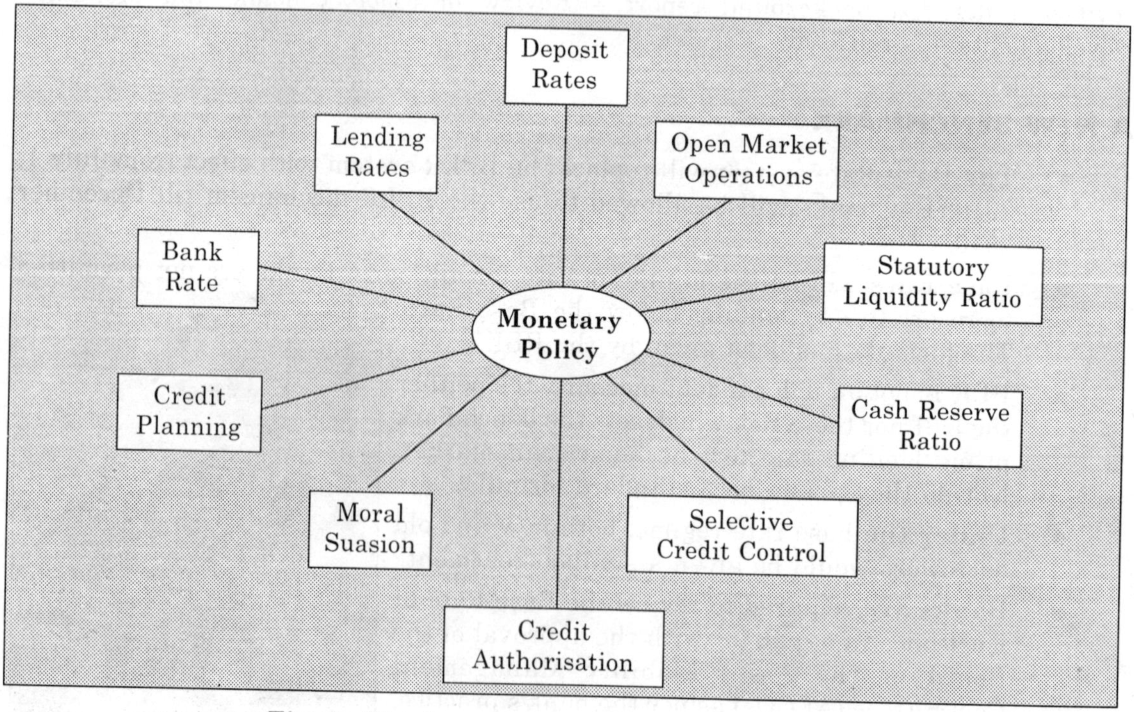


**Fig. 3 : The Instruments of Monetary Policy**

## (i) Bank Rate and the Banks' Lending Policy:

Although the Bank Rate was intended to be used primarily as the rate for buying or rediscounting bills of exchange or other eligible commercial paper, in the absence of a genuine market in India for such credit instruments, the Bank Rate has been used mainly as the rate governing the Reserve Bank's lending policy. A consequence of this has been that the Bank Rate, instead of being the leader of short-term rates in the system, since bonds have generally been the predominant collateral against which advances are taken by banks from the Reserve Bank.

One of the factors which limits the use of frequent variations in the Bank Rate as a technique for controlling credit is the imperfection of the money market resulting in a rather wide spectrum of interest rates in the economy and the lack of cohesion amongst them. It has been the endeavour of monetary authorities to reduce the disparities in interest rates in different sectors of the market for funds, more particularly with a view to lessening the high cost of credit to the weaker sectors of the economy. Hence, while the bank's lending rate to the organized money market has been stepped up in the manner described above, efforts have been made to reduce the cost for agriculture and small-scale industries by giving them finance at concessional rates.

In addition, for influencing the cost of bank credit, the Reserve Bank relies on direct control over the lending rates of banks. It derives its authority to regulate the interest rates of banks under Sections 21 and 35A of the Banking Regulation Act.

## (ii) Open Market Operations:

The use of this technique of controlling credit through its direct impact on the bank's liquidity position has been circumscribed by different factors at different periods in its history. In the early years of its existence, the scope for these operations was limited by the state of the economy. After the War, the cheap money policy coincided with the Government securities, to revert to a more normal pattern of distribution of their assessment through a liquidation of a part of these holdings. As mentioned earlier, late in 1951, the bank replaced the cheap money policy with that of discriminating support to the market. Thereafter, the growing needs of development, necessitating increasing efforts on the part of the authorities to sell more and more government debt management have tended to become a one-way affair.

Amongst the factors which limit the scope for a greater use of open market operations in India may be cited the absence of a well-developed market for Treasury and commercial bills, and the predominance of certain types of institutional investors like banks, the Life Insurance Corporation, provident funds and trusts which are required by statute to hold a certain proportion of their assets in the form of Government securities. The first has meant that the Reserve Bank use its lending policy rather than open market operations at the short end of the market to control short-term fluctuations in credit. The Reserve Bank's open market operations have, therefore, to be in medium and long-term securities. Here, the latter factor necessitates a policy of gradualness in effecting changes in the long-term interest rate structure. Yet, open market operations are the best way to conduct monetary policy.

### (iii) Variable Reserve Requirements:

Until October 1956, the Reserve Bank did not possess powers to vary the reserve requirements of banks, which were fixed at 5 per cent of demand liabilities and 2 per cent of time liabilities. The powers which it then acquired permitted the Bank to vary these up to 20 per cent of demand liabilities and 8 per cent of time liabilities. Also, it obtained powers to vary incremental reserve requirements, i.e., the proportion to be maintained as reserves of increments after a certain date to deposits, up to 100 per cent of the increase in deposits to the overall maxima mentioned above. These powers were used in 1960 under conditions of a rapid rise in the liquidity of the banking system. In March 1960, scheduled banks were required to maintain with the Reserve Bank 25 per cent of the increase in their deposit liabilities over and above the minimum statutory reserves, *viz.,* 5 per cent of demand liabilities and 2 per cent of time liabilities. From 6 May, 1960, the requirement was raised to 50 per cent of the additions to deposit liabilities after that date. The measure was operative mainly over the slack season of 1960, towards the end of which came the fundamental change in the Bank's lending policy with the introduction of the three-tier system of lending rates. The measure was, therefore, withdrawn and the impounded deposits released in two instalments, one in November 1960 and the other in January 1961. It may be noted that banks were compensated by the Reserve Bank in respect of the interest lost by them following the impounding of additions to deposits. The compensation was initially equal to the average rate of interest paid by banks during the corresponding quarter, subject to a ceiling equal to the Bank Rate. Later, it was raised by 1/2 per cent with a corresponding increase in the ceiling.

In September 1962, the distinction maintained between demand and time liabilities for purposes of reserve requirements was abolished. The minimum requirements, with effect from 4th February, 1984 are 9 per cent of demand and time liabilities taken together, and they can be varied between 3 per cent and 15 per cent. This change was necessitated by the increasingly important role played by time deposits in the Indian money market. With the constantly increasing tempo of economic activity, there has been a very keen competition for funds, which has found expression in the growth of the volume, and a tendency towards the shortening of the maturity of time deposits. A sizable part of time deposits held by the banking system now partakes of the character of demand deposits.

The Regional Rural Banks, have been allowed to maintain a lower level of cash reserve, *viz.,* 3 per cent, as in the case of scheduled State co-operative banks. This concession has been deemed necessary to increase their lending operations by not impairing their resources position. The exemption from the application of the provisions of Sub-section (1) of Section 42, insofar as they require a scheduled bank to maintain a cash reserve in excess of 3 per cent, is granted by notifications issued by the Bank from time-to-time under Sub-section (7) of that section which empowers it to extempt any scheduled bank with reference to the whole or any part of its reference to all or any of its offices or with reference to the whole or any part of its assets and liabilities.

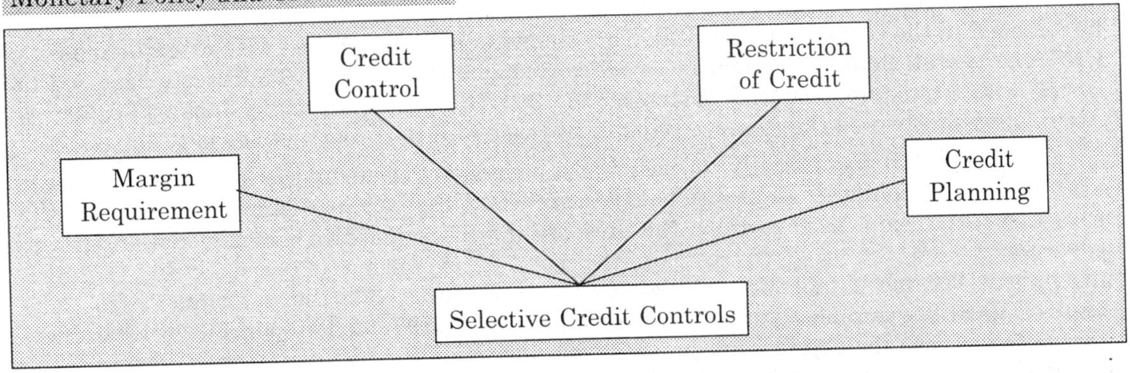


**Fig. 4 : Forms of Selective Credit Controls**

The cash reserve requirements for non-scheduled banks have been put down in Section 18 of the Banking Regulation Act. These banks have to maintain in cash with themselves or in current account with the Reserve Bank, the State Bank of India or any other notified in this behalf; or partly in cash and partly in such account, a minimum of 3 per cent of their total demand and time liabilities in India. The associate banks of the State Bank of India and all 20 nationalised banks have been notified by the Central Government for this purpose (as well as for the purpose of compliance with the liquid assets requirement under Section 24 (2A) of the Banking Regulation Act).

## STATUTORY LIQUIDITY RATIO: GENESIS AND FUNCTIONS — BOX : 3

Commercial banks in India have traditionally been subject to two types of reserve requirements. *viz.*, the CRR and the SLR. While the former is a stipulation under Section 42 of the Reserve Bank of India Act, 1934, the latter is specified in Section 24 of the Banking Regulation Act, 1949 under which all banking companies are required to hold a minimum stipulated proportion of their demand and time liabilities is India in the form of cash, gold, balances with the Reserve Bank, current account balances with other banks, money at call and short notice and unencumbered government and other approved securities. The primary objective of the stipulation of liquidity ratio was to ensure that banks hold sufficient liquid reserves to meet any unexpected drain. Thus, it sought to impose financial discipline on banks and provide some protection to depositors. Commercial Paper (CP) being short-term money market instrument, could have qualified as a 'liquid asset'. However, paucity of good quality CP, necessitated inclusion of Government securities, even though they may have a medium to long-term tenor, in the definition of SLR as they have a gilt edged character and are the easiest stock to liquidate in a crisis (Balachandran, 1998).

Cash maintained with the Reserve Bank for the purpose of meeting CRR requirement formed part of the overall liquidity ratio until 1962. This enabled banks to liquidate their government security holding whenever the marginal reserve requirement was raises, thereby blunting the effectiveness of this instrument. During the early 1960s while average overall liquidity ratio continuously declined, the credit to deposit ratio increase, raising apprehensions of bank credit outpacing deposit growth and eroding the liquidity position of the banks. The Banking Regulation Act was, therefore, amended in 1962, raising the minimum SLR of banks from 20 per cent to 25 per cent of their demand and time liabilities in India. The SLR to be maintained was made exclusive of balances maintained for the purpose of meeting cash reserve ratio requirements. Any balances in excess of the prevailing CRR requirements could, however, be included in the computation of SLR. This amendment ensured that with every increase in CRR, the overall liquidity obligations were correspondingly raised. Banks were required to comply with this requirement from September 16, 1964. The amendment of the Banking Regulation Act in 1983 empowered the Reserve Bank to increase SLR of banks up to 40 per cent.

Although SLR was initially conceived as a measure of securing the liquidity of banks, it also had implication for their ability to expand credit to the private sector. In the light of the monetary expansion triggered by the Reserve Bank's unbridled accommodation of the government and the need to restrain the pace of expansion of bank credit, the SLR instrument became a tool for mobilizing greater resources for the government from the banks. The SLR was raised gradually from 25 per cent in 1970 to 38.5 per cent in 1990. This served to increase the captive investor base for Government securities, thereby reducing the pressure on the Reserve Bank to absorb these securities. However, the incidence of macroeconomic crisis in the early 1990s and the emphasis of the role of SLR as a prudential instruments rather than an instrument for accommodating fiscal deficit led to scaling down of the SLR back to the statutory minimum of 25 per cent in October, 1997. SLR was scaled down to 24 per cent in November 2008, it was restored to 25 per cent in 2009.

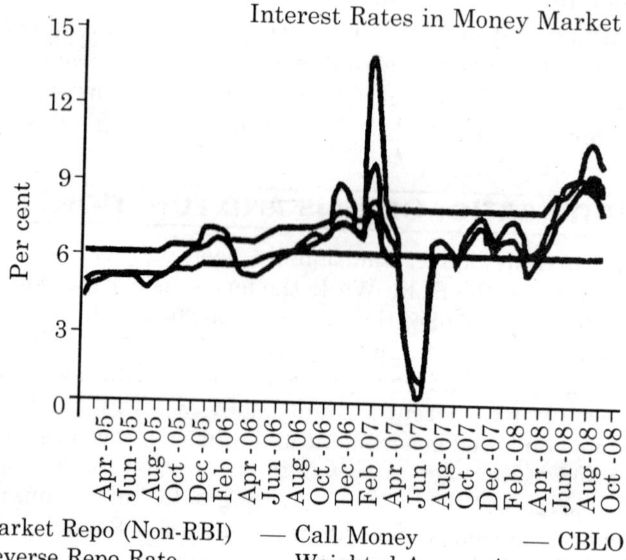

* : Weighted average of interest rate in the call money, CBLO and market segments.

**Table 2: Changes in Policy Rates and Cash Reserve Ratio**

| Effective From | Reserve Repo Rate | Repo Rate | Cash Reserve Ratio |
|---|---|---|---|
| 1 | 2 | 3 | 4 |
| March 31, 2004 | 4.50 | 6.00 | 4.50 |
| September 18, 2004 | 4.50 | 6.00 | 4.75 (+ 0.25) |
| October 2, 2004 | 4.50 | 6.00 | 5.00 (+ 0.25) |
| October 27, 2004 | 7.75 (+ 0.25) | 6.00 | 5.00 |
| April 29, 2005 | 5.00 (+ 0.25) | 6.00 | 5.00 |
| October 26, 2005 | 5.25 (+ 0.25) | 6.25 (+ 0.25) | 5.00 |

| | | | |
|---|---|---|---|
| January 24, 2006 | 5.50 (+ 0.25) | 6.50 (+ 0. 25) | 5.00 |
| June 9, 2006 | 5.75 (+ 0.25) | 6.75 (+ 0. 25) | 5.00 |
| July 25, 2006 | 6.00 (+ 0. 25) | 7.00 (+ 0. 25) | 5.00 |
| October 31, 2006 | 6.00 | 7.25 (+ 0. 25) | 5.00 |
| December 23, 2006 | 6.00 | 7.25 | 5.25 (+ 0.25) |
| January 6, 2007 | 6.00 | 7.25 | 5.50 (+ 0.25) |
| January 31, 2007 | 6.00 | 7.50 (+ 0.25) | 5.50 |
| February 17, 2007 | 6.00 | 7.50 | 5.75 (+ 0.25) |
| March 3, 2007 | 6.00 | 7.50 | 6.00 (+ 0.25) |
| March 31, 2007 | 6.00 | 7.75 (+ 0.25) | 6.00 |
| April 14, 2007 | 6.00 | 7.75 | 6.25 (+ 0.25) |
| April 28, 2007 | 6.00 | 7.75 | 6.50 (+ 0.25) |
| August 4, 2007 | 6.00 | 7.75 | 7.00 (+ 0.50) |
| November 10, 2007 | 6.00 | 7.75 | 7.50 (+0.50) |
| May 24, 2008 | 6.00 | 7.75 | 8.25 (+ 0.25) |
| June 11, 2008 | 6.00 | 8.00 (+ 0.25) | 8.25 |
| June 24, 2008 | 6.00 | 8.50 (+ 0.50) | 8.75 (+ 0.50) |
| July 29, 2008 | 6.00 | 9.00 (+ 0.50) | 8.75 |
| August 30, 2008 (Peak) | 6.00 | 9.00 | 9.00 (+ 0.25) |
| October 11, 2008 | 6.00 | 9.00 | 7.50 (- 1.50) |
| October 14, 2008 | 6.00 | 9.00 | 6.50 (- 1.00) |
| October 20, 2008 | 6.00 | 8.00 (- 1.00) | 6.50 |
| October 25, 2008 | 6.00 | 8.00 | 6.00 (- 0.50) |
| November 1, 2008 | 6.00 | 7.50 (- 0.50) | 6.00 |
| November 8, 2008 | 6.00 | 7.50 | 5.50 (- 0.50) |
| December 8, 2008 | 5.00 (– 1.000 | 6.50 (- 1.00) | 5.50 |
| January 2, 2009 | 4.00 (– 1.00) | 5.50 (- 1.00) | 5.00 (-50) effective from 17.01.2009 |
| March 4, 2009 | 3.50 (– 0.50) | 5.00 (- 0.50) | |
| April 21, 2009 | 3.25 (– 0.25) | 4.75 (- 0.25) | 5.00 |
| February 13, 2010 | 3.25 | 4.75 | 5.50 (+ 0.50) |
| February 27, 2010 | 3.25 | 4.75 | 5.75 (+ 0.25) |
| March 19, 2010 | 3.50 (+ 0.25) | 5.00 (+ 0.25) | 5.75 |
| April 20, 2010 | 3.75 (+ 0.25) | 5.25 (+ 0.25) | 5.75 |
| April 24, 2010 | 3.75 | 5.25 | 6.00 (+ 0.25) |
| July 2, 2010 | 4.00 (+ 0.25) | 5.50 (+ 0.25) | 6.00 |
| July 27, 2010 | 4.50 (+ 0.50) | 5.75 (+ 0.25) | 6.00 |
| September 16, 2010 | 5.00 (+ 0.50) | 6.00 (+ 0.25) | 6.00 |
| November 02, 2010 | 5.25 (+ 0.25) | 6.25 (+ 0.25) | 6.00 |
| Januray 25, 2011 | 5.50 (+ 0.25) | 6.50 (+ 0.25) | 6.00 |
| March 17, 2011 | 6.00 (+ 0.25) | 6.75 (+ 0.25) | 6.00 |

**Note 1:** Over the fiscal year 2010–2011 the Reserve Bank of India (RBI) has increased eight times its repo and reverse repo rates by 175 and 250 basis points (bps), respectively. The Cash Reserve Ratio (CRR) has been retained at 6 per cent for over ten months. The baby steps of the RBI have little effect on the inflation since market rates have accelerated more than the RBI's policy rates.

2: With effect from October 29, 2004, the nomenclature of repo and reverse repo was changed in keeping with international usage. Now, reverse repo indicates absorption of liquidity, while reverse repo meant injection of liquidity. The nomenclature on this Report is based on the new usage of terms even for the period prior to October 29, 2004.

3: Figures in parentheses indicate change in policy rates.

**Changing Stance of RBI: Ploicy by Policy**

| October 2008 Crisis MGMT | January 2009 Accommodative | April 2009 Accommodative | July 2009 Neutral Stance | October 2009 Exit Stance | January 29, 2010 Tightening |
|---|---|---|---|---|---|
| Ensure a monetary and interest rate environment that optimally balances the objectives of financial and price stability and well-anchored inflation expectations and growth | Provision of comfortable liquidity...Ensure a monetary and interest rate environment consistent with price stability, well-anchored inflation expectations... | Ensure a policy regime that will enable credit expansion at viable rates... in order to support the return of the economy to a high-growth path | Manage liquidity actively so that the credit demand of the government is met while ensuring the flow of credit to the private sector at viable rates | Keep a vigil on the trends in inflation and be prepared to respond swiftly and effectively through policy adjustments to stabilise inflation expectations | Anchor inflation expectations and keep a vigil on the trends in inflation and be prepared to respond swiftly and effectively through policy adjustments as warranted |

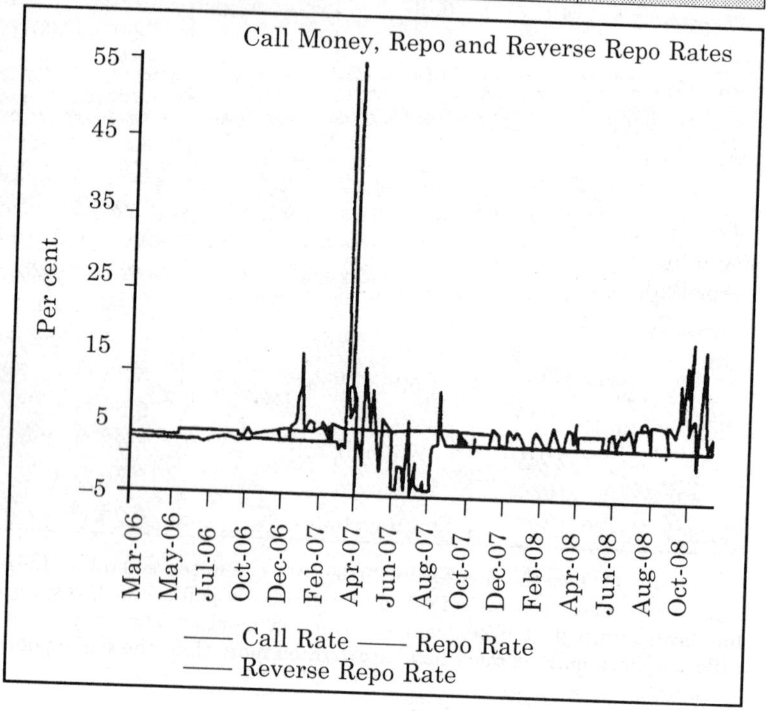

### (iv) Selective Credit Controls:

Selective credit controls have been used by the bank mainly with a view to restraining excessive speculative stock-building of commodities in short supply either as a result of a crop shortage or as a result of a fall in the production of manufactured articles following raw materials shortages, etc. The commodities in respect of which these articles of consumption or items important for exports are foodgrains, oilseeds, jute, cotton textiles and sugar.

These controls have taken the form of objectives to increase the margin requirements, to regulate the size of credit limit per borrower with a view to ensure maintenance of an aggregate level of credit against a particular commodity at a certain level which may have reference to the level of credit maintained in the corresponding period in the past, etc. Adjustments to suit the needs of the economy in a particular region have also been incorporated in these controls. Besides exercising control on bank credit against the security of particular commodities in short supply, the Reserve Bank has also endeavoured to control excessive borrowing from the banking system by way of clean advances or against the security of other assets, such as shares and stocks. Initially, it took some time for the banking system to get accustomed to these techniques. Extensive branch network and difficulties of communication as well as differences in the efficiency of the branches of different sizes and in different areas were some of the problems which had to be overcome.

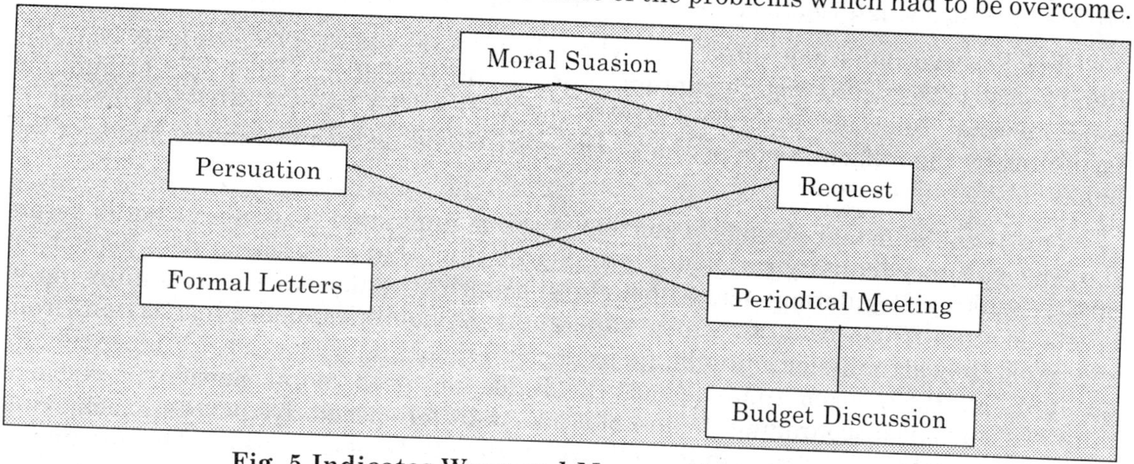


**Fig. 5 Indicates Ways and Means of Moral Suasion**

The main instruments of selective controls in India are:

(a) Minimum margins (in a secured advance, the "margin" represents a portion of the value of the security charged to the bank, which is expected to have been paid for by the borrower out of his own resources) for lending against selected commodities;

(b) Ceilings on the levels of credit; and

(c) Charging minimum rate of interest on advances against specified commodities. While the two instruments control the quantum of credit, the third instrument works as a leverage on the cost of credit. On the whole, the banking system in India has shown a good appreciation of the needs of such controls and has co-operated quite well. As regards their overall efficiency, the experience in India has been the same as that of most other countries, namely, that their effectiveness in general is comparatively limited. Generally, they are successful if employed in combination with measures of general credit control.

### (v) Moral Suasion:

Moral suasion refers to the advice or indication given by the central bank, generally to banks and sometimes to other financial institutions also, in the matter of their lending and other operations with the objective that they might implement or follow it. Moral suasion may be quantitative in content, such as fixation of the aggregate amount of credit to be granted by banks during a period, or caution to be exercised in granting advances against commodities whose prices are subject to speculative tendencies. Periodically, letters are issued to banks urging them to exercise control over credit in general or advances against specified commodities or unsecured advances in particular. Discussions are also held from time-to-time with banks with the same objective. Wherever the use of moral suasion is possible, it makes it easier for the central bank to secure the willing and active co-operation of commercial banks in complying with the regulatory measures, both in letter and in spirit; it also enables the central bank to exert influence not only on the borrowing banks (which is possible by direct action) but also on the non-borrowing banks, and other credit and financial institutions, whose operations are significant enough to affect the credit policy of the central bank.

The Reserve Bank has found the technique of moral suasion, backed as it is by the Bank's vast powers of direct regulation, quite useful; and it has been able to build-up good informal relations with banks over the years. The use of this instrument is facilitated by the concentration of almost the entire banking business in the hands of the banks in the public sector.

One notable instance of moral suasion is the maintenance by banks of liquid assets (*i.e.*, the statutory liquidity ratio) at a level higher than that prescribed under Section 24 of the Banking Regulation Act. Although, statutorily, banks have to maintain liquid assets equal to 25 per cent of their demand and time liabilities, under instructions from the Bank, they actually maintain liquid assets at a much higher level, *e.g.*, 35 per cent as on June 30, 1982. From time-to-time, the Bank has used moral suasion for various purposes, such as discouraging the use of bank credit for speculative purposes, achieving the desired degree of contraction in bank credit during the slack season, checking undue expansion of clean advances, helping government's borrowing programme, etc. This has been done through both informal consultation and issuance of formal letters by the Governor of the Bank to scheduled banks. The fact that 10 to 15 banks account for most of the deposit resources of the banking system makes frequent consultations easier between the Reserve Bank and the former and ensures the success of this method. Even when using other instruments of control, the Bank has endeavoured to explain the problem to the banking system and enlist their co-operation in achieving its objective.

The task of the central bank becomes easier, however, if there is a proper understanding and respect between it and the banking system as to the responsibilities and capabilities of each. Above all, it must be realized that, in countries following a broad-based warfare policy, there is a fundamental community of interest between the central bank and the banking system. The latter is the essential medium through which a central bank's monetary

policy can make itself effective. A well-organized banking system is, therefore, the first requirement of the success of a central bank. It need not then always use controlling instruments which force the banking system to act in the desired direction. It can achieve the same object through what is called "moral suasion", i.e., informing the banks what the central bank considers to be a desirable line of action and leave them to do the rest. For underdeveloped countries, the significance of this is that the central banks have to devote a considerable part of their energies to the provision of an efficient banking system. In some countries, this is done by the central bank itself undertaking either the whole business of commercial banking or at least such aspects of it as are immediately relevant in the interests of the development of the country. In others, it is attempted by offering various facilities to the banking system to enable it to expand and diversify its services, and if necessary, by subsidizing it up to ancillary money and capital market institutions.

A system of administered interest rates has also had an impact on the instruments on credit control. Since the interest rates offered on deposits and charged on lending are directly controlled by the monetary authorities, bank rate as an instrument of credit control has not much significance. Open market operations in Government securities have also become less relevant as instrument of credit control since the rates of interest offered on Government securities though reasonable are not truly competitive. It is in this context as mentioned earlier, the variable reserve ratio has emerged as an important instrument of credit control.

**TRANSITION FROM AUTOMATIC MONETISATION TO WAYS AND MEANS ADVANCES** — **BOX : 4**

Monetary policy had to contend with the imperatives of automatic monetisation through accommodating Government of India's *ad hoc* Treasury Bills up to March 1997. In order to check this unbridged automatic monetisation of government deficits, the First Supplemental agreement between the Reserve Bank and the Government of India on September 9, 1994 set out a system of limits for creation of *ad hocs* during the three-year period ending 1996-97 before being completely phased out from April 1997. It was agreed during 1994-95 that the net issue of *ad hoc* Treasury Bills would not exceed ₹ 6,000 crore as end-of the year, whereas it would not exceed ₹ 9,000 crore for more than 10 continuous working days during the year. It was further agreed that if the net issue of *ad hoc* Treasury Bills exceeded ₹ 9,000 crore for more than the stipulated period, the Reserve Bank would automatically reduce the excess amount of the *ad hoc* Treasury Bills beyond the prescribed level by auctioning of Treasury Bills or floatation of Government of India dated securities. While the year-end limit was lowered further to ₹ 5,000 crore for 1995-96 and 1996-97, the 'within-the-year' limit was retained at ₹ 9,000 crore for these two years. It was agreed that a suitable daily monitoring mechanism would be put in place by the Reserve Bank so as to furnish an updated position of the net issue of *ad hoc* Treasury Bills to the government. Accordingly, the Reserve Bank was responsible to advise the government about the net increase in *ad hocs* on a daily basis and the number of consecutive working days when the net issue of *ad hocs* exceeded the stipulated level, while on receipt of this information the government had to convey to the Reserve Bank its views and instructions on regularisation or the extent to which market borrowings had to be raised.

In pursuance of the Second Supplemental Agreement between the Reserve Bank and the Government of India on March 6, 1997, *the ad hoc* Treasury Bills were completely phased out by funding *ad hoc* Treasury Bills as on end-March 1997 into special undated securities at an interest rate of 4.6 per cent on April 1997 and were replaced by a system Ways and

Means Advances (WMA) commencing April 1, 1997. In order to smoothen the transition, the proportion of auction 91-day Treasury Bills was increased. Under the WMA system the Reserve Bank has ben extending short-term advances only up to the pre-announced half-yearly limits, at a mutually agreed rate of interest rate and fully payable within three months. The Government of India was also allowed to incur overdraft but an interest rate higher than that of the WMA which, effective April 1, 1999 has ben restricted to a maximum of 10 working days. Furthermore, it was also agreed that the Reserve Bank would trigger fresh floatation of Government securities whenever 75 per cent of the WMA limit was reached. It was also agreed that the government's surplus cash balances with the Reserve Bank beyond an agreed level would be invested by it in its own paper. With the depletion of Government securities from the reserve Bank's protfolio on account of its sterilisation operations, investment of Central Government's surplus cash balances in dated securities was temporarily suspended between April and June 2004 before being partially restored with a ceiling of ₹ 10,000 crore (enhanced to ₹ 20,000 crore in October 2004.

## CREDIT AUTHORISATION SCHEME

The Credit Authorisation Scheme was introduced by the Reserve Bank in November 1965 as an additional measure of credit regulation in the context of the Bank's policy of keeping inflationary pressures under check. The other main objectives of the scheme were to enforce financial discipline on the larger borrowers and ensure that they did not pre-empt scarce bank resources. Under the scheme, the Reserve Bank regulates not only the quantum but also the terms on which credit flows to the different large borrowers, in order that credit is directed to genuine productive purposes, that it is in accord with the needs of the borrowers, and that there is no undue channelling of credit to any single borrower or group of borrowers.

Originally, the scheduled commercial banks were required to obtain the Reserve Bank's prior authorisation for sanctioning any fresh working capital limit (including commercial bill discounts) of ₹ 1 crore or more to any single party or any limit that would take the total limits enjoyed by such a party from the entire banking system to ₹ 1 crore or more on secured and/or unsecured basis. The scheme has been modified from time-to-time in the light of the prevailing economic situation. Thus, in exceeding ₹ 25 lakh and repayable over a period of more than 3 years sanctioned (singly or jointly with other banks or financial institutions) to any single party, irrespective of the totality of the credit limits available to it from the banking system as a whole. This modification was made in order that borrowers might not avoid the discipline sought to be enforced by the specialised term-lending institutions. Further, borrowings by the public sector undertakings, including State Electricity Boards, advances against the guarantees of Central and State Governments, which were exempted from the requirement of the Reserve Bank's prior authorisation was required for sanctioning any credit limit (including commercial bill discounts) of ₹ 3 crore or more to any single borrower, or any limit that would take the total limits enjoyed by such a borrower from the entire banking system to ₹ 3 crore or more on secured and/or unsecured basis.

## INTEREST RATE REFORM

Policies on the level and structure of interest rates have implications for both monetary control and savings mobilization and allocation. While fund-supported programmes typically focus on the level of interest rates, which should reflect market conditions, reforming the interest rate structure increasingly receives more attention, because such reforms could help improve the allocation of credit. Bad debt and high operating costs can lead to low deposit rates and high lending rates, often with inappropriate distribution of risk. For example, distortions in credit allocation result from prime customers paying for risks of default arising elsewhere in the system. A term structure of interest rates that offers insufficient returns to longer maturity deposits could reduce the availability of term finance for investment. Policies to improve the structure of interest rates include measures to reduce interest subsidies, based on an assessment of their incidence and effectiveness (in redirecting resource flows); modify the sectoral distribution of subsidies to ensure consistency with external adjustment objectives; introduce a prime rate or base lending rate system; improve the operating efficiency of financial institutions; and minimize the incidence of bad debt through legal, regulatory and institutional changes.

A full-scale liberalization of interest rates requires prior implementation of structural policies to eliminate or substantially reduce selective credit policies based on below market interest rates; homogenize portfolio regulations; modify rules and regulations on mergers, licensing, and branching; and improve the soundness of the banking system and the adequacy of bank supervision. Without these policy changes, there would be inefficient and unequal competition in the loan and deposit markets. Interest rate liberalization under such circumstances could produce excessive fluctuations and significant distortions in the level, structure and responsiveness of interest rates. Moreover, in the absence of a well developed money market and of measures to strengthen the monetary policy instruments, the national authorities would be hard-pressed in influencing the marginal cost of funds to banks, much less its speed of response to monetary policy.

### ISSUES IN MONETARY AND FISCAL CO-ORDINATION — BOX : 5

There are several merits in co-ordinating fiscal and mometary policies. First, they interact to affect aggregate demand and determine output and interest rates in the short run. Second, in an open economy context, while higher interest rates arising out of tight monetary policy can adversely influence the cost of production of tradable goods, fiscal policy measures through tariffs, quotas and customs duties can alleviate the burden of producers of such goods. Third, monetary-fiscal co-ordination ensures the optimal mix of bond and money financing of government deficits as open market operations of the Central Bank determines the extent of money/bond financing. Fourth, political pressures may impose co-ordination as governments, in a democracy, enjoy popular mandate in setting economic policy objectives, which the monetary authority has to adhere to. Fifth, timing considerations and variable lags with which fiscal and monetary policy instruments impact upon targets in the short-and long-run also necessitate some co-ordination between the two arms of economic policy. Finally, uncertainty about unco-ordinated policy outcomes may be minimised through active co-ordination, as co-ordination failures often result in large losses of social welfare.

The moot question, however, is whether more co-ordination is necessarily better. If the Central Bank and the government agree on what needs to be done, but a co-ordinated approach cannot be put things, whereby the sensible policymaker must dominate the perverse one. In reality, however, fiscal and monetary policies are often poorly co-ordinated. If both authorities take consistent and credible actions, then the lack of co-ordination can stem from one of three causes, *viz.*, *(i)* the fiscal and monetary authorities might have different objectives, *i.e.*, different conceptions of what is best for society; *(ii)* the two authorities might have different opinions about the likely effects of fiscal and/or monetary policy actions on the economy, *i.e.*, they might adhere to different economic theories; and *(iii)* the two authorities might make different forecasts of the likely state of the economy in the absence of policy intervention. The co-ordination problem can be solved by vesting the powers of decision-making in the hands of the authority with the proper objective or corect theory or accurate forecast, if it is known which of the two authorities is correct. In reality, this is rarely known in advance. The best strategy, therefore, is to give some power to each authority and also to give each some ability to cancel out the actions of the other, although this may result in a conflict of interest in the worst case or, more often, end in a stalemate.

*Source :* RBI

## CO-ORDINATED ACTIVITIES

The Reserve Bank has continued its efforts at co-ordination with the Central and State Governments to bring about an improvement in the structure and working of the banking institutions at different levels and to stimulate and increase their own resources in the form of share capital and deposits. From this point of view, it is significant that, during the year 1971, an action programme for the reorganization and development of co-operative credit was drawn up on the basis of discussions held between representatives of the Bank, the concerned Union Ministers and the Planning Commission, and was thereafter circulated by the Government of India to State Governments for implementation in the districts selected for the Intensive Agricultural Areas Programme.

## LIMITATIONS OF MONETARY POLICY IN THE CONTEXT OF DEVELOPMENT

The central banking authorities can operate the monetary policy effectively only if they are fully aware of the limitations of the monetary policy in bringing about development. Effectiveness of their policy would also depend upon the extent to which they are able to convince the governmental authorities about the true role of money. Central banks and central banking policies can play no more than a modest role in promoting economic development and growth. For, money cannot be a substitute for real resources. It is, of course, true that money — either in the form of cash or bank credit — is necessary to bring together and render effective the sinews of growth, i.e., the real inputs such as raw materials, labour, enterprise and technology. But money, by itself, cannot add either to their supply or to their real productivity. Finance whether from budgetary or banking sources — is a necessary but not sufficient input. And, therefore, mere spending does not produce real inputs. If money could buy development, no central bank is so underdeveloped as to be unable to create any amount of money needed. But the central banker is painfully aware of the limitations and more importantly

the dangers of excessive money. Real output or real income can be produced only with real resources. These real factors in production or growth are: full and efficient utilisation of existing productive resources; improved technology in agriculture and industry; scientific attitudes and practices; increased productivity of workers through improved nutrition, health and education; development of spirit of enterprise; creation of an enterprising and able managerial class; encouragement to innovation and productivity; an increased rate of real saving and capital formation; a stable, honest, and efficient government, etc. In short, it implies reconstruction of the entire society in all its aspects. Obviously, such a process cannot be purchased with money alone.

It is, unquestionably true that inadequate monetary policy can seriously retard growth. But, it is still more important a truth that even the most powerful monetary policy cannot be a substitute for the various real factors mentioned above. "Therefore, to rely too heavily on monetary policy, and to try to substitute it for other necessary measures, is to invite disappointment and failure."

This, however, does not mean that monetary policy has no important role in development far from it. In fact, central banks can and should make important contribution to growth. Monetary policy, together with fiscal policies, can ensure adequate demand to help growth of output. Monetary policy can help provide adequate finance for bringing together the various real inputs of production. It may also increase real savings through a forced saving programme under which increases in money supply may be used to force the community to consume a smaller part and save a larger part of its income. The process is indeed inflationary and, therefore, needs to be resorted to with utmost care. The monetary policy can also use selective controls to channelise funds in desired direction to be in alignment with planned policy objectives. It can foster the growth of financial institutions and promote savings and investment media. It can influence the saving habits of the people by providing institutional saving devices at their doorsteps and thus divert funds away from dead assets like land and gold towards financial assets which would help productive effort. Thus, the potential of monetary policy for bringing about economic development is as important but its contribution becomes more effective and tangible, if its limitations are not lost sight of.

## ASSESSMENT OF REFORMS

Structural reforms initiated in the Indian economy since the early 1990s have encompassed all spheres of economic activity. Reforms included industrial deregulation, liberalisation of the foreign trade and investment regime, public enterprises reform and financial sector liberalisation. These reforms, aimed at reorientation of the Indian economy from a centrally directed command and control economy to a market-oriented economy so as to foster greater efficiency and growth, have contributed to a sustained pick-up in growth.

The conduct of monetary policy during the 1990s was geared to supporting the overall economic reforms with a view to creating a competitive environment as a means of improving productivity and efficiency and ensuring macroeconomic stability. While the twin objectives of monetary policy remained the pursuit of price stability and ensuring credit availability for growth, the operating procedure of monetary policy underwent significant changes in response to the challenges of financial liberalization, this also entailed reforms in the monetary and fiscal interface in order to ease the fiscal constraint. This process was well supported by structural measures, through the dismantling of administered interest rates and the deregulation of credit markets. Given the changes in the monetary landscape, the process of adjustment has been reasonably smooth. The Reserve Bank was successful in achieving the objective of a phased scaling down of statutory pre-emotions unimportant macroeconomic development was the sharp decline in the inflation rate during the second half of the 1990s attributable to better monetary management as well as generally favourable supply side factors, an empirical assessment of the monetary policy transmission mechanism suggests that the output and inflation variations, particularly in the second half of the 1990s largely emanated from non-monetary factors and the contribution of the monetary policy shocks has further declined during the 1990s as compared with the 1980s.

Monetary management increasingly assumed a market orientation. Switch over to indirect instruments of monetary control was consistent with the objective of rekindling the process of price discovery in the financial markets for the purpose of efficient resource allocation. Besides, the opening up of the economy required the Reserve Bank to counterbalance the domestic and the external sources of monetisation in order to maintain stable monetary conditions. The Reserve Bank gradually put in place a liquidity management framework in which monetary conditions are harnessed to the final objectives through a range of instruments, such as open market (including repo) operations and changes in reserve requirements, reinforced by interest rate signals through the bank rate and the repo rates. In the process, the liquidity adjustment facility (LAF) has emerged as the principal operating instrument of monetary policy. Besides, the growing macroeconomic complexities required a shift from the earlier monetary targeting framework to a multiple indicator approach in which a host of macroeconomic variables are now monitored for the purpose of monetary policy formulation.

The deregulation of interest rates and the evolution of inter-linked financial markets facilitated the gradual emergence of an interest rate channel of monetary policy transmission. There is increasing evidence that the Reserve Bank is now able to effectively influence movements in short-term interest rates in the money markets and by extension, prices in the Government securities markets. The pass through to the credit markets is, however, still very weak. The deposit and lending rates of scheduled commercial banks continue to be relatively sticky, largely reflecting structural constraints in the form of a large order of NPAs and the continuation of government administered interest rates in small saving instruments. This had led to downward rigidity in real interest rates blunting the effectiveness of monetary policy. It may be mentioned here that this rigidity in the small savings rate has been partially addressed as the Union Budget, 2002-03 announced that the interest rate on small savings would be linked to the average annual yield on Government securities in the secondary market. Corresponding adjustments in these rates have been announced in the Union Budget, 2003-04. To promote flexibility in interest rates, issues such as asset quality of banks, adoption of floating deposit rates and strengthening of asset liability and risk management by banks, and rigidities in the interest rates of competing assets need to be addressed.

Wide-ranging structural reforms have inevitably impacted upon the conduct of macroeconomic policy in India. Monetary policy framework, in particular, had to contend with a number of changes in its operating environment. These changes have been brought about primarily by financial and external sector liberalization. First, the process of financial liberalization now necessitates a greater market orientation of the process of monetary policy formulation than ever before in view of the shift to a market-oriented economy from a control-oriented regime. Second, financial liberalisation has led to emergence of financial conglomerates with implications for financial stability. Third, the globalization of economies, while essential for greater competition and hence for efficiency, has posed several challenges for monetary management emanating, *inter alia,* from swings in international commodity prices, and, more importantly, from large and sudden movements in capital flows and exchange rates. Finally, advances in information technology are not only revolutionising payment and settlement practices but also speeding up the spread of information. For all these reasons, during the 1990s, monetary policy in India, like other countries, revisited issues related to objectives, intermediate targets, instruments and operating procedures of monetary policy.

In the monetary policy arena, a significant success has ben in respect of reigning in inflation since the second half of the 1990s. This has also enabled lower inflationary expectations. Efforts to improve the credit delivery mechanism have also begun to indicate some success recently. Real interest rates for borrowers have also softened. A noteworthy achievement, despite progressive opening up of the Indian economy has been the maintenance of financial stability in the country. In contrast to the Indian experience, financial crises were endemic in many developing and emerging market economies during the 1990s. These issues have been addressed in detail in earlier chapters. This concluding chapter provides an overall assessment of the dynamics and challenges for monetary policy in India.

## MONETARY POLICY AND PUBLIC DEBT

The conduct of monetary policy during the 1990s was geared to supporting the overall economic reforms with a view to creating a competitive environment as a means of improving productivity and efficiency and ensuring macroeconomic stability. While the twin objectives of monetary policy remained the pursuit of price stability and ensuring credit availability for growth, the operating procedure of monetary policy underwent significant changes in response to the challenges of financial liberalisation. This also entailed reforms in the monetary and fiscal interface in order to ease the fiscal constraint. This process was well supported by structural measures, through the dismantling of administered interest rates and the deregulation of credit markets. Given the changes in the monetary landscape, the process of adjustment has been reasonably smooth. The Reserve Bank was successful in achieving the objective of a phased scaling down of statutory pre-emptions. An important macroeconomic development was the sharp decline in the inflation rate during the second half of the 1990s attributable to better monetary management as well as generally favourable supply side factors. An empirical assessment of the monetary policy transmission mechanism suggests that the output and inflation variations, particularly in the second half of the 1990s, largely emanated from non-monetary factors had the contribution of the monetary policy shocks as further declined during the 1990s as compared with the 1980s.

Monetary management increasingly assumed a market orientation. Switch over to indirect instruments of monetary control was consistent with objective of rekindling the process of price discovery in the financial markets for the purpose of efficient resource allocation. Besides, the opening up of the economy required the Reserve Bank to counterbalance the domestic and the external sources of monetisation in order to maintain stable monetary conditions. The Reserve Bank gradually put in place a liquidity management framework in which monetary conditions are harnessed to the final objectives through a range of instruments, such as open market (including repo) operations and changes in reserve requirements, reinforced by interest rate signals through the Bank Rate and the repo rates. In the process, the liquidity adjustment facility (LAF) has emerged as the principal operating instrument of monetary policy. Besides, the growing macroeconomic complexities required a shift from the earlier monetary targeting framework to a multiple indicator approach in which a host of macroeconomic variables are now monitored for the purpose of monetary policy formulation.

In addition, the Reserve Bank, like many other central banks in emerging market economies, has had to increasingly contend with maintaining financial stability. Besides, the Reserve Bank's role as manager of public debt also implies that the internal debt management function gets inextricably mixed with the monetary management function. In view of the limited number of instruments, the Reserve Bank has to prioritise its objectives given the circumstances. This constrains the degree of flexibility available to monetary policy in a complex macroeconomic environment.

Fiscal dominance continues to be the critical issue. Capital inflows coupled with weak credit demand enabled the Reserve Bank to trade surpluses of the banking system with the deficits on the government account and thereby ease the fiscal constraint on monetary policy. In the process, net domestic assets of the Reserve Bank have been shrinking and this could impose limits on the scope for sterilisation in the future. At the same time, in view of the burgeoning fiscal deficit, the situation could change very quickly in case there is a pick-up in industrial activity or if capital flows dry up, especially as banks continue to hold a large portfolio of government securities well beyond the statutory prescriptions. It is in this context that the need is sometimes felt to separate the internal debt and monetary management functions. At the same time, even if the Reserve Bank does not directly subscribe to market borrowings, the fiscal impact on bank liquidity would still constrain monetary policy.

There is thus a limit to which a central bank can ease the fiscal constraint through liquidity management operations. The proposals advocated by the proposed FRBM legislation for reducing the role of the Reserve Bank in primary subscriptions and limiting the fiscal deficit, thus, assume particular significance.

The deregulation of interest rates and the evolution of inter-linked financial markets facilitated the gradual emergence of an interest rate channel of monetary policy transmission. There is increasing evidence that the Reserve Bank is now able to effectively influence movements in short-term interest rates in the money markets and by extension, prices in the Government securities markets. The pass through to the credit markets is, however, still very weak. The deposit and lending rates of scheduled commercial banks continue to be relatively sticky, largely reflecting structural constraints in the form of a large order of NPAs and the continuation of government administered interest rates in small saving instruments. This had led to downward rigidity in real interest rates blunting the effectiveness of monetary policy. It may be mentioned here that this rigidity in the small savings rate has been partially addressed as the Union Budget, 2002-03 announced that the interest rate on small savings would be linked to the average annual yield on Government securities in the secondary market. Corresponding adjustments in these rates have been announced in the Union Budget, 2003-04. To promote flexibility in interest rates, issues such as asset quality of banks, adoption of floating deposit rates and strengthening of asset-liability and risk management by banks, and rigidities in the interest rates of competing assets need to be addressed.

Unlike in the past when bank balances with the Reserve Bank were largely governed by reserve requirements, the demand for bank reserves in the future, in the context of a declining cash reserve ratio (CRR), are likely to depend on banks' requirements in respect of settlement balances. Day-to-day monetary management would thus require a closer assessment of market liquidity. It is in this connection that the Reserve Bank has initiated a process of liquidity forecasting. While the gradual institution of a real time gross settlement (RTGS) system would control domino risks of default, this is also likely to exert pressure on liquidity management.

The monetary policy framework has been shifting course throughout the 1990s. The break down of a stable relationship between money, output and prices as a result of financial innovations coupled with high inflation rates led to the adoption of an inflation targeting framework in many economies. While the pursuit of price stability could be a sound proposition in itself, there continue to be many constraints in the Indian economy, as in many other emerging market economies, which prevent the switch to an inflation-targeting framework. At the same time, it must be recognised that the current anti-inflationary stance was largely built in the backdrop of the high inflation of the 1980s. Since inflationary pressures have been subdued in the recent past, the co-existence of low inflation and low growth in the past two years poses a fresh challenge to the conduct of monetary policy.

The issue of growing public debt is another area of serious concern and it has a close bearing on the sustainability of fiscal policy. An assessment of the public debt in terms of both the 'accounting approach' and the 'present value constraint approach' indicates that continuation of current fiscal stance could make public debt of both Central and State Governments unsustainable unless corrective measures are undertaken to rein in fiscal deterioration. The persistent rise in interest payments particularly in the 1990s, has been a key factor for widening of fiscal deficit and consequent steep rise in public debt. The proposal to swap states' outstanding liabilities to Central Government on account of small savings could make a major dent in the growth of interest payments. For the Central Government, aggressive restructuring and divestment in unviable public sector units could bring in sizable resources to redeem a part of outstanding liabilities and consequent reduction in interest payments.

The policy initiatives undertaken for the development of the government securities market phasing out of automatic monetisation and reduction in pre-emption of institutional resources have provided a level-playing field to the private investor. The widening fiscal gap, however, could hamper the maintenance of low interest rate regime, which is vital in the context of the revival of economic activity.

In such an eventuality, it would not only crowd out investment, but would also make public debt highly unsustainable given the level of returns on government investments. Adoption of rules based fiscal policies could facilitate the path for durable fiscal consolidation through mandatory fiscal discipline. Speedy implementation of the provisions of the proposed Fiscal Responsibility and Budget Management (FRBM) Bill is critical for achieving the goal of ensuring inter-generational equity in fiscal management and long-term macroeconomic stability. It should not only help in attaining sustainability, but should also enhance the level of accountability and transparency in fiscal operations of the Central Government. Similarly, efforts should also be initiated at the sub-national level towards rule based fiscal policies for long-term fiscal sustainability.

## CONCLUSION

Money is a facilitating device. Too much of it can cause distortions in the economy through price increase just as too little can hinder the smooth functioning. The process of money creation is a process of credit creation. Money comes into existence because credit is given either to the government or to the private sector or to the foreign sector. Since credit facilitates the production process, it has a favourable impact on output. But at the same time, the increased money supply raises demand with an upward pressure on prices. The output effect and the price effect must be taken together to judge the overall impact on the economy. A model built on these postulates for India indicates that the price effect of money supply is greater than the output effect.

With the growing globalization and integration of economies, monetary authorities are now required to pay greater attention to external developments. Swings in trade flows and, especially capital flows are quite common and these impart a high degree of volatility to exchange rates. Even in an environment of price stability, the 1990s witnessed episodes of financial instability. The presumption that price stability ensures financial stability is thus not true, at least in the short-run. Ensuring orderly conditions in financial markets and maintenance of systemic financial stability has thus emerged as an important objective of monetary policy, even for central banks not involved with banking regulation and supervision.

Financial innovations have also impacted upon the conduct of monetary policy. In consonance with the preference for a degree of operational flexibility in a complex macroeconomic environment, most central banks are beginning to eschew setting unique intermediate targets or following some fixed rule of monetary policy. They, instead, prefer to monitor a range of macroeconomic indicators, which carry information about the ultimate objectives. Short-term interest rates have emerged as operative target/instruments of monetary policy. Most central banks now prefer to manage liquidity to steer monetary conditions in consonance with the overall policy objectives of price stability and growth. Central banks usually forecast market liquidity and then conduct open market operations to impact the interest rate structure to affect the real economy. Along with these developments, central banks have strengthened their balance sheets in order to be able to meet unforeseen contingencies that may arise from their market operations.

In India, the opening up of the economy in the early 1990s had a significant impact upon the conduct of monetary policy. Price stability remains the key objective of monetary policy and there is virtually a national consensus that high inflation is not good. Inflation expectations and inflation tolerance have come down. Adherence to the Fiscal Responsibility and Budget Management Act should stabilize inflation expectations and hence contribute to the objective of price stability. While adequate availability of credit to meet investment demand continues to remain an important objective, the growing integration of the Indian economy with the global economy has led to financial stability emerging as a key consideration in the conduct of monetary policy. Although there are complementarities between the objectives in the long-run, there are certain trade-offs in the short-run.

In order to meet challenges thrown by financial liberalization and the growing complexities of monetary management, the Reserve Bank switched from a monetary targeting framework to a multiple indicator approach. Short-term interest rates have emerged as indicators of the monetary policy stance. A significant shift is the move towards market-based instruments away from direct instruments of monetary management. In line with international trends, the Reserve Bank has now put in place a liquidity management framework in which market liquidity is now modulated through a mix of open market (including repo) operations and changes in reserve requirements and standing facilities, reinforced by changes in the policy rates, including the LAF rates and the Bank Rate. These arrangements have been quite effective in the recent years in managing liquidity in the system, especially in the context of persistent capital flows. The introduction of the Market Stabilisation Scheme has provided further flexibility to the Reserve Bank in its market operations.

As monetary policy emerges as the primary instrument of macroeconomic stabilisation, the Reserve Bank, like most other central banks, has initiated several measures to strengthen the health of its balance sheet. Over the past few years, the process of monetary policy formulation has become relatively more articulate, consultative and participative with external orientation, while the internal work processes have also been re-engineered. The stance of monetary policy and the rationale are communicated to the public in a variety of ways, the most important being the monetary policy statements. The communications strategy and provision of information have facilitated conduct of monetary policy in an increasingly market-oriented environment.

While financial and external liberalization present opportunities, they also throw challenges for policy authorities. Monetary authorities are increasingly required to take cognizance of not only domestic shocks but also external shocks. Given their objectives, central banks are required to monitor various segments of financial markets to ensure orderly conditions. Given the random nature of the shocks hitting the economy, central banks are increasingly acting as shock absorbers. In order to manage these shocks effectively, a steady stream of innovations is required by central banks in terms of instruments and operating procedures while strengthening their balance sheets.

The demand function for money provides a convenient starting point for understanding what is a desirable order of increase in money supply in the context of expected growth in income. As non-monetary factors play an important role in influencing the price variations in India, these are also taken into account while determining the tolerable limit to monetary expansion exercises. While the Reserve Bank of India has not formally adopted a system of monetary targeting, it nevertheless indicates to the banking system at the beginning of each year the expected increase in deposits. In fact, the Committee to Review the Working of the Monetary System appointed by the Reserve Bank of India in 1983 suggested the adoption of a flexible system of monetary targeting with appropriate feedback for the purpose of regulating the volume of money and credit and for ensuring effective co-ordination between monetary and fiscal policies. In a situation where the bulk of the primary money expansion comes as a consequence of the central bank credit to government, the system of monetary targeting can succeed only if there is a close understanding between the government and the central bank.

Fiscal discipline creates enabling conditions for monetary and financial stability. Monetary policy will have, however, still to grapple with uncertainty in the environment it operates. Incoming economic data — crucial for the conduct of monetary policy – provide, at best, incomplete coverage of economic activity; are subject to substantial sampling errors; become available with only a lag; and, are subject to substantial revisions (Bernanke, 2004). Despite substantial empirical research, there is still no unanimity on the channels through which monetary policy affects output and prices. Lags with which monetary policy works remain uncertain and can vary from one business cycle to another. Therefore, policymakers are unable to predict with great confidence how – and how quickly – their own actions are likely to affect the economy. Divergent movements in alternative indicators of inflation in the short-run – for instance, between wholesale and consumer prices in India, as at the present juncture – pose further challenges for the monetary authority in gauging underlying inflationary conditions in the economy. In addition to these uncertainties, short-term risks to monetary management emerge from global macroeconomic imbalances and the associated possibility of disruptive currency adjustments. In the medium – and long-term, evolving demographic patterns and the electronic money revolution will add to uncertainties of the transmission mechanism. In the context of these uncertainties, a risk-management approach involving a judgement about the probabilities, costs and benefits of the various possible outcomes has been recommended for the conduct of monetary policy (Greenspan, 2004).

Uncertainty about how economies operate and about monetary policy itself is, however, no excuse for not pursuing price stability. While year-to-year inflation may vary depending upon the intensity of supply shocks, monetary policy can stabilize inflation expectations at low levels. An environment of sustained low and stable inflation is conducive for financial savings, with beneficial impact on investment in the economy and for sustained growth and employment. Price stability is all the more important for an economy like India, with a large proportion of poor population that has no hedges against inflation.

The monetary authorities in India besides regulating the overall volume of money and credit have also been concerned with the allocation of credit. This is so because of the imperfections in the credit market. In view of the rigidities present in the credit market, special measures have to be taken to ensure the flow of credit to the needy and the priority sectors. Thus, credit policy in the Indian context becomes as relevant as the overall monetary policy.

The 1990s marked a fundamental shift in the role of the monetary and financial system from a passive channel of resource mobilization and disbursal guided by the planning process to an active role in resource allocation in accordance with market signals. The reforms were enabled by fundamental shifts in the monetary-fiscal interface. Moreover, in the context of the growing openness of the Indian economy, the absorption of excess foreign exchange supply in the market led to significant compositional shifts in the Reserve Bank balance sheet and the reserve money analytics. This necessitated recourse to open market operations to achieve the monetary policy objectives. Coupled with the ongoing financial deregulation and its possible implications for stability of money demand, the monetary targeting framework evolved into a multiple indicator approach in 1998-99. In addition, a framework of liquidity management in the form of Liquidity Adjustment Facility was put in place in June 2000.

The monetary policy reforms facilitated a significant reduction in pre-emption of resources. A noteworthy development was the lowering of inflation in the economy in the second half of the 1990s attributable, *inter alia*, to better monetary management. This, in turn, led to a concomitant softer interest rate environment, especially in the Government securities market. The LAF was able to maintain stability in money market conditions. Finally, monetary policy was successful in sterilisation of capital flows in consonance with domestic requirements. An empirical assessment of the monetary transmission mechanism suggests that the output and inflation variations are largely on account of non-monetary factors and the contribution of the monetary policy shocks declined further during the 1990s as compared with the 1980s.

A few issues emerge from the analysis. An important factor determining the effectiveness of the monetary transmission process is the degree of 'pass-through'. In view of the weak sensitivity of the bank lending rates to changes in the Bank Rate, the efficacy of the monetary policy in reinvigorating growth runs up against a constraint. Second, the shrinking net domestic assets of the Reserve Bank in the context of sustained capital flows brings into focus the limits of sterilisation on an ongoing basis.

Finally, a key objective of macroeconomic policy, including monetary policy, must be the avoidance of resurgence of inflationary expectations. In this context, despite a significant improvement in the monetary-fiscal interface during the 1990s, fiscal dominance continues to persist with growing volume of gross market borrowings. The burden of directly financing the fiscal deficit could easily revert to the Reserve Bank in case of a reversal in the liquidity conditions, especially as banks' investments in Government securities are already far in excess of their statutory SLR requirements. Therefore, the issue of separation of debt management function from the monetary authority needs to be addressed. The proposed Fiscal Responsibility and Budget Management Legislation and the need to accord greater operational flexibility to the Reserve Bank, could have far-reaching ramifications on the operational framework of monetary policy in India.

❖❖❖

CHAPTER 5

# DEVELOPMENT FINANCE INSTITUTIONS

## INTRODUCTION

Development Finance Institutions (DFIs), a heterogeneous group of diverse institutions form an integral part of the Indian financial system providing a range of financial services. They form an important segment of the financial sector.

DFIs in India have had a long and successful history and were visualised in a role complimentary to commercial banks and other private financial agents in lending activities of long gestation that were not catered to by the commercial banks. In particular, in the key segments of agriculture, micro, small and medium enterprises, housing, infrastructure, irrigation, power and exports and imports.

DFIs form a diverse group not only in terms of size and nature of incorporation, but functionally as well. Apart from enhancing competition in the financial system, these institutions play a crucial role in broadening the access of a vast section of the population to financial services by offering a variety of products and services. The role that some of the DFIs play acquired greater significance in view of the emergence of financial inclusion as one of the major policy objectives since they can play a critical role as an instrument of credit delivery, particularly in the small-scale retail sector and in fostering entrepreneurship in the country.

The concept of development banking was used for the first time in the post-Second World War period to refer to the institutional financial machinery built for fostering industrial growth in the country. In the post-Second World War period, several newly liberated underdeveloped countries in Asia, Africa and Latin America wanted to solve their chronic problems of squalor and poverty and in their anxiety to hasten the pace of industrialisation, they established special financial institutions to supply the basic ingredients of development — capital, know-how and entrepreneurship for the rapid growth of the country.

The concept of development banking is based on the assumption that mere provision of finance will not bring about entrepreneurial development. More importantly, development banks play an important role in using mobilised resources effectively to help meet the development needs of the country/region or state.

It is difficult to imagine the course of economic growth which has taken place in the world without the significant contribution made by these financing institutions. Their catalytic importance should not be underestimated. They have been able to make an impact on employment and have also stimulated small-scale and medium enterprises. As experience is gained by these agencies, they are themselves evolving and are able to take new initiatives to further the wider cause of development, as may suit the growing needs of their respective economies.

Development banking, as it exists today, had no fixed pattern, and has taken many norms. There are varying structures and forms of organisation, whether private sector, public sector, joint sector, or many variants of these categories, not excluding commercial banks. The organisation of development banks and the pattern of their financing all over the developing world, present a kaleidoscopic view, in regard to ownership of the initial equity capital by the government, government agencies and non-government agencies. What is ultimately important is, not so much their form, as the spirit inspiring their functioning and the dedication of the executives to attain their basic development objectives. For example, the World Bank has financed a wide variety of development banks, including mixed commercial and development agencies, large government banks that undertake a sizeable range of programmes on behalf of the government, banks that specialise in financing state enterprises and multi-sector institutions that perform not only a banking but also a promoter/holding company function.

## SOME OTHER CONCEPTS OF DEVELOPMENT BANK

"It may be said with a claim to generality that a 'development bank' which deserves its name legitimately, will give priority to development objectives, while other selection criteria, though not excluded at all, will clearly range second to the aims of development policies."

— *H.E. Bachem*

"The developmental role of a development bank is precisely that mix of functions or tasks which called for linking the words 'development' and 'bank' together and which justified governments is sponsoring and financing them."

— *William Diamond*

"Financial institutions need not be passive instruments of economic activity. With dynamic management and an adequately permissive environment of available opportunities and of favourable policies, they can be active engines of economic development."

— *William Diamond*

"If among financial institutions, one particular type — the development bank — has been singled out for discussion, it is not because it is unique in the opportunities or it has to foster economic development. It is rather because the development bank has, aside from the conventional function of providing finance, an explicit, special task. It has been created generally with community support, to do something which needs to be done to foster development and which is being done by others. The development bank cannot avoid the responsibility to behave accordingly."

— *William Diamond*

"A development bank has the opportunity to promote enterprises, i.e., to conceive investment proposals and to stimulate, to pursue them or itself to carry them through, from 'conception' to 'realisation'. In principle, a development bank is well suited to assume the kind of role. Yet, enterprise creation is fraught with costs and risks which development bank cannot neglect. Development banks can prudently undertake them only when they have the requisite financial strength, technical expertise and the managerial skill to deal with them effectively."

— *William Diamond*

"A development bank is like a living organism that reacts to its socio-economic environment and its success depends on reacting most aptly to that environment."

— *A.G. Kheradjou*

'There should be a determined and conscientious effort on the part of the Development Financing Institutions (DFIs) as well as those entities that are interested in DFIs, to search out for the methods by which they can participate effectively in the task of rural mobilisation for national progress. DFIs can undertake programmes of action-oriented research as to how best they can contribute to the strengthening of inter-sectoral linkages between industry and agriculture."

— *C.S. Krishna Moorthi*

"There is a convincing reason for planning institutions as well as for development banks to evaluate especially the use of power for productive purpose with regard to the contribution which the output of an angry-using project, directly or indirectly, makes to agreed development goals."

— *H.D. Krukenberg*

"The future industrialisation of Asian countries rests in large measure in their own hands, i.e., in mobilising domestic resources.... Although external borrowing is necessary, it should be noted that the higher the average level of domestic savings, the lighter will be the burden of external debt."

— *Masao Fujioka*

## OPERATIONAL PRIORITIES

The Development Banks (DBs) are a multilateral development finance institutions engaged in promoting the economic and social progress in the areas of their operation in the post-Independence era.

The strategic development objectives continue to promote economic growth, reduce poverty, support human development, promotion of trade infrastructural development as well as accelerate industrialisation and agricultural development.

Over the years, Development Banks have played a key role in the economic and social development through their operational priorities.

## DEFINITION

Development Bank has been defined as: "A bank whose main objective is to promote industrial development, encourage industrial ownership, and mobilise financial, managerial and entrepreneurial resources so as to increase long-term wealth and well-being."

William Diamond and Shirley Bosky consider industrial finance and development corporations as 'development banks'. Dr. Desai defines development bank as, "a financial institution concerned with providing all types of financial assistance to enterprises in the form of loans, underwriting, investment, guarantee operations and promotional activities to accelerate the process of sustainable socio-economic development and fosters growth and co-operation". Dr. K.V. Prabhakar observes, "a development bank is a multi-purpose institution which shares entrepreneurial risks, changes its approach in tune with the industrial climate and encourages new industrial projects to bring about speedier economic growth".

The concept is interrelated with industrial development, entrepreneurship, leadership vision and efficient management. Truly, during the last century, industrialisation has been given the highest priority in development. The concept also lays equal emphasis on mobilisation of resources both from savings, borrowings and investment, improve managerial and encore entrepreneurship for the accelerated process of economic growth and all-round development.

Development is synonymous with industrial development which is *inter alia* linked with the economy. Thus, development bank is the kingpin in the process of economic growth. In short, all financial institutions which are development-oriented may be called as a development bank. The development bank is essentially a multipurpose financial institution with development outlook.

## CHARACTERISTICS OF DEVELOPMENT BANKS

The creation of development banks has been one of the most widespread and highly useful efforts to solve the problems of industrial and agricultural development. And, the working of development banks depend on the synthesis of the skills of various disciplines like finance, economics, engineering, accountancy, law, etc. In recent years, development banks have extended their professional services to other sectors for promoting sustainable economic growth. In some countries, emphasis is being laid on to expand investment in social infrastructure, in particular public health and education, both to enhance the quality of life directly and to promote economic growth in the longer term. Social infrastructure is vital not only for humanitarian reasons, but also for economic growth and development.

To pursue development goals, the banks will need to build on their multilateral character. More specifically, development banks modify the environment in which they work, as well as provide finance for it. The distinctive characteristics of development bank lingers around promotion or "motivate", "encourage" and "stimulate"; and their public declarations and policy statements generally express their intentions to 'encourage, stimulate or promote' development in one sector or another. Promotion is, in effect, the carrying out of the entrepreneurial function. In other words, the development banks are institutional entrepreneurs engaged in the process of enterprise creation.

Thus, the characteristics of development banks are visionary, promoter, technically competent, mobiliser of resources, innovator, creative, leader as well as entrepreneur. In a way, banks play a catalytic role in development.

**CORPORATE FINANCE IN THEORY AND PRACTICE** **BOX : 1**

Much attention has been paid in academic circles to identifying the factors that influence corporate financial structure and dividend policies. The seminal article by Modigliani and Miller in 1958 demonstrated that in a world with perfect capital markets a corporation's debt-to-equity ratio is irrelevant to the firm's market value. In such a world the value of the firm is determined entirely by its investment decisions, which can therefore be completely separated from financing decisions. But markets are never perfect, and in practice financing decisions are not irrelevant. Subsequent developments in corporate finance theory relaxed some of the explicit or implicit conditions underpinning the assumption of perfect capital markets.

Corporate taxes and the worldwide practice of tax deductibility of interest payments provide an incentive for debt finance. This incentive is weakened, however, by the direct and indirect costs of financial distress and bankruptcy, which are more likely to be encountered in a highly leveraged company. Information flows are not perfect, and this has an important influence on financing decisions. In particular, managers have better information on a firm's performance and prospects than do outside creditors and shareholders. By maintaining stable dividends, firms help to signal their confidence about future prospects. This may explain why firms continue to pay dividends even if they need additional external finance or if taxes on capital gains are lower than those on dividend income.

Furthermore, since the interests of managers may differ from those of creditors and shareholders, the latter group must incur costs in trying to monitor and affect the way the company is run. Decisions on capital structure will be influenced by the ability of creditors and shareholders to get the information they need in order to exercise control over managers.

Recent theories have provided some plausible explanations for the differences in corporate financing patterns between the bank-based systems of Germany and Japan, on the one hand, and the market-based systems of the United States and United Kingdoms, on the other. The two bank-based systems involve greater corporate indebtedness (although the difference is not as large as suggested by reported accounting data). This may be explained by the close relations between banks and industry — that is, by the ability of bankers to influence the decisions of managers.

A development bank which has a high level of administrative ability, innovative ideas, vision about economic development, technical capability, trained professional and dedicated management team, effective communication, organisational ability, prudent capacity stands a much better chance of success in the process of development.

Some other characteristic features of a development bank are:

(1) It is a multi-purpose specialised financial institution.

(2) It strives to promote economic development.

(3) It provides refinance to other financial institutions.

(4) It provides a package of services from identification to management.

(5) It arranges for a package of incentives to entrepreneurs.

(6) It brings in institutional innovations entrusted with development.

(7) It is a visionary institution.

(8) It is a link that spurs all-round development.

**Chart 1**

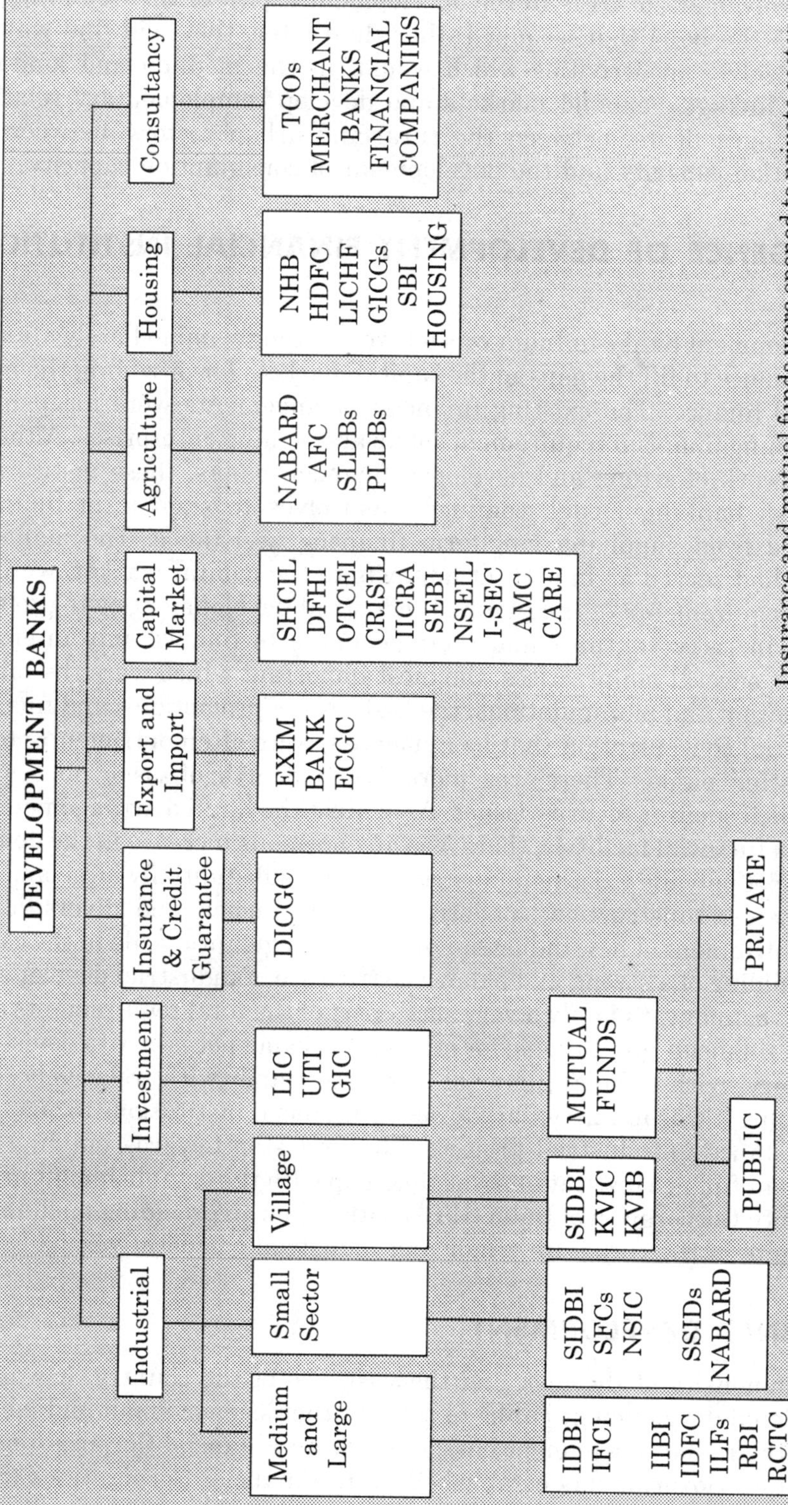


Insurance and mutual funds were opened to private sector. As on March 2009, there were 21 insurance companies in the life segment and 15 in the general insurance segment and 36 in mutual funds segment are in operation.

ICICI and two of its subsidiaries merged with ICICI Bank on March 30, 2002
IDBI was merged with IDBI Bank on April 2, 2005

The increasing involvement of DFIs in the development aspect of their banking and financial function gives the hope that, sooner rather than later, they will find ways in which to involve themselves in activities which would, in the medium and long-run, promote inter-sectoral linkages, expand markets and develop complementary relations between industry and agriculture, between the rural and urban sectors, between the development of production capacity and the development of consumption capacity.

## NEED AND EMERGENCE OF DEVELOPMENT FINANCIAL INSTITUTIONS IN INDIA

The need for development banks in India was felt very strongly immediately after the attainment of independence to fill the gaps in the capital markets for providing the needs of long-term industrial finance. The existing financial arrangements were incapable of coping with the burgeoning financial requirements of up and coming enterprises. Although the country had a network of strong and developed financial banks, these institutions, working on the British banking model, confined themselves to short-term financing activity, and abstained from supplying long-term financial assistance. The managing agency houses, which had served as important adjuncts to the capital market, were not able to cope with the requirements of the planned industrial development owing to their apathy to investment in risky ventures and their keenness to finance only interested concerns. Furthermore, several malpractices, the most important which were the misuse of funds, excess speculation and manipulations, the high cost of promotions, and financial and marginal managerial concentration that had emerged, were often detrimental to the interests of the investing public. There was moreover, a dearth of issue houses and underwriting firms which sponsor security issues. As against the limited arrangements for the supply of long-term financial facilities, there was an enormous increase in the demand for long-term capital. Not only did existing industries require substantially large amounts of capital to meet their reconstruction, modernisation, expansion and diversification programmes, the establishment of new industrial projects on a gigantic scale in the capital goods sector for the building of a strong and balanced structure of industrial development, called for enormous investment. But only a very small part of the total requirements could be met by the existing financial institutions; for others, it became necessary to devise new institutional machinery with ample financial resources and with relatively more comprehensive functions. It was felt necessary to set up financial institutions to ensure an adequate flow of assistance to industrial projects. The first step towards building up a structure of development finance institutions was taken up with the establishment in 1948 of the Industrial Finance Corporation of India (IFCI) with a view to providing medium and long-term credit to units in the corporate sector and industrial co-operatives.

## AN ERA OF PLANNED DEVELOPMENT

In view of the immensity of the task and the vast size of the country, it was also decided to set up regional development banks to cater to the needs of small and medium enterprises. In 1951, the Indian Parliament passed the State Financial Corporations Act. Under the Act, the State Governments established State Financial Corporations (SFCs) for their respective regions. By 1955-56, 12 SFCs were set up and by 1967-68, all the 18

SFCs now in operation came into existence. SFCs grant financial assistance to public limited companies, private limited companies, partnership firms and proprietary concerns.

The role of an integrated financial infrastructure in stimulating and sustaining economic growth is well recognised now. A network of financial institutions helps an economy to augment its savings. At the same time, it leads to a more efficient utilisation of the available investible resources. There is a well-integrated network of financial institutions in the country comprising 44 institutions at the national level and 82 at the state-level. Broadly, they are classified as follows:

(1) All India Development Banks (AIDBs)

(2) Specialised Financial Institutions (SFIs)

(3) Investment Institutions (IIs)

Financial institutions with their role as a mobiliser of the community's savings and a channeliser of these savings into productive outlets, play a crucial role in the economic development of a country. As a matter of fact, economic and industrial development of a country depends, in the main, upon how efficiently funds are managed by the banks. Like other businesses, financial institutions must be managed efficiently. Efficacious management of these institutions will not only improve their profitability but also enhance their contribution to industrial and financial development of the country. Management should, therefore, be well-versed in problems, principles, policies and techniques involved in mobilisation of funds and their channelisation.

Among the AIDBs, IDBI, IFCI, ICICI, IIBI and DFC provide financial assistance to medium and large industries. SIDBI and SFCs cater to the needs of small and tiny industries.

Of the SFIs, RCTC and TDICI provide risk capital, venture capital and technology development finance and TFCI extends finance to hotels and tourism-related projects. LIC takes care of the business of life insurance. GIC offers general insurance facilities. UTI mobilises savings and channelises them into corporate investments.

**INDUSTRIAL FINANCE CORPORATION OF INDIA** **BOX : 2**

The Industrial Finance Corporation of India was established on 1st July, 1948 under the Industrial Finance Corporation Act, 1948 as the first development financial institution in the country to make the medium – and long-term finance more readily available to industrial concerns in India.

To provide IFCI greater flexibility to respond to the needs of the rapidly changing financial system and an access to the capital markets, the constitution of IFCI was changed from a statutory corporation to a company under the Companies Act, 1956. The Company was incorporated on the 21st May, 1993, under the Companies Act, 1956 in terms of Section 4(2) of the Industrial Finance Corporation (Transfer of Undertaking and Repeal) Act, promulgated on the 2nd April, 1993 and obtained Certificate of Commencement of Business on 24th June, 1993. The objective *inter alia*, was to takeover the assets and liabilities, business and functions of the erstwhile Industrial Finance Corporation of India (IFCI), established under the Industrial Finance Corporation Act, 1948 (IFC Act). Accordingly, the undertaking of IFCI under IFC Act stands transferred to and vests in the Company with effect from the 1st July, 1993, vide notification issued by the Government of India, Ministry of Finance, Department of Economic Affairs (Banking Division) on the 7th June, 1993.

**Main Objects of the Company**

The main objects of the Company include *inter alia:* (*i*) providing financial assistance to industrial and service sector in the form of Short, Medium or Long-term Loans or Working Capital facilities or Equity Participation, and (*ii*) To carry on the business of leasing and hire purchase finance company and to acquire to provide on lease or to provide on hire purchase basis all types of industrial and office plant, equipment, machinery, vehicles, buildings and real estate, required for manufacturing, processing, transportation and trading business and other commercial and service business.

## FUNCTIONS

Functions mean activity. The functions of development banks foster economic growth and co-operation in the country. The six all-India development banks are specialised development banks. IDBI, IFICI, ICICI and IRBI cater to the needs of industry, SIDBI is designed to function as the principal financial institution for the small-scale sector and NABARD caters to the needs of agricultural and rural development.

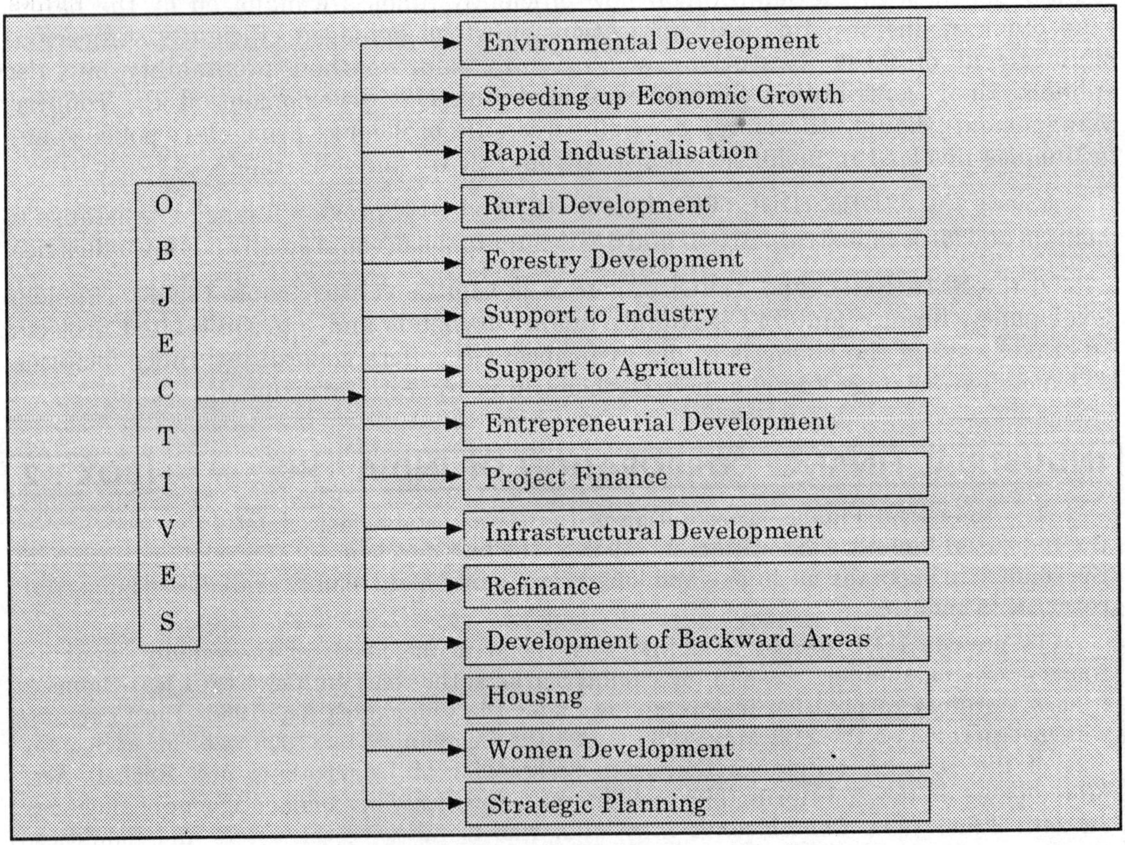


**Fig. 1 Objectives of Development Banking**

Development banks are not only financial agencies which are engaged in providing medium and long-term assistance to business undertakings in the form of loans, underwriting and investment, but which act as catalytic agents in promoting balanced and viable development by assuming the promotional role of discovering project ideas, undertaking feasibility studies, providing technical, financial and managerial assistance for the implementation of projects, and on some occasions, for the establishment and management of industrial units.

Providing financial assistance and rendering promotional services are the minimal functions of development banks, besides a number of other activities, such as the development of infrastructure and social utilities, which are also included among the functions of development banks. The emphasis on its various activities has shifted from one country to another, depending on its peculiar needs and circumstances. In some countries the stress has been on finance; in some others on promotion; in yet others on technical know-how; and elsewhere on economic planning itself.

## OBJECTIVES

The main objectives of a development bank is to serve as an agent of development in various sectors, viz., industry, agriculture and international trade.

Their first and foremost task is to accelerate the growth of the economy.

Rapid industrialisation, particularly in the private sector, so as to provide additional employment opportunity as well as higher production.

Development of backward areas.

To take up rural development and agriculture.

To finance projects which are of great importance to the economy.

To finance housing and small-scale industries.

To foster entrepreneurship

To promote innovative practices

To develop diversified economic activities in the country in the ever-changing economic environment.

In addition, they are assigned a special role in: (i) planning, promoting and developing industries to fill the gaps in the industrial structure; (ii) co-ordinating the working of institutions engaged in financing, promoting or developing industries, agriculture or trade; (iii) providing technical and administrative assistance; and (iv) undertaking marketing and investment research and surveys.

## PRINCIPAL FUNCTIONS

The functions of development banks have been attuned to the needs of industry, small-scale industries including traditional ones and agriculture.

The principal functions common to all development banks are:

(*i*) Promoting investment of public and private capital for development;

(*ii*) Mobilising resources and use them judiciously and productively;

(*iii*) Providing technical assistance to help prepare, finance and carry-out development projects and programmes;

## RETALING BANKING

Home Loans

Car Loans

Consumer Loans

Savings and Term Deposits

Power Pay

Business Multiplier

Investment Products

Private Banking

NRI Sevices

Demat Services

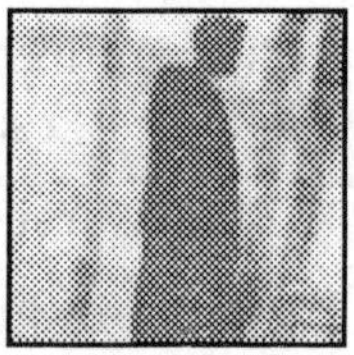

Credit Cards

Debit Cards

Smart Cards

E-cheques

Branches

ATMs

Internet

Call Centres

Agriculture

Emerging Corporates

Capital Markets

Government Enterprises

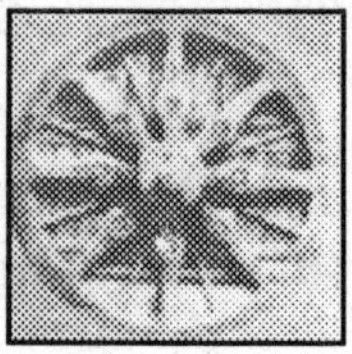

(*iv*) Co-operating with the governments, Reserve Bank of India, with development banks and other organisations that are concerned with the investment of development funds;

(*v*) Promoting institutional infrastructure to accelerate the process of economic development;

(*vi*) Train entrepreneurs and professional managers.

The promotional activities of the bank cover a wide range of functions including identification and training of new entrepreneurs through Institutes of Entrepreneurship Development and other accredited agencies, self-employment/wage employment in industrial sector for weaker sections of society through voluntary agencies, support to Science and Technology, Entrepreneurs' Parks, energy conservation, provision of consultancy services, etc. Besides providing support to specific schemes and programmes in these areas, it has been the endeavour of the bank to strengthen and upgrade institutional infrastructure for undertaking promotional activities.

- Commercial banks provide development finance, venture capital, extension work, entrepreneurship development and management consultancy.
- Mutual funds provide easy accessibility to the investing public.
- Merchant banks provide professional advice and services to industry for raising resources from the market, acquisition of assets on lease and mergers/ takeovers of existing units.
- Finance companies offer the entire range of financial services to individuals and corporates.
- Leasing companies operate four types of lease, viz.: (*i*) operating lease, (*ii*) financial lease, (*iii*) sale and lease back transaction, and (*iv*) the leveraged lease.
- Technical Consultancy Organisations (TCOs) cater to the consultancy needs of small and medium industry and also for the new entrepreneur.
- Management institutes sponsored by development banks are engaged in developing and upgrading the managerial ability and managerial talents of the practising managers.
- STEPS interface between Science and Technology institutes and industry.
- Entrepreneurial development institutes sponsored by financial institutions are engaged in the crucial task of entrepreneurship development and research.

## EXTENSION OF OPERATION

Assistance sanctioned by financial institutions rose manifold from one plan to another. While it was ₹ 37.47 crore in the First Plan, assistance rose to ₹ 53,608.50 crore in the Seventh Plan. As against this, during the year 2006-07, financial institutions sanctioned ₹ 31,238 crore and disbursed ₹ 38,656 crore. Over the years, the institutions have developed and introduced a variety of products and services to meet the growing needs of the corporate sector. Besides expanding the scope of their financing activity, the institutions have diversified into newer fee-based services offering an array of services such as banking, debenture trusteeship and forex services, etc.

**Table 1 : Financial Assistance Sanctioned and Disbursed by the Financial Institutions**

| | | | *(₹ in Crore)* |
|---|---|---|---|
| **Period** | **Assistance Sanctioned** | **Assistance Disbursed** | **Proportion Disbursement to Sanction (%)** |
| Pre-plan Period (1948-1951) | 8.13 | 5.79 | 71.1 |
| First Five-Year Plan (1951-56) | 37.47 | 15.22 | 40.6 |
| Second Five-Year Plan (1956-61) | 212.24 | 142.02 | 66.9 |
| Third Five-Year Plan (1961-66) | 471.91 | 422.84 | 89.6 |
| Three Annual Plans (1966-69) | 374.78 | 335.93 | 89.6 |
| Fourth Five-Year Plan (1969-74) | 1,452.61 | 984.20 | 67.7 |
| Fifth Five-Year Plan (1974-79) | 4,737.90 | 3,092.10 | 65.3 |
| Sixth Five-Year Plan (1979-84) | 18,153.80 | 12476.40 | 68.7 |
| Seventh Five-Year Plan (1985-90) | 53,608.50 | 36405.30 | 67.9 |
| (1990-91) | 19,196.10 | 12,810.10 | 66.7 |
| Eighth Five-Year Plan 1991-96 | 2,19,883.10 | 1,38,267.30 | 62.9 |
| Ninth Five-Year Plan 1996-97 | 52,033.62 | 45,020.58 | 76.5 |
| 1997-98 | 76,427.33 | 55,865.13 | 73.1 |
| 1998-99 | 85,909.55 | 61,262.94 | 71.3 |
| 1999-2000 | 1,08,688.12 | 72,941.67 | 67.1 |
| 2000-01 | 1,29,337.79 | 81,047.03 | 62.6 |
| 2001-02 | 72,613.00 | 56,685.00 | 78.1 |
| 2003-04 | 41,407.00 | 27,032.00 | 65.3 |
| 2004-05 | 19,606.00 | 15,323.00 | 78.1 |
| 2005-06 | 27,666.00 | 21,146.00 | 76.7 |
| 2006-07 | 31,238.00 | 38,656.00 | 123.5 |

## ROLE OF DEVELOPMENT BANKING

Development banking in India has witnessed a sea change having undergone radical transformations in its structure and organisation as well as in the scope and contents of its business operations.

In the following pages, an attempt is made to examine the role of development banks in the process of change in which the exploitation of resources, the direction of investment, the orientation of technological development and institutional change accelerate economic growth. Economic growth, poverty alleviation and proper management of natural resources must be viewed as mutually interdependent facts of ultimate development goal.

The term role is often used in different contexts especially that of acting. Role is the set of expectations, behaviour of individual and/or organisation. Expectations about role playing are closely associated with the group norms and the culture of a group. In India, development banks have developed a distinctive culture and thus they stand distinct from all other financial institutions. The technique of role-playing can be adopted for various purposes and the nature of the technique would differ for different purposes. The main focus here is on role clarity, effectiveness and improved fit between the institution and the role. By sharing common role problems, development banks may develop alternating solutions which result in better performance.

## FINANCIAL SECTOR

Financial sector development is not an end itself. It is to promote and sustain productive activities in various economic sectors by providing needed financial products and services. For the financial system to perform this function adequately and effectively, individual institutional efficiency alone would not suffice. There should also be a conducive policy environment, political stability, political will and entrepreneurship. In addition, financial institutions should have adequate autonomy to bring in initiative and innovations to growth. More importantly, the financial institutions should be flexible in establishing backward and forward linkages for all-round growth of the economy.

## DEVELOPMENT GOALS

The overriding objective of the development bank, is to promote the development of industry, agriculture, trade as well as capital market. Development in this sense implies a steady improvement of living standards achieved through increases in income, improvement in social conditions and protection of the natural environment. Economic growth is fundamental to development.

Economic growth, while important, has not been seen as an end in itself; in line with this perception, the Asian Development Bank (ADB) has become increasingly aware that its efforts should contribute to overall development. Expansion of social infrastructure, poverty alleviation and conservation of the natural resources receive more attention, as the ADB seeks to help improve living standards and quality of life generally. Faced by this showing diversity, the ADB has sought to respond appropriately by extending the scope of its activities beyond the confines of the traditional approach.

In the nineties, development banks are competing with each other for good business. Further, they have become increasingly conscious of the need for improving the quality of their portfolio. They are adopting prudential exposure norms and are classifying their assets into four groups — standard, sub-standard, doubtful and loss — a classification internationally followed for determining loan provisioning.

Development banks seeking new growth paths should not be deviated from their responsibility of promoting projects and encouraging new generation entrepreneurs. More importantly, worthwhile projects should be allowed to flounder for want of finance.

## PROJECT FINANCING

Financial assistance from IFCI is available to industrial and service concerns as rupee loans, foreign currency sub-loans, underwriting and direct subscription to shares/ debentures, and guarantees for deferred payments and foreign currency loans. The assistance is provided for setting up of new units, expansion, diversification and modernisation schemes.

## FINANCIAL SERVICES AND MERCHANT BANKING

A number of schemes are offered by IFCI like Equipment Leasing, Equipment Procurement, Equipment Credit, Instalment Credit, Suppliers' Credit, Buyers' Credit and finance to Leasing and Hire Purchase Concerns. Other services offered are project counselling, credit syndication, corporate counselling for financial reconstruction and rehabilitation of old, ailing or sick industrial units, assistance in the negotiation of foreign collaborations, technology, finance and arrangements for risk/venture capital.

Today, IFCI's role extends to the entire industrial spectrum of the country. While it continues to be one of the important surveyors of direct financial assistance to eligible industrial concerns, no less important is its promotional role whereby it has been helping and developing the small and medium-scale industrial entrepreneurs by providing them the much needed guidance through its recently set-up specialised agencies in project identification, formulation and implementation, development of ancillary and small-scale industries, encouraging the adoption of indigenous technology, etc.

## FUNCTIONS OF THE IFCI

The activities of the IFCI include the following:

(*a*) Granting loans or subscribing to debentures repayable with a period not exceeding 25 years.

(*b*) Underwriting the issue of shares or debentures by industrial concerns, subject to their disposal by the Corporation within a period of seven years. This limit may be waived with the permission of the Union Government.

(*c*) Guaranteeing loans:

  (*i*) raised by industrial concerns which are repayable within a period not exceeding 25 years and are floated in the market;

  (*ii*) raised by industrial concerns from scheduled banks or state co-operative banks.

(*d*) Guaranteeing deferred payments due from any industrial concern:

  (*i*) in connection with the import of capital goods from outside India;

  (*ii*) in connection with the purchase of capital goods within India.

(*e*) Guaranteeing loans in foreign currency (with the prior approval of the Central Government) raised from or credit arrangements made with any bank or financial institution in any country outside India by industrial concerns.

(*f*) Acting as agent for the Central Government or with its approval, for the World Bank in respect of loans granted or debentures subscribed by either of them.

(*g*) Subscribing to the shares of any industrial concern.

(*h*) Acquiring, with the approval of the IDBI, an undertaking including the business assets and liabilities of any institution, the principal object of which is the promotion or development of industry in India or the grant of financial assistance for such promotion or development.

## FINANCIAL ASSISTANCE

Direct financing is the Corporation's main business, the assistance under which can be any one or more of the following forms:

(1) Rupee loans;

(2) Sub-loans in foreign currencies out of the foreign exchange lines of credit made available to it;

(3) Underwriting of and/or Direct Subscription to the shares and debentures of public limited companies; and

(4) Guaranteeing of: (*a*) deferred payments for machinery imported from abroad or purchased within the country; (*b*) foreign currency loans raised by industrial concerns from foreign institutions; and (*c*) rupee loans raised by industrial concerns from Scheduled Banks or State Co-operative Banks or the public market.

Industrial concerns which are eligible for financial assistance under the IFC Act, 1948 are —

(*a*) Limited Companies (whether in private, joint or public sectors) incorporated in India; and

(*b*) Co-operative Societies registered in India;

which are engaged or propose to engage themselves in any of the following activities, namely, (*a*) manufacture, preservation or processing of goods; (*b*) shipping; (*c*) mining; (*d*) hotel industry; and (e) generation or distribution of electricity or any other form of power.

Financial assistance is available from the IFCI to industrial concerns regardless of their size. Nevertheless, having regard to the scope and operations of the various other institutions operating at the all-India and state levels as also some of them specifically meeting the financial requirements of cottage and small-scale sectors, IFCI has been largely catering to the needs of medium and large-sized projects either singly or jointly with other all-India Financial institutions like the Industrial Development Bank of India (IDBI), Industrial Credit and Investment Corporation of India Ltd., (ICICI), Unit Trust of India (UTI); Life Insurance Corporation of India (LIC) and General Insurance Corporation of India (GIC).

Assistance from IFCI singly or jointly with other institutions, is available for: (a) setting up of new industrial projects, (b) expansion of existing units or for diversification into new lines of activity, and (c) for renovation and modernisation of existing units.

IFCI does not ordinarily grant assistance for purposes of working capital, as it is a normal function of the commercial banks to provide such capital. IFCI does not also allow its funds to be utilised for meeting existing liabilities of the industrial concerns, save in exceptional circumstances, or for acquisition of capital goods for commercial or trading purposes. Likewise sub-loans in foreign currencies are granted only for the import of capital goods and not for financing import of raw materials or maintenance of spares or payment of royalties, dividends, etc.

Project finance, which accounted for 86.6% of the total sanctions and 89.9% of the disbursements, has always been the sheet anchor of the IFCI's business, but in the past seven years, financial services have been an important growth area. The Merchant Banking and Allied Services Department has diversified both fund-based and non-fund-based activities, and taken up project counselling, loan syndication and debenture trusteeship assignments. Schemes like equipment leasing, equipment procurement, equipment credit, suppliers' credit, buyers' credit, finance to hire-purchase and leasing companies, and instalment credit have been introduced. IFCI is to be merged with the Punjab National Bank.

## EXPORT-IMPORT BANK OF INDIA

Economic development is characterised by the growth of the foreign trade sector. Finance is one of the key aspects of export promotion. The Export-Import Bank of India aims to promote India's international trade. It also functions as the principal institution for co-ordinating the working of institutions engaged in financing exports and imports of goods and services. In a way, the EXIM-Bank has been changing the outlook of Indian exports by reaching new markets and extending services beyond banking. In fact, the bank has created a dynamic environment for Indian exports to grow and exploit new opportunities.

### Objectives

Export-Import Bank of India, set up in 1982, for the purpose of financing, facilitating, and promoting foreign trade of India, is the principal financial institution in the country for co-ordinating working of institutions engaged in financing exports and imports.

### Operation

*(i) Finance:* The present focus of EXIM Bank is on export finance. The Bank finances export of Indian machinery, manufactured goods, consultancy and technology services on deferred payment terms. EXIM Bank finance is also available at export production stages. EXIM Bank undertakes co-financing with global and regional development agencies and assists Indian exporters in their efforts to participate in such overseas projects. The Bank has diversified into all stages preceding export of goods, on credit terms.

*(ii) Services:* EXIM Bank provides information, advisory services to enable exporters to evaluate the international risks, export opportunities and competitiveness. These

include country studies, merchant banking services, advice on international marketing and data to enable effective participation in opportunities offered by projects by multilateral institutions.

*(iii) Research and Analysis:* Research and analysis is carried out on specific industry subsectors with export potential, and international trade related subjects. These are widely disseminated amongst exporters, academicians, industry and trade organisations and government. EXIM Bank thus follows a three-pronged strategy to promote Indian exports. More than export finance, the Bank is engaged in export capability creation.

**A Variety of Programmes**

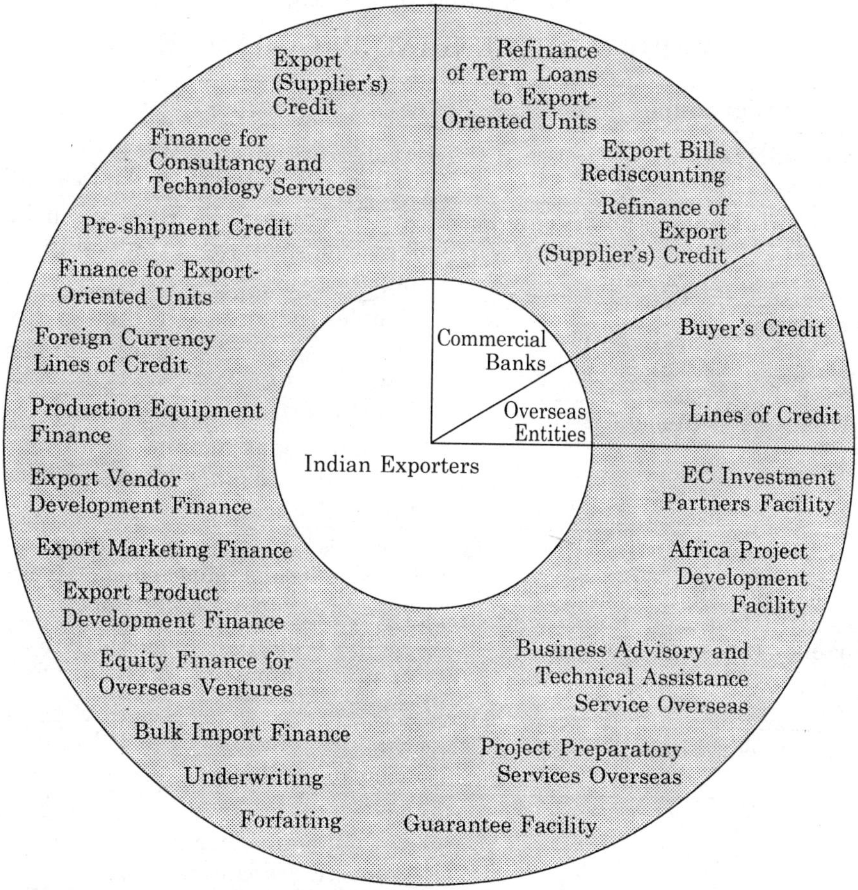


EXIM Bank promotes exports through a variety and a range of lending programmes. These programmes are tailored to meet the needs of different customer groups, viz. Indian exporters, overseas entities and commercial banks.

## We are at all stages of the export cycle

EXIM Bank offers competitive finance at various stages of the export cycle, viz.: export product development, export production, export marketing and export credit at pre- and post-shipment stages.

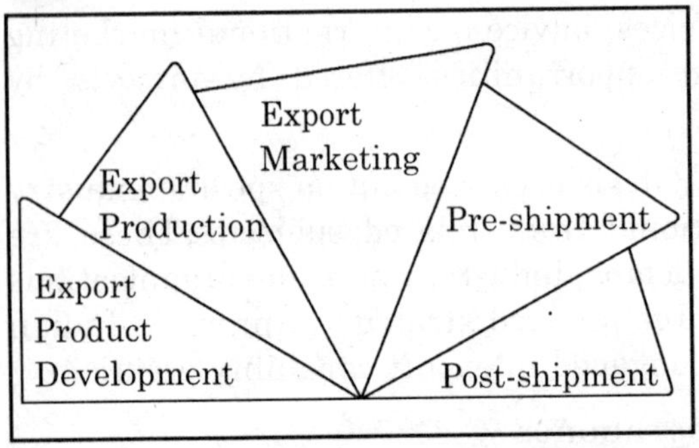


The Bank now has a distinctive group of knowledge workers. It represents perhaps the only experiment where strengths of the public sector have been blended with features of professional private sector work culture. The results so far are there to be seen. The Bank now has the capabilities to exceed its original limits. It has been a privilege to lead in contributing to the growth of a new National Financial Institution designed for trade finance and related capabilities.

## A VARIETY OF LENDING PROGRAMMES

| Programme | Use |
|---|---|
| **For Indian Exporters**<br>Export (Supplier's) Credit | Enables Indian exporters to extend term credit to importer overseas, of eligible Indian goods. |
| Finance for Consultancy and Technology Services | Enables Indian exporters of consultancy and technology services to extend term credit to importers overseas. |
| Pre-shipment Credit | Enables Indian exporter to buy raw material and other inputs for export contracts involving cycle time exceeding six months. |
| Foreign Currency Pre-shipment Credit | Enables eligible exporters to access finance through commercial banks for import of raw materials and other inputs needed for export production. |
| Finance for EOUs and Units in EPZs | Enables Indian companies to acquire indigenous and imported machinery and other assets for export production. |
| Foreign Currency Lines of Credit for Imports | Enables eligible export-oriented units to acquire imported machinery for export production. |
| Production Equipment Finance | Enables eligible export-oriented units to acquire equipment. |
| Export Marketing Finance | Enables exporters to implement market development programmes and finances productive capabilities through loan financing. |
| **Loan** finance for modernisation, capacity creation, quality upgradation, product development and marketing.<br>**Grant** finance on matching basis for market entry, ISO 9000 certification, minor product adaptation, consultancy for productivity improvement. | |
| Export Product Development | Enables Indian firms undertake product development, R&D for exports. |
| Overseas Investment Finance | Enables Indian promoters to finance equity contribution in joint ventures set up abroad. |

| | |
|---|---|
| Strategic Market Entry Support | Enables Indian project exporters to seek reimbursement of tendering cost incurred in respect of successful bids for MFPO projects. |
| Project Preparatory Services Overseas | Enables Indian Consultancy firms undertake prefect preparatory studies in developing countries by grant/loan financing. |
| Business Advisory and Technical Assistance Services Overseas | Enables Indian Consultancy firms undertake specific assignments in select countries through grant financing. |
| Africa Project Development Facility | Enables Indian Consultancy firms undertake specific assignments in sub-Saharan Africa through grant financing. |
| EC Investment Partners Facility | Enables setting up of joint ventures in India between Indian companies and enterprises in the European Community. |
| Forfaiting | Enables Indian exporter to convert credit sale to cash sale without recourse to the exporters. |
| **For Commercial Banks** Refinance of Export (Supplier's) Credit | Enables banks to offer credit to Indian exporters of eligible goods, who extend term credit over 180 days to importers overseas. |
| Relending Facility | Enables banks overseas to make available term finance to their clients, for import of eligible Indian goods. |
| Refinance of Term Loans to EOUs | Enables banks to offer credit to eligible export-oriented units to acquire indigenous and imported machinery and other assets for export production. |
| Refinance of Term Loans for Computer Software Exports | Enables acquisition of imported and indigenous computer systems, and project related assets. |
| Bulk Import Finance | Enables banks to offer finance to importers for bulk import of consumable inputs. |
| **For Overseas Entities** Lines of Credit | Enables overseas financial institutions, foreign governments, their agencies to on lend term loans to finance import of eligible goods from India. |
| Buyer's Credit | Enables overseas buyer to import eligible goods from India on deferred credit terms. |

## SMALL INDUSTRIES DEVELOPMENT BANK OF INDIA

Small Industries Development Bank of India (SIDBI) was set up as a wholly-owned subsidiary of Industrial Development Bank of India (IDBI) in April 1990 under an Act of Indian Parliament as the principal financial institution for:

- promotion,
- financing,

- development of industry in the small-scale sector, and
- co-ordinating the functions of other institutions engaged in similar activities.

SIDBI has completed 12 years of service to the small-scale sector. Consequent upon amendment in the SIDBI Act, the Bank has been delinked from IDBI with effect from March 27, 2000. The SIDBI (Amendment) Act, 2000 has changed the provisions relating to capital structure, shareholding pattern, management, business, borrowings, etc. The authorised capital of the Bank has been increased from ₹ 4.5 billion to ₹ 10 billion, divided into 750 million equity shares of ₹ 10 each and 250 million redeemable preference shares of ₹ 10 each. The amended Act provides for divesting of 51 per cent of the equity share capital of ₹ 4.5 billion subscribed and held by IDBI in favour of Life Insurance Corporation, General Insurance Corporation, public sector banks and other institutions owned or controlled by the Government of India. Presently, shares of the Bank are held by 36 such institutions. While IDBI continues to be the single largest shareholder of SIDBI, the State Bank of India and Life Insurance Corporation of India follow as the next two large shareholders in that order.

Since its inception, SIDBI has been assisting the entire spectrum of the SSI sector including the Tiny, Village and Cottage industries through suitable schemes tailored to meet the requirements of the setting up of new projects, expansion, diversification, modernisation and rehabilitation of existing units.

## DOMAIN OF SERVICE

The Small Scale Industries (SSI) sector is a vibrant and dynamic sector of the Indian economy. The sector presently occupies an important place and its contribution in terms of generation of employment, output and exports is quite significant. For the purpose of defining an SSI unit in India, the original purchase value of plant and machinery installed in a unit has been adopted as the sole criterion. The ceiling on investment in plant and machinery has undergone periodical change from time-to-time since after the introduction of this concept. For a unit to be considered as SSI unit, the current ceiling on investment in plant and machinery is ₹ 10 million. For a tiny unit, the said ceiling is ₹ 2.5 million. The limit in select subsectors, such as, knitwear, hosiery and handtools is ₹ 50 million. The Small Scale Industries sector including tiny units comprises the domain of SIDBI's business. Besides, the projects in the services sector with total cost up to ₹ 250 million are also taken within the area of SIDBI's operations. The Bank also finances industrial infrastructure projects for the development of SSI sector.

## CHANNELS OF ASSISTANCE

SIDBI's financial assistance to small-scale sector have three major dimensions:

(*i*) Indirect assistance to primary lending institutions (PLIs)

(*ii*) Direct assistance to small units

(*iii*) Development and Support Services

## INDIRECT ASSISTANCE

SIDBI's schemes of indirect assistance envisage credit to SSIs through a large network of 913 PLIs spread across the country with a branch network of over 65,000. The assistance is provided by way of refinance, bills rediscounting and resource support in the form of short-term loans/line OT credit in lieu OT refinance, etc.

## REFINANCE

The main objective of SIDBI's refinance schemes being enhancement of flow of credit to the SSI sector and augmenting the resources of PLIs, the Bank provides refinance to PLIs against the term loans granted by them for:

- setting up of new SSI projects and for expansion, technology upgradation, modernisation, quality promotion, diversification by existing units and rehabilitation of sick SSI units.
- small road transport operators, qualified professionals for self-employment, small hospitals and nursing homes, cybercafes, marketing, industrial infrastructure and to promote hotels and tourism-related activities.

SIDBI extends Financial Support (Short Term Loans) to scheduled banks in respect of their outstanding portfolio relating to SSI sector against which no financial support has been availed of from other institutions.

## REDISCOUNTING

In order to help the machinery manufacturers in the SSI sector and to maximise their sales by offering deferred payment credit to the prospective purchaser users, the Bank operates a Bills Rediscounting Scheme where bills arising out of sale/purchase of machinery discounted by scheduled commercial banks are rediscounted by SIDBI. Facilities under the Scheme are also extended to cover purchases of machinery by Small Scale Industries.

## DIRECT ASSISTANCE

The objective behind SIDBI's direct assistance schemes has been to supplement the efforts of PLIs by identifying the gaps in the existing credit delivery mechanism for Small Scale Industries. Direct assistance is provided under several tailor-made schemes through SIDBI's 41 Regional/Branch Offices spread across the country.

### Assistance is provided directly for

- Setting up of new SSI units, small hotels, hospitals/nursing homes
- Technology upgradation and modernisation, expansion, diversification
- Quality upgradation/acquiring of ISO 9000 series certification
- Development of markets for SSI products

- Development of infrastructure for SSI sector
- Pre-shipment and Post-shipment Credit and Export Bill Finance
- Discounting of bills of manufacturer-seller in SSI sector, selling either equipment or components
- Factoring services.

## SIDBI offers

- Financial assistance to SSI units under Technology Development and Modernisation Fund (TDMF) Scheme.
- Financial assistance to SSI units in the textile and cotton ginning and pressing sectors for taking up technology upgradation and modernisation under Technology Upgradation Funds Scheme (TUFS).
- Financial assistance to tanneries for taking up modernisation under the Tannery Modernisation Scheme (TMS).
- Twelve per cent capital subsidy on loans advanced to SSI units engaged in select product subsectors for technology upgradation by scheduled commercial banks, SFCs and NSIC under Credit Linked Capital Subsidy Scheme.
- Short-term loans to State Electricity Boards to facilitate their purchases from SSIs and effect payment in time. Discounting of invoices of SSIs supplying their products to large purchaser companies in the public/private sector.
- Interest subsidy in respect of certain hotel projects under one, two and three star and heritage category, where loans are sanctioned after approval of projects from the Department of Tourism.
- Support to obtain credit rating from accredited rating agencies.

## SIDBI's Foreign Currency Assistance includes

- Foreign currency loans to import equipment by existing export-oriented SSI units and new units having definite plans for entering export markets.
- Foreign currency loans to execute confirmed export orders by way of pre-shipment credit/letter of credit and post-shipment credit facilities.
- Pre-shipment and Post-shipment Credit in rupee terms to exporting SSIs for greater flexibility.
- Export bills financing in foreign currency.

## SIDBI's Venture Capital includes

- Assistance to small-scale entrepreneurs using innovative indigenous technology and expertise.
- Contribution to corpus of other venture funds.

- Promotion of State level Venture Capital Funds and a National Venture Fund for Software and IT industry dedicated to small-scale units in Software/ IT industry.
- SIDBI has entered into a Memorandum of Understanding with Small Enterprise Assistance Funds of United States of America.

## Lines of Credit are established by SIDBI in favour of

- State Financial Corporations.
- State Industrial Development Corporations.
- State Small Industries Development Corporations (for supplying raw material and extending marketing support to SSI units).
- Factoring Companies (to factor receivables of SSIs).
- National Small Industries Corporation Ltd.

## Development and Support Services

- The Bank extends development and support services in the form of loans and grants to different agencies working for the promotion and development of SSIs and tiny industries. Over the years, the initiatives of SIDBI under promotional and developmental activities have crystallised into the following important areas:
- Enterprise Promotion with emphasis on Rural Industrialisation.
- Human Resource Development to suit the SSI sector needs.
- Technology Upgradation.
- Quality and Environment Management.
- Marketing Promotion, and
- Information Dissemination.

## Enterprise Promotion is supported through

**Micro Credit Scheme:** Having encouraged by the results and to accord focused attention for increasing flow of funds to the poor through sustainable microfinance institutions (MFIs), SIDBI launched a SIDBI Foundation for Micro Credit on November 27, 1998. The foundation presently functioning as a department of the Bank commenced its operations in January 1999 with an initial corpus of ₹ 1 billion. The mission of the Foundation is "to create a national network of strong, viable and sustainable micro-finance institutions from the informal and formal sectors to provide microfinance services to the poor, especially women". The new approach not only envisages financial assistance but also strives to build and strengthen the management capabilities of the microfinance practitioners and related institutions through customised capacity building inputs for achieving sustainability, economies of scale, desired outreach, etc. SIDBI foundation has taken a lead in the country by initiating a pioneering effort for 'capacity assessment rating' of NGOs/MFIs.

The foundation has entered into an agreement with International Fund for Agricultural Development (IFAD), Rome for upscaling its operations. Earlier, SFMC had signed an MoU with Department for International Development (DFID), UK for granting support for financing various capacity building initiatives of the Foundation as well as MFIs. The Foundation has drawn up a comprehensive action plan with a view to mainstreaming the microfinance and providing capacity building support to the micro-finance institutions.

**Rural Industries Programme:** Rural Industries Programme (RIP) has been designed to provide a cohesive and integrated package of basic inputs like information, motivation, training and credit, backed by appropriate technology and market linkages. The programme is executed through Non Governmental Organisations, Technical Consultancy Organisations and development professionals.

**Mahila Vikas Nidhi:** Mahila Vikas Nidhi Scheme is aimed at the economic empowerment of women, especially from the weaker strata in rural areas by providing them with avenues for training and employment by creation of infrastructure in the form of Training-cum-production Centres. The projects are implemented through accredited NGOs with good track record in the field of enterprise development for women.

**Entrepreneurship Development Programmes:** The programmes aim at training various target groups with entrepreneurial traits so that they obtain necessary information, motivation and guidance in setting up their own enterprises. Specialised Entrepreneurship Development Agencies are supported to conduct programmes for specific target groups such as rural youth, women, SC/ST, ex-servicemen, etc.

## Human Resources Development of the SSIs is pursued through

- Small Industries Management Programme (SIMAP), and
- Skill-cum-Technology Upgradation Programme (STUP).

While SIMAP is designed to develop a cadre of second line industrial managers, specifically trained to assist SSI entrepreneurs in discharging multiple responsibilities, STUP has been formulated to improve the performance of existing SSI units by developing/strengthening managerial skills and technical competence of entrepreneurs and senior executives. The reputed management/technical institutes are provided grant/ corpus support to conduct these programmes.

## Programmes for Technology Upgradation include

- Technology upgradation in identified industry clusters
- Technology transfer
- Quality improvement.

## Quality and Environment Management Programmes Aim at

- Making the SSI units aware of the importance of environmental issues and providing them with necessary technical support to implement projects which can provide relative social and environmental benefit as compared to financial cost incurred, and
- Educating the SSI units about environmental regulations, which need to be adhered to and the steps required to operate within prescribed norms.

## Marketing Promotion Initiatives include

- Sponsoring/organising exhibitions in India and abroad with intention of subsidising participation costs for SSIs.
- Tying up with renowned organisations to provide market information at concessional rates.
- Rating services to export-oriented SSI units, and
- Sponsoring market studies.

## Information Dissemination Initiatives include

- Promoting new units by identification and publicity of viable project ideas and business opportunities through project profiles, Udyog Sadhana Radio Programme and Udyog Sadhana Television Series.
- Publication of "SIDBI Report on Small Scale Industries Sector" on an annual basis.
- Publication of theme-based reports for SSI sector such as "Technology for Small Scale Industries — Current Status and Emerging Needs".
- Product specific sectoral studies to assess the impact of policy changes.
- WTO impact studies.

## SIDBI's National Programme on Innovation and Incubation for Small Industries includes

- Memorandum of understanding signed with Indian Institute of Technology, Kanpur and Birla Institute of Technology, Mesra, Ranchi for setting up of Innovation and Incubation centres.
- Centre at IIT, Kanpur became operational and at BIT, Mesra to commence operations shortly.

## NEW INITIATIVES

### Fast Track Financing Scheme

The scheme aims to provide assistance on a fast track basis without subjecting the existing clients to detailed procedures applicable to the new clients, thus improving relationship banking and promoting good clientele.

### Credit Linked Capital Subsidy under Technology Upgradation Fund Scheme

The scheme envisages an option to the small-scale textile industries to avail of either one time 12 per cent Credit Linked Capital Subsidy or the existing 5 per cent interest reimbursement under the Technology Upgradation Fund Scheme for textile industries.

### Financing Service Sector

SIDBI has included the activities of establishing cinema theatrer, multiplexes and restaurants, as eligible activities for direct assistance from the Bank.

### Interest Subsidy on Hotel Loans

SIDBI has been notified as an eligible institution for the availment of interest subsidy in respect of certain hotel projects under one, two and three star and heritage category where loans were sanctioned after approval of projects from the Department of Tourism. Accordingly, an interest subsidy of 3 to 5 per cent is being extended on loans sanctioned by SIDBI to approved projects at notified places, with effect from October 1, 2001.

As on March 31, 2009, the Authorized Capital of SIDBI is ₹ 1,000 crore and paid-up Capital is ₹ 450 crore. SIDBI is the principal financial institution for financing (direct, indirect and refinance) and promotion and development of Micro, Small and Medium Enterprises (MSME) sector. The Bank also co-ordinates the functions of institutions engaged in similar activities. Presently, the Bank provides refinance support through a network of eligible member lending institutions for onward lending to MSMEs and direct assistance is channelised through SIDBI's 100 branch offices. SIDBI also extends financial assistance in the form of loans, grants, equity and quasi-equity to NGOs/Micro Finance Institutions (MFIs) for lending to micro enterprises and economically weaker sections of society, enabling them to take up income generating activities on a sustainable basis.

SIDBI has initiated various schemes for upliftment of the MSME sector and continues to be a prime lending institution for MSME sector.

**(a) SME Refinance/Risk Capital Funds:** During the Budget for the year 2008-09, two funds of ₹ 2,000 crore each *viz.:* SME (Refinance) Fund and SME (Risk Capital)

Fund under SIDBI were announced. Accordingly, MSME (Risk Capital) Fund with an initial corpus of ₹ 1,000 crore was created with SIDBI. RBI has so far released ₹ 250 crore in respect of MSME (Refinance) Fund, RBI had initially allocated ₹ 1,600 crore, which was enhanced to ₹ 3,600 crore and against this, SIDBI has drawn an amount of ₹ 3,325 crore as on March 31, 2009.

**(b) Special Refinance Facility:** RBI had provided a special refinance facility of ₹ 7,000 crore @ 5.5% to SIDBI on December 7, 2009. SIDBI had earmarked an amount of ₹ 6,390 crore for Public Sector Banks (PSBs) and ₹ 610 crore for State Financial Corporations (SFCs). Banks had availed ₹ 4,336 crore up to March 31, 2009 which indicates an increase in credit flow by banks to Micro Enterprises of about ₹ 8,650 crore as refinance to banks is provided at 50% of the incremental credit. As on March 31, 2009, SIDBI had availed the RBI line to the extent of ₹ 6,269 crore of which ₹ 4,336 crore was for PSBs, ₹ 420 crore for SFCs and ₹ 1,513 crore for SIDBI's own incremental credit.

**(c) Credit Guarantee Fund Trust for Micro and Small Enterprises (CGTMSE):** The Ministry of Micro, Small and Medium Enterprises, Govt. of India, (the then Ministry of SSI) and Small Industries Development Bank of India (SIDBI), established a Trust named Credit Guarantee Fund Trust for Small Industry (CGTSI) which was subsequently renamed as "Credit Guarantee Fund Trust for Micro and Small enterprises (CGTMSE) to implement the Credit Guarantee Scheme for Micro and Small Enterprises". The scheme was formally launched on August 30, 2000. Under the scheme, credit facilities, which are extended without collateral security by eligible lending banks/Financial Institutions, are covered. Numerous initiatives have been taken by the government to enhance the coverage of credit guarantee to incentives collateral-free lending to the MSE Sector. The initial corpus of CGTMSE of ₹ 125 crore has gradually increased and as on March 31, 2009, it was ₹ 1,740.14 crore. It is proposed to be raised to ₹ 2,500 crore overtime.

During the FY 2008-09 numerous changes were made to enhance the coverage under the scheme, which are as follows:

Credit facility eligible for guarantee cover was enhanced to ₹ 100 lakh.

The lock-in period for filing claims against loans covered under the existing credit guarantee scheme was reduced from 24 to 18 months, to encourage banks to cover more loans under the guarantee scheme.

Guarantee coverage for loans up to ₹ 5 lakh was increased to 85%, and guarantee fee was reduced for loans up to ₹ 5 lakh.

As on December 2009, guarantees were extended to 2,49,000 proposals covering credit assistance of ₹ 9,200 crore under CGTMSE. The enterprises covered under the scheme employed 4,58,629 persons having aggregate turnover of about ₹ 21,548 crore. In addition, as on March 31, 2009, the membership of CGTMSE comprised 81 banks and Financial Institutions.

**(d) Venture Capital Fund:** In order to provide risk capital to the SME sector, a SIDBI Venture Capital Limited (SVCL) with a corpus of ₹ 500 crore has been set up, which is presently managing national SME Growth Fund for biotech, food processing, pharmaceuticals, light engineering and knowledge-based industries.

The total commitments under SME Growth Fund as on March 31, 2009 stood at ₹ 446.34 crore and total investment was ₹ 353.02 crore. SVCL has successfully implemented the first Fund, viz., National Venture Fund for Software and IT industry (NFSIT) with a corpus of ₹ 100 crore benefiting 31 MSME units as on March 31, 2009.

**(e) SME Rating Agency (SMERA):** SMERA, operational from September 2005, is a third party credit rating agency for MSMEs. It provides ratings that are comprehensive transparent and reliable and which would enable the rated units to borrow funds at competitive rates of interest.

As on March 31, 2009, SMERA had completed 3,438 cumulative ratings for MSMEs. It had completed 1,742 MSMEs ratings during FY 2008-09, thus exhibiting 55 per cent growth in comparison to the previous year.

Risk profiling studies in respect of BMSME clusters have been completed.

SMERA has signed MoU with 24 banks for offering interest rate concession to the better rated units RBI has been requested for accreditation to SMERA.

## STATE INDUSTRIAL DEVELOPMENT CORPORATIONS

The investment institutions are major players in the secondary market; they also extend assistance to the corporate sector by way of term loans/underwriting/direct subscription to equity and debentures. The SFCs provide finance mainly to small and medium enterprises, whereas SIDCs cater to the needs of medium and large industries in their respective states. Apart from providing financial assistance, the SFCs and SIDCs also play a promotional and developmental role.

The increasing involvement of DFIs in the development aspect of their banking and financial function gives the hope that, sooner rather than later, they will find ways in which to involve themselves in activities which would, in the medium and long-run, promote inter-sectoral linkages, expand markets and develop complementary relations between industry and agriculture, between the rural and urban sectors, between the development of production capacity and the development of consumption capacity.

State Industrial Development Corporations (SIDCs) were established under the Companies Act, 1956 in the sixties and early seventies as wholly-owned State Government undertakings for the promotion and development of medium and large industries. SIDCs act as catalysts for industrial development and provide an impetus to further investment in their respective states.

The SIDCs/SIICs have been promoted by the States and Union Territories as promotional bodies entrusted with the major task of promoting industries and ensuring balanced regional growth with each state.

For efficiently carrying out the functions of promotion, improvement and development of industries, these corporations are empowered to plan, formulate and execute an industrial undertaking, project or enterprise which is likely to accelerate industrial development.

SIDCs provide assistance by way of term loans, underwriting and direct subscription to shares/debentures and guarantees. They undertake a variety of promotional activities such as preparation of feasibility reports, industrial potential surveys, entrepreneurship development programmes and developing industrial areas/estates. SIDCs' activities also include setting up of medium and large industrial projects in the joint sector in collaboration with private entrepreneurs or as wholly-owned subsidiaries. The SIDCs' activities have now widened to include equipment leasing, providing tax benefits under State Governments' Package Scheme of incentives, merchant banking services and setting up of mutual funds. Some of the SIDCs also offer a package of developmental services such as technical guidance, assistance in plant location and co-ordination with other agencies.

Of the 28 SIDCs operating in the country, eleven SIDCs function as SFCs to provide assistance to small-scale sector as well as act as promotional agencies. The twin-function of the SIDCs are in the Andaman & Nicobar, Arunachal Pradesh, Daman, Diu, Dadra & Nagar Haveli, Manipur, Meghalaya, Mizoram, Nagaland, Tripura, Goa, Pondicherry and Sikkim. Seven SIDCs are also involved in infrastructure development and other extension services for the small sector.

The functions of SIDCs include the following:

(*a*) Industrial promotion activities such as project identification, preparation of feasibility reports, identifying entrepreneurs and assisting them in project implementation.

(*b*) Setting up of industrial projects in the medium and large sectors either in the joint sector, i.e., in partnership with private entrepreneurs, or as wholly-owned subsidiaries.

(*c*) Provision of infrastructure facilities and market intelligence services.

(*d*) Granting of financial assistance by way of term loans/bridging loans and underwriting of subscription to equity/preference shares.

(*e*) Acting as agents of State/Central Governments in respect of growth of subsidiaries, incentives, etc., as also IDBI for provision of seed capital assistance.

(*f*) Undertaking the business of equipment leasing, hire-purchase and venture capital, etc.

(*g*) Undertaking merchant banking and mutual funds activities in tune with the changing economic scenario and financial sector environment.

SIDCs/SIICs grant financial assistance to industrial concerns in the form of:

(*a*) direct subscription to their equity;

(*b*) loans, term loans and short-term loans.

(*c*) extension of guarantees for loans and deferred payments;

(*d*) underwriting and subscriptions to the issue of shares, bonds and debentures;

(*e*) equipment leasing;

(*f*) hire-purchase;

(*g*) venture capital;

(*h*) merchant banking services;

(*i*) seed capital assistance to technically-qualified entrepreneurs and persons having relevant experience or skills;

(*j*) equipment finance;

(*k*) project identification;

(*l*) plant location service; and

(*m*) industrial escort services.

Corporations in states like Karnataka and Bihar are empowered to undertake special activities like establishing and managing industrial estates, development of industrial areas, generation, transmission and sale of electricity, etc.

### Main Activities:

(*a*) Development of industrial areas by acquiring land.

(*b*) Preparing layout with suitable grouping of plots of various sizes and allotment of land.

(*c*) Construction of roads, drainage system, provision of street lights in the industrial areas.

(*d*) Planning implementing and managing of water supply schemes.

(*e*) Establishing common facility centres (CFC) by providing accommodations for bank, post office, telecom facilities, police station, fire station, medical facilities, canteen, etc.

(*f*) Implementing government/semi-government projects.

SIDCs have initiated a number of measures during the last three years, in response to the changing business environment. *Conscious efforts are being made to alter the product mix and develop business other than term-lending such as merchant banking, leasing, portfolio investment, commercial paper, etc.* Even in the case of project finance, the range of projects has been widened to include projects higher than ₹ 5 crore and the upper limit on the quantum of loans has been removed.

## MEETING THE CHALLENGES

**PICUP:** Accent on infrastructure. Promoting an infrastructure leasing company in the private sector for building roads and bridges in UP. Floating multi-crore "integrated industrial townships" which will have all facilities — power, water supply, roads, telecom facilities, schools and hospitals. Also launching a mutual fund and seeking membership of the over-the-counter Exchange of India.

**SICOM:** Planning to market Bombay's advantages — major banking presence and twin ports — to draw investors to Maharashtra, especially in petrochemicals. Has engaged consultants McKinsey to help determine Maharashtra's unique selling proposition (USP) in the domestic and international markets. Has contributed to Indus Venture Capital Fund's equity and is planning a mutual fund.

**GIIC:** Moves afoot to encourage capital-intensive projects like coke and pig iron following the discovery of lignite deposits in Gujarat. Will continue to promote petrochemical, chemical and drug and pharmaceutical units. A software park planned at Gandhinagar. Additional USP: trouble-free labour and adequate power in the state. Has plans for a mutual fund.

**RIICO:** Successful in encouraging industry-specific complexes — gemstone park, hosiery complex and software park. Stress on export-oriented units; other thrust areas include the tertiary sector (hospitals, hotels), mineral resource-based projects (granite, marble, cement), and agro-based industry (oil mills, solvent extraction and edible oil refineries).

**HSIDC:** Intends to provide project and financial consultancy services, and establish a strong database and market research facility for pre-feasibility studies of projects in Haryana. The aim of the organisation is to cut expenses and reduce response time with the help of external agencies. Organisational changes are also planned for quicker responses.

**WBIDC:** Changes in the Centre's freight equalisation scheme and steel decontrol have improved West Bengal's competitive edge. The proposed Haldia petrochemicals complex and its proximity to steel manufacturing units are additional advantages. Industry is being lured to 10 new growth centres with the promise of zero power cuts. A venture capital fund is on the cards.

As the end of March 1994, the total sanctions of financial assistance of SIDCs amounted to ₹ 8,110 crore and disbursements ₹ 6,302 crore. Of the total assistance, sanctioned by the SIDCs, rupee loans accounted for 85.5%, followed by underwriting/ direct subscription 10.7% and guarantees 3.0%.

The private sector enterprises received 84%, joint sector 10.2% and the public sector 4.9% of the total assistance. The share of the co-operative was very negligible (0.6%).

The bulk of assistance sanctioned by the SIDCs was claimed by chemicals and chemical product (15.6%), followed by textiles (14.8%), food products (9.0%) and electrical and electronic equipment (5.5%).

More importantly, sanctions to backward areas accounted for ₹ 4,393 crore (54.2%) and disbursement to ₹ 3,456 crore (54.9%).

Assistance sanctioned to new enterprises absorbed 63.5% of the total sanctions, followed by expansion/diversification 22.6% and modernisation 7.6%.

## MAJOR RECOMMENDATIONS OF THE WORKING GROUP FOR HARMONISING THE ROLE AND OPERATIONS OF DFIs AND BANKS — BOX - 3

**Role, Structure and Operations**

- To enable Indian financial institutions and commercial banks to compete in a deregulated and increasingly global marketplace, a progressive move towards universal banking subsidiary (with holdings up to 100 per cent); DFIs themselves to continue to play their existing role.
- The appropriate corporate structure for the universal bank should be an internal management/shareholder decision. The structure can be a single company or a holding company with individually capitalised but wholly-owned subsidiaries, a group of entities with cross holdings or a flagship company with subsidiaries which may or may not have independent shareholders.
- Keeping in view the importance of size, expertise and reach for sustained viability and future survival in the financial sector, management and shareholders of banks and DFIs should be permitted to explore and enter into gainful mergers. Such mergers can be between banks or between banks and DFIs. However, restructuring/ consolidation should be brought about in a market-oriented fashion and led solely by considerations of viability and profitability.
- DFIs in India have started moving in the direction of universal banking and increasingly operate on commercial as opposed to developmental considerations. Development obligations would require financial support from RBI/government.

**Regulatory and Legal Framework**

- Establish a 'super regulator' to supervise and co-ordinate the activities of multiple regulators.
- Undertake legal reforms with focus on debt recovery areas of banks and FIs; thorough revamp of the 1993 Act on Recovery of Debts from Banks and DFIs.

**Supervisory Practices**

- Supervisory framework be risk-based with focus on macro-management.
- Consolidated supervision for financial subsidiaries and conglomerates and global consolidated suppression by banking supervisor.

**Statutory Obligations**

- CRR should be confined to cash and cash-like instruments: it should be brought down progressively within a time-bound frame to international levels.
- Given the stringent asset classification and provisioning norms and government borrowing at market determined rates, the need or SLR has declined; SLR may therefore be phased out in line with international practice.
- There is a need to develop an alternative mechanism for financing specific sectors which require concessional funds which can be provided by specifically targeted subsidies rather than, viz., statutory obligation on the entire banking system.
- Definition of priority sector should be modified to reflect the growing importance of infrastructure finance. However, infrastructure lending may not be included in the definition of "net bank credit" used in computing priority sector obligations.

- To facilitate sound credit planning and efficient disbursal of loans, priority sector obligation should be linked to the net bank credit at the end of the previous financial year.

**State Level Institutions (SLIs)**

- Eventual merger of SFCs, SIDCs and SSIDCs in each state into a single entity.
- Strong SFCs to go public with state government holdings gradually brought down to below 50 per cent.
- Transfer of present shareholdings of IDBI in SLIs to SIDBI.
- Ownership of SIDBI to be transferred to RBI/govt. on the same lines as NABARD.

**Harmonising the Role, Operations and Regulatory Framework**

- In view of the large amount of funding required, both DFIs and Banks have a role in working capital finance and long-term funding with different levels of emphasis on each segment. Since the basic functional differences will continue (at least for the present), removal of the following restrictions/stipulations be considered:
  - (*i*) Prior approval for bond issues by DFIs with either maturity of less than 5 years or maturity of 5 years and above but with interest rate exceeding 200 basis points over the GoI securities of equal residual maturity.
  - (*ii*) Overall ceiling for DFIs' mobilisation of resources by way of term money bonds, CDs, term deposits and inter-corporate deposits at 100 per cent of net owned funds of DFIs.
  - (*iii*) Maturity ceiling of five years on deposits from the public and the capping of interest rate on deposits of DFIs at interest rate offered by SBI for similar maturities.
  - (*iv*) Minimum size of deposits to be accepted by DFIs.

## NEED AND EMERGENCE OF DEVELOPMENT FINANCIAL INSTITUTIONS IN INDIA

The need for development banks in India was felt very strongly immediately after the attainment of independence to fill the gaps in the capital markets for providing the needs of long-term industrial finance. The existing financial arrangements were incapable of coping with the burgeoning financial requirements of up and coming enterprises. Although the country had a network of strong and developed financial banks, these institutions, working on the British banking model, confined themselves to short-term financing activity, and abstained from supplying long-term financial assistance. The managing agency houses, which had served as important adjuncts to the capital market, were not able to cope with the requirements of the planned industrial development owing to their apathy to investment in risky ventures and their keenness to finance only interested concerns. Furthermore, several malpractices, the most important which were the misuse of funds, excess speculation and manipulations, the high cost of promotions, and financial and marginal managerial concentration that had emerged, were often detrimental to the interests of the investing public. There was moreover, a dearth of issue houses and underwriting firms which sponsor security issues. As against the limited arrangements for the supply of long-term financial facilities, there was an enormous increase in the demand for long-term capital. Not only did existing industries require substantially large amounts of capital to meet their reconstruction, modernisation, expansion and diversification programmes, the establishment of new industrial projects on a gigantic scale in the capital goods sector for the building of a strong and balanced structure of industrial development, called for enormous investment. But only a very small part of the total requirements could be met by the existing financial institutions; for the others, it became necessary to devise new institutional machinery with ample financial resources and with relatively more comprehensive functions. It was felt necessary to set up financial institutions to ensure an adequate flow of assistance to industrial projects. The first step towards building up a structure of development finance institutions was taken up with the establishment in 1948 of the Industrial Finance Corporation of India (IFCI) with a view to providing medium and long-term credit to units in the corporate sector and industrial co-operatives.

## AN ERA OF PLANNED DEVELOPMENT

In view of the immensity of the task and the vast size of the country, it was also decided to set up regional development banks to cater to the needs of small and medium enterprises. In 1951, the Indian Parliament passed the State Financial Corporations Act. Under the Act, the State Governments established State Financial Corporations (SFCs) for their respective regions. By 1955-56, 12 SFCs were set up and by 1967-68, all the 18 SFCs now in operation came into existence. SFCs grant financial assistance to public limited companies, private limited companies, partnership firms and proprietary concerns.

The role of an integrated financial infrastructure in stimulating and sustaining economic growth is well recognised now. A network of financial institutions helps an economy to augment its savings. At the same time, it leads to a more efficient utilisation of the available investible resources. There is a well-integrated network of financial institutions in the country comprising 44 institutions at the national level and 82 at the state-level. Broadly, they are classified as follows:

(1) All India Development Banks (AIDBs)
(2) Specialised Financial Institutions (SFIs)
(3) Investment Institutions (IIs)

Financial institutions with their role as a mobiliser of the community's savings and a channeliser of these savings into productive outlets, play a crucial role in the economic development of a country. As a matter of fact, economic and industrial development of a country depends, in the main, upon how efficiently funds are managed by the banks. Like other businesses, financial institutions must be managed efficiently. Efficacious management of these institutions will not only improve their profitability but also enhance their contribution to industrial and financial development of the country. Management should, therefore, be well-versed in problems, principles, policies and techniques involved in mobilisation of funds and their channelisation.

## NEED TO ACTIVISE CAPITAL MARKET

The development banks have been in the forefront in strengthening the capital market with a view to give a much needed impetus to the growth of private sector activities.

All the development banks established in the country since independence are expected to encourage and promote healthy growth of the capital market with a view to mobilising private savings into industrial securities. The respective charter of IFCI, IDBI, ICICI, SFCs/SIDCs, LIC and UTI enjoin on them supporting issues of industrial securities through underwriting and/or direct subscription.

It was expected that the mere support of the financial institutions to the equity issues would act as an indicator that such industrial ventures were supportworthy in view of the thorough investment appraisal by the institutions that is involved before the institutions extending their underwriting support.

Over the last two decades, however, the experience of the institutions in regard to their underwriting operation has been somewhat different. The mere fact that an issue has been underwritten by the institutions no longer provides an assurance to the investor that the industrial security is worth purchasing. In reality what has happened is that whenever the major term lending institutions are involved, an impression prevails in the market that the industrial security being issued is not necessarily attractive from the point of view of the private investors but that institutions have offered the underwriting support in the national interest, as an exercise for tying up the entire financing plan for the project.

The trends in sanctions and disbursements against underwriting/direct subscriptions to equity and debentures in relation to the trends in equity and debenture capital raised from the market indicate that institutional support to the capital markets has grown and is growing overtime. The institutions, therefore, are obliged to absorb growing proportion of the issues coming to the market with their underwriting assistance.

A number of measures are being suggested for activising the market for industrial securities so that a larger flow of household sector's savings is available to the corporate sector. The several areas in which some positive action is called for relate largely to suitable changes in direct and indirect taxes, and the policy of the term lending institutions relating to their investment in industrial securities.

In conformity with their major objectives, the term lending institutions need to give greater importance than in the past for encouraging growth of the capital market. As a first major step in this direction, the institutions need to reconsider their policy of holding on to their sizeable investments in easily marketable industrial securities. Bulk of the investment of the institutions in shares and debentures are as a result of development of part of the issues underwritten by them in the past as also due to an exercise of their convertibility rights in respect of the loans to assisted concerns. With a view to creating a wider market for industrial securities and also for recycling the funds required for their growing volume of operations, institutions should, more than ever in the past, give greater attention to unloading of their holdings. As a matter of policy, the preference of the institutions should be one of not holding on to the securities in which investors are interested.

The disinvestment operations by the institutions could be undertaken in an orderly fashion without creating unstable trading conditions in the stock markets. Institutions could offer for sale these securities in the same manner as some companies do whenever they are expected to broad-base their shareholding through the sale of part of the large block of shares held by one or a few shareholders with controlling interest. I am sure such a measure would not at all affect the sentiment of the market whenever such orderly disinvestments are undertaken by the institutions.

## DISPERSAL OF ASSISTANCE

Sometimes, it is pointed out that institutional assistance flows largely to states which are already industrially well developed. Apparently this may be true but one should not try to draw wrong conclusions from the trends in institutional assistance. It is true that industrially more developed states, particularly Maharashtra, Gujarat and Tamil Nadu continue to receive major chunk of assistance extended by the institutions.

In this context, the basic operational objective of the all-India financial institutions needs to be taken into account before drawing any conclusions about their inter-state distributional pattern of assistance. The institutions, no doubt, accord priority to the major socio-economic objective and to more even distribution of assistance particularly in favour of the relatively less developed regions, but they consider that overall viability of assisted projects based on economic, financial and technical considerations should be accorded due importance.

It may be noted that flow of institutional assistance depends essentially on the level of entrepreneurial activity in different states. The locational decisions of industrial units are largely outside the purview of financial assistance. As far as the all-India institutions are concerned, they would prefer to go by the locational decisions of entrepreneurs and of the licensing authorities. The institutions offer incentives to influence location of projects as between backward areas and others but not between states. Different states and their SIDCs offer attractive participation terms in respect of their assisted/joint sector projects. Competition among states to attract industrial units by offering incentives quite often results in more or less equalisation of incentives, leaving the locational decision finally to the entrepreneurs than to the inter-state incentive patterns. Hence, the flow pattern of institutional assistance among different states is the outcome of the relative advantages, real or fancied, perceived by the entrepreneurs in locating their units in particular states.

## DEVELOPMENT OF BACKWARD AREAS

Industrial dispersal coupled with development of relatively less developed areas has been the integral policy of the national development plans as also the lending policies of the financial institutions. But a specific incentive framework designed exclusively for the development of identified backward areas was adopted by the institutions only since the beginning of 1970s.

There are a number of fiscal concessions for investment in backward areas which are important for attracting investment in the earlier neglected areas. The financial institutions offer concessions in terms of lower interest rates, longer moratorium period, easier repayment schedule and more favourable treatment in regard to promoter's distribution and debt-equity norms.

With a view to making the national policy for development of backward areas more purposeful and effective, Planning Commission had set up a high powered committee called the "National Committee on Development of Backward Areas", which submitted its report in October 1980. Recognising the inadequacies of existing incentive framework, the Committee was in favour of giving focal attention to growth of certain identified centres around which further growth of certain identified centres needs to be accelerated. To begin with, the Committee recommended adoption of 100 suitable locations as growth centres (70 of which would be in industrially backward states), each under the charge of a developmental authority that would be created to provide a package of services, infrastructure and incentives conducive to healthy growth of industries within the defined boundaries of the growth centre.

## GROWING INDUSTRIAL SICKNESS

There is a fallacious assumption that finance would be the panacea for industrial sickness in the country. The nursing of sick units is necessary in the country, in the interests of sustaining production and employment, but is it the sole responsibility of the banks and the financial institutions? The attitude of most of the State Governments in this regard is apathetic.They are concerned more with sustaining employment than production and very often the pressures of labour unions weigh more in their consideration than viability of the unit. There are also cases where the management of sick units throw them in the laps of banks and merrily start new and more profitable ventures. The promoters and managements of sick units believe that banks will not be allowed by the governments to close an industrial unit.

Rehabilitation of sick units calls for a concerted and co-ordinated approach on the part of all concerned, financial institutions, banks, State and Central Governments, other creditors and more particularly the promoters and labour who are directly concerned with the unit. There is a tendency to pass the burden of revival of the unit on the others, with the result that banks which have large stake in the unit have to bear the heaviest burden in the form of the reliefs and provision of further finance. The ultimate objective of reviving an otherwise viable unit is conveniently forgotten. Thanks to the inordinate delays that ensue, the unit is allowed to become more sick and even reach a stage of irretrievability. On the other hand, an irretrievable unit is compelled to stretch its parasitic existence. Surely, in an environment where survival of business is impossible, there should be freedom to close shop. The decision to nurse a sick unit should be taken purely on professional considerations. While social considerations cannot be ignored, they cannot be the sole guiding factor and in any case, the entire burden of 'social cost' should not be passed on to the banking industry.

On an average, an investment of ₹ 7.38 lakh in gross fixed assets is required to create one job in 2007-08 as against ₹ 2.95 lakh per job in 1990-91. Even taking into consideration the latest figure of 2006-07, the investment by development banks would generate employment opportunities around 55 million. On the other hand, SIDBI has envisaged that their operation is expected to catalyse an aggregate investment of ₹ 66,229 crore and create additional employment of 100 lakh in the small-scale sector on completion of the assisted projects. Here, the per person investment is as low as ₹ 39,959. If this is materialised, the development banks' contribution to human development will be quite unique. They will be setting to enforce a chain of positive activities, which will boost the economy. More importantly, they will improve the living standards of the people.

This apart, in the process, the financial institutions have helped create additional capacities in a large number of industries. Again, there will also be a spurt of new industries, new services, innovative products and large turnover, higher sales, higher profits. In this sense, the role of development banks is not only catalytic but also unique and significant.

## ELIGIBILITY FOR BANK'S ASSISTANCE

The bank's assistance may be considered for projects to establish, expand, diversify and modernise productive facilities in various sectors, including energy, manufacturing, transportation, forestry, fisheries, mining, tourism, health and agriculture. The project should produce or provide essential goods or services and serve national development objectives. Projects to produce non-essential or luxury consumer goods may be eligible provided the products are primarily for export. The Banks prefer projects which use domestic raw materials, create jobs, employ modern management techniques and technology and those which are export-oriented or lead to efficient import substitution, induce foreign investment and provide wider dispersal of ownership.

## ASSISTANCE TO SMALL-SCALE INDUSTRIES

Small-scale industries are provided finance and extension on service support by development banks such as SFCs, NSICs, SSIDCs, KVIC, NABARD and SIDBI. While other agencies are serving the small-scale enterprises at the grassroots level, NABARD has its focus on rural areas through linkages with the banking system. SIDBI has been set up as a principal financial institution for promotion and financing of the small-scale sector.

## NEW GROWTH PATHS

In recent years, the very character and complexion of development banks are undergoing change. One such is the change in the composition of business and assets of development banks with greater emphasis on non-project assistance. Non-project finance in the form of equipment finance, leasing, asset credit and bridge loans against public or rights issue of shares and debentures is now on the increase. Of late, development banks have become more selective and cautious in respect of project finance. In fact, non-project finance is less risky, there is assured repayment, for shorter duration with higher rates of return and thus more profitable.

DFIs also took several steps to reposition themselves and reorient their operations in the competitive environment by offering innovative products and diversifying their activities into new areas of business (such as investment banking, stock broking, custodial services, etc.), so as to harness the synergies and to reduce the risk arising out of narrow specialisation. DFIs were reasonably successful in diversifying into some non-traditional products, especially fee and commission based business.

Another development related to raising resources at reasonable cost is the strategic decisions taken by IDBI, ICICI and have resorted to the public issue of unsecured bonds, certificates of deposits and public deposits. The equity base of development banks is being broadened.

In the nineties, development banks are competing with each other for good business. Further, they have become increasingly conscious of the need for improving the quality of their portfolio. They are adopting prudential exposure norms and are classifying their assets into four groups — standard, sub-standard, doubtful and loss — a classification internationally followed for determining loan provisioning.

Development banks seeking new growth paths should not be deviated from their responsibility of promoting projects and encouraging new generation entrepreneurs. More importantly, worthwhile projects should be allowed to flounder for want of finance.

## CATALYTIC AGENT

In six decades, the new species of development banking has emerged as a powerful instrument of economic development in several developing countries including India. The concept of development banking and the areas of activities that are rightly said to be belonging to development banks has proved to be ever growing. While increasingly new demands are being made on them, both in regard to volume of finance and on their multifarious developmental and promotional services, it is not being adequately appreciated that there is always an inevitable and unavoidable time lag between the point of time when new demands are made and the minimum time required by the development banks to equip themselves organisationally to cater to new demands. Some of the problems arising out of industrial sickness and entrepreneurial behaviour or the developmental and promotional tasks of building up entrepreneurial cadre among sections of society, not usually supply effective entrepreneurial talent, or orderly development of relatively backward areas, etc., are all relatively new and challenging areas. Since all these are complex and onerous tasks not always assuring quick results, the rate of progress of development banks as seen by outsiders, may perhaps appear to be slower than what they would like. It, however, needs to be appreciated that development banking is not a technology but an art which tells us as to what our goals are but does not provide us unambiguous and readymade solutions. Hence, our search for satisfactory solutions has to continue.

Development banks today have come of age. They are, and have been acknowledged to be the prime movers of change. They have been and remain, in the vanguard of professionalised management as well as of better systems of management. They are promoters and vehicles of more rapid and broad-based economic growth through wide ranging stimulus to entrepreneurship development in their respective economies.

Development banking has, indeed, travelled a long way. One of its durable concerns, indeed, is to assist in setting on foot viable productive projects with supplementation of capital. Time was when the assistance given by a development bank was related primarily to the security that a borrower could offer. In this respect, the shift to the wide considerations of profitability and productivity of a venture and its contribution to the economic strategies of the country, as well as furtherance of the objectives of its social policy, is now an accomplished fact.

Over the years, the DFIs have come to occupy a place of importance in the planning and promotion of industries in the country. Responding to the emerging requirements of industrial and economic growth, they have not only constantly increased the flow of assistance, but developed a co-ordinated approach to industrial financing. Within a span of 45 years or so, a wide network of DFIs has been established; and some of these have specialised in particular areas of development finance. At the same time, all DFIs have introduced important organisational changes, including decentralisation and delegation of powers to their branch offices. Lending procedures have undergone changes in response to emerging requirements. As a result, the process of appraisal of project finance proposals as well as of sanctioning and disbursal of assistance has become considerably simpler and quicker. Simultaneously, consistent with their role as catalysts in economic development, the financial institutions have been continuously enlarging the scope of their operations — from providing financial assistance to identification of industrial opportunities, identification and training of entrepreneurs, provision of techno-economic consultancy facilities, industrial research and other promotional activities.

Thus, institutions are playing a significant role in creating fresh capacity in a large number of new projects as also the expansion/diversification of existing units. There is hardly any project in the private sector especially the larger ones, which could materialise without substantial support from the institutions. Even as regards the small- and medium-scale projects financed by the state-level institutions their financial support varies from 50% to 75% of the total project cost.

With an increasingly important role played by the financial institutions in industrial investment, during the last decade, institutions are becoming aware of some of the inadequacies that exist in their lending strategies, support to capital market, development of backward areas and effective follow-up of assisted projects.

## CHALLENGES IN THE NEW CENTURY

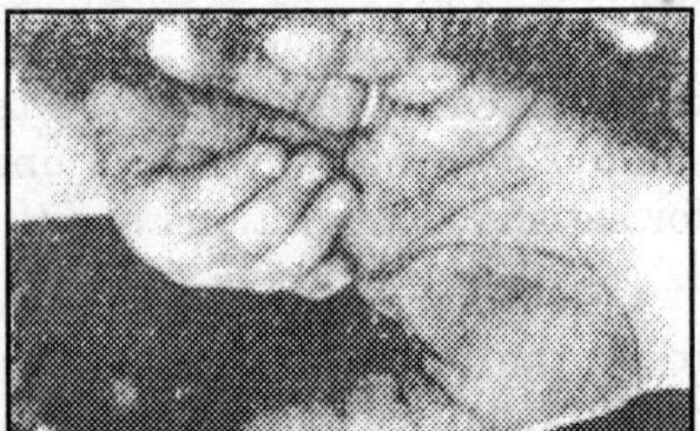

The challenges currently faced by Development Banks differ from those in the past. In particular, globalisation, led by trade and financial liberalisation and increasingly rapid changes in information and communication technology, is having a deed impact on Indian economy and society. Globalisation changes not only the markets work but also low governments, the private sector and civil society work and interact. In recent years, development thinking has also changing, with approaches emphasising a broader view of development. Globalisation opens up opportunities for developing countries, facilitating wider and faster access to resources, capital, technology know-how, and markets, thereby expanding development options and increasing the potential for participation in the development process. On the other hand, globalisation also involves risks that have to be managed. Globalisation can generate social and economic stresses as well as financial volatility.

## TOWARDS PROSPERITY

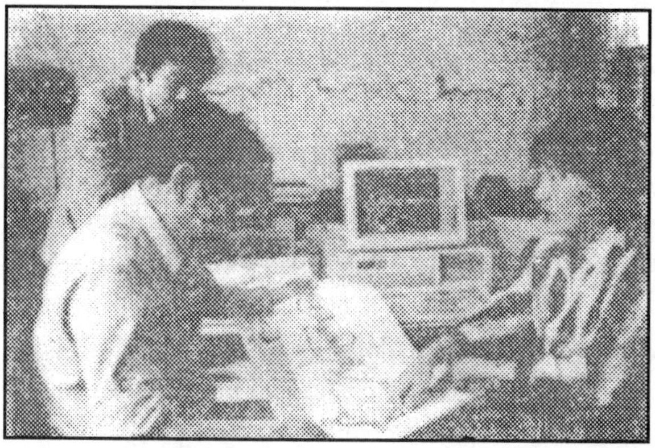

To ensure project quality, technical assistance is provided to prepare detailed engineering, including designs, specifications, cost estimates, sectoral surveys or master plans.

The Bank promotes policy reforms that will have a lasting impact on future generations.

The vision of Development Banks is the socio-economic growth. Economic growth can reduce poverty by generating employment and income, labour intensive growth can reduce it even faster. Promoting sustainable economic growth relies on the successful pursuit of the other pillars of Development Banks strategy: Social development and good governance.

These challenges have made economic development even more daunting. To be more effective and responsive, Development Banks have to change their directions, approaches and commitment.

The strategic focus will be on achieving sustainable economic growth, inclusive of social development and good governance. In particular, the framework embraces the philosophy and thrusts of the new private sector development strategy, and it recognizes the importance of regional development activities and DB's unique role as the region's development bank. It also reaffirms commitment to the international development goals. Core medium-term poverty targets for 2005 are for each state to implement national sustainable development strategies and eliminate gender disparities in primary and secondary education. The fundamental long-term target is to reduce the incidence of extreme poverty by 2015, compared with 1990.

Progress is contingent on clear objectives, an over-arching vision and an ability to care. Without caring little is achievable. Governance is about caring. The Development Banks have to imbibe and remain committed to their values as they develop into an integrated financial conglomerate.

Finally, Development Banks can play a large role in helping states increase the efficiency and effectiveness of their own lending through greater selectivity, better co-ordination with other lenders, and more effective monitoring of performance. The fundamental factors of success are:

- A commitment to sound macroeconomic policies,
- Free trade and open investment policies that exposes companies to international competition,
- Generally low levels of taxation,
- High levels of investment in human capital through sustained public sector commitment to health and basic education,
- A strong sense of entrepreneurship, and
- A high propensity to save.

Apart from repositioning, re-organisation, promoting better partnerships, efficient and effective use of savings, ensuring adequate financial and human resources, Development Banks must secure adequate financial resources by maintaining sound financial management of existing resources, and maximising internal efforts to utilise them to their fullest extent before taking any other actions. Development Banks are firmly committed for translating vision into action and achieving the goal.

Up to end March 2000, sanctions and disbursements of all financial institutions aggregated to ₹ 6,52,799.26 crore and ₹ 6,54,911.67 crore respectively.

In line with the emerging needs of industry in the new competitive and deregulated financial environment, institutions have reoriented their policies by drawing up their prospective mission and strategy so as to make themselves globally competitive. An important effect of the entire process is a movement towards 'Universal Banking' encompassing a wide range of products to suit the varied needs of clients and investors so as to be internationally competitive. This would be an ideal route to becoming an efficient service provider committed to maximising stakeholders' value.

Clearly, a sustained pro-growth strategy requires power sharing among major sectors in the economy and stronger public institutions to prevent private sector excesses. Good governance determines the quality of growth in the 21st century.

## FUTURE ROLE OF DFIs

The DFIs have been facing stiff competition ever since the entry of commercial banks into the medium and long-term loan sector. Now the boundaries between the commercial banks and the development financial institutions have blurred considerably. As a result, the DFIs have concentrated on more profitable areas so as to increase their income. Their focus seems to have shifted from the very purpose for which they had been set up. While all of them had been set up for the same purpose, IDBI is now concentrating on wholesale term lending, whereas ICICI is all set to enter the retail segment with its strategic tie-ups. IFCI, despite being the oldest DFI in the country, has not been able to report positive net cash flows. The profitability of these FIs have also been eroded because of the lack of control on the growing non-performing assets (NPAs). In the wake of all this, these institutions might face an increasing problem in servicing their debt in the future. If it continues growing at such a rate, it might not be in a position to sustain the growth rate and might have to keep borrowing heavily from the market to service their debt in the future.

With the growth of universal banking, the future role of the Development Financial Institutions (DFIs) also needs to be re-examined. Many of them are entering into commercial banking business. The logical culmination of this should be that they be converted into banks and subject in a phased manner to the same regulatory and prudential norms as are applied to the banking system. We would thus have only two classes of financial institutions, namely, banks and non-banks, and it is for the DFIs to decide whether they wish to continue to be non-banking or become banking institutions. Even if they were in the process of becoming universal banks, to take up normal commercial banking functions, the specialist expertise which they have acquired over the years in investment funding and term capital finance should not be lost.

In future, the participation and involvement of DFIs in the process of economic development will be still deeper as they intensify their efforts at the development of entrepreneurs, backward areas, small industries and export-oriented units as well as at the upgradation of technology in the traditional sectors. The tasks ahead are varied and challenging. Fresh demands may not only call for a substantial step up in resource mobilisation efforts to keep pace with growth in the volume of financial assistance but may also require a orientation of the policies and priorities for allocation of assistance. Equally important will be the demands for multifarious promotional and developmental activities. Considering the strength and flexibility of the development finance system that has been built-up over the years, the DFIs in India should be able to respond competently and adequately to future demands and add newer dimensions to the field of development banking.

## MERGERS

On March 30, 2002, when ICICI and two of its subsidiaries merged with ICICI Bank, it marked the beginning of a new era for the Bank and for the financial sector in India — the era of universal banking. The era when players recognize the plurality of customer preferences and strive to fulfil them.

The merger has created the country's largest private sector bank and the second largest bank in terms of assets, with a growth model that bring together complementary capabilities and provides opportunities hitherto unavailable as separate entities. The merger has combined two organisations with complementary strengths and products and similar processes and operating architecture. The merger has combined the large capital base of ICICI with the strong deposits raising capability of ICICI Bank, giving ICICI Bank improved ability to increase its market share in banking fees and commissions, while lowering the overall cost of funding through access to lower-cost retail deposits. ICICI Bank would now be able to fully leverage the strong corporate relationships that ICICI has built, seamlessly providing the whole range of financial products and services to corporate clients. The merger has also resulted in the integration of the retail finance operations of ICICI, and its two merging subsidiaries, and ICICI Bank into one entity, creating an optimal structure for the retail business and allowing the full range of asset and liability products to be offered to all retail customers.

Similarly, IDBI merged its IDBI Bank and formed IDBI Bank on April 2, 2005. Further took over United Western Bank in its fold on October 2006. And, actively negotiated making a private bank to expand its base in the country.

## CRITICAL APPRAISAL

A plethora of financial corporations catering to the financial needs of a variety of industries, had come into existence, each one functioning within the narrow framework set down by the statute or the memorandum that accredited it. The multiplicity of financial institutions operating in the same field with hardly any demarcation in their specific activities led to overlapping and duplication of their efforts with the result that financially well off concerns could manage to procure financial assistance from a number of institutions, while the weaker concerns were left high and dry. A co-ordination of functions and working of financial institutions was, therefore, considered necessary so that they might play a more useful role in the industrial development of the country. Many gigantic projects of national importance were held up because of the absence of financial arrangements. Furthermore, a large number of industrial projects were envisaged to be set up during the fourth and succeeding plans to achieve self-sufficiency in the industrial sector; and this called for a substantially large amount of capital provision, which the existing institutions were not able to supply in view of their own limited resources. The establishment of a financial institution with a substantially larger amount of resources and capable of functioning undeterred by statutory rigidities, therefore, became inevitable.

The DFIs were set up to provide the necessary capital and know-how to business enterprises so as to bolster the industrial growth of the country. Till 1991, they had been functioning in a highly regulated environment and had enjoyed a comfortable spread since the cost of their borrowings had been considerably lower than the return on their financing. Since deregulation, and after the easing out of cheap SLR funds from the government, there has been an increasing funds in the market. As a result, these institutions have resorted to heavy borrowing from the market. In the past few years, they have borrowed large amount of funds by floating a number of innovative debt and equity issues catering to the needs of various kinds of investors.

Over the years, the development banks have failed in these crucial areas:

(1) DFIs have financed industrial groups rather than new entrepreneurs.

(2) Entrepreneurship development lacked commitment and innovation.

(3) Inordinate delay in sanction and disbursement.

(4) Emphasis on plurality of institutions assisting the same project.

(5) Dilution of the standards of scrutiny of project proposals.

(6) Absence of project monitoring and implementation.

(7) Inability to build-up adequate expert staff, both technical and financial.

(8) Their incapacity to advise the new entrepreneurs on various matters from project idea, formulation, execution and implementation.

(9) Distortion in the growth of a developed capital market.

(10) The development financial institutions in India lack in vision, innovation and enterprise. In the process, they have inherited the bureaucratic attitude.

Judged in these terms, although the quantity of funds flowed through these channels is huge, but it failed to generate sources of savings to retain the qualitative tempo of industrial development on a sustainable basis. It is right time to reorganise the development institutions to accelerate the process of equitable and healthy industrial development in the future.

In the changed operating environment, development finance institutions (DFIs), which have traditionally been among the main sources of long-term finance for the corporate sector in India, are finding it increasingly difficult to maintain their viability. In view of this, the future role of these DFIs needs to be addressed urgently as the alternative source of long-term funds has not developed. As some DFIs convert themselves into banks or NBFCs, an important source of long-term funds would dry up. Thus, there is a concern regarding the vacuum which would be created by the withdrawal of DFIs from the scene. Although banks have entered the domain of term-lending, there are limits on the extent to which commercial banks may be able to fill this vacuum. The shift from fixed to flexible interest rate regime, development of instruments for hedging interest rate risk, and effectiveness of timely resolution of NPA-related problems would influence the flow of funds from banks for meeting long-term financing requirements. Banks alone, however, may not be able to compensate the decline in long-term funds by DFIs to the corporate sector. To fill the gap, the development of a private corporate debt market is of crucial importance. The development of a benchmark in the fixed securities market and development of secondary market for corporate debt would also stimulate banks' investment in corporate securities.

DFIs were set up with the specific objective of meeting the medium to long-term requirement of funds. However, DFIs in the present form are finding it difficult to sustain their operations. Their business has slowed down and their operations have become less profitable. This has raised issues relating to the viability of DFIs. It is not clear, however, whether the perceived lack of viability emanates from the structural constraints under which they operate or simply from the legacy of the past.

The Narasimham Committee II (1988) had recommended that DFIs should, over a period of time, convert themselves into banks or NBFCs. There would then be only two forms of intermediaries, i.e., banks and NBFCs. The Reserve Bank in the Discussion Paper released in January 1999 indicated that DFIs should have the freedom to retain their status and specialised in their own activities. However, if a DFI chooses to become a bank, that option should also be available. In response to interest evinced by DFIs the Reserve Bank issues guidelines setting out various operational and regulatory parameters that need to be complied with by DFIs if they are to become banks. ICICI, one of the major DFIs, along with two of its subsidiaries has recently merged with the ICICI Bank. However, to fill the void being created by the disappearance of DFIs, urgent steps are required to be taken to develop the private corporate debt market and introduce appropriate instruments to reduce the risk arising out of long-term financing by other players such as banks.

## REGULATION AND SUPERVISION

The Reserve Bank started monitoring the operation of DFIs in 1990 with a view to taking on integrated view of the operations of financial institutions and commercial banks. DFIs were brought within the supervisory jurisdiction of the Board for Financial supervision from April 1995.

The main objectives of reforms in the case of DFIs were to impart market orientation to their operations and strengthen them by applying prudential norms.

- DFIs are being covered by an on-site supervisory process (CAMELS standards) since 1995.
- The resource mobilisation by DFIs was brought under the purview of regulations in 1998.
- The RBI will continue to supervise DFIs on-site and off-site surveillance system.
- To follow uniform accounting standards similar to those followed by banks.
- Norms for income recognition, asset classification, provisioning and other related matters regarding grantees are spelt out by the RBI.

## CONCLUSION

With the adoption of planning for economic development, the building up of an appropriate structure of development finance institutions has been of crucial importance. The first decade of Indian planning witnessed the emergence of a number of development banks, both at the all-India and regional levels. Overtime, as the industrial structure of the country became more diversified, the activities of development finance institutions not only widened, keeping pace with the growing needs of industry, but became increasingly complex and wide-ranging. In recent years, while efforts at filling the gaps in the institutional structure for the promotion and financing of industry have been intensified, a need has arisen for a more effective co-ordination of activities of the different institutions and for evolving integrated financing institutions for the industrial sector. In addition, new development institutions have been established to cater the needs of agriculture, and foreign trade in the eighties. New guarantee institutions too, were moulded to cater to the needs of the weaker sections of society.

Financial institutions, which historically played an important role in meeting the medium to long-term requirements of the economy, have been repositioning themselves in the changed operating environment. Two large FIs (ICICI and IDBI) have already converted into banks and another FI IIBI has been wound up by the government.

With a view to strengthening FIs, the Reserve Bank has been focusing on imparting greater operational flexibility, while strengthening the regulatory and supervisory framework. Prudential norms for FIs have been broadly brought on par with commercial banks. Recently, a modified approach for supervisory assessment of these institutions has been introduced, wherein only four FIs, *viz.* NABARD, SIDBI, NHB and EXIM Bank are subjected to full-fledged regulation and supervision by the Reserve Bank. FIs not accepting public deposits by the Reserve Bank. FIs not accepting public deposits, but having asset size of ₹ 500 crore and above, are subjected to only limited off-site supervision by the Reserve Bank. At present, the major AIFIs are in the nature of refinance institutions, which do not have significant exposure to direct finance. To that extent they pose less of a supervisory concern in comparison with FIs undertaking direct finance.

At present, the country is served by over 428 development banks with a wide network of branches, and supported by technical consultancy organisations. The Industrial Development Bank of India is acting as the apex institution for co-ordinating their diverse financing and promotional activities. The strategies, policies and industrial promotional efforts of these institutions subserve the larger national objective of rapid industrial growth, balanced regional development, self-reliance, employment generation and equitable distribution of income and means of production.

CHAPTER 6

# INSURANCE AND MUTUAL FUNDS

## INTRODUCTION

The structure of development banks, besides the all-India development financial institutions, also consists of three investment institutions comprising Life Insurance Corporation of India (LIC), Unit Trust of India (UTI), and General Insurance Corporation of India (GIC).

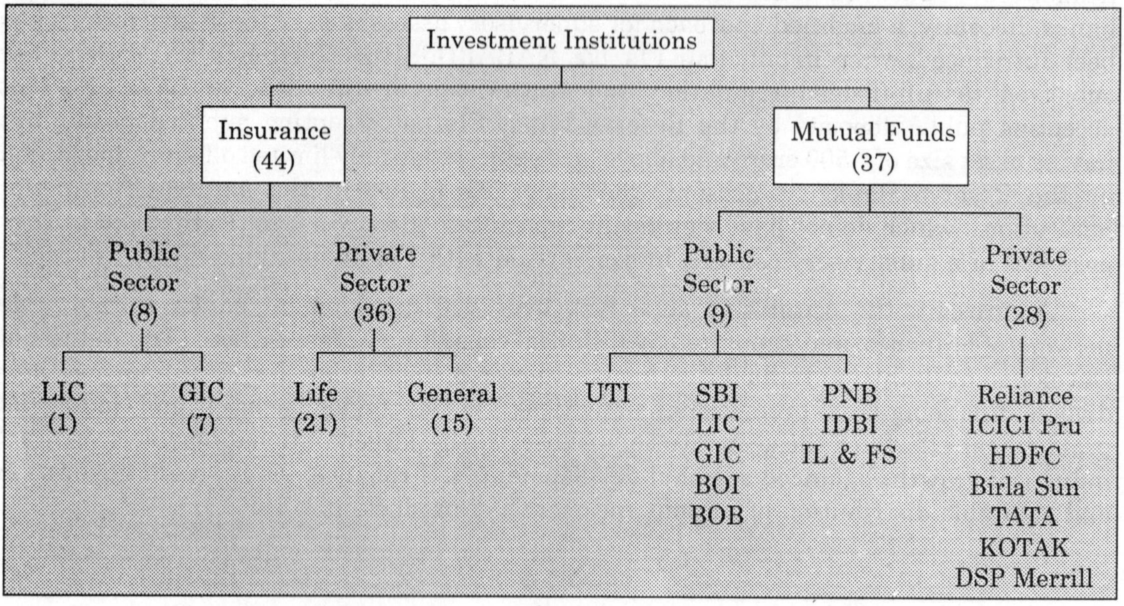


**Fig. 1**

Of the investment institutions, LIC and GIC which primarily take care of the life and general insurance needs of the society and UTI which is a mutual fund mobilises the savings of the community for channelising into productive sectors, are active participants in providing finance to industry both by way of term loans and subscription to equity and debentures. They are also principal players in the primary and secondary markets, besides extending assistance to industry through loans and by way of underwriting/ direct subscription to equities and debentures.

## INSURANCE SECTOR

In the Indian financial sector, insurance sector is the second largest group of financial institutions. In the Indian financial landscape, the insurance sector accounts for around 15 per cent, next only to banking. Further more, India has been ranked amongst the top ten life insurance markets worldwide. The insurance sector in India offers immense growth opportunities. The potential can be judged by the fact that today life insurance premiums account only 2.5% of the country's GDP, while general insurance premiums are at only 0.65%.

Insurance business in India has had a long history since 1818. Life insurance and general insurance were a mixed business and were decentralised until the entire insurance business as brought under social control — Life Insurance in 1956 and General Insurance in 1972.

Insurance basically is sharing of loss of a few individuals by a large group of persons. It is an arrangement by which a large number of persons agree to share the loss which a few of them are likely to incur in future, with the advantage that the individual share of the loss is small and remains fairly steady over a number of years. Such association of persons is organised by an insurance organisation.

**RISK:** For insurance purpose risk means uncertainty about loss, i.e., financial loss.

**PERIL:** The term "Peril" may be defined as the cause of loss.

### HOW IT ALL STARTED — BOX : 1

Life insurance in its modern form is a Western concept. Although it has been taking shape for the last 300 years, it came to India with the arrival of the Europeans. The first life insurance company was established in India in 1818 as Oriental Life Insurance Company, mainly to provide for widows of Europeans. The companies that followed mainly catered to Europeans and charged extra premium on Indian lives. The first Indian company insuring Indian lives at standard rates was Bombay Mutual Life Insurance Company, which was formed in 1870. This was the year also when the first Insurance Act was passed by the British Parliament. The years subsequent to the Swadeshi Movement saw the emergence of several insurance companies. At the end of the year 1955 there were 245 insurance companies and provident societies out of which 16 were non-Indian companies. All the companies were nationalised in 1956 and brought under one umbrella — The Life Insurance Corporation of India (LIC) — which enjoyed a monopoly of the life insurance business till near the end of 2000. By enacting the Insurance Regulatory and Development Authority (IRDA) Act, (2000), the Government of India effectively ended LIC's monopoly and opened the doors for private insurance companies.

Insurance eliminates risk and substitutes certainty for uncertainty. Insurance is the protection of the economic value of assets. Basically, insurance is a protection against financial loss arising on the happening of an unexpected event. Besides, insurance policy helps in not only mitigating risks but also provides a financial cushion against adverse financial burdens suffered.

Insurance is a contract between two parties, the insurer or the insurance company, and the insured, the person seeking the cover. Within this contract, the insurer agrees to pay the insurer for financial losses arising out of any unforeseen events or risk in return for a regular payment of premium.

But why should one insure? One of the main reasons one should insure is to protect one's belongings and assets against financial loss. When one has earned and accumulated property, protecting it is prudent.

## LIFE INSURANCE AND GENERAL INSURANCE

Insurance policies cover the risk of life as well as other assets and valuables, such as home, automobiles, jewellery, etc. On the basis of the risk they cover, insurance policies can be classified into two categories: Life insurance and general insurance. As the term suggests, life insuarnce covers the risk involved in a person's life, while general insurance provides financial protection against unforeseen events, like accident, flood, earthquake, disease, fire and burglary. General insurance also covers injury due to accident or hospitalisation for illness and surgery can also be insured. Your liabilities to others arising out of the law can also be insured and is compulsory in some cases like motor third party insurance.

Besides, term 'life insurance' or term 'assurance' is life insurance which provides coverage for a limited period of time, the relevant term. In fact, term life insurance is the original form of life insurance and is considered to be the pure insurance protection because it builds no cash value. Should the insured person pass away, the family is protected by a certain amount.

There are three key factors to be considered in term insurance: face amount (protection or death benefit); premium to be paid (cost to the insured); and length of coverage (term).

| Life Insurance | Non-life or General Insurance |
|---|---|
| 1. Risk is certain under life insurance.<br>2. It is a long-term contract.<br>3. Difficult to determine the value of human life.<br>4. Life insurance and personal accident insurance are not contracts of indemnity.<br>5. The right to renew life policy on payment of premium is automatic throughout the agreed period.<br>6. Principle of subrogation does not apply.<br>7. Once the contract is entered into the insured generally has no duty to report any event affecting the risk insured.<br>8. Premium remains constant throughout the period of policy. | 1. Risk is not certain.<br>2. Usually one year contract.<br>3. It is not difficult to determine the value of subject matter of insurance.<br>4. These are contracts of indemnity.<br>5. Each renewal constitutes a new contract.<br>6. When the insurer makes good the loss offered by a person, he acquires the rights and remedies of that person.<br>7. Duty of utmost good faith arises at every renewal. Certain policies prescribe disclosure of material changes in the risk.<br>8. Premium may vary at each renewal (depending upon the changed nature of risk or loss experience.) |

**INSURANCE SPEAK** **BOX : 2**

**Get to know the jargon: only way you'll know a whole-life plan from a hole in the ground.**

Let's begin at the beginning. Life insurance is a legal contract between you and an insurer, under which you pay the insurer a premium, or a periodic payment, in return for covering the risk of your death. Think of it as a game: every year. you're betting that you won't live another year; the insurer is betting that you will. If you live (and therefore lose the bet), you pay him a small premium; if you die (and the insurer loses the bet), he pays your nominee the jackpot (that's because you won't be around to collect it).

There are, broadly, four types of life insurance policies. **Term plans** are the cheapest, purest form of insurance, which cover the risk of death for a specified period. If you survive the policy, you get no returns; if you die during the policy tenure, your nominees get the **sum assured**, or the amount for which you are covered. Endowment plans are insurance-cum-investment vehicles: they cover the risk of death for the policy tenure and, additionally, offer a return on investment. Moneyback plan are Endowment plans in which the policy tenure and additionally, offer a return on investment. **Moneyback plans** are endowment plans in which the policyholder receives a part of the return on investment during the policy tenure. **Whole-life plans** are policies that, as the name suggests, cover you for your whole-life, not just for a fixed tenure.

**Human life value** is, in life insurance parlance, the present value of your family's share of your earnings over a lifetime. It's one measure of how much life insurance you need.

There are other kinds of insurance policies that cover you for various other risks. A **Personal Accident Insurance Policy** (PAIP), offered by the general insurers, covers you for one or more of four contingencies in the event of an accident: death, permanent total disability, permanent partial disability and temporary total disability (these last three terms involve graphic — and morbid — descriptions of body parts, particularly what happens to them in the event of an accident). The PAIP provides for payment of lump sum of either the sum assured or a percentage of it — in the event of your being permanently or temporarily disabled owing to an accident. In addition, one variant of the PAIP provides for a weekly compensation for the period you are unable to return to work, subject to a maximum of 104 weeks. This policy costs the same across all ages — as low as ₹ 150 a year for every ₹ 1 lakh of cover.

Then there's **Mediclaim**, which covers your health insurance needs: It lets you claim reimbursement for hospitalisation or 'domiciliary' (treatment at home) expenses up to a specified limits. A variant of this plan provides for **cash less settlement** of your hospital bills.

**Householder's insurance** covers your home and everything that's in it against loss or damage. A particularly useful plan, available at low premiums.

**Liability insurance** covers you for legal liabilities arising from a third party in certain uncommon circumstances. Some insurance plans also serve as retirement financing vehicles. For instance, an **annuity** is a contract between you and an insurer, which allows you to accumulate money for retirement or generate an income stream in retirement. A **deferred annuity** is a long-term retirement planning vehicle in which your accumulation in your earning years are not subject to tax — and, therefore, grow faster. In recent years, insurance products have undergone marked innovations that add value to customers. One of them is the **rider**. It's an add-on provision, available at the policyholder's option and for an additional premium, and alters certain features of a policy to provide an element of customization to suit specific needs. Another such innovation is the **decreasing term insurance plan**. It's essentially a term insurance policy with a level premium and a death benefit that decrease overtime. This plan is most commonly used as 'debt insurance': the death benefit reduces as the loan amount declines over its tenure.

## LIFE INSURANCE CORPORATION OF INDIA

There were a large number of companies of varying age, size and pattern of organisations — 245, on the eve of nationalisation in 1956, which conducted life insurance business in India. There were also other companies which had main business of general insurance but also undertook life insurance. On nationalisation, a single monolithic organisation, the Life Insurance Corporation of India (LIC), was set up in 1956. Almost the entire life insurance business is now in the hands of the LIC. The Post and Telegraph Department conducts such limited business for its employees on a negligible scale.

The objective of the nationalisation of life insurance business was to take insurance to the neglected areas in the country and utilise the savings of the people in such activities as would ensure not only the safety of the capital, but also help in the rapid economic development of the nation. As a matter of fact, it is the largest single investor in the country today. It invests its funds in well-established joint-stock companies which have been regularly paying a good dividend to their shareholders.

The LIC operates a variety of schemes so as to benefit individuals and groups from the urban and rural areas.

According to the Investment Policy of LIC, out of the accretions to the Controlled Fund, not less than 75% has to be invested in Central and State Government securities, including government-guaranteed marketable securities and in the socially-oriented sectors. Besides Life Insurance made its debut in India well over 100 years ago. But strangely enough even its salient features are not as widely understood in our country as they ought to be. What follows is an attempt to acquaint readers with some of the concepts of life insurance, with special reference to LIC. It should, however, be clearly understood that the following narration is by no means an exhaustive description of the terms and conditions of an LIC policy or its benefits or privileges. For more details, please refer to our Prospectus or contact our Branch or Divisional Office. Any LIC agent will be glad to help you choose the life insurance plan to meet your needs and render policy servicing.

## WHAT IS LIFE INSURANCE?

Life Insurance is a contract for payment of a sum of money to the person assured (or failing him/her, to the person entitled to receive the same) on the happening of the event insured against. Usually, the contract provides for the payment of an amount on the date of maturity or at specified dates at periodic intervals or at unfortunate death, if it occurs earlier. Among other things, the contract also provides for the payment of premium periodically to the Corporation by the assured. Life insurance is universally acknowledged to be an institution which eliminates 'risk', substituting certainty for uncertainty and comes to the timely aid of the family in the unfortunate event of the death of the breadwinner. By and large, life insurance is civilisation's partial solution to the problems caused by death.

Life insurance, in short, is concerned with two hazards that stand across the life-path of every person: that of dying prematurely leaving a dependent family to fend for itself and that of living to oldage without visible means of support.

## WHY IS IT SUPERIOR TO OTHER FORMS OF SAVINGS?

**(i) Protection:** Savings through life insurance guarantee full protection against risk of death of the saver. In life insurance, on death, the full sum assured is payable (with bonuses wherever applicable), whereas in other savings schemes, only the amount saved (with interest) is payable.

**(ii) Aid to Thrift:** Life Insurance encourages 'thrift'. Long-term savings can be made in a relatively 'painless' manner because of the 'easy instalment' facility (method of paying premium either monthly, quarterly, half-yearly or yearly) built into the scheme. Take for example, *Salary Savings Scheme.* This scheme provides a convenient method of paying premium each month by deduction from one's salary. The deducted premium is remitted by the Employer to the LIC. The Salary Savings Scheme can be introduced in an institution or establishment subject to specified terms and conditions.

**(iii) Liquidity:** Loans can be raised on the sole security of a policy which has acquired loan value. Besides, a life insurance policy is generally accepted as security for a commercial loan.

**(iv) Tax Relief:** Considerable tax relief in Income Tax and Wealth Tax is available to an individual or a Hindu Undivided Family for amounts paid by way of premium for life insurance. Individual and HUF assessees can avail themselves of provisions in the law for tax relief. In such cases the assured in effect pays a substantially lower premium for his insurance than he would have to pay otherwise.

Life Insurance policies can be classified as shown in the following chart:

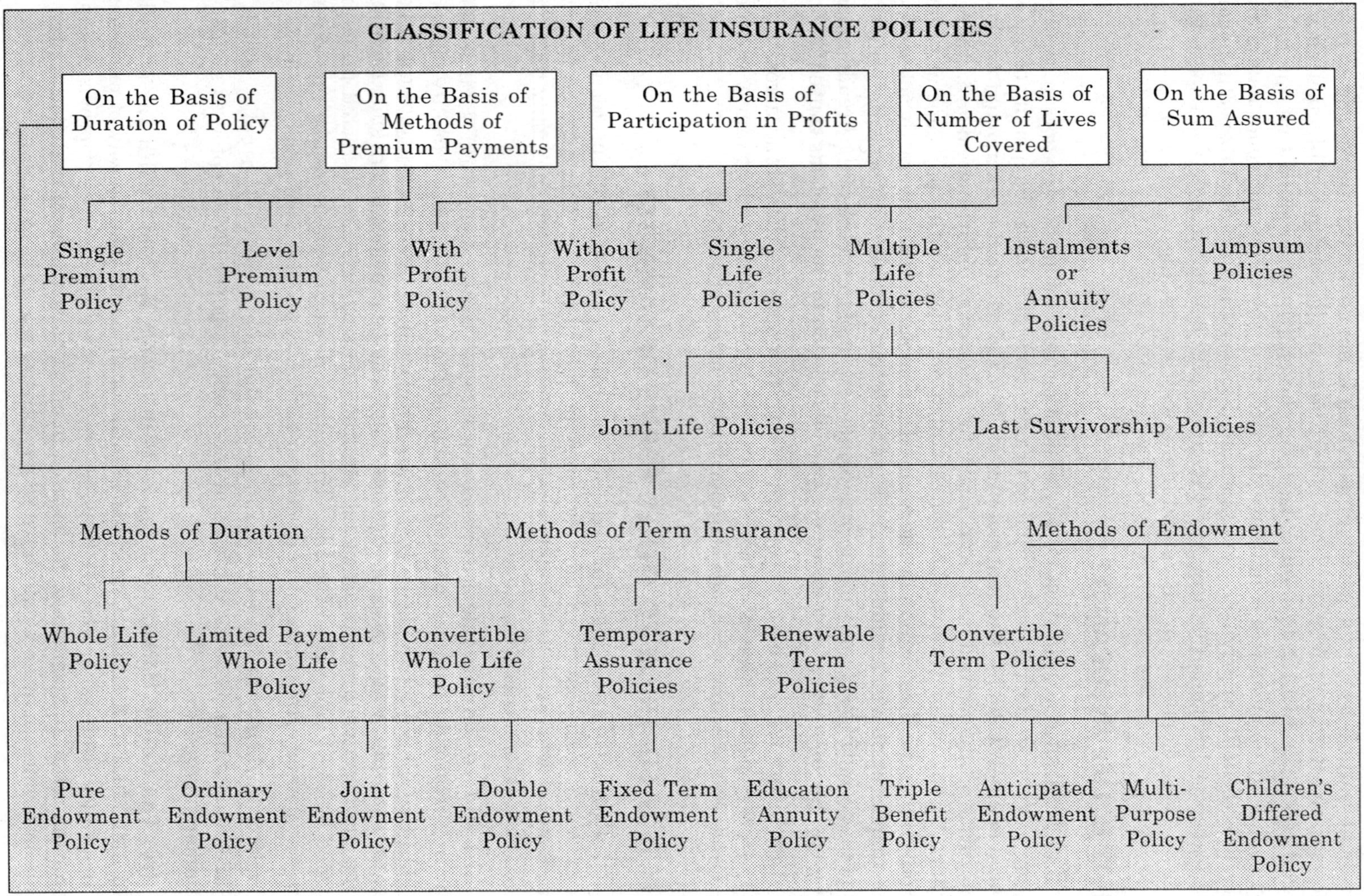

**(v) Money When You Need It:** A suitable insurance plan or a combination of different plans can be taken out to meet specific needs that are likely to arise in future, such as children's education, start-in-life or marriage provision or even periodical needs for cash over a stretch of time. Alternatively, policy moneys can be so arranged to be made available at the time of one's retirement from service to be used for any specific purpose, such as for the purchase of a house or for other investments. Subject to certain conditions, *loans are granted to policyholders for house building or for purchase of flats.*

## MEANING OF LIFE INSURANCE

According to Sec. (2) (11) of the Insurance Act, Life Insurance business means "the business of effective contracts upon human life. It includes.

(a) Any contract whereby the payment of money is assured upon death (except death by accident only) or the happening of any contingency dependent on human life;

(b) Any contract which is subject to the payment of premiums for a term dependent on human life;

(c) Any contract which includes the granting of disability and double or triple indemnity, accident benefits, the granting of annuities upon human life, and the granting of superannuation allowance."

## ESSENTIAL FEATURES OF LIFE ASSURANCE

Essential Features

The following are the essential features required for a valid contract of life insurance:

(1) Elements of a Valid Contract
(2) Insurable Interest
(3) Utmost Good Faith
(4) Warranties
(5) Assignment and Nomination
(6) Cause is Certain
(7) Premium
(8) Terms of Policy
(9) Return of Premium

After a long period of a monopolistic environment, the insurance sector was opened to private participation with the enactment of the Insurance Regulatory and Development Authority Act in 1999. Since then, the number of participants has increased from one wholly public-owned insurer to 22 insurers operating in life segment. Apart from LIC, there are twenty one life insurance companies that have setup operations in the life segment post opening of the sector nineteen are in joint ventures with foreign partners.

Participation by foreign joint venture partners through the FDI route is limited to 26 per cent of the paid-up capital under the current legislation. Through this route, foreign players have also entered the Indian insurance market. There are proposals under consideration to increase this FDI cap to 49 per cent (Insurance Laws Amendment Bill, 2008 has been tabled in the Parliament). The CFSA notes that the government has for quite sometime been emphasising the need to enhance the limits for FDI ceilings. Though, in the immediate future, this would present difficulties owing to the global financial turmoil and the absence of an enabling statutory framework, it needs to be addressed in the medium-term.

The presence of new players in the market has resulted in enhanced product innovation, better services and value-added benefits. A significant component of growth in the life sector has been savings-linked insurance products. Public sector companies require time to mould themselves to the competitive environment and associated contemporary structural changes, though the post-deregulation period has seen greater diversification in their product offerings, with added stress on marketing and distribution strategies. The regulatory policy has taken a cautious and calibrated approach in sequencing various elements of the reform process, which aims not only at a level playing field, but also takes into account the structural constraints in the insurance sector.

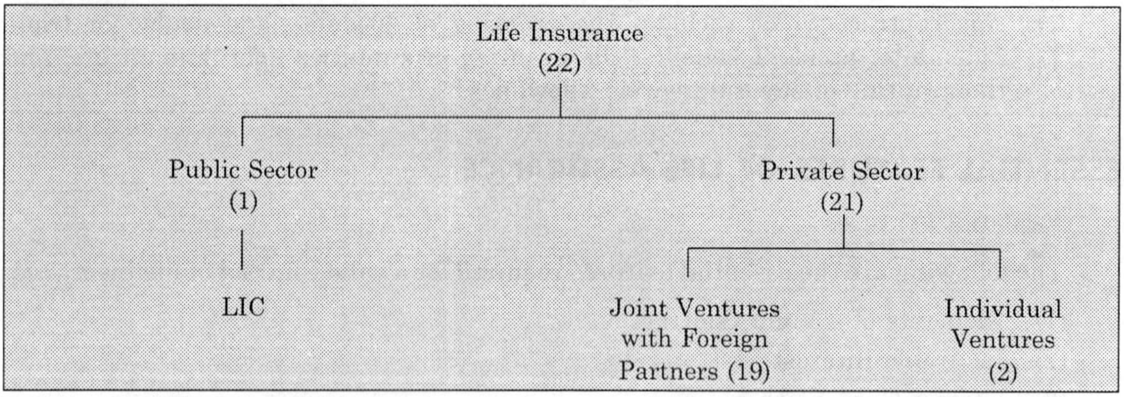


## LIFE INSURANCE INDUSTRY

The post-liberalization period has witnessed tremendous growth in the insurance industry, more particularly so in the life segment. The total premium underwritten by the industry has grown from ₹ 34,898.47 crore in 2000-01 to ₹ 2,23,555.79 crore in 2008-09. The first year premium, which is a measure of new business secured, underwritten by the life insurers during 2008-09 was ₹ 87,107.62 crore as compared to ₹ 9,708 crore in 2000-01. During the financial year 2008-09, the life insurance industry has reported negative growth of 6.32% in new business premium underwritten as against growth of 23.88% in 2007-08.

In terms of linked and non-linked premium, during 2008-09, 51.30% of the first year premium was underwritten in the linked segment while 48.70% of the premium was in the nonlinked segment. The corresponding previous year proportion was 75.34:24.66 respectively.

An analysis of key indicators for financial soundness shows that the life insurance segment is reasonably comfortable as regards solvency, though the solvency ratio of the largest life insurance company (LIC) is barely at the stipulated regulatory minimum. Capital adequacy, due to low capital base of LIC, is low. Though there has been increase in asset quality ratios, they are within the regulatory stipulation. Profitability and liquidity indicators do not throw up any cause for concern. There is a general trend to increase link-based business in the life sector.

## THE WAY FORWARD

The Indian life insurance sector has been experiencing robust growth since it was opened up in 1999 – both in the public and the private sector companies. The nature of the product mix has changed significantly.

In order to enhance their market share and to have a sustainable premium growth, companies have started expanding presence, bringing other innovative forms of distribution channels, sell health and pension products.

However, the companies will have to pay more attention in expense management. And also institute an asset-liability management (ALM) framework in order to measure and manage the market risk and the interest rate risk, as these can have a pronounced impact on the financial stability for life insurance companies.

Finally, though the performance of the insurance companies in India has been satisfactory on account of various prudential policies pursued by IRDA, there is more need to invest in capital and also need for more trained actuaries as acturial skills are fundamental to development of risk management capacity – further opening up and the entry of more players would increase the range of competitive products and the development of human and professional skills which would also help complement the growth of the financial sector.

### INSURANCE TERMINOLOGY — BOX : 3

Typically, there are three points of the matrix along which insurance products evolve and are marketed. The most fundamental is term insurance. It is a pure risk product, in that it offers protection cover during a limited number of years in case of death. But if the policyholder survives the stated term or period, no amount is payable on maturity, irrespective of premium payments made earlier. That's because reserves are not accumulated and the premium is meant for offering protection alone. For that reason the product offers high cover on payment of a small premium, as compared to whole Life and Endowment policies. Typically, for a Term Policy of ₹ 1 lakh, one has to pay between ₹ 250-₹ 500, annually.

It is normally availed of for short tenures to cover against mortgages and other temporary liabilities. Term Insurance is also aimed at the young.

Next product along the matrix is Whole Life. Like Term Insurance, it too primarily caters to protection, but for one's entire life. The fundamental difference with Term Insurance is that it also builds up a cash surrender value (which typically gets eroded by 30 per cent if premium payments are stopped). The cost of insurance is higher in this case. For a sum assured of ₹ 1 lakh, one has to pay an annual premium of ₹ 3,000 a year, which is still far less than the payments for Endowment and Moneyback policies. A variable in the Whole Life policy is divided, which could vary depending on how well the insurer is doing.

At the other end of Term Insurance products are Endowment and Moneyback policies which serve as savings instruments since only a small portion of premium income is meant for protection. The bulk is meant to contribute towards savings. The insured amount is payable either at the end of a specified number of years or upon the death of the insured person — or in periodic intervals in case of Moneyback — whichever is earlier. These are by far the most expensive products.

Clearly, both Term Insurance and Whole Life policies are protection-oriented plans, in terms of end objective, and are reinforced by low premium payments. Moneyback and Endowments by reverse logic are savings products. A combination of more than one of he above are also on offer.

A pension plan enables the insured to build-up a corpus of savings against which he can purchase annuities for fixed income after retirement.

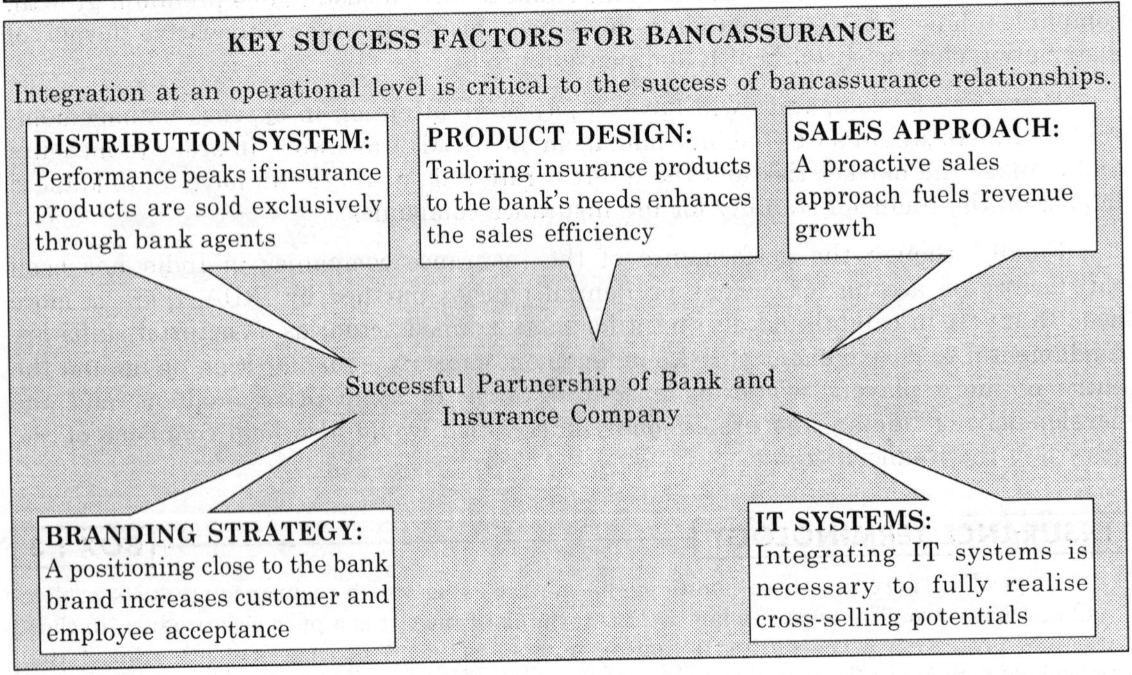


*Source:* Monitor – J.P. Morgan Study on Bancassurance.

The general insurance is also a key component of the financial system. In fact, India is at a much earlier stage of development for general insurance – an overwhelming majority of the demand is still generated by some form of mandatory or regulatory requirement.

The general insurance industry in India has currently about ₹ 12,000 crore of premium income, with a five-year compounded annual growth rate in the 11 per cent range. The first important issue with the market is that GIC's book of business is not profitable at the underwriting level. The general insurance business – before accounting for the investment income that the GIC companies make — is in the red, and has been so for the last few years. This is of critical importance to all participants in the business.

As was the case with life insurance, general insurance was also handled by a number of Indian and foreign companies, till nationalised in 1972. At the time of nationalisation, there were 68 Indian companies (including the LIC) and 45 non-Indian companies in the field. Their business was nationalized and vested in the General Insurance Company (GIC) and its four subsidiaries, viz., National Insurance Co. Ltd., New India Assurance Co. Ltd., Oriental Fire and General Insurance Co. Ltd., and United India Insurance Co. Ltd. The GIC is the holding company and its direct business is restricted only to aviation insurance; general insurance is handled by the subsidiaries of GIC. The premia income of GIC accrues through obligatory reinsurance premia from the four subsidiaries on their direct business, on a quota share basis.

## Objectives of the Act

(1) To provide for the acquisition and transfer of shares of Indian Insurance Companies and undertakings of other existing insurers.

(2) To serve better the needs of the economy by securing the development of general insurance business in the best interests of the community.

(3) To ensure that the operations of the economic system does not result in the concentration of wealth to the common determinants.

(4) For the regulation and control of such business and for matters connected therewith or incidental thereto.

### THE NEW INDIA ASSURANCE CO. LTD.: BORN TO LEAD — BOX : 4

*Inception:* The New India Assurance Company Limited was incorporated on July 23, 1919, and commenced operations on October 14, 1919.

*The Pioneers:* In the field of insurance, there was no Indian company of sufficient size and resources catering for general insurance business in India up to 1919. Insuarnce, a highly intricate and technical business, was then new to this country. True to the pioneering traditions of the House of Tata, the late Sir Dorab Tata conceived the idea of establishing a great and truly Indian composite insurance company and undertook the responsibility of promoting 'New India'.

*The Early Days:* Within a span of less than 10 years 'New India' became a leader in the insurance market. This was mainly the result of the drive and enthusiasm of its directors, and its people, the goodwill and patronage of the Indian business community.

*Nationalisation of General Insurance:* General insurance industry had a metamorphic change in 1972 when the Government of India passed the General Insurance Business (Nationalisation) Act and it was made into a public sector enterprise. But the most important object of the Act was "to serve better the needs of the economy by securing the development of general insurance business in the best interests of the community".

After the state takeover, 107 companies including branches of foreign companies operating in the country were grouped into – National Insurance Co. Ltd., Calcutta; The New India Assurance Co. Ltd., Bombay; The Oriental Insuarnce Co. Ltd., New Delhi, and United India Insuarnce Co. Ltd., Madras. The General Insurance Corporation was incorporated in November 1972 as a holding company and the above four companies were formed as its subsidiaries from January 1, 1973.

*The Position as it is Today:* Amongst the four subsidiaries of GIC, New India has been leading because of its performance. The gross direct premium in India which was ₹ 44.45 crore in 1973 has risen to ₹ 2,979 crore in 1999-2000.

The company has a strong organisational base consisting of 26 regional offices, 383 divisional offices and 714 branches in the country. It has a trained manpower of 24,000 employees who are committed to provide the best service to the customers.

The company also operates abroad and has 39 offices in 23 countries. Gross direct premium earned for the year ended 31st March, 2000 ₹ 326.96 crore (US $ 74.9 mm). New India has etched an enviable name for itself amongst leading insurers in the world.

## Establishment of General Insurance Corporation of India (GIC)

The General Insurance Business (Nationalisation) Act, 1972 provides that the Central Government shall form a Government Company in accordance with the provisions of the Companies Act, 1956 to be known as General Insurance Corporation of India for the purpose of superintending, controlling and carrying on the business of general insurance.

The authorized capital of ₹ 75 crore of the Corporation out of which ₹ 5 crore is the subscribed capital wholly contributed by the Central Government.

## Function of GIC

The functions of the Corporation shall include:

(a) the carrying on of any part of the general insurance business, if it thinks it desirable to do so.

(b) aiding, assisting and advising the acquiring companies in the matter of setting up of standards of conduct and sound practice in general insurance business.

(c) rendering efficient service to holders of policies of general insurance.

(d) advising the acquiring companies in the matter of controlling their expenses including the payment of commission and other expenses.

(e) advising the acquiring companies in the matter of investing of their funds.

(f) issuing directions to acquiring companies in relation to the conduct of general insurance business.

*(g)* issuing directions and encouraging competition among the acquiring companies in order to render their services more efficiently.

## GIC Companies: The Distribution System

Multi-layered distribution and support set-up impedes decision-making and adds unnecessary costs.

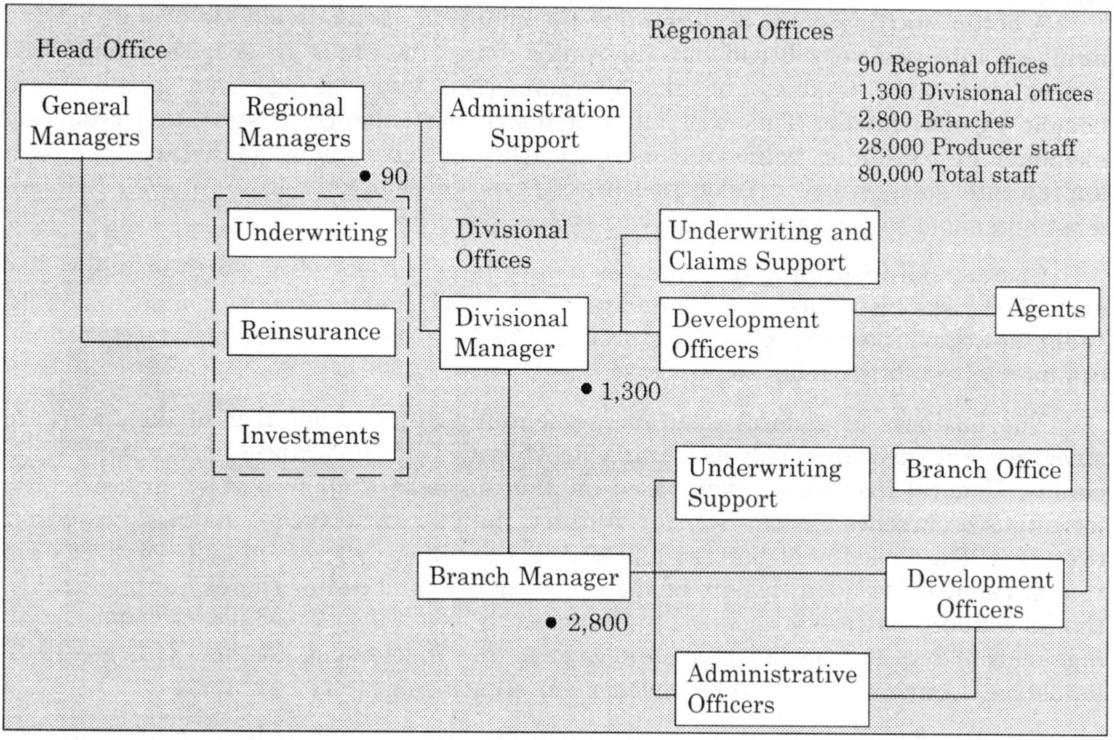


Sales: Other functions

*Source:* GIC Publications, Expert Interviews, Monitor Analysis

## CLASSIFICATION

The general insurance business is broken into three product lines – fire and allied perils (25 per cent), marine (10 per cent) and miscellaneous (65 per cent). However, this classification is not meaningful as it clubs many diverse lines of business into one large block – miscellaneous – and does not offer any insights into distinctive diverse of various businesses within any of the three classes.

In modern times General Insurance is classified as follows:

(i) Insurance of person — Personal Accident and Personal Accident along with Sickness Insurance are included under this classification.

(ii) Insurance of Property — Buildings, machinery, aircraft, steamers, stock of business, cash, securities come under the heading property and therefore Fire Insurance, Marine Hull Insurance, Marine Cargo Insurance, Burglary Insurance, Engineering Insurance, Crop Insurance and Aviation Hull Insurance fall under this classification.

(iii) Insurance of Interest — Fidelity Guarantee Insurance and the Guarantee Insurance fall under this classification.

(iv) Insurance of Liability — Public (third party) Liability Insurance. Professional Indemnities fall under this classification.

A better starting point of examining the challenges is to divide the overall market numbers into two very broad but internally consistent areas — one, that comprises general insurance products bought by commercial undertakings and second, those bought by individuals. This will allow industry participants to start understanding elements of consumer behaviour more clearly and give them an ability to design appropriate measures to develop and profit from sub-segments of the market that are most amenable to providing attractive business potential.

Commercial insurance encompasses a very large variety of products including fire and allied risks insurance, marine insurance, casualty, and workmen's compensation. In India, however, the most 'developed' product-lines are those that are mandatory for the commercial establishments to purchase.

The business of general insurance essentially differs from that of life insurance since general insurance policies, unlike most under life insurances, are not financial claims. General insurance cover based on sharing risks that may arise on accidental, fortuitous occurrences, is of a shorter duration than life insurance — normally a year or even less. The investment pattern followed by the GIC is, therefore, quite distinct from that of the LIC. As liabilities are of short-term nature and claims thereby unpredictable, the investment pattern is dictated by the need to have fairly liquid assets coupled with higher returns. The most important avenue for investment for the GIC is, thus, industrial securities, followed by government securities.

GIC and its subsidiaries, apart from offering insurance cover in such areas as fire, automobile, ocean, and inland marine, theft, loss, damage, etc., have introduced quite a few non-traditional schemes suitable to Indian conditions. An example of such insurance schemes is the Comprehensive Crop Insurance Scheme introduced by the government and being managed by GIC since 1985, in respect of summer and winter crops. GIC also operates cattle and livestock insurance schemes. Other innovative scheme recently introduced are Mediclaim, Householders' Comprehensive Insurance Policy, Professional Products, Nuclear Insurance Pool for insurance on nuclear power plants and other nuclear related risks, Personal Accident and Insurance Social Security Scheme, etc. Although general insurance business, unlike life insurance, does not collect savings of the community, it does collect pools of funds from premia and investment income, to provide cover to various types of activities in the economy.

The General Insurance Industry in India offers a wide range of policies to cover risks associated with industrial, commercial, social and personal activities. General Insurance indemnifies the policyholder for financial losses suffered as a result of the occurrence of an insured peril.

A criticism is often voiced that the LIC's investment policies have not benefited the policyholders. Policyholders, it is argued, pay high premia but receive bonus at low rates. The criticism is not entirely misplaced. But the major factors responsible for high premia and low bonus rates are the high expense ratio, premia rates not being correctly adjusted to actual mortality experience — mortality rates have gone down but premia rates have not come down corresponding — and, more importantly, lower returns on LIC investments. Bulk of LIC investments going into low-yield Government securities has, as mentioned, led to lower aggregate returns on investments resulting in higher premia rates being levied. With higher interest being offered on Government securities now, it is expected, henceforth, greater benefits would accrue to policyholders.

The General Insurance Industry in India offers a wide range of policies to cover risks associated with industrial, commercial, social and personal activities. General Insurance indemnifies the policyholder for financial losses suffered as a result of the occurrence of an insured peril.

| | |
|---|---|
| **Industry and Trade** | To cover risks of fire and allied perils, erection of plant and machinery, machinery break down, boiler explosion, business interruption, inland and overseas transit risks for goods, insurance on hull and machinery of ocean going vessels, including country craft, sailing and fishing vessels, liability — public, product, employer, burglary, loss of cash, etc. Low cost covers specially designed for the small-scale sector are also available. |
| **Individual/Family** | Covering personal accident including air travel, medical insurance in India and while on travel abroad, baggage insurance, insurance of valuables, etc. Package cover for householders are also available. |
| **Rural Sector** | Covering cattle, livestock, poultry, plantations, agricultural pumpsets, failure of new wells, village artisans, cottage industries, etc. |
| **Economically Weaker Sections** | Personal Accident Insurance Social Security Scheme (PASS) and the Scheme for insurance of rural huts and its contents against fire. Both these are social security schemes covering poor families and premium is paid by the government for these covers. |

## NEW PRODUCT DEVELOPMENT

GIC and its four subsidiary companies have developed several innovative covers to suit the Indian market. Cover offering insurance protection for rural assets, small-scale workers and women are the first of their kind in the world.

Some of the latest products include:

- *'Videsh Yatra Mitra', 'Suchana Safar'* and *'Marga Bandhu'*
  — a total package of travel insurance
- *'Rajrajeshwari'* and *'Bhagyashree'*
  — Two trail blazing new covers for women and for the girl-child
- *Industrial All Risks Policy*
  — a comprehensive new cover to meet the needs of a wide spectrum of industries
- *Other milestones*
  — Advance Loss of Profit
  — Seafarer's Health Policy
  — Long-term retirement medical plan
  — *'Nadha Lahari'* for performing artists

The future is filled with even more possibilities as each company now innovates to meet diverse local needs.

**New Entrants in the General Insurance Segment**

Since opening up, the number of participants in the general insurance segment has gone up from five — General Insurance Coopration and its four subsidaries — in the year 2000 to 22 as on March, 2009 operating in the non-life and re-insurance segments including specialized insurers, viz.: Export Credit Guarantee Corporation and Agriculture Insurance Company of India Limited (AICIL). Two of the general insurance companies, viz.: Star Health and Alliance Insurance Company and Apollo DKV Health Insurance Company function as standalone health insurance companies. Of the fifteen who have commenced operations in the non-life segment, fourteen had been set up in collaboration with the foreign partners.

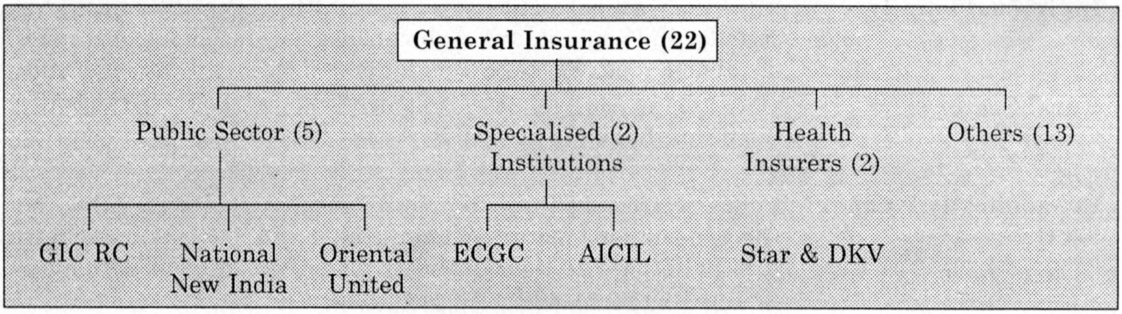


## NON-LIFE INSURANCE INDUSTRY

The non-life insurance excluding specialized institutions like Export Credit Guarantee Corporation (ECGC) and Agriculture Insurance Company of India Limited (AICIL) and the standalone health insurance companies underwrote premium within India ₹ 6,061.20 crore in 2008-09, as against ₹ 9,806.95 crore in 2001-01. During the year, the non-life industry reported growth of 9.09% in Gross Direct Premium as against 12.63% in 2007-08. Two of the fastest growing segments are Motor and Health. The said segments accourted for 42.92% and 19.97% of the premium underwritten in India during the period April-December 2008 as against 44.26% and 17.11% respectively during the corresponding period of 2007-08. Post-detariffing, while the growth in premium as slowed down during the last two years (other than in Health and Motor segments) on account of reduction in rates, the number of policies underwritten have exhibited an increase.

The non-life segment also displays comfortable solvency. The capital base of private non-life sector shows a declining trend. There are, also, some concerns in relation to actuarial issues of the public sector. There are also concerns on the earnings and profitablility front, which point to the need for better quality control in underwriting new business, better risk management and increasing re-insurance. The adequacy of premium, particularly in public sector companies, also needs to be looked into. There are some liquidity concerns in the non-life insurance sector, as current assets are not sufficient to cover all current liabilities.

## INVESTMENT POLICIES

The investment policies of the GIC and its subsidiaries have been evolved within the ambit of Section 27(B) of the Insurance Act, 1938, and the guidelines issued by the Government of India from time-to-time. The objective is to maximise income, ensure the safety and liquidity of funds, and deploy resources consistent with the national objectives and priorities. According to Government guidelines, 70% of the annual accretion to the investible funds of the general insurance industry are required to be invested in socially-oriented sectors of the economy. Such investments include Central and State Government securities, bonds and debentures of public sector undertakings and loans on soft terms to State Governments and other agencies engaged in housing and urban development. The GIC's market operations (sales and purchase of corporate securities) have a stabilising effect on the stock market. GIC has been providing financial assistance to the industrial sector by participating with other AIFIs in consortium financing of industrial projects since 1976, by extending term loans and underwriting of equity shares/preference shares/debentures of both existing and new industrial undertakings.

The different types of schemes prevalent in India are:

**(1) Growth Schemes:** The objectives of these schemes is to provide maximum capital appreciation to the investor through investments mainly in equities. The capital appreciation is due to sizable investments in equity shares. Income by way of dividends may or may not be declared.

**(2) Income Schemes:** The objective of these schemes is to generate a high regular income by investing in interest-bearing and money market instruments. They can be cumulative or non-cumulative income schemes. In case of non-cumulative schemes, dividends are declared either yearly or monthly. In case of cumulative schemes, the returns are accumulated in the scheme itself, instead of being distributed to the investor.

**(3) Income-cum-growth Schemes:** The aim of these schemes is to provide income as well as capital appreciation, by investing part of the funds in fixed-interest instruments and the rest in equity shares.

**(4) Tax Shelter Schemes:** These schemes offer tax exemption to the investor. Investors in these units qualify for a tax rebate of 20% of the amount invested in these units up to an investment of ₹ 10,000. They are usually growth-oriented and provide capital appreciation. These schemes are characterised by an initial lock-in period of three years.

All schemes can be either open-ended or close-ended.

Close-ended schemes are open for subscription only for a specified period at the start of the scheme. These schemes offer redemption facility to the investor after a specified period — usually four to seven years. These schemes may also offer a repurchase facility to the investor. The redemption or repurchase of these schemes is made at the then existing net asset value (NAV) of these schemes minus cost of liquidation of the scheme.

Open-ended schemes are open for purchase and sale throughout the life of the scheme. The sale and repurchase of these schemes by the mutual funds are made at a marginal discount or premium to the existing NAV.

## INSURANCE INTERMEDIARIES

The primary difference between a broker and an insurance agent is that the former is an agent of the insured, whereas the latter acts for the insurer. In countries like Australia, insurers are responsible for the conduct of their agents even if the latter do not operate within the purview of their authority. Although both insurance brokers and consultants represent the insured, the former have to be registered after meeting the eligibility criteria. The relationship between the broker and the client is subject to a code of conduct imposed by the registering authority. But the consultant does not have to be registered. His relationship with the client is governed by the contract between them.

Brokers have been in business since the 17th century. The concept of insurance gradually evolved from sharing losses to transferring the risks to professional financiers of underwriters. As the market grew, merchants began the complicated, time-consuming exercise of looking out for the best bargain. To resolve this was born the insurance broker: a middleman between the buyer, or the insured, and the seller, or the insurer.

In most developed markets, insurance brokers are regulated in the following areas:

- Registration.
- Experience, training and qualification, and other restrictions on entry into the profession.
- Solvency requirements.
- Professional indemnity, or a minimum level of errors. There is also a central fund to protect clients against broker malpractice.

**The Insurance Brokers**

Service Portfolio

- Advise clients on product selection with an indepth knowledge of the market process
- Provide a one-stop for clients seeking insurance and risk-management advice
- Process insurance papers and claims and provide service beyond premium collection
- Provide specialised services by concentrating on single lines of business like fire insurance
- Assist insurers on new products through an intimate knowledge of market needs
- Develop risk-management strategies by providing clients links with insurance firms.

Internationally, insurance brokerages are more than just distribution intermediaries. Broking companies provide a host of insurance-related services to their clients including loss control, risk management, etc. While these are specialized services, most Indian insurance customers get only "seat-of-the-pants" advise on these issues from sales employees of GIC. Based on selected target customer segments, new intermediaries will have to assess appetite for such services and provide these. Not only will this add fee-based income to the intermediary (substantial portion of income for international brokers), it also gives the new entrants an opportunity to differentiate by adding significant value.

## THE CHANGING FACE OF GENERAL INSURANCE

Most general policies have undergone a defining change in recent years – in the way they are structured, the range and extent of cover, how the premiums are computed and how settlements are made. Here's how they have evolved, and here's what you can expect in this space.

| | Past | Present | Present |
|---|---|---|---|
| Health | Single standard plane ● No cover for pre-existing diseases ● Available only from insurer/agent ● Pay and get reimbursed. | ● Product differentiation and addon like hospital cash ● Pre-existing diseases covered after 3-5 years of no claims ● Cashless claims via TPAs | ● Pre-existing diseases covered from day 1 at higher premium ● More hospital in cashless network ● Policy transferable across insurers |
| Automobile | Premium based on market value of car ● Unlimited third-party cover ● Pay and get reimbursed ● Not deductible ● No-claims bonus lowered after claim | Premium based on IEV, vehicle c.c., city ● ₹ 7.5 lakh limit on third-party cover ● Cashless settlements ● No-claim bonus ends after claim ● Mandatory deductible | ● Customisation via. 'detariffing' : literate/safe/better drivers to pay less premium ● Policy transferable across insurers. |
| Overseas Travel | ● One-size-fits-all plans; ● PSU insurers had tie-up with only one global partner for settlements; ● Min. deductible: $ 150; ● Sold by insurer alone. | ● Tailor-made covers for tourist, executives and students; ● Country-specific tie-ups for claims settlement ● Min. Deductible: $; ● Also sold by travel agents/airlines | ● Wider claims settlement network; ● More toll-free helplines to help with claims settlement. |
| Householder | ● Policy an all-or-nothing cluster of assorted clauses; ● No no-claims benefit | ● Freedom to choose assets you want covered; ● No-claims benefits in the form of higher cover or lower premium | ● Higher cover for expensive electronic gadgets; ● Free pricing as opposed to regulator-defined tariffs. |

In terms of the number of players entering the insurance market, general insurance has seven new entrants in the post-liberalisation period.

Fuelled by competition, increased awareness will bring the customers on to centre-stage. The customer will be the single most important factor and will drive change in the life insurance business. The customer in India is increasingly becoming aware and is actively managing his/her financial affairs. Today, while boundaries between various financial products are getting blurred, people are increasingly looking not just at products but at integrated financial solutions that can offer them stability of returns along with total protection. The key to success therefore would be in providing insurance solutions, not insurance products.

In an increasingly competitive scenario the key differentiator will be the customer experience that each life insurance player can offer in terms of quality of advice, product choice, policy servicing, and settlement of claims. Service would focus on enhancing the customer experience and maximizing customer convenience.

For new entrants, to convert the opportunity into profits need to make considered choices in selecting their customers, the portfolio of services they offer and the capabilities they need to acquire or build.

First, it will be important to target the right customer segments. Consider segmentation based on industry sector — most of the old economy companies with traditional insurance needs are being served reasonably well by GIC producers. However, as mentioned earlier, emerging sectors such as software, telecom services, life sciences and others are under-served. Next, if one were to segment the universe of commercial insurance buyers on the basis of their size, while the concentration of premiums in large corporate entities make them an attractive target, these are the accounts that GIC will compete most fiercely for. In contrast, the small and medium enterprises will emerge as a group that is very dissatisfied with both pre- and post-sale service standards of GIC companies (the targets and incentive system for development officers and divisional managers at GIC companies are based on growth in premium collection and therefore the good producers do not "waste their time" on small and medium enterprises) and may be an interesting segment for new channels to focus on.

For any new entrant, it is critical to address these issues — making integrated choices across these will help it win against incumbent and emerging competition. Simultaneously, from an industry perspective, entry of players who make such co-ordinated and distinct choices will hasten the shift of premiums from high cost and inefficient traditional channels to alternate ones — to the benefit of both insurance carriers and their end-customers.

## MALHOTRA COMMITTEE

The major recommendations of Malhotra Committee on the reforms in the insurance sector are as follows:

(1) A strong and effective Insurance Regulatory Authority is to be set up on the lines of SEBI for the capital market, which is already done.

(2) LIC should be registered as a company under the Companies Act and its paid-up capital raised from ₹ 5 crore to ₹ 200 crore with government holding only 50% and the rest by the public at large.

(3) LIC zonal offices should have more powers and there should be greater decentralisation of decisions and authority along with a reorganisation of both the central office and zonal offices and branches.

## ECONOMIC CHANGE

The Indian economy is depicting a qualitative change in its composition. Essentially built on agricultural wealth, the Indian economy has transformed itself in stages over the period of the Five-Year Plans. A perceptible change in the last few years has also been observed with an emphasis on information technology and other service sectors.

At present, the Gross Domestic Product (GDP) of the country is predominantly derived from the services sector of which the insurance sector is an integral part. As more than 42 per cent of the country's current GDP is being generated by the services sector, it becomes essential that necessary steps are taken to sustain this process of growth. A co-ordinated approach to enhance economic growth is necessary under the current circumstances and the insurance sector, an important component of the service industry, could drive growth.

In this regard, the history of the development of insurance industry in India has been one of under-performance and under-achievement. Appreciation for the necessity to cover risks of both personal lives and property has been very poor. In fact, growth in the life insurance sector has been mainly driven by the need to avail concessions in income tax. This has been the primary reason why the urban population has shown interest in purchasing life policies.

## THE INSURANCE REVOLUTION

However, the insurance industry in India is undergoing a drastic transformation, albeit slowly. This transformation is being driven by reasons like changes in consumer psyche and changing socio-economic conditions in the country. This led the government to realise the need to provide consumers with opportunities to choose from a larger and a more competitive market and an array of risk bearers. This resulted in the entry of several new players in the insurance industry – a small step, but nevertheless a significant one.

THE INSURANCE INDUSTRY STRUCTURE

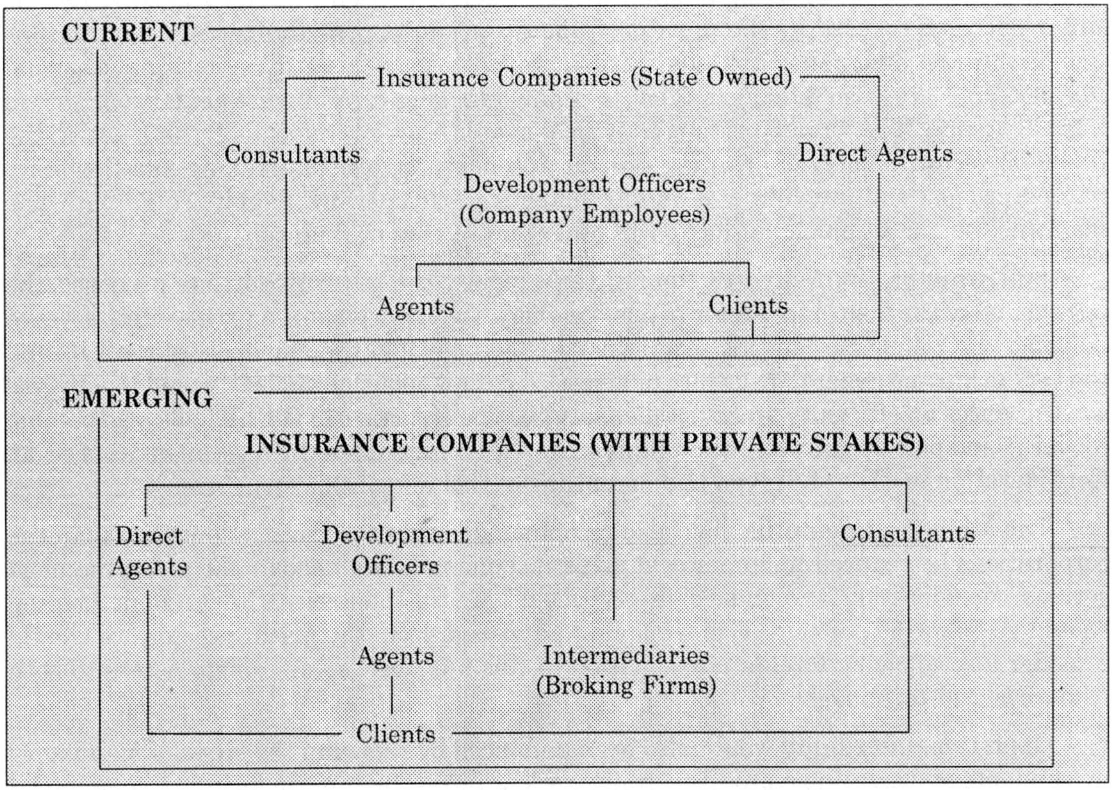

## REFORM PROPOSALS

As part of the financial sector reforms programme, the government has appointed a committee to go into issues concerning the insurance industry in detail and submit recommendations on the structure and efficiency of the sector. Reforms in the insurance sector would cover identification of risk exposure and risk management, pricing, methodology of claim settlement and speedy payments. There have been suggestions on denationalisation of the general insurance business to open it to private and foreign competition. This and other issues like setting up a separate regulatory body for the insurance sector to supervise adherence to prudential norms, setting up a National Fund for social insurance, etc., are within the committee's brief. Reducing the share of direct investment by the General Insurance Corporation in its total investment would also be looked into.

The insurance sector serves as an important financial intermediary providing insurance cover, both on life and other risks. It is also an important source of funds for the corporate sector as also the government to direct investment into socially desired sectors. On removal of the shortcomings observed to have crept into the working of the sector in the past, the insurance sector is expected to function more efficiently in the year ahead, once the reforms' agenda on hand is launched.

## LIBERALISATION OF INSURANCE

No financial sector reform can be complete without encompassing a major constitution like the insurance sector. Despite laudable statements of intent, the insurance sector has so far not been covered by the process of liberalisation. Contractual savings institutions like insurance and pension funds have a major role to play in mobilising financial savings and are also ideally suited to financing long-term investments such as in infrastructure. The broad principles which should govern reform of the rest of the financial sector, namely of granting greater autonomy in decision-making and flexibility in operations, and providing a more competitive framework, apply equally to the insurance sector as much as they do to other sub-sectors of finance.

Following on the Malhotra Committee's report, the government has proposed the opening up of the insurance sector to private entry, though legislation to this effect is yet to be enacted. Competition in this sector would effectively end the monopoly of the LIC and the GIC in life and general insurance business. This monopoly has had its attendant adverse consequences on efficiency and customer service. The structure of the LIC has also become too large and perhaps unwieldy and represents the emergence of the diseconomies of scale. Consideration needs to be given to dismantling of this monolithic structure.

The Malhotra Committee has 'also recommended that the governments' stake in the corporations be reduced to 50 per cent. This recommendation needs to be given the most serious consideration and indeed in respect of general business. Government holding should go below 50 per cent. While opening up insurance to the private sector, we should consider also allowing foreign participation in this business, so as to help access to both resources and technology.

Operational flexibility would also been enhanced by reducing the scope of mandatory investments and creating a proactive framework or infrastructure financing on commercial principles. With the opening up of this sector, attention has to be paid to the scope and content of prudential regulation, covering solvency margins, capital adequacy, investment norms and other aspects as well as regulation of tariffs. An Insurance Regulatory and Development Authority (IRDA) has been set up so as to provide such a framework of regulation but vesting this authority with statutory status and other aspects of reform await legislative action. It is to be hoped that the necessary legislation would be enacted soon. In the new liberalised economic environment, general insurance has greater scope for expansion and focus. The thrust areas are widening and as such, it plays a catalytic role in accelerating the process of industrialisation.

The process of liberalisation gathered momentum in the Indian insurance market during 2001-02 with the entry of a number of private life and general insurers. The Insurance Regulatory and Development Authority (IRDA) has registered 13 life insurance companies and 10 non-life insurance companies so far. The insurance market witnessed the introduction of a number of investment-linked products in debt and equity markets.

**The Insurance Regulatory and Development Authority Act (IRDA), 1999**

The insurance sector was opened up to private participation with the enactment of the Insurance Regulatory and Development Authority Act, 1999. The core functions of the Authority include: (i) licensing of insurers and insurance intermediaries; (ii) financial and regulatory supervision; (iii) protection of the interests of the policyholders. With a view to facilitating development of the insurance sector, the Authority has issued regulations on protection of the interests of policyholders; obligations towards the rural and social sectors; microinsurance and licensing of agents, corporate agents, brokers and third party administrators. This is in addition to the regulatory framework provided for registration of insurance companies, maintenance of solvency margin, investments and financial reporting requirements.

## CONSTITUTION OF THE IRDA

The IRDA shall consist of not more than nine members, not more than five members of whom, including the chairperson to be full-time. The whole-time members shall hold office for five years or until the age of 62 *(65* in the case of chairperson) whichever is earlier, part-time members will hold office for not more than five years. The above said members to be appointed by the Central Government from among persons of ability and standing who have knowledge or experience in life insurance, general insurance, actuarial science, finance, economics, law, accountancy, administration or any other discipline which would, in the opinion of the Central Government, be useful to the Authority.

**THE INSURANCE OVERVIEW**

| Individual New Life Business* | Individual Pension Business* |
|---|---|
| Private Insurers: ₹ 285.29 crore<br>9%<br>91% LIC: ₹ 2,790.38 crore | Private Insurers: ₹ 39.95 crore<br>33%<br>67%<br>LIC: ₹ 82.76 crore |

Figures are for April to December 2002.

* Premium Income.

## Objectives of IRDA

The main objectives of the Insurance Regulatory and Development Authority are:

(1) To take care of the policyholders interest.
(2) To open the insurance sector for private sector.
(3) To ensure continued financial soundness and solvency.
(4) To regulate insurance and re-insurance companies.
(5) To eliminate dishonesty and unhealthy competition.
(6) To supervise the activities of intermediaries.
(7) To amend the Insurance Act, 1938, the Life Insurance Corporation Act, 1956 and the General Business Nationalisation Act, 1972.
(8) Clear appointments to top post.
(9) Issue guidelines to insurance intermediaries.
(10) To grant licences to new companies to operate in the insurance sector.
(11) Prescribe prudential norms to insurance companies.
(12) Ensure transparency in the working of insurance companies; and
(13) Facilitate new products, and
(14) Build-up systems and infrastructure, that allow effective monitoring.

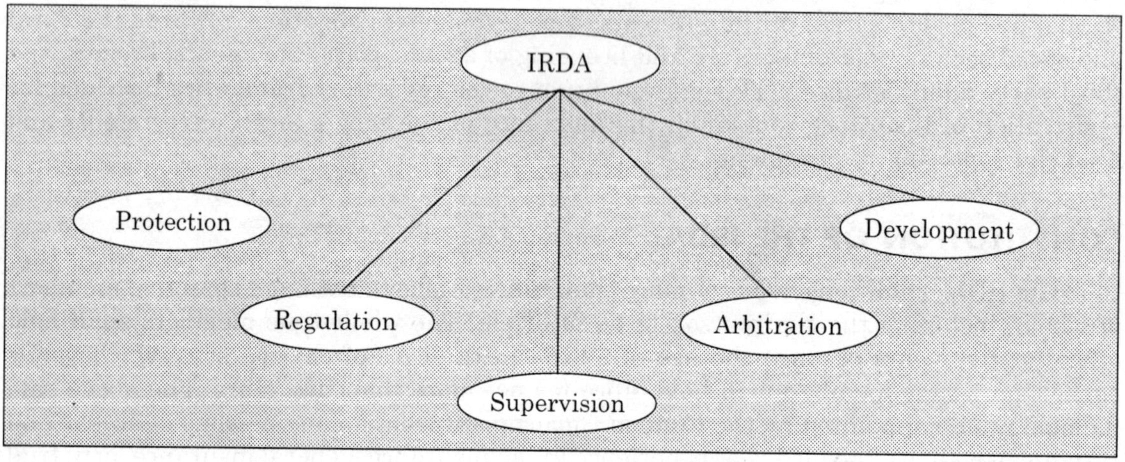


**Fig. 1 : Objectives of IRDA**

## DUTIES AND POWERS OF IRDA

For smooth running of insurance business, the regulatory authority has vested with adequate power and duties. The duties and powers of the IRDA are:

(1) To regulate, promote and ensure orderly growth of the insurance business.
(2) To exercise all powers and functions of the controller of insurance:
(3) To protect the interest of the policyholders in settlement of claims and terms and conditions of policies.

(4) To promote and regulate professional organisations connected with insurance business.

(5) To call for information from, undertake inspection and conduct investigations including audit of the insurer, intermediaries and other connected organisations and persons.

(6) To control and regulate the rates and terms and conditions that may be offered by the insurers in respect of general insurance matters, not so controlled by the Tariff Advisory Committee under Section 64(U) of the Insurance Act.

(7) To prescribe the manner and form in which accounts will be maintained and submitted by insurers and intermediaries.

(8) To regulate investment of funds.

(9) To regulate margins of solvency.

(10) To adjudicate disputes between insurers and intermediaries.

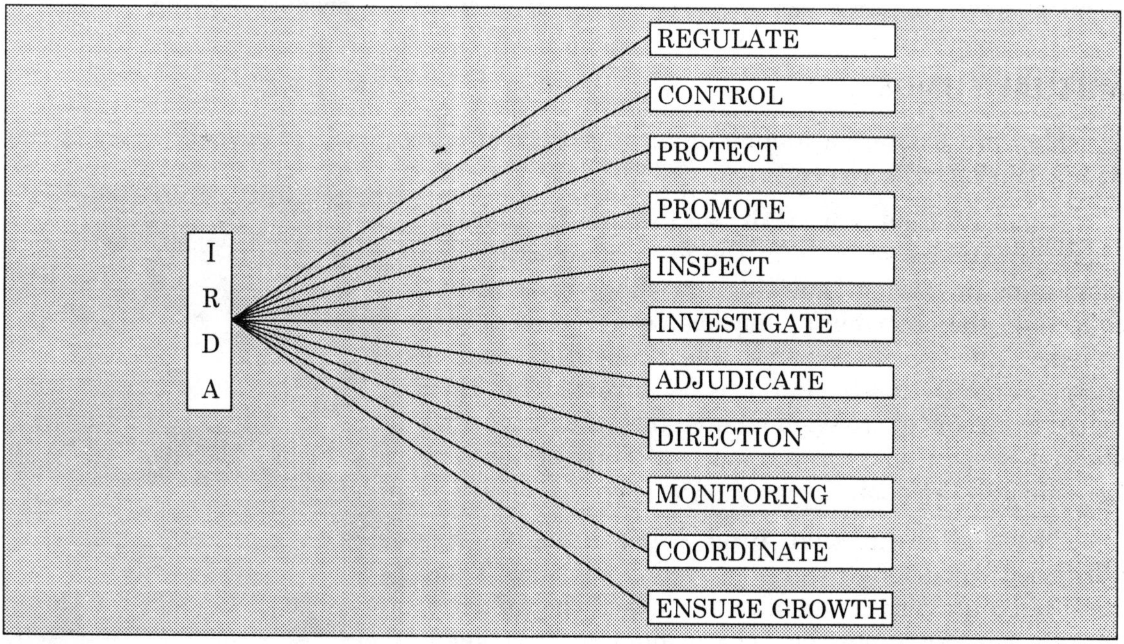


**Fig. 2: Duties of IRDA**

## THE PRODUCT RUSH

The disparity in initial performance, however, masks the marked similarity in the new entrants' route-to-market choices. A quick look at the product and distribution configurations highlights this phenomenon.

The private players have introduced 70 odd "new" products in all. A portfolio can shows up two important conclusions — first, endowment and moneyback products (historically, mainstay of LIC's business) constitute almost half of the total and second, much of the actual business transacted has been through their assured return, single premium policies. In pushing a combination of standard products and assured benefits, the new entrants have elevated to tread safe ground (though the emphasis on assured return products has already invited cautionary comment from IRDA).

Not surprisingly, the starting point of such strategies is a superior understanding on part of companies of customers and the market realities. Conventional segmentation approaches utilising one or more variables of income classification, age group, and level of education sometimes succeed in identifying groups of customers who share the same basic needs and beliefs. But the segmentation is almost invariably done in a manner that no one can ever find such groups.

For instance, a study that concludes that "self-assured young women are looking for a high-value term policy" might have an assertion that is quite accurate on its own but will likely prompt some sales managers to justifiably ask: How do I find these people?

The game is to find customer segments that are relevant to the realities of the company and also economically well-defined, in the sense that all members of the same segment have similar needs and experiences concerning the product offering.

## MUTUAL FUNDS

Mutual funds are a unique financial service offering people to save and play in the equity market collectively.

A mutual fund is basically an investment route. It offers investment services in the form of selecting and monitoring investment, marking and selling investments, collecting and distributing income, etc. It is really a collective investment scheme where investors pool in their investible funds and this is invested on their behalf by a team of professional investors. Each investor's share is proportionate to the amount of investments he has made in the pool.

The Indian mutual fund (MF) industry has witnessed some tough times in recent memory. There has been quite a churn in several parts of the industry, though this might not be very evident at first sight. Currently, the perennial favourite – the debt mutual fund scheme – is facing rough weather as the debt market has taken a hit in the last one year. All this led to investors deserting income schemes for better opportunities. The equity market, indirect contrast, was riding the crest of a bull wave. It evoked a lot of investor interest both in existing and new MF schemes. These schemes, on their part, had also performed very well, helping their investors to make smart gains.

Globally, mutual funds have long been a popular investment option. In developed markets such as the US, the assets under management (AUM) of mutual funds are more than 60 per cent of the gross domestic product (GDP) as compared to a little above 10 per cent in India. Even in other emerging markets it is a lot higher. Brazil for example has a ratio of 39 per cent.

We take a look at the several aspects of the MF industry and how developments have shaped up in the recent past.

The economic progress of a country is, to a certain extent, linked with the growth of the capital market. Capital market growth depends on the savings of the nation. In India, notwithstanding a high rate of savings by the community, the capital market is not in a position to grow fast because the common man has not acquired the necessary know-how himself to select appropriate avenues of investment which will serve his needs. Therefore, the savings are mainly directed towards bank deposits/real estate/gold, etc. If he is assured that there are organisations of repute which have necessary expertise to select appropriate avenues of investment where the yield is attractive enough, with utmost security of the capital invested, it would create a proper climate for diversion of a part of the savings which at present goes into sectors, where there is either only capital appreciation but with little or no scope for regular periodical return on investment or no capital appreciation at all, but with a periodical small return on the investment.

In these circumstances, there is enough scope for mutual funds to operate, which would not only assure a reasonable capital appreciation on his investment but also provide a regular dividend at periodical intervals with also a facility for easy encashment of the principal.

## Evolution of Mutual Funds

Historically, mutual fund investment traces its origins to the early pioneering investments of Scottish and English investors in the American West in the 1800s, and later of the early global portfolio investors in Japan in the 1960s.

## The Origins of Mutual Funds

Sure, the stock market is the best place for your money to make more money. But only if you start out with a lot of money in the first place, and if you understand financial manoeuvring. In 1822, royalty (in the form of King William I of the Netherlands) came up with an option for the rest of us. The closed-end fund. It was a startlingly simple idea. A group of investors, individuals and institutions with common investment goals, pooled their investment and placed them with fund managers. These professional money managers then invested these funds in securities, and distributed the profits among the fund members. The 'investment trust' concept spread rapidly through Europe, and the first American fund was created in 1893. The idea spread quickly around the world, but it came to India only in the 1960s. Today, there are over 100 distinct schemes in the market, and more being introduced every year.

## What is a Mutual Fund?

Mutual fund units are investment vehicles that provide a means of participation in the stock market for people who have neither the time, nor the money, nor perhaps the expertise to undertake direct investment in equities successfully. On another level, they also provide a route into specialist markets where direct investment often demands both more time and more knowledge than an investor or his financial adviser may possess.

The basic idea is simple: a large number of investors pool their money in order to obtain a spread of professionally managed stock exchange investments that they cannot obtain individually. The advantage is that the investor in a mutual fund is taking much less of a risk than a direct equity investor, because increase in the number of stocks held obviously reduces the effect that any one stock can have on the overall performance of the equity portfolio. Professional management has two main benefits: it provides specialist investment expertise which should ensure greater success than the inexperienced investor can achieve on his own and it reduces the administrative burden of investment.

A mutual fund is divided into equal portfolios called units. The price of units is calculated regularly by the managers, rather than being determined by supply and demand in the market. The prices are quoted for units — the higher (offer) price being the price the investor pays to buy units, and the lower (bid) price being the price he will receive for units sold back to the managers.

Mutual fund managers are the only people allowed to make a market in mutual fund units, and they must be prepared to buy units from and sell units to the public at any time.

The price of the units in any mutual fund is governed by the value of the underlying securities. The price will therefore fluctuate with the movements of the market sector in which a fund is invested. The value of an investor's holding in a unit can therefore, like an investment in shares, go down as well as up.

## Types of Mutual Fund

No single gun is suitable for all types of hunting. Nor is one fishing rod suitable for all types of fishing. Similarly, no one mutual fund is suitable to the vast variety of investors' needs and objectives. The needs and the risk-taking capacity of an old widow may differ significantly from those of a young businessman. In the funds market, many types of funds are offered to the investor. His choice of a fund will depend on what he wants his money to earn for him and how much risk he is willing to take. Most of the funds will fall in one of the following four categories:

**(i) Open and Close-ended Funds:** If the period and/or target amount of the fund is definite, the fund is called close-ended. If indefinite, it is called open-ended. For instance, the Unit Scheme (1964) of the Unit Trust of India (UTI) is an open-ended fund, both in terms of period as well as target amount.

**(ii) Income and Growth-oriented Fund:** The income-oriented fund aims at distribution of income periodically amongst investors. Consequently, its investment strategy conforms to the fund objective by deployment of investors' monies into fixed income yielding securities. On the other hand, the growth-oriented fund meets the investors' need for appreciation, high risk-bearing capacity and ability to defer liquidity. As such, the investment by growth-oriented funds are predominantly made in equities. The fund which partially meets the needs for income and growth are called 'balanced' or 'income-cum-growth' fund.

**(iii) Area, Industry, Customer Group Funds:** The funds may have, at the international level, investments in securities of specified areas, e.g., Japan Fund, Thailand Fund or South Korea Fund, etc. These funds provide access to foreign investors into domestic securities of these countries. Similarly, certain funds may invest their resources in specified industry or industries like Rail / Road or Petroleum Industry funds in the US. Certain mutual funds may be confined to a high-tech and high-growth industry, which may attract risk taken in such cases. The fund may also aim at a specific customer target group to meet their major needs, like funds for pensioners, widows, etc.

**(iv) Taxation Funds:** Certain funds are designed to avail certain tax exemptions, whether in the domestic or foreign capital markets. Tax Saving Magnum of SBI Capital Markets Limited is an example of the domestic type. UTI's US $60 million India Fund, based in the US, is an example of the latter type offshore mutual fund to avail the tax exempt status in tax havens.

## Sector Mutual Funds

Sector funds are mutual funds that invest in stocks of a particular sector. This is both their biggest advantage and disadvantage. By investing in a single sector, these funds are well-placed to cash in when the sector does well. On the contrary, when a sector does not do well, the performance of these funds takes a beating as it happened with investors who had invested in technology funds before the sector went bust.

Sector mutual funds are categories into Auto, Banking, Fast Moving Consumer Goods, Petroleum, Pharma, Technology and others.

Evidence suggests that in case of sector funds, it is the leaner funds that have been giving greater returns. As assets under management increase, it leaves a fund manager with fewer options to invest money in. This becomes an even bigger factor to reckon with in case of sector funds because the fund manager has a smaller universe of stocks to choose from. If he decides to retain the money as cash and not to invest, the returns of the fund go down. If he decides to invest in a stock which he already owns and which would have probably gone up by then, his returns are again less.

According to experts, different sectors tend to perform well at different points of time. So, it's very important to enter the sector fund at the right time. And to be able to do that, an investor needs to understand the sector very well.

**ULIPs vs. Mutual Funds**

| | ULIPs | Mutual Funds |
|---|---|---|
| Insurance cover | Provide insurance cover. | Don't provide insurance cover. |
| Expenses | Expenses ratio are much higher in the initial years, but reduces to 2% p/a levels over 15 years and above. | Expenses ratio is capped at around 2.5% p/a by SEBI. |
| Investment horizon | Suits only long-term investors – 10 years or more. | Suits short-term as well as long-term investors |
| Tax benefit | All ULIPs enjoy Sec. 80C benefit up to ₹ 1 lakh. | Only ELSS funds enjoy Sec. 80C benefit up to ₹ 1 lakh. |
| Liquidity | Liquidity comes at higher cost (in case of premature exit) though the exit is at NAV value. | After 3 years lock-in (for all ELSS funds) redemption is at NAV values.<br>Monthly portfolios are disclosed by most MFs. |
| Portfolio disclosure | Only quarterly portfolios are disclosed by insurance companies. | Comparatively more 'active' in fund management. |
| Investment style | Generally, less aggressive and resort to less churning. | Equity funds have long history of fund performance. |
| Track record | Not more than 3 years of fund performance is available for most insurance companies. | |

## Twin Benefits

What do you get when you opt for insurance from MFs as compared to ULIPs.

| ULIPS | MFs |
|---|---|
| • Do not overtly encourage monthly payments; usually favour annual or half-yearly payments | • Payments through auto debit or ECS route on a monthly basis. Monthly SIPs create wealth more efficiently. |
| • Investors can switch between plans like debt or equity, but the life cover won't lapse | • Investors don't have such an option and are tied to one fund, |
| • If you miss a premium payment, life cover stays if there are funds in your account | • If you delay payment more than three times, the cover lapses |
| • Overheads are high, resulting in lower sums invested | • Overheads are in line with MF norms and much lower than that of a ULIP Plan |
| • Partial withdrawals are allowed without affecting cover. | • Cover lapses if units are redeemed even partially |
| • ULIP schemes are usually segregated as high risk, balanced or low risk schemes | • MF schemes vary depending on the product range of the fund house. But you can choose only one fund. |
| • Investor can opt for bigger life covers without huge payouts | • MFs place a limit on the maximum cover. Birla Sun Life MF, for instance, offers a maximum cover of ₹ 20 lakh. |

**The advantages of investing in mutual funds are:**

(1) *Professional Management:* You avail of the services of experienced and skilled professionals who are backed by a dedicated investment research term which analyses the performance and prospects of companies and selects suitable investments to achieve the objectives of the scheme.

(2) *Diversification:* Mutual Funds invest in a number of companies across a broad cross-section of industries and sectors. This diversification reduces the risk because seldom do all stocks decline at the same time and in the same proportion. You achieve this diversification through a Mutual Fund with far less money than you can do on your own.

(3) *Convenient Administration:* Investing in a Mutual Fund reduces paperwork and helps you avoid many problems such as bad deliveries, delayed payments and unnecessary follow-up with brokers and companies. Mutual Funds save your time and make investing easy and convenient.

(4) *Return Potential*: Over a medium to long-term, Mutual Funds have the potential to provide a higher return as they invest in a diversified basket of selected securities.

(5) *Low Costs:* Mutual Funds are a relatively less expensive way to invest compared to directly investing in the capital markets because benefits of scale in brokerage, custodial and other fees translate into lower costs for investors.

(6) *Liquidity:* In open-ended schemes, you can get your money back promptly at net asset value related prices from the Mutual Fund itself. With close-ended schemes, you can sell your units on a stock exchange at the prevailing market price or avail of the facility of direct repurchase at NAV related prices which some close-ended and interval schemes offer you periodically.

(7) *Transparency:* You get regular information on the value of your investment in addition to disclosure on the specific investments made by your scheme, the proportion invested in each class of assets and the fund manager's investment strategy and outlook.

(8) *Flexibility:* Through features such as regular investment plans, regular withdrawal plans and dividend reinvestment plans, you can systematically invest or withdraw funds according to your needs and convenience.

(9) *Choice of Schemes:* Mutual Funds offer a family of schemes to suit your varying needs over a lifetime.

(10) *Well Regulated:* All Mutual Funds are registered with SEBI and they function within the provisions of strict regulations designed to protect the interests of investors. The operations of Mutual Funds are regularly monitored by SEBI.

## Choosing a Fund

The investor may either directly choose a fund or if his portfolio is substantial, he may hand over this responsibility to an adviser. In either case, he has to be clear in his objectives: What does he want from the fund?

Before choosing a fund, the investor or his adviser should assess the performance of the fund. A good historical record, though not a guarantee for similar future trend, could, among other things remaining the same, be a better horse to bet on than new funds. Fund's overall performance in all schemes, rather than one or two schemes, will indicate its investment expertise.

Also, worth looking at is a fund's consistency in beating the index representing the market in which it is invested. Yet another rule of thumb for the investor is that traditionally the stock market index and inflation rate have moved in unison. On the other hand, the interest rates and stock markets have moved in the opposite direction. The investor may, therefore, time his entry and exit into the fund market accordingly.

## Key 'Take Aways'

- Start investing early
- Approach Financial Planner to know risk appetite
- Use the 'SIP' route to investing
- Don't ignore asset allocation
- Diversify portfolio across equity and debt schemes
- Don't take undue risks
- Stay invested over the long-term in equities
- Don't time the equity market
- Create a basket of tax-efficient debt-oriented schemes
- Invest in equities – the great Indian story lies ahead
- Double-digit returns from income funds are over
- Diversified equity funds are better than sector funds
- Avoid fashionable schemes
- IPG of MFs are different from those of companies
- Don't underestimate the power of compounding.

## Goals

Different goals may be set apart for each class of fund. Some may be income-oriented; some growth-oriented and some a combination of both. Depending upon the goal set for the fund, the nature of investment to be made is decided.

The units are sold or bought back on the basis of an offer price and a bid price. The former is the price at which the managers are prepared to sell the units and the latter is the price at which they are prepared to repurchase them. The difference in prices would reflect the income accrued on the fund and the same belongs to the managers to give them a profit after they have met the associated cost, commission and the management expenses.

Where the demand for units exceeds the purchases, new units are created. Otherwise, some units are cancelled. This new creation or cancellation will involve adjustment to the Net Asset Value (NAV) which would take care of the expenses of acquiring or realising the investment. Any difference between this adjusted NAV and the offer and the bid prices accrues to the managers. The NAV will be worked out and published at regular intervals so as to enable the unitholders to know the growth of their investment in units.

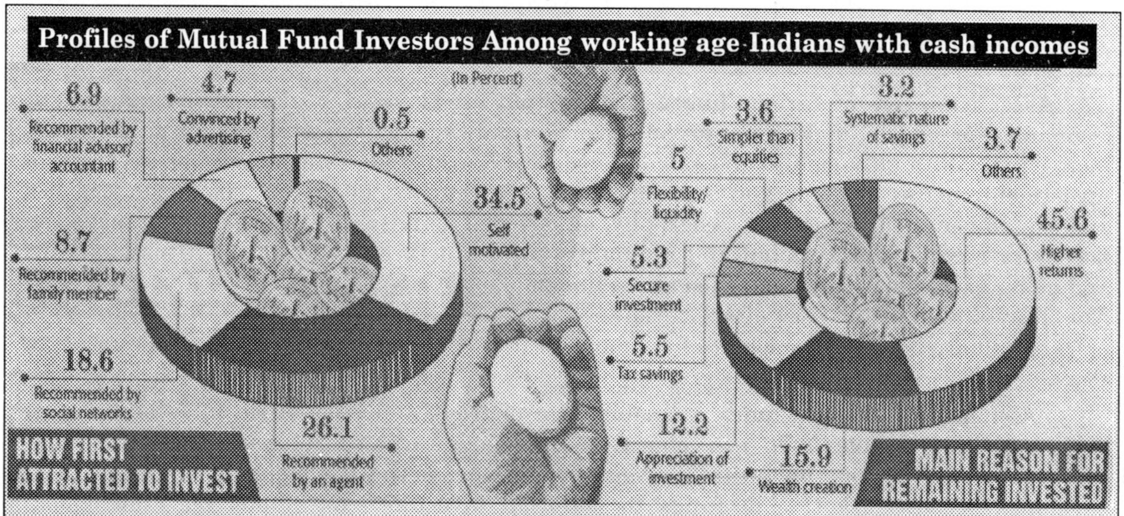


Source: Invest India Incomes and Savings Survey 2007; IIMS Dataworks

## Funds Dawn Over India

In India, The Unit Trust of India was established by an Act of Parliament in 1963. The Trust has, over a period spanning quarter of a century, successfully launched a variety of schemes to meet the diverse needs of lakh of investors. Recently, a growth-cum-income fund, called the 'Mastershare', was launched by the Trust. This was followed by two India Funds: the first trade in the London Stock Exchange (India Fund Unit Scheme 1986) and the second in New York Stock Exchange (India Fund Unit Scheme 1988). Today, the total investible funds of UTI exceed ₹ 68,000 crore.

With a view to providing a wider choice to small investors, the government has now permitted banks to launch mutual funds in the country. The entry of banks and financial institutions in this vital field will provide, in the first place, the much-needed competition. This will show a positive trend in terms of improved customer service and widen customer choice.

Secondly, the inherent strength of banks in India is their branch network and their ability to tap business in rural, semi-urban, urban and metropolitan areas can be fully exploited to the advantage of the mutual funds industry. Thirdly, banks/institutions may provide a wider range of products/services in mutual funds by introducing innovative schemes built around their regular services and extend their professionalism to the mutual funds industry.

Following UTI, Public Sector Institutions (LIC, GIC, SBI, BOI, BOB, Canara, Indian, PNB, IDBI) also operate mutual funds. Since November 1993, 12 mutual funds have been set up in the private sector.

Among the competing mutual fund products available in the Indian market, the investors have a good choice to meet their expectation of security, growth and liquidity.

**GLOBAL ASSET MANAGEMENT** **BOX : 5**

Asset managers of various hues – i.e., mutual funds, open or close ended investment companies or trusts, public or private pension funds, insurance premium funds, and, increasingly, of highly mobile and flexible hedge and arbitrage funds – look for an array of investment choices at home and overseas, including equities, bonds, property, commodities and cash diversified in terms of geography, or sector of activity. A viable IFC must have the necessary market, institutional and regulatory infrastructure to attract asset management and global portfolio diversification services undertaken by a variety of national, regional and global asset managers. Very often, revenues from asset management are directly linked to market valuations, so in the event of a major fall in asset prices, revenues decline relative to costs.

Asset management includes a combination of front and back-office functions. Front-office activities include *inter alia:* objective setting for targeted returns, risk and capital preservation, based on the future pay-out obligations of the funds being managed (e.g., pensions); active marketing of funds to potential investors; continuous real-time global research into individual assets and asset classes across all sectors and geographies; indepth financial analysis; asset selection; plan implementation; buy-sell trading/dealing/transacting; and continuous monitoring of investments to keep pace with domestic and global changes in financial and demographic environments and circumstances. Back-office functions (i.e., tracking and recording of all buy/sell transactions, and minute-to-minute fund valuations, for thousands of different clients per institution) usually involve activities such as: payment and settlements for billions of daily transactions; ensuring increasingly complex national and global compliance for a variety of purposes; bookkeeping and financial control; trade confirmations; fault correction and dispute resolution; continuous real-time internal auditing; and the preparation of a variety of internal and external reports (by day, week, month, quarter, year) for managers and clients.

## The LIC Mutual Fund Difference

The investors may be aware that a few other institutions are also operating mutual funds which offer some combination of liquidity, return and safety.

LIC Mutual Fund is in operation to offer investment options with a fourth dimension — *insurance protection.* Many of the specific products that will be offered by the LIC Mutual Fund will offer some life cover (of course not unlimited cover).

In concept, it works like this. The investor can set a goal to build a corpus of savings within a certain timeframe. Contribution(s) to the Mutual Fund is (are) made to achieve this. Should the unforeseen happen, and the investor dies during the specified time-frame, the Mutual Fund will pay the investor's nominee the full amount originally set as the goal.

It must also be mentioned here that the LIC Mutual Fund will launch products which will be based on the three pins of safety, liquidity and returns and, to take care of pure investments alone.

The LIC Mutual Fund pledges to serve the investors to the best of its ability. This service will be rendered through an innovative set of products meeting specific investor needs and facilities made available at the doorstep of the investors, as far as practicable.

In short, the LIC Mutual Fund will help investors to meet their cherished expectations of a peaceful, secure and good life — present and future.

## Present Scenario

There are two fundamental dynamics in the Indian mutual fund industry today.

- The trend towards open-ended funds.
- Greater awareness among individual investors about how mutual funds work and the value they add.

| Features | Mutual Fund | Pension Scheme | Provident Fund |
|---|---|---|---|
| Investor | Individual | Individual | Company |
| Objective | Variety of purposes | Retirement planning | Retirement planning |
| Time Horizon | Variable | Long-term | Long-term |
| Participation | Voluntary | Voluntary | Mandatory |
| Contribution to Fund | Initial investment | Regular payments | Regular payments |
| Exit | At will | Penalised | Penalised |
| Tax Concessions | None | None | Contributions tax-deductible |
| Fund Manager's Discretion | High | High | Limited |
| Investments | Debt + Equity | Debt | Debt |

The rest are:

- The combined effect of these trends will result in more benefits.
- More money flowing into mutual funds as investors realise the futility and difficulty in direct primary and secondary market investments.
- The narrowing of the gap between the net asset value of many close ended funds and their market price, as the more educated investors seize this opportunity to buy funds trading at discounts.
- The emergence of a class of educated intermediaries who will sell mutual funds by taking on the role of financial planners/counsellors rather than mere purveyors/sellers of financial products.
- The start of a new industry in mutual fund rating agencies as investors look for an unbiased source of information on the performance of various funds.
- The professionalisation of the secondary market brokers as they cater to demands of savvy institutional investors.

- Creation of more sophisticated infrastructure such as custodians, depositories, screen-based confirmations, jumbo lots and inter-institutional trading.
- The emergence of industry specific funds as well as the launch of many more income and money market funds.

## THE UNIT TRUST OF INDIA

The Unit Trust of India, established by an Act of Parliament in 1984, plays an important role in tapping the savings of the small investors through the sale of units and channelising them into corporate investments, so as to provide for growth and diversification of the economy. The UTI has introduced new schemes at regular intervals to meet the need of diverse sections of investors. From April 1986, after an amendment to its Act, UTI can extend assistance to the corporate sector by way of term loans, bills rediscounting, equipment leasing and hire-purchase financing.

The Unit Trust of India provides attractive investment opportunities to the community through the sale of units under its various schemes. The funds so mobilised are invested, largely in corporate securities, with a view to fetching maximum return to the primary investors, simultaneously keeping in view the element of safety of their investments. Consequent upon the amendment to the UTI Act, effective April 23,1986, UTI grants term loans, rediscounts bills, undertakes equipment leasing and hire-purchase financing.

### Investment Strategy of the Fund

The main objective of the fund has been to attain higher appreciation with a minimum risk through a diversified portfolio of securities. It has been our endeavour to achieve this by spreading the investment over different industries and scrips. The Mastershare portfolio is now spread over carefully selected scrips, covering selected industries.

High growth sectors of the economy like automobiles, basic metals, cement, consumer products, dyes and chemicals, engineering, tea and plantations and textiles form about three-fourths of the total investment.

UTI's investment strategy is backed by continuous research and analysis on trends and forces within the economy, capital market, and corporate sector. UTI closely monitors the performance of companies in the portfolio and studies the market trends to take advantage of the ups and downs of the market. Its investment is expected to cover a judiciously selected diverse portfolio of securities designed to give to the unitholders security of capital, besides reasonable return and capital appreciation.

Underwriting the public issues of shares and debentures, direct subscription to the shares and debentures and subscription to the privately placed debentures are the usual forms of assistance provided by the UTI to the industries.

### Pattern of Investment

The UTI's total investible funds crossed the ₹ 50,000 crore mark to reach ₹ 51,709 crore as at end-March 1994, with 3.6 crore unitholding accounts. The total investments in the corporate sector amounted to ₹ 40,761 crore, constituting 78.8 per cent of the total investible funds. Equity shares accounted for 51.8 per cent of corporate investments, followed by debentures 27 per cent, and term-loans 10 per cent.

The UTI plays a unique role in the rapid growth of the corporate sector. Mainly, the UTI subscribes to bonds/debentures, underwriting, direct subscription and special deposits. As at end-March 1994, assistance by way of underwriting/direct subscriptions, firm allotment and rights constituted 47%, followed by privately-placed debentures/loans 32.3% and special deposits 20.7%.

## The Future of Mutual Funds

The future of mutual funds in India is inextricably linked to the growth of the Indian economy, savings and investment patterns, government policy towards private sector and the development of capital market. The government has provided the initial impetus for launching of the funds by providing tax concessions and tax exemptions. The creators of the funds are trusted banks with a good track record. The first step has, therefore, been taken very carefully, ensuring success and building up investor confidence in the new instrument.

Mutual funds in India have a significant and centre-stage role to play in spreading equity cult. The wider range of products/services offered by the funds will make the investor quality-conscious. He will now be able to assess comparable competing products in the market. The government will have to enact a 'Mutual Fund Act' to regulate the industry in the interest of investors and the promoting banks and institutions. Initially, the industry may be confined to the public sector only. But a logical extension to the joint sector and thereafter to the private sector could follow in due course.

In the context of recent developments in the Indian capital market, the advent of mutual funds has augured well for small investors who had suffered grievously during the last two years. On the other hand, the genuine and good entrepreneurs did not enter capital market with their public issues because of near-certain failure of the new issues during 1987 and early 1988. The lack of investor-confidence in capital market on the one hand, and the fear of the promoters to enter the new issue market on the other, had to be corrected immediately, before serious and any irreparable damage could be done to the capital market. Among the many effective measures taken by the government, permitting banks to form a trustworthy bridge between investors and promoters was a very timely and wise step.

Mutual funds in India provide safety, liquidity and growth to investors. They are safe and readily available conduits for channeling savings into investments yielding income and growth. The funds provide stability to share prices, safety to investors and resources to promoter entrepreneurs.

Capital markets are operationally efficient if financials intermediaries who provide the service of channeling funds from savers to investors do so at the minimum cost which provides them a fair return for their services. A narrow spread between the rate at which funds are raised and the rate at which they are lent is considered an indicator of efficiency. In the Indian context; most financial institutions face an administered interest rate structure covering both their borrowing and lending operations. As such the spread between costs and earnings does not provide an indication of the operational efficiency of the system. There must therefore be a conscious effort at reducing the cost per unit of operation whether it be in raising funds or in lending. The costs must be taken to include not only administrative and operating costs but also the cost arising from defaults.

Ensuring the proper end use of funds lent is an important aspect of operational efficiency. However, it is only an efficiently administered financial system that can impose the necessary financial discipline on the borrowing units. If capital is scarce, so are financial resources. The financial institutions owe it to the community of savers whose funds have been placed at their disposal to see that these funds are prudently managed and purposefully utilised.

## CONCLUSION

A total approach to the financing needs of a growing enterprise may be more efficient than compartmentalisation between short-term and long-term needs. In any case, such an approach will ensure a single point monitoring and timely corrective action than the present dichotomy, the lack of co-ordination between different lenders being one of the important weaknesses of the existing system.

Mutual funds having tapped over ₹ 8,00,000 crore, have emerged as a major vehicle for mobilisation of savings, particularly from the small and household sectors for sustained investment in the stock market. In view of their growing importance in the capital market, their expanding investor base and the decision to allow mutual funds to be set up in the joint and private sectors. It has become necessary to evolve a comprehensive set of prudential guidelines for the all-round development and regulation of mutual finds and for ensuring investors' protection.

Mutual funds in India provide saftey, liquidity and growth to investors. They are safe and readily available conduits for channeling savings into productive investments yielding income and growth. With greater flexibility in operation, the mutual funds are expected to play its desired role to harness savings for sustained economic development, inculcate equity culture and strengthen the capital market. With the growth of the economy mutual funds play a unique role in mobilising savings in India.

Some of the prerequisites for success in the Indian mutual funds space are, innovative marketing, brand building, distribution network, high quality of fund management, new products, excellent customary service, killed manpower, right risk management, targeting, research and investors' continued confidence.

The institutional infrastructure in India has stood the test of time and performed well in mobilisation of resources and their allocation. It is remarkable that not only has it helped to subserve the multiplicity of policy objectives but also ensured that no viable investment proposal languishes for want of funds. However, partly in an endeavour to reach out to all viable investment proposals and in part because of the rapid growth in the size of their operations and regional spread of lending agencies, the performance of the financial system with regard to co-ordination, particularly in dealing with problem projects is far from satisfactory.

## An MF Investor's Check List

**Systematic Investment Plan (SIP):** Instead of investing at one go, an investor here commits to invest in a selected scheme at regular intervals – say, on 10th of every month – a predefined amount of money for a stipulated period of time, say, one year. This helps him build an investment over a period of time taking advantage of market volatility employing rupee-cost averaging.

**Systematic Transfer Plan (STP):** Investors transfer a fixed amount of money or appreciation enjoyed by them on the unit value in one scheme to another at regular intervals with an intention such as profit booking or step-by-step exposure to a new asset class. STP is done for a specific period of time.

**Systematic Withdrawal Plan (SWP):** Investors can redeem their investments using SWP. A fixed sum or a specific number of units can be redeemed at regular intervals. This is exactly opposite to an SIP. It helps an investor encash his investments without getting exposed to timing risk. Income need of an investor can also be met using SWP.

**Trigger:** Investors can instruct the fund house to redeem their investments or transfer their investments to another scheme if an event takes place. Such events can be appreciation in value of investments, NAV movement or market index movement.

## ANNEXURE : 1

### METHODS OF VALUATION IN INSURANCE

As a consequence of the level premium system, the premiums received by an insurer during the early years of a policy are in excess of those actually required. These excess premiums of early years are to be accumulated and kept in reserve to meet the shortfall in future years when premiums receivable will be less than those actually required. All premiums received for various types/plans of policy contracts are pooled together in Life Fund. From the common pool payments claims are made and expenses of the insurer are met, and no individual account is maintained for each policy. The excess of the premiums and interest income over the outgo from claims and expenses is to be invested with security and to the best advantage.

It is necessary to have periodic investigation into the financial position of the insurer, the principal feature of which is valuation of his assets and liabilities. In this lesson we shall deal only with the valuation of liabilities. The valuation of assets is beyond the scope of this course. However, it should be noted that the method chosen to value assets should be consistent with the method used for the valuation of liabilities.

The valuation of liabilities of an insurer is the process of arriving at the policy values of various contracts in existence on the date of valuation. As the values can be arrived at in two ways, methods of valuation are of two kinds; prospective and retrospective according as policy values are arrived at prospectively or retrospectively. If the mortality rates, interest rates and expense provision assumed in the valuation are identical with those in the premium basis, the two methods would give the same result. Normally, the prospective method of valuation is adopted.

The excess premiums accumulated will be equal to the prospective value of the policy at any point of time provided the premiums are adequate and if the business progresses as anticipated as per the basis on which the premiums are computed. The premiums charged by an insurer include provision for expenses. Thus, the Life Fund which is built-up by the accumulations of balance of premiums will be sufficient to meet the future liabilities only if the outgo from office premiums on account of expenses and claims and additions to the premiums on account of interest earnings are exactly those anticipated. Such conditions rarely exist in practice. As such, the Life Fund on hand will never be exactly sufficient to meet the future liabilities. It may either be in excess or in deficit. The necessity of valuation is, therefore, to ascertain the adequacy of the Life Fund on hand.

**Prospective Method of Valuation**

The formula for a prospective policy value for a Whole Life assurance is

$$_{t}V_{x} = A_{x+t} - P_{x}\,\ddot{a}_{x+t}$$

where age as on the valuation date, known as the 'valuation' age, is x + t and it is obtained by adding the duration elapsed t, to the age x, as on the date of commencement of policy. The age x which may be age nearer birthday or next birthday according to the practice of the office, will be integral number of years and the duration t, will also be reckoned in integral number of years. The value of 't' is generally obtained by taking the difference between the calendar year of valuation and calendar year of commencement with suitable adjustment to allow for the month of valuation and month in which policy commenced.

In case of an Endowment Assurance the prospective policy value is

$$_{t}V_{x:n} = A_{x+t:\overline{n-1}} - P_{x:n}\,\ddot{\alpha}_{x+t:n-t}$$

The valuation age, x + t, is reckoned in the same way as in case of Whole Life Assurance, the outstanding term n -1 may be arrived at by subtracting the calendar year of valuation from the maturity year with suitable adjustment to allow for month of valuation and month in which policy matures.

**Methods of Valuation**

We now discuss the following methods of valuation:

(i) Net premium method of valuation,

(ii) Modified net premium method of valuation,

(iii) Gross premium method of valuation,

(iv) Gross premium bonus reserve method of valuation.

**Concepts of Estate and Trading Profit**

A valuation is an exercise in estimating probable future trends in respect of two very uncertain factors, viz.: trend of interest rates and of expenses of management over a very long period. For this reason, the valuing actuary has to take a conservative view of the future trends, specially as the premium rates are fixed for whole duration of the contract which may last over several decades. Consequently, the reserves brought out by the formal valuation may be larger than what would be really required. The 'estate' is defined as the difference between the value of assets held by the office and the assets which will in fact be required to meet the liability, including future bonuses, in respect of existing policies. It is not possible for the insurer to forecast accurately as on what assets will in fact be required to meet the liability under existing policies, because such forecast would require an exact determination of the future experience in the matter of mortality; interest and expenses. It is therefore possible to make only a tentative estimate of the size of the estate. For this purpose, along with normal valuation (done on any method) which will be on a conservative basis, the insurer does an internal valuation by the bonus reserve method on somewhat closer to the current experience basis. In such a valuation, future bonuses at the rates being declared currently would also be provided for as a liability. The difference between the reserve brought out by such a valuation and by normal valuation can be treated as the estate. Thus, the estate is in the nature of a general reserve for a trading company, and provides a cushion against possible adverse experience in future. It also provides necessary security for payment of both the basic sum assured and current level of bonuses.

It is essentiai that the insurer distributes only the trading profit of the inter-valuation period as bonus. It should be understood that the trading profit itself is a product of the valuation method and bases and could alter if the valuation method and bases are changed. Even in respect of the current valuatior, method, the bonus that can be supported by the trading profit will depend to a considerable extent on the changes made in the valuation bases. When the rate of interest assumed in the valuation is increased with a corresponding increase in the provision for expenses and future bonuses, the surplus disclosed may be the same as the trading profit. However, because interest rate has been increased, the bonus that can be supported by the same amount of surplus will be at a higher rate. Thus, even if it is accepted that the surplus disclosed at the valuation by the method adopted correctly represents the trading profit of the inter-valuation period, the valuation method by itself distorts and considerably reduces the actual bonuses that can be supported by surplus disclosed.

In making the valuation and deciding upon the level of reversionary bonus, the insurer should keep in mind the "over-riding need" to ensure complete security both for the basic sum assured and bonuses and also for maintaining the present level of reversionary bonuses in future. At the same time the bonus system should also ensure the full return to the policyholder of the contribution made by him to the estate during the currency of his policy when the policy goes out of the fund by way of a claim. This can be done by declaring a terminal bonus in addition to the normal simple reversionary bonus. The terminal bonuses, i.e., bonuses which would be payable only to policies which result into claims by death or maturity during the inter-valuation period, should be so determined as to ensure the principle of full return to the policyholders of contribution made by them to the estate during the currency of the policies. How to arrive at the level of terminal bonuses for different types of policies with different durations is beyond the scope of this course.

**Insurance Act, 1938**

Requirements of Indian Insurance Act, 1938, more or less govern the method of valuation in our country. Section 13 of this Act requires the submission of returns to the Government of India in Form H whenever a valuation is made, setting forth the values of sums assured and bonuses, if any, the values of office premiums and net premiums and policy values as net liability.

The above particulars cannot be supplied if retrospective method of valuation is adopted as it gives policy values, i.e., net liability as a difference between accumulations of past premiums and accumulations of last expected claims. Thus, out of necessity, prospective method of valuation has become prevalent.

**Special Use of Retrospective Method**

In case of Pure Endowment policies and Children's Deferred policies during deferment period, there is no risk cover. Provisions are usually made for return of premiums with or without interest in the event of death of life assured. As the policy value at any time should not be less than the benefits guaranteed, a retrospective method of valuation is best suited.

The policy values are calculated as accumulation of certain percentage of premiums paid. The percentage is so chosen that policy values are not less than the guaranteed returns and that the margins left cover the expenses also.

**Data for Valuation**

For carrying out the valuation, the insurer compiles the requisite data in respect of all the policies which are in force on the valuation date. Prior to the advent of computers and microprocessors, policy servicing was done with the help of Unit Record (Punched Card) equipment. For each policy two cards were prepared, one for the purpose of premium accounting and related functions and the other for the purpose of valuation and mortality investigation. The latter cards, known as "Valuation and Mortality Cards" were grouped according to the following criteria:

(i) Policy class, i.e., Whole Life, Endowment, etc.

(ii) Bonus Group, i.e., With Profits or Without Profits.

(iii) Integral age of the life assured on the valuation date, i.e., year of valuation less office year of birth.

(iv) Integral outstanding term of assurance on the valuation date, i.e., office year of maturity less year of valuation.

After preparation of the relevant schedules for each rounds with details such as sum assured, vested bonus, annual premium, outstanding premium, etc., the valuation liability as obtained separately for each groups. The results for all the groups were aggregated for deciding the amount of bonus to be allocated and also for preparation of the statutory returns. This process took considerable time.

When the Unit Record equipment were replaced by microprocessors, the valuation process underwent a sea-change. Now a single record containing all the basic data in respect of a policy is available on the magnetic tape. It is therefore possible to build a valuation extract relevant to any valuation date. The use of microprocessor has made it possible to compute valuation liability policywise and aggregate the results in respect of all the 'in force' policies for the purpose of analysis and statutory groupings. Further, it is possible to obtain the results quickly on different methods of valuation and different basis of valuation. At the same time additional items necessary for an analysis of surplus can also be produced.

Life Insurance Corporation of India introduced microprocessors in a phased manner from the year 1981. Since the Branch Offices carry out the policy servicing with the support of microprocessor the valuation extract is generated in the standard format at the level of Branch Offices and consolidated at the Divisional Offices. The Zonal Offices have also been carrying out a part of valuation processing from the year 1988. The final valuation is done at the Central Office. The LIC has been conducting an annual valuation from the year 1986 onwards.

The computer programes relating to the valuation process carry-out the following functions:

(a) Check the data for validity.

(b) Compute valuation parameters such as valuation age, outstanding term of assurance, premium paying term, etc., for each policy.

(c) Group the "like" policies aggregating the sum assured, vested bonus, annual premiums, outstanding premium, extra premium, etc.

(d) Compute the assurance factors and annuity factors having regard to the valuation parameters and generate the value of sum assured, value of vested bonus, value of future bonus, value of annual premium, value of expenses, etc.

(e) Print the accumulated group totals according to plan of assurance annuity.

The final valuation results are presented as per the statutory requirements in the form H given in Annexure to this lesson. The policywise data obtained on the magnetic tape comprise the following:

(1) Policy Number.

(2) Date of commencement: Only month and year of commencement are recorded.

(3) Plan of assurance/annuity.

(4) **Original premium paying term:** In case of Whole Life policies and Convertible Whole Life policies (during the first five years or even at the end of five years, if they are continuing as Whole Life policies), the premium paying term is dependent on age at entry. In these cases, even if the premium paying term is not stated, the valuation programme calculates the same. In respect of all other cases, the actual premium paying term is stated.

(5) **Additional term:** This refers to policy term–when policy-term is different from premium paying term. In case of Children Deferred Assurance plans, this refers to deferment period. Whenever the policy term and premium term are the same, this data is not required. Even in case of Whole Life, Limited Whole Life, Convertible Whole Life (during the first five years or even at the end of five years, if the policy continues as Whole Life) plans, even though the policy term is different from premium term, it can be determined on the basis of age at entry and hence it is not stated.

(6) **Sum assured:** In case of 'in force' policies, the sum assured is to be stated. When a policy becomes paid-up, the paid-up sum assured and vested bonuses can be calculated on the basis of first unpaid premium. Therefore, even under paid-up policies, the original sum assured is to be stated.

But in paid-up cases if the basic records do not contain the original sum assured, this data may not be furnished; because the data of paid-up sum assured and vested bonuses in such cases are obtained separately.

(7) **Mode:** In case of premium paying policies mode will be monthly, quarterly, half-yearly or yearly. In case of other policies, what is stated is a paid-up policy or single premium policy.

(8) **Status of the policy:** Whether reduced paid-up, fully paid-up, claim has arisen and it is pending, etc.

(9) Due date of first unpaid premium.

(10) Age on the date of commencement.

(11) Extra premium.

(12) Accident premium.

(13) **Vested bonuses:** This is to be stated in respect of paid-up policies where the paid-up sum assured and not the original sum assured is available from original records.

(14) Whether participating policy or non-participating policy.

(15) **Paid-up sum assured:** This is to be stated only in respect of paid-up policies where the paid-up sum assured and not the original sum assured is available from original records.

(16) **Entry particulars:** Whether the policy has come on the books due to new business, revival, reinstatement of surrendered policy, missing policy reincluded or 'transfer in'.

(17) **Exit particulars:** The particulars to be furnished are date of exit and mode of exit. The mode of exit may be lapsed without paid-up value, lapsed with paid-up value, surrendered towards, loans (foreclosure action), surrendered, maturity, death claim, cancellation or transfer out.

### Valuation of Non-standard Plans

In case of Children's Deferred Assurance policies, there is no risk on the life of the child during the deferment period. The liability is the cash option payable at the end of the deferment period. The usual method of valuing these policies is by accumulating office premiums at such rate of interest as will produce the cash option at the end of the deferment period (that is, vesting date).

In the case of Temporary Assurances the sum assured is payable only if death occurs within the selected term. The value of the policy will therefore be quite small. A reserve equal to one half of the annual office premium under the policy will suffice. If the policy is a long-term policy a reserve of one year's premium may be made.

### Special Reserves and Adjustments

Policy value in respect of each policy is calculated as per the method of valuation adopted by the insurer. Valuation liability is the total of such policy values in respect of contracts in force on the date of valuation. It is necessary to provide for special reserves and adjustments asunder to arrive at the final valuation liability:

(i) Allowance for actual incidence in premium income,

(ii) Adjustment for outstanding premiums,

(iii) Reserve for early payment of claims,

(iv) Reserve for revival of lapsed policies,

(v) Provision for expenses in respect of fully paid-up policies,

(vi) Provision for expenses in respect of reduced paid-up policies,

(vii) Reserve for elimination of negative values, and

(viii)) Exchange fluctuation reserve.

**Profit:** In life Insurance business, profit arises, broadly, because of the margins provided, in the bases adopted for premium calculations regarding mortality, interest and expense and also on account of other factors such as lapses, surrenders, etc. Profit also arises when actual experience is more favourable than that assumed at the time of premium calculations. Valuation of the policy contracts of an insurer is made at intervals to ascertain the financial effect of the actual experience in comparison with that initially assumed.

If the experience of an insurer is the same as that assumed while calculating premiums, in a valuation subsequently made on the basis on which premiums were calculated, the difference between Life Fund and valuation liability represents the profit arising out of margins provided in premiums. On the other hand, if subsequent experience was more favourable than the original estimates, valuation on the same basis as for the premiums, would reveal not only the profit arising out of margins in the premiums but also the profit arising out of favourable experience up to the time of valuation. This is because of the fact that Life Fund at any time is the result of accumulations of balances of premiums already received. These balances are the excess of premiums after meeting the claims and expenses of respective years. Because of favourable experience, claims were less and probably expenses also were less i.e., the outgo from income was much less than was anticipated. Prospective valuation on the basis adopted for calculation of premiums brings about the liability that would arise if premium assumptions are to be realised in future. The excess of the Life Fund over the valuation liability is the result of margins in the premiums and also the favourable past experience.

If valuation of the contracts is made on favourable experience basis, valuation liability takes into account the continuation of the existing favourable experience in future also. Thus, a still lower liability is shown. The excess of Life Fund over this liability consists of margins in premiums, past favourable experience and also future favourable experience.

Life Fund which is the result of accumulation of excess of income over outgo is always kept in the form of various investment which yield regular interest income. Life Fund at anytime depends on the value of the investments constituting the fund. If current rates of interest are higher than those prevailing at the time of investments of Life Fund, investments depreciate in value. If interest rates have fallen there may be appreciation in the value of investments. Thus, if values of investments are always revised to bring them in line with current market conditions, Life Fund varies from time-to-time and these variations affect the profit. Usually, an investment reserve fund is built-up out of the incomes, of various years. All minor changes in the values of investments are met from this fund without writing up or down the Life Fund. A detailed discussion of the valuation of investments is, however, beyond the scope of this course.

**Surplus:** Valuations are very rarely done on the basis assumed for calculation of premiums. In selecting the basis for valuation regard is always had to the actual experience. Even if the experience assumed in premium calculations has been reproduced, it is not usual to adopt the same rates of mortality, interest and expenses in the valuation of net liability. The present experience may not be reproduced in future. A proper valuation has to take into account not only the actual mortality experience but also future trends of mortality. This is necessary, because of the fact that the existing contracts will subsist for varying periods as future. Even if an attempt is made to forecast the future experience as closely as possible on the basis of past experience and future trends it is not possible to predict it with any degree of certainty. It is possible that the future experience may turnout to be worse. In such an event losses may easily arise. To prevent such a contingency the practice is to use, for this purpose of valuation a life table based on heavier rates of mortality than those that are actually being experienced. This method provides a safety margin for adverse fluctuations.

Sufficient time has, therefore, to be allowed between valuation and valuation to make sure that the growth of the Life Fund is steady. In the case of small insurers a longer period is needed to make sure about the progress of their funds. Whereas in the case of a big insurer like Life Insurance Corporation of India with millions of policies on books, a smaller period should be sufficient to ascertain the distributable surplus.

Rates of bonus declared as a result of the surplus revealed at the time of valuation, are usually for full year's premiums, paid during the inter valuation period. If on the date of valuation full year's premium is not yet paid in respect of any policy, the bonus allowed for that year is subject to the payment of the premium for the current year in full. If valuation date is 31st March, 1990 and if the anniversary of a policy, with quarterly mode of payment of premiums, fell due on, say, the 18th day of January, 1990, the bonus for the policy year current on the date of valuation is payable in full, only if the three remaining premiums due in April, July and October 1990 are also paid. Otherwise the bonus may be either proportional or nothing at all.

Because of the necessity of preserving the stability of Bonus rates once declared, valuations with a view to distribute bonus are always done on a stringent basis leaving sufficient margins in the rate of interest, expenses and also possibly in the rates of mortality. These margins act as a buffer against any adverse experience that may result under unfavourable conditions not anticipated in advance. Without such margins future bonus rates are likely to fluctuate depending on the experience of individual years.

Valuations are performed to ascertain the distributable surplus only if the financial stability is beyond doubt. When the financial stability is suspected, it is necessary to know the actual position whether the liabilities can be met in full, with the assets available. There is no need in such cases to have any margins in the bases adopted for valuation of liabilities. The actual experience, after taking into consideration the distribution of the assets and the possibility of the continuation of the present experience, should be the basis for valuation to decide solvency of the insurer. A valuation for this purpose is known as 'solvency valuation'.

## ANNEXURE : 2

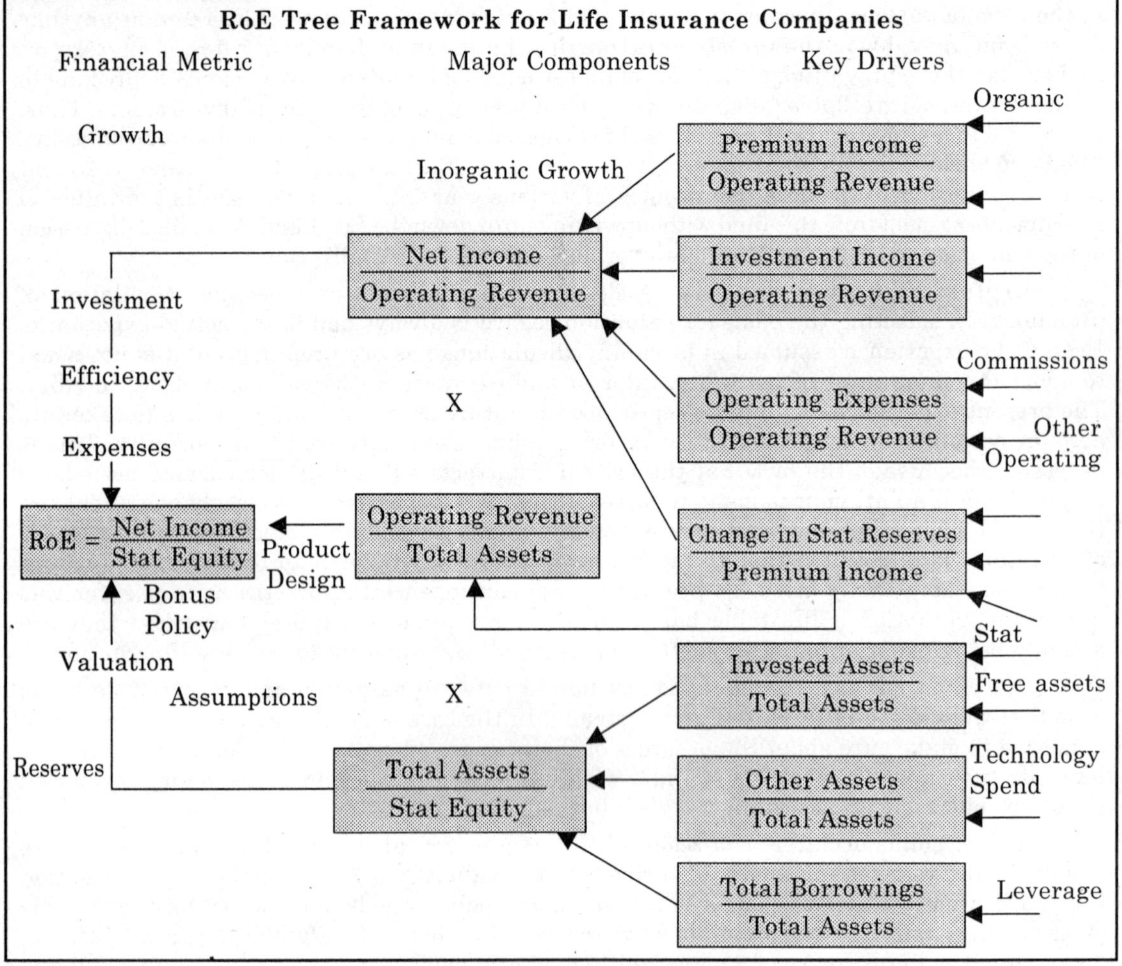


**Notes:**

(1) Net Income = Profit after Tax

(2) Stat Equity = Statutory Equity = Share Capital + Reserves and Surplus – Accumulated Losses – Miscellaneous Expenditure not written off – fictitious assets, if any, not written off

(3) Operating Revenue = Premium Income (First Year and Renewal) + Investment Income + Other Miscellaneous Income

(4) Total Assets = Net Fixed Assets + Investments + Current Assets

(5) Premium Income = First Year Premium Income + Renewal Premium Income

(6) Operating Expenses = Commissions + Other Selling. Distribution and Administration Expenses

(7) Other Assets = Net Fixed Assets + Current Assets

(8) Total Borrowing = Long-term Borrowings (= Secured Loans + Unsecured Loans) + Current Liabilities and Provisions

(9) RoE = Return on Equity

(10) The term "statutory equity" has been used in this framework because of this equity which is used to demonstrate statutory solvency is usually different from the GAAP equity that would be reported in the published financial statements.

## ANNEXURE : 3

IRDA (Obligation of insurers to rural/social sector) Regulations 2002, States that:

Every insurer, who begins to carry on insurance business alter the commencement of the IRDA Act, 1999 shall ensure that he undertakes the following obligations, during the first five financial years, pertaining to the persons in —

**(a) Rural Sector**

(1) in respect of a Life Insurer

(*i*) 7% in the first financial year
(*ii*) 9% in the second financial year
(*iii*) 12% till the third financial year
(*iv*) 14% in the fourth financial year
(*v*) 16% in the fifth financial year
of total policies.

(2) in respect of a General Insurer

(*i*) 2% in the first financial year
(*ii*) 3% in the second financial year
(*iii*) 5% in the third financial year
of gross premium income.

**(b) Social Sector**

In respect of all insurers, the obligation is

(*i*) 5,000 lives in the first financial year
(*ii*) 7,500 lives in the second financial year
(*iii*) 10,000 lives in the third financial year
(*iv*) 15,000 lives in the fourth financial year
(v) 20,000 lives in the fifth financial year

**Obligation of Existing Insurers**

The obligations of existing insurers as on the date of commencement of IRDA Act, shall be decided by the Authority after consultation with them and the quantum of insurance business to be done shall not be less than what has been recorded by them for the accounting year ended 31st March, 2002.

Also, the Authority shall view such quantum of insurance business periodically and give directions to the insurer for achieving the specified targets.

***Note:*** for the purpose of the above regulations, rural sector means — any place which meets the following criteria

(*i*) A population of less than 5,000
(*ii*) A population density of less than 400 per square km.
(*iii*) Male working population engaged in agricultural pursuits not less than 25%

Agricultural pursuits means agricultural labour, workers in livestock, forestry, fishing, plantation, orchards, etc.

For the purpose of these regulations social sector means

(*i*) Unorganised sector
(*ii*) Informal sector
(*iii*) Economically vulnerable sections or backward classes.

CHAPTER 7

# INTEREST RATE STRUCTURE

## INTRODUCTION

Interest rate acts both as a motivator and cost-effective. As such a study of interest rate structure is quite essential. Broadly, interest rates are classified into Bank rate, Call rate, Saving bank rate, Term-deposit interest rate, loan rate. Interest rates on deposits and loans are not uniform. They reflect both the characteristics of the individual loan and the general conditions of supply and demand for credit in the money market. Rates vary with the degree of credit risks associated with the loan, its maturity, the size of the borrower and of the loan, the cost of making the loan, the compensating balance of the borrower, and security deposit rates vary for different period. There are several short-term rates such as the treasury bill rate, call money rate, short-term deposit rate and so on. Similarly, there are many medium and long-term interest rates such as term loan rate, yield rate on long-term Government bonds, industrial debenture rate, etc. Besides, there are various concepts like the ceiling rate of interest, coupon rate, dividend yield and, so on.

## INTEREST RATES IN THE INDIAN FINANCIAL SYSTEM

From 1961 onward till recent years, interest rates in India were primarily administered; that is, not determined by market forces. The preponderance of controls were exercised by various authorities. Let us present a brief outline of the controls in force at different levels of our financial system prior to recent deregulatory measures.

(*i*) The RBI began fixing the maximum and minimum lending rates of commercial banks in 1964 and 1969 respectively.

(*ii*) Deposit rates of commercial and co-operative banks first came to be regulated in 1966. The RBI fixed different rates (both deposit and lending) for different types of banks.

(iii) The Indian Bank's Association had been fixing the ceiling on call money rates from 1973 until 1988 when it was freed,

(iv) The Controller of Capital Issues fixed the coupon rates on industrial debentures and preference shares.

(v) The government fixed the rate of Treasury Bills and long-term Government securities.

(vi) The RBI put in place a very complex and elaborate interest rate regime for borrowers (from the commercial banks), based on the sectors to which the borrower belongs or the purpose for which the loan is taken.

(vii) The RBI also fixed the interest rates of different financial instruments.

(viii) The government exerted considerable influence on the interest rates on term loans given by DFIs.

**INTEREST RATES POLICY** **BOX : 1**

Before 1997, the Reserve Bank of India regulated interest rates for bank under Section 21 and 35A of the Banking Regulation Act. The power to fix interest rates covered both advances and deposit rates. Rates on loans and advances were controlled mainly to influence the demand for credit and to an extent discipline the use of bank funds. This was generally done by stipulating minimum rates of interest. Minimum lending rates were prescribed for extending credit against commodities covered under selective credit control. Also, there were concessional interest rates to advances for certain sectors to reduce the interest burden and thus facilitate their development. The purpose behind fixing the rates on deposits was to avoid unhealthy competition among banks for deposits, keep the level of deposit rates in alignment with the lending rates of banks, especially with other market rates of interest and aid in deposit mobilisation.

The prescription of minimum lending rates for advances to be adhered to by scheduled banks was resorted to by the Reserve Bank as far as in October 1960. The rate then was 5% on all kinds of advances. This measure, which was adopted concurrently with the system of slab rates for the banks' borrowings from RBI, was intended to ensure that the higher cost of borrowing from the central bank was transmitted to the ultimate borrower, thus dampening the demand for bank credit. However, in 1997, the Reserve Bank of India liberalised deregulated interest rates and gradually allowed banks to fix their own rates on loans and deposits. Currently, only interest rates on savings deposits is fixed by RBI.

## YIELD VS. COST

Interest is capable of giving a return as well as be cost to the other. For investors yield relates to return on investment and/or a return on savings. Likewise to a borrower it turns to be a cost. The borrower has to pay a contracted amount on the money received. The interest structure thus influences savings, investment and other economic activities by striking an equilibrium.

**THE CONCEPT OF YIELD** **BOX : 2**

Yield relates to return on investment made in any security or financial instrument and is linked with the interest rate. Yields may be classified into different categories. In the case of equities, the yield refers to the ratio between current dividend cum capital appreciation on the one hand and the purchase price of the share on the other. In case of bonds, we have some coupon rates, which specify the interest payable on the face-value, whatever be: (*i*) the market price of the bond, and (*ii*) the current market rate of interest. In that case, yield should be calculated as follows: Let a 10% bond (of face-value ₹ 100) be purchased at ₹ 80, then the yield = $\frac{10}{80} \times 100 = 12.5\%$. These yields are known as current yields. It does not take into consideration any capital gains.

Redemption yield refers to yield to maturity. It is the average rate of return comprising return in the form of interest and capital gain (loss) over the period till maturity. The formula for deriving redemption yield is as follows:

$$V = \sum_{n=1}^{N} \frac{In}{(1+i)^n} + \frac{P_N}{(1+i)^N}$$

where $i$ = the yield to be derived.

$I_n$ = Absolute interest amount paid in the nth year.

$P_N$ = Face value of the bond to be received at maturity.

$V$ = Current value of the bond

$N$ = Number of years remaining to maturity.

Thus, the yield to maturity on a three-year bond with annual interest payments of ₹ 100, a principal payment of ₹ 1,000, and a current value of ₹ 9,000 is given by :

$$900 = \frac{100}{1+i} + \frac{100}{(1+i)^2} + \frac{100}{(1+i)^3} + \frac{1{,}000}{(1+i)^3}$$

Thus, $i$ = 14.3%

Let the holder of an instrument does not hold it till it matures. Thus, if $P_K$ is the price at the beginning of the holding period. $P_i$ is the price at the end of that period and $I$ is interest payment. Holding Period Yield simply equals.

$$\frac{(P_i - P_K)+1}{P_K}$$

## DETERMINANTS OF THE INTEREST RATE STRUCTURE

How are interest rates determined? There are several theories on interest rate determination. We shall discuss briefly, three such theories — (*a*) The Classic Theory, (*b*) The Loanable Funds Theory, and (c) The Keynesian Theory. But before that, let us explain the concepts of nominal and real interest rates.

What is an interest rate? According to the Macmillan Dictionary of Model Economics, it is the price of money services. The 'pure' rate of interest is the price that would have to be paid to borrow money in order to take a completely riskless enterprise.

Now the sum of money received on holding a bond is the nominal interest, which expressed as fraction of the face-value of the bond gives the nominal interest rate. Let R be the nominal rate of interest. If P is the rate of inflation, the real interest rate r is given by $r = R - P$.

The intuition behind this relationship is simple to follow. If a person lends ₹ 100 this year and gets back ₹ 110 next year, it might appear that he receives a 10% return, but if at the same time the general price level also rises by 10%, he gets no real return. This is because his purchasing power remains the same: goods worth ₹ 100 this year will cost ₹ 110 the next year and the person will find that he is able to purchase the same bundle of goods with ₹ 110 as he could buy with ₹ 100 last year. Similarly, in times of deflation, the real return will exceed the nominal return.

## THE CLASSICAL THEORY

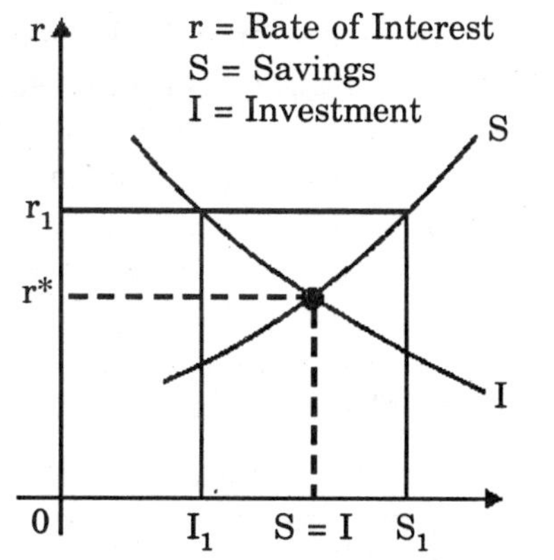

**Fig. 1**

According to the classical theory, the rate of interest is determined through the interaction between the supply of savings on the one hand, and demand for investment on the other. Savings are generated by foregoing current consumption expenditure. The households, the firms, the government — all contribute to this savings. Now foregoing current consumption involves a 'sacrifice' and interest is considered to be a reward for such sacrifice. Thus, the 'time preference' of present consumption over future consumption is a key factor influencing the supply of savings, which is positively related to the rate of interest. This is because, with higher interest rates, the opportunity cost of current consumption rises, that is, one unit of current consumption involves a larger foregoing of future consumption. On the demand (investment) side, firms require capital to undertake projects which would yield profits to them. A higher interest rate would reduce profits, thus making some projects enviable: as a result of which aggregate demand for investment will fall. The classical theory can be succinctly expressed in terms of a simple diagram.

Equilibrium is obtained at the rate of interest r*, where supply of savings just equal the demand for investment. At other rates, there would be a mismatch between the two, and assuming perfect flexibility of the interest rate, it will either rise or fall to bring about the desired equilibrium. For example, at $r_1$, $S_1 > I_1$, that is, the supply of savings exceeds the demand for investments and thus, the frustrated savers will bring down the rate of interest.

## THE LOANABLE FUNDS THEORY

The Loanable Funds Theory makes some important modifications in the classical theory. Firstly, it incorporates a dynamic aspect; secondly, it combines real and monetary factors and thirdly, it takes a more short-run view of the problem.

This theory, due to such classical economists as Wicksell, Ohlin and Robertson, is also formulated in terms of the flow of demand for and supply of loanable funds. Now, however, we take account of two sources of demand and two sources of supply. The source of loanable funds now consists of *planned savings plus any increase in the stock of money over the relevant (short-term) period.* Similarly, the demand for loanable funds is assumed to arise from the demand for finance in order to *invest in capital goods plus the demand for loans from those who wish to build-up their stock of money balances.* Equilibrium is obtained when the two sides match.

Thus, this theory emphasises the role of the banking sector and credit creation in respect of the determination of interest rate. So, it offers a real-cum-monetary explanation and also considers a more short-term view of the determination of the rate of interest.

## CRITICAL APPRAISAL OF THE LOANABLE FUNDS THEORY

Keynes has criticised the loanable funds theory bitterly. His first basic criticism is about the assumption that saving is interest-elastic. According to him, saving will depend upon the level of income of the people and not upon the rate of interest. For instance, the rich persons in a community will save automatically even if the rate of interest is zero, since they have too much money. Middle income group will also save, even if the rate of interest is zero, for they save to provide security for their family. The low income groups have such low incomes that they may not be in a position to save even if the rate of interest is very high. Thus, the level of saving in a country depends upon the level of income and has nothing to do with the rate of interest.

Secondly, Keynes rejects the classical view that the level of investment in a country depends upon the rate of interest in such a way that at a lower rate of interest, investment demand will be larger. According to Keynes, investment does not depend upon the rate of interest alone. For instance, investors may be prepared to borrow more and invest more, even if the rate of interest is high, provided they anticipate a still higher margin of profit. On the other hand, investors will not be tempted to borrow even when the rate of interest is very low, or even zero, if they are afraid that they may lose their capital. In other words, investment depends upon the rate of return in a particular industry or what Keynes calls the marginal efficiency of capital rather than upon the rate of interest. Recent empirical studies have proved that Keynes is correct on this point.

Thirdly, Keynes does not agree with the classical and neo-classical theory that the rate of interest equates saving and investment. According to Keynes, equality of saving and investment is brought about by changes in the level of income and expenditure.

Fourthly, Keynes questions the following conclusions of the classical theory, viz.:

(*a*) the rate of interest brings about the equality of saving and investment;

(*b*) equality of saving and investment establishes stability of business conditions in a country; and

(*c*) stability in business conditions takes place at the level of full employment.

Keynes agrees with the second conclusion that equality of saving and investment brings about stability in income, employment and production in the economy. But he does not believe that a stable economy need necessarily be a full employment economy. According to him, an economy may be stable, but it may be functioning at a low level of employment.

Finally, Keynes rejects the policy importance given to the rate of interest in the classical theory. He believes that by simply manipulating the rate of interest, it is not possible to bring about expansion or the desire to hold wealth in the form of cash with the available quantity of cash. While wages, land rent and profit are payments in money but for services rendered by the factor units, interest is the only case of payment in money and for the use of money. It is for this reasons that Keynes regards interest as a purely monetary phenomenon, not related to or dependent upon real factors. But the Keynesian theory of liquidity preference of interest may be criticised on the following grounds:

## LIQUIDITY PREFERENCE THEORY

This celebrated model is due to Keynes, who considered the rate of interest as a purely monetary phenomenon. The demand for money is considered to be the sum of three components, (*i*) the transaction demand for money, (*ii*) the precautionary demand for money, and (*iii*) the speculative demand for money. The first two (often clubbed together and referred to as the *transaction-cum-speculative demand*) are function of national income while the third one negatively related to the rate of interest. This is the quantity of idle cash balances people hold, anticipating a future rise in interest rates (that is, a decline in bond prices).[1] Thus, people's *liquidity preference* (*L, say*) (*i.e.*, demand for money) is a function of the rate of interest r, and national income (Y, say). Given the value of Y, we therefore have a downward-sloping L-schedule (drawn as function of r). The supply of money, on the hand, is taken to be exogenously given. Given the value Y, L is downward sloping. Money supply is exogenously fixed at M and money-market equilibrium is established at the rate of interest r*.

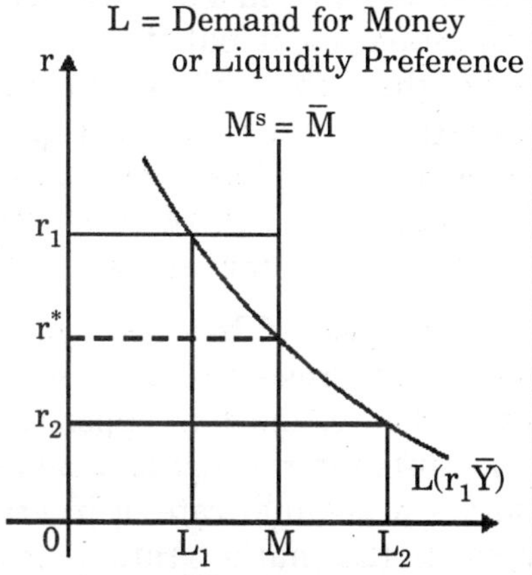

**Fig. 2**

## SOME IMPLICATIONS OF LIQUIDITY PREFERENCE THEORY

Some of the important implications of the liquidity preference theory of interest are as follows:

**(i) Rate of Interest and the Supply of Money:** Under the Keynesian system, the monetary authority is expected to stimulate employment by following a cheap money policy which implies the lowering of the rate of interest through increasing the supply of money. The idea behind an easy money policy is that an increase in the total supply of

1. It is quite a well-known relationship in respect of financial as well as macroeconomic theory. Let us explain this with the help of an example. Consider a bond with a face value of ₹ 100 and a coupon rate of 10%. The holder of the bond will get a stream of earnings at the rate of ₹ 10 per year. Now, if the market rate of interest comes down to 5%, only a bond with a face value of ₹ 200 (and a coupon rate of 5%) will yield the same stream of earnings. Therefore, not considering the issue of redemption value, we may reasonably suppose that the two bonds will have equal market prices. So, a halving of the rate of interest doubles the price of the ₹ 100 (10%) bond.

money (other things — remaining the same) will increase the money available for speculative motive ($M_2$), thereby causing a fall in the rate of interest and stimulating investment which, in turn, will increase income. How effective monetary stimulation will be depends on: (*a*) how much the rate of interest falls in response to an increase in $M_2$, (*b*) how responsive investment is to a fall in the rate of interest, and (*c*) how much a given increase in investment will increase the income.

An increase in the quantity of money (other things remaining the same) will lower the rate of interest; it will not do so if the liquidity preference is increasing more than the quantity of money. Similarly, a fall in the rate of interest will increase investment and employment but it may not be so if the marginal efficiency of capital is declining more than the rate of interest. When an economy is passing through a chronic depression, when liquidity preference is high and expectations of profitability low, monetary policy may prove quite ineffective to break the economic deadlock. Thus, from the practical point of view, monetary policies based on Keynes' liquidity preference analysis encounters serious limitations.

**(ii) Rate of Interest and Bond Prices:** Liquidity preference theory shows clearly how bond prices are inversely related to the interest rates or how bond prices and interest rates move in opposite directions. When interest rates fall, bond prices rise and when interest rates rise, bond prices fall. Suppose a bond of the nominal value of ₹ 1,000 carries a nominal rate of interest of 5 per cent; it will yield a fixed income of ₹ 50 per year. If the market rate of interest is 4 per cent, the price of the bond will rise to ₹ 1,250; and if the market rate rises to 6 per cent, the price of the bond will fall to about ₹ 850 — so that the bond income is ₹ 50.

The changes in the prices of the bonds reflect the changes in the liquidity preference of the people. An increased desire of the people to buy bonds implies a decline in liquidity preference — the price of bonds will rise and the yield rate of interest will fall. On the other hand, if the people have a stronger liquidity preference, they would like to part with their bonds; this implies that bond prices will decline and the interest rate will rise.

**(iii) Emphasis on Long-term Rate of Interest:** The rate of interest differs depending upon the length and maturity of loans or securities. The rate of interest on money at call and short notice (i.e., daily or weekly loans) will be different from the rate of interest on bills of three months maturity, which, in turn, will be different from the rate of interest on long period advances. Though normally we speak of the rate of interest, as if there is only one rate of interest, in practice, there are many types of rates of interest. However, we broadly distinguish two types of rates of interest — short-term and long-term rates of interest. The short-term rate of interest is generally on bills of three months maturity (or 90 days paper) and short-term advances, and the long-term rate of interest is on bonds and securities. In Keynes' analysis the long-term rate of interest has more relevance than short-term rate of interest. For, according to him, real investment in durable capital assets plays an important role in influencing the level of business activity and these investments are financed through long-term rate of interest on loans, bonds and securities.

**(iv) Liquidity Trap:** We have already referred to the concept of liquidity trap in Chapter 5 of Part 1. It is shown there that the liquidity preference curve becomes perfectly elastic after a point, indicating that no further reduction in the rate of interest is possible merely by increasing the quantity of money. At this point, the demand for cash balances is perfectly elastic. The rate of interest is so low at the point of liquidity trap that the wealthholder will prefer to keep cash rather than securities, for the low rate does not adequately compensate him for the incidental expenses and inconveniences of buying bonds. Further, the rate of interest is so low that the people come to be convinced that the rate of interest has fallen to the minimum and do not expect it to fall further, Or, the bond prices are so high (when the interest rate will be low, the prices of bonds are high) that the wealthholders believe that if bond prices change at all, they must decline. Thus, according to Keynes, the rate of interest becomes sticky and gets trapped at about the level of 2 per cent and does not — or cannot — fall to zero.

Prof. J. R. Hicks gives a different reason for the liquidity trap. Hicks points out that money is the most liquid asset and is the only medium of exchange to obtain goods and services. The demand for and the supply of money is basically different from the demand for and supply of any other commodity. An excess of supply over demand of a commodity may cause its price to fall to zero but excess of money over its demand will not cause its price (*viz.,* the rate of interest) to fall to zero. So long as money serves as the only medium of exchange, it is bound to be demanded and carry a price, however low it may be. The question of zero rate of interest does not arise. If zero rate of interest is not possible the question of negative rate of interest does not arise at all.

## CRITICISMS OF THE LIQUIDITY PREFERENCE THEORY

Like the other theories of the rate of interest, the liquidity preference theory of interest is also not free from certain weaknesses and limitations.

(*i*) If the demand for money is largely a demand for idle balances and if interest is the price paid for parting with liquidity, then nothing other than cash balances which satisfy the desire for liquidity should be included in the supply of money. But there is a contradiction in the statement of Keynes, as he includes in the idle cash balances "any command over general purchasing power which the owner has not parted with for a period in excess of three months".

(*ii*) According to Keynes, the rate of interest is not a reward for waiting or saving. However, he forgets that saving or waiting is a necessary means to obtain funds for liquidity. As Jacob Viner has clearly pointed out, "there can be no liquidity without saving". It is a commonly observed fact that a man first earns an income, then saves a part of it, and thereafter decides whether to keep it in liquid (cash) form or illiquid form (bonds and securities). There can be no liquidity without saving.

(*iii*) Keynes' distinction between liquidity and illiquidity is too simple. He ignores the time element involved and, therefore, ignores the complex system of interest rates depending upon the differences in the degree of liquidity. According to him, the rate of interest will have to be entirely uniform due to the perfect uniformity of the cash balances. In the words of Prof. George Halm, Keynes' theory does not explain the time element in credit transactions, as well as the existence of different rates of interest.

(*iv*) According to Keynes, the rate of interest is independent of the demand for investment funds, but this is not so. The cash balances of businessmen and industrialists are largely influenced by their demand for purposes of investment. The demand for capital being dependent upon the marginal productivity of capital, the rate of interest is not determined independently of the marginal efficiency of capital.

(*v*) While the liquidity preference plays an important role in the determination of the rate of interest, it is not inclusive enough. The supply of and the demand for cash balances are factors which along with many others, determine the rate of interest. It is true that interest is the price paid for parting with liquid funds because hoarding is one of the determinants of the supply of loanable funds. However, by excluding all other factors in determining the rate of interest, Keynes' theory becomes as much one-sided as was the classical theory which concentrated attention only on saving as the single source of the supply of loanable funds. As D. H. Robertson has pointed out: "the fact that the rate of interest measures the marginal convenience of holding idle balances need not prevent it from measuring also the marginal inconvenience of abstaining from consumption."*

(*vi*) Keynes' liquidity preference theory is indeterminate, as the liquidity preference curve shifts up and down with changes in the level of income and it is difficult to locate it without knowing the level of income. Keynes' liquidity preference curve includes all the motives [$L_1$ (Y)+$L_2$ (r)]. The first part of the liquidity preference curve ($L_1$) comprising transactions and precautionary motives cannot be known unless we know the level of income; therefore, we cannot know the relevant liquidity preference curve and hence the rate of interest.

(*vii*) The liquidity preference theory is wrong since it goes .against the facts it attempts to explain. According to this theory, the short-term rates of interest should be highest at the bottom of a depression because at that time, people would like to be highly liquid and they would be reluctant to part with their cash balances unless the price they received for parting with their cash balances was high. In other words, during depression the liquidity preference of wealthholders is very high. Holding cash balances becomes more attractive than holding non-cash assets. But during depression all prices, including the rate of interest, are low. Similarly, if the Keynesian theory were right, then the rate of interest during recovery and the peak of boom will be the lowest because everybody would be wishing to invest in the non-money assets. But during this period, the rate of interest is quite high.

(*viii*) Keynes ridiculed the earlier theories of the rate of interest which brought to the fore *real* factors. He wrote: "The perplexity which I find in Marshall's account of the matter is fundamentally due, I think, to the incursion of the concept of 'interest', which belongs to a monetary economy, into a treatise which takes no account of money, "Interest has really no business to turn up at all in Marshall's *Principles of Economics*, — it belongs to another branch of the subject". According to Keynes, interest is purely a monetary phenomenon emerging from the intersection of the demand for and the supply of money curves. But Keynes' theory is just superficial for we must explain what determines the demand for and the supply of money. The explanation will have to be

* D. H. Robertson: "Alternative Theories of the Rate of Interest", *Economic Journal,* 1937.

largely in real terms, even though Keynes denies the relevance of real factors. True, monetary factors have to be considered in the determination of the rate of interest, but the mistake of Keynesis that he excludes real factors altogether.

According to many modern authorities, Keynes did not really formulate a new theory of the rate of interest. On the other hand, his emphasis on the influence of hoarding on the rate of interest constituted an invaluable addition to the theory of interest as it was developed before Keynes. In fact, D. H. Robertson and many others successfully incorporated much of Keynes' ideas into the loanable funds theory to make it more complete.

The modern or the neo-Keynesian theory of the rate of interest is superior to either the classical or the Keynesian theory because it successfully integrates all the four factors — saving, investment, the demand for money, and the money supply — which were crudely combined by the loanable funds theorists. The modern theory looks at the determination of the rate of interest by considering both the monetary and the non-monetary or real sectors of the economy. The classical theory considered equilibrium of only the real variables ignoring the monetary variables, while the Keynesian theory went to the opposite extreme, declaring that saving and investment had nothing to do with the determination of the rate of interest. 'Although the loanable fund theorists recognised that a complete theory of interest rate must include the real as well as the monetary variables, they could not succeed in integrating the two sectors. This difficulty has been successfully removed by the modern neo-Keynesian economists.

## THEORIES ON THE TERM STRUCTURE OF INTEREST RATES

The above discussion on different theories on interest rate determination tells us that whatever may be the differences in approach among the models, they have one remarkable common feature — all are framed in terms of only one rate of interest. In other words, these theories describe a world where a single rate of interest prevails. In reality, however, there are a number of interest rates prevailing in any economy at any one point of time. So, we should attempt lo explain such *differentials in the interest rate.*

Now, different debt instruments can have different interest rates due to a variety of reasons. For example, the rates may be administered (see the next section) and the authorities may fix different rates for different instruments on grounds of social justice. The government may wish some sector(s) to have cheaper credit, or it may be desirous of providing a particular class of savers a higher return. Such decisions are basically *ad hoc* in nature and so we really cannot offer a theory behind such differentials.

A more fundamental reason behind a differentiated interest rate structure is the difference in riskiness among the various bonds. The lender may be less sure in respect of one class of bond (than in respect of another) about the prospect of timely repayment of principal and interest. In that case, a risk-premium may be charged for the riskier bond, which will then bear a higher interest rate.

There are other factors which may result in interest rate differentials. One important feature of a bond is its liquidity (or lack of it). Bondholders typically want flexibility in portfolio, so that they can quickly switch from one instrument to another (or to cash). Therefore, a lower degree of liquidity is considered to be a disadvantage and as a result, a relatively illiquid bond will usually carry a higher rate of interest.

Another factor which may lead to an interest rate differential is the buyback or callback clause (at a specified price) carried by some bonds. The holders of such bonds run the risk of their bonds being repurchased at times when interest rates are low. In that case, the bondholder will lose out on capital gains and will have to redeploy his funds at lower yields. Therefore, a bond which can be called back by the issuer will have a higher interest rate than the one which cannot be so repurchased.

Besides these factors, the tax incentives/liabilities carried by different bonds/may be different. Such heterogeneity will also lead to interest rate differentials.

In this section, however, we shall not be concerned with the explanation of interest differentials due to risk differentials or the other factors mentioned above. Instead, we shall assume bonds to be homogeneous except for *one feature*, which is their *term to maturity*. This is nothing but the time between now and the time when a purchaser may expect it to be redeemed. In other words, we are concerned with the *term structure or maturity structure of interest rates.*

## THE EXPECTATION THEORY

The Expectation Theory of the term structure is based on the following assumptions:

(*a*) There are no costs/taxes involved in holding or trading bonds. This means that the net income from a bond consists of interest receipts and capital gains.

(*b*) There is no default risk.

(*c*) The bondholder is a profit (or net income) maximiser.

(*d*) The bondholder has an expectation about the future levels of interest rates on bonds of different maturity.

Based on the above set of assumptions, the Expectation Theory considers an individual who has some fund to invest in bonds and who will not sell the same before N (say) years. Now, he may buy a bond which matures in year N, or he can buy several short-term bonds over N years. For simplicity, consider that there is only one other type of bonds — bonds with one year maturity periods. Let R be the interest rate on the N-year bond. Then he will receive at the end of the Nth year a sum of $P (I + R)^N$ where P is the principal invested.

So, $V_1$ (optional) = $P (I+ R)^N$ ... (*i*)

In case of the second option, his wealth at the end of the Nth year will be given by

$V_2 = P (I + R_1) (1 + R_2^e) (I + R_3^e) .... (I + R^e_{N-1})$ ... (*ii*)

Where $R_1$ is the current rate of interest on a one year bond and $R^e_j$ is the current expectation about the rate of interest on a one year bond at period j.

The result is easily derived. Let an amount P be invested in a one year bond now (period 1). At the beginning of period 2, the (certain) amount available for reinvestment will be $P (I + R_1)$. If the entire amount is actually reinvested, the expected amount available for reinvestment at the beginning of period 3 will be P $(1 + R_1)$ $(I + R^2{}_e)$. Proceeding this way we finally arrive at the above result.

Now clearly, the prospective bondholder's decision will depend on whether $V_1$ > or = <$V_2$. If $V_1 > V_2$, people will invest only in N-year bonds and R will then go down. On the other hand, if $V_2 > V_1$, there will be a rush for one year bonds and the $R^e{}_j$s must be downgraded. Only in equilibrium we shall find $V_2 = V_1$ From (*i*) and (*ii*), we then get

$$R = \sqrt[N]{(1+R_1)(1+R_2^e)....(1+R_{N-1}^e)} - 1 \qquad ...(iii)$$

If now people expect one year interests ($R_j^e$s) to go up in the future, R will be greater than $R_1$ and the yield curve will be upward sloping.

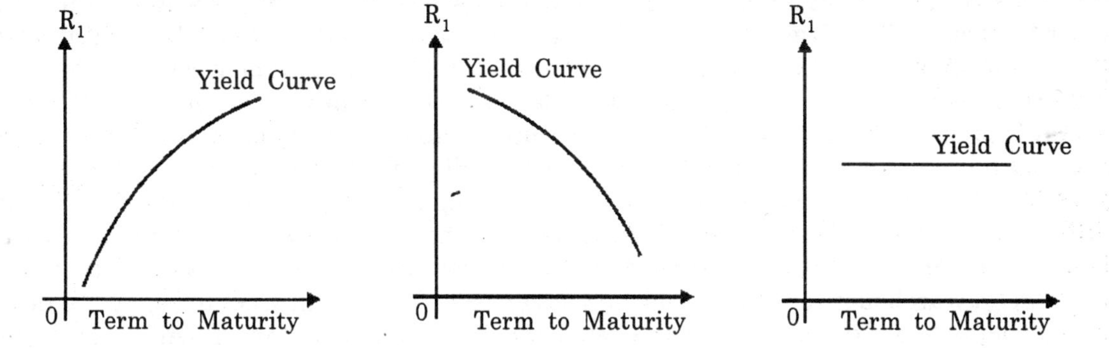


**Fig. 3**

Therefore, the Expectation Theory tells us that as long as people expect short-run rates to rise, the long-term rate R will be greater than $R_j$. In other words, and as a general principle, if people expect the short-term rates to go up with time, the current long-term rate will be greater than the current short-term rate. On the other hand, if they expect the rates to be falling, R will be less than $R_j$. Finally, if people anticipate no change in the short rates, $R = R_j$ this is also clear from equation (*iii*). Let, $R_1 = R_2{}^e = R^e{}_3 = R^e{}_{N-i}$.

Then $R = \sqrt[N]{(1+R_1)^N} - 1 = 1 + R_1 - 1$ that is, $R = R_1$

## SEGMENTATION THEORY

In the 'Expectation Theory' we assumed that expectations about future rates are held with certainty. Thus, the individual was concerned about only one value of $R^e{}_i$. However, when we introduce uncertainty, his expectations of future short-term rates will take the form of a probability distribution.

We assume that our individual is a risk-averter of an extreme kind: he maximizes utility by reducing the risk on his portfolio to zero irrespective of the expected return. Borrowers and lenders of this model hedge their risks by matching the maturity of assets to that of liabilities. In such a model, the term structure of rates is determined by the demand for and supply of each maturity. If lenders with short liabilities and borrowers with long assets (such as firms with long-term investment projects) are more in in number than those with opposite characteristics, there will be: (*i*) an excess demand for short bonds, and (*ii*) an excess supply of long bonds if the rates (of the two types of bonds) are equal. This will cause the price of short bonds to rise (i.e., short rates to fall) and that of long bonds to fall (i.e., long rates to rise). This will restore equilibrium with an upward-sloping yield-course, because some short lenders will withdraw from the market and some short borrowers will enter the market. Exactly, the opposite will hold in the long bond market and equilibrium will obtain.

Let us now explain this theory with the help of an example.

The segmentation market theory has its origin in the observation that many lenders/borrowers have strong preferences for some specific maturity period so that they care little about rate differentials existing between debts of different maturities. Consider a life insurance firm collecting premium (for a long-term policy) from a 30-year-old person with a normal health. The firm will naturally anticipate that no payment will be needed over the next 25/30 years in the least. Now the firm will invest the premium in some bonds. Will it go for a 25/30 years bond or will it buy successive short-term bonds over the next 25/30 years? It is clear that as long as the current coupon rate on a 30 years bond is higher than the return promised to the policyholder, the firm will go for the long-term bond. For, if it goes for short-term bonds, and the coupon rates begin to decline, the firm will find it difficult to meet its obligation. So, the insurance firm has a strong preference for long-term bonds. Similarly, a manufacturing firm borrowing from the market to buy some machinery, warehouse (or some other long-term assets), etc., will wish to repay the debt over a long period of time as long as the long-term rate is not exorbitant. It will avoid short-term loans because any upward fluctuation of the short rates will reduce its profitability.

## LIQUIDITY PREMIUM THEORY

This theory is mainly due to Hicks, though Meiselman and Leijonhufvud also elaborated on it. We recall equation (iii) of the Expectation Theory:

$$R = \sqrt[N]{(1+R_1)(1+R_2^e)...(1+R_{N-1}^e)} - 1$$

Hicks introduces the idea that (here is a liquidity or risk premium in each rate of interest to reflect the riskless of bonds of different maturities. In other words, (iii) must be written in the following modified form:

$$R = \sqrt[N]{(1+R_1)(1+R_2^e)...(1+R_{N-1}^e)} - 1 + (L_N - L_1) \qquad ... (iv)$$

Where $L_i$ is a liquidity or risk premium that is zero on a risk-free asset (such as money). The liquidity premium reflects the fact that the risk of an N-year bond differs from the risk on a sequence of short bonds. The extent and nature of risk differ from one borrower (and lender) to another because of differences in encashment periods.

Hicks assumed that, in general, $L_i$ increases with the length of maturity of the bond. In other words, long bonds have a higher liquidity premium than short bonds: $L_1 < L_2 < ... L_N$. Hicks argued that this characteristic arises because lenders, in general have short encashment periods and hence they prefer to buy short-period bonds to reduce their capital risk. Borrowers, on the other hand, generally issue bonds in order to finance their long-term investment projects and therefore prefer long-period bonds. As a result, there is an inherent weakness in the bond market and short-period bonds will be in excess demand and long-period bonds in excess supply unless the relative interest rates reflect the relationship $L_1 < L_2 < ... < L_N$.

## FUNCTIONS OF THE RATE OF INTEREST

We are now in a position to describe the functions of the rate of interest in a modern economy. According to the classical and neo-classical economists:

(*a*) The rate of interest influences saving in a community, i.e., given the levels of income, the higher the rate of interest, the more will be the volume of saving.

(*b*) The rate of interest determines the volume of investment in an economy. If the rate of interest is lowered, businessmen and industrialists will like to borrow more and expand their investment. This will promote economic growth.

(*c*) The rate of interest brings about the equality of saving and investment, which in turn will stabilise the level of business activity.

Keynes, of course, does not believe that the rate of interest performs all these functions. According to him, the rate of interest along with marginal efficiency of capital determines the volume of investment, but the more important determinant is the marginal efficiency of capital. If there are different alternative types of investment, with different productivities, the rate of interest will help to determine as to which type of investment should be undertaken and which should be rejected. In the case of planned socialistic economies, this is the role which the rate of interest performs. It will help to ration out the limited amount of loanable funds between different public enterprises on the basis of their productivities.

The rate of interest influences the movement of capital between countries. A high bank rate and consequently high interest rates in a country will attract short-term capital from other countries which have low rates of interest. Such an inflow of capital into a country could be used to correct balance of payments deficits. But the rate of interest can have such a function only in countries with well developed money markets like London and New York. In undeveloped money markets such as India, a high rate of interest cannot generally attract capital from foreign countries.

Finally, the rate of interest is supposed to influence the level of business activity. A low rate of interest and cheap money policy will help the economy to expand, while a high bank rate will reduce borrowing and, therefore, investment. There are, however, considerable differences of opinion on this aspect of the question. This subject is dealt with elaborately in Section 4 of this chapter.

## RECENT CHANGES IN THE INTEREST RATE STRUCTURE

As noted earlier, interest rates were largely administered in India. With the ushering in of the New Economic Policy, there has been a gradual deregulation in the interest rate structure (as in every sphere of economic life). We discuss below some recent changes in some of the important interest rates in India.

In case of Prime Lending Rates (PLRs) of scheduled commercial banks, the RBI used to prescribe both minimum lending rate and the ceiling rate during 1975-76 to 1980-81. During 1981-82 to 1987-88, RBI prescribed only the ceiling rate which was progressively reduced in three steps from 19.5 per cent in 1982-83 to 16.5 per cent in 1987-88. During the period 1988-89 to 1994-95, RBI switched from a ceiling rate to a minimum lending rate.

The minimum lending rate, which was initially fixed at 16.0 per cent, was raised to 19.0 per cent in 1991-92 in response to a rise in the inflation rate. With the gradual arrest in inflation rates, the minimum lending rate was also reduced to 14.0 per cent in 1993-94.

With effect from October 18, 1994, the lending rate was deregulated in respect of loans above ₹ 2 lakh. Thereafter, it is observed that lending rates have gradually come down and was at 12.0-12.5 per cent levels during 2000-2001.

**Table 1 : Trend in Nominal and Real PLR during the Period 1994-95 to 2003-04**

| Period | 1994-95 | 1995-96 | 1996-97 | 1997-98 | 1998-99 | 1999-2000 | 2000-01 | 2001-02 | 2002-03 | 2003-04 |
|---|---|---|---|---|---|---|---|---|---|---|
| Nominal PLR | 15.00 | 16.50 | 14.50 | 14.00 | 12.00 | 12.50 | 11.00 | 11.00 | 11.00 | 10.75 |
| Real PLR | 2.4 | 8.50 | 10.1 | 9.60 | 6.10 | 9.20 | 8.50 | 8.50 | 8.25 | 8.00 |

***Source:*** Economic Survey, 2003-2004.

## INTEREST RATE DEREGULATION

The deregulation of interest rates was central to the new market-oriented monetary strategy in terms of rejuvenating the price discovery process, on the one hand and in terms of developing an interest rate channel of monetary transmission on the other. The process of interest rate liberalisation began in the mid-1980s. The initial initiative to introduce a degree of flexibility by allowing banks to set interest rates for maturities between 15 days and up to one year subject to a ceiling of 8.0 per cent, effective April 1985, however, had to be withdrawn in the face of an ensuing price war by end-May 1985.

The dismantling of the administered interest rate structure gathered momentum during the 1990s. The first step in this direction was taken in September 1991 with the discontinuation of sector-specific and programme-specific prescriptions excepting for a few areas like agriculture and small industries, the Differential Rate of Interest (DRI) scheme and export credit. Loans above ₹ 2 lakh were freed from various prescriptions, subject to the minimum lending rate prescribed by the Reserve Bank. By linking the concessionality in interest rates to the size of the loan, the new structure ensured that the basic societal concerns were taken care of while significantly reducing the multiplicity and complexity of the rate structure.

The process of deregulation was carried forward with the withdrawal of the minimum lending rate in October 1994, thereby providing banks full freedom to determine lending rates for loans above ₹ 2 lakh. Banks were only required to announce their prime lending rates (PLR); subsequently, in October 1996, in view of the high spreads over the PLR and to impart a degree of transparency, banks were advised to announce the maximum spread over the PLR. Banks were later permitted to operate different PLRs for different maturities and lend at sub-PLR to creditworthy borrowers.

Deposit rate deregulation was more gradual as it was considered prudent to free deposit interest rates at the end of the process of deregulation and at a time when inflation was under control. The process began in April 1992 by replacing the existing maturity-wise prescription by a single ceiling rate, which was subsequently varied in line with the modifications in the minimum lending rate and the evolving macro-economic developments followed by complete deregulation in October 1997. At present, the only domestic deposit rate that continues to be prescribed is the savings deposit rate (fixed at 3.5 per cent, effective March 2003). The deposit rates in respect of non-resident rupee deposits were also deregulated on broadly similar lines while that on foreign currency deposits are subject to a ceiling rate linked to LIBOR.

**Table 2 : Interest Rates on Domestic Term Deposits: Deregulation**

| Month | Measure |
|---|---|
| April 1992 | The existing maturity-wise prescription replaced by a single ceiling rate of 13 per cent for all deposits above 46 days of maturity. |
| November 1994 | The ceiling rate brought down to 10.0 per cent. |
| April 1995 | The ceiling rate raised to 12.0 per cent. |
| October 1995 | Deposits of maturity of over two years exempted from the ceiling. |
| July 1996 | Deposits of maturity of over one year exempted from the ceiling. |
| April 1997 | The ceiling rate for deposits of 30 days up to one year linked to the Bank Rate *less* 200 basis points. |
| October 1997 | Deposit rates fully deregulated by removing the linkage to the Bank Rate. |
| April 1998 | Banks allowed to offer differential rates of interest depending upon the size of the deposit. |

While bank term deposit rates stand deregulated, small savings continue to be administered, thereby imparting a degree of rigidity to the interest rate structure. The Expert Committee to Review the System of Administered Interest Rates and Other Related Issues (Chairman: Y.V. Reddy) (RBI 2001c) recommended that interest rates on small savings and other administered instruments of various maturities needed to be benchmarked to the secondary market yields of Government securities of corresponding maturities. In pursuance of these recommendations, the Union Budget 2002-05 announced that interest rates on small savings would be henceforth linked to the average annual yield of Government securities in the secondary market for the corresponding maturities, with an annual adjustment on an automatic and non-discretionary basis. This measure is expected to enhance the flexibility of the interest rate structure in the economy. Interest rates on small savings instruments were cut by 50 basis points in the Union Budget, 2002-03 and by another 100 basis points in the Union Budget, 2003-04.

## INTEREST RATE PASS-THROUGH

While the Reserve Bank is increasingly able to ensure orderly conditions in the financial markets, the critical issue in determining the effectiveness of the signals emanating from the changes in the policy rate is the degree of 'pass-through', i.e., the speed and the magnitude of the response of the market interest rate spectrum to the monetary policy signals (RBI, 2002d). Between March 1998 and February 2003, the Bank rate and the repo rate were cut by 425 basis points and 250 basis points, respectively. In addition, the CRR was reduced by 550 basis points over the same period. The repo rate was cut by a further 50 basis points in March 2003. The easing of the monetary policy stance was mirrored in a general softening of interest rates in the money markets (with call rates declining by almost 325 basis points) and in the Government securities markets (with the yield on 10-year Government securities

**Chart : 1**

**Borrowing Costs of the Government and Others**

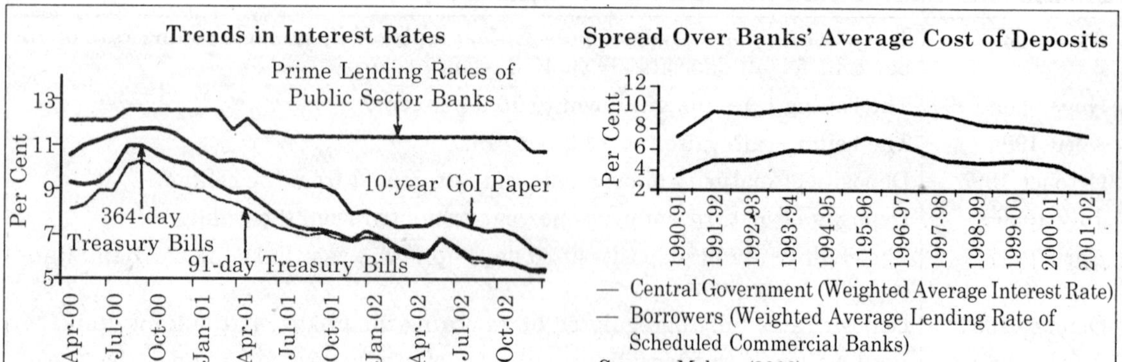


*Source:* Mohan (2002)

The figures in brackets are t-values; *, ** and *** denote significance at 1, 5 and 10 per cent level, respectively. DNDA, DNFA, DIIP and DCRRAVG denote monthly variations in net domestic assets, net foreign assets, index of industrial production and average CRR, respectively. DWPIA is year-on-year inflation rate. In addition, monthly dummies for March, April, May, October and November turned out to be significant and were included in the estimated equation. The variable DCRRAVG captures the reduction in NDA over the sample period that was due to the lowering of CRR.

declining by almost six percentage points). However, the prime lending rates of major banks remained sticky. This suggests a low level of pass-through of the changes in the policy rates on to the lending rates, thereby blunting the efficacy of the monetary policy. Over a medium-term horizon, the spreads of lending rates of commercial banks over their average costs of deposits reveal a marginal narrowing down since 1996-97. The spreads, however, still continue to be fairly large. The spread of the Central Government's market borrowings over the banks' average cost narrowed from 5.2 per cent during 1990-96 to 4.4 per cent during 1996-2002 while that of other borrowers declined from 9.2 per cent to 8.1 per cent over the same period.

**DISMANTLING OF THE ADMINISTERED INTEREST RATES** **BOX : 3**

In order to improve flexibility, banks were given freedom to decide the period of reset on variable rate deposits.

In order to ensure appropriate pricing of loans, banks were encouraged to review both their PLRs and spreads and align spreads within reasonable limits around PLR subject to approval of their Boards.

RRBs/LABs and co-operative banks were encouraged not to pay any additional interest on the savings bank accounts over and above what is payable by commercial banks.

Co-operative banks were encouraged not to pay interest on current accounts.

Sponsor banks were encouraged not to pay interest on the current accounts maintained by RRBs with them.

With a view to encouraging competition among banks and to increase the flow of credit to export sector, the interest rates on export credit in rupee terms were proposed to be liberalised in two phases:

In the first phase, the ceiling rate of PLR plus 0.5 percentage point on pre-shipment credit beyond 180 days and up to 270 days and post-shipment credit beyond 90 days and up to 180 days will be deregulated with effect from May 1, 2003. Banks would have freedom to charge PLR or sub-PLR rates subject to approval of their Boards.

In the second phase, with effect from a date to be announced later, it would be considered whether the ceiling rates on pre-shipment credit up to 180 days and post-shipment credit up to 90 days should also be discontinued to encourage greater competition in the interest of exports.

This relative downward inflexibility in the commercial bank interest rate structure can be attributed to a number of structural factors in the Indian banking system (RBI, 2002e):

- Average cost of deposits for major banks continues to be relatively high (6.25 to 7.25 per cent). This could be attributed partly, in turn, to the returns on alternative savings instruments in the country. Despite reductions in the administered interest rates on small savings and provident funds in the recent period, these instruments still yield higher returns than bank deposits, which are made even more attractive by tax benefits. This, therefore, constrains the banks' ability to reduce deposit rates. Furthermore, in the absence of a well-developed pension market, bank deposits continue to be the dominant source of income for senior citizens. This hinders sharp cuts in interest rates on bank deposits. Moreover, although the inflation rate has declined in the recent period, its year-to-year variability, as noted earlier, remains high. This might have prevented a commensurate decline in inflation expectations and thus, keeping nominal rates high.
- Substantial portion of bank deposits remains in the form of long-term deposits at fixed interest rates. This limits the flexibility available to banks in reducing their lending rates in the short-run without adversely affecting their return on assets.
- Relatively high overhang of non-performing assets (NPAs) further pushes up the average cost of funds for banks, particularly public sector banks.
- Non-interest operating expenses of banks workout to 2.5 to 3.0 per cent of total assets, putting pressure on the required spread over the cost of funds.

- In view of legal constraints and procedural bottlenecks in recovery of dues by banks, the risk-premium tends to be higher resulting in a wider spread between deposit rates and lending rates.
- In the context of the current cyclical slow down of the economy, especially the industrial sector, the probability of defaults and late payments by borrowers increases; this could lead to an increase in risk premium and hence a stickiness in the PLR.
- The large borrowing programme of the government, over and above SLR requirements, gives an upward bias to the interest rate structure.

In order to overcome these rigidities and to impart more flexibility to the interest rate structure, the Reserve Bank has recently initiated a number of measures. Banks were encouraged to introduce a flexible interest rate system option for all new deposits and urged to review and announce the maximum spreads over PLR. To have a greater degree of transparency with regard to actual interest rates for depositors as well as borrowers, banks were asked to provide information on deposit rates for various maturities, the effective annualised return to the depositors and maximum and minimum interest rates charged to their borrowers. These factors are expected to increase the degree of pass-through overtime. For instance, the median range of interest rates at which at least 60 per cent of business is contracted narrowed from 12.75-14.00 per cent as at end-June 2002 to 12.00-14.00 per cent as at end-September 2002.

It would be useful to compare the Indian experience of pass-through with that of a developed economy. In contrast to the Indian experience, the pass-through in USA is almost instantaneous and complete. For instance, between January 2001 and January 2003, the Fed Funds rate declined by 474 basis points; the prime rate over the same period declined by 480 basis points. The correlation coefficient between the two rates was therefore, nearly unity. The spread of the prime rate over the Fed Funds rate was almost constant at 300 basis points in the US as compared with almost 600 basis points over the Bank Rate in India at present. The pass-through is relatively lower on to the long-rates. For instance, the correlation coefficient of 10-year Treasury yields with the Fed Funds rate was 0.70 over the period January 1997 to January 2003. On the other hand, in India, although long-term yields fell in line with the monetary easing, the prime lending rate did not show much co-movement. This brings into sharp focus the importance of a faster pass-through for an effective monetary policy.

## REAL INTEREST RATES

The real interest rate is defined as the difference between nominal rate of interest and the expected rate of inflation.

Real interest rates are determined by a conjunction of several factors, such as:

- Productivity and thrift,
- The monetary policy regime,
- Stance of other policies, i.e., fiscal policy,
- Investors' risk perception,
- Market interest rates,

- Regulation/Deregulation of capital market
- Structural rigidities
- Sensitivity of various interest rates,
- System of administered rates.

Real interest rates also reflect the availability of lendable resources with respect to the demand for investment. They also have implications for public finances and capital flows. It has been well recognized that there is a vicious circle between interest rates and the fiscal deficit and that fiscal restraint/consolidation accompanied by effective debt management would greatly alleviate the problem of high interest rates.

## REAL AND NOMINAL INTEREST RATES IN THEORY — EXAMINED IN INDIAN CONTEXT

Fisher, Wicksell and Keynes provided the main contributions to the traditional theory of real and nominal interest rates.

The distinction between real and nominal interest rates was clearly drawn by Fisher in 1930 and his work has been the starting point for most modern studies. He defined the real rate of interest as the money rate of interest adjusted for the effects of changes in the price level.

According to the classical monetary theory, the forces of productivity and thrift determine the real rate of interest. It should not be affected in the long-run by nominal variables, such as, monetary growth or inflation. A higher rate of inflation should be reflected in a higher level of nominal interest rates, leaving the real rate of interest, defined as the nominal interest rate less the expected rate of inflation, unchanged.

Fisher found that the adjustment of the nominal interest rate to changes in the price level was highly imperfect in practice: "when the cost of living is not stable, the rate of interest takes the appreciation and depreciation into account to some extent, but only slightly and in general, indirectly. That is, when prices are rising, the rate of interest tends to be high but not so high as it should be to compensate for the rise: and when prices are falling the rate of interest tends to be low, but not so low as it should be to compensate for the fall. That is what exactly is happening in India at present time, where inflation rate is falling steadily but real interest rates continues to remain high to borrowers which discourages investments in the global competitive environment. Earlier, when long-term inflation rate in India was high, nominal rates were not very high.

To examine the above aspect of interest rate behaviour in the Indian context, interest rates were analyzed for the past 32 years, from 1970-71 to 2001-02. It was observed that when rate of inflation was 8 to 10%, nominal interest rates were not very high around 11 or 12%. And when rate of inflation started falling after 1995-96 and came down to around 3 or 4%, nominal interest rates, until recently, were 9 or 10% for depositors.

Fisher argued that agents suffered from money illusion in failing to adjust interest rates fully for inflation. He suggested that interest rates would adjust gradually to rate of change of prices.

Wicksell (1898-1958) explained the behaviour of the price level in terms of the relationship between the return on capital or the natural rate of interest and the rate of interest in the money market. If the natural rate were raised by improved opportunities for investment, as in the boom of the mid-nineteenth century, it would exceed the market rate of interest and both the level of demand and the price level would rise. If the natural rate were depressed by reduced investment prospects, it would fall below the market rate of interest and prices would decline. The impact of market rate of interest on the price level did not depend on its absolute level, but rather on whether it was high or low relative to the natural rate of interest.

Keynes in 'A Treatise on Money' (1930-71) used a theory which was similar to that by Wicksell. Keynes argued that capital accumulation would gradually bring about a decline in the natural rate of interest, defined as the rate, which equates investment and savings. As in Wicksell's theory, an excess of the natural rate over the maket rate of interest caused prices to rise and an excess of market rate over the natural rate caused prices to fall. The normal process of capital accumulation led to a gradual fall in the natural rate of interest, calling for a decline in the market rate which might not occur because of its stickiness, causing savings to exceed investment and prices to fall.

**Table 3 : Trends in Interest Rates**

(per cent per annum)

| Interest Rate | 30-3-01 | 11-1-02 | 29-3-02 | 10-1-03 |
|---|---|---|---|---|
| 1 | 2 | 3 | 4 | 5 |
| Bank Rate | 7.00 | 6.50 | 6.50 | 6.25 |
| IDBI[1] | 12.50 | 12.50 | 12.50 | 12.50 |
| PLR[2] | 11.0 - 12.0 | 11.0 - 12.00 | 11.00 - 12.00 | 10.75 - 11.50 |
| Deposit Rate[3] (> one year) | 8.50 - 10.0 | 7.50 - 8.50 | 7.50 - 8.50 | 5.50 - 6.50 |
| Call Money (Borrowings) (low/high)[4] | 6.80/13.50 | 4.54/7.30 | 5.00/19.00 | 3.50/7.00 |
| CDs | 6.30 - 11.50 | 6.20 - 9.50 | 5.00 - 10.03 | 4.71 - 6.50* |
| CPs | 8.75 - 11.25 | 7.40 - 9.75** | 7.41 - 10.25 | 5.70 - 7.50# |
| 91-day T-Bills | 8.50 | 6.83 | 6.13 | 5.39 |
| 364 days T-Bills | 8.96 | 7.00 | 6.16 | 5.41 |

\# Relates to January 15, 2003

* Relates to December 27, 2002.

** Relates to January 15, 2002.

*Notes:* 1. Minimum Term Lending Rate (MTLR).
2. Prime Lending Rate relates to five major banks.
3. Deposit rate relates to major banks for term deposits of more than one year maturity.
4. Date cover 90-95 per cent of total transactions reported by participants.

The low interest pass-through, in the context of a decline in the inflation rate, is reflected in a hardening of the real interest rate (Table 4). The impact differed across various sectors in view of divergent trends in the pass-through as well as the relevant inflation rates. In particular, the appropriate real interest rate for borrowers increased significantly as manufacturing inflation declined more sharply than the headline inflation while the nominal rates remained relatively sluggish. The sluggishness of nominal rates, in turn, emanated from a combination of downward rigidity of deposit rates, low pass-through and risk-aversion by banks in view of the prudential norms. In the case of the Central Government, the increase in real interest rates could be attributed partly to the fact that the administered interest rate mechanism continued during the first few years of the 1990s. For the Central Government, real interest rates, in fact, fell sharply in 2002-03 on the back of a substantial decline in nominal yields. The key issue, in terms of the growth objective, is the impact of the structure of real interest rates, especially as the interest cost as a proportion of sales of corporates is much higher as compared with many emerging market economies (Mohan, 2002).

**Table 4 : Real Interest Rates**

*(Per cent)*

| Category/Period | 1990-91 to 1995-96 | 1996-97 to 2001-02 |
|---|---|---|
| | 1 | 2 |
| Depositors | – 0.3 | 1.9 |
| Central Government | 1.8 | 6.8 |
| Borrowers | 6.5 | 12.5 |

***Note:*** Real interest rates calculated as the weighted average lending rate of scheduled commercial banks *less* manufacturing inflation, for borrowers; weighted average interest rate on Central Government securities *less* WPI inflation, for the Central Government; and average cost of time deposits *less* CPI-IW inflation for depositors.

***Source:*** Mohan (2002).

For India, econometric evidence suggests that a 100 basis points rise in real interest rates depresses the real GDP and hence widens the output gap (actual *less* trend output) by six basis points in the short-run and almost 60 basis points in the long-run. Available empirical evidence also suggests that the response of output to monetary policy signals is asymmetric with a tight monetary policy being more effective than an easy monetary policy.

## FACTORS AFFECTING LOWERING OF INTEREST RATES

Banks in India are facing a number of difficulties in bringing lending rates down to the level comparable with other countries of the world. These problems are mainly due to the structural rigidities prevailing in the system, which is again due to the difficulties in pushing reforms in banking and other sectors due to democratic set-up, causing political compulsions. Although, the RBI has spelled out structural rigidities, a quick recapitulation is nevertheless needed.

- Although interest rates on deposits have been brought down considerably from 12-13% in 1996-97 to 7-7.5% at present, still cost of deposits for banks is high around 7%. The reason being, cut in interest rates affects only incremental deposits and not old term deposits. In the Monetary and Credit Policy of April 2002, although banks have been permitted to issue floating rate deposits, still such products are at the budding stage. It needs proper marketing in the competitive product markets. Moreover, banks are not sure about its success in the falling interest rate scenario.
- Interest on small savings are still high, which limits banks' ability to make downward adjustment in the deposit rates.
- High level of NPAs with banks in India is another major problem. After introduction of stricter prudential norms, assets were classified, higher

provisions were made, write-off and compromise proposals were encouraged, and recoveries were speeded up. Consequently, the proportion of gross and net NPAs to advances came down, but still gross NPAs of banks, in absolute terms, are increasing year-after-year. It is necessary to bring down gross NPAs of banks from the present 11% to around 5% and net NPAs from 6.2% to around 2% to bring interest rates close to the international level. It is hoped that the new Securitisation Bill 2002 will see the light of the day in its present form. Of course, the Bill will not be a panacea for all recovery problems being faced by banks, but it will certainly improve recovery of bank dues.

- In this context, it would be worthwhile to quote a comprehensive study, published recently in October 2002. The study was carried out jointly by the United Nation's Economic and Social Commission for Asia and the Pacific (ESCAP) and the Asian Development Bank. According to the study, the high levels of NPAs are the bane of the entire banking spectrum in the Asian region. Banks in Asia are afraid to lend, companies are reluctant to borrow and the region's monetary authorities have given little or no indication as to how they will solve this credit crunch. The report states that most countries are at present experiencing 'ample liquidity with low and declining interest rates' but there exists a shortage of 'creditworthy' corporate borrowers. The impact of current reluctance to lend or borrow could have even more negative effect on the region's economy. Until banks regain their ability and willingness to lend and become less risk-averse, the pace of economic growth is likely to remain muted, as the banks will avoid many less creditworthy customers, warns the study.
- High fiscal deficit of the government and increasing market borrowings year-after-year are the major difficulties in bringing interest rate down in the country. There is a need to introduce fiscal reforms. It is observed that more than 60-70% of the incremental deposits of the banks go in for financing government deficits.
- As stated earlier, reforms initiated since 1991 in the banking and financial sector are on half way. Number of structural changes including amendment to the various Acts are yet to get the Parliament's nod.
- Technological initiatives taken in the recent years are picking up and will take few more years to accrue real benefits to banks.
- The area of 'labour reform' is more or less untouched, except some stray measures here and there like allowing banks to recruit certain percentage of people from business schools, abolition of BSRBs, VRS, etc. According to the available statistics, establishment cost of public sector banks is high. It was nearly 20% in 2000-01 as against 9-9.5% in foreign banks in India and 12-13.5% in private banks. However, after the VRS exercise in PSBs, establishment cost has come down to 18% in 2001-02. Even 18% establishment cost is high compared to other banks in the world. Without taking radical reform measures in this particular area it is difficult to reduce high establishment cost, change overall work culture which can ultimately help in bringing down interest rates to the desired level.

- Intermediation cost of Indian banks is high at around 2.5-3% due to inefficiencies prevailing in the system. It is imperative to bring it down to around 1% for further softening of lending rates on sustainable basis.
- As compared to strong well-capitalized international banks, banks in India are operating with a weak capital base. In the circumstances to survive under post-Basel Capital Accord, banks are required to generate its additional capital requirement to take care of business growth from profit plough-back. This phenomenon has compelled banks to operate with a high spread of around 3%. However, competitive forces have compelled public sector banks to bring down interest spread from 3.08% in 1995-96 to 2.84% in 2000-01.
- Interest spread in respect of old private sector banks have come down from 3.14% to 2.51%, while for new generation private sector banks it came down from 2.84% to 2.14% in the same period. If the real interest rates have to come down, it is necessary that banks should operate with even lower spread.
- Interest rates are mostly deregulated. It is, therefore, necessary to deregulate interest rates on savings bank deposit accounts also which is being considered as one of the impeding factors in lowering interest rates.
- Priority sector lending rate should be delinked from PLR of banks as it is considered as one of the factors discouraging banks from lowering of PLRs.

## CONCLUSION

The interest rate structure is a complex subject. To a greater extent, they are regulated and not determined by the market variables alone. However, in recent years greater flexibility is given to the interest rate structure with a preference for soft interest rate regime. Yet, reduction in lending rates has not kept pace with the deposit rates.

The moot point is unless banks are able to cover their operating cost through other income, pressure on spreads will continue. It will create difficulties in lowering of nominal and real interest rates in the country. The structural rigidities with regard to interest rates should be removed. For that banking reforms in critical areas, such as, NPA management restructuring, right sizing, technology related issues and HRM needs to be pushed up in the right direction as it will have a positive impact on lowering of interest rates on a sustainable basis in future.

An important financial market prices channel is the interest rate channel. A contractionary monetary policy leads to a hike in nominal short-term interest rate, which given nominal rigidities (sticky nominal wages and prices) and the expectations model of the term structure, translates into higher real interest rates. The resultant increase in the price of currently purchased goods as compared with goods purchased in the future reduces investment and consumption and contracts output. As wages/goods prices adjust overtime, real GDP returns to the potential level and the real interest rate and the real exchange rate also return to their fundamental levels.

The efficacy of the interest rate channel would, however, be reduced in case banks rations credit. But even though interest rates charged by banks do not change, the amount of lending by banks would increase if the supply curve of funds shifts to the right; to that extent, even with unchanged interest rates, the economic activity will have a positive effect.

## ANNEXURE : 1

### REAL INTEREST RATES WORKED OUT FOR DEPOSITORS AND BORROWERS

| Year | Call Rates (%) Average | Deposit Rates Time Period in Years (%) | | | Avg. Inflation WPI | Avg. Inflation CPI | Real Interest Rate to Depositors SBI | | | General Real Int. to Lending Borrower | |
|---|---|---|---|---|---|---|---|---|---|---|---|
| | | 1 to 3 yr. | 3 to 5 yr. | Over 5yrs. | (%) | (%) | WPI | CPI | SBAR | Rates | WPI |
| 1970-71 | 6.38 | 6.00-6.50 | 7.0 | 7.25 | — | — | — | — | 7.0-8.5 | — | * |
| 1971-72 | 5.16 | 6.0 | 6.5 | 7.25 | 5.6 | 3.2 | 1.65 | 4.05 | 8.5 | — | 2.9 |
| 1972-73 | 4.15 | 6.0 | 6.5 | 7.25 | 10.1 | 7.8 | −2.85 | −0.55 | 8.5 | — | −1.6 |
| 1973-74 | 7.83 | 6.0 | 7.0 | 7.25 | 20.2 | 20.8 | — | — | 8.5-9.0 | — | — |
| 1974-75 | 12.82 | 6.75-8.0 | 7.75-9.0 | 8.0-10.0 | 35.2 | 26.8 | — | — | 9.0-13.5 | — | — |
| 1975-76 | 10.55 | 8.0 | 9.0 | 10.0 | −1.1 | −1.3 | — | — | 14.0 | 16.5 | 15.1 |
| 1976-77 | 10.84 | 8.0 | 9.0 | 10.0 | 2.1 | −3.8 | 7.9 | 13.8 | 14.0 | 16.5 | 11.9 |
| 1977-78 | 9.28 | 6.0 | 8.0 | 9.0 | 9.2 | 7.6 | -0.2 | 1.4 | 13.0 | 15.0 | 3.8 |
| 1978-79 | 7.57 | 6.0 | 7.5 | 9.0 | — | 2.2 | — | 6.8 | 13.0 | 15.0 | — |
| 1979-80 | 8.47 | 7.0 | 8.5 | 10.0 | 17.1 | 8.8 | — | 1.2 | 16.5 | 18.0 | — |
| 1980-81 | 7.12 | 7.5-8.5 | 10.0 | 10.0 | 18.2 | 11.4 | — | — | 16.5 | 19.4-19.5 | — |
| 1981-82 | 8.96 | 8.0-9.0 | 10.0 | 10.0 | 9.3 | 12.5 | 0.7 | −2.5 | 16.5 | 19.5 | 7.2 |
| 1982-83 | 8.78 | 8.0-9.0 | 10.0 | 11.0 | 4.9 | 7.8 | 6.1 | 3.2 | 16.5 | 19.5 | 11.6 |
| 1983-84 | 8.63 | 8.0-9.0 | 10.0 | 11.0 | 7.5 | 12.6 | 3.5 | −1.6 | 16.5 | 18.0 | 9.0 |
| 1984-85 | 9.95 | 8.0-9.0 | 10.0 | 11.0 | 6.5 | 6.3 | 4.5 | 4.7 | 16.5 | 18.0 | 10.0 |
| 1985-86 | 10.0 | 8.5-9.0 | 10.0 | 11.0 | 4.4 | 6.8 | 6.6 | 4.2 | 16.5 | 17.5 | 12.1 |
| 1986-87 | 9.99 | 8.5-9.0 | 10.0 | 11.0 | 5.8 | 8.7 | 5.2 | 2.3 | 16.5 | 17.5 | 10.7 |
| 1987-88 | 9.88 | 9.0-10.0 | 10.0 | 10.0 | 8.1 | 8.8 | 1.9 | 1.2 | 16.5 | 16.5 | 8.4 |
| 1988-89 | 9.77 | 9.0-10.0 | 10.0 | 10.0 | 7.5 | 9.4 | 2.5 | 0.6 | 16.5 | 16.0 | 9.0 |
| 1989-90 | 11.49 | 9.0-10.0 | 10.0 | 10.0 | 7.5 | 6.1 | 2.5 | 3.9 | 16.5 | 16.0 | 9.0 |
| 1990-91 | 15.85 | 9.0-10.0 | 11.0 | 11.0 | 10.3 | 11.6 | 0.7 | −0.6 | 16.5 | 16.0 | 6.2 |
| 1991-92 | 19.57 | 12.0 | 13.0 | 13.0 | 13.7 | 13.5 | -0.7 | −0.5 | 16.5 | 19.0 | 2.8 |
| 1992-93 | 14.42 | 11.0 | 11.0 | 11.0 | 10.1 | 9.6 | 0.9 | 1.4 | 19.0 | 17.0 | 8.9 |
| 1993-94 | 6.99 | 10.0 | 10.0 | 10.0 | 8.4 | 7.5 | 2.6 | 2.5 | 19.0 | 14.0 | 10.6 |
| 1994-95 | 9.40 | 11.0 | 11.0 | 11.0 | 12.5 | 10.1 | −1.5 | 0.9 | 15.0 | 15.0 | 2.5 |
| 1995-96 | 17.73 | 12.0 | 13.0 | 13.0 | 8.1 | 10.2 | 4.9 | 2.8 | 16.5 | 16.5 | 8.4 |
| 1996-97 | 7.84 | 11.0-12.0 | 12.0-13.0 | 12.5-13.0 | 4.6 | 9.3 | 8.4 | 3.2 | 14.5 | 14.5-15.0 | 9.9 |
| 1997-98 | 8.69 | 10.5-11.0 | 11.5-12.0 | 11.5-12.0 | 4.4 | 7.0 | 7.6 | 5.0 | 14.0 | 14.0 | 9.6 |
| 1998-99 | 7.83 | 9.0-11.0 | 10.5-11.5 | 10.5-11.5 | 5.9 | 13.1 | 5.6 | −1.6 | 12-14 | 12.0-13.0 | 6.1 |
| 1999-00 | 8.87 | 8.5-9.5 | 10.0-10.5 | 10.0-10.5 | 3.3 | 3.4 | 7.2 | 7.1 | 12.0 | 12.0-12.5 | 8.7 |
| 2000-01 | 9.15 | 8.5-9.5 | 9.5-10.0 | 9.5-10.0 | 7.1 | 3.7 | 2.9 | 6.3 | 11.5 | 11.0-12.0 | 4.4 |
| 2001-02 | 7.32 | 8.0-8.5 | 8.25-9.0 | 8.25-9.0 | 3.7 | 4.3 | 5.3 | 4.7 | 11.5 | 11.0-12.0 | 7.8 |
| 2002-03 | 5.00 | 6.5-7.5 | 7.0-7.5 | 7.0-7.5 | 2.4* | 4.2* | 5.1 | 3.3 | 11.0 | 11.0-12.0 | 8.6 |

* (up to October)

*Source:* RBI Handbook of Statistics on Indian Economy 2001, Table No. 57, 28 and 29.

## ANNEXURE : 2

### HUME AND THE QUANTITY THEORY

David Hume, in his *Political Discourses* (1752) skilfully exposed fallacies then current. By and large, his analysis was a good corrective, and, moreover, it fitted passably well the conditions of his time.

Put in technical terms, Hume denied that the demand function for money was interest-elastic. In his view the demand for money was elastic only with respect to the "price of labour and commodities".

He begins his discourse "Of interest" by denying that the "lowness of interest" can be ascribed to "plenty of money". Money, however plentiful, will have no other effect than to "heighten the price of labour and commodities". He allowed that in the process of adjustment "the augmentation may have some influence[1] by exciting industry". But the rate of interest is not derived from the quantity of money.

High interest, he says, arises from three circumstances: (1) a high rate of profit, (2) a large volume of investment — a "large demand for borrowing", and (3) a low volume of saving — "little riches to supply the demand". Landlords are typically prodigal, and beggarly peasants have no means. Merchants alone — "the most useful races of men"— compose a great monied interest. Thus, there arises a great number of lenders, which tends to reduce the rate of interest. But money in the hands of landlords and peasants "could never gather into sums, and would only serve to increase the prices of everything". Thus, it depends upon who it is that gets the "plentiful" money supply; if it gets into the hands of merchants, it will be gathered into large sums to be lent out and so will tend to reduce the rate of interest; if it gets into the hands of landlords and peasants, it will be spent and so raise prices.

The rate of interest, says Hume, depends upon: (1) industry, and (2) frugality — or in other words, upon productivity and thrift. Commerce increases industry. "Commerce alone assembles it [money] into considerable sums." The increase of commerce "raises a great number of lenders". But the great increase in commerce also diminishes profit. This is due to the "rivalry among merchants, which diminishes the profits from trade". Low interest and low profit both arise from extensive commerce. Thus, if we consider the whole connection of causes and effects, interest is the barometer of the economy, and its lowness is a "sign almost infallible of the flourishing condition of a people". Translated into modern terminology, he means to say that a high development of industry and commerce tends to promote the expansion of investment and capital formation to a point at which the marginal efficiency of capital is low.

Now the expansion of industry and commerce "will require a great quantity of these metals (money) to represent a great quantity of commodities and labour". Thus, "low interest and plenty of money are in fact almost inseparable". Both are concomitant effects of a high state of industry and commerce.

"[A sudden] new acquisition of money will fall into a few hands, and be gathered into large sums, which seeks a secure revenue, either by the purchase of land or by interest... The

---

1. In his essay "Of Money" he says it is of no consequence "whether money be in a greater or less quantity. The good policy of the magistrate consists only in keeping it, if possible, still increasing; because by that means he keeps alive a spirit of industry in the nation... In my opinion, it is only in the interval or intermediate situation, between the acquisition of money and the rise in prices, that the increasing quantity of gold and silver is favourable to industry... The farmer or gardener, finding that all their commodities are taken off, apply themselves with alacrity to the raising of more:.. It is easy to trace the money in its progress through the whole commonwealth; where we shall find that it must first quicken the diligence of every individual, before it increase the price of labour."

increase of lenders above borrowers sinks the interest... But after this new mass of gold and silver has been digested, and has circulated, through the whole state, affairs will soon return to their former situation. ... The whole money may still be in the state, and make itself felt by the increase of prices."

Thus, in the end the increase in the money supply affects the price level, but not the rate of interest.[1]

The reduction of interest might indeed prove to be permanent, but not "from the increase of money, considered merely in itself". The natural effect of an increase in money "in that interval, before it raises the price of labour and provisions" is to increase industry.[2] And this increase in industry concentrates large sums in the hands of merchants and lowers the rate of interest; on the other hand, it pushes investment to a low profit rate. Thus in so far as the increase in the money supply in the *short run* stimulates industry, the effect is to promote fundamental *long-run* conditions favourable to a low rate of interest.

"Suppose four-fifths of all the money in Great Britain to be annihilated in one night... Must not the price of all labour and commodities sink in proportion?" Or suppose the opposite — money "multiplied five-fold in a night... Must not all labour and commodities rise to such an exorbitant height, that no neighbouring nation could afford to buy from us; while their commodities ... would be run in upon us, and our money would flow out." Thus, the money supply of each nation will be "nearly proportional to the art and industry each nation". The level of money is always in "proportional level to the commodities, labour, industry, and skill, which is in the several states".

Industry and commerce may indeed "be promoted by the right use of paper money. It is well known of what advantage it is to a merchant to be able to discount his bills..." As "his bank credit is equivalent to ready money, a merchant does hereby in a manner coin the goods in his warehouse ... and can, upon occasion, employ them in all payments, as if they were the current money of the country." Thus, Hume regards the monetization of private credit as advantageous to industry and commerce. Here we have an early statement of the banking principle.

Money and bank credit are useful institutions. But their importance is secondary.

"In short, a government has every reason to preserve with care its people and its manufactures. Its money, it may safely trust to the course of human affairs, without fear or jealousy. Or if it ever give attention to this latter circumstance, it ought only to be so far as it affects the former."

Here are the root ideas that permeated monetary thinking in much of the nineteenth century. Thrift and productivity determine the rate of interest; the money supply determines the level of prices. The demand for money is interest-inelastic. Internationally, gold and silver are distributed in proportion to the level of industry and commerce in each country and thereby the price levels of different countries are kept in line.

1. Changes in the quantity of money "are not immediately attended with proportionable alterations in the price of commodities. There is always an interval before matters can be adjusted to their new situation..." But in the end he thinks that "prices of commodities are always proportional to the plenty of money..."
2. This comes to much the same thing as the Wicksellian analysis: investment is stimulated when the market rate of interest falls below the productivity rate.

## IMPLICATIONS OF REAL INTEREST RATES TURNING NEGATIVE

**Negative real interest rate:** The real interest rate is the effective rate after adjusting for inflation and is considered a true measure of the cost of funds for the borrower or the return to the lender. It is calculated approximately by subtracting the rate of inflation from the nominal interest rate. When inflation is higher than the interest rate, the real interest rate becomes negative. If the one year interest rate is 8% and average inflation over this period is 10% then the real interest rate is negative 2%.

**Implication of a negative real interest rate:** Savers of lenders are losers in a negative real interest rate situation. Take the same example of bank deposit rate for one year of 8% and the average rate of inflation over this period 10%. At the end of one year, you are left with ₹ 108. But what ₹ 100 could purchase a year ago will now take ₹ 110 to purchase, so your interest earning has failed to protect your saving, because it earned a negative rate of interest, the nominal rate of 8% was lower than the rate of inflation of 10%. However, the borrowers benefit in a negative real interest rate regime. The money used to repay loan will have lesser value than the original amount borrowed because of the high inflation. In this case, the borrower should have been paying back more than ₹ 110 to give him a real return of money but he only paid ₹ 108. This is how the idea of inflating debt away has come.

**The situation in India:** The widely followed measure of inflation in India, the wholesale price index, was 10.55% for June and is expected to climb further. The rate of interest on a ten-year benchmark government paper is about 8%. This implies that the difference between the long-term interest rate and inflation is about 2.5 percentage point, or a negative real interest rate of that much.

**Is the negative real interest rate a concern?:** The real interest rates need to be seen over a longer period. The rate of inflation has been high in India in recent months, causing the real rate of interest to be negative. However, over a longer period the average inflation is likely to be much lower, even if we went by the wholesale price index. If the GDP deflator, a more comprehensive measure of inflation, was considered the inflation for the year would be lot less, which will give a positive real rate of interest.

## INTEREST RATE SWAP

**What is an interest rate swap?:** An interest rate swap is an over-the-counter (OTC) derivative instrument available in the currency market where counterparties can exchange a floating payment for a fixed payment and *vice versa* related to an interest rate. Financial institutions going for foreign borrowings usually buy interest rate swaps to hedge their interest rate exposure due to fluctuating interest rates.

These were originally created to allow multinational companies to evade exchange controls. Today, they are used to hedge against or speculate on changes in interest rates.

Interest rate swaps are also used speculatively by hedge funds or other investors who expect a change in interest rates or the relationships between them. Traditionally, fixed income investors who expected rates to fall would purchase cash bonds, whose value increased as rates fell. Today, investors with a similar view could enter a floating-for-fixed interest rate swap; as rates fall, investors would pay a lower floating rate in exchange for the same fixed rate.

**How does it work?:** In an interest rate swap, each counterparty agrees to pay either a fixed or floating rate denominated in a particular currency to the other counterparty. The fixed or floating rate is multiplied by a notional principal amount (say, $1 million). This notional amount is generally not exchanged between counterparties, but is used only for calculating the size of cash flows to be exchanged.

The most common interest rate swap is one where one counterparty A pays a fixed rate (the swap rate) to counterparty B while receiving a floating rate (usually pegged to a reference rate such as LIBOR — London Inter Bank Offered Rate).

A pays fixed rate to B (A receives floating rate)

B pays floating rate to A (B receives fixed rate).

Consider the following swap in which Party A agrees to pay Party B periodic fixed interest rate payments of 3.784%, in exchange for periodic floating interest rate payments of LIBOR + 70 bps (0.70%). There is no exchange of the principal amount and that the interest rates are on a notional principal amount. The interest payments are settled in net. The fixed rate (3.784% in this example) is referred to as the swap rate.

**What are the different types of swaps?:** Being OTC instruments, interest rate swaps can come in a huge number of varieties and can be structured to meet the specific needs of the counterparties. By far the most common are fixed-for-floating, fixed-for-fixed or floating-for-floating. The legs of the swap can be in the same currency or in different currencies. The above example is a specimen of fixed-for-floating swap. Fixed-for-fixed works the same way except that there is no change in the rate used during the date of payment, as does floating-for-floating swap.

❖❖❖

CHAPTER 8

# FINANCIAL SECTOR REFORMS

## INTRODUCTION

The financial sector plays a major role in the mobilisation and allocation of financial savings in the economy and in facilitating funds flow among the various sub-sectors. Financial institutions, instruments and the financial markets together act to transfer financial resources from net savers to net borrowers. The resultant gains to the real sector of the economy depend on the efficiency of the financial sector to perform the function of financial intermediation.

The major aim of financial sector reforms in India has been enhancing efficiency and profitability while maintaining stability to the financial sector.

The core issue of financial sector reform is to ensure that the financial services industry operates on the basis of operational flexibility and functional autonomy, with a view to enhancing efficiency, productivity and profitability. A vibrant and competitive financial system is also necessary to sustain the ongoing reform in the structural aspects of the real economy. We believe that ensuring the integrity and autonomy of operations of banks and DFIs is by far the more relevant issue at present than the question of their ownership.

The Indian banking and financial system has made commendable progress in extending its geographical spread and functional reach. The spread of the banking system has been a major factor in promoting financial intermediation in the economy and in the growth of financial savings. The credit reach also has been extensive and the banking system now caters to several million borrowers especially in agriculture and small industry. The DFIs have established themselves as major institutions that support for investment in the private sector. The last decade has witnessed considerable diversification of the money and capital markets. New financial services and instruments have appeared on the scene.

Despite this commendable progress, serious problems have emerged reflected in a decline in productivity and efficiency, and erosion of the profitability of the banking sector.

The major factors responsible for these are: *(a)* directed investments; and *(b)* directed credit programmes. In both these cases, rates of interest that were available to banks were less than the market related rates or what they could have secured from alternate deployment of funds. There has been a deterioration in the quality of the loan portfolio which in turn has come in the way of banks' income generation and enhancement of their capital funds. Inadequacy of capital has been accompanied by inadequacy of loan loss provisions.

The accounting and disclosure practices also do not always reflect the true state of affairs of banks and financial institutions. The erosion of profitability of banks has also emanated from the side of expenditure as a result of fast and massive expansion of branches, many of which are unremunerative especially in the rural areas, a considerable degree of over-manning especially in the urban and metropolitan centres and inadequate progress in updating work technology. Both management weaknesses and trade union pressures have contributed to this. There have also been weaknesses in the internal organisational structure of the banks, lack of sufficient delegation of authority and inadequate internal controls and deterioration in what is termed 'housekeeping' such as balancing of books and reconciliation of inter-branch and inter-bank entries. The DFIs also suffer from a degree of portfolio contamination. This is more pronounced in the case of the SFCs. Being smaller institutions, the internal organisational problems of the DFIs have been less acute than those of the banks. However, both banks and the DFIs have suffered from excessive administrative and political interference in individual credit decision-making and internal management. The deterioration in the financial health of the system has reached a point where unless remedial measures are taken soon, it could further erode the real value of and return on the savings entrusted to them and even have an adverse impact on depositor and investor confidence. This diagnosis of the problems indicate the lines of solution which the committee proposes with a view as much to improving the health of the system, as for making it an integral part of the ongoing process of economic reforms.

The reform approach thus seeks to consolidate the gains made in the Indian financial sector while improving the quality of the portfolio, providing greater operational flexibility and most importantly greater autonomy in the internal operations of the banks and financial institutions so as to nurture a healthy, competitive and financial sector. This will, above all else, require depoliticisation of appointments, implying at the same time a self-denial by government and the perception that it has distanced itself from the internal decision-making of the banks and the financial institutions. The proposed deregulation of the financial sector and the measures aimed at improving its health and competitive vitally would, in the Committee's view, be consistent with the steps being taken to open up the Indian economy, enable the Indian financial sector to forge closer links with the global financial markets, and enhance India's ability to take competitive advantage of the increasing international opportunities for Indian trade, industry and finance.

The major aim of financial sector reforms in India has been enhancing efficiency and profitability, while maintaining stability in the financial sector. Financial sector reforms, going ahead, will focus on bank consolidation, containing the systematic risks arising out of inter-connectedness of the banking sector with other components of the financial sector, and laying down the road map for furthering foreign banks participation.

## THE FINANCIAL SECTOR

The Indian financial sector comprises an impressive network of banks, other financial and investment institutions and a range of financial instruments, which together function in fairly developed capital and money markets. Short-term funds are mainly provided by the commercial and co-operative banking structure. Banking business is managed by twenty-eight banks in the public sector, private sector banks and RRBs. In addition to commercial banks, there is the network of co-operative banks and land development banks at state, district and block levels. With around two-thirds share in the total assets in the financial system, banks play an important role. Of late, Indian banks have also diversified into areas such as merchant banking, mutual funds, leasing and factoring.

**STRUCTURAL POLICIES IN THE FINANCIAL SECTOR**

| *Objectives* | *Measures* | *Countries* |
|---|---|---|
| To improve the monetary control system | Improvements in financial programming framework | Algeria, China, and Egypt |
| | Adequacy of monetary policy instruments; switch from direct to indirect controls | Botswana, China, Costa Rica, Hungary, Indonesia, Mauritius, the Philippines, and Sri Lanka |
| To improve the mobilization and allocation of domestic savings | Development of money and Government securities markets | Indonesia, Malaysia, Oman, Sri Lanka, Yemen, Arab Republic, and Zaire |
| | Reduction of selective credit policies; integration of unregulated financial institutions; promotion of term finance and capital market development | Costa Rica, Dominican Republic, Indonesia, Malaysia and Papua New Guinea |
| | Improvement in supervision of financial institutions and creation of deposit insurance schemes | Chile, Dominican Republic, Panama, and Trinidad and Tobago |
| | New financial institutions and instruments, and adequacy of bank regulation and legislation | Aruba, Bolivia, Hungary, Kenya, and Nepal |
| To improve the level and structure of interest rates | Reduction of interest rate subsidies and of bad debts | Bangladesh, Chile, Malaysia, Mauritania, Senegal, and Uruguay |
| | Liberalization of interest rates; introduction of prime rate or base lending rate system | Bolivia, Burundi, The Gambia, Haiti, Indonesia, Malaysia, the Philippines, and Sierra Leone |

***Source:*** International Monetary Fund.

The list under each category comprises countries which have received advice in the indicated areas, either in the context of the use of Fund resources and consultation missions, or direct Fund technical assistance. Countries receiving technical assistance through the placement of experts are not covered in the list.

Medium-and long-term finance is provided mainly by a few large development banks with all-India status, and state level institutions in the various states. For each category of term financing activity, an apex all-India development bank has been promoted — Industrial Development Bank of India, National Bank for Agriculture and Rural Development (NABARD), Export-Import Bank of India, National Housing Bank, etc. Besides these development banks, all-India investment institutions such as Unit Trust of India, Life Insurance Corporation, General Insurance Corporation also play a major role in channeling financial savings to the industrial and other sectors. There are, besides, institutions exclusively supporting tourism, small-scale industry, etc. In recent years, a number of public sector mutual funds set up by banks and financial institutions have been added to the institutional framework. Para-banking activities, mainly in the area of hire-purchase and leasing are undertaken by newly set up large number of private sector non-bank financial companies.

The vital capital market has evidenced tremendous growth in the last decade in terms of resource mobilisation, listing and market capitalisation. Activities in a network of twenty-four stock exchanges listing over six thousand companies, are being regulated by the special purpose institution — Securities and Exchange Board of India (SEBI). The development of short-term money market has, however, lagged behind that of other sub-sectors of the market. It comprises five segments — the call money market, inter-bank term deposit market, bills rediscounting market, treasury bills market and the inter-corporate funds market. Discount and Finance House of India (DFHI) a specialised money market institution has been positioned in an effort to provide liquidity to money market instruments and develop an active secondary market. The trends indicate the increasing market role of institutions in allocating resources and the growing separation of saving and investment functions of the economic units, evidencing widening and deepening of the financial system.

A feature of the Indian financial system is the dominance of public sector institutions be it in banking, term lending or insurance. The financial system has thus been subjected to a high degree of regulatory control. This regulatory mechanism, originally devised keeping in view certain socio-economic considerations, defined the various activities in the financial sector. Thus, both entry and expansion of the financial institutions remained for a long time subjected to control. Credit deployment policies were determined at the apex, with mandatory allocations for specific sectors such as government, small-scale industries, agriculture, etc. An element of cross subsidisation was introduced, providing concessionality in interest rates, within the overall framework of the administered interest rate structure. The regulatory policy and the direct controls placed in the planning process were necessary during the initial underdeveloped state of the financial sector to ensure flow of necessary funds to the socially desirable sub-sectors of the real economy.

The progress made thereafter by the financial sector in terms of growth as well as in meeting the financial needs of the economy has certainly been commendable. Banking statistics (number of offices, population per bank office, overall business growth, financial assistance to weaker sections of society, etc.), performance of term lending and investment institutions and the growing equity cult reflected in capital market activities, indicate the tremendous strides the financial sector has taken in facilitating economic growth.

In the process of this growth, the financial system, however, developed certain rigidities and deficiencies, hampering operational efficiency. In particular, the banking industry witnessed perceptible decline in productivity and profitability and a substantial increase in its Non-performing Assets (NPAs). This led to inadequate provisioning for bad and doubtful assets making the financial position of some of the banks delicate. Incidence of sickness in the industrial sector and tardy recovery of agricultural and other rural advances largely contributed to the problem, resulting in large accumulation of bank losses. The term lending and investment institutions performed better in comparison, probably due to the limited nature of their operating activities. Capital markets (both primary and secondary) also showed differing performance. The heartening response from the investing public in the capital market was not matched by removal of inadequacies in the market operations. As such, investor protection, settlement system, and inculcation of uniform trading practices left much to be desired. In the absence of a proper regulatory system and a single regulatory authority, in the aftermath of sizeable expansion in the volume of business, the market witnessed events which could not be adequately controlled. The development of the short-term money market has, besides, picked up only over the last 5 to 6 years.

Financial sector reforms in India are grounded in the belief that competitive efficiency in the real sectors of the economy will not be realised to its full potential unless the financial sector was reformed as well. Thus, the principal objective of financial sector reform was to improve the allocative efficiency of resources and accelerate the growth process of the real sector by removing structural deficiencies affecting the performance of financial institutions and financial markets.

The main thrust of reforms in the financial sector was on the creation of efficient and stable financial institutions and markets. Reforms in respect of the banking as well as non-banking financial institutions focussed on creating a deregulated environment and enabling free play of market forces while at the same time strengthening the prudential norms and the supervisory system. In the banking sector, the particular focus was on imparting operational flexibility and functional autonomy with a view to enhancing efficiency, productivity and profitability, imparting strength to the system and ensuring financial soundness. The restrictions on activities undertaken by the existing institutions were gradually relaxed and barriers to entry in the banking sector were removed. In the case of non-banking financial intermediaries, reforms focussed on removing sector-specific deficiencies. Thus, while reforms in respect of DFIs focussed on imparting market orientation to their operations by withdrawing assured sources of funds, in the case of NBFCs, the reform measures brought their asset side also under the regulation of the Reserve Bank. In the case of the insurance sector and mutual funds, reforms attempted to create a competitive environment by allowing private sector participation.

## FINANCIAL SECTOR REFORMS: THEORETICAL RATIONALE AND INTERNATIONAL EXPERIENCE

The financial system acts as an efficient conduit for allocating resources among competing uses. The role and importance of the financial sector in the process of economic growth has evolved overtime along with the changing paradigms. Till the late 1960s, the role of financial intermediaries in general, and banks in particular, in the process of economic growth of a country was largely ignored. The views on neutrality of financial intermediaries to economic growth, however, came under attack during the late

1960s. It was pointed out that there exists a strong positive correlation between financial development and economic growth of a country (McKinnon, 1973; Shaw, 1973). The McKinnon-Shaw paradigm highlighted the negative impact of 'financial repression', under which the government determined the quantum, allocation and price of credit, on the growth process. They argued that credit is not just another input and instead, credit is the engine of growth. Subsequently, the proponents of endogenous growth theories argued that with positive marginal productivity of capital, development of financial market induces economic growth in the short as well as long-run by improving efficiency of investment (Bencivenga and Smith, 1991). Under this approach, efficient financial intermediation is growth-inducing through its role in allocating financial resources in the best possible uses. This approach challenged the McKinnon-Shaw paradigm that efficient financial intermediation results in positive real interest rate and that this enhances both saving and investment and thereby economic growth.

Notwithstanding the debate over the relative significance of the channels of financial intermediation in promoting economic growth, an efficient financial system is regarded as a necessary precondition for higher growth. Several developing countries, therefore, undertook programmes for reforming their financial systems. In the initial stages of the development process, the financial sector in developing countries was characterised by directed credit allocation, interest rate restrictions and lending criteria based on social needs, etc. These policies retarded the nature of financial intermediation in developing countries and the recognition of the same paved the way for financial sector reforms.

**FINANCIAL SECTOR REFORMS: CROSS-COUNTRY EXPERIENCES — BOX : 1**

The guiding objectives of financial sector reforms in several countries were to improve financial sector efficiency while strengthening financial stability. It was believed that stable and efficient financial systems provided the foundation for implementing efficiency of investment, all of which help in achieving sustainable and higher rates of economic growth.

Cross-country experiences relating to financial sector reforms exhibited significant diversity, both overtime and across countries. Despite the evolving consensus on the underlying rationale of a robust financial system, there was no unique approach that was uniformly applied across countries. Significant differences could be observed in respect of the content, pace and sequencing of reforms, which, to some extent, were due to the reason that some countries experienced financial crises after implementation of liberalization measures.

**FINANCIAL LIBERALISATION IN SELECT COUNTRIES: 1973-2002**

| *Country* | *Year* | *Credit Controls* | *Interest Rates* | *Entry Barriers* | *Government Regulation of Operations* | *Privatisation* |
|---|---|---|---|---|---|---|
| | 1 | 2 | 3 | 4 | 5 | 6 |
| United States | 1973 | B:L; S&L:R | LL | PR | L | L |
| | 2002 | L | L | LL | L | L |
| United Kingdom | 1973 | LL | B:LL | B:LL | L | L |
| | 2002 | L | L | L | L | L |
| Korea | 1973 | R | R | R | R | R |
| | 2002 | LL | LL | B:PR NBFI:LL | PR | LL |

(Contd.)

| | | | | | | |
|---|---|---|---|---|---|---|
| Philippines | 1973 | R | R | R | PR | PR |
| | 2002 | PR | LL | LL | PR | LL |
| Thailand | 1973 | R | R | R | — | PR |
| | 2002 | LL | L | LL | — | LL |
| Argentina | 1973 | R | R | R | — | R |
| | 2002 | LL | LL | L | — | PR |
| Brazil | 1973 | R | R | R | — | PR |
| | 2002 | PR | LL | LL | — | PR |
| India | 1973 | R | R | R | R | R |
| | 2002 | LL | LL | PR | LL | PR |

L: Liberalized – A liberalized system is one where the role of the government has been largely curtailed.

LL: Largely liberalized – Largely liberalized denotes a system governed more by market forces, with government role in certain important spheres.

R: Repressed – A repressed system is one in which virtually all decisions in the relevant dimension are made by the government.

PR: Partly repressed – A partly repressed system is one where repression is not complete, but the system is closer to that end of the spectrum.

B: Banks; NBFIs: Non-banking financial institutions; S&L: Saving and Loan Associations.

*Note/Source:* The position for 1973 is from Williamson and Mahar (1998). The position for 2002 is compiled based on information from central bank websites, IMF reports, etc.

There was significant liberalization of the financial sector both in industrial and developing countries over the period 1973-2002 (Table 1). Interest rate controls were almost universally eliminated and barriers to entry for most non-bank financial institutions were lowered, and in certain instances, rationalized. Most Latin American economies eliminated directed credit programmes and interest rate controls (exceptions being Brazil and Venezuela). Competition in the commercial banking sector was permitted in Latin American economies in the late 1970s and more recently in several Asian countries. Privatisation of state-owned banks accounted for at least 40 per cent of the total banking sector assets. In several Asian (Korea, Taiwan and Indonesia) and Latin American countries (Chile and Mexico), the share of state-owned banks was higher than 70 per cent. However, recent evidence suggests a significant scaling down of government ownership in the banking sector.

As regards the pace of reforms, Asian countries like Japan, Korea, Malaysia and Indonesia followed a gradualist approach to financial liberalization in contrast to transition economies of Eastern Europe and some of the Latin American countries which adopted the 'big-bang' approach. While the Asian countries could afford a gradualist approach and maintain a system of financial repression because it did not reduce their ability to mobilise savings for economic development, some of the Southern Cone countries needed to liberalise rapidly to encourage greater mobilization of savings to finance development. The pace of liberalisation tended to be faster in the Latin American countries, although there were instances of reversal. For example, Chile first liberalised with a big-bang in the 1970s when it privatised nationalised banks and removed control on interest rates. Argentina also eliminated directed credit and interest rate controls in the late 1970s. However, both Chile and Argentina re-imposed controls during the financial crisis of the early 1980s, although they were subsequently relaxed. Chile, for instance, removed most controls by 1984 and reprivatised the nationalised

(Contd.)

banks in the mid-1980s. Argentina, on the other hand, embarked on a course of bank regulatory reform in the early 1990s albeit at a slower pace. The major elements of the reforms comprised privatisation, free entry, limited safety net support and a mix of regulatory and market discipline to ensure stable growth of the banking system during the liberalisation process (Calomiris and Powell, 2000). Mexico's liberalisation in the late 1980s was punctuated by four turning points: 1982 (exchange rate crisis and bank nationalisation ), 1988-89 (interest rate liberalisation), 1991-92 (bank privatisation) and 1994 (Tequila crisis). The financial liberalisation process culminated into transfer of ownership of state-owned banks to the private sector in 1991-92 and elimination of most of the entry barriers.

A number of countries in Asia, following the gradualist approach, progressively dismantled their directed credit programmes by introducing market-based rates on directed loans and increasing the number of categories eligible for special credit access. In Thailand, for instance, directed credit was eased in 1987 by widening the definition of agricultural credit to include wholesale and small-scale industrial activities. In Indonesia, Malaysia and South Korea, targeted lending programmes were reduced in scope, and subjected to market rates in the 1980s and the 1990s. In Philippines, however, the government exerts influence over credit allocations through commercial banks' dependence on central bank rediscount window. Indonesia, Malaysia and Philippines assumed the lead in interest rate deregulation, beginning the process in the early 1980s.

Following the macroeconomic crisis in the early 1980s in Argentina and Chile and subsequent to the initiation of financial sector reforms, a strand of literature evolved which sought to explain the failure of reforms in terms of incorrect sequencing of the reform programmes (McKinnon, 1993). According to the conventional wisdom, stable macroeconomic environment and a sound system of prudential supervision are prerequisites for domestic financial deregulation. In practice, however, several countries implemented macroeconomic reforms prior to, or in tandem with, financial liberalisation.

Chile, Peru and Turkey began financial sector deregulation under conditions of macroeconomic instability, but implemented their reforms as part of a larger stabilization effort. Argentina, Brazil and Mexico, however, deregulated their financial sectors during periods of high inflation ahead of stabilization programmes.

The apprehension that financial liberalisation is destined to breed crises has been documented in an influential study (Diaz-Alejandro, 1985). Several developing and industrial countries experienced episodes of systemic or borderline banking crises of varying magnitude and frequency, although in several instances they were not associated with financial liberalisation. Most developing countries, in particular, witnessed some financial instability, following liberalisation, including those in Latin America (Argentina, Chile, Brazil and Mexico) and Asia (Indonesia, Malaysia, Philippines, Sri Lanka, Thailand and Turkey). Banks generally found their existing loan portfolios to be less sound in a liberalised environment, because borrowers were not able to service debts due to higher interest costs or simply because implicit guarantees from government on these debts were no longer available.

Thus, the evidence suggests that there are no iron cast formulae for financial liberalisation. A strategy adopted by a country could largely depend on the initial conditions of its financial infrastructure and extent of repression, the response of monetary and credit aggregates to monetary reforms and the health of its banking sector. Recent studies indicate that banking crises tend to precipitate balance of payments crises, but not *vice versa* (Kaminsky and Reinhart, 1999). The analysis of the experience of over 50 countries during 1980-1995 reveals that banking crises are more likely to occur in liberalised financial systems, but not where the institutional environment is strong in terms of respect for the rule of law, low level of corruption and good contract enforcement (Demirguc-Kunt and Detragiache, 2002).

## POLICY INSTRUMENTS

Effective monetary control through reserve money management requires the development of adequate instruments and their proper use and co-ordination. For instance, reserve requirements for banks and other financial institutions may be ineffectual because penalties for reserve shortfalls are set too low. In any case, the lack of co-ordination of reserve requirements with the management of the discount window allows banks to borrow easily and cheaply from the central bank to meet reserve needs. (Credit is channeled by the central bank through its discount window by rediscounting particular types of eligible bills and securities). If required reserves earn little or no interest, an increase in reserve requirements may cause banks to raise effective loan rates, for example, through higher service charges and/or lower deposit rates, with adverse effects on savings mobilization and allocation. Structural measures to tighten penalties for reserve shortfalls, to improve co-ordination with the discount window, and to pay appropriate interest rates on required reserves will make reserve requirements an effective instrument of monetary control and promote the efficiency of financial intermediation.

A reform of the discount window operations of central banks can also enhance the efficiency of short-term bank liability management, and encourage the use of money markets.

The key objective of reforms in the financial sector in India has been to enhance the stability and efficiency of financial institutions. To achieve this objective, various reform measures were initiated that could be categories broadly into three main groups: enabling measures, strengthening measures and institutional measures. The enabling measure were designed to create an environment where financial intermediaries could respond optimally to market signals on the basis of commercial considerations. Salient among these included reduction in statutory pre-emptions so as to release greater funds for commercial lending, interest rate deregulation to enable price discovery, granting of operational autonomy to banks and liberalisation of the entry norms for financial intermediaries. The strengthening measures aimed at reducing the vulnerability of financial institutions in the face of fluctuations in the economic environment. These included, *inter alia,* capital adequacy, income recognition, asset classification and provisioning norms, exposure norms, improved levels of transparency, and disclosure standards. Institutional measures were aimed at creating an appropriate institutional framework conducive to development of markets and functioning of financial institutions.

## RECENT REFORMS

To analyse problems which the financial sector faced and to suggest remedial measures, various study groups and committees were set up in the recent past which went into the problems and suggested steps to vitalise the underdeveloped sub-sectors of the system to function in a deregulated environment. A major committee to go into the functioning of the system was appointed in 1985 with late Prof. S. Chakravarty as its chairman. It studied various aspects of the Indian monetary system and proposed measures to improve its functioning. The other major committee, which had a wider canvass was set up in 1991 under the chairmanship of Mr. M. Narasimham. It went into the different aspects of the entire financial system and offered suggestions to revamp it, to improve its functioning. There were also the various study groups which suggested setting up new institutions, introduction of new products, regulation of capital market institutions and, so on. Many of the recommendations of these committees and groups have been implemented; a few are at different stages of implementation.

## BANKING INSTITUTIONS

The measures adopted aim at introducing an element of competitive efficiency in the Indian banking system. It would improve their operational efficiency and strengthen the financial position of banks, which is a prerequisite of their exposure to the globalised banking environment. Banking, nine-tenth of which is in the public sector, has been subjected to administrative controls in respect of interest rates, directed lending, personnel policies, expansion of offices, etc., over the years. These controls are now sought to be eased in a gradual manner.

Both the deposit rates structure and the lending rates structure were determined by the regulatory authority in the past. In addition, banks used to be subjected to various guidelines on priority sector lending, investment in government securities, etc., which were a part of the policy to ensure that a certain percentage of credit went to specified sub-sectors. Till recently, banks were required to keep investment in government and other approved securities at 38.5% of their net demand and time liabilities by way of Statutory Liquidity Ratio (SLR), which investments in effect were banks' funds lent to the government at concessional rates. In the 'private' sector category also, banks were required to dispense 40% of credit to 'predefined' priority sectors, again most of it at concessional rates. The concessionality in interest charged and a high level of pre-empted funds, affected bank profitability adversely, despite a measure of cross-subsidisation. Under the new policy regime, the SLR has been reduced in stages. As to the interest structure, fixed rates have been done away with. Banks enjoy the freedom to offer deposit rates subject to a maximum and charge lending rate subject to a minimum on their non-priority advances. Significantly, the banks can now charge interest at commercial rates on priority advances, if the amount advanced exceeds ₹ 2,00,000. These steps should help banks shore up profitability to a large extent. In respect of larger industrial advances, the erstwhile Credit Authorisation Scheme has been replaced by a relaxed Credit Monitoring Arrangement which permits individual banks to avail of the opportunity to tone up their credit appraisal skills.

To rationalise banking presence on efficient lines, banks have been given permission to open, close or relocate branches in non-rural areas without prior approval of the Reserve Bank of India subject to their fulfilling certain norms, thus virtually doing away with the branch licensing policy. A proposal is also under active consideration to segregate the regional rural bank subsidiaries of the commercial banks and reorganise them into separate units with different norms to judge their viability.

To restore financial health of banks, prudential norms have been set, adherence to which will reflect, in the first phase, the true picture of their financial condition. Guidelines have been issued on the transparency of their financial statements, on income recognition, asset classification as well as on provisioning for bad and doubtful assets. Simultaneously, capital adequacy norms have been prescribed for various banks (please see box given below).

The guidelines are to be implemented over a period of time. One other important aspect of banks' health which will need to be dealt with is the present accumulation of their Non-performing Assets (NPAs) and their present comparatively weak capital base. It is essential that the accumulated NPAs be removed from the banks' balance sheets by means of a mechanism like the Asset Reconstruction Fund, recommended by the Narasimham Committee. This undoubtedly would involve substantial separate funding. But, without it, touching capital adequacy norms will pose a very difficult problem for banks.

**BANK CAPITAL ADEQUACY** **BOX : 2**

In the past, Indian banks were subjected to varying capital requirements stipulated under the statutes. On the pattern of Basle Committee recommendations, RBI has now stipulated that commercial banks should attain capital adequacy in a phased manner. For the purpose, guidelines have been issued on risk weights to be assigned to assets (both funded and off-balances sheet) and banks are required to maintain minimum unimpaired capital funds to conform to the set norms. For Indian banks which have branches abroad, the norm of 8 per cent was to be met by March 31, 1994, foreign banks operating in India were to meet this norm by March 31, 1993. Other Indian banks were asked to attain the adequacy norm of 4 per cent by March 31, 1993 (tier 1 capital should not be less than 50 per cent of the total capital) and the 8 per cent norm by March 31, 1996. The total tier 11 elements will be limited to a maximum of 100 per cent of total tier 1. Banks were also advised to review the existing level of capital funds *vis-a-vis* the prescribed level and plan increase in capital funds in a phased manner.

A major structural change in our financial system is the infusion of competition. The enabling conditions for a more competitive environment initially took the form of shifts in the policy regime. Statutory pre-emptions were progressively lowered, interest rates were deregulated and restrictions on entry and exit were eased. Financial markets were developed to enable financial intermediaries to deal in assets and liabilities of varying maturities and risk profiles. Activity restrictions were eased and banks can now undertake various types of activities reserved earlier for development financial institutions. Likewise, the term-lending financial institutions have been allowed to undertake working capital financing. Elements of this growing convergence have determined the pace and sequencing of the approach to universal banking in the recent years.

Within the banking system, there is heightened competition with the introduction of new generation private sector banks. Foreign banks have also been a source of competition, at least potentially, given their use of sophisticated technology, risk monitoring analysis and exposure management. In recent years, the policy thrust has been to level the playing field for domestic and foreign banks. For example, foreign banks that were earlier allowed to operate only branches but not subsidiaries, are now free to choose to set up either branches or subsidiaries under common banking regulations including lending norms. Appropriate legislative changes are also under consideration of the government. Foreign direct investment up to 49% has been allowed in private sector banks and up to 20% in nationalized banks. Guidelines have been issued for the entry of banks into insurance business for providing infrastructure and services support without any contingent liability.

## ISSUES IN SUPERVISION AND REGULATION

Recent international financial developments have underscored the critical role of the regulatory and supervisory function in ensuring the health and stability of the financial system. There is now a worldwide debate on how to strengthen financial regulation even further, including proactively, to contend with the dangers posed by creative accounting practices, even as the depressed state of economic activity exerts conflicting pulls on the extent of supervisory rigour. At the same time, the impact of technological advancement, financial liberalisation and the degree of integration between domestic and international financial markets has rendered the conduct of oversight of the financial system a highly complex task.

Regulatory and supervisory authorities need to be regarded as providing a range of services to the community. This includes the establishment of specific rules of behaviour for participants in the financial system, monitoring the observance of the rules, and general supervision of the behaviour of financial entities. The primary need for regulation arises from the fact that consumers of financial services are not in a position to evaluated the soundness and safety of financial entities since even the most stringent laws regarding enforceability of contracts cannot protect for post-contract-signing behaviour. Therefore, the rationale for financial regulation lies in the economic costs imposed on society by the external effects of financial market failure which can threaten systemic stability. There is also a potential for gridlocks in the financial system due to adverse selection and moral hazard problems. At the same time, substantial benefits can accrue from correction of market imperfections, reduced transaction costs, and in general, providing people with a financial system they can trust.

In India, progressive strengthening of the regulatory and supervisory framework has been a key element of financial sector reforms since their inception. There has been progress in achieving international best practices in banking supervision and this has been noted even convergence with the best practices, fine-turning is undertaken keeping in view the country-specific circumstances. An example of this is the approach being evolved towards consolidated supervision and the compliance of banks with accounting standards.

In recent years, there has been a shift in emphasis from microregulation to macro-management, supported by a tightening of prudential norms and improvements in the functioning of financial markets. A clearer definition of the regulatory role of the Reserve Bank is also being considered within the broader debate on the conflict of interest between ownership and regulation. The supervisory strategy of the Board for Financial Supervision, which is entrusted with the supervision of banks, all-India financial institutions, non-bank financial companies and systemically important institutions, consists of combining a restructured system of onsite inspection with off-site surveillance, enhancing the role of external auditors and strengthening corporate governance, internal controls and audit information on exposure to sensitive sectors, market risks and macro-prudential early warning indicators. Banks need to prepare for switching to risk-based supervision by 2003 by identifying information gaps in the compilation of risk profiles and training to personnel. The supervisory follow-up process will then involve a monitorable action plan including remedial actions and timely corrective steps.

Banks are being encouraged to improve the reliability and robustness of their risk management, management information and supervisory reporting systems. A scheme of prompt corrective action based on early warning triggers is being developed as a supervisory tool. Trigger points would be set for three parameters — capital, non-performing assets, return on assets — and for each trigger a set of mandatory and discretionary prompt corrective actions would be laid down. Financial soundness indicators have been proposed for monitoring the health and soundness of financial institutions and markets. The legal reforms to enable the regulatory and supervisory regime to keep pace with advancements in information and communication technology. The envisaged reforms relate to electronic cheques, cheque truncation, securitisation and reconstruction of financial assets, the payment system and money laundering. With regard to the co-operative banking sector, the Reserve Bank has proposed that there is a need for an apex supervisory body to deal with the existing regulatory overlap among multiple agencies. In respect of the financial institutions, the Reserve Bank has been in favour of divesting all or part of its holdings to mitigate the conflict of interest that could potentially arise in regulating the entities. However, it is necessary to recognise that there are distinct limits to what regulation and supervision can achieve. In particular, it does not provide a fool-proof of assured contract of safety and does not absolve either management or consumers of their responsibilities.

## CAPITAL MARKET

Reforms in financial markets focussed on removal of structural bottlenecks, introduction of new players/instruments, free pricing of financial assets, relaxation of quantitative restrictions, improvement in trading, clearing and settlement practices, more transparency, etc. Reforms encompassed regulatory and legal changes, building of institutional infrastructure, refinement of market microstructure and technological upgradation. In the various financial market segments, reforms aimed at creating liquidity and depth and an efficient price discovery process.

With activity on the capital market increasing, consistent with government's liberalisation policy in other spheres, liberalised operations were permitted on the capital market and the market was opened to potential global investment. Over the past 3-4 years, major liberalisation measures were taken in this regard.

(*a*) The office of the controller of capital issues was disbanded. Corporates are now allowed to enter the market directly, without prior approval. For the purpose of control and regulation in the process, SEBI has laid down certain guidelines for disclosures, etc.

(*b*) A new company set up by an existing company with a five-year track record of consistent profitability is now free to price its issue (in the past, such issues used to be at par). Similarly, private or closely held companies, with a 3-year track record of consistent profitability, can now price their issues freely.

(*c*) Stringent disclosure norms have been prescribed for compliance by corporates by SEBI.

(*d*) For debentures, companies are now allowed to determine interest rates, the premium amount on fully convertible debentures, etc. Credit rating has been made mandatory for issue of debentures or any debt instrument by a company.

(*e*) The capital market has now been opened to foreign institutional investors. An earlier issue of this publication carried a feature on the scheme.

(*f*) New institutions, *viz.*, Stock Holding Corporation of India Ltd., Over the Counter Exchange of India (OTCEI) have been set up to cater to investor requirements and improve the working of stock exchanges.

**INCOME RECOGNITION, ASSET CLASSIFICATION AND PROVISIONING FOR BAD ASSETS** — **BOX : 3**

With a view to bringing consistency and uniformity in the accounting policies of all the banks, so as to reflect the real position of banks' financial performance and strength, guidelines have been issued for compliance by banks in a phased manner, in three years beginning 1992-93.

Interest income on loan assets is now to be reckoned on realisation basis and not on accrual basis, as per standard international accounting practice. Some banks (e.g., State Bank of India) have already been following the 'realisation' practice for quite sometime. Income from advances in respect of codes five to eight is not recognised until it is realised. The new guidelines clearly define the procedure for classifying advances into 'past due' and 'non-performing' for income recognition.

Similarly, for provisioning for loan losses, detailed guidelines have been issued to banks. Assets are to be classified into four categories, *viz.*, standard, substandard, doubtful and loss assets. Instructions for provisioning in respect of assets falling under the categories substandard, doubtful and loss assets have been issued. Separate instructions have also been issued for provisioning for losses on investment and other assets.

With growing equity cult and investment awareness among savers, the capital market is poised to play a much enlarged role in the financial sector.

In the short-term money market, many new instruments have been introduced such as certificates of deposit, commercial paper, up to 364 days treasury bills, etc. To regulate activities in the money market, which is not as developed as the capital market, Discount and Finance House of India was set up. Commercial banks and financial institutions have been permitted to set up Money Market Mutual Funds. Steps have also been taken to regulate the activities of Mutual Funds set up by banks and financial institutions. They have been brought under the purview of SEBI.

## PRIVATE SECTOR NON-BANK FINANCIAL COMPANIES (NBFCs)

A committee recently went into the functioning of NBFCs and its recommendations are under consideration. Major recommendations are: enactment of suitable new legislation, compulsory registration with SEBI for NBFCs of certain minimum size, stipulations regarding profit appropriation, risk exposure, portfolio management, etc. A policy announcement is expected shortly.

The financial sector plays an important role as fulcrum for the activities in the real sector of the economy. It has to perform its functions most efficiently. Alive to this need, many structural and operational reforms have been and are being implemented and the financial system is being liberalised to let market forces determine their operational efficiency. The sector has an ambitious agenda ahead whose objective is a vibrant, internationally competitive financial system which is adequately responsive to the needs of India's economic and social development.

The financial sector has a vital role in promoting efficiency and growth. It intermediates in the flow of funds from those who want to save a part of their income to those who want to invest in productive assets. The efficiency of intermediating depends on the width, depth and diversity of the financial system. Till about two decades ago, a large part of household savings was either invested directly in physical assets or put in bank deposits and small saving schemes of the government. Since late eighties, however, equity market started playing an important role. Other markets such as the medium to long-term debt markets and short-term money market remained relatively segmented and underdeveloped. In the past decades, the government and its subsidiary institutions and agencies had an overwhelming and all encompassing role, which has played a part in slowing the evolution and development of these markets. The extensive system of controls, rules, regulations and procedures, directly or indirectly affected the development of these markets.

Major problems in the financial system were lack of flexibility in intermediary behaviour and segmentation of various markets and sets of financial intermediaries. Well developed markets are inter-connected; demand-supply imbalances in one market overflow into related markets, thereby dampening shocks and disturbances. The interconnection also ensures that interest rates and returns in any market, reflect the broad demand supply conditions in the overall market of savings. A rise in the demands for funds for investment, above the existing flow of funds from savings, leads to rise in the interest rate or rate of return in all markets. The time lag may differ from market-to-market depending on economic factors. Conversely, a decline in demand for funds for investment below savings leads to a fall in interest rates across the board. This does not happen in segmented markets. Adjustment in interest rates is also delayed by the slow speed of response of intermediaries and their lack of flexibility.

## DEREGULATION OF INTEREST RATES

Rationalisation of the interest rate structure has been carried out gradually with the ultimate objective of total deregulation of interest rates. The most important reform in interest rate structure was the deregulation of lending rates on advances above ₹ 2 lakh. With predominant portion of loans falling in this category, banks have been given freedom to fix the interest rates, depending upon the risk-perception of the loan. For this, banks are to evolve a Prime Lending Rate (PLR) which will be the rate offered to the first-class clients of the banks and peg the interest rates to be charged for other borrowers to this base rate. Banks have been required to declare the maximum spread they earn over the PLR. Loans in the ₹ 25,000 - ₹ 2 lakh category are to be charged at PLR.

In order to switch to signal-based tools of monetary control, the RBI has more recently activated the bank rate which is the rate at which the central bank discounts eligible bills. Interest rates are getting gradually linked to the bank rate and with inflation at low levels in the recent period, the bank rate has been reduced to 7%. Keeping with such a falling interest rate regime, many banks have also reduced their PLR to the lowest at 1-1.5%. Loans up to ₹ 2 lakh will be charged not beyond PLR. More recently, keeping with international practice, RBI has provided freedom to banks to provide loans at sub-PLR rates to exporters and other creditworthy borrowers. Thus, lending rates have been deregulated for all loans and advances excepting those under Differential Rate of Interest (DRI) scheme, export credit and advances up to ₹ 2 lakh. Banks have also been permitted to announce their prime term lending rate (PTLR) for term loans over ₹ 2 lakh.

In respect of deposit rates also, interest rates have been mostly deregulated with banks given freedom to determine interest rates on term deposits of all tenors. Interest rates on saving deposits, however, continue to be regulated and this is also expected to be deregulated eventually.

Thus, the process of deregulation of interest rates has been more or less achieved, save for certain categories of loans and saving deposits. The deregulation process during the last decade has provided valuable lessons to banks, particularly in regard to the cost-consciousness in resource mobilisation.

## DIRECTED CREDIT AND RURAL FINANCE

Considering the contribution of agriculture and the rural sector to the national economy, a multi-agency approach to rural credit and development has been adopted. The rural credit system in the Indian context has been a product of both *evolution* and active *intervention* by the government. Bank credit to the rural sectors are denominated under "Priority Sector" credit under which various target groups of beneficiaries are included. These *inter alia* include credit to agriculture and allied activities, small-scale industries, credit to weaker sections, professionals and self-employed. At the end of March 2001, lending to priority sector credit extended by public sector banks amounted to ₹ 1,47,478 crore and formed 43.2% of net bank credit as against the national goal of 40%. Advances to agriculture stood at ₹ 54,100 crore, while SSI credit was to the tune of ₹ 48,000 crore.

Important changes have been brought in the definition of priority sector by broadening the coverage and combining sub-goal relating to direct/indirect agriculture credit. Concessionality element in interest rates on these loans have also been largely done away thereby reducing the burden of cross-subsidisation. To provide a level playing field, foreign banks are also now required to dispense PS credit as will be the new private sector banks. Balancing social orientation with achievement of adequate profits is a challenge before the banks.

## FINANCIAL SUPERVISION

With deregulation, the supervisory role of the Reserve Bank of India has been enhanced. Following the recommendations of the Narasimham Committee, a separate Board for Supervision (BFS) has been established. Besides, a Department of Supervision (DoS) headed by a Deputy Governor has been established. The DoS has been entrusted with the task of supervising the banks and other non-banking financial companies. A process of rating banks on the *CAMELS (Capital Adequacy, Management, Earnings, Liquidity and Systems)* format has been put in place.

Keeping with the shift towards prudential regulation, emphasis is being laid on off-site supervision which will supplement onsite supervision. The offsite supervision system comprises 12 returns focussing on the supervisory concerns like capital adequacy, asset quality, credit concentration, connected lending, risk exposure, etc. The role of reporting accountants has been enhanced so as to improve the authenticity of the data reported, while measures have also been initiated to strengthen internal governance in banks. Particular mention may be made of the system of Concurrent Audit of large branches of banks and the constitution of the Audit Committee of the Board (ACB). Banks have already the system of Executive Committee (EC) and Management Committee (MC) to make important operational decisions.

Following the adoption of international financial standards and codes, the RBI has put in place a system of Prompt Corrective Action (PCA) which will help in addressing financial distress in banks in a proactive manner. Under the PCA framework, which is modelled on the lines existing in USA, three main parameters have been proposed *viz.*, Capital to Risk Asset Ratio (CRAR), Net NPAs and Return on Asset (RoA). Trigger points have been set up under these three parameters and for every trigger point, a set of mandatory and discretionary preventive corrective actions have been prescribed. The PCA will pre-empt further deterioration in the soundness of the banks and bring about improvement in their functioning. RBI has also proposed to move over to risk-based supervision which aims at allocation of supervisory resources according to the risk perception of the supervised institution. This will also facilitate adoption of one of the pillars of the New Capital Accord, *viz.,* Supervisory Review. Also, the RBI has proposed to adopt Consolidated Supervision which will allow bank supervisors to get a consolidated view of the operations of banking groups, apart from that of the parent bank.

## FINANCIAL MARKET INTERLINKAGES

Indian financial market till recently was characterized by market segmentation among its various constituents on account of variety of regulations including barriers to entry. This impaired free flow of resources. Since the introduction of reform measures in early 1990s, broad segments of the market, viz., money market, Government securities market, and foreign exchange market have responded favourably with growing interlinkages among them, thus facilitating faster liquidity pass-through. This is borne out by the fact that improvements in liquidity in 1996-97 were translated in significant softening of various money market rates, interest rates on Government Papers, particularly those on shorter end, and forward premia in the foreign exchange market.

The increasing complementarity between credit market and capital market on the one hand, and credit market and external sources of financing on the other, has become evident in the availability of a wider choice among alternate sources of funds to the corporates. The integration between yield rates of Government Papers and those of other debt market instrument is, however, currently at a formative stage on account of, *inter alia*, narrow investor base and lack of depth in secondary markets. While these changes are symptomatic of a greater interplay of market forces, the thrust of the present policy is on elimination of the factors constraining free flow of resources among these segments and to facilitate opportunities for larger arbitrage, so that pricing and allocation of resources become more efficient. These interlinkages, however, have also added another dimension to the conduct of monetary policy in view of the necessity to assess, on a continuous basis, the liquidity in the system and to adopt appropriate measures minimizing volatility in financial markets.

## CHALLENGES OF FINANCIAL SECTOR

The India financial system has shown considerable widening and deepening since the initiation of the present phase of financial sector reforms in 1992-93. In the years to come, the financial sector would grow not only in size but also in complexity as the forces of reform gather momentum. Over the last few years, the macropolicy framework conducive to growth and development of the financial system has been put in place. Now a range of issues relating to micromanagement need to be addressed. In this regard, improving organizational effectiveness of banks and financial institutions assumes importance.

Risk management is an important area where improvements are needed. All major components of risk, *viz.*, credit risk, interest rate risk and foreign exchange risk will become much more critical than in the past. Credit risk will call for tackling the risk of non-performance and non-repayment by improving management efficiency. For managing interest rate risk, necessity expertise will have to be developed for asset-liability management. Exchange rate risk will call for developing appropriate risk-hedging techniques. Banks and financial institutions, therefore, need to develop relevant expertise in risk management backed by appropriate management information system and sound treasury management framework.

From the policy perspective, maintaining integrity and credibility of financial entities is a crucial pre-requisite for smooth functioning of the financial system. In a competitive environment wherein profits are subject to pressures from assets as well as liability sides, financial entities often tend to venture into new areas of activities which are disproportionately risky relative to capital deployed, which may, if unimpeded, affect the financial system. For avoiding such occurrence, strict adherence to prudential norms and effective system of supervision are necessary.

Over the last few years, Indian financial system has been going through a process of transformation. To match with the changing environment, the financial entities have to readjust their system of functioning. It calls for shifting emphasis from traditional areas of financing and venturing into new areas, improving efficiency level by inclusion of trained manpower and restructuring their organizations.

The reform process so far can be considered as first phase of reform. The thrust of the second phase of reforms is on improvement in the organizational effectiveness of banks and other financial entities. More specifically, future trends of banking development will be: (*i*) greater specialization by banks in different niches of the market such as retail, agriculture, export, small-scale and corporate sector, (*ii*) greater reliance on non-fund business such as advisory and consultancy services, guarantee and custody services, (*iii*) greater overlap in product coverage between commercial banks and non-bank financial intermediaries, (*iv*) greater financial disintermediation with large companies accessing securities debt domestically and in the financial market abroad. The areas needing special attention are: asset-liability management, risk management, ability to work under deregulated interest rate environment, customer-service and housekeeping. In other words, the banks are to revamp their structure and system of functioning to meet the challenges of reform.

## THE SECOND PHASE

The first phase of India's financial reforms highlighted above may be termed as "Curative" inasmuch as they were addressed to the issue of cleansing the balance sheet of banks and putting them on recovery path. The second generation reforms will be "Preventive", aimed at building a strong and robust banking system which can withstand the pressures of globalisation.

The broad tenor of the recommendations of the second Narasimham Committee (1998) is to move towards universal banking. This view has also been echoed by the RBI also. The opening of the Indian insurance sector will usher in bancassurance. The Development Finance Institutions (DFIs) like IDBI, ICICI have moved for converting themselves into universal banks. They have already set up commercial bank ventures. Commercial banks, especially in the private sector, have entered the insurance business with joint ventures. Some of the public sector banks have also taken up distribution of insurance products, so as to realise cross-sell opportunities by leveraging on their large branch network. In a way, it also indicates that the Indian banking system is not immune from the trends holding sway in the global financial scenario.

It has been suggested that the twin forces of consolidation and convergence need to be reckoned in the Indian context. Possibilities of convergence have been envisaged through universal banking to lead to one-stop financial supermarkets providing a range of services such as commercial, merchant and investment banking and even insurance. Risk diversification is also expected to be achieved through convergence resulting in strengthening of the system. In essence, the suggestions are aimed at establishing financial conglomerates through a process of mergers and diversification.

The first and foremost condition for attainment of capital account convertibility will be strengthening the banking system, which in turn would call for higher size of balance sheet so that Indian banks can withstand the pressures of international competition. But it is felt that attainment of bigger size should not be seen as a major driver of consolidation, especially from the point of view of systemic soundness.

At the same time, supervisory structure will have to allow financial diversification and innovation while attempting to contain risks within individual financial affiliates and preferably prevent any spillage of financial difficulties originating in a non-bank affiliate overflowing into the parent bank. It may be mentioned that Reserve Bank of India, following the BIS model has started moving towards the *Three-Pillar Approach* to regulation by strengthening internal governance, official oversight and market discipline.

With interest rates more or less deregulated, competition gaining is apace in different market segments. So far, the public sector banks have been beneficiaries of state protection and rule-based regulation and direction from the monetary authority. With the reforms and the gradual freedom that they have now been bestowed with, adjustment to the market-led conditions will have to be completed. The logical outcome of the strategy of deregulation and competition will be financial innovations and introduction of risk hedging mechanisms.

The process of financial innovations has also commenced recently with the introduction of interest rate swaps. But this needs to be followed up by other derivative instruments. However, development of full-fledged OTC market will take longer time. Near absence of technology and skills have impaired the development of such markets and these impediments cannot just be wished away. There is a need to systematically address the structural issues so that the financial markets can attain full integration. With suitable supervisory structure including proper legal systems and investor protection measures, Indian financial market can graduate from an "emerging" market to an "efficient" market. It may be noted that the bi-annual Monetary and Credit Policy announced by the RBI in the recent period has shown a pronounced shift towards addressing the structural issues.

As part of rationalisation of manpower in public sector banks, the Narasimham Committee has suggested scheme for voluntary separation. Following the government's encouragement, public sector banks have implemented, the Voluntary Retirement Scheme (VRS). This has been a major step as this was one of the most contentious issues facing the banking industry. Nearly one lakh employees of banks, constituting about 11% of the total staff strength have accepted VRS, the severance package has been estimated to cost over ₹ 10,000 crore. Although, banks have been allowed to amortise the VRS outgo over a period of five years, the financial burden has been significant. This has reflected in the profit performance of most of the banks during 2000-01. No doubt, the reduction in staff is likely to reduce establishment expenses over the medium-term. With this, the 'golden handshake' has been accepted as a downsizing (rightsizing) tool in the public sector. The real managerial challenge lies in the aftermath of the VRS. Firstly, rationalisation of manpower will have to be achieved at the earliest so that the vacuum arising out of the exit of employees is filled up. This could also require relocation of staff in large numbers. Secondly, this could lead to 'delayering' aimed at cutting down organisational tiers and closure of unviable branches and merger of branches. With interest rates moving southwards, banks will have to learn to work with leaner staff and thinner margins. Banks should also ensure that due to shortage of manpower, the quality of customer-service does not suffer. In balance, it appears that VRS could at best provide a partial solution to the issue of reduction in intermediation costs as banks which are burdened with a backlog of NPAs will not be in a position to cut interest rates to the desired extent.

But so far, the most challenging task before banks in the post-VRS situation will be changing the mindset of employees to face the competitive pressures. This will call for thorough reorientation of the HR initiatives in the banks. The HR strategy, *inter alia,* will have to deal with career path, provision of incentives for better performance, training in areas like risk management, technology, marketing, relationship management, etc. In other words, employees should be able to adopt a commercial orientation to business so that they can service existing clients well and recruit new customers.

The reduction in manpower could also give a push to the use of technology. Public sector banks have been relatively late entrants in respect of technology, with the result, their level of technology absorption has been low. However, recognising the need for using IT, the banks have gone for large-scale computerisation of branches in a rapid pace. Almost all the public sector banks have been able to capture 70% of their business through computerisation in compliance with the guidelines of the Central Vigilance Commission. They are offering various electronic banking products like Electronic Fund Transfer (EFT), Electronic Clearing Services, Electronic Data Interchange, etc. Besides, as part of alternative channels of delivery, they have established ATMs and in a limited scale offer telebanking and remote access facility to customers. Some of the banks have also established connectivity between select branches and provide "Anytime Anywhere" banking. However, considering the vast customer base they serve, such strategies are inadequate. Further lack of standardisation and non-availability of a reliable and safe inter-bank and intra-bank communication backbone have hampered any significant development of technology. With the establishment of INFINET (Indian Financial Network) by RBI, using V-SAT technology has begun. The INFINET will provide inter-bank connectivity and would eventually help introduction of various electronic banking products addressed to different market segments. It is also envisaged that the implementation of the Real Time Gross Settlement (RTGS) system will be completed soon bringing the payment systems in the country on par with other developed countries. It may be mentioned that the Information Technology Bill, 1999 *inter alia* provides for legal recognition of electronic records, digital signatures and books of account maintained in electronic form by a bank.

While the efforts of banks to evolve alternative channels of service delivery like ATMs, internet banking, etc., is laudable, adding another channel of delivery without pruning the existing channels like branch will only add to overheads. Since electronic service channels will drastically cut costs of transactions, banks will be required to optimise their branch network.

Closely linked to the use of technology is innovations. In fact, in the developed economies, technology has been a key-driver of financial innovations. It was the advancement in computing and communications technology that spurred the growth of derivative instruments and cross-border transactions. In fact, technology is credited with 'ending geography', as funds today flow in a seamless world. In fact, unbundling of risks has become possible by use of technology-based solutions, a task which derivatives perform. As the process of deregulation is pursued and structural barriers are lowered, new opportunities will emerge. But in every opportunity, there is an inherent risk as well. Banks cannot perform in a competitive environment unless there are means of mitigating the inherent risks. Derivative instruments like swaps, options, futures, etc., enable such risk mitigation. As the Indian financial market moves towards more sophistication, some of these instruments have emerged as in the case of interest rate swaps, futures, etc. Securitisation is in its infancy. But there is a need for more such instruments considering globalisation of the corporate sector and as the Indian economy integrates with the world economy. Acquiring the skills to offer such products will pose a major challenge to the public sector banks. But as mentioned earlier, development of full-fledged OTC markets will take sometime till the structural rigidities in the financial markets are addressed.

At the retail level, public sector banks will have to make further inroads into electronic banking. It could be through card-based mechanisms like Stored-value products (Smart Cards), internet-based banking, telebanking, remote banking, etc. This will lead to innovative technology-based products and services.

As the Indian banks move gradually towards universal banking and as they position themselves as financial service providers, banking business is getting redefined. Technology is unsettling the earlier business processes and customer behaviour is undergoing change. To survive under these conditions, the public sector banks will have to undertake business process re-engineering, redefine their strategy and align their organisational structure. They have to understand their core competencies and dovetail their strategies to exploit such strengths. Besides, banks will have to develop IT and HR strategies which are aligned to the overall business strategy. Banks which are successful in restructuring their operations will be better placed to face the onslaught of competition.

## CONTINUING PROCESS

There can be no finite end to the process of financial sector reform and liberalisation. Financial sector reform is a process rather than an event. Strengthening the financial system has to be a continuing effort. If India has been spared the ravages of the type of financial crisis that has overtaken some countries as far apart as East Asia, Russia and some Latin American countries, it is because of an element of prudence that has marked our policies. Our banks have not been exposed to lending to the bubble sectors such as real estate and the stock market nor have they been involved in the dangerous type of assets, liability mismatches that characterised the financial systems in some East Asian countries.

The Indian financial services sector is witnessing unprecedented changes, fuelled by economic deregulation and technological and financial innovation. The emergence of the internet as an alternative service delivery platform has profound implications for the way that business is conducted. The availability of online real-time information implies considerably lower switching costs for customers and places a premium on customer retention. Also, traditional entry barriers are rendered redundant to a large extent. As a result, traditional entities increasingly have to focus on technology adoption as a means of retaining competitive advantage.

The internet has changed the competitive dynamics of the financial services business in the United States with nearly all traditional service providers setting up parallel online delivery channels. Competition has been heightened by the emergence of certain internet-only banks and online brokerage service providers. However, the internet has not yet had the same kind of impact in India, owing to the absence of an enabling regulatory framework and a lack of adequate infrastructure, resulting in low levels of internet penetration particularly in rural areas.

Following a decade of reform, the Indian financial sector is gradually moving towards attainment of global standards, through the proactive role played by the RBI and other regulatory bodies. The RBI has adopted the Core Principles for Effective Banking Supervision suggested by the Basle Committee and is working out further improvements to prudential norms, particularly in the areas relating to asset classification and provisioning standards. It has also brought disclosure standards almost at par with global best practices by requiring data on important performance indicators including provisions and non-performing loans to be added as notes to accounts. In a free-interest-rate regime, asset-liability management (ALM) is of paramount importance, and the RBI has instituted an ALM reporting system beginning this financial year. Further, the RBI has also moved towards more stringent capital adequacy norms and adopted the CAMELS (capital adequacy, asset quality, management, earnings, liquidity and systems and control) system for evaluating the soundness of banks. All these measures are aimed at ensuring the stability and health of the Indian financial system, which is imperative in a global financial environment marked by increasing capital mobility.

## FINANCIAL REFORMS VS. ECONOMIC REFORMS

The financial sector reforms in India is an integral part of the overall programme of economic reforms aimed at improving productivity and efficiency. A major lesson to be learnt from the experiences of other countries which have gone through a programme of financial sector reform is that reforms are successful only if accompanied by fiscal consolidation, moderate inflation and no sharp appreciation in the real effective interest rate. The problem into which the financial sector reforms ran into in the Southern countries were because of uncontrolled inflation and sharp appreciation in real exchange rates. In those circumstances, interest rate deregulation faced even more difficulties. Also, in those countries, no effective prudential guidelines had been put in place either prior to or simultaneous with the introduction of the reforms.

On the contrary, the Indian financial sector reform has gone hand-in-hand with fiscal reforms, trade reforms and exchange rate reforms. The three major building blocks of the financial sector reform in our country have been: (*i*) removing or relaxing the external constraints; (*ii*) introduction of prudential norms; and (*iii*) institutional strengthening. The chief merit of our reform process has been the cautious sequencing of reforms and the consistent and the mutually reinforcing character of the various measures taken. Even as the new prudential norms are reportedly being introduced, the capital base of the banks has been strengthened and organisational improvements are said to be in place.

Improving the profitability and viability of banks is only one aspect of enhancing their performance. The other is how adequately and satisfactorily banks are able to meet the demand of customers. The ultimate test of success of the financial sector reforms is truly customer satisfaction; customer — as a borrower and a depositor. Through the various reform measures, we are laying the foundation for an efficient and a well-functioning banking system. A renewed and a reinvigorated banking system can play an important role in accelerating economic growth. Significant changes have already taken place. It has however miles to go. But the steps that are being taken are in the right direction. The first phase of the banking sector reform concentrated on such factors as pre-emptions, interest rate structure, prudential norms and supervisory oversight. The second phase of banking reform must lay stress on the improvement of the organisational effectiveness of banks, for which the initiative has to come largely from banks themselves.

The financial system should have to redouble efforts to adapt to the advances in technology which are changing the contours of financial intermediation worldwide. Unless they catch up, the technology lag could widen with adverse implications for efficiency and costs, the system also need to imbue our financial institutions with flexibility to absorb and adapt to institutional change. Banks must shed their inward-looking focus and develop an outward orientation. And, most important of all, we have to invest more resources into human resource development with a focus on the quality, timeliness and delivery of financial services. The human resource model of the future will require professionals to be both driving and anticipating change, understanding the complexities of the new business environment and forces shaping it.

In financial systems worldwide, today's buzzwords are competition, consolidation and stability. Proactive strengthening of prudential regulations, enhanced transparency and accountability, initiatives in setting best practices of corporate governance, and comprehensive, sound and effective regulation and supervision have together played a key role in creating a secure and conducive environment for the functioning of the financial system. There is currently a strong emphasis on upgrading the technological infrastructure for our financial institutions and markets. This is expected to provide significant gains in terms of the efficiency and cost of intermediation. The full benefits of technological transformation, especially in terms of dealing with the vulnerabilities that persist in our system, will hinge upon enabling changes in the legal architecture.

Financial sector reforms have supported the transition of the Indian economy to a higher growth path while significantly improving the stability of the financial system. In comparison of the pre-reform period, the Indian financial system today is more stable and efficient. However, the gains of the past decade have to be consolidated, so that these could be translated to drive the institutions, markets and practices into a mature financial system that can meet the challenges of sustaining India on a higher growth trajectory. The financial system would, therefore, not only need to be stable but would also need to support still higher levels of planned investments by channeling financial resources more efficiently from deficit to surplus sectors. The banks would need to reassess their core banking business to view how best they could undertake maturity transformation to step up the lendable resources in support of real economic activity. Competitive pressures as well as prudential regulatory requirements have made banks risk-averse and their investment in relatively risk-free gilt instruments have far exceeded the stipulated requirements. The behaviour and strategies of bank business would need to change from the present so that they can factor in their own risk assessment even while performing their core activities. There is a need to ensure long-term finance to support development and growth in the economy, even as restructuring takes place through mergers and universal banking. Also, the functioning of the capital markets requires to be toned up so that the levels of primary resource mobilisation seen in the early years of reform period are reached and perhaps surpassed. The key to attaining higher levels of investments by way of direct finance routed through capital markets lie in bringing about institutional improvement. Improved corporate governance practices can go a long way in bringing the retail investors back to capital markets. Institutional reforms supporting risk capital is important in broad-basing the entrepreneurship culture in the economy. While financial sector reforms till date have been helpful, more needs to be done so that greater gains from the financial sector reforms could be realised for the real economy.

## FINANCIAL GLOBALISATION

During the past two decades, financial markets around the world have become increasingly interconnected. Financial globalization has brought considerable benefits to national economies and to investors and savers, but it has also changed the structure of markets, creating new risks and challenges for market participants and policymakers.

Globalization — the process through which an increasingly free flow of ideas, people, goods, services, and capital leads to the integration of economies and societies — has brought rising prosperity to the countries that have participated. It has boosted incomes and helped raise living standards in many parts of the world, partly by making sophisticated technologies available to less advanced countries.

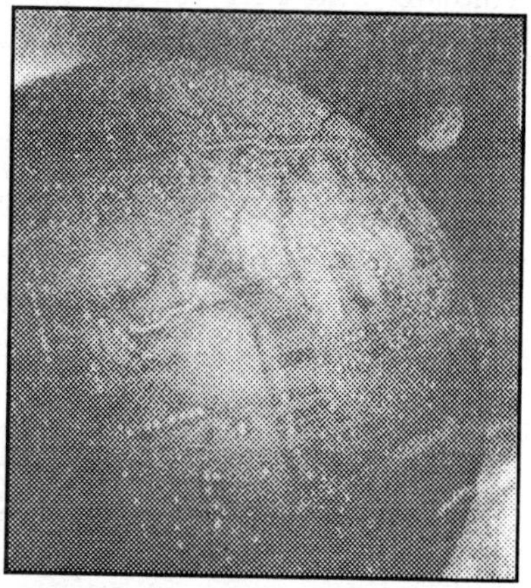

The *globalization of national economies* has advanced significantly as real economic activity — production, consumption, and physical investment — has been dispersed over different countries or regions. Today, the components of a television set may be manufactured in one country and assembled in another, and the final product sold to consumers around the world. New multinational companies have been created, each producing and distributing its goods and services through networks that span the globe, while established multinationals have expanded internationally by emerging with or acquiring foreign companies. Many countries have lowered barriers to international trade, and cross-border flows in goods services have increased significantly.

*The liberalization of national financial and capital markets,* coupled with the rapid improvements in information technology and the globalization of national economice, has catalyzed financial innovation and spurred the growth of cross-border capital movements. The globalization of financial intermediation is partly a response to the demand for mechanisms to intermediate cross-border flows and partly a response to declining barriers to trade in financial services and liberalized rules governing the entry of foreign financial institutions into domestic capital markets.

*Competition among the providers of intermediary services* has increased because of technological advances and financial liberalization. The regulatory authorities in many countries have altered rules glooming financial intermediation to allow a broader range of institutions to provide financial services and new classes of non-bank financial institutions, including institutional investors, have emerged. Investment banks, securities firms, asset managers, mutual funds insurance companies, speciality and trade finance companies hedge funds, and even telecommunications, software and food companies are starting to provide services similar to those traditionally provided by banks.

## BENEFITS VERSUS RISKS

All in all, the radical change in the nature of capital markets has offered unprecedented benefits. But it has also changed market dynamics in ways that are not yet fully understood. One of the main benefits of the growing diversity of funding sources is that it reduces the risk of a "credit crunch". When banks in their own country are under strain, borrowers can now raise funds by issuing stocks or bonds in domestic securities markets or by seeking other financing sources in international capital markets. Securitisation makes the pricing and allocation of capital more efficient because changes in financial risks are reflected much more quickly in asset prices and flows than on bank balance sheets. The downside is that markets have become more volatile, and this volatility could pose a threat to financial stability. For example, the OTC derivatives markets, which accounted for nearly $100 trillion in notional principal and $3 trillion in balance sheet credit exposures in June 2001, can be unpredictable and, at times, turbulent. Accordingly, those in charge of preserving financial stability need to better understand how the globalization of finance has changed the balance of risks in international capital markets and ensure that private risk-management practices guard against these risks.

Another benefit of financial globalization is that, with more choices open to them, borrowers and investors can obtain better terms on their financing. Corporations can finance physical investments more cheaply, and investors can more easily diversify internationally and tailor portfolio risk to their preferences. This encourages investment and saving, which facilitate real economic activity and growth and improves economic welfare. However, asset prices may over-shoot fundamentals during booms and busts, causing excessive volatility and distorting the allocation of capital. For example, real estate prices in Asia soared and then dropped precipitously before the crises of 1997-98, leaving many banks with non-performing loans backed by collateral that had lost much of its value. Also, as financial risk becomes actively traded among institutions, investors, and countries, it becomes harder to identify potential weaknesses and to gauge the magnitude of risk. Enhanced transparency about economic and financial market fundamentals, along with a better understanding of why asset market booms and busts occur, can help markets better manage these risks.

Finally, creditworthy banks and firms in emerging market countries can reduce their borrowing costs now that they are able to tap a broader pool of capital from a more diverse and competitive array of providers. However, as we saw during the Mexican crisis of 1994-95 and the Asian and Russian crises of 1997-98, the risks involved can be considerable — including sharp reversals of capital flows, international spillovers, and contagion. (Even though the extent of contagion seems to have decreased, for reasons that are still unclear, since the 1997-98 crises, the rise of contagion cannot be ruled out). Emerging market countries with weak or poorly regulated banks are particularly vulnerable, but such crises can threaten the stability of the international financial system as well.

In response to reforms, the Indian financial sector has undergone radical transformation over the 1990s. Reforms have altered the organisational structure, ownership pattern and domain of operations of institutions and infused competition in the financial sector. The competition has forced the institutions to reposition themselves in order to survive and grow. The extensive progress in technology has enabled markets to graduate from outdated systems to modern market design, thus, bringing about a significant reduction in the speed of execution of trades and the transaction costs. However, despite substantial improvements in the financial sector, some issues have to be addressed overtime as the reform process is entrenched further. Whether the public sector character of the banking sector is affecting its performance adversely? Whether dilution of the government stake would have a positive impact on the efficiency of the banking sector? As a result of various reform measures aimed at enhancing stability of financial institutions, there is a possibility that such measures might have affected the efficiency of financial institutions. Whether DFIs have lost their relevance? The relevant issue, however, is how to fill the vacuum that would be created when DFIs withdraw from the scene. The role of mutual funds in promoting savings continues to be insignificant. There is also an issue of availability of adequate risk capital with the resource mobilisation from the primary capital market showing a sharp decline in the second half of 1990s and the early 2000s. It has also been argued by some that various markets are still segmented. With blurring of boundaries among providers of various financial services, the issue as to what should be the appropriate supervisory framework for regulating them has also arisen.

As wide ranging reforms have been initiated in the financial sector with a view to making it more efficient and stable, the main focus of this chapter is to assess the impact of reforms on efficiency and stability of financial institutions and financial markets. Besides, this chapter attempts to seek answers to the following three questions: (*i*) whether ownership pattern (public or private) impinges on the efficiency of the banking sector; (*ii*) whether various stability enhancing measures introduced in the Indian banking system have had any adverse impact on its efficiency; and (*iii*) whether the various market segments have become integrated.

## AN ASSESSMENT OF REFORMS

While financial institutions and financial markets are two generic mechanisms for transferring resources from the surplus sectors to deficit sectors, their relative significance varies from country-to-country. In the context of the underdeveloped capital market in India, financial intermediaries or institutions have traditionally played a predominant role in meeting the fund requirements of various sectors in the form of credit and investment. The major institutional purveyors of credit in India are banks (commercial banks and co-operative banks), DFIs and NBFCs. Traditionally, banks and MBPCs predominantly extended short-term credit and DFIs mainly provided medium and long-term loans. Insurance companies and mutual funds provided medium to long-term funds mainly in the form of investments. This distinction has got somewhat blurred in recent years. While financial intermediaries play an important role in the growth process by encouraging saving and investment and by improving the allocative efficiency of resources, this role is performed well only when financial intermediaries are sound, stable and efficient.

The key objective of reforms in the financial sector in India has been to enhance the stability and efficiency of financial institutions. To achieve this objective, various reform measures were initiated that could be categorised broadly into three main groups: enabling measures, strengthening measures and institutional measures. The enabling measures were designed to create an environment where financial intermediaries could respond optimally to market signals on the basis of commercial considerations. Salient among these included reduction in statutory pre-emptions so as to release greater funds for commercial lending, interest rate deregulation to enable price discovery, granting of operational autonomy to banks and liberalisation of the entry norms for financial intermediaries. The strengthening measures aimed at reducing the vulnerability of financial institutions in the face of fluctuations in the economic environment. These included, *inter alia,* capital adequacy, income recognition, asset classification and provisioning norms, exposure norms, improved levels of transparency and disclosure standards. Institutional measures were aimed at creating an appropriate institutional framework conducive to development of markets and functioning of financial institutions.

Financial sector reforms have been successful in bringing significant improvements in various market segments by effecting regulatory and legal changes building up of institutional infrastructure, constant fine-tuning in market microstructure and substantial upgradation of technological infrastructure. Efficient stable and healthy financial markets constitute the bedrock for successful conduct of monetary policy; hence, improving the effectiveness of the transmission channel of monetary policy necessitated significant reforms in the money and Government securities markets. Facilitating integration of domestic financial markets was the other major objective of financial market reforms.

Reforms in the financial markets have encompassed all segments. The development of financial markets in India has been pursued to bring about a transformation in the structure, efficiency and stability of the markets as also to facilitate their integration. The emphasis has been on strengthening price discovery, easing restrictions on flows or transactions, lowering transaction costs, and enhancing liquidity. During the post-reform period, the structure of financial markets has witnessed a significant change in terms of financial instruments traded in various segments of the financial market and market participants. The development of these markets has been done in a calibrated, sequenced and careful manner in step with those in other markets in the real economy.

Sequencing has also been informed by the need to develop market infrastructure, technology and the capabilities of market participants and financial institutions in a consistent manner.

The gradual removal of structural bottlenecks in the Indian financial markets and a shift away from the erstwhile administered rates has led to greater domestic market integration. This has also benefited from a series of other policy initiatives overtime which included enabling market-determined price discovery through interest rate deregulation: expansion and diversification of the investor base; introduction of a variety of instruments of varying features and tenor; and improvement in market infrastructure. Some of the markets which show strong co-movement are money and Government securities markets, exchange rate and stock markets, and foreign exchange forward and money markets.

These developments have facilitated the growth of deeper and more efficient domestic markets, facilitating a more effective channel for transmission of monetary and financial policy impulses.

India's experience once again demonstrates that the development of financial markets is an arduous and time-consuming task that requires conscious policy actions and effective implementation. Financial markets have to be created, nurtured and monitored on a continuous basis, as they attain maturation.

Financial market reforms have helped in improving the price discovery in the primary market, while the secondary markets have attained greater depth and liquidity. The number of instruments and participants has also increased. The capital market has become a safer place for investors as various risks involved at various stages of trading and settlement have been either completely eliminated or reduced considerably. Liquidity in the stock market has improved considerably. The Government securities market has witnessed a transformation from a captive bank-dominated market to an active debt market operating at market related/determined interest rates.

Among the financial market segments, the linkages among the money, government securities and foreign exchange markets have been established and are growing. The presence of foreign institutional investigators strengthened the integration between the domestic and international capital markets.

The Reserve Bank's short-term liquidity management is centred around the LAF operations through repo reverse repo transactions. However, certain impediments need to be overcome for the smooth operation of LAF. These include the presence of non-bank players in the call market and skewed distribution of liquidity among market players. Further development of the term money market would help in removing the segmentation in the yield curve. This is crucial for effectiveness of monetary policy transmission. Placing limits on banks' exposure to call money market, making call money market a purely inter-bank market, encouraging development of the collateralised repo market, adherence to prudential asset-liability and risk management guidelines, and online connectivity between major bank branches are expected to preserve the integrity of financial markets and facilitate emergence of term money/repo markets in the near future. Significant achievements have been made through the operationalisation of the

Clearing Corporation of India Ltd., (CCIL) and the Negotiated Dealing System (NDS). The wider accessibility of NDS to facilitate the development of a repo market in a risk-free environment for settlement would need to be expedited.

Future developments in the Government securities market hinge on legislative changes consistent with modern technology and market practices. Other measures include the introduction of an RTCS system, integration of the payment and settlement systems for Government securities, standardisation of practices with regard to manner of quotes, conclusion of deals and code of best practices for repo transactions and retailing of Government securities. The introduction of trading in Government securities through a nationwide, anonymous, order-driven, screen-based trading system of the stock exchanges, in the same manner in which trading takes place in equities, would further enhance the operational and informational efficiency of the market as well as its transparency, depth and liquidity, thereby providing for a countrywide retail investor base.

Derivatives can play an important role in risk mitigation. There has been a substantial increase in Interest Rate Swaps (IRS — Forward Rate Agreements (FRA) transactions in 2002. With the increased popularity of the derivatives, a range of possibilities for efficient pricing, hedging and managing of interest rate risks will open up. These would raise new issues like counterparty risks and liquidity risks. For optimising the capital charges, the clearing and settlement of contracts could increasingly be through a centralised counterparty. It may, however, be noted that derivatives market is in an evolving stage in India. A cautious, gradual and sequenced approach to introduction of derivatives instruments to avoid pitfalls is in order. Like derivatives, introduction of floating rate bonds can promote effective management of balance sheet risks, when interest rate outlook is uncertain.

Depth and liquidity in the spot as well as forward segments in the foreign exchange markets need to be enhanced further. A way to address these concerns lies in the further development of the money market as well as in assumption of the role of 'market makers' by large public sector banks who handle the major portion of the export-import transactions. The preconditions for the pick-up of activity in forex derivatives include sequentially, the development of: (*i*) a deep and liquid inter-bank term money market, (*ii*) a liquid forward dollar-rupee market, and (*iii*) rupee-based derivatives. Expeditious development of these market segments would remove the irritants in the healthy development of the foreign exchange market. In the light of the experience of the East Asian crisis, the movement would need to be 'gradual' as the 'big-bang' approach could have adverse repercussions for the exchange rate regime, foreign exchange reserves, BoP situation and the overall growth prospects of the economy.

Although the capital market has made significant strides in information acquisition, processing and dissemination, there is little evidence that it is now processing the information more efficiently than before the reforms. Both, the primary market for private debt (with preponderance of privately placed debt issues) and the secondary market are tagging behind the equity markets in terms of transparency, thus adversely affecting the process of price discovery. Preponderance of the private placement market can potentially strip the market of its ability to discipline issuers and thereby enhance systemic risk. Not all privately placed issues are listed. As a result, investors cannot signal their changing evaluation of the business prospects of the issuers. Some recent regulatory initiatives have been taken to contain risks. In addition, norms for corporate disclosure would also require to be strengthened that would enable investors to take informed decisions as well as to promote transparency. Measures to revive the public issues segment of the primary market could also be contemplated.

## CONCLUSION

The financial system in India is undergoing structural transformation under the influence of globalization, deregulation, technological advances and institutional and legal reforms. While the liberalized environment has opened new avenues of business for financial institutions, it has led to intensified competition. To survive in a competitive environment, financial institutions have been diversifying into non-traditional activities, altering their pricing strategies and looking for non-fund based sources of income. As a result, operations of financial institutions are becoming increasingly complex and, correspondingly, exposed to greater risks. In order to ensure that financial institutions grow along sound lines, a robust prudential regulatory framework has been put in place.

Globalisation, financial deregulation and improvement in technology have had a profound effect on the financial landscape in recent years. These developments have intensified competition and resulted in financial engineering through product innovation and business strategies. While market participants have now greater scope to diversify risk and manage it efficiently, this has also posed new risks and challenges to the financial system. Growth of financial firms across different business lines and across national boundaries has made the task of designing appropriate policies more challenging. Regulatory and supervisory policies are, therefore, constantly assessed regarding their capabilities to meet the challenges of containing systemic risk in the financial system. The main challenge for the supervisory authorities has been to maintain financial stability without curtailing the incentive to innovate.

Financial sector reforms, going ahead, will focuss on bank consolidation, containing the systemic risks arising out of inter-connectedness of the banking sector with other components of the financial sector.

Keeping in view the changing landscape in the financial sector, the Reserve Bank has been suitably focusing its regulatory and supervisory framework to promote a stable and efficient financial sector.

Financial regulation and supervision has been progressively aligned with international best practices with suitable adaptations. Calibrated deregulation, prudential regulation and supervision and a responsive policy environment have resulted in significant improvement in the efficiency, stability and resilience of financial institutions. This is reflected in their profitability, improved asset quality and higher capital levels. As the economy grows and becomes more sophisticated, the banking sector has to develop in a manner that supports and stimulates such growth. There are, however, several challenges in future which may require new technologies, better processes of credit and risk appraisal, product diversification, robust internal controls and corporate governance and efficient human resource management.

Financial sector reforms in India is a continuous process in the changing milieu for a safe and sound financial sector for sustained growth of the economy. The stability of the financial system is the prerequisite to financial institutions to respond effectively to the growing competition while taking advantage of business opportunities and technological developments.

## LOOKING AHEAD

Looking ahead, there is a growing recognition that openness matters and globalisation is an irreversible process entailing both opportunities as well as challenges. With increasing openness, monetary and fiscal policies are expected to play a key role in ensuring macroeconomic stability while facilitating sustained economic growth within the framework of a market economy, in view of increased uncertainty, central banks need to take into account developments in the global economic situation, the international inflationary situation, interest rate situation, exchange rate movements and capital movements while formulating policy responses. The maintenance of financial sector stability has assumed much greater importance with opening up of the economy to the influence of globalisation.

Monetary policy would have to play an important role in this context by ensuring appropriate real interest rates and low and stable inflation. The key challenge for macroeconomic policies would be to ensure that the anticipated expansion in saving in developing countries is productively utilised within the economy and not exported abroad so that the investment rate rises in close co-movement with the saving rate. As sustainable growth hinges around the existence of a critical minimum in terms of physical infrastructure, an acceleration of growth in the future requires massive investments to close the gaps between demand and supply in key infrastructural areas such as power, roads and highways, ports and telecommunication, cities and urban utilities. More rational user charges have to be levied to finance the restoration of public investment in agriculture.

Real sector developments have close connection with the process of opening up. In order to reap the fruits of opening up, enabling conditions need to be created. Illustratively, decisive actions are required to promote agricultural diversification and active investment in rural infrastructure to enable greater food processing and value addition to agricultural products. A proper incentive structure needs to be put in place to encourage private investment in hi-tech horticulture with micro propagation, protected cultivation, drip irrigation, and integrated nutrient and pest management. A progressive correction is required in the incentive structure for agriculture so that the excessively high minimum support prices that currently exist for wheat and rice do not continue to distort resource allocation in agriculture as a whole. Corresponding changes would also need to be made in the current policies related to other subsidies, particularly those related to fertiliser, power and water. The reduction in various subsidies in these areas will provide a very significant fiscal dividend for the country enabling higher public investment where it is required, and particularly in .agriculture. In view of the relatively high level of food security, the climate is now right for further policy reforms in agriculture. Similarly, the absorption capacity of the industrial sector has increased after initiation of the liberalisation process, which has impacted on its size and spread. The globalisation process brought about changes in the expenditure pattern of the industries, as there are evidences that the costs of production, including interest payments declined which resulted in increased profitability of the factory sector. The fact remains that whole package of reforms that has been carried out over the past 12 years was expected to lead to significant industrial restructuring. Resources should have moved from the more capital-intensive sectors to the more labour using ones, leading to both higher output and employment growth. It is felt that industrial restructuring in terms of more rapid bankruptcy procedures, easier reallocation of capital, faster transformation of urban land use, and flexibility in labour use, legislative changes, social security mechanism, and technological upgradation need priority.

The process of opening up of the Indian economy has given birth to a host of new challenges and opportunities. The spirit of the liberalisation process entails a conscious effort on the part of the policymaker(s) *to* optimise on these opportunities-challenges trade-offs. When a definitive history of the reform process pursued in the Indian economy will be written, it would probably hinge on the synergy between the domestic and external sectors, each throwing up its strengths and threats.

## ANNEXURE

### ASSESSMENT OF REFORMS: FINANCIAL INSTITUTIONS

In line with the deregulation and liberalisation policies of the 1990s, financial sector reforms were undertaken in the early phase of reforms. The basic objectives of the reforms were to enhance stability and efficiency of the financial system. It was felt that directed allocation of resources during the pre-reform period, although in accordance with the Plan priorities, was not conducive to allocative efficiency, and the higher rate of growth of financial saving was not matched by a proportionate increase in the rate of growth. The recurrence of domestic banking crises in developed and developing economies alike during the 1980s, and the financial crises in a host of countries in the 1990s underscored the necessity of financial stability for sustained growth. It was recognised that a vibrant, resilient and competitive financial sector is vital for sustaining the reform process in the real sectors of the economy.

The most significant achievement of the financial sector reforms has been the marked improvement in the financial health of the commercial banking sector, in terms of asset quality, capital adequacy and profitability. Despite these improvements, the commercial banking sector continues to face several challenges. First, a major concern for the banking system has been the high cost and low productivity as reflected in relatively high spreads and cost of intermediation. An important challenge for the banking sector, therefore, remains in transforming itself to a more efficient, productive and competitive set up.

Second, although the capitalisation level of almost all banks operating in India is above the prescribed minimum levels, banks may face difficulties to maintain their capital levels in coming years. The capital requirement of banks is likely to increase with pick-up in credit demand and the implementation of the New Capital Accord sometime in 2006, which has accorded greater emphasis on risk-sensitivity in credit allocation. Banks would need to consider these factors while estimating their capital requirements. Given depressed capital market conditions and banks' limited ability to generate sufficient funds internally, maintaining the capital position in line with the prescribed norms would be a major challenge.

Third, commercial banks continue to face the problem of overhang of NPAs, attributable, *inter alia* to systemic factors such as weak debt recovery mechanism, non-realisability of collateral and poor credit appraisal techniques. Policy measures have yielded mixed results. The recent enactment of the Securitisation and Reconstruction of Financial Assets and Enforcement of Security Interest Act, 2002 has increased the momentum for the recovery of NPAs. However, banks need to intensify their efforts to recover their overdues and prevent generation of fresh NPAs.

Fourth, in a regulated regime, risks were essentially compartmentalised with various categories of market and credit risks being managed separately. Increasingly, risk is viewed as multi-dimensional. To enable banks to cope with risks, the Reserve Bank has been engaged in preparing banks for proactive risk management. Banks would need to establish technical systems and management processes necessary not only to identify risks associated with their activities, but also to effectively measure, monitor and control them.

Fifth, it is important that financial institutions possess means and measures of corporate governance. The quality of corporate governance would become critical as competition intensifies, ownership is diversified and banks strive to retain their client base. Banks would be required to further improve their internal management systems in terms of housekeeping, audit practices, asset-liability management and systems management to attain international best practice levels.

Sixth, a sound and well-diversified banking system envisages development of a banking sector with a diverse array of well-capitalised and healthy banks. As the dynamics of reforms gathers momentum, the coming years are likely to witness consolidation in the banking sector. Such consolidation will be driven by market forces in an enabling environment, which brings together willing institutions. A related issue is that of ownership of banks. Public Sector Banks (PSBs) continue to dominate the Indian banking sector and progressively the ownership needs to be diversified to make them more amenable to market discipline and reduce the possibility of regulatory forbearance.

Finally, bank lending tends to be pro-cyclical while the level of NPAs tends to behave in a counter-cyclical fashion. Consequently, in a downturn, as this condition of borrowers deteriorates, they tend to be downgraded by banks with the consequence that extra provisioning has to be set aside, potential exacerbating the capital shortage. Such behaviour of the part of banks tends to accentuate cyclical fluctuations. In these circumstances, dynamic or forward-looking provisioning by banks may be useful for circumventing such outcome.

With the phased withdrawal of government from direct intervention in the financial sector and gradual divestment of government ownership in major financial institutions, the importance of deposit insurance arrangements has increased in the context of attainment of financial stability. Introduction of risk based deposit insurance premium, separation of deposit insurance arrangements for co-operative and commercial banks and introduction of co-insurance among others, would help foster greater systems stability as also provide a safety net for depositors.

In co-operative banks, the impact of reforms appears to be limited, if assessed in terms of stability and efficiency parameters. One of the reasons for this appears to be delay in the initiation of reforms and the slow paced reform in the sector. Duality of control has also posed concern over the sharing of responsibilities among the regulatory and supervisory authorities. The current duality of control over co-operative banks by the Reserve Bank and the respective State Governments is impeding effective supervision of such entities, which needs to be resolved.

In the changed operating environment, Development Finance Institutions (DFIs), which have traditionally been among the main sources of long-term finance for the corporate sector in India, are finding it increasingly difficult to maintain their viability. In view of this, the future role of these DFIs needs to be addressed urgently as the alternative source of long-term funds has not developed. As some DFIs convert themselves into banks or NBFCs, an important source of long-term funds would dry up. Thus, there is a concern regarding the vacuum which would be created by the withdrawal of DFIs from the scene. Although banks have entered the domain of term-lending, there are limits on the extent to which commercial basis may be able to fill this vacuum. The shift from fixed to flexible interest rate regime, development of instruments for hedging interest rate risk, and effectiveness of timely resolution of NPA-related problems would influence the flow of funds from banks for meeting long-term financing requirements. Banks alone, however, may not be able to compensate the decline in long-term funds by DFIs to the corporate sector. To fill the gap, the development of a private corporate debt market is of crucial importance. The development of a benchmark in the fixed securities market and development of secondary market for corporate debt would also stimulate banks' investment in corporate securities.

In the case of mutual funds, while reforms have been successful in creating a competitive environment, the growth of mutual funds slowed down sharply partly due to depressed market conditions and partly due to the problems faced by the Unit Trust of India. Reforms in the insurance sector, which are of recent origin, have also been successful in enhancing competition even as the impact of increased competition on the insurance penetration is yet to be felt.

***Source:*** RBI

## ROBUST CREDIT CULTURE

Despite good progress, Asia-Pacific still has a long way to go before its local bond markets realise their potential. Fostering national credit cultures built on transparency, creditor rights and independent credit analysis is essential. Nearly every Asia-Pacific government has started building local corporate debt markets. In the region, annual domestic corporate bond issuance reached $758.4 billion in 2009, an increase of 1.5x since 2005. Last year alone, local issuance jumped 38%.

This momentum, partly reflects concerns about the future ability of banks to meet borrower needs as banks conserve balance sheets to comply with Basel III capital adequacy requirements. Governments are also looking to local corporate bond markets to bolster resilience to future global shocks. They recognise the role well-functioning corporate debt markets play in allocating capital and aiding the common goal of regional financial integration. Robust credit cultures are built on key elements: fostering a credit culture goes hand-in-hand with bond market development. A global best-practice credit culture would produce an attractive and rewarding environment in which investors can operate. In our opinion, chief elements include:

*Transparency:* Disclosure, high and consistent reporting standards, and good corporate governance.

*Independent and objective credit analysis:* High-quality and credible research and analysis in a competitive environment.

*Risk-based pricing:* Compensation for investor's risk-taking.

*Creditor rights:* Bankruptcy laws and a legal system that enforces the rights.

*Arm's-length relationships:* Between issuers and investors, and between governments and banking systems.

A healthy credit culture thrives on a bottom-up approach in which investors drive the market. It is based on free flow of reliable and independent information. It is also about equal treatment and a level-playing field. In countries where relationship-driven preferential treatment has taken precedence, regulators and policymakers will have to eradicate entrenched sub-part practices.

Big issues driving the momentum include investor's need to grow wealth more rapidly to offset global ageing and likely rising living costs; the region's generally urgent need for infrastructure investment; and the need for companies to diversify funding sources in bank-dominated environments.

**Credit Culture:** India has a sound and improving credit culture. Objective and independent credit analysis has increased investor comfort in the debt markets, and the rating agencies have helped the market to move from relationship- and name-based pricing to arm's-length pricing that factors in underlying credit it and liquidity risks.

**Local bond market development:** India's corporate bond market is small but growing rapidly. The outstanding stock of corporate bonds in June 2010 was $156 billion, about 12% of India's GDP. Public debt issuance is limited. India requires $1 trillion in infrastructure investment over the five years from 2012, mostly as specialised debt. Bankruptcy laws limit a lender's ability to enforce securities in a timely manner.

**The investor's perspective:** India's strong and improving credit culture is attractive to investors. Information is transparent and readily available, and arm's-length relationship exist between investors and issuers. The removal of investment rules that constrain insurers and pension funds would greatly benefit the Indian bond market. Most bond market investors in India operate in buy-and-hold mode. Such investors typically look for highly-rated paper; which dampens demand at the lower end of rating scale.

## PROPOSED BASEL III GUIDELINES

### A Credit Positive for Indian Banks

The proposed Basel III guidelines seek to improve the ability of banks to withstand periods of economic and financial stress by prescribing more stringent capital and liquidity requirements for them. ICRA views the suggested capital requirement as a positive for banks as it raises the minimum core capital stipulation, introduces counter-cyclical measures, and enhances banks' ability to conserve core capital in the event of stress through a conservation capital buffer. The prescribed liquidity requirements, on the other hand, are aimed at bringing in uniformity in the liquidity standards followed by banks globally. This requirement, in ICRA's opinion, would help banks better manage pressures on liquidity in a stress scenario.

The capital requirement as suggested by the proposed Basel III guidelines would necessitate Indian banks[1] raising ₹ 6,00,000 crore in external capital over next nine years, besides lowering their leveraging capacity. It is the public sector banks that would require most of this capital, given that they dominate the Indian banking sector. Further, a higher level of core capital could dilute the return on equity for banks. Nevertheless, Indian banks may still find it easier to make the transition to a stricter capital requirement regime than some of their international counterparts since the regulatory norms on capital adequacy in India are already more stringent, and also because most Indian banks have historically maintained their core and overall capital well in excess of the regulatory minimum.

As for the liquidity requirement, the liquidity coverage ratio as suggested under the proposed Basel III guidelines does not allow for any mismatches while also introducing a uniform liquidity definition. Comparable current regulatory norms prescribed by the Reserve Bank of India (RBI), on the other hand, permit some mismatches, within the outer limit of 28 days.

The key elements of the proposed Basel III guidelines include the following:

(1) Definition of capital made more stringent, capital buffers introduced and loss absorptive capacity of Tier 1 and Tier 2 Capital instrument of internationally active banks proposed to be enhanced.

(2) Forward looking provisioning prescribed.

(3) Modifications made in counterparty credit risk weights.

(4) New parameter of leverage ratio introduced.

(5) Global liquidity standard prescribed.

An Illustration on Movement of Capital Requirement and Triggers Under Various Scenarios Regulatory Capital = Core Capital + Capital Conservation Buffer + Countercyclical Buffer (if any)

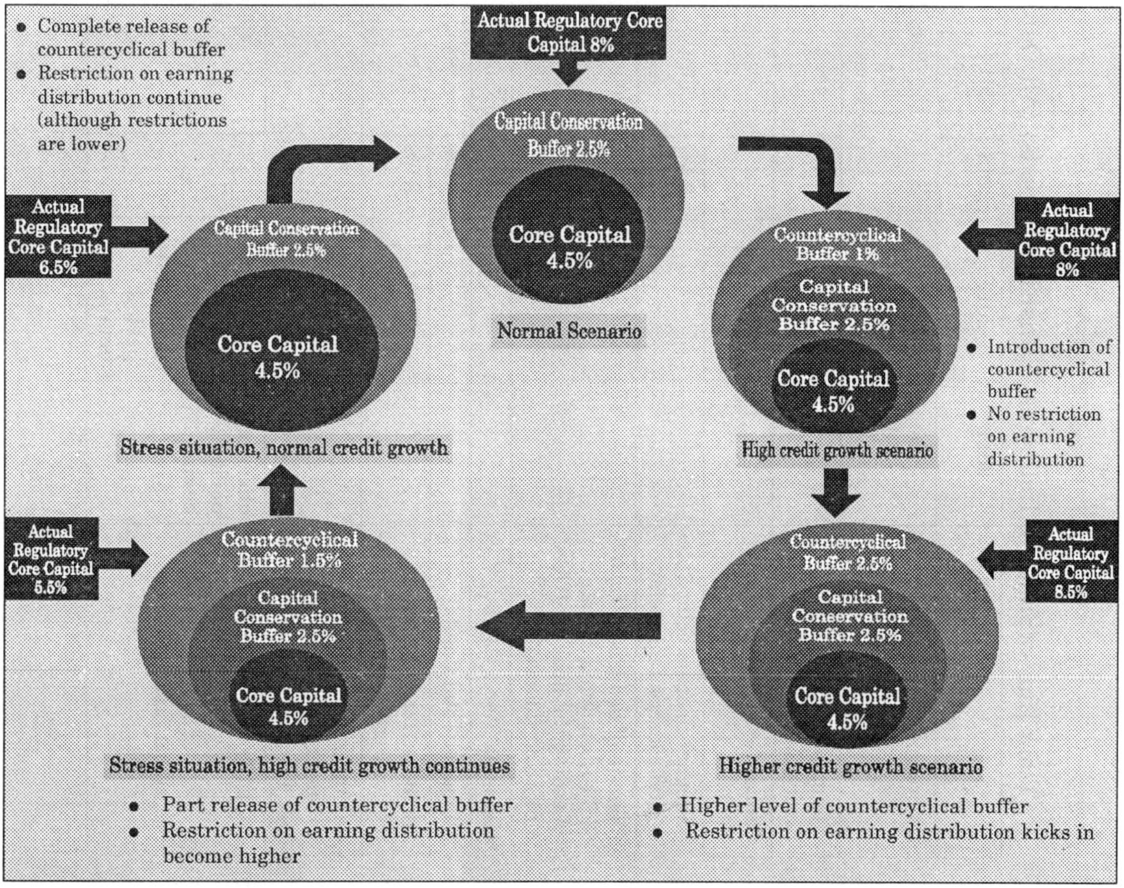


***Note:*** Figures in circles represent the minimum regulatory requirement.

Time Lines (Shading Indicates Transition Periods) (All Dates are as of 1st January)

| | 2011 | 2012 | 2013 | 2014 | 2015 | 2016 | 2017 | 2018 | As of 1 Jan. 2019 |
|---|---|---|---|---|---|---|---|---|---|
| Leverage Ratio | Supervisory Monitoring | | Parallel run 1 Jan 2013-I Jan 2015 Disclosure Starts 1 Jan 2015 | | | | | Migration to Pillar 1 | |
| Minimum Common Equity Capital Ratio | | | 3.5% | 4.0% | 4.5% | 4.5% | 4.5% | 4.5% | 4.5% |
| Capital Conservation Buffer | | | | | | 0.625% | 1.25% | 1.875% | 2.50% |
| Minimum common equity plus capital conservation buffer | | | 3.5% | 4.0% | 4.5% | 5.125% | 5.75% | 6.375% | 7.0% |
| Phase-in of deductions from CET1 (including amounts exceeding the limit for DTAs, MSRs and financials) | | | | 20.0% | 40.0% | 60.0% | 80.0% | 100.0% | 100.0% |
| Minimum Tier 1 Capital | | | 4.5% | 5.5% | 6.0% | 6.0% | 6.0% | 6.0% | 6.0% |
| Minimum Total Capital | | | 8.0% | 8.0% | 8.0% | 8.0% | 8.0% | 8.0% | 8.0% |
| Minimum Total Capital plus conservation buffer | | | 8.0% | 8.0% | 8.0% | 8.625% | 9.25% | 9.875% | 10.5% |
| Capital instruments that no longer qualify as non-core Tier 1 capital or Tier 2 capital | Phased out over 10-year horizon beginning 2013 | | | | | | | | |
| Liquidity coverage ratio | **observation period begins** | | | | **Introduce minimum standard** | | | | |
| Net stable funding ratio | | **Observation period begins** | | | | | | **Introduce minimum standard** | |

❖❖❖

# PART II

## LEAPING TO FINANCE MARKET

## FINANCIAL MARKET OPERATIONS

## FINANCIAL MARKETS

Financial markets are never perfect. In allocating credit, they can make two mistakes: funding low-yielding projects and failing to fund high-yielding ones. In the early stages of development, the governments of developing countries fearing that the costs of failing to fund good projects were likely to be high, intervened to direct credit. Perhaps that assessment was sound at the time, but experience has since revealed too many errors of the first kind — funding low-yielding projects. With time, economies have become more complex, information flows have improved, and financial managers have become more skilled. In most countries, errors can be minimized by leaving more decisions to a diverse and competitive financial system that responds to market signals. The primary role of the government then shifts to making market signals more meaningful and, in particular, to preventing its own actions from distorting them.

On occasions, the government may have a role to play as a promoter of financial institutions and markets in order to create a diversified and competitive financial system. Many high-income and developing countries have used fiscal incentives to favour particular institutions and markets. Such incentives may be justified to encourage financial diversity, particularly if the existing markets are dominated by large banks and are uncompetitive. Fiscal incentives, however, should be used only moderately, should have clear objectives, and should be withdrawn once those objectives are achieved. In the long-term, countries should opt for regimes that do not favour one type of instrument or institution over others.

To improve competition and efficiency, some small countries have opened their markets to foreign banks or have encouraged joint ventures between foreign and domestic institutions. Many small and medium-size countries could buy the specialised financial services they need (such as reinsurance, swaps, and forward contracts) from abroad. Small, specialised institutions and foreign competition can force even big oligopolistic banks to behave competitively — although not necessarily across the full range of financial services.

## THE HISTORY OF STOCK MARKETS IN INDIA

A brief history of the rise of equity trading in India: July 9, 1875 to July 9, 2008.

- **July 9, 1875** : The Stock Exchange at Bombay was established in 1875 as "The Native Share and Stockbrokers Association". The exchange was established with 318 members with a fee of rupee one.

  : Admission fee, which is the price of card for membership was originally ₹ 15, raised to ₹ 20 in 1877 and ₹ 51 in 1886. The number of brokers in 1878 was 318.

- **January, 18, 1899** : Bombay Stock Exchange acquires own premises.

  : The 1st building of the Stock Exchange Sir Dinshaw Petit native brokers' Hall was inaugurated.

  : Clearing Houses are established for settlement of trades as volumes increase.

- **February 2, 1921** : The first Clearing House was known as BOISL (BSE & Bank of India Shareholding Limited) came into being, promoted jointly by BSE & Bank of India.

**The earlier Bombay Stock Exchange Building**

- **1923** : K.R.P. Shroff becomes the Honorary President of BSE.
- **1925** : Bombay Securities Contract Control Act (BSCCA) comes into force.
- **December 1, 1939** : Stock exchange building is acquired on Dalal Street, Fort, Mumbai.
- **1943** : Forward trading banned till 1946. Only ready-to-delivery and hand-delivery contract were permitted.
- **1956** : Securities Contract Regulation Act, drafted on the lines of BSCCA, comes into force. Stock Exchanges in India are governed by this Act.
- **1957** : BSE becomes the first exchange in India to get permanent recognition.
- **1964** : Unit Trust of India (UTI) was established as the first Mutual Fund in the country.
- **April 1, 1966** : K.R.P. Shroff retires and Shri Pheroze J. Jeejeebhoy becómes the Chairman.
- **June 29, 1969** : Morarji Desai bans forward trading.

- **1970** : Participation certificates and commercial bills (under bills rediscounting schemes) were introduced in the money market.
- **1973** : Construction of P.J. Towers, named after late Phiroze Jamshedji Jeejeebhoy starts.
- **January 2, 1986** : BSE Sensex launched as the first Stock Market Index with 1978-79 as the base year.
- **November 1987** : SBI Mutual Fund launches Magnum regular income scheme.
- **April 1988** : Securities and Exchange Board of India was set up as a non-statutory body. S.A.Dave, SEBI's First Chairman.
- **1990** : The Over-the-Counter Exchange of India (OTCEI) was incorporated and fully operationalised in September 1992. OTCEI is the national ringless and computerised exchange. It deals in equity, preference shares, bonds, debentures and warrants.
- **January 1992** : Securities and Exchange Board of India given statutory powers for regulating the securities market.
- **May 1992** : Harshad Mehta's securities scam rocks the market.
- **May 27, 1992** : Reliance is the first Indian company to make a GDR issue.
- **May 30, 1992** : The Capital Issues Control Act, 1947 was repealed paving the way for market forces in the determination of pricing of issues and allocation of resources for competing uses.

  : The functions of capital issues controller were entrusted to SEBI.
- **September 1992** : Foreign institutional investors are permitted to invest in Indian securities market.
- **November 1992** : National Stock Exchange was established.
- **October 30, 1993** : The First private sector mutual fund — Kothari Pioneer MF begins operations.
- **1993** : SEBI bans badla trading on BSE and a modified Badla was introduced by SEBI in July 1995.
- **May 1994** : BSE 200 Index with 1989-90 as the base year was introduced.
- **June 1994** : NSE commences operations in wholesale debt market segment.
- **November 1994** : Capital Market segment of NSE goes on stream. Trading is screen-based for the first time in India.

A slice of history: the old Trading Ring

- **January 1995** : BSE Online Trading System (BOLT) replaces open outcry system and became operational from May 1995.
- **June 1995** : NSCCL, India's first clearing Corporation was set up.
- **October 1995** : National Stock Exchange overtakes the Bombay Stock Exchange as the largest stock exchange in terms of volumes of trading.
- **March 1996** : The system of primary dealers in Government securities was introduced to provide two-way quotes and develop the market.
- **April 1996** : S&P CNX Nifty was introduced by NSE Ltd.

  S&P CNX stands for : S&P = Standard & Poor

  C = CRISIL N = NSE X = INDEX

  All NSE indices are prepared by the India Index Services & Products Ltd., (IISL), which is a joint venture of NSE, CRISIL and Standard & Poor.
- **November 1996** : The National Securities Depository Ltd., (NSDL) was established.
- **February 1997** : SEBI releases norms for takeovers and acquisitions.
- **May 1997** : BSE introduces screen-based trading.
- **December 1997** : Capital indexed bonds were issued to broaden the market.
- **November 1998** : SEBI gives recognition to integrated stock exchanges founded by 16 regional stock exchanges.
- **February 1999** : Launch of automated lending and borrowing mechanism (ALBM), on NSE.
- **1999** : BSE introduced BSE 500 index.
- **March 11, 1999** : Infosys Technologies is the first company to list on NASDAQ through a public offering of American Depository Receipts.
- **March 22, 1999** : Central Depository Services (India) promoted by BSE commenced operations enabling paperless trading in the exchanges.
- **1999** : The Electronic Fund Transfer (EFT) facility combined with dematerialisation of shares created a conducive environment for reducing the settlement cycle in stock markets.
- **September 1999** : ICICI is the first Indian company to list on NYSE.
- **October 11, 1999** : For the first time in BSE's history, the Sensex closed above 5,000, mark at 5,031.78.
- **January 2000** : BSE creates 'Z' category of Scrips, in addition to A, B1, and B2, comprising scrips that breached or failed to comply with the listing agreement.
- **February 2000** : Internet trading commences on NSE. On February 21, NSE records peak market capitalization of ₹ 11,94,282 crore. On February 14, 2000, BSE Sensex hits an all-time high of 6,150.
- **April 10, 2000** : The Sensex is revamped to include Dr. Reddy's Lab, Reliance Petroleum, Satyam Computers and Zee Telefilms, replacing Indian Hotels, Tata Chemicals, Tata Power, and IDBI.

- **June 2000** : BSE and NSE introduce derivatives trading in the form of index futures.
- **July 9, 2000** : BSE turns 125.
- **October 19, 2000** : WIPRO Company lists on the NYSE.
- **January 22, 2001** : Borrowing and Lending Securities Scheme (BLESS) launched on BSE to promote securities lending and borrowing activities.
- **2001** : BSE introduced trading in the Debt segment.
- **March 2001** : Ketan Parekh scam breaks. SEBI suspends all the broker-directors of the BSE in relation to the KP scam on March 13.
- **May 2001** : BSE advises compulsory demat for B2 scrips.
- **June 2001** : Index options start trading on NSE.
- **July 2001** : A SEBI directive bans carry-forward. All major securities are moved to rolling settlement. Options of individual scrips start trading on NSE.
- **November 9, 2001** : BSE and NSE launch futures in individual stocks.
- **July 2, 2001** : The age-old *badla* system was abolished and replaced by rolling settlement and options trading.
- **January 1, 2002** : Account period settlement system in vogue was discontinued.
- **February 2, 2002** : The Indian companies were allowed to raise funds from abroad, through American/Global Depository Receipts (ADRs/GDRs), foreign currency convertible bonds (FCCBs) and external commercial borrowings (ECBs). The Reserve Bank allowed two-way fungibility of ADRs/GDRs in February 2002.

  : Insider trading was made a criminal offence. The regulations governing substantial acquisition of shares and takeovers of companies were also introduced aimed at protecting the interests of minority shareholdeers by making the takeover process more transparent.

  : For providing market participants instruments for hedging and risk management, several types of derivative products on equities were introduced. Non-transparent products like 'badla' were banned.
- **February 15, 2002** : The Negotiated Dealing System (NDS) was operationalised to provide, *inter alia,* online electronic bidding platform for primary auctions and OMO/LAF auctions.
- **April 1, 2002** : The trading and settlement cycles were initially shortened from 14 days to 7 days. Subsequently, to enhance the efficiency of the secondary market, rolling settlement was introduced on a T + 5 basis.
- **August 2002** : Government announces ₹ 500 crore bailout package for UTI.
- **January, 2003** : Collateralised Borrowing and Lending Obligations (CBLO) was launced by CCIL for the benefit of non-bank participants.
- **February 2003** : SEBI directs exchanges to monitor the "possibility of price manipulations".

- **April, 2003** : The settlement cycle for all listed securities was shortened to T + 3 and further to T + 2.
- **September 2003** : BSE Sensex moves to "free float market capitalization" from the earlier "full market capitalization".
- **2004** : The entry of FIIs has strengthened the diversity of views and compulsions, and helped full market liquidity.
- **April 2004** : The Market Stabilisation Scheme (MSS) was introduced as a special scheme to absorb liquidity of a more enduring nature.
- **January 2005** : Only ten of the original Sensex 30 survive. TCS and NTPC added to the list.
- **August 19, 2005** : Bombay Stock Exchange transformed into a corporate entity BSE Ltd., with Rajanikant Patel as its first CEO.
- **September 2005** : The Sensex crossed the 8,000 mark and closed at 8,052.56 mark on 08-09-05, raising the investor's wealth to ₹ 22 lakh crore.
- **2006** : At the end of 2006, the number of FIIs stood at 1,044 and sub-accounts at 3,045. Total Fll investment (Net) amounted ₹ 41,294 crore (US $ 9,031 million).
- **2006** : The Sensex gained 4,389 points and appreciated by 46.7 per cent.
- **April 20, 2006** : The stock market breached the milestone with the benchmark sensex surging past the 12,000 point mark on 20-04-2006 for the first time in history.
- **September 18, 2006** : A screen-based negotiated quote-driven system for dealings in Call/Notice and term money market (NDS-CALL) was launched on voluntary basis.
- **2006-07** : The private placement market in India, which shot into prominence in the early 1990s, has grown sharply in recent years. The resource mobilisation by way of private placements increased from ₹ 13,361 crore in 1995-96 to ₹ 1,11,838 crore at end November 2007.
- **February 6, 2007** : The Sensex closed at 14,652. The journey from 13,000 to 14,000 mark, achieved in 26 trading sessions.
- **July 2, 2007** : SEBI stipulated that Permanent Account Number (PAN) as the sole identification number.
- **August - September, 2007** : Sixteen stock exchanges completed their demutualization process.

  : The climb of BSE Sensex was the fastest ever in 2007. It crosses 20,000 mark between June and December.
- **December 2007** : SEBI permits short selling by institutional investors.

  : SEBI approved the introduction of seven new products. (1) Mini contracts on equity indices, (2) Options with longer life/tenure, (3) Volatility Index and Futures & Options (F&O) contracts, (4) Options or futures, (5) Bond indices, (6) Exchange-traded currency (foreign exchange) futures and options, and (7) Exchange traded products to cater to different investment strategies.

: BSE issued show cause notice to 800 companies for violating the listing agreement. Over 4,000 companies are listed on BSE. Trading in shares of 1,564 companies is suspended for violation of listing norms.

- **January 4, 2008** : Entry load by mutual funds was waived for investors making applications for investment in mutual fund schemes directly.
- **January 11, 2008** : BSE-30 index crossed 21,000 mark to peak of 21,207 in an intra-day trading and closed at 20,873.33. Between March 26, 2007 and January 08, 2008, the BSE Sensex rose by 7,649.01points.

Jagdish Capoor, Chairman

- **2008** : Reliance Power IPO set the benchmark in mobilisation of resources in the world. The scrip was over-subscribed by 73 times.
- **June 25, 2008** : Jagdish Capoor replaced Sekhar Dutta as elected chairman of BSE.
- **July 11, 2008** : Since its peak of 21,207 on January 11, 2008, the stock market has lost 7,738 points or 38.6 per cent by July.
- **August 10, 2008** : An alternate payment system for public issues, which will not debit money from retail investors' account unless shares are actually allotted to them, is launched by SEBI as a pilot project.
  - Rajanikant Patel stepped down as the CEO of BSE.
  - Trading in futures contracts in Rupee - US dollar began on the NSE on August 29, 2008, followed by MCX-SX and BSE.
- **2009** :
  - Madhu Kannan was appointed as the CEO and MD of BSE.
  - MCX-SX, India's new Stock Exchange was launched.
  - The United Stock Exchange (USE) opened for trading in financial derivatives.
- **2010** : The National Stock Exchange (NSE) and the Bombay Stock Exchange started trading at 9 a.m. from Monday, January 4, 2010.

  : Regulators (SEBI and RBI) allowed Indian bourses on Jan 19, 2010 to start trading in derivatives contracts in three more currency pairs – Rupee – Euro. Rupee – Japanese Yen (JPY) and Rupee – British Pound (GBP). The three new pairs introduced from February 1 to add depth to the currency futures markets.

**Madhu Kannan,**
CEO, BSE

## MCX-SX, INDIA'S NEW STOCK EXCHANGE

**First stock exchange to roll our pioneering market development initiatives**

- Reducing the gap of collections of mark-to-market (M2M) margins to same day.
- Deploying superior technology for continued operation during some outages.
- Signing MoU with partners for Financial Literacy to enable Financial Inclusion.
- Releasing 1st handbook on currency futures and interest rate futures.
- Providing price updates of currency futures via SMS.
- Launching website in 11 regional languages.

**Exchange Operation Performance**

| Operation Parameters | Oct 08 - Oct 09 |
|---|---|
| Number of members | 626 |
| Number of banks | 23 |
| Geographic spread across cities and towns | 478 |
| Highest Open Interest (industry record) | 6,12,560 |
| Highest turnover (₹ crore) (industry record) | 10,798.05 |
| Highest number of contracts traded (industry record) | 23,07,868 |
| Market Share (in %)* | 50.43% |
| Number of corporate houses participating | 1,167 |
| Education programes across India | 225 |

**Elements of Market Design in Indian Securities Market, 1992 and 2007**

| Features | 1992 | 2007 |
|---|---|---|
| | **Corporate Securities Market** | |
| Regulator | No specific regulator, Central Government oversight | A specialized regulator for securities market (SEBI) vested with the powers to protect investors' interest and to develop and regulate securities market, SROs strengthened |
| Securities | Limited number of traditional instruments | Expanded to cover Government securities, units of CISs and MFs, derivatives of securities, security receipts, etc. |
| Form of Securities | Physical | Dematerialised |
| Regulatory Approach | Merit-based regulation | Disclosure-based regulation |
| Intermediaries | Some of the intermediaries (stock brokers, authorized clerks and remisiers) regulated by the SROs | A variety of specialized intermediaries emerged. They are registered and regulated by SEBI (also by SROs in some instances). They as well as their employees are required to follow a code of conduct and are subject to a number of compliances. All participants are |

| | | |
|---|---|---|
| | | identified by a unique indentification number |
| Access to Market | Granted by the Central Government | Eligible issuers access the market after complying with the issue requirements |
| Disclosure | Voluntary, vague, scanty and non-standardised | Standardised, systematic and at par with the international standards. A dedicated website for corporate disclosures, EDIFAr, operationalised |
| Pricing of Securities | Determined by the Central Government | Determined by market, either by the issuer through fixed price or by the investors through book building |
| Access to International Market | No access | Corporates allowed to issue ADRs/GDRs and raise ECBs. ADRs/GDRs have two way fungibility. FIIs allowed to trade in Indian market. MFs also allowed to invest overseas |
| Corporate Compliance | Very little emphasis | Emphasis on disclosures, accounting standards and corporate governance |
| Mutual Funds | Restricted to public sector | Open to private sector and emergence of a variety of funds and schemes |
| Exchange Structure | Mutual not-for-profit exchanges | For profit corporate, demutualised exchanges |
| Trading Mechanism | Open outcry, available at the trading rings of the exchanges; opaque, auction/negotiated deals | Screen-based trading system; orders are matched on price-time priority; transparent, trading platform accessible from all over the country |
| Aggregation of Order of Flow | Market fragmented by geographical distance. Order flow observed. | Order flow observed. The exchanges have open electronic consolidated limit order book (OECLOB) |
| Anonymity in Trading | Absent | Complete |
| Settlement Cycle | 14-days account period settlement, not adhered to always | Rolling settlement on T + 2 basis |
| Counterparty Risk | Present | Absent |
| Form of Settlement | Physical | Mostly electronic |
| Basis of Settlement | Bilateral netting | Multilateral netting |
| Transfer of Securities | Cumbersome. Transfer by endorsement security and registration by issuer | Securities are freely transferable. Transfers are recorded electronically in book entry form by depositories |
| Risk Management | No focus on risk management | Comprehensive risk management system encompassing capital adequacy, limits on exposure and turnover, VaR-based margining, client level gross margining, online position monitoring, business continuity plans, etc. |

| | | |
|---|---|---|
| Derivatives Trading | Absent | A wide array of exchange traded derivatives such as Futures and Options on indices and select securities and Futures on interest rate available |
| Research | very little | Many market participants have full-fledged research departments. Some of them have schemes/initiatives to promote research |
| | **Government Securities Market** | |
| Securities | Plain vanilla securities | Expanded to include zero coupon bonds, floating securities rate bonds, capital indexed bonds, bonds with embedded derivatives, interest rate futures, etc. |
| Form of Securities | Physical | Demat holding by RBI regulated entities |
| Pricing of Securities | Administered interest rates | Issue at market related rates (auction) |
| Participation | Captive investors (mostly banks) | Expanded to allow primary dealers, FIIs, retail investors |
| Trading Mechanism | Through telephone | Negotiated Dealing System which provides negotiation and screen-based trading |
| Counterparty Risk | Present | Clearing Corporation provides novation and guarantees settlement |
| Mode of Settlement | – | Delivery-versus-payment (DVP-III) |

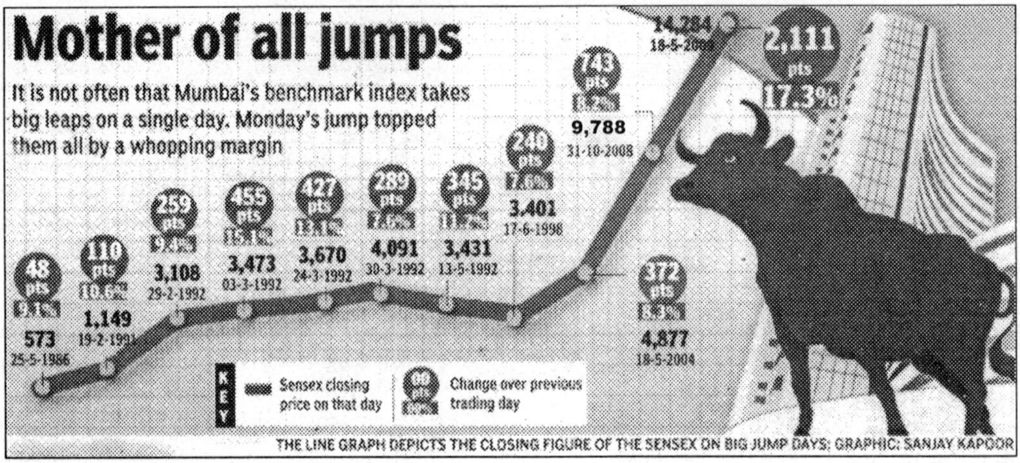


## DECODING CIRCUIT BREAKER

**What is a circuit breaker?**

A circuit breaker helps check abnormal movement in indices, and alsó stock manipulation. The breaker is applied in three stages of movement — 10%, 15% and 20% — either up or down.

**How's the circuit limit fixed?**

A circuit limit is fixed on the basis of the indices' closing values at the end of the previous quarter. Monday's limits were based on the closing values of the Sensex and the Nifty on March 31, 2009.

| | |
|---|---|
|  | Nifty touches 15% circuit within **60 seconds** of opening; Trading suspended for two hours |
|  | Trading resumes but **suspended** for the rest of the day after indices hit **20% circuit** |

**Ben S Bernanke & Toshihiko Fukui**

**Jean-Claude Trichet & Mervyn King**

- **For the first time** in Indian stock market history, trading suspended for hitting the Upper Circuit
- **Only 845 companies** were able to trade on BSE while the number on NSE was just 587

# CHAPTER 9

# MONEY MARKET

## INTRODUCTION

The money market is a key component of the financial system. It is a market for short-term funds with maturity ranging from overnight to one year. It includes instruments that are deemed to the close substitutes of money or near money like trade bills, promissory notes and Government Papers drawn for a short period not exceeding one year. These short-term instruments can be converted into cash readily without any loss and at low transaction cost.

Money market is the centre for dealing mainly in short-term money assets. It meets the short-term requirements of borrowers and provides liquidity or cash to lenders. It is the place where short-term surplus funds at the disposal of financial institutions and individuals are borrowed by individuals and also the government.

The money market does not refer to a particular place where short-term funds are dealt with. It includes all individuals, institutions and intermediaries dealing with short-term funds. The transactions between borrowers, lenders and middlemen take place through telephone, telegraph, mail and agents. No personal contact or presence of the two parties is essential for negotiations in a money market. However, a geographical name may be given to a money market according to its location. For example, the London money market operates from Wall Street. But, they attract funds from all over the world to be lent to borrowers from all over the globe. Similarly, the Mumbai money market is the centre for short-term loanable funds of not only Mumbai, but also the whole of India.

Money market is the fulcrum of monetary operations conducted by the central bank (RBI) in its pursuit of monetary policy objectives. An objective analysis of the structure of the Indian money market, therefore assumes great importance in the study of monetary policy and central banking activities. In this chapter the concept, structure and management are discussed in brief.

## THE CONCEPT

At the outset, it is necessary to examine what we mean by the term *money market,* which has sometimes been defined as an organisation for dealings in loan money or borrowed funds. This is a very broad definition and has been adopted by a number of writers. It is also defined as follows:

*A money market is a mechanism through which short-term funds are loaned and borrowed and through which a large part of the financial transactions of a particular country or of the world are cleared.* Broadly conceived, it includes the entire mechanism employed in financial business of all types. In the narrower sense, in which the term is generally used, however, a money market includes only dealings in more or less standardised types of loans, such as call loans and in credit instruments, such as acceptance and Treasury Bills, in which personal relations between lender and borrower are of negligible importance. In this sense, a money market is distinct from, but supplementary to the commercial banking system.[1]

Money market has no geographical constraints and relates to all dealings in money or monetary assets. J.S.G. Wilson defined the money market as a "centre in which financial institutions congregate for the purpose of dealing impersonally in monetary assets". This is giving too literal an interpretation of money market. In fact, 'money market' is a wide term and encompasses a variety of transactions, instruments and institutions. Money market is a centre where borrowers and lenders of money and near money assets are put together. It may comprise a group of such markets for various types of money assets characterised by relative liquidity or nearness to money. Such assets may be called call money, treasury bills or bills of exchange, etc. Secondly, although there are various centres of money market such as Mumbai, Kolkata, Chennai, etc., they are not separate independent markets but are interlinked and related. Thirdly, in a true sense of free and perfect competition, there should be only one price for each category of money assets, which would result from dealing of purchase and sale made on a purely impersonal basis and through blind economic forces. The financial institutions dealing in these assets may be spread over so wide a geographical area that it would be impossible to specify the geographical limits of the market. The fact that there are some geographical centres does not limit the operations to these centres.

According to Geottery Crowther, "The money market is the collective name given to the various firms and institutions that deal in the various grades of near money".

The RBI defines the money market as, a 'market for short-term financial assets that are close substitutes for money, facilitates the exchange of money for new financial claims in the primary market as also for financial claims, already issued, in the secondary market'.

Traditionally, the money market in India comprised mainly the call money market. Although other money market segments, *viz.,* commercial bills market and inter-

---

1. Madan, J.T. and Nadler, M.: *The International Money Markets,* 1935, p. 108. See also Wilson, J.S.G.: 'The Business in India', in *Banking in the British Commonwealth,* edited by R.S. Sayers, 1952, p. 102, where Wilson writes: "In essence, a money market is a place where the borrowers and lenders of short-term funds are brought together".

corporate deposits market have been in existence for a long time, there has not been much activity in these segments. Therefore, for assessing the impact of reforms on the money market the focus is mainly on the call money market. The impact of reforms is assessed in terms of behaviour of the call money market and the market growth related parameters, including those instruments, which were introduced in the 1990s.

The development of securities markets usually starts with trading in a short-term money market instrument, often a Government security. Other money market instruments are inter-bank deposits, bankers' acceptances, certificates of deposit and commercial paper issued by non-financial corporations. Money markets provide a non-inflationary way to finance government deficits. They also allow governments to implement monetary policy through open market operations and provide a market-based reference point for setting other interest rates. Furthermore, money markets are a source of funds for commercial banks and other institutions with limited branch networks, including foreign banks and leasing and factoring companies. By enabling large corporations to issue short-term securities in the form of commercial paper, money markets make the corporate loan market more competitive and reduce the market power of large commercial banks.

## ROLE OF THE MONEY MARKET

The money market forms an important part of the financial system by providing an avenue for equilibrating the surplus funds of lenders and the requirements of borrowers for short periods ranging from overnight up to a year. It also provides a focal point for central bank's intervention for influencing the liquidity in the financial system and thereby transmitting the monetary policy impulses.

The money market performs three broad functions.

One, it provides an equilibrating mechanism for demand and supply of short-term funds.

Two, it enables borrowers and lenders of short-term funds to fulfil their borrowing and investment requirements at an efficient market clearing price.

Three, it provides an avenue for Central Bank (RBI) intervention in influencing both quantum and cost of liquidity in the financial system.

From the point of view of monetary and financial stability, an effective functioning of the money market is very important.

## IMPORTANCE OF MONEY MARKET

A developed money market plays an important role in the financial system of a country by supplying short-term funds adequately and quickly to trade and industry. The money market is an integral part of a country's economy. Therefore, a developed money market is highly indispensable for the rapid development of the economy. A developed money market helps the smooth functioning of the financial system in an economy in the following ways:

**(i) Development of Trade and Industry:** Money market is an important source of financing trade and industry. The money market is an integral part of country's economy. The money market, through discounting operations and commercial papers, finances the short-term working capital requirements of trade and industry and facilitates the development of industry and trade both — national and international.

**(ii) Development of Capital Market:** The short-term rates of interest and conditions that prevail in the money market influence the long-term interest as well as the resource mobilization in capital market. Hence, the development of capital market depends upon the existence of a developed money market.

**(iii) Smooth Functioning of Commercial Banks:** The money market provides the commercial banks with facilities for temporarily employing their surplus funds in easily realisable assets. The banks can get back the funds quickly, in times of need, by resorting to the money market. The commercial banks gain immensely by economising on their cash balances in hand and at the same time meeting the demand for large withdrawal of their depositors. It also enables commercial banks to meet their statutory requirements of Cash Reserve Ratio (CRR) and Statutory Liquidity Ratio (SLR) by utilizing the money market mechanism.

**(iv) Effective Central Bank Control:** A developed money market helps the effective functioning of a central bank. It facilitates effective implementation of the monetary policy of a central bank. The central bank, through the money market, pumps new money into the economy in slump and siphons it off in boom. The central bank, thus, regulates the flow of money so as to promote economic growth with stability.

**(iv) Formulation of Suitable Monetary Policy:** Conditions prevailing in a money market serve as a true indicator of the monetary state of an economy. Hence, it serves as a guide to the government in formulating and revising the monetary policy then and there depending upon the monetary conditions prevailing in the market.

**(vi) Non-inflationary Source of Finance to Government:** A developed money market helps the government to raise short-term funds through the Treasury Bills floated in the market. In the absence of a developed money market, the government would be forced to print and issue more money or borrow from the central bank. Both ways would lead to an increase in prices and the consequent inflationary trend in the economy.

## SUB-MARKETS

However, with the development of the economy and techniques, the money market is composed of money sub-markets of a sort in almost every country in the form of institutions that lend and borrow money for short periods. Some of these markets, for example, the call money market, short-term market, capital market, stock market or bond market, commercial bill market, treasury bill market, discount market, etc., are highly developed and well organised. The larger the number of sub-markets, the broader and more developed is the structure of the money market. In developed money markets, large varieties of sub-markets have been organised for specialised dealings in almost all sources of loanable funds. Money markets that are undeveloped generally lack such of a variety of sub-markets.[2]

The Indian money market has generally been divided into two watertight compartments: that which concerns itself with modern commercial banking and that which derives from indigenous practice with a tradition going back many hundred years.[3] The "black market money" or "unaccounted money" is made up of accumulated gains, largely of illegal transactions which cannot be brought into account books or into bank accounts.[4]

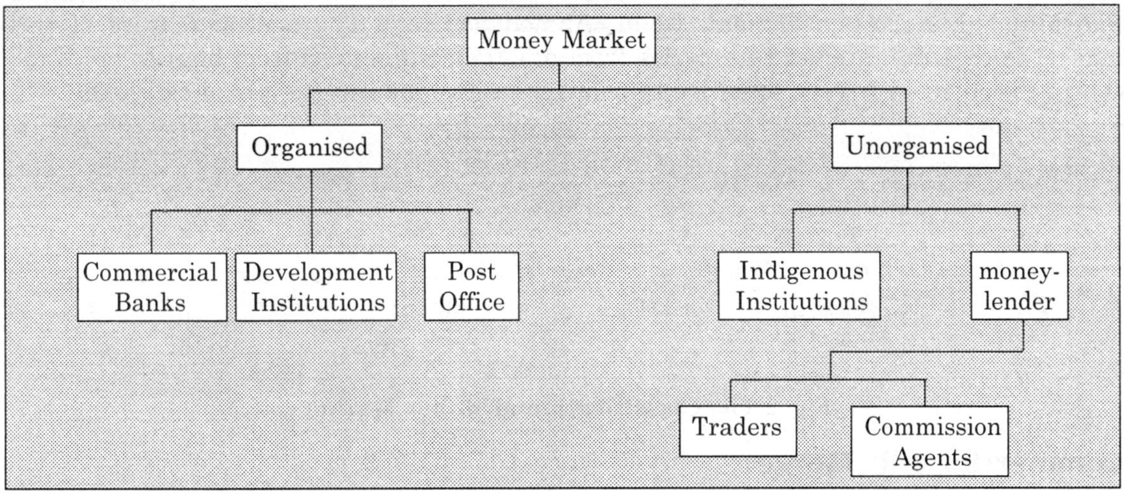


**Fig. 1 The Institutionalisation of Money Market**

## ORGANISED SECTOR

The organised sector of the money market consists of the Reserve Bank of India, commercial banks, large-sized joint stock companies lending money, financial intermediaries such as the Life Insurance, Credit and Investments Corporation of India, the Unit Trust of India, the Agricultural Refinance and Development Corporation, Land Mortgage Banks, Co-operative Banks, Insurance Companies, etc., and call-loan brokers, general finance brokers and stock brokers. The unorganised sector of the money market is largely made up of indigenous bankers, moneylenders, traders, commission agents, etc., some of whom combine moneylending with trade and other activities. Then there are the co-operative credit institutions set up mainly with a view to supplanting the indigenous sources of rural credit, particularly the moneylenders. These co-operative institutions are liberally assisted by the Reserve Bank and are being brought into closer contact with the commercial banks. Generally speaking, these two sectors in the Indian money market — those institutions which come directly or indirectly under the broad regulations of the Reserve Bank constitute the organised sector, while the others, which

2. Sen, S.N.: *Central Banking in Undeveloped Money Markets,* 1961, p. 17.
3. See Gupta, G.P.: *Reserve Bank of India and Monetary Management,* 1962, p. 234.
4. Gadgil, D.R.: "Effectiveness of Credit Regulation by the Reserve Bank of India," *Artha-Vijnana,* March 1963, p. 2.

fall completely outside the purview of the central banking regulations, make up the unorganised sector.

## Call Money Market

The call money market is a market for extremely short period loans say one day to fourteen days. So, it is highly liquid. The loans are repayable on demand at the option of either the lender or the borrower. In India, call money markets are associated with the presence of stock exchanges and hence, they are located in major industrial towns like Mumbai, Kolkata, Chennai, Delhi, Ahmedabad, etc. The special feature of this market is that the interest rate varies from day-to-day and even from hour-to-hour and centre-to-centre. It is very sensitive to changes in demand and supply of call loans.

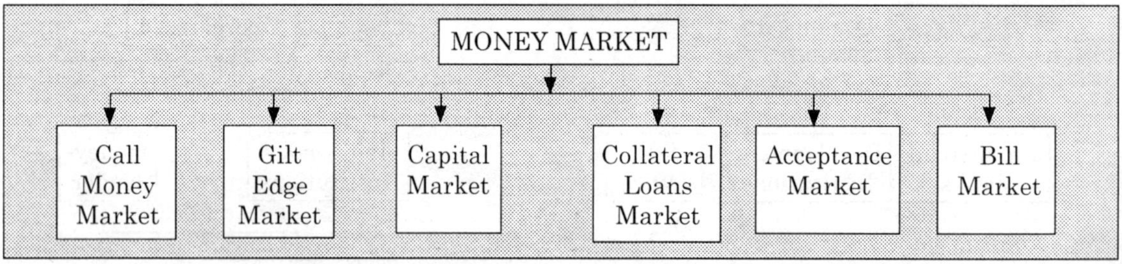


**Fig. 2 The Classification of Money Market**

## Commercial Bills Market

It is a market for Bills of Exchange arising out of genuine trade transactions. In the case of credit sale, the seller may draw a bill of exchange on the buyer. The buyer accepts such a bill promising to pay at a later date the amount specified in the bill. The seller need not wait until the due date of the bill. Instead, he can get immediate payment by discounting the bill.

In India the bill market is underdeveloped. The RBI has taken many steps to develop a sound bill market. The RBI has enlarged the list of participants in the bill market. The Discount and Finance House of India was set up in 1988 to promote secondary market in bills. In spite of all these, the growth of the bill market is slow in India. There are no specialised agencies for discounting bills. The commercial banks play a significant role in this market.

## Treasury Bills Market

It is a market for treasury bills which have 'short-term' maturity. A Treasury Bill is a promissory note or a finance bill issued by the government. It is highly liquid because its repayment is guaranteed by the government. It is an important instrument for short-term borrowing of the government. There are two types of treasury bills namely: (i) ordinary or regular, and (ii) *ad hoc* Treasury Bills popularly known as *'ad hocs'*.

Ordinary treasury bills are issued to the public, banks and other financial institutions with a view to raising resources for the Central Government to meet its short-term financial needs. *Ad hoc* Treasury Bills are issued in favour of the RBI only. They are not sold through tender or auction. They can be purchased by the RBI only. *Ad hocs* are not marketable in India but holders of these bills can sell them back to RBI. Treasury Bills have a maturity period of 91 days or 182 days or 364 days only. Financial intermediaries can park their temporary surpluses in these instruments and earn income.

## Short-term Loan Market

It is a market where short-term loans are given to corporate customers for meeting their working capital requirements. Commercial banks provide short-term loans in the form of cash credit and overdraft. Overdraft facility is mainly given to business people, whereas cash credit is given to industrialists. Overdraft is purely a temporary accommodation and it is given in the current account itself. But cash credit is for a period of one year and it is sanctioned in a separate account.

The organised sector of the Indian money market is comparatively well-developed in terms of organised relationships and specialisation of functions. It more or less centres round the Reserve Bank of India; and the State Bank, commercial banks and co-operative banks are associated with it. The policies and operations of the State Bank and the co-operative banks are governed by the Reserve Bank and are also dependent on it for direct financial assistance. In fact, a substantial portion of the funds which co-operative credit agencies lend out is provided by the Reserve Bank. Financial intermediaries, such as the Industrial Financial Corporation, the Industrial Development Bank of India, State Financial Corporation, the Agricultural Refinance Corporation, etc., derive most of their resources from the Reserve Bank. The policies of these financial intermediaries are enunciated with the approvals of the Reserve Bank; even the personnel of some of them are supplied by the Reserve Bank. More important than all the above-mentioned institutions, is the inter-bank call-money market, which is regarded as the core of the Indian money market. "*Although the magnitude of funds dealt in this market is not large in relation to the deposit resources of banks, perhaps this is the most sensitive sector of the money market.*" Then there are the Treasury Bills and bills of exchange, which absorb the surplus liquidity of the institutions in the organised sector.

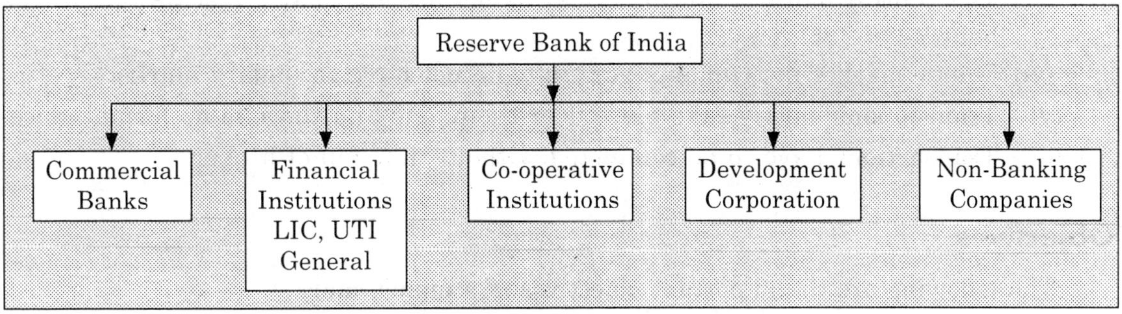


**Fig. 3 Institutions in the Organised Sector under the Control of the Reserve Bank of India**

## FEATURES OF A MONEY MARKET

The following are the general features of a money market:

(i) It is a market purely for short-term funds or financial assets called near money.

(ii) It deals with financial assets having a maturity period up to one year only.

(iii) It deals with only those assets which can be converted into cash readily without loss and with minimum transaction cost.

(iv) Generally, transactions take place through phone, i.e., oral communication. Relevant document and written communications can be exchanged subsequently. There is no formal place like stock exchange as in the case of a capital market.

(v) Transactions have to be conducted without the help of brokers.

(vi) It is not a single homogeneous market. It comprises several sub-markets, each specializing in a particular type of financing, e.g., Call money market, Acceptance market, Bill market and, so on.

(vii) The components of a money market are the Central Bank, Commercial Banks, Non-banking financial companies, discount houses and acceptance houses. Commercial banks generally play a dominant role in this market.

**Other features of the money market are:**

(i) It is a market for short-term loanable funds for a period of not exceeding one year.

(ii) This market supplies funds for financing current business operations, working capital requirements of industries and short period requirements of the government.

(iii) The instruments that are dealt in a money market are bills of exchange, treasury bills, commercial papers, certificate of deposit, etc.

(iv) Each single money market instrument is of large amount. A TB is of minimum for rupees one lakh. Each CD or CP is for a minimum of ₹ 25 lakh.

(v) The central bank and commercial banks are the major institutions in the money market.

(vi) Money market instruments generally do not have secondary markets.

(vii) Transactions mostly take place over-the-phone and there is no formal place.

(viii) Transactions have to be conducted without the help of brokers.

### Objectives

The following are the important objectives of a money market:

(i) To provide a parking place to employ short-term surplus funds.

(ii) To provide room for overcoming short-term deficits.

(iii) To enable the central bank to influence and regulate liquidity in the economy through its intervention in this market.

(iv) To provide a reasonable access to user of short-term funds to meet their requirements quickly, adequately and at reasonable costs.

## Characteristic Features of a Developed Money Market

In order to fulfil the above objectives, the money market should be fully developed and efficient. In every country of the world, some type of money market exists. Some of them are highly developed while others are not well developed. Prof. S. N. Sen has described certain essential features of a developed money market. They are as follows:

**(i) Highly Organised Banking System:** The commercial banks are the nerve centre of the whole money market. They are the principal suppliers of short-term funds. Their policies regarding loans and advances have impact on the entire money market. The commercial banks serve as a vital link between the central bank and the various segments of the money market. Consequently, a well developed money market and a highly organized banking system co-exist. In an underdeveloped money market, the commercial banking system is not fully developed.

## FUNCTIONS OF MONEY MARKET

As the Reserve Bank of India observes, "A well-developed money market is the basis for an effective monetary policy. It is in the money market that the central bank comes into contact with the financial sectors of the economy as a whole and it is through varying the liquidity in the market and thereby influencing the cost and availability of credit that the bank achieves its economic objectives."

The important functions of a well developed money market may be listed down in more precise terms as follows:

(1) By providing various kinds of credit instruments suitable and attractive for different sections, a money market augments the supply of funds.

(2) Efficient working of a money market helps to minimize the gluts and stringencies in the money market due to the seasonal variations in the flow of and demand for funds.

(3) A money market helps to avoid wide seasonal fluctuations in the interest rates.

(4) A money market, by augmenting the supply of funds and making them readily available to the legitimate borrowers, help in making funds available at cheaper rates.

(5) A well organized money market, through quick transfer of funds from one place to another, helps to avoid the regional gluts and stringencies of funds.

(6) It enhances the amount of liquidity available to the entire country.

(7) A money market, by providing profitable investment opportunities for short-term surplus funds, helps to enhance the profit of financial institutions and individuals.

## MONEY MARKET INSTRUMENTS

A variety of instruments are available in a developed money market. In India, till 1986, only a few instruments were available. They were:

(i) Treasury Bills in the treasury market.

(ii) Money at call and short notice in the call loan market.

(iii) Commercial bill, promissory notes in the bill market.

Now, in addition to the above, the following new instruments are available:

(i) Commercial papers (CPs)

(ii) Certificate of deposit (CD)

(iii) Inter-bank participation certificates

(iv) Repo instruments.

## CHARACTERISTICS OF MONEY MARKET

A major characteristic of the Indian money market each year is the pronounced swing from 'busy' to 'slack' times and *vice versa*.[5] The Reserve Bank provides accommodation to the commercial banks, especially during the busy season; and the treasury bills issued by the Reserve Bank provide an important outlet for the surplus funds of the commercial banks during the slack season. In the same way, other financial institutions, such as hire-purchase companies, insurance companies, etc., place their surplus funds with commercial banks or co-operative banks in short-term deposits; and they borrow from the commercial banks in case of need. The noteworthy feature is that one does not find a clear-cut demarcation of functions among the institutions comprising the organised money market in India, as one finds, for example, among the financial institutions in UK, where the commercial banks, discount houses, acceptance houses, etc., perform a highly specialised set of functions, and their spheres of operations are well defined and co-ordinated. But in India, the Reserve Bank is not only the lender of the last resort, but provides capital to co-operative banks, refinance facilities for export and special accommodation to banks financing small industries. Commercial banks in India directly undertake the discounting of commercial bills. In UK, however, such bills are initially taken up by the discount houses. Therefore, in India, there is a considerable overlapping of functions among the institutions comprising the organised money market, which perhaps is the outcome of the peculiar circumstances under which they have developed.

The Indian banking structure possesses a heterogeneous mass of indigenous banks, joint stock banks and co-operative banks as its base layers; the highly organised, developed and nationalised banks, State Bank as its middle layer and a state-owned central bank, namely, the Reserve Bank of India, as its apex.[6]

The organised sector is principally composed of the commercial banks, the co-operative banks and the land mortgage banks. Considering the continental character of

5. *Tata Quarterly*, April/July, 1964, p. 43.
6. Ghosh, Alak: *Indian Economy*, 1963, p. 468.

the country, the banking development is most inadequate for the needs of trade and industry, largely because of the hoarding habit among the people. J.S.G. Wilson remarks: "*The hoarding habit appears to provide an almost bottomless pit for the absorption of gold and silver*".[7]

With a view to strengthening the organised money market in India, new institutions have been established and consolidated to either lend on long-term basis or regulate credit in a prescribed manner. The new institutions which have come up after independence are the Industrial Finance Corporation (1948); the National Industrial Development Corporation (1954); the Industrial Credit and Investment Corporation of India, Ltd., (1955); State Financial Corporations (1951); the National Small-scale Industries Corporations (1955); the Agricultural Refinance and Development Corporation; the Unit Trust of India (1964) and the Industrial Development Bank of India (1964), which incorporates the Refinance Corporation and the Industrial Reconstruction Corporation (1971).

## GROWTH OF MONEY MARKET: POST REFORM

The money market in India witnessed significant progress particularly from the mid-1990s in terms of refinements in money market instruments, introduction of new instruments and supplementary measures to add depth and liquidity to the market. The money market instruments in India during the period mainly consisted of: *(i)* Call/Notice Money, *(ii)* Term Money, *(iii)* Certificates of Deposit, *(iv)* Commercial Paper, *(v)* Treasury Bills, *(vi)* Repurchase Agreements (Repos), *(vii)* Interest Rate Swaps/Forward Rate Agreements, and *(viii)* Rediscounting of commercial bills scheme.

During the 1990s, the participation in the call money market was widened to cover primary and satellite dealers and corporates (through primary dealers) besides other participants. While banks and primary dealers are permitted to lend and borrow in the market, other entities could participate only as lenders. Following the recommendations of the Narasimham Committee (1998) and the Reserve Bank's Internal Working Group-1997, steps were initiated to reform the call money market and make it a pure inter-bank market, in a phased manner starting in 1999. With the development of the repo market since the late 1990s, the call money market has gradually been transformed into a pure inter-bank market including primary dealers. This process which was initiated in 1999, was completed in August 2005.

A significant development in the Indian money market has been the introduction of rupee derivatives, i.e., Interest Rate Swaps (IRS) /Forward Rate Agreements (FRA) in 1999 to further deepen the money market and enable market participants to hedge their risks. In addition to several other measures taken since its introduction, with effect from May 20, 2005, market participants were advised to use only domestic rupee benchmarks for interest rate derivatives. Market participants were however, given a transition period of six months for using Mumbai Inter-bank Forward Offered Rate (MIFOR) as a benchmark, subject to review. However, on request from the Fixed Income Money Market and Derivatives Association (FIMMDA), market participants have been allowed to use MIFOR swaps in respect of transactions having underlying permissible forex

7. *Op. cit.*, p. 151. Wilson also gives some of the reasons for the strength of the hoarding habit in India.

exposures, for market making purpose, subject to appropriate limit as may be approved by the Reserve Bank.

## UNORGANISED SECTOR

As regards the agencies constituting the unorganised money market, it is necessary at the outset to clarify one important point regarding the nomenclature used to designate them. The term *unorganised money market* conveys the impression that indigenous agencies providing credit have neither any system nor any organisation among themselves, nor any definite procedure regulating their lending practices. In fact, these agencies have been functioning for ages in almost all parts of this country, and have a time-tested organisation. They follow well-set patterns, both as regards their lending policies and their interest rates. Their native origin is mainly responsible for some of their unique features, which have few parallels among similar agencies in Europe.

## INDIGENOUS BANKING

The system of indigenous banking in India is of ancient growth and dates back to Vedic times, which may be taken to range between 2000 B.C. and 1400 B.C. Moneylending was regarded as an ancient practice. That it was practised even in the early Aryan days is evident from the references to moneylending as one of the four honest callings, the other three being tillage, trading and harvesting. The researches of MacDonnell and Keith provide the main source of information regarding moneylending during the Vedic and Pre-vedic periods. *Rina* (debt) is often mentioned in the Rig Veda and in late Vedas, and indicates a normal condition in the Vedic society. On the subject of interest, the available information is sketchy. That interest was charged may be inferred from the fact that the usurer (kusidin) is referred to in the Shatapatha Brahmana and the Sutras. However, little is known about the rate of interest prevailing in Vedic times or the terms and conditions on which loans were advanced. The available evidence shows that rather low rates were generally prevalent and usurious rates were frowned upon.

The money market in India is dominated by the unorganised sector. The only link that exists between the organised and unorganised sectors is through the commercial banks. Indigenous shroffs carry on their activities through the media of these commercial banks. In rural areas, they do so through co-operative credit societies. However, a number of credit societies are under the control of moneylenders. In fact, the Rural Credit Survey Report gives instances of moneylenders who are actively associated with co-operative credit agencies either as members or as office-bearers. Recently, more instances of their active interest have come to light. It seems that a growing number of spurious co-operative societies have been organised solely to enable these moneylenders to take advantage of the concessions they offer. The indigenous bankers use banks as intermediate agencies of their transactions and yet remain outside the orbit of central bank control.

The unorganised market has of late been strengthened with the addition of unaccounted money, variously known as black money or unaccounted gains or untaxed

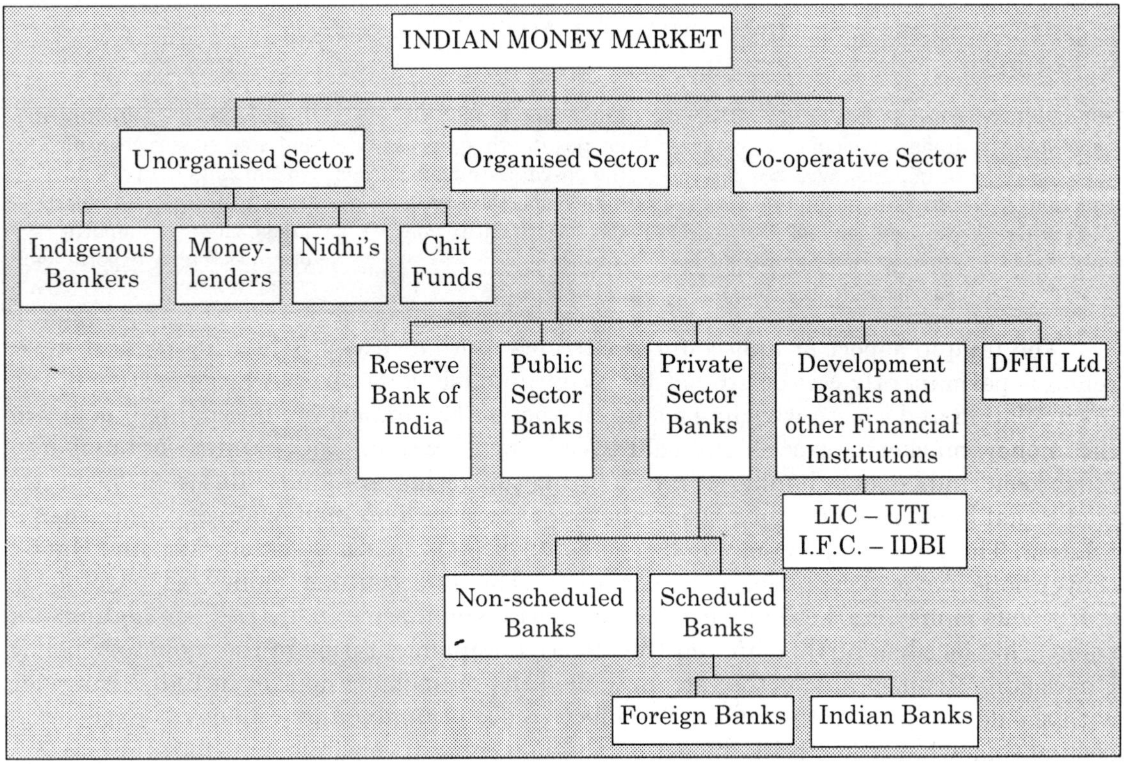


**Fig. 4.4 The Indian Money Market.**

assets. A conservative estimate places this amount at between ₹ 2,500 crore and ₹ 4,000 crore or more.

As a result of the income velocity of money, considerable savings will be accruing in the unaccounted income sector. These savings seek outlets which again escape from the tax-net and thus enlarges the unaccounted sector. In view of the plethora of liquid funds in the unaccounted sector and the high rates of return in the speculative holding of goods, the production circuit is severely disturbed. In an international context, there are high returns from in-smuggling and out-smuggling of goods, drugs and precious metals. These high-staked, high-return activities are invariably financed from the unaccounted money. Likewise, unaccounted money is also found in real estate and also a useful source of finance for the political process. In the process, the unaccounted sector has acquired respectability and at the same time, running a parallel money market with a continued drain to the exchequer and violation of foreign exchange laws. The operation of the unaccounted income (money) sector is illustrated as follows:

**UNACCOUNTED MONEY MARKET**

| | | | | | |
|---|---|---|---|---|---|
| Speculative holding, gold, silver, diamonds, and other jewellery | Foreign Exchange, under-invoicing of imports, over-invoicing of inputs, over-invoicing of exports. Hotel and Tourist Industry | Growth, Stocks, Invent-ories of Commo-dities | Financing of political parties (by this process the operators have acquired high respectability in the society with wide contacts) | Real Estate, building sites, vacant flats, agricultural lands, sites of mines, etc. | Holding of government permits, transport, imports, exports, etc. |

The unique aspect of unaccounted currency is that, except when hoarded, it never remains permanently concealed, not for a continuously long-term. A large portion of it is in circulation and constantly changes its character. The impact of unaccounted money on the money market is very significant. With its growth in the country, a number of mushroom indigenous bankers have sprung up, who are quite different from the traditional bankers; and it has been reported that they lend money at very high rates of interest. The indigenous money market has itself become a lawless market, and the old conventions have very little relevance to it. The unaccounted money as part of the indigenous money market is invested in property, small-scale industries, smuggling, and trade. This fact has further limited the effective implementation of the monetary policy. Unaccounted money has further strengthened the indigenous market in India. However, with the devaluation of the rupee, the effective use of unaccounted money is expected to decline somewhat, though its impact on the market will continue as before (Fig. 5).

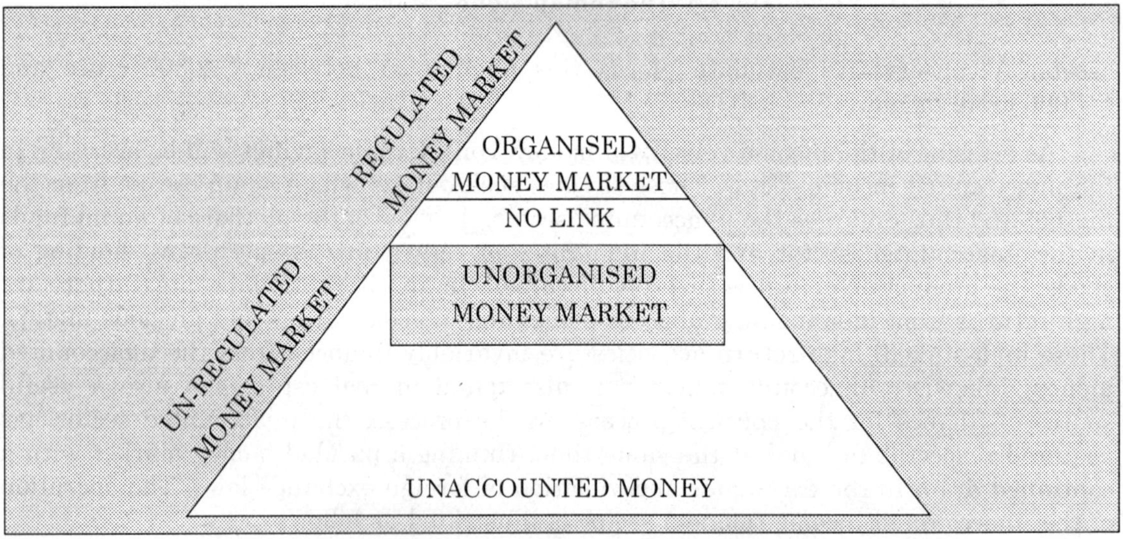


**Fig. 5 The broad-basing of the unorganised money market with the growth of unaccounted money**

Since there is no direct link between the unorganised and organised money markets, it is essential to establish such a link. The link of commercial banks between the two markets is so weak that it is more advantageous to the unorganised market than to the organised sector.

## EFFECTIVE MANAGEMENT

The money market performs three broad functions. One, it provides an equilibrating mechanism for demand and supply of short-term funds. Two, it enables borrowers and lenders of short-term funds to fulfil their borrowing and investment requirements at an efficient market clearing price. Three, it provides an avenue for central bank intervention in influencing both quantum and cost of liquidity in the financial system, thereby transmitting monetary policy impulses to the real economy. The objective of monetary management by the central bank is to align money market rates with the key policy rate. As excessive money market volatility could deliver confusing signals about the stance of monetary policy, it is critical to ensure orderly market behaviour, from the point of view of both monetary and financial stability. Thus, efficient functioning of the money market is important for the effectiveness of monetary policy.

In order to meet these basic functions efficiently, money markets have evolved over time spawning new instruments and participants with varying risk profiles in line with the changes in the operating procedures of monetary policy. Changes in financial market structures, macroeconomic objectives and economic environment have called for shifts in monetary regimes, which, in turn, have necessitated refinements both in the operating instruments and procedures, and in institutional arrangements by central banks.

Internationally, following the break down of the Bretton Woods system, there was a shift from rule-based frameworks towards discretion in the use of monetary policy instruments, which ultimately led to the gradual abandonment of exchange rate targets. Changes in financial structures and financial innovations also rendered monetary targeting ineffective by making the money demand functions unstable. Accordingly, since the early 1990s there has been a shift towards greater exchange rate flexibility and adoption of inflation targeting by some central banks partly because of increased capital mobility, greater financial market integration and repeated episodes of currency crises. Commensurate with these changes, central banks have moved away from conventional (direct) instruments of monetary control (working through the quantum channel towards more use of indirect instruments (operating through the price channel). Accordingly, the use of reserve requirements and direct credit controls has been gradually de-emphasized, while relying more on interest rates for signalling the monetary policy stance. As central banks have only limited control over long-term interest rate, the most commonly adopted strategy has been to extert direct influence only on short-term interest rates and permitting market expectations to influence long-term interest rates through financial market inter-linkages. Thus, the choice of monetary policy instruments is guided by the structure of the money market.

## MONEY MARKET DEVELOPMENT

The development of the money market contributes to the efficiency of the financial sector by allowing financial institutions to transfer surplus funds to other financial institutions instead of directly financing inefficient borrowers or discouraging depositors; and by facilitating the management of bank liabilities through refinancing, thereby increasing the availability of long-term finance for investment. In addition, open-market operations could be conducted more effectively and their effects on banks' marginal cost of funds felt more rapidly. Specific policies to develop and strengthen money markets have been addressed in fund programmes of technical assistance. Such policies include strengthening broker-dealer services and their regulation, introducing money market instruments, reforming the central bank's discount window operations to support money market development consistent with monetary control, setting up auction systems in the primary market for money market financial instruments, and favourable tax treatment of interest income of financial assets.

The Indian money market prior to the 1980s was characterized by paucity of instruments, lack of depth and dichotomy in the market structure. The money market consisted of the inter-bank call market, Treasury Bills, Commercial Bills and participation certificates. Historically, the call money market has constituted the core of the money market structure in India due to lack of other instruments and strict regulations on interest rates and participation.

In the call/notice money market, overnight money and money at short notice (up to a period of 14 days) are lent and borrowed without collateral. This market enables banks to bridge their short-term liquidity mismatches arising out of their short-term operation. The call money market in India was purely an inter-bank market until 1971 when the erstwhile Unit Trust of India (UTI) and Life Insurance Corporation (LIC) of India were allowed to participate as lenders. The interest rate in the call money market was freely determined by the market till December 1973. However, as call money rates sharply to touch 25-30 per cent, the Indian Banks Association (IBA) instituted an administered system of interest rates by imposing a ceiling interest rate of 15 per cent in December 1973 so as to maintain systemic stability and quell any abnormal rise in the call rates. The ceiling was subject to several revisions but there were several instances of violation of the ceiling rates through other means (like buyback arrangements) during phases of tight liquidity.

Treasury Bills constituted the main instrument of short-term borrowing by the government and served as a convenient gilt-edged security for the money market. The characteristics of high liquidity, absence of default risk and negligible capital depreciation of Treasury Bills made them another attractive instrument for short-term investment by banks and other financial institutions. The Reserve Bank, being the banker to the government, issued Treasury Bills at a discount. The issuance system of Treasury Bills migrated from an auction to tap basis in July 1965 with the rate of discount administratively fixed at 3.5 per cent per annum, which was raised to 4.6 per cent by July 1974 and remained at that level, in respect of 91-day Treasury Bills till 1991. There was also a system of *ad hoc* Treasury Bills from 1955, which were created by the Central Government in favour of the Reserve Bank to automatically restore its cash balances to the minimum stipulated level, whenever there was excess drawdown of cash.

Participation Certificates (PCs) and commercial bills (under bills rediscounting scheme) were introduced in the money market in 1970. PCs were utilised mostly by financial institutions to park their funds for longer maturities and could not be developed for meeting liquidity mismatches between financial institutions and/or banks. Under the bills rediscounting scheme, the Reserve Bank rediscounted genuine trade bills

**STRUCTURE OF MONEY MARKETS**

| Instruments | Tenor | Major Participants |
|---|---|---|
| Call Money | Overnight | Scheduled commercial banks (excluding RRBs), co-operative banks, primary dealers (PDs) and till August 5, 2005 select all-India FIs, insurance companies and mutual funds. |
| Notice Money | 2 to 14 days | |
| Term Money | 15-days to 1 year | Banks, all-India financial institutions and PDs. |
| Certificates of Deposit (1989) | Minimum 7 days | Scheduled commercial banks (excluding RRBs and Local Area Banks) and select all-India financial institutions. |
| Commercial Paper (1990) | Minimum 7 days | Corporates, all-India financial institutions and PDs. |
| Forward Rate Agreements/ Interest Rate Swaps (1999) | Contracts are available for maturities up to 10 years | Scheduled commercial banks, PDs and all-India financial institutions. |
| Bills Rediscounting | | Banks, PDs, select all-India financial institutions, insurance companies and mutual funds. |
| Repurchase Agreements (1992) | | Banks, PDs, all-India financial institutions, insurance companies, mutual funds and listed corporates. |
| Market Repo | 1 day to 1 year | |
| RBI Repo (LAF) | 1 day* | Banks and PDs. |
| Treasury Bills | 91, 182 and 364 days | Banks, PDs, financial institutions and other non-bank entities. |
| Inter-bank Participation Certificates (1988) | 91 to 180 days | Scheduled commercial banks. |

* The Reserve Bank retains the option to conduct longer term repo under LAF depending on market conditions and other relevant issues.

at the Bank rate or at a rate specified by it. The underlying purpose of developing the bill market was to enable banks and other financial institutions to invest their surplus funds profitably by selecting appropriate maturities. Over the years, the rediscounting facility became restrictive and was made available on a discretionary basis. The main factors inhibiting the development of bill finance were lack of a bill culture, non-availability of stamp papers of required denominations, absence of specialized credit information agencies and an active secondary market. Both these instruments (participation certificates and commercial bills), however, did not develop any activity in these instruments remained insignificant.

Since the early 1990s, the money market has undergone a significant transformation in terms of instruments, participants and technological infrastructure. Various reform measures have resulted in a relatively deep, liquid and vibrant money market. The transformation has been facilitated by the Reserve Bank's policy initiatives as also by the shift in the monetary policy operating procedures from administered and direct to indirect market-based instruments of monetary management. The changes in the money market structure and monetary policy operating procedures in India have been broadly in step with the international experience and best practices.

Along with the shifts in the operating procedures of monetary policy, the liquidity management operations of the Reserve Bank have also been fine-tuned to enhance the effectiveness of monetary policy signalling. The increasing financial innovations in the wake of greater openness of the economy necessitated the transition from monetary targeting to a multiple indicator approach with greater emphasis on rate channels for monetary policy formulation. Accordingly, short-term interest rates have emerged as key instrument of monetary policy since the introduction of LAF, which has become the principal mechanism of modulating liquidity conditions on a daily basis.

In line with the shifts in policy emphasis, various segments of the money market have been developed. The call money market was transformed into a pure inter-bank market, while other money market instruments such as market repo and CBLO were developed to provide avenues to non-banks for managing their short-term liquidity mismatches. Furthermore, issuance norms and maturity profiles of other money market instruments such as CPs and CDs were aligned for effective transmission of policy intent across various segments. The abolition of *ad hoc* Treasury Bills and introduction of Treasury Bills auction have led to the emergence of a risk-free rate, which acts as a benchmark for pricing other money market instruments. The increased market orientation of monetary policy and greater integration of domestic markets with global financial markets however, have necessitated the development of an institutional framework for appropriate risk management practices.

**DEVELOPMENT OF A SHORT-TERM YIELD CURVE — SOME ISSUES** **BOX : 1**

The existence of a wide, deep and liquid money market is critical for the development of a smooth yield curve, which facilitates the conduct of monetary policy. As money market determines the cost of liquidity and anchors the short-end of the yield curve, the development of a deep and liquid money market is imperative for the emergence of a yield curve which would credibly transmit monetary policy signals. In this regard, the Reserve Bank has taken several measures since the mid-1990s to develop a short-term yield curve with deep liquidity. These are : *(i)* exempting inter-bank liabilities from the maintenance of CRR, *(ii)* operationalising the LAF whereby the reverse repo and repo rates are used as policy instruments to modulate liquidity conditions and stabilize call rates within the LAF corridor; *(iii)* transforming the call money market into a pure inter-bank The full implementation of the real time across settlement (RTGS) would further aid this process by contributing to systemic stability market by phasing out the non-bank lenders; *(iv)* developing other market segments with adequate access for non-banks; *(v)* developing a relatively vibrant non-RBI repo market; and *(vi)* developing the CBLO market as yet another instrument of overnight borrowing/lending facility.

Notwithstanding these initiatives, a short-term yield curve which is readily amenable for policy purposes is yet to emerge. In this regard, the single largest impediment for the emergence of a short-term yield curve has been the non-existence of a vibrant and liquid term-money market, mainly due to the inability of market participants to build long-term interest rate expectations, skewed distribution of market liquidity, reduction in the minimum maturity period of term deposits of banks, and tendency on the part of banks to deploy their surplus funds in LAF auctions rather than in term money market.

As a result, the yield curve has been flattening in recent years; it even remained inverted for a very brief period. For instance, the absorption of liquidity through sterilization operations had led the call rates and the cut-off yield on 91-day Treasury Bills to edge above the yield of 364-day Treasury Bills, leading to an inversion of a segment of the yield curve for a few days in October 2003.

The prolonged flattening of the yield curve has, however, been influenced by structural factors such as considerable softening of yields due to dismantling of administered interest rate regime, favourable inflationary expectations and excess liquidity in the wake of capital flows. The moderation in yields has also been supported by rationalization of small savings interest rates administered by the government. The stickiness of the reverse repo/repo rate could also have contributed to the flattened yield curve. Maintaining the reverse repo/repo rate at the unchanged level for an extended period of time could have also led to distortions in the term structure of interest rates. This can be understood by the fact that while the 10-year gilt yield declined by 257 basis points during May 2002 to April 2004, the reverse repo rate declined by 150 basis points while call money rates declined by 180 basis points during the same period. These structural factors appeared to have contributed to the flattening of the yield curve. Owing to these distortions, the Indian yield curve does not fully reflect the market expectations on inflation and growth prospects.

An important objective of money market reforms by the Reserve Bank in recent years has been to facilitate transparency in transactions in order to reduce transactions cost and improve price discovery. The Clearing Corporation of India Limited (CCIL) by providing for guaranteed settlement of all trades, ensures prevention of grid-lock in financial transactions. Furthermore, the introduction of CBLO by the CCIL in January 2003 and operationalisation of an order matching (OM) anonymous trading screen has made trading transparent and on a real time basis, thereby making the money market more efficient. In order to further enhance transparency in the money market, screen-based trading through the NDS-CALL was operationalised in September 2006. The full implementation of the real time across settlement (RTGS) would further aid this process by contributing to systemic stability.

Notwithstanding considerable progress, a proper short-term yield curve, which facilitates the transmission of monetary policy signals and provides a benchmark for the pricing of other short-term debt instruments, is yet to emerge fully. In this regard, the constant interaction between the Reserve Bank and market participants through frequent meetings, speeches, interviews, press releases and publications is progressively expected to mute the surprise element of monetary policy and facilitate the process of formation of market expectations, which would increasingly get captured in the yield curve.

## INSTRUMENTS

In view of the rapid changes on account of financial deregulation and global financial markets integration, central banks in several countries have striven to develop and deepen the money markets by enlarging the ambit of instruments, and participants so as to improve the transmission channels of monetary policy. The structure of money markets determines the type of instruments that are feasible for the conduct of monetary management. Evidence and experience indicate that preference for market-oriented instruments by the monetary authorities helps to promote broader market development (Forssbaeck and Oxelheim, *op. cit.*).

The diminishing role of quantitative controls and search for alternatives gave rise to three major market-oriented instruments, *viz.*, short-term securities, repurchase operations and swaps. Theses instruments prompted the central banks to create, stimulate and support the development of markets particularly, inter-bank deposit market and short-term securities market. In the absence of an efficient inter-bank market, there was a pressing need for the central banks to create adequate instruments to absorb liquidity and stimulate the formation of markets for alternative short-term assets. The emergence of the short-term securities market added a new dimension to liquidity management by central banks. In the absence of outright transactions in the securities market, the existence of a liquid securities segment in the money market is often believed to facilitate the central bank's operations by providing collateral to repurchase agreements and similar collateralized transactions.

Notwithstanding depressed conditions in the capital market in the last few years, significance of the capital market in meeting the financing requirements of the corporate has generally improved. Since the initiation of the reforms, the reliance of the corporate sector on the capital market for funds increased markedly.

In the secondary market, the move to an electronic trading system has resulted in transparency in trades, better price discovery and lower transaction costs. The efficiency of the market has improved through faster execution of trades. The operational efficiency of the stock market has also been strengthened through improvements in the clearing and settlement practices and the risk management process. Almost the entire delivery of securities now takes place in dematerialized form. During the last four years or so, there has been no instance of postponement or clubbing of settlements at two main stock exchanges (BSE and NSE) despite defaults by brokers. The cases of bad deliveries have become almost nil. The setting up of trade/settlement guarantee funds in most of the exchanges has considerably reduced the settlement risk for investors. The corporate governance practices and disclosure norms have led to transparency in information flows, which, in turn, have improved the price discovery process.

## ROLE OF THE RESERVE BANK

The first thing to which the Reserve Bank of India has to assign top priority is the introduction of effective monetary management and the co-ordination of the money market with a view to bringing indigenous bankers within the fold of its central banking policy. Even before the Reserve Bank was established, the Central Banking Enquiry Committee considered it to be a matter of paramount importance. It had recommended the development of direct links between moneylenders and the Reserve Bank of India, in the same way in which it had established links with the joint-stock banks. "*Such indigenous bankers as are engaged in banking proper or are prepared to shed their business other than banking should be eligible to be placed on the approved list of the*

*Reserve Bank in the same manner as joint-stock banks.*" Some of the Provincial Banking Enquiry Committees had also suggested that:

(*i*) Indigenous bankers should be linked with the central banking institutions;

(*ii*) They should be treated as member banks on the approved list of banks;

(*iii*) Commercial banks might discount their bills more easily; and

(*iv*) Indigenous bankers should be licensed.

The scheme suggested by the Central Banking Enquiry Committee was that the Reserve Bank should prescribe a standard which indigenous bankers must follow before they are given the concessions recommended. The maintenance of proper books of accounts in the recognised manner and the submission of these books to the Reserve Bank for inspection and audit were two of the important eligibility conditions.

Although commercial banks are expected to pay much greater attention than they did in the past to the needs of small borrowers of various types, it is unlikely that they will be able to displace indigenous bankers altogether. The Banking Commission does not think that such displacement is ever possible or practicable. A more useful course would be to adopt measures which would enable these agencies to work in conformity with the overall credit policy of the Reserve Bank.

The Reserve Bank of India is the central bank of the country. In order to exercise effective monetary management, the Bank has to introduce monetary discipline in the money markets. In this connection, its first and foremost task has been to consolidate commercial banking and extend banking facilities in the country. The apex bank stands committed today in this task. The mergers introduced by the Bank since 1970 should be strengthened and extended to more scheduled and non-scheduled banks, particularly to those that are sick. The branch expansion programme should be planned so as to meet the needs of the various regions. The State Bank and its associates should be merged, the nationalised banks should be reorganised into viable units, and the link between the State Bank and commercial banks should be codified. Again, the Reserve Bank should acquire powers to control the other financial institutions in the country which substantially influence the money market. A direct link between the unorganised and organised money markets must be established. Co-operative banks should be brought within the full control of the Reserve Bank. Only then the Central Bank will be able to implement its monetary policy more effectively.

In a country like India, with large geographical dimensions, a huge population of over 68 crore and a large number of banking offices, co-operative banks and indigenous bankers, it is necessary that there should be regional central banks which would be effective with their constituents, subject to the overall control of the Central Monetary Authorities.

The regional central banks thus established should be co-ordinated, guided and controlled by a Central Monetary Board, like the Federal Reserve Bank in the USA. A leading banker observes: "*There may be, say, four or five autonomous regional reserve banks, co-ordinated by a central board, which will evolve policies and take important decisions, the execution being entrusted to the regional banks. Such decentralisation will bring the local management in closer and more intimate contact with the respective regions; this will facilitate not only better appreciation of the local problems and needs but also the development of the desired relationship between the regional reserve banks and commercial banks.*[8]

**ROLE OF THE MONEY MARKET IN THE MONETARY TRANSMISSION MECHANISM** **BOX : 2**

The money market forms the first and foremost link in the transmission of monetary policy impulses to the real economy. Policy interventions by the central bank along with its market operations influence the decisions of households and firms through the monetary policy transmission mechanism. The key to this mechanism is the total claim of the economy on the central bank, commonly known as the monetary base or high-powered money in the economy. Among the constituents of the monetary base, the most important constituent is bank reserves, i.e., the claims that banks hold in the form of deposits with the central bank. The bank's need for these reserves depends on the overall level of economic activity. This is governed by several factors: *(i)* Banks hold such reserves in proportion to the volume of deposits in many countries, known as reserve requirements, which influence their ability to extend credit and create deposits, thereby limiting the volume of transactions to be handled by the bank; *(ii)* Bank's ability to make loans (asset of the bank) depends on its ability to mobilize deposits (liability of the bank) as total assets and liabilities of the bank need to match and expand/contract together; and *(iii)* Bank's need to hold balances at the central bank for settlement of claims within the banking system as these transactions are settled through the accounts of banks maintained with the central bank. Therefore, the daily functioning of a modern economy and its financial system creates a demand for central bank reserves which increases along with an expansion in overall activity (Friedman, 2000b).

The central bank's power to conduct monetary policy stems from its role as a monopolist, as the sole supplier of bank reserves, in the market for bank reserves. The most common procedure by which central banks influence the outstanding supply of bank reserves is through 'open market operations' – that is, by buying or selling Government securities in the market. When a central bank buys (sells) securities, it credits (debit) the reserve account of the seller (buyer) bank. This increases (decreases) the total volume of reserves that the banking system collectively holds. Expansion (contraction) of the total volume of the reserves in this way matters because banks can exchange reserves for other remunerative assets. Since reserves earn low interest, and in many countries remain unremunerated, banks typically would exchange them for some interest bearing asset such as Treasury Bill or other short-term debt instruments. If the banking system has excess (inadequate) reserves, banks would seek to buy (sell) such instruments. If there is a general increase (decrease) in demand for securities, it would result in increase (decline) in security prices and decline (increase) in interest rates. The resulting lower (higher) interest rates on short-term debt instruments mean a reduced (enhanced) opportunity cost of holding low interest reserves. Only when market interest rates fall (rise) to the level at which banks collectively are willing to hold all of the reserves that the central bank has supplied will the financial system reach equilibrium. Hence, an "expansionary" (contractionary) open market operation creates downward (upward) pressure on short-term interest rates not only because the central bank itself is a buyer (seller) but also because it leads banks to buy (sell) securities. In this way, the central bank can easily influence interest rates on short-term debt instruments, In the presence of a regular term structure of interest rates and without market segmentation such policy

8. B. K. Dutt's Prof. Benoy Kumar Sarkar's Memorial Lectures (1960) at the Calcutta University, *Commerce*, October 15, 1960.

impulses get transmitted to the longer end of the maturity spectrum, thereby influencing long-term interest rates, which have a bearing on household's consumption and savings decisions and hence on aggregate demand.

There are alternative mechanisms of achieving the same objective through the imposition of reserve requirements and central bank lending to banks in the form of refinance facilities. Lowering (increasing ) the reserve requirement, and , therefore, reducing (increasing) the demand for reserves has roughly the same impact as an expansionary (contractionary) open market operation, which increases (decreases) the supply of reserves creating downward (upward) pressure on interest rates. Similarly, another way in which central banks can influence the supply of reserves is through direct lending of reserves to banks. Central banks lend funds to bank at a policy rate, which usually act as the ceiling in the short-term market. Similarly, central banks absorb liquidity at a rate which acts as the floor for short-term market interest rates. This is important, since injecting liquidity at the ceiling rate would ensure that banks do not have access to these funds for arbitrage opportunities whereby they borrow from the central bank and deploy these funds in the market to earn higher interest rates. Similarly, liquidity absorption by the central bank has to be at the floor rate since deployment of funds with the central bank is free of credit and other risks. Typically, the objective of the central bank is to modulate liquidity conditions by pegging short-term interest rates within this corridor.

While the above mechanism outlines how central banks can influence short-term interest rates by adjusting the quantity of bank reserves, the same objective can be achieved by picking on a particular short-term interest rate and then adjusting the supply of reserves commensurate with that rate. In many countries, this is achieved by targeting the overnight inter-bank lending rate and adjusting the level of reserves which would keep the inter-bank lending rate at the desired level. Thus, by influencing short-term interest rates, central banks can influence output and inflation in the economy, the ultimate objectives of monetary policy.

## LIQUIDITY MANAGEMENT

Although significant progress has been made in refining the liquidity management practices in India, several new challenges have emerged. First, during periods of abundant liquidity, the LAF window becomes a first resort for parking surplus funds by banks. Second, the Reserve Bank has developed the MSS as a sterilisation mechanism for arresting the liquidity impact of foreign exchange inflows of a more enduring nature, while the LAF continues to be used for managing liquidity at the margin. There is, however, no way of knowing *ex-ante* whether the liquidity situation is temporary or permanent. Furthermore, the MSS remains immobilized for the entire period of its maturity. There is, therefore, a need to explore further instruments/options to undertake liquidity management, particularly in the context of a move to fuller capital account convertibility. Third, the Reserve Bank may not be in a position to conduct sterilisation operations indefinitely as its inventory of government paper is limited. There is also a limit on MSS issuances. Furthermore, the Reserve Bank has withdrawn from primary market auctions of Government Paper from April 1, 2006 in terms of provisions of the Fiscal Responsibility and Budget Management (FRBM) Act, 2003. Fourth, the absence of a vibrant corporate debt market continues to impede further refinements in liquidity management in terms of eligible instruments as collaterals. In this context, it may be noted that State Development Loans, which are treated as eligible securities for collaterals under LAF operations effective April 3, 2007, have widened the collateral base for LAF. Fifth, as many banks are now operating close to the prescribed levels of SLR securities, in case of liquidity tightness, banks may find it difficult to approach the LAF window in the absence of sufficient collateral securities. Sixth, while the Reserve Bank now holds the auctions twice on each working day to facilitate intra-day liquidity, a moral hazard issue arises as some market participants may not be actively managing their own liquidity in the wake of the Reserve Bank's market operations.

The above issues need to be addressed, especially in the wake of a progressive move to fuller capital account convertibility. First, there is a need to further refine the system of assessing liquidity conditions, which calls for an improved framework of liquidity forecasting. The short span within which liquidity conditions have been changing by large amount has posed a major challenge for targeting short-term interest rates. The understanding of the fiscal position and the government's cash balances as also the timing and extent of capital inflows assumes added significance. In this context, there may be a need to consider the regular release of information on government cash balances held with the Reserve Bank. Second, progressively more weightage needs to be given to movements in international interest rates in view of increased capital mobility. Third, destabilizing large and sudden capital flows call for more flexible and swift monetary policy responses through small and gradual changes in policy rates, as has been practised in recent years, as large changes can be disruptive. Fourth, open market operations (OMOs), apart from being used for modulating liquidity conditions, could also be used to correct any serious distortions in the yield curve.

Finally, while the Reserve Bank has progressively deemphasized the use of reserve requirements as an instrument of monetary policy, given the present state of market development, it is necessary to retain the flexibility of using reserve requirements, as and when necessary.[9]

## MARKET-MAKERS

Market-makers are entities who give a two-way quote in the market. This means that they are willing to buy and sell the shares in a particular company. The price on both the buy and sell sides are announced by them and this keeps on changing with conditions.

### What is their role in the share market?

The main role of the market-maker is to create an opportunity for trading in shares and hence increase liquidity in the area. Any investor who wishes to buy or sell the shares would be sure that they would be able to transact at the prices that are available.

9. The provisions of Section 3 of the Reserve Bank of India (Amendment) Act, 2006 came into force effective April, 2007, which provides the necessary flexibility to the Reserve Bank in the use of the CRR.

### When does the demand for them peak?

Earlier there were several market makers who were appointed for specific issues that hit the market but this has been rare in recent times. Usually, such demands come up when times are tough in the primary market and investor confidence is shaken.

### How do they quote their price?

There will be a difference between the buy price and sell price, which becomes the earning for the market maker. The price at which shares are sold to other investors would be slightly higher than the price at which they are bought.

## MONEY MARKET BEHAVIOUR AND MONETARY POLICY

The effectiveness of monetary policy hinges on the ability of the monetary authority to communicate with the public in a clear and transparent manner. In this regard, the signalling of policy assumes key importance as it conveys the stance of monetary policy. While the signalling mechanisms in developed countries are quite robust, they tend to be weak in emerging market economies, particularly in the wake of market segmentation and absence of a well-defined transmission mechanism.

Financial markets are typically characterized by asymmetric information, where some agents are better informed than others, that gets reflected in the problems of moral hazard and adverse selection. Seminal research on the economic theory of information has demonstrated that better-informed agents in a market could credibly "signal" (transmit) their information to less informed agents, so as to avoid some of the problems associated with adverse selection and improve the market outcome (Spence, 1973).

The effectiveness of monetary policy is strongly related to the signalling of policy, the reason being that important variable such as the exchange rate and long-term interest rates reflect expectations about future monetary policy. Central banks usually consider, *viz., (a) speeches* of executives, *(b)* views about future inflation, *(c)* changes in policy instruments, and *(d)* publication of the minutes of policy meetings. In particular, the announcement of an inflation forecast or a monetary condition's index (MCI) is used to signal central bank's intentions.

In India, several measures have been initiated in the post-reform period to develop indirect instruments for transmitting policy signals. An important measure was the introduction reactivation of the bank rate in April 1997 by initially linking it to all other rates, including Reserve Bank's refinance rates. The introduction of fixed rate reverse repo helped in creating an informal corridor in the money market with the reverse repo rate as the floor and the bank rate as the ceiling, which enabled the Reserve Bank to modulate the call rate within this informal corridor. Subsequently, the introduction of the Liquidity Adjustment Facility (LAF) from June 2000 facilitated the modulation of liquidity conditions and also short-term interest rates on a daily basis through the LAF window, while signalling the medium-term stance of policy through changes in the bank rate.

An increase in the bank rate, as the signalling mechanism of policy stance over the medium-term, appears to have a instantaneous effect on call, Government securities and forward premia because of the news effect. The long-term impact, however, gets muted as refinance at the bank rate is formula driven and not adequate to have a liquidity impact. In the stock market, hardening of the bank rate is construed as restrictive monetary policy, which dampens the market sentiment.

The instantaneous impact of monetary policy signals on most financial market segments points towards increasing integration and sophistication of markets. Therefore, increasing reliance on direct instruments, greater market integration and technological innovations *prima facie* have improved the channels of communication between the Reserve Bank and the financial market and facilitated the conduct of monetary policy.

The liberalisation of capital controls resulted in increased integration of the Indian economy with the global economy, however, posed new challenges and dilemmas for monetary management. These developments called for a greater emphasis on orderly conditions in financial markets for ensuring financial stability. In this context, the need for developed and well-integrated money market also assumes critical importance.

In the emerging scenario of increasing integration of domestic and international markets, several issues have come to the fore. First, the absence of a developed term money market is one of the important gaps in the development of domestic financial markets. This is affecting the development of a money market yield curve, and, in turn, the development of the derivative market and the integration of the foreign exchange market and the domestic currency market. Accordingly, greater efforts would be required to expedite the development of the term money market in the country, given the critical role of this market in the development of other segments. Well-developed term money market would, *inter alia,* contribute to the emergence of deep and vibrant markets for interest rate derivatives and provide useful inputs of market expectations for the conduct of monetary policy.

Second, in view of the transformation of the money market into a pure inter-bank market, there may be a need to provide greater flexibility to banks and PDs to borrow or lend in this market, depending on the robustness of the risk management practices being followed by them. Prudential limits on borrowing and lending in the inter-bank market could be replaced, in stages, by a system where such limits are taken care of by the banks' own internal ALM framework.

Third, in view of sustained credit demand in recent years, there has been some revival of interest in Inter-Bank Participation Certificates (IBPCs). IBPCs, by enabling banks to even out their short-term liquidity mismatches, provide greater degree of flexibility in banks' credit portfolios. Accordingly, the IBPC scheme needs a thorough review to improve asset liability management and liquidity management. This will also help in developing a market for credit risk transfer instruments.

Fourth, the Reserve Bank in its operations would have to progressively give somewhat more weightage than hitherto to international interest rates in view of increased capital mobility. Fifth, potentially destabilising large and sudden capital flows may call for more flexible and swift monetary policy responses. Sixth, open market operations (OMO), apart from being used for modulating liquidity conditions, could also be used to correct any serious distortions in the yield curve. Seventh, although the Reserve Bank has progressively de-emphasised reserve requirements as an instrument of monetary policy, given the present state of market development, it may be necessary to keep the option of flexible use of reserve requirements. Finally, as the banking system is moving to maintenance of SLR securities close to the prescribed minimum levels, liquidity provision would become more difficult unless the instrument set is widened to facilitate market participants to even out liquidity mismatches.

## MONEY MARKET REFORMS

A major objective of reforms is to develop the money market eliminate segmentation and smoothen the process of transmission, easing the liquidity management process and making resource allocation process more efficient.

Since the early 1990s, the RBI and the government have taken various measures to strengthen and improving depth and liquidity in the money market. The reforms also emphasised on improving the transparency and efficiency of the money market. The key reform measures undertaken are briefly presented below:

- A ceiling of 10 per cent on call money rates imposed by the Indian Banks Association was withdrawn in 1989.
- Initially, the participation in the call market was gradually widened by including non-banks, such as, financial institutions, non-banking finance companies, primary/satellite dealers, mutual funds, corporates (through primary dealers), etc. The process of transformation of call money market to a pure inter-bank market commenced effective May 2001.
- The 182-day Treasury Bills were introduced effective November 1986, followed subsequently by phasing out of on-tap Treasury Bills, introduction of auctioning system in 91-day Treasury Bills since January 1993, and introduction of 14-day and 364-day Treasury Bills. The system of *ad hoc* Treasury Bills (with a fixed 4.6 per cent interest rate since July 1974), which were issued by the Central Government to the Reserve Bank, was abolished effective April 1997. Currently only the 91-day and 364-day Treasury Bills exist.
- The Discount and Finance House of India (DFHI) was set up in April 1988, and was allowed to participate in the call/notice money market both as a borrower and lender commencing from July 1988.
- Several new financial instruments were introduced, such as inter-bank participation certificates (1988), certificates of deposit (June 1989), commercial paper (January 1990) and repos (December 1992).
- Derivative products like forward rate agreements and interest rate swaps were introduced in July 1999 to enable banks, FIs and PDs to hedge interest rate risks.
- A full-fledged Liquidity Adjustment Facility was introduced on 5$^{th}$ June, 2000 with a view to modulating short-term liquidity under diverse market conditions.

- With a view to adopting the sound risk management procedures and eliminating counterparty risk, the Clearing Corporation of India Ltd., was set up on February 15, 2002. The CCIL acts as a central counterparty to all trades involving foreign exchange, Government securities and other debt instruments routed through it and guarantees their settlement.
- The segment refinance facility for banks is gradually being phased out. Collateralised Borrowing and Lending Obligations (CBLO) was launched by CCIC in January, 2003.
- Institutionalisation of the Clearning Corporation of India Limited (CCIL) as a central counterparty.
- Issuance norms have been modified to encourage wider participation while strengthening the transmission of policy signals.
- Upgradation of payment system technologies.

During 2009-10, the money market interest rates stayed closer to the lower bound of the liquidity adjustment facility (LAF) rate corridor as the overall liquidity conditions remained in surplus mode. The key drivers of liquidity were Central Government balances with the Reserve Bank, open market operations (OMO) and market stabilisation scheme (MSS) unwinding.

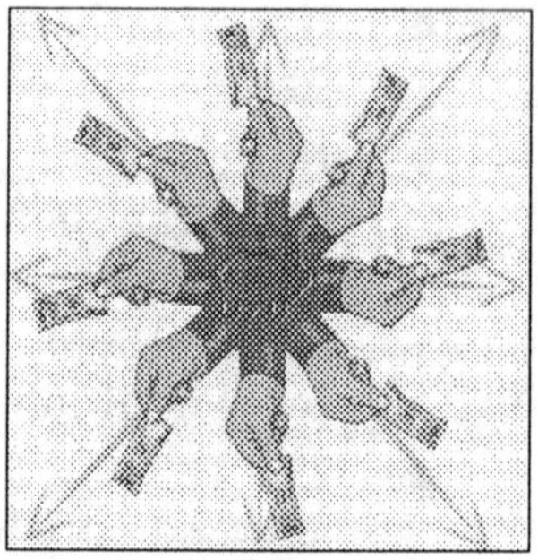

As the Indian economy grows, the quantum of resources required places the development of the financial sector in a vital position. Well-developed and linked financial markets can facilitate the flow of funds from savers to investors and producers, and reduce the cost of intermediation and borrowing. The efficiency of intermediation depends on the width, depth and diversity of the financial system. It can play a critical role in improving macroeconomic policy setting as well as transmission mechanism.

For a well functioning financial market, efficiency and liquidity are critical. The Indian financial markets, except equities to some extent, lack both efficiency and liquidity, leading to high transaction cost. Indian markets lack a well-functioning corporate bond market. Almost 91% of the debt market is government funding market. During 2008-09, average daily volume in corporate bonds was merely ~0.1% of total issuances.

In the recent past, policymakers have opened up the interest rate futures market, allowed repo in corporate bonds, established clearing and settlement mechanism and compulsory reporting of corporate bond trades. But we need to educate retail investors, permit institutional investors to participate in all markets and remove quantitative ceilings.

Regulators should remove investment restrictions on long-term institutional investors such as life insurance and pension funds. Life insurance companies are not allowed to participate in equity derivatives while pension funds have restricted participation in equities itself. The Employees' Provident Fund Organisation (EPFO) manages funds totalling more than ₹ 2.5 lakh crore with investments limited to Government securities and state-level bonds. New pension scheme has been launched but its linkages are weak. Currently, only 2% of Indian pension-fund assets are in equities, compared to 40% in developed markets and over 20% in other emerging markets.

Well-developed markets should be inter-connected so that demand-supply imbalance in one market can overflow into related markets, dampening the shocks. An inter-connection also ensures that the interest rates and returns in any market reflect the broad demand-supply conditions in the market of savings. But such adjustment of interest rates is delayed when the intermediaries lack flexibility. There is an urgent for a strong integration of bonds-currency-derivatives-equity (BCDE) markets. Full integration of BCDE markets will reduce spreads, impact cost and ensure better price discovery for all asset classes. It can play an important role in shaping the long-end curve in the Indian bond market that is currently missing. It will also strengthen financing for leveraged infrastructure projects.

## CONCLUSION

The money market, which is the market for short-term funds with maturity ranging from overnight to one year, provides an avenue for the central bank intervention in influencing both quantum and cost of liquidity in the financial system, thereby transmitting monetary policy impulses to the real economy. The central bank strives to align money markets rates with the key policy rate. Ensuring stability in the money market is critical

Since the early 1990s, the money market has undergone a significant transformation is terms of instruments, participants and technological infrastructure. Various reform measures have resulted in a relatively deep, liquid and vibrant money market. The RBI's approach has been to foster balanced development of the money market, introduce new innovative instruments and make the existing instruments more flexible, reduce dependence of participants on uncollateralised exposures, facilitate price discovery in the short-end and upgrade the payment system infrastructure. The RBIs strategy has focused on instituting full-fledged liquidity adjustment facility, developing infrastructure, promoting transparency and initiating various measures pertaing to instruments for non-bank participants.

These measures have helped in containing volatility in the 'money market, improved significantly the depth and liqudity in the market, and also improved the signalling mechanism of monetary policy while ensuring financial stability. However, there is a need to develop the money market further, particularly in the context of a move towards fuller capital account convertibility.

Notwithstanding the considerable progress made so far, there is a need to develop the money market further, particularly in the context of a move towards fuller capital account convertibility.

Further development of the money market participants which would enable banks to evolve appropriate prudential limits on their money exposures from their internal control systems. In order to develop the term money market, participants need to take a long-term view on interest rates. Furthermore, there is a need to expand the eligible set of underlying collateral securities for repo transactions. This would not only facilitate liquidity management but also promote the development of underlying debt instruments. Finally, liquidity forecasting techniques need to be further refined for proper assessment of liquidity conditions by the Reserve Bank. This would facilitate finer changes in the operating procedures of liquidity management and enable the Reserve Bank to flexibly meet the emerging challenges. As these developments take place, it needs to be understood that monetary will continue to be conducted in and intermediate regime that will have to respond creatively and carefully to the emerging and evolving monetary and macroeconomic conditions, both domestic and global.

In India, although the ultimate goals of monetary policy, *viz.,* growth and price stability, have remained unchanged over the years, the Reserve Bank has modified its operational and intermediate objectives of monetary policy several times in response to changes in the economic and financial environment. For instance, in the mid-1980s, the Reserve Bank formally adopted monetary targeting with feedback as a nominal anchor to fight inflation, partly induced by the large-scale monetisation of fiscal deficits. The operating procedure in this regime was modulation of bank reserves by varying reserve requirements. In order to meet reserve requirements, banks borrowed primarily from the inter-bank (call money) market. Hence, these transactions were reflective of the overall liquidity in the system. Accordingly, the Reserve Bank focussed on the money market, in particular, the call money market by using various direct instruments of money control to signal the policy stance consistent with the overall objectives of achieving growth and price stability. As interest rates were regulated, monetary management was undertaken mainly through changes in the Cash Reserve Ratio (CRR), which was used to influence indirectly the marginal cost of borrowing by having an initial impact on the call money market.

Accordingly, the Reserve Bank's emphasis has been on encouraging migration towards the collateralized segments and developing derivatives for hedging market risks. This has been complemented by the institutionalization of CCIL as a central counter party to mitigate the settlement risk. The upgradation of payment technologies has further enabled market participants to improve their asset liability management. Cumulatively, these measures have helped in containing volatility in the money market, thereby improving the signalling mechanism of monetary policy while ensuring financial stability.

In the money market, the policy thrust of the Reserve Bank would continue to encourage the development of collateralized market, broad-base the pool of securities to act as collateral for repo and CBLO markets and provide avenues for better risk management with further improvements in the ALM framework.

The money market provides a focal point for the central bank's operations in influencing liquidity and thereby transmitting monetary policy impulses. The Reserve Bank of India (RBI) has been playing a proactive role in developing the money market for ensuring stability, avoiding volatility, minimizing default risk and achieving a balanced development of various segments. In the process, the RBI has introduced new instruments, broadened the participants' base and strengthened institutional infrastructure. The policy thrust given to the growth of the collateralised segment has improved options for liquidity management while reducing risks. Likewise, developments in institutional and technological infrastructure have also helped in improving transparency, facilitating price discovery process and providing avenues for better liquidity and risk management.

# CHAPTER 10 THE CAPITAL MARKET

## INTRODUCTION

The process of industrial development requires, as one of its accompanying structural changes, the development of a capital market. The capital market should be capable of meeting the requirements of credit and finance of the private entrepreneurs. The capital market should also help in sustained national industrial development.

The capital market provides an alternative mechanism of reallocating resources; it channelises household saving to the corporate sector and allocates funds among firm. In this process, it allows both firms and households to share risk. The capital market enables the valuation of firms on an almost continuous basis and it plays an important role in the governance of the corporate sector.

Indian capital market has been experiencing metamorphic changes for the last few years. The changes have become more pronounced in the last couple of years with the advent of liberalisation pertaining to the industrial policy, licensing policy, financial services industry, interest rates, etc. The competition has become very intense and real, thus affecting the industrial sector and financial services industry. As a result of this, in the area of capital market, and the more and more new financial instruments have been introduced by the companies accessing capital markets.

Sound development of various segments of the capital market is a prerequisite for a well functioning financial system. The capital market in India has been modernized over the past 17 years and is now comparable with the international markets. There has been a visible improvement in trading and settlement infrastructure, risk management systems and levels of transparency. These improvements have brought about a reduction in the transaction costs and led to improvement in liquidity.

Over the years, the development banks have been playing a major role and continued actively to participate in the development of capital market. Thus, development banks, capital markets and industry are inter-linked and inter-dependent. The economic growth reflects the combined effort and strength of these institutions. As such, the capital market in the 1980s has emerged as a rapidly growing source of investible funds to the corporate sector. The total amount of capital raised through different market instruments during 2007 was 31.5 per cent higher than in 2006. Component-wise, private placement accounted for ₹ 1,11,838 crore (up to Novemeber 2007). The total equity issues mobilized was ₹ 58,722 crore, of which, one hundred Initial Public Offerings (IPOs) mobilized ₹ 33,912 crore on an average, there were around eight IPOs per month. The buoyant equity markets also helped the mutual funds to raise ₹ 1,38,207 crore in 2007 as compared to ₹ 4,775 crore in 2004. Further, Indian companies are also raising more and more funds from the EURO markets.

## CAPITAL MARKET FOSTERS ECONOMIC GROWTH

The capital market fosters economic growth in various ways such as by augmenting the quantum of saving and capital formation and through efficient allocation of capital, which in turn, raises the productivity of investment. It also enhances the efficiency of a financial system as diverse competitors vie with each other for financial resources. Further, it adds to the financial deepening of the economy by enlarging the financial sector and promoting the use of innovative, sophisticated and cost-effective financial instruments which ultimately reduce the cost of capital. Well-functioning capital markets also impose discipline on firms to perform (Beck *et. al.*, 2000; Bandiera *et. al.* 2000). Equity and debt markets can also diffuse stress on the banking sector by diversifying credit risk across the economy.

Although the capital market in India has a long history, during the most part, it remained on the periphery of the financial system. Various reforms undertaken since the early 1990s by the Securities and Exchange Board of India (SEBI) and the government have brought about a significant structural transformation in the Indian capital market. As a result, the Indian equity market has become modern and transparent. However, its role in capital formation continues to be limited. The private corporate debt is yet to pick-up. It is the primary equity and debt markets that link the issuers of securities and investors and provide resources for capital formation. In some advanced countries, especially the US, the new issue market has been quite successful in financing new companies and spurring the development of new technology companies. A growing economy requires risk capital and long-term resources in the form of debt for enabling the corporates to choose an appropriate mix of debt and equity. Long-term resources are also important for financing infrastructure projects. Therefore, in order to sustain India's high growth path, the capital market needs to play a major role. The significance of a well-functioning domestic capital market has also increased as banks need to raise necessary capital from the market to sustain their growing operations.

## INDIA INC RELIES MORE ON BANKS THAN CAPITAL MARKETS

**The Reserve Bank of India** raised key policy rates by over 300 basis points in FY11. A basis point is 0.01 percentage point. This has prompted banks to push up lending rates during the year. Despite the rise in borrowing costs, Indian firms have relled more on bank funds to finance their businesses rather than tapping the capital market directly. As a result, loan growth rose sharply – about 22% – higher than the central bank's comfort level of 20% for 2010-11

**Flow of financial resources to the commercial sector (₹ Crore)**

**2008-09 2009-10 2010-11**

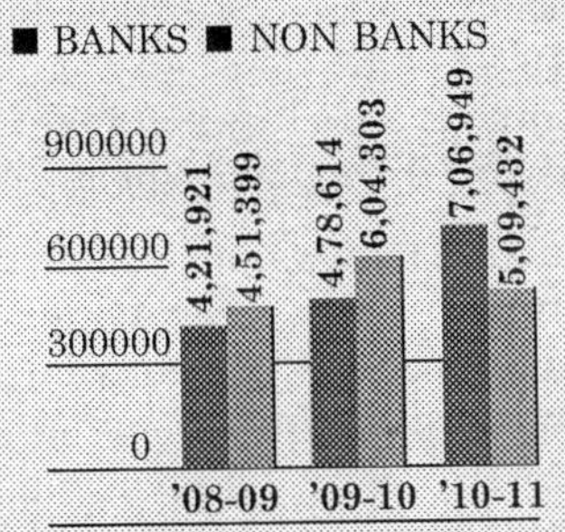


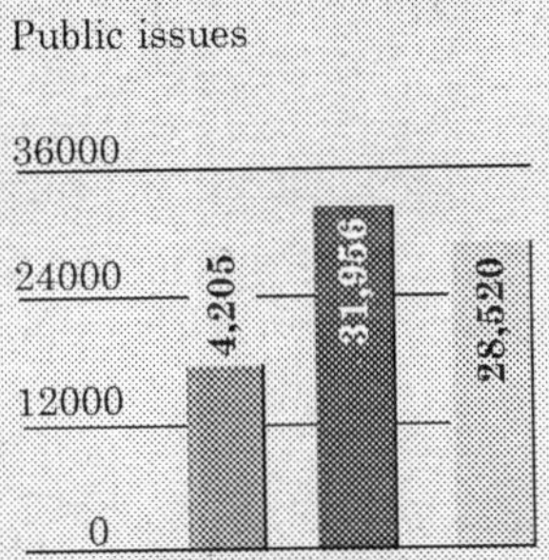


There are several factors responsible for this. Though there was a huge response to many equity issuances by a few public sector companies during the year, the private sector had little success in raising funds from the primary market during the year

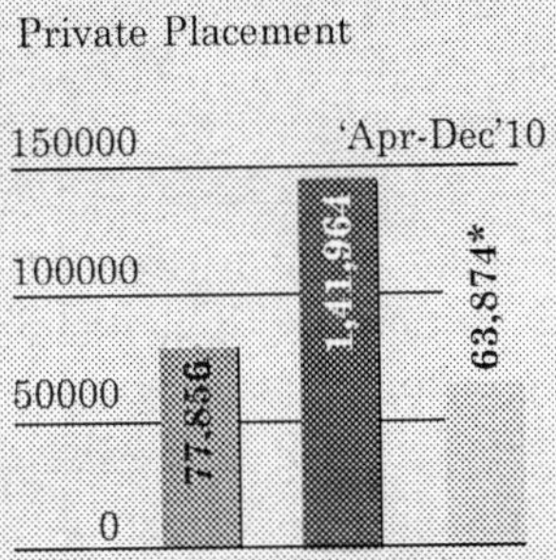


Recourse to bank financing was also higher during the last fiscal as investor response to private placement of debt was lukewarm compared to the huge response a year ago

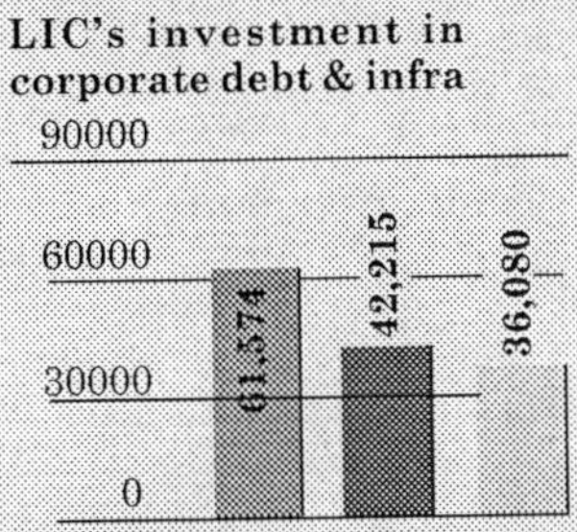


That is because the biggest institutional investor – LIC was not an aggressive buyer of corporate debt during the year

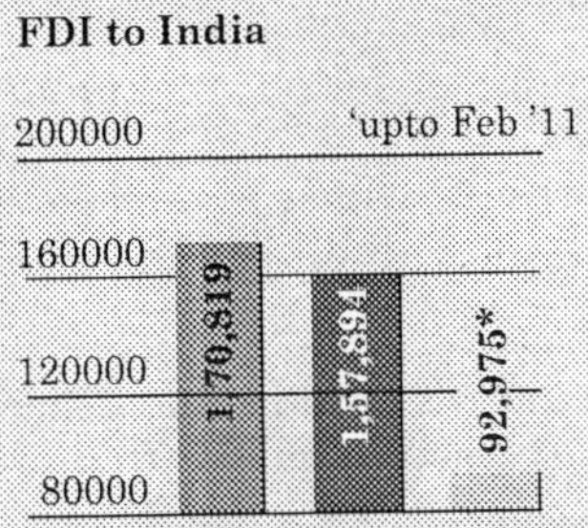


From a broader macro economic and policy point of view, what is worrying is the fact that a stable form of foreign investment – foreign direct investment, or FDI– dipped sharply during the year

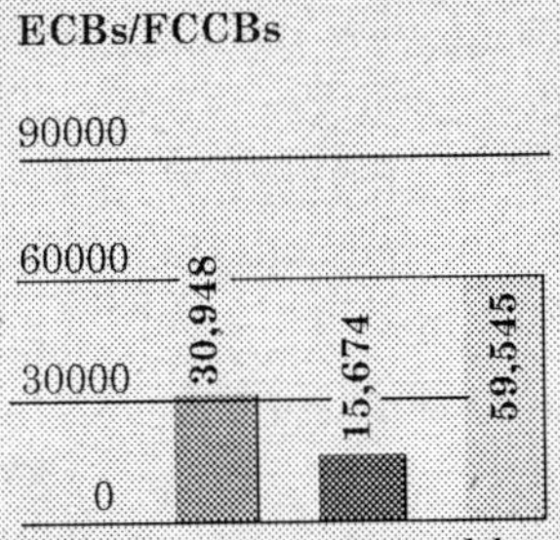


This was compensated by a sharp uptick in foreign borrowings and foreign currency convertible bonds, or FCCB, during the year

*Source:* RBI

## LONG-TERM FINANCE AND INSTITUTIONAL DEVELOPMENT

The promotion of long-term finance and capital markets is essential to improve investment incentives consistent with external adjustment, as well as to avoid excessive reliance on short-term funds to finance investments — a practice which in the past led to liquidity crisis (and at times bankruptcies) of enterprises and financial institutions. Because of their expertise in development finance, the World Bank Group and, in particular, the International Finance Corporation have played a leading role in this

| STOCK-PICKING TECHNIQUES-I | STOCK-PICKING TECHNIQUES- II | STOCK-PICKING TECHNIQUES- III |
|---|---|---|
| **Value Investing** | **Intangible Advantage** | **Discounted Cash Flow** |
| Is the company's price-to-earnings ratio lower than the markets and sectoral averages? **YES** | Do the company's products have many substitutes? **NO** | Calculate the free cash Flow (FCF), deducting tax on operating income, increase in working capital, and capital expenses from operating profits |
| Does the company's current price-to-book value ratio workout to less than one? **YES** | Does the company have strong, easily-recognized brands? **YES** | Calculate the net present value of Future Cash Flow (NPVFCF), by discounting the free cash flow for the life of the company and adjusting it of liquid assets currently on the balance sheet. |
| Is the company's price-to-earnings ratio less than its expected earnings growth **YES** | Does the company have deep distribution reach? **YES** | Calculate the total value by adding the NPVFCF, the aggregate cash flow discounted to its present value, and non-operating investments. |
| Do the company's strategy, market shares, and cost structure suggest intrinsic strengths? **YES** | Calculate aggregate sales for 20 years at the current growth rate | Calculate the future cash flow by subtracting total loan funds from the total value |
| Buy the scrip<br>Keep calculating the above indicators | Discount the figure at the company's rate of return on equity | Calculate the fair value of the scrip by dividing the total value by the number of equity shares |
| Have any of the above indicators become adverse? **YES** | Call the result, which is the net present value, brand value | Is the result higher than the market price? **YES** |
| Sell the scrip and book profits. | Is the company's brand value greater than its market capitalisation? **YES**<br>Buy the scrip | Buy the scrip |

area. In a supplementary role, recent fund technical and economic issues relating to policies aimed at lengthening the maturities of loans and deposits.

## What is Capital Market?

It is an organised market mechanism for effective and efficient transfer of money capital or financial resources from the investing class (a body of individual or institutional savers) to the entrepreneur class (individual or institutions engaged in industry business or service) in the private and public sectors of the economy.

In a very broad sense, it includes the market for short-term funds. H.T. Parikh has referred to it as, "*By capital market, I mean the market for all the financial instruments, short-term and long-term as also commercial, industrial and Government Paper*".

In the words of Goldsmith, "the capital market of a modern economy has two basic functions: first the allocation of savings among users and investment; second the facilitation of the transfer of existing assets, tangible and intangible among individual economic units".

Grant defines capital market in a broad sense as "a series of channels through which the savings of the community are made available for industrial and commercial enterprises and for public authorities. It embraces not only the system by which the public takes up long-term securities directly or through intermediaries but also the elaborate network of institutions responsible for short-term and medium-term lending."

From the above definitions, it may be deducted that the function of capital market is the collection of savings and their distribution for industrial investment. Thus, capital formation is *sine qua non* of economic development. As such, the relationship between the market, instrument, and services are integrated as well as inter-dependent.

Capital market is generally understood as the market for long-term funds. The capital market provides long-term debt and equity finance for the government and the corporate sector. By making long-term investments liquid, the capital market mediates between the conflicting maturity preferences of lenders and borrowers. The capital market also facilitates the dispersion of business ownership and the reallocation of financial resources among corporations and industries.

Capital market facilitates capital formation, where borrowing and lending of funds takes place. It plays an important role in the development of economy. Two important operations are carried out by capital markets, raising the new capital (Primary Market) and trading in securities already issued by the companies (Secondary Market). For development and economic growth, existence of a sound capital markets is an essential prerequisite.

Three major stock exchanges are functioning in the State viz. Bombay Stock Exchange (BSE), National Stock Exchange (NSE) and Pune Stock Exchange (PSE). In addition to these, three other stock exchanges namely Over The Counter Stock Exchange of India (OTCEI), Inter Connected Stock Exchange (ICSE) and United Stock Exchange of India Limited (USE) are also functioning in the State.

The market capitalization of equity shares available for trading on Indian bourses experienced considerable growth during 2009-10 with increase of 107.5 per cent and 99.8 per cent respectively over the previous year. The Market Capitalization of NSE and BSE during April to October, 2010 amounted to ₹ 70,55,094 crore and ₹ 72,24,908 crore.

## DIMENSIONS OF CAPITAL MARKET

The capital market is directly responsible for the following activities: (1) Mobilisation or concentration of national savings for economic development, (2) Mobilisation and import of foreign capital and foreign investment capital plus skill to fill up the deficit in the required financial resources to maintain the expected rate of economic growth, (3) Productive utilisation of resources, and (4) Directing the flow to funds of high yields and also strive for balanced and diversified industrialisation.

A nation embarking upon accelerated economic development and industrialisation has to make planned efforts to develop an organised and healthy money and capital markets with an adequate institutional set-up. Market for credit (money and capital market) and business enterprises must go hand-in-hand to ensure quick industrialisation in a developing democratic country.

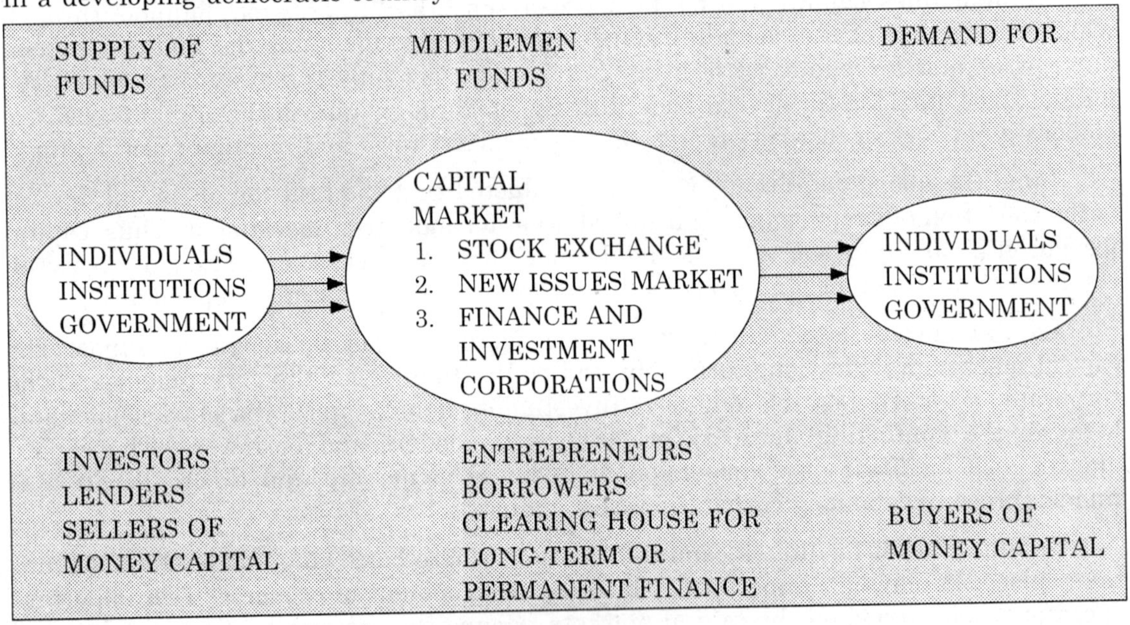


**Fig. 1 Capital Market Mechanism**

## CAPITAL MARKET STRUCTURE

An important segment of the organised financial system comprises the new issues market and stock market. The term capital market is a wide term, encompassing all long-term claims of moneylendings and borrowings. It thus includes all term lendings by banks and financial institutions and long-term borrowings from foreign markets and new issues by companies and raising of all resources from public through issue of new securities, deposits, loans, etc.

As chart 1 shows, capital market includes issues of two major categories — marketable and non-marketable. Whether marketable or not, these are issued by government and government departments, companies, public sector units, mutual funds, UTI, etc. LIC and GIC sell policies and collects savings from public, which are not marketable. The other non-marketable securities or claims are issued by post offices as savings certificates, deposit receipts, etc., non-securitised loans and advances of banks and financial institutions, deposits with banks and companies and securities of private limited companies and finance company deposits/loans, chit funds, etc. The marketable securities are issued through the new issues market and are traded through the stock market.

The contributors to new issues are promoters, collaborators, if any, employees, NRIs, banks, FIs, Mutual Funds and the public at large. The players through whom these issues are managed are mainly merchant bankers, registrars, brokers, mutual funds, etc., which are dealt within detail in later chapters. The ancillary functions and complementary to the above are those of underwriters, collecting bankers, printers, advertising agents, etc. The main players in the stock market, namely, brokers, investment consultants, portfolio managers, investment managers, etc., are also discussed in later chapters.

The capital market study should authentically encompass both the marketable and non-marketable segments. In view of the fact that demand and supply forces and trading activity is confined only to the segment of marketable securities, this book is using the term 'Capital Market' in the sense of marketable securities. Thus, more prominent issuers of such securities are public limited companies and, government and the more popular instruments traded in the market are equity, debentures, bonds, etc., which are discussed in this book. UTI and the mutual fund schemes being popular for trading, they are also dealt with. Briefly the major players — instruments and activity in capital market are covered from the point of management.

## CONSTITUENTS OF CAPITAL MARKET

The constituents of the capital market comprise development banks, specialised financial institutions, investment institutions, state level development banks, mutual funds, lease companies, financial service companies, commercial banks and other specialised institutions were set up by development banks for the growth of the capital market, notably, SEBI, SHCI, CRISIL, IICRA, I-Sec, AMC, OTCEI and the National Stock Exchange.

### Highlights

(*i*) There has been an accelerated growth of the long-term capital market in India in the recent years. But the absolute size in relation to the economy is still small and the institutional structure inadequate.

(*ii*) In this purpose, we must reach out and activate the potential investors in parts of the country other than the Western region and in rural and semi-urban areas. This could be done, if a few large reliable national level private sector investing or promoting companies are established, which would have the capability of establishing branches in several centres and in training and appointing its own agents in the smaller towns.

(*iii*) The desirability of introducing the new instruments. In this, the non-voting shares and the equity warrant may be considered. With the introduction of non-voting shares in a company, the controlling groups could be persuaded to reduce their holdings correspondingly.

(*iv*) Supply of venture capital is high risk business, but the reward would also be high. Government must allow private investing agencies to be set up which could supply this capital to new ventures.

(*v*) A major deficiency in our capital market is the absence of a well developed housing finance system. In relation to demand, the flow of institutional funds into the housing sector has been quite meagre. The housing finance system that we build-up must facilitate an adequate flow of institutional finance to the housing sector as one of the priority sectors.

(*vi*) "Commercial Paper" having maturity period ranging from 30 days to a year may be introduced, as it would relieve pressure in the long-term or medium-term funds.

The healthy growth of the capital market rests on broadbasing and mature development of the banking system in the country. As such, both are complementary and supplementary. The term capital market is used to designate activities in long-term credit, which is characterised by securities. It comprises specialised financial institutions including investment and trust companies, banks, stock exchanges and other institutions.

The capital market is classified into two categories, *viz.,* organised and unorganised. With the emerging of development banks, commercial banks, Life Insurance, Unit Trust, the unorganised sector seems to have become isolated. In the organised sector, development banks are the key institutions.

## ROLE OF THE CAPITAL MARKET

The capital market play a vital role in providing liquidity and investment instruments. It fosters economic. growth in various way such as by augmenting the quantum of savings and capital formation and through efficient allocation of capital, which, in turn, raises the productivity of investment. It also enhances the efficiency of a financial system diverse competitors vie with each other for financial resources. The domestic capital market can help financial stability by reducing currency mismatches. The capital market also provide an alternative means of long-term resources for development. It also improves economic efficiency by generating market determined interest rates that reflect the opportunity costs of funds at different maturities. Further, it adds to the financial deepening of the economy by enlarging the financial sector and promoting the use of innovative, sophisticated and cost-effective financial instruments, which ultimately reduce the cost of capital. Well-functioning capital markets also impose discipline of firms to excel in performance. And, also diffuse stress on the banking sector by diversifying credit risk across the economy.

The capital market also enables the valuation of firms on an almost continuous basis and plays an important role in the governance of the corporate sector.

## IMPORTANCE OF CAPITAL MARKET

The pace of economic development is conditioned, among other things, by the rate of long-term investment and capital formation. And capital formation is conditioned by the mobilization, augmentation and channelisation of investible funds. The capital market serves a very useful purpose by pooling the capital resources of the country and making them available to the enterprising investors. Well-developed capital markets augment resources by attracting and lending funds on a global scale. The Euro-currency and Euro-bond markets are international finance markets in terms of both the supply and demand for funds.

CHART 1
CAPITAL MARKET STRUCTURE

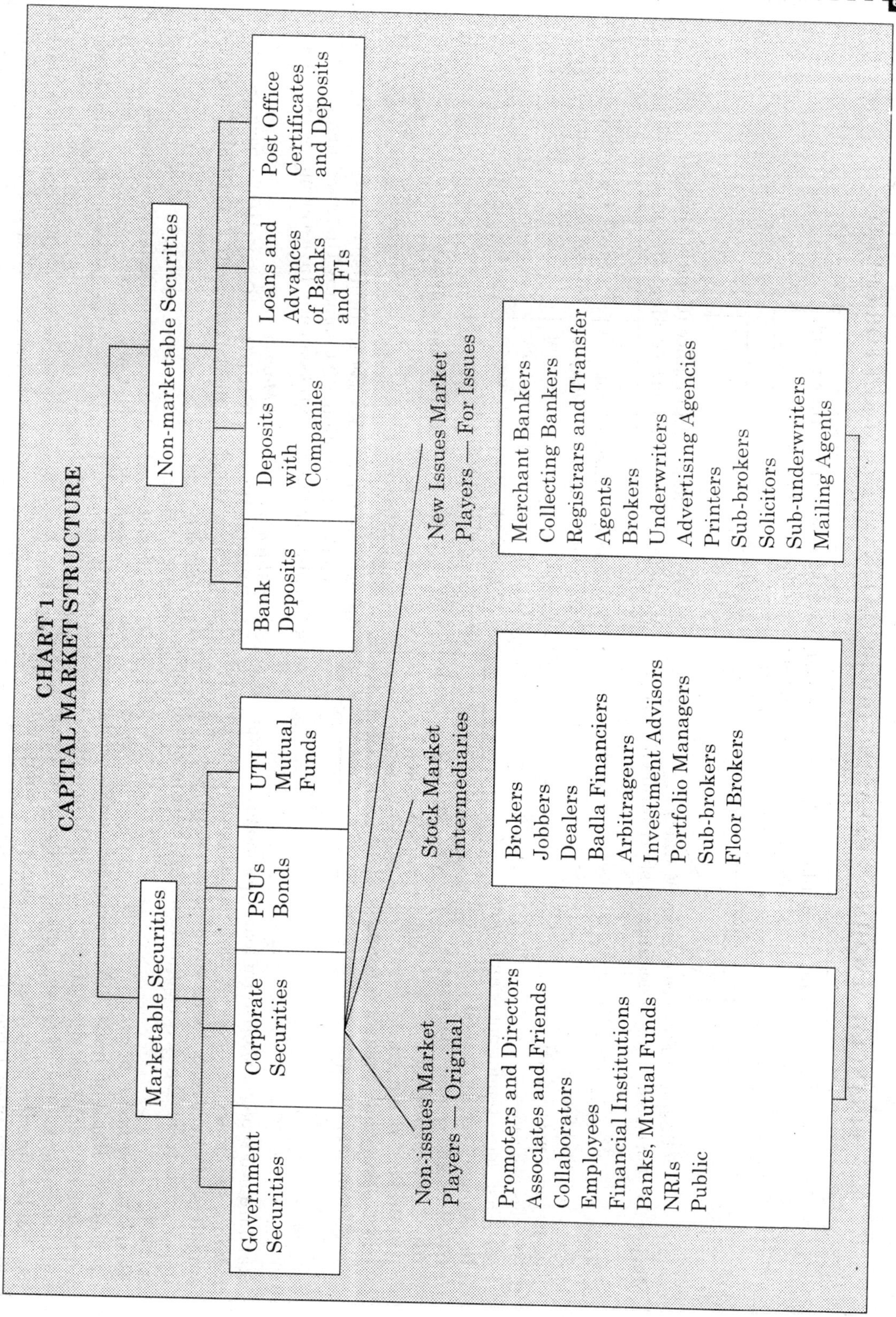

## CHART 2

## FINANCIAL MACHINE — CLEARING HOUSE OF FINANCE (MARKET FOR CREDIT)

Capital formulation depends upon supply of saving for investment and adequate institutional set-up in Credit Market

### Business Finance (Money Market)

Market for short-term finance dealings in short-term obligations

1. Reservoir of short-term or liquid funds.
   Money and near money
2. Articles of Trade:
   (*a*) Cash-legal tender notes and coins
   (*b*) Money Market Assets:
   (*i*) Bills and commercial papers
   (*ii*) Call-loan market
   (*iii*) Brokers loan market
   (*iv*) Treasury bills and short bonds financial government deficits

(*i*), (*ii*) and
(*iii*) for Financing Trade
1. Bills Market
2. Stock Exchange
3. Commodity Markets

Standardised types of short-term loans are money market assets forming secondary reserves of commercial banks, the greatest suppliers of short-term loans in the money market. They are impersonal, transferable, negotiable assets having broad open market.

*Money Market Institutions*

(1) Reserve Bank of India, (2) Deposit or Commercial banks, (3) Merchant banks and discount houses, (4) Co-operative banks, (5) Foreign banks, (6) Indigenous banks, (7) Non-banking agencies, e.g., sales finance companies, hire-purchase companies, life insurance companies, large business houses, etc.

### Industrial Finance (Capital Market)

Market for long-term finance dealings in long-term obligations

Financial Institutions
They are specialised Finance Corporations and Investment Institutions as underwriters, promoters and financiers of enterprises

Stock Exchanges
(For existing securities)

New Issues market

Underwriters | Sharebrokers

Functions of Capital Market Institutions
(1) Company Promotion, (2) Company Underwriting, (3) Company Finance, (4) Company Investment

*Constituents of Capital Market*

(1) IDBI (2) IFCI (3) ICICI (4) LIC (5) GIC (6) UTI (7) SIFC (8) SICO (9) Merchant Banks (10) SCICI (11) TDICI (12) NSE (13) OTCEI

*Articles of Trade*

(1) Debt and Bonds (2) Equity and Preference Shares

*Components of Stock Exchange*

(1) Market for listed industrial securities — Two-way Auction Market
(2) Market for Government securities — Over-the-counter Market for non-listed industrial securities — Over-the-counter Market

The increase in the size of the industrial units and business corporations due to technological developments, economies of scale and other factors has created a situation wherein the capital at the disposal of one or few individuals is quite insufficient to meet the growing investment demands. A developed capital market can solve this problem of paucity of funds. An organized capital market can mobilise and pool together even the small and scattered savings and augment the availability of investible funds. While the rapid growth of joint stock companies has been made possible to a large extent by the growth of capital markets, the growth of joint stock companies has in its turn, encouraged the growth of capital markets. A well developed capital market provides a number of profitable investment opportunities to the investors.

The importance of capital market can be briefly summarised as follows:

*(i)* The capital market serves as an important source for the productive use of the economy's savings. It mobilises the savings of the people for further investment and thus avoids their wastage in unproductive uses.

*(ii)* It provides incentives to savings and facilitates capital formation by offering suitable rates of interest as the price of capital.

*(iii)* It provides an avenue for investors, particularly the household sector to invest in financial assets which are more productive than physical assets.

*(iv)* It facilitates increase in production and productivity in the economy and thus, enhances the economic welfare of the society. Thus, it facilitates "the movement of stream of command over capital to the point of highest yield" towards those who can apply them productively and profitably to enhance the national income in the aggregate.

*(v)* The operations of different institutions in the capital market induce economic growth. They give quantitative and qualitative diretions of the flow of funds and bring about rational allocation of scarce resources.

*(vi)* A healthy capital market consisting of expert intermediaries promotes stability in values of securities representing capital funds.

*(vii)* Moreover, it serves as an important source for technological upgradation in the industrial sector by utilising the funds invested by the public.

Thus, a capital market serves as an important link between those who save and those who aspire to invest their savings.

The pace of economic development is conditioned, among other things, by the rate of long-term investment and capital formation. And capital formation is conditioned by the mobilisation, augmentation and channelisation of investible funds. The capital market serves a very useful purpose by pooling the capital resources of the country and making them available to the enterprising investors. Well-developed capital markets augment resources by attracting and lending funds on a global scale. The Euro-currency and Euro-bond markets are international finance markets in terms of both the supply and demand for funds.

The increase in the size of the industrial units and business corporations due to technological developments, economies of scale and other factors has created a situation wherein the capital at the disposal of one or few individuals is quite insufficient to meet the growing investment demands. A developed capital market can solve this problem of paucity of funds. An organised capital market can mobilise and pool together even the small and scattered savings and augment the availability of investible funds. While the rapid growth of joint stock companies has been made possible to a large extent by the growth of capital markets, the growth of joint stock business has in its turn, encouraged the development of capital markets.

A developed capital market provides a number of profitable investment opportunities for the small savers.

## Money Market vs. Capital Market

In this context, it is imperative that one should know the distinction between a money market and a capital market. The distinction is briefly shown in the following table:

| Money Market | Capital Market |
|---|---|
| (i) It is a market for short-term loanable funds for a period not exceeding one year. | (i) It is a market for long-term funds for a period exceeding one year. |
| (ii) This market supplies funds for financing current business operations, working capital requirements of industries and short period requirements of the government. | (ii) This market supplies funds for financing the fixed capital requirements of trade and commerce as well as the long-term requirements of the government. |
| (iii) The instruments that are dealt in a money market are bills of exchange, treasury bills, commercial papers, certificate of deposit, etc. | (iii) This market deals in instruments like shares, debentures, government bonds, etc. |
| (iv) Each single money market instrument is of large amount. A TB is of minimum for rupees one lakh. Each CD or CP is for a minimum of ₹ 25 lakh. | (iv) Each single capital market instruments is of small amount. Each share value is ₹ 10. Each debenture value is ₹ 100. |
| (v) The Central Bank and commercial banks are the major institutions in the money market. | (v) Development banks and insurance companies play a dominant role in the capital market. |
| (vi) Money market instruments geneally do not have secondary markets. | (vi) Capital market instruments generally have secondary markets. |
| (vii) Transactions mostly take place over-the-phone and there is no formal place. | (vii) Transactions take place at a formal place *viz..*, stock exchange. |
| (viii) Transations have to be conducted without the help of brokers. | (viii) Transactions have to be conducted only through authorised dealers. |

## THE INDIAN CAPITAL MARKET TODAY

The Indian capital market with over 7,500 listed companies and 23 stock exchanges is second in size only to that of the USA, in terms of availability of industrial securities. The Indian capital market offers good potential for further expansion in terms of absorption of large capital flows. It is noteworthy that despite problems faced on account of irregularities in security transactions earlier this year, the Indian stock markets have shown creditable business resilience and recovery. As per the review published by

*Fortune International* in its Autumn Special 1992 number, the Indian capital market has appreciated by 44 per cent in US dollar terms an appreciation rate which was second only to that of the Philippines at 71%. Comparable statistics for other emerging markets are: South Korea (–)24 per cent, Indonesia (–) 5 per cent, Singapore 5 per cent, Malaysia 9 per cent, Hong Kong 39 per cent, etc. It is true that the price-earning ratio of 29 is comparatively high when compared with the prevailing ratios in the afore-mentioned markets. But it needs mention that in the Indian market, the PE ratio is influenced to a very large extent by 4 or 5 leading scrips. If one leaves out these scrips, the PE ratio would certainly compare favourably with those prevailing in other emerging markets. In fact, considering that active trading is confined to few hundred scrips, it is conceivable that with substantial inflow of foreign capital, many of the currently dormant scrips, mainly of medium-sized corporate bodies, would show growth potential.

There are a couple of areas where some improvement will be necessary. The first is the factor of a long time between the transaction and the actual registration of transfer of securities at present.

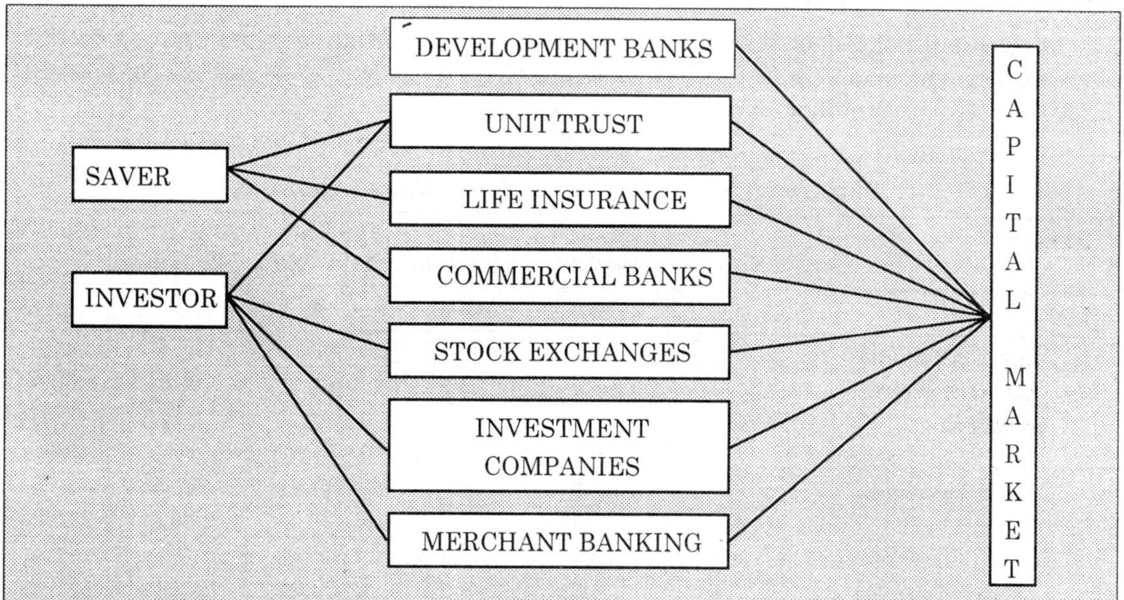


**Fig. 2**

Secondly, the reporting and controlling system will have to be geared up to ensure compliance with the stipulations regarding upper limit for investment in a domestic company (24%) and by a particular investor (5%). The Reserve Bank authorities confirm that steps are being taken to overcome these problems.

Following the recommendations of Chakravarty Committee Report on Monetary System, the RBI during the year, began the auction of 182 days Treasury Bills in the money market. The objective of this measure has been to broadbase the development of money market by introducing new instruments, create an active secondary market, bring the interest rates on Treasury Bills to the market level and gradually reduce the monetisation of public debt.

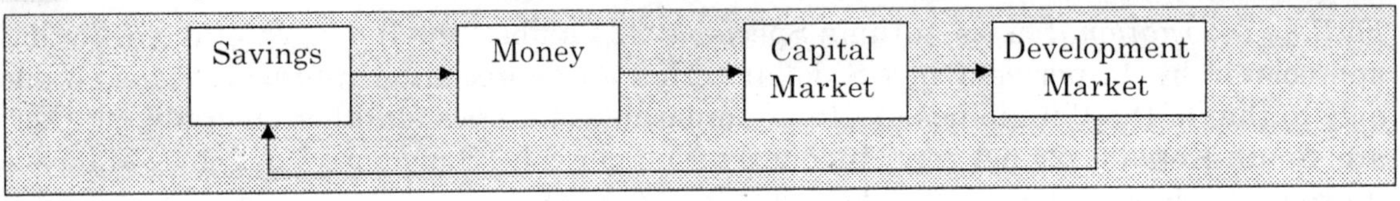


**Fig. 3**

The steady increase in the capital formation, which is slightly higher than the level of gross domestic savings, indicates that the development banks have been playing a significant promotional role in mobilising resources and channeling savings into productive investment. The enlargement of their coverage will definitely accelerate the growth process.

Over the years, the corporate sectors share of internal resources increased from 31.9 per cent during the period 1985-86 to 1989-90 to 60.7 per cent during 2000-01 to 2004-05. As such, the dependence on market-based financing declined from 18.2 per cent to 8.6 per cent respectively. The share of capital market related instruments (Debentures and Equity Capital) in total external financing peaked at 26.0 per cent during 1990-91 to 1994-95. It was around 14.3 per cent in 2005-06.

As a result, the debt-equity ratio declined sharply from 88.4 per cent to 61.6 per cent during the same period. This has enabled to corporate sector to significantly improve their profitability and their resilience.

**Table : 1**
**Pattern of Sources of Funds for Indian Corporates**

| Item | 1985-86 to 1989-90 | 1990-91 to 1994-95 | 1995-96 to 1999-2000 | 2000-01 to 2004-05 | 2005-06 |
|---|---|---|---|---|---|
| 1 | 2 | 3 | 4 | 5 | 6 |
| 1. Internal Sources | 31.9 | 29.9 | 37.1 | 60.7 | 43.6 |
| 2. External Sources | 68.1 | 70.1 | 62.9 | 39.3 | 56.4 |
| of which: | | | | | |
| (a) Equity capital | 7.2 | 18.8 | 13.0 | 9.9 | 17.0 |
| (b) Borrowings | 37.9 | 32.7 | 35.9 | 11.5 | 24.4 |
| of which: | | | | | |
| (i) Debentures | 11.0 | 7.1 | 5.6 | –1.3 | –2.7 |
| (ii) From Banks | 13.6 | 8.2 | 12.3 | 18.4 | 23.8 |
| (iii) From FIs | 8.7 | 10.3 | 9.0 | –1.8 | –2.4 |
| (c) Trade dues and other current liabilities | 22.8 | 18.4 | 13.7 | 17.3 | 14.7 |
| **Total** | **100.0** | **100.0** | **100.0** | **100.0** | **100.0** |
| Memoranda: | | | | | |
| (i) Share of Capital Market Related Instruments (Debentures and Equity Capital) | 18.2 | 26.0 | 18.6 | 8.6 | 14.3 |
| (ii) Share of Financial Intermediaries (Borrowings from Banks and FIs) | 22.2 | 18.3 | 21.3 | 16.6 | 21.4 |
| (iii) Debt-Equity Ratio | 88.4 | 85.5 | 65.2 | 61.6 | 43.0 |

**CAPITAL MARKETS IN INDIA** **BOX : 1**

In the 1950s India's capital markets helped to mobilize financial resources for the corporate sector. The importance of these markets then diminished, because subsidized credits were available from commercial and development banks, equities had to be issued at a discount substantially below market value, the capital market lacked liquidity, and investor safeguards were inadequate.

A reform of the Foreign Exchange Regulation Act in the early 1970s limited the expansion of foreign-owned and foreign-controlled companies. In response, many companies decided to become Indian companies. This led to the issue of substantial quantities of company shares at low prices, the market's revival continued in the 1980s, as various measures were introduced to stimulate both demand and supply. Incentives for equity and debenture issues included reducing the corporate rate of tax of listed companies and fixing the permitted interest rate for debentures above that of fixed deposits but below that for bank loans. The government also authorized the use of cumulative, convertible preference shares and equity-linked debentures and gave generous fiscal incentives to investors.

The growth of the Indian capital markets has been impressive. Equity market capitalization on the Bombay stock exchange increased from \$11.8 billion to \$ 19.4 billion between the end of 1980 and 1987; average capitalization ratios remained roughly equal to 6.5 per cent of increased from 2,114 in 1981 to 6,017 in 1987. New issues of debentures also multiplied. However, there were also abuses, such as the use of misleading prospectuses and insider trading. In addition, the processing of new issues, which were heavily oversubscribed because of their low prices, was plagued by delays in share allocation.

In April 1988 the Securities and Exchange Board of India was established to oversee and regulate the market. In August 1988 a credit rating agency was established to grade capital issues. In January 1989 proposals were published regarding the appointment of market makers offering bid-and-asked quotations, the responsibility of stock brokers for vetting companies before listing, the opening of stock broking to banks and other financial institutions, and the creation of a second-tier market for smaller enterprises, with less onerous listing requirements. The measures were intended to improve market liquidity and transparency and to provide adequate protection to investors.

## Capital Market Instruments

The following instruments are being used for raising resources:

(1) Equity shares
(2) Preference shares
(3) Non-voting equity shares
(4) Cumulative convertible preference shares
(5) Company fixed deposits
(6) Warrants
(7) Debentures/bonds
(8) Secured premium notes (SPNs)
(9) Euro Convertible Bonds (ECBs)/Global Depository Receipts (GDRs).

## CAPITAL MARKET DEVELOPMENTS

The capital market has passed through a phase of substantial adjustment and advancements in recent years. A significant development was the entry of public sector enterprises in the power and telecommunication sectors in the capital market to raise larger resources by issue of tax-free bonds. Although this did not have any crowding out effect on the private sector borrowers, they faced stiffer competition in the market and had to come out with more attractive features attached to their issues.

The drop in the stock prices experienced during the year also the marked a corrective phase, following the boom in 1985-86. However, it is seen as a temporary phase which would in no way deter the long-term development of the market. High rate of savings, increasing presence of households for investment in financial assets, increasing diversity of financial instruments and growing securitisation of the financial market have been the basic factors providing enduring strength to the capital market. Besides, the need to raise the rate of industrial growth would require larger financial resources to be raised from the market. The market capitalisation of equity shares quoted on stock exchanges is currently estimated to be around 9 per cent of GNP. This is a relatively low figure by international comparison. The share of market capitalisation in GNP is 160 per cent in Japan, 65 per cent in the USA, 122 per cent in UK, 42 per cent in Taiwan, 95 per cent in Malaysia and 23 per cent in South Korea. The average price-earning (PE) ratio in India is currently in the range of 9 to 10 compared to 91 in Japan, 67 in South Korea, 32 in Malaysia and 15 in USA and Hong Kong. The lower size of market capitalisation and PE ratio in India are thus indicative of the potential for further development of the capital market in India.

## INSTITUTIONAL INVESTMENT IN INDIAN CAPITAL MARKET

Indian capital market had been kept insulated from global capital markets and cross-border movement of capital all these years, as a matter of policy. Recent changes have made the economy more open to the international markets. Access to India's markets has been made easier for foreign capital, technology and goods. It is natural that the Indian capital market should have been thrown open to the overseas investors.

In the past, overseas investments had been mainly in the shape of direct foreign investment in specific approved industrial ventures. The capital market was open to non-resident Indians and, more recently, to overseas corporate bodies of Indian nationals in a restricted way. In conformity with various policy measures taken during the past year-and-a-half, which cover India's external trade, collaboration and technology policies, financial restructuring, etc., the government has since announced a new policy, welcoming Foreign Institutional Investors (FIIs) to invest in the Indian capital market, both primary and secondary.

The salient features of the recently announced policy are:

(1) Foreign institutional investors (FIIs) including pension funds, mutual funds, investment trusts, asset management companies, nominee companies and incorporated/institutional portfolio managers or their attorneys (providing

discretionary and non-discretionary portfolio management services) would be welcome to make investments under the new guidelines.

(2) Investment in all securities traded on the primary and secondary markets, including the equity and other securities/instruments of companies which are listed/to be listed on the stock exchanges in India including the OTC Exchange of India is permitted. The instruments would include shares, debentures, warrants and schemes floated by domestic mutual funds. Government may even add further categories of securities from time-to-time.

(3) FIIs would be required to obtain an initial registration with Securities and Exchange Board of India (SEBI) to enter the market. Nominee companies, affiliated and subsidiary companies of an FII will be treated as separate FIIs for registration and may seek separate registration with SEBI.

(4) Since there are foreign exchange controls in force, FIIs shall also seek various permissions under FEMA from the Reserve Bank of India. Both SEBI and RBI registrations will be under a single window approach.

(5) FIIs seeking initial registration with SEBI shall be required to hold a registration from the Securities Commission, or such other regulatory organisations for the stock market in their country of domicile/incorporation.

(6) SEBI's initial registration would be valid for five years. RBI's general permission under FEMA to the FII will also hold good for five years. Both will be renewable for similar five-year periods later on.

(7) Under the FEMA permission, FII will be able to buy, sell and realise capital gains on investments made through the initial corpus remitted to India, subscribe/renounce rights offerings of shares, invest on all recognised stock exchanges through a designated bank branch and appoint a domestic custodian for custody of the investments.

(8) The general permission from the RBI will enable the FII to:

(*a*) Open foreign currency account(s) in a designated bank. (There can be more than one account in the same bank branch, in different currencies, if so required by the FII for its operational purposes).

(*b*) Open a special non-resident rupee account to which all receipts from the capital inflows, sale proceeds of shares, dividends and interest could be credited.

(*c*) Transfer sums from the foreign currency accounts to the rupee account and *vice versa*, at the market rates of exchange.

(*d*) Make investments in securities in India out of the balances in the rupee account.

(*e*) Transfer repatriable (after tax) proceeds from the rupee account to the foreign currency accounts.

(*f*) Repatriate the capital, capital gains, dividends, incomes received by way of interest, etc., and any compensation received towards sale/renouncement of rights offerings of shares subject to the designated branch of a bank/ the custodian being authorised to deduct withholding tax on capital gains and arranging to pay such tax and remitting the net proceeds at market rates of exchange.

(g) Register FIIs holdings without any further clearance under FERA.

(9) There would be no restriction on the volume of investment — minimum or maximum — for the purpose of entry FIIs, in the primary/secondary market and also on the lock-in period prescribed for the purpose of such investments made by FIIs. However, portfolio investments in primary or secondary markets will be subject to a ceiling of 24% of issued share capital for the total holdings of all registered FIIs in any one company. Conversions, out of the fully and partly convertible debentures issued by the company will also be taken into account for the purpose. The holding of a single FII in any company would be subject to a ceiling of five per cent of total issued share capital, for which purpose, holdings of an FII group will be counted as holdings of a single FII.

(10) The maximum holding of 24% for all non-resident portfolio investments, including those of the registered FIIs, will also include NRI corporate and non-corporate investments, but will not include: direct foreign investments (which are permitted up to 51% in all priority areas) and investments by FIIs through the following alternatives: Offshore single/regional funds, global depository receipts and Euro-convertibles.

(11) Disinvestment will be allowed only through stock exchanges in India including the OTCEI. In exceptional cases, SEBI may permit sales other than through stock exchanges, provided the sale price is not significantly different from the stock market quotations, where available.

(12) All secondary market operations would be only through the recognised intermediaries on the Indian stock exchange, including OTCEI. FIIs would not be expected to take delivery of purchased and give delivery of sold securities.

(13) FIIs can appoint as custodian an agency approved by SEBI to act as a custodian of securities and for confirmation of transactions in securities, settlement of purchase and sale and for information reporting. Such a custodian shall establish separate accounts for detailing on a daily basis the investment capital utilisation and securities held by each FII for which it is acting as custodian. The custodian will report to the RBI and SEBI semi-annually, as part of their disclosure and reporting guidelines.

(14) RBI may at anytime request by an order, a registered FII to submit information regarding the records of utilisation of the inward remittances of investment capital and the statement of its securities transactions. RBI and/or SEBI may also at anytime conduct a direct inspection of the records and accounting books of a registered FII.

(15) FIIs investing under this scheme will benefit from a concessional tax regime of a flat tax rate of 20% on dividend and interest income and a tax rate of 10% on long-term (one year or more) capital gains.

The capital market in the present decade has magnificently responded to meet the evergrowing capital needs of both the private and public sectors. Despite the ten-fold increase in the total capital raised from the market in the short span of seven years by the private sector alone, the total mobilisation was only 5% of the net household savings. There is no reason why the share of the household savings flowing into the capital market should not increase substantially in the coming years. The other factor which must be kept in view is that yield and earnings on equities in India are far higher than in most other countries where stock exchanges are fairly developed. Given the improvement in the general economic environment and better corporate results which are likely to follow in the wake of the massive investments in plant and technology that has taken place in the last five years, interest in corporate securities is likely to widen.

The capital market has also undergone a sea change with its scale and scope of its activities also diversified in a multi-directional way. With the establishment of new institutions, the edifice of the capital market is strengthened and broad-based. With the significant increase in savings, many investment avenues have opened up in recent years. The review shows that the capital market in India has grown on its own impetus. The changes brought about in it since independence have strengthened it. The potential of the Indian capital market is immense which can help a great deal in establishing a welfare state in India by tapping public savings, engendering a sense of public participation as also management accountability to the public.

Financial innovation has brought undoubted benefits to the customers of financial services. The markets have shown that they can adapt quickly and flexibly to changing circumstances; they will probably continue to do so. Achieving the objective of bringing immediate benefits to individual firms requires continued alertness to ensure that risks are adequately assessed and controlled and are priced appropriately. The technology which has nurtured these innovations is also available to help in controlling them, for efficient markets require not only the absence of distorting restrictions but also good information on which to base decisions and allocate resources. Experience has proved that no amount of fiscal and financial incentives alone, or even easy availability of finance, can bring success in industrialisation efforts, unless other inputs like resourceful entrepreneurship, latest and efficient technology/know-how, professionalised management, well-motivated and skilled manpower coupled with project counselling facilities and extension services are available at every stage during the life cycle of a project. In its promotional and developmental role, it has been, and continues to be, the endeavour of development banks to provide these non-financial inputs to the best possible extent, consistent with their resources and capability. This apart, the development banks will continue to play a significant role in widening the savings market and capital market, and at the same time providing equal opportunities to employ the savings protectively thereby increasing employment, raising the level of income, reducing poverty and improving the standard of living of the people.

In South Asia, India is the only capital market capable of growing into an international centre with its inherent strength which very few markets possess. Both Singapore and Hong Kong are highly developed, but they do not possess inherent strength. With the centre of financial gravity shifting to the Middle East, India is sure to command increasing interest. But this can happen only if we are able to redesign our complex structure of regulations affecting the flow of capital. This would call for a new vision and a new strategy. We would have to emerge out of the maze we have built for ourselves. A new order is emerging. We have opened up our closed economy on a selective basis. We have to cast our sight to a new horizon. Let us hope that we will be able to see the new vision and endeavour to achieve it in the coming years.

## STRENGTHENING THE CAPITAL MARKET

The Abid Hussain Committee on development of capital market has suggested creation of two-tier stock exchanges along with a number of fiscal measures to streamline the stock market for bringing stability and restoring investors' confidence.

It has recommended long-term policy measures to bolster the capital market so that industries with a proven track-record could meet their financial needs from the growing capital market.

The public sector financial institutions could then be made to cater to the needs of the newly emerging companies for survival and sustenance during their nascent phase.

During the stock exchange boom of 1985-86, a number of listed companies disappeared overnight giving rise to the 'fly by night' phenomenon. The committee noted that most of these companies were largely promoted by merchant banks, which were found to have received commission in the process.

The Committee recommended that all the companies should go through the registered merchant banks when they went public. The merchant banks should scrutinise the new companies entering the capital market, besides certifying that they were viable. This would act as a safeguard on the listing of new companies.

Yet another major recommendation dealt with the development of market makers, not prevalent in the exchanges now. The report proposed that merchant banks enter into a tie-up with the brokers to quote a cost-effective floor price.

To finance the buying or selling of shares, it called for provision of institutional financing through commercial banks.

The Committee recommended simplification of procedures involved in transferring of shares, which are considered to be complicated and cumbersome at present.

This included the creation of a network of corporations akin to the proposed Stock Holding Corporation of India (SHCL) under the leadership of the IDBI so that private investors could freely transfer the shares.

The report urged that a highly reputed national level institution be set up to undertake multiple membership in stock exchanges throughout the country.

The Committee also underlined the need to open new instruments such as non-voting shares with higher dividends than the voting shares. This would remove the fear of capture of managements of the companies as harboured by some efficiently run units.

In case dividends were not declared for three consecutive years, these non-voting shares would automatically be declared as voting shares, thereby providing an element of control over the management for those non-voting shares.

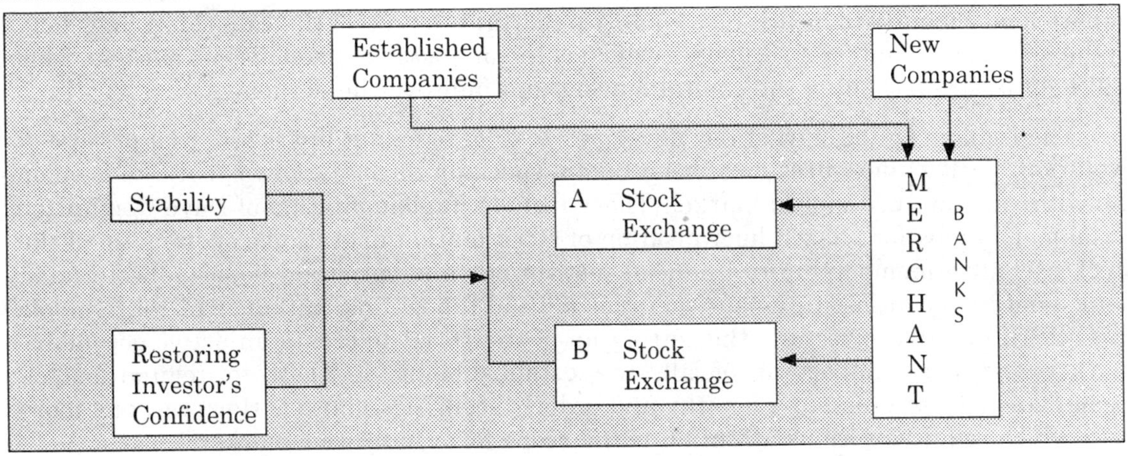


**Fig. 4 Development of Capital Market: Structural Changes**

This would also facilitate Non-resident Indians (NRIs) to come forward and participate in portfolio investment in the Indian market.

For the profit-making public sector companies, entering the capital market with tax concessions, the Committee suggested unitisation by which a public financial institution would act as an intermediary in creating units through selling of 25% of the share capital. As and when there are dividends, the value of these units would automatically go up.

The Committee also suggested that guidelines be evolved for the proper utilisation of mutual funds for equity raising instead of buying debentures as had been done by the State Bank of India and the Canara Bank in some cases.

Apart from making equity a worthwhile investment, it is important that the share base itself is widened. At present, the market for shares is limited to only urban areas and that too to a few major cities. There is considerable scope for raising resources from semi-urban markets and even in the rural sector. The equity culture is almost absent in these areas. There is an acute need to educate the public about the advantages of equity holding as also to provide facilities for purchases and sale of securities. For this purpose, the following steps have been necessary:

(*i*) Investment trusts or mutual funds have to be set up in semi-urban and even rural areas to be run on the same lines as the UTI to garner resources.

(*ii*) The number of stock exchanges for cash transactions has to be increased.

(*iii*) The financial institutions who also undertake underwriting operations have to undertake a publicity campaign to inculcate public interest in equity investment.

## CAPITAL MARKET IN THE PROCESS

The important task of the economy has always been to strengthen the capital market largely through stimulation of private investment. This could be achieved by effecting structural changes to the capital market, widening the scope of fiscal incentives and to impart some mobility to it. It is also equally important to protect the value of savings held in the form of fixed interest securities, which is the mainstay of fixed income earners. This will help in strengthening the capital market and improve the economy.

The Indian capital market has developed to a large extent but is still in a process of evolution. Various measures have been taken, specially in the last two years, to develop a healthy and mature capital market. These include implementation of Dave Committee recommendations for phased liberalisation of stock market operations, opening up of the stock exchange membership to financial institutions and corporate bodies, encouraging banks and financial institutions to go in for mutual funds, finalisation or rating symbols by CRISIL to guide investors, the setting up of the DFHI to create an active secondary market and most important of all, the establishment of SEBI to regulate stock exchanges so as to promote a healthy and orderly securities market. However, one more area which requires serious attention is the scope for a multi-tier market.

**WHAT INVESTMENT BANKS DO IN GLOBAL CAPITAL MARKET** — **BOX : 2**

Capital markets permit investment bankers to provide users of funds with greater flexibility (in terms of instrumentation, timing and risk management appurtenances) in: *(a)* accommodating how much money is required and when; *(b)* what type of security should be sold and to whom, in order to maximize efficiency and minimize costs of fund-raising; *(c)* what special features such securities might be depending on the credit rating and cash-flow circumstances of the entity concerned; *(d)* at what price it should be sold and when; and *(e)* how much the fund raising activity will cost.

To reduce its own uncertainty and risk, a user-of-funds may decide to go in for an underwriting agreement with its investment bank. Under this arrangement, called the firm commitment, the investment bank buys the new securities for an agreed price and resells the securities to the public at a mark-up, bearing all of the expenses associated with the sale. Usually, the investment bank becomes a broker-dealer or market-maker in the new security sold. Through underwriting the issuer (user-of–funds) gets the funds on a guaranteed basis even if the investment bank does not succeed in selling all of the securities issued. Thus, the investment banks takes a calculated risk for a short period. But it can also profit significantly if the issue is greatly desired by investors, allowing the investment bank to charge a higher mark-up and book an immediate profit. Under stable market conditions, knowledgeable investment banks are rarely trapped into having to hold underwritten securities for long. But sometimes market conditions can change suddenly in response to an unforeseeable shock. Investment banks can then be caught holding the bag for longer than they wanted, thus tying up capital that could be used for other (higher-return) purposes.

Direct responsibilities in an underwriting include registering new securities with the concerned regulator, deciding the offer price, and forming/managing a syndicate to market the new securities. Often the investment bank pegs the price of a new issue by buying in the open market. Successful underwriting is about selecting the right issue, offering it at the right price, and selling it at the right time. The investment bank may have to lower the price of the new issue to below what it paid for it, thereby resulting in a loss. Furthermore, the initial customers who paid a higher price for the new issue will be disappointed that they paid a higher price, and the investment bank may lose these customers in a future offering.

Investment banking is a very competitive business in global capital markets and established IFCs. Every deal forms an input for future business possibilities for the banker both from the issuer and other companies.

Most agreements for the sale of new securities get underwritten. But when the issuer is perceived as risky, the investment bank may use a best efforts approach; i.e., it undertakes to do its best to sell all of the new securities, but does not guarantee it. The issuer bears the risk that the investment bank may fail to sell all of the new issue, thereby reducing the amount of money that the company receives. Underwriters make money by selling the new securities at a mark-up from what they paid for it, known as the underwriting discount, or underwriting spread. The underwriting discount is set by bidding and negotiation, but is influenced by the size of the new issue, whether it is equities or bonds, and the perceived difficulty of selling the new issue. More speculative issues require a larger underwriting spread for the increased risk involved.

The liquidity risk taken in an underwriting transaction can be 'laid-off' in the risk market using derivatives. Investment banks utilize sophisticated financial economics in quantifying their exposure. They establish a set of exchange-traded and OTC positions in derivatives markets (for credit, interest rate, and currency risks) through which the bulk of their risk is transferred to buyers of risk in the derivatives market. The residual risk is borne by investment banks against equity capital, and is required to earn a high rate of return. Hence, to the extent that risk-markets support laying-off through exposure hedging, the lower is the unhedged component of the risk, and thus the lower is the cost of capital for the unhedged portion.

The total floatation costs of bringing new issues to the capital market also includes legal, accounting, and other costs borne by the issuer in addition to the underwriting discount. Economies of scale result in floatation costs for small issues generally being a larger percentage of the total sale of new securities than for larger issues. They are also greater for equities than for bonds. The underwriting spread may vary from about 1% for investment-grade bonds to almost 25% for the stocks of small unknown companies. As additional compensation, the underwriting firm may get rights to buy additional securities at a specified price (pre-negotiated call options), or receive a membership on the board of directors of the issuing company. The underwriting firm frequently becomes a market maker in the new security, keeping an inventory and providing a firm bid and offer price for the new security to provide a secondary market, so that investors can buy or sell the new securities after primary sale. This ensures liquidity for investors and thus increases the value of the primary offering, since few investors would buy a new security if they couldn't sell it at will.

Sometimes investment banks form syndicates and enlist the help of other investment banks to sell securities. The 'lead' investment bank selects the members of the syndicate and determines how many shares each will get and manages the overall process. In addition, each member of the syndicate, including the originating investment bank may have selling groups, consisting of other investment bankers, dealers, and brokers that may also sell to investors. The main advantage of syndication is that it reduces risk by sharing it among the syndicate members, and each syndicate member and their selling groups have their own customers to whom they can sell the new issues.

Overtime, while the securities market has expanded manifold, the structure and working of the market has remained unchanged. At present though, various securities traded in the stock exchanges are different in nature they are all subject to the same listing requirements. The size, liquidity, floating stock, volume of trade, company's performance, etc., of listed companies differ widely, still they are all treated at par. The existing uniform listing requirements are neither suitable to the investor, who is not aware of the differences in securities, nor to the issuing companies whose needs are diverse.

The SEBI, in its approach paper, has referred to its plans to seek and promote a multi-tier market structure, with different tiers having distinct characteristics suited to the differing needs of issuers and investors. Each tier would have its own listing requirements. The primary objective of such a structure would be to ensure that the market is attractive to issuers of different sizes and is suited to their needs to impart liquidity to issues and to provide appropriate incentives to elicit good response from the investors.

There is no doubt that there is need for a multi-tier market. However, as a first step, it would be advisable to have a two-tier market. It has been suggested that public issues below ₹ 3 crore should form one tier of the market, while those above ₹ 3 crore can form the other elevated tier of the market. Such bifurcation would help the smaller companies to mobilise resources at a lower cost, with less stringent requirements, and provide a way for companies to gradually move up to the elevated market as they grow. The higher tier would be subject to stringent requirements of disclosure to stock exchanges and investors. These shares would obviously be more liquid. The investors on their part would be aware of the relative liquidity and risk and the reward profile of alternative investments.

The idea behind the introduction of a two-tier market is to insulate the general public from the relatively high risk shares in the lower market. This should be possible since only those persons having the capacity to take risks and the necessary expertise to make professional judgement would operate in this market. Mainly financial institutions, banks and their subsidiaries and brokers would actively participate in this market. The companies with relatively few shareholders, with no recent trading history or those having only local or regional investor interest, would be attracted to this lower tier of the market. The envisaged two tiers of the market would continue to form part of the existing securities exchange market.

Another type of secondary securities market being envisaged is the Over-the-counter (OTC) market. The difference between the two is that a securities exchange market operates on auction basis, whereas an OTC market functions on the negotiation principle. In an exchange market, many buyers and sellers compete for the best share price through agents, whereas in an OTC market, intermediaries (brokers/dealers) for one buyer and one seller seek each other and agree on a trade price. In the OTC market, there is no physical meeting place for buyers and sellers. Instead they find each other through an electronic network or by telephone or telex. There is no double auction method as practised by the exchanges. Instead the market in a stock is maintained by firms that act as dealers by establishing positions in a security.

An important and unique characteristic of the Indian capital market, that has been lost as a result of globalisation of the market, is the isolated nature of the markets. The Indian markets till now were neither linked to global markets nor were affected by ups and downs being experienced by global markets. As a result, the markets continued to remain buoyant even during Gulf War and other world crisis. However, now the markets are reportedly more volatile and more prone to economically beneficial happenings overseas. This would necessitate a need for greater intervention and stricter policing and hence there is a need to give greater freedom and more powers to SEBI, the supervising authority in the Indian market.

The volume of capital market activity has increased substantially over the last couple of decades though in the most recent period, for various reasons, activity has been somewhat subdued both in the primary and secondary markets. The period has also witnessed some widening and deepening of the market and the emergence of new institutions, such as merchant banks and mutual funds as well as new market instruments. Venture capital companies have also made their appearance but they have not grown anywhere near their potential, as exemplified in the US or the need for them given the contribution they can make to convert innovative scientific ideas into commercial propositions and for their role in promoting techno-entrepreneurship. This calls for proactive policies such as fiscal concessions and a supportive set of operational guidelines including encouraging foreign venture companies to set up in India.

The expansion of capital markets to meet successfully the challenges of the future requires the correction of some long standing systemic deficiencies stemming from institutional and procedural aspects of the functioning especially of secondary market institutions. This is being done and there is now a greater measure of transparency as a result of the requirement of fuller disclosure and the arrival on the scene of investment oriented research agencies. Reform of the stock exchanges is also under way. A depository system has been introduced and dematerialised trading is picked up. Computerised online trading between different markets is gathering momentum and the presence of the National Stock Exchange has made an enormous difference acting as it does as a pace setter for improved market procedures.

The reform in the Indian capital market would gain added significance in the context of a measure of internationalisation of Indian capital markets. For the Indian system to derive the full benefits and avert risks involved in the process, a structured and sequenced integration would be needed. The greater interaction of Indian and international markets would necessarily involve further improving our procedures and practices. Foreign investors are used to open trading systems within the framework of prudential regulation. Their markets are also characterised by adequate disclosure and research based information and severe penalties for insider trading. Our markets would need, both for their own development and to promote fruitful linkages with foreign capital market, to conform to these principles.

## CONCLUSION

The liberalisation in the primary capital market was mainly aimed at greater autonomy to corporates and better transparency for investors. These included free pricing norms for issues, removal of interest ceiling on debentures, abolition of the position of Controller of Capital Issues and dropping of mandatory conversion of debt to equity by term lending institutions. Statutory powers were conferred on the Securities and Exchange Board of India (SEBI) and comprehensive measures were taken for investor protection in the form of laying down disclosure norms, allotment procedures, control over insider trading, rights issue norms, handling of investor complaints, etc. The OTCEI was set up in February 1992 to trade in the scrips of middle market corporates. The National Stock Exchange (NSE) has been set up recently, with nation-wide stock trading facilities, electronic display, efficient clearing and settlement facilities.

The Indian capital market has undergone a sea change in the post-independence era. More particularly, the Stock (Share) Operations have witnessed a spurt of activities with the liberalisation of the economy and active participation of development banks.

The important task of the economy is to strengthen the capital market largely through stimulation of private investment. This could be achieved by effecting structural changes to the capital market, widening the scope of fiscal incentives and to impart some mobility to it. It is also equally important to protect the value of savings held in the form of fixed interest securities, which is the mainstay of fixed income earners. This will help in strengthening the capital market and improve the economy.

In recent years, various reform measures for blending market to freedom and regulation of the market on prudential lines were introduced. The measures include abolishing government control over capital issues and pricing, allowing mutual funds to be set up in the private sector, freeing of interest rates on debentures, excluding financial instruments from the purview of wealth tax and permitting foreign institutional investment directly in the capital market. All-India development banks have promoted individually and collectively, new institutions to help investors and entrepreneurs.

Building a capital market more responsive to the needs of lenders and borrowers would require substantial improvements in the macroeconommic, legal, and regulatory environments.

To operate efficiently, capital market and financial institutions have to be guided by market forces rather than government directives. Competition needs to be strengthened by encouraging the entry of new and innovative providers of financial services. And all the players of the capital market need to introduce discipline in their activities and transparency in their transactions.

Towards this end, the development banks have a lead responsibility and mutual funds, the merchant bankers and the stock exchanges have to play a crucial role with efficiency and credibility of a sound and vibrant capital market to promote investments and thereby accelerate the process of industrial development and at the same time push up exports to new heights.

The future of the capital market holds promise on account of the fact that India is expected to continue to grow aggressively at 8% plus for several years ahead. Further, the Indian growth story is domestically inclined (infrastructure, rural development, retail spending, etc.), and as such, external factors are likely to have rather less impact on the overall growth prospects. Morever, the corporate India is gaining global credibility with improved visibility, productivity and performance. However, the global oil prices and possibility of rising interest rates pose constraining factors for sustained future rise.

## ANNEXURE I

### THE HIGHLIGHTS OF THE MALEGAM COMMITTEE REPORT ON REFORMS IN THE PRIMARY MARKET

| *Issue* | *Current Status* | *Committee Recommendations* |
|---|---|---|
| Information on use of proceeds of the issue on the project | At present, the issuer is required to indicate project cost as well as means of financing. | Indicate actual expenditure incurred on the project up to the date of filling the draft prospectus with SEBI or up to a date two months earlier with the Registrar of Companies — whichever is later — and the sources from which such expenditure is financed, as also a year-wise break-up of the expenditure yet to be incurred. |
| Financial information regarding the issuer | Financial information for five preceding years and for the period not earlier than six months before the filling of the prospectus of an audited statement of profit and loss and also an audited statement of assets and liabilities of the issuer as at the balance sheet date is mandatory. | It should be mandatory for all necessary adjustments, wherever possible, to be made in the statement itself and not indicated by way of notes. |
| Other income | There is no provision currently for a company to disclose how much of its turnover arises from activities outside its main lines of business. Current SEBI guidelines require that if the total amount under other income exceeds 10 per cent of the total income, the sources and other particulars of such income should be disclosed. | The statement of profit or loss and turnover should be bifurcated into a turnover of the products manufactured by the company and the turnover of products traded by the company. The committee recommends that such disclosure should be made in all cases where other income (net of related expenses) exceeds 20 per cent of the profit after tax. |
| Future Prospects | The issuer can have a project appraised, and if the appraisal has been made by a financial institution, bank, or one of the lead managers, the same may be relied upon to make adequate and appropriate disclos-ure in the offer documents. Normally, only companies setting up new projects or major capacity expansion publish projections of future profits. | Companies taking on large expansions or new projects should make complete disclosures about technology, market, competition, managerial competence, and capacity build-up. Potential future earnings are to be published only if appraised by a bank, financial institution, or lead manager contributing five per cent of the project cost or ₹ 10 crore, whichever is less, as equity or underwriting. The projection period should not extend beyond two years after the expected date commercial production begins or three years after the issue closes. |

| | | |
|---|---|---|
| Stock market data | Part I of Schedule II requires disclosure of the high/low price in each of the last three years and the monthly high/low during the last six months. SEBI requires the disclosure of the average market value during the last three years, the number of shares traded on the day of the high and low in the last six months, and the volume of business during each period. | Disclosure should be made separately for each period which commences with a change in the capital structure, with effect from the date of the concerned stock exchange recognises the change. The volume of business must be shown not merely for the last three years, and for the six-month period preceding the issue, but also for each month during such monthly roundups. |
| Justification of price | There is currently no guidance about the manner in which the justification of the price at which the issue is made. | For justifying the price, the prospectus must disclose the EPS for the three years preceding the issue adjusted for capital changes. The pre-issue PE ratio should be compared with the average industry PE ratio. It should also show the average return on net worth in the three preceding years, and the minimum return on net. |

## ANNEXURE II

### MAPPING GLOBAL CAPITAL MARKETS

*In-depth analysis of the financial assets of more than 100 countries shows that financial markets are becoming deeper, more liquid and increasingly integrated.*

The world's capital markets now enjoy unprecedented breadth and strength. Financial institutions routinely move trillions of dollars of assets — stocks, bonds, and other instruments — around the globe. Cross-border capital flows and foreign holdings of financial assets continue to grow rapidly, linking individual financial markets into an increasingly integrated global one.

Executives who seek to raise money, institutions hoping to shape the global capital market, and policymakers who regulate it must all understand its evolution. The McKinsey Global Institute (MGI) has conducted a year long research effort on the world's financial markets and created a comprehensive database of the financial assets of more than 100 countries since 1980. Together, these assets make up the global financial stock.

This research yielded several notable observations. One of them is simply that global capital markets are huge: we calculate that the world's financial assets now total more than $118 trillion and will exceed $200 trillion by 2010 if current trends persist.

The stock of global financial assets has grown faster than the world's GDP, indicating that financial markets are becoming deeper and more liquid.

With a few qualifications, this trend bodes well for the world's economies, since deeper markets provide better access to capital and improve the allocation of risk.

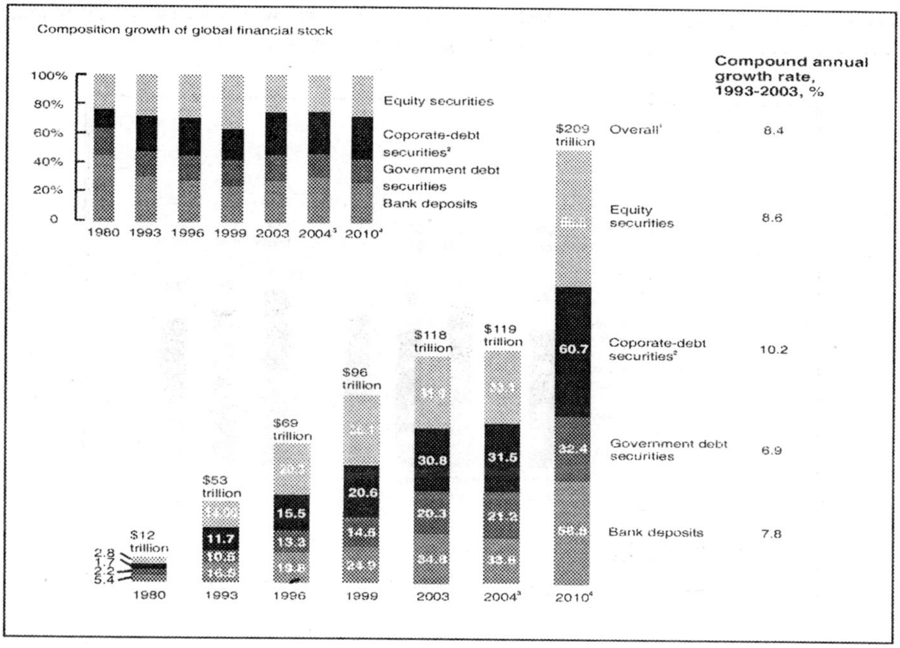


Much of the growth in global financial assets comes from rapid expansion of corporate and government debt, with all of the attendant benefits and risks. Last, the roles that major countries and regions play in capital markets are changing. The United States has the largest of them, which attracts foreign issuers and investors alike. European markets are becoming more integrated, however, and gaining in market share and depth. Meanwhile, Japan's role in global capital markets is diminishing and China has become a new force.

**$ 118 trillion and growing**

The total value of the world's financial assets (including bank deposits, Government debt securities and corporate debt securities, and equity securities) stood at $118 trillion at the end of 2003, up from $53 trillion in 1993 and from just $12 trillion in 1980. This $118 trillion is the total amount of capital intermediated through the world's banks and capital markets, and made available by them to households, businesses, and governments. A simple extrapolation indicates that the value of global financial assets will exceed $200 trillion by 2010. The growth so far has been accompanied by a striking shift away from banks and toward market institutions as the primary financial intermediaries. That change can be seen in the declining share of bank deposits in the global financial stock — to 30 per cent today, from 45 per cent in 1980— and in the corresponding increase in the share of debt and equity securities. The liquidity of world capital markets has increased as a result.

**Different profiles in different regions...**

Although we talk about a global capital market, just four areas account for more than 80 per cent of the world's financial stock: the United States, the euro zone, Japan, and the United Kingdom. Furthermore, regions differ starkly. The market of the United States — which, with $44 trillion in financial assets, accounts for 37 per cent of the world's financial stock – is dominated by private debt and equity. In Europe, banks play a larger role in finance. Asian financial markets are relatively isolated from one another and differ in important ways. Japan has the region's largest financial stock, but it is relatively stagnant and only the expansion of government debt fuels its growth. China's financial market, though less than one-third the size of Japan's, is among the world's fastest growing, and the country has amassed a sizable portion of the world's bank deposits.

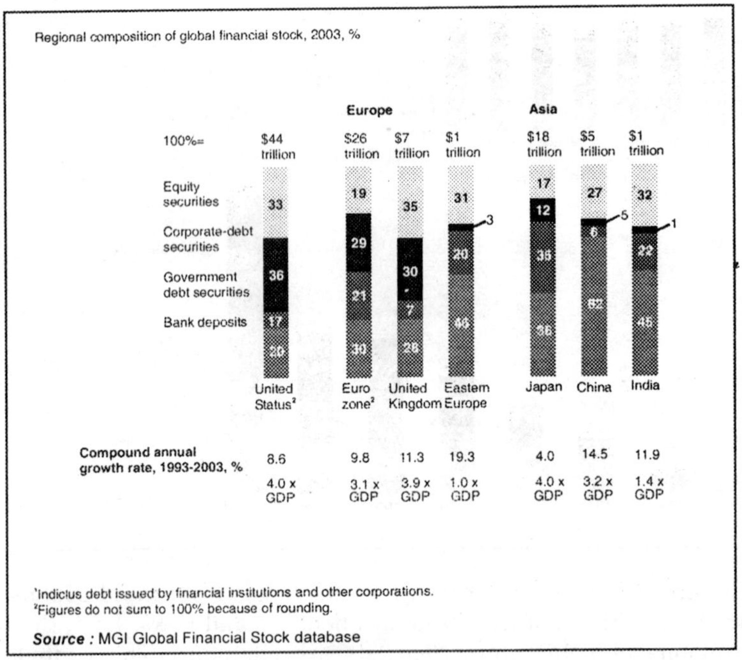


### ... and divergent growth patterns

Patterns of growth in financial assets vary across geographies. Corporate debt is expanding fast in both the United States and Europe. In the United States, initial public offerings are a significant source of growth in equities, as are higher price-to-earnings ratios. In Europe, by contrast, earnings and newly floated shares from the privatisation of state-owned companies explain most of the growth in equities. In Japan, a huge expansion of public debt is the only source of growth in the financial stock; equities and corporate-debt securities haven't changed. And in China and Eastern Europe all asset classes are growing quickly.

### Steadily deeper

An important measure of the development of financial markets is depth: the ratio between the financial stock and the size of the underlying economy as measured by GDP. Because financial assets reflect the expectation of future value, a country's financial stock can be many times larger than its GDP, which reflects current economic activity. Since 1980, the value of global financial assets has grown from an amount roughly equalling the global GDP to three times its size. Financial deepening is usually beneficial, giving households and businesses more choices for investing their savings and raising capital as well as promoting a more efficient allocation of capital and risk.

Compound annual growth rate by asset class, 1993-2003, %

| | United States | Euro zone | United Kingdom | Eastern Europe | Japan | China | India |
|---|---|---|---|---|---|---|---|
| Equity securities | 11 | 12 | 8 | 56 | 0 | 13 | 11 |
| Corporate-debt securities[1] | 11 | 11 | 21 | 25 | 0 | 18 | 0 |
| Government debt Securities | 2 | 8 | 5 | 17 | 12 | 28 | 14 |
| Bank deposits | 7 | 9 | 13 | 14 | 3 | 14 | 12 |

< 1% 1-7% 8-16% >16%

## Depth does not equal wealth

Financial depth alone, however, doesn't indicate the strength of an economy or its financial system. The financial depth of the United States is nearly twice that of Norway, for example, though both countries have similar GDPs per capita. Germany and Thailand, by contrast, have similar financial depth at greatly different income levels. Financial depth also doesn't necessarily mean that an economy's financial system is in relatively good health. Japan, for instance, has great financial depth but struggles with non-performing bank loans and with shrinking corporate-bond and equity markets. Asset price bubbles and the issuance of excessive government debt can lead to an unhealthy financial deepening – and painful corrections.

## Debt, debt and more debt

One of the biggest stories of the past decade was the growth of the world's debt levels. Corporate-debt securities are the largest — and fastest-growing— component of the global financial

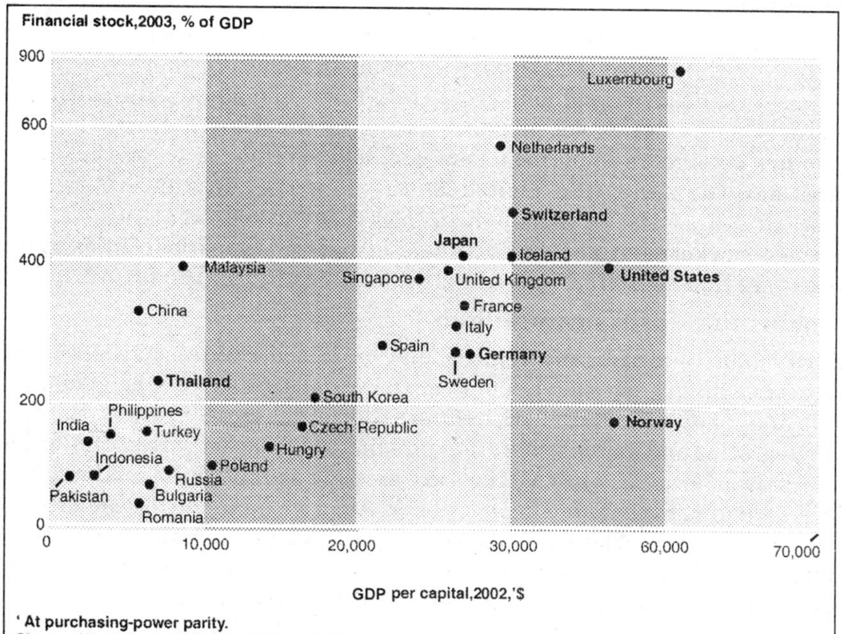


' At purchasing-power parity.
Source : World Bank; MGI Global Financial Stock database

Contribution to growth of global financial stock by asset class,[1] 1993-2003, $ trillion

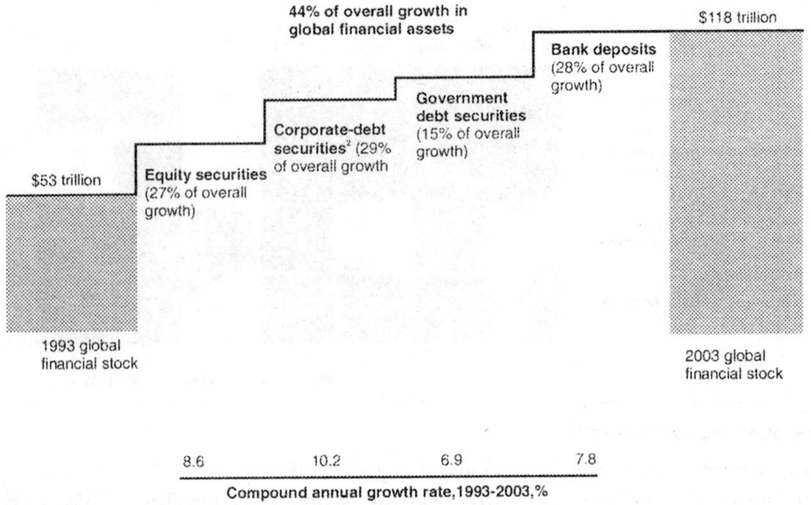


[1] Figures do not sum to 100%, because of rounding.
[2] Includes debt issued by financial institutions and other corporations.
**Source:** MGI Global Financial Stock database.

stock. Together with Government debt securities, they account for nearly half of the overall growth in global financial assets from 1993 to 2003. Debt has increased across all major countries and regions. International issues of corporate debt, though still small, are growing more than three times as fast as domestic issues (22 and 7 per cent a year, respectively), reflecting the increasing globalisation of capital as companies seek funds outside their domestic borders.

**What drives debt?**

The relative role of Government debt securities and corporate debt securities in explaining the overall increase in debt varies among countries. Higher government borrowing accounts for most of the growth of debt in France, Italy, and Japan. By contrast, an increase in corporate debt securities is the primary factor in the United Kingdom. The process of securitisation has become an important source of debt, as illustrated by the experience of the United States and Germany. The United States is at the forefront of the trend, with $7 trillion in securitised assets: $5.3 trillion in mortgage-backed securities (fuelled by a $9.9-trillion mortgage market) and $1.7 trillion in asset-backed securities. Other countries are far behind, suggesting that this market could grow significantly in the future.

**The US remains the world's capital hub**

The roles major countries and regions play in global capital markets are in flux. The United States has a unique position not only as the world's largest financial market but also as the global hub and conduit of capital. With the creation of the euro, however, European financial markets are integrating and gaining share. Japan's financial markets are becoming less important in the global financial system, while China's are growing rapidly. Financial markets in the rest of the world — including Singapore and all of Latin America — are negligible in a global context. Latin America's financial markets are notably underdeveloped compared with those of middle-income countries in other regions: despite representing over 4 per cent of global GDP, Latin America has less than 2 per cent of the world's total financial assets.

Contribution to overall increase in outstanding debt securities by component, 1990-2003

| | United States | United Kingdom | France | Germany | Italy | Japan | China[2] | India[2] |
|---|---|---|---|---|---|---|---|---|
| Government debt securities | 21 | 14 | 61 | 35 | 59 | 75 | 60 | 100 |
| Corporate-debt securities | 42 | 82 | 39 | 29 | 39 | 24 | 40 | 0 |
| Securitization | 36 | 4 | <1 | 36[3] | 2 | 1 | Negligible | |

< 5% 5-50% >50%

[1]Includes debt issued by financial institution and other corporations.
[2]Earliest available data shown: 1993-2003
[3]Predominantly pfandbriefe-covered bounds collateralized by long-term assets; traditionally issued by German mortgage banks.

**Source** : Deutsches Bundesbank; Standard & Poor's Thomson; US Bureau of Labour Statistics; MGI Global Financial Stock database

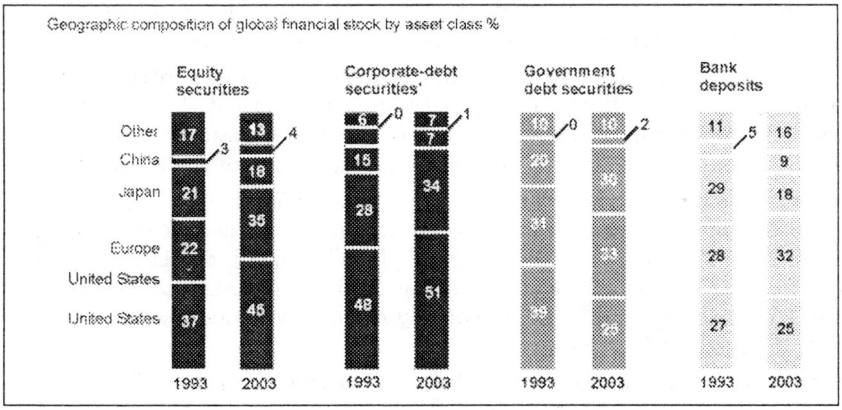


## A Weaker but still Dominant Dollar

Notwithstanding the recent decline in the value of the US dollar, it continues to dominate global financial markets. For starters, it is the world's most heavily traded currency and the preferred one for issuing equities and bonds. Many other countries, including China and Malaysia, have tightly linked their domestic currencies to it.

Although the euro is gaining notice among the world's central bankers, it is a long way from matching, let alone surpassing, the dollar's role in international finance.

## Growing Cross-border Capital Flows

With a few exceptions, it no longer makes sense to think in terms of national financial markets: they are increasingly being integrated into a single global one as cross-border holdings of financial assets and cross-border flows of capital grow. Today, for example, foreigners hold 12 per cent of US equities, 25 per cent of US corporate bonds, and 44 per cent of treasury securities, up from 4, I, and 20 per cent, respectively, in 1975. Since 1995, cross-border capital flows have more than tripled, and they now total upward of $4 trillion annually, including foreign purchases of equity and debt securities, foreign direct investment by corporations, and cross-border bank lending. These flows create stronger links among national markets and clearly show that despite the past decade's financial crises and the backlash against globalisation, the world capital market continues to integrate and evolve.

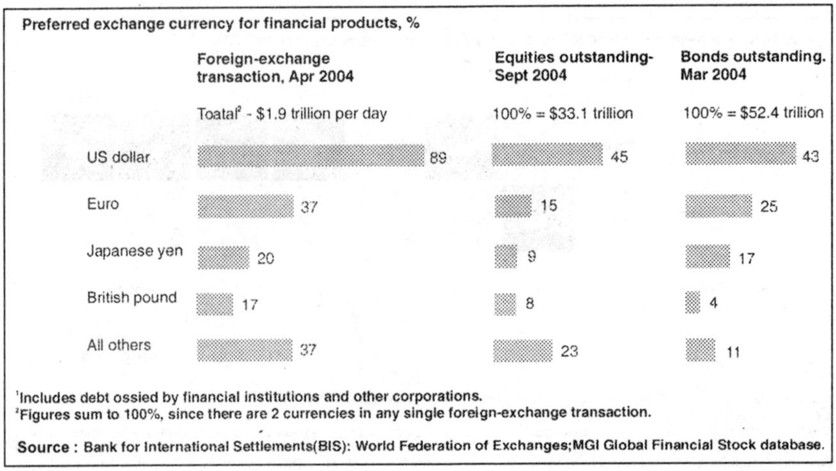


*This article was originally published in The McKinsey Quarterly, 2005 Special Edition, and can be found on the publication's Website, www.mckinseyquarterly.com.* 

Excluding cross-investment between them, oil investors, Asian central banks, hedge funds and private equity firms collectively held $8.7 trillion in assets at the end of 2006. Together, they represent some 5 per cent of the world's $167 trillion in financial assets – a considerable leap forward, given that five years ago, they were on the fringe of the global financial system.

The size of the four new power brokers, and their influence on global capital markets, will continue to expand. Given current growth trends, their assets are expected to reach $20.7 trillion by 2012, 70 per cent of the size of global pension funds. But even if oil prices fall, China's current account surplus declines, and growth in hedge funds and private equity slows, the assets of these four players will nearly double over the next five years increasing to as much as $15.2 trillion by 2012.

**New Power Brokers are Emerging in Global Capital Market**

Petrodollar investors, Asian Central Banks, hedge funds, and private equity firms are playing an increasingly important role in the world's financial markets, says a research paper by McKinsey Global Institute.

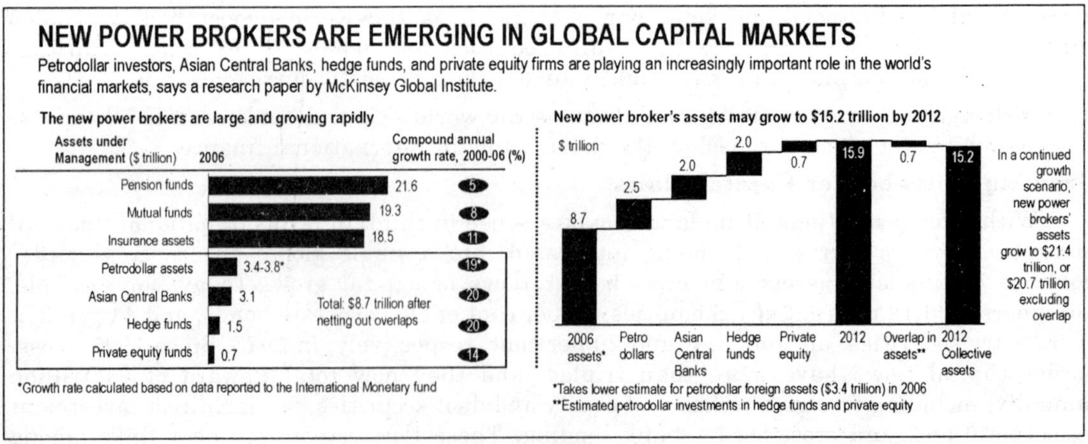

# CHAPTER 11 RECENT TRENDS IN THE CAPITAL MARKET

## INTRODUCTION

From its formal inception in the 19th century, the Indian capital market has come a long way and can be said to be in a maturing stage, backed by a developed legal system and an evolving regulatory framework.

The term *'capital market'* is generally understood as the market for long-term funds. In its broad sense, it embraces the new issues market and the money market also. In this sense both primary and secondary markets are covered. In fact, the money and capital markets are inter-dependent.

The capital market consists of individuals and institutions. The stock exchange, mutual funds, commercial banks, cooperative banks, development banks, insurance companies, investment trusts, merchant banks, finance companies, etc., are the important constituents of the capital market.

## RECENT TRENDS

The latter half of the 1980s witnessed a dramatic upsurge in the capital market in India and this has given rise to a general euphoria about the future development of the capital market. The various measures taken to open up the economy since mid-1991 like trade liberalization, industrial decontrol and measures to attract foreign investment–all these have given further boost to this euphoria. The Memorandum to the IMF on Economic Policies is unequivocal in its commitment to the development of the capital market. To quote: *"To continue the process of developing more competitive capital markets, the government has decided to promote the development of private sector and joint-venture mutual funds:* a *comprehensive set of policies and guidelines that will apply equally to both public and private sector mutual funds is being developed. The government also intends to introduce legislation ... that would allow the Securities and Exchange Board of India to function as an autonomous body with full statutory powers to regulate equity markets."*

The healthy growth of the capital market rests on broadbasing and mature development of the banking system in the country. As such, both are complementary and supplementary. The term capital market is used to designate activities in long-term credit, which is characterised by securities. It comprises specialised financial institutions including investment and trust companies, banks, stock exchanges and other institutions.

**HIGHLIGHTS**

(*i*) There has been an accelerated growth of the long-term capital market in India in the recent years. But the absolute size in relation to the economy is still small and the institutional structure inadequate.

(*ii*) In this purpose, we must reach out and activate the potential investors in parts of the country other than the Western region and in rural and semi-urban areas. This could be done, if a few large reliable national level private sector investing or promoting companies are established, which would have the capability of establishing branches in several centres and in training and appointing its own agents in the smaller towns.

(*iii*) The desirability of introducing the new instruments. In this, the non-voting shares and the equity warrant may be considered. With the introduction of non-voting shares in a company, the controlling groups could be persuaded to reduce their holdings correspondingly.

(*iv*) Supply of venture capital is high risk business, but the reward would also be high. Government must allow private investing agencies to be set up which could supply this capital to new ventures.

(*v*) A major deficiency in our capital market is the absence of a well developed housing finance system. In relation to demand, the flow of institutional funds into the housing sector has been quite meagre. The housing finance system that we build-up must facilitate an adequate flow of institutional finance to the housing sector as one of the priority sectors.

(*vi*) "Commercial Paper" having maturity period ranging from 30 days to a year may be introduced, as it would relieve pressure in the long-term or medium-term funds.

The term *'Capital Market'* is used here in the wider sense of the term as to include both the new issues market and the stock market. In this sense, both primary and secondary markets are involved in terms of transactions made on the exchange.

The tone of the capital market depends on the available savings and investment in the economy, on the one hand, and the performance of the industry and the economy in general, on the other. Among others, the monsoon and agriculture, industrial growth and performance of the corporate sector in particular, reflecting the fundamentals in the economy would influence the tone of capital and stock markets. In particular, the government policy, the psychological expectations and a host of other factors play a role in influencing the capital market.

## NEW CAPITAL ISSUES

The main indicator of the state of the capital market is the quantum of new capital issues floated or raised. There has been a quantum jump in the amount of new issues raised in the market over the last decade. From hardly ₹ 100 crore per annum in the seventies, the amount of capital issues increased to ₹ 5,651 crore in 1988-89 and it further rose to ₹ 10,120 crore, including PSU Bonds in 1989-90. Over the decade of eighties, capital issues rose by nearly 10 times.

## Capital Market

Various measures announced by the government during the year had their impact on the capital market. The severe import and credit squeeze imposed in July 1991 resulted in the postponement of investment programmes by promoters. However, this did not have an impact on the extent of capital raised from the market. During 1991-92, capital raised from the market aggregated to ₹ 7,473 crore as compared to ₹ 4,754 crore in 1990-91. Among the issues made in 1991-92, equity issues amounted to ₹ 2,235 crore, convertible debentures to ₹ 3,486 crore and non-convertible debentures to ₹ 1,752 crore. An amount of ₹ 486 crore was mobilised by lOBI through the issue of unsecured bonds. Amount raised through PSU bonds aggregated ₹ 5,721.7 crore during 1991-92 as compared to ₹ 4,933 crore in 1990-91; a major portion of which was through private placement. A noteworthy feature of public issues in 1991-92 was their number which at 499, was substantially more than in the previous year. With the lifting of credit and import curbs in December 1991, public issue-activity increased considerably. Currently, several companies have plans to enter the market with rights issue to get the benefit of the pricing freedom given recently.

The secondary market also witnessed a period of continuous boom during 1991-92, in response to the liberalization measures announced by the government. The boom was fuelled by intense speculative activity, shortage of floating stock in the market and the expectation of further scarcity of such stock with the anticipated large demand for equity from domestic mutual funds and from potential FIIs. However, various irregularities in the money market operations revealed recently have subsequently brought down stock prices and caused fluctuations and uncertainty in the markets.

The capital market is classified into two categories, *viz.*, organised and unorganised. With the establishing of development banks, commercial banks, Life Insurance, Unit Trust, the unorganised sector is isolated. In the organised sector, development banks are the key institutions.

## Savings Market

Indian economy continues to maintain high savings rate. Although there has been some decline in gross domestic savings rate in recent years from the highest level of 24.7 per cent so far achieved in 1978-79, it remained at 22.8 per cent in 1985-86 and 21.7 per cent in 1986-87. Out of total estimated gross savings of ₹ 63,413 crore, the household sector contributed ₹ 50,788 crore, amounting to 80 per cent. The share of household sector in net domestic savings, however, remained at 90.8 per cent. Growing preference of the household sector for financial investment was witnessed in recent years. Financial savings, of the household sector, increased to 58 per cent of its net savings in 1986-87 from 45 per cent in 1979-80. These trends indicate financial deepening of the economy and healthy environment for the growth of financial instruments.

During the year, the public sector enterprises in telecommunications and power sectors were permitted to enter the capital market by issuing tax free bonds to raise resources from the public for their expansion/modernisation plans are to thereby reduce the deficit in the budget. While 14 per cent public sector bonds were only free of wealth tax, 10 per cent bonds were totally tax free. The market response including that from the financial institutions to these bonds was favourable and the bonds are estimated to have mobilised about ₹ 1,516 crore, during 1986-87. The Central Government also floated Indira Vikas Patra, a new financial instrument, to provide remunerative return on investment for small savers. These Patras, made available through post offices, are bearer instruments, doubling the investment in 5½ years.

The New National Savings Scheme, 1987 was introduced from April 1, 1987 with Section 80CCA of the Income Tax Act, 1961 benefits. The scheme is administered through post offices. Under this scheme, a deposit per month in multiples of ₹ 100 is permitted with a ceiling of ₹ 20,000 in a year. Fifty per cent of the deposits in a year are eligible for Income Tax deduction under Section 80C of the Income Tax Act, 1961. This is in addition to the existing ceiling of ₹ 40,000 per year available under Section 80C of the Income Tax Act. The lock-in period of the investment is 3 years and one withdrawal per annum would be permitted. An interest rate of 9 per cent was fixed for the year 1987-88. However, in the year of withdrawal, 50 per cent of the amount withdrawn would be added to the taxable income. In addition to the existing National Rural Development Bonds and Capital Gains Unit Scheme of UTI, IDBI launched capital bonds carrying exemption from capital gains tax.

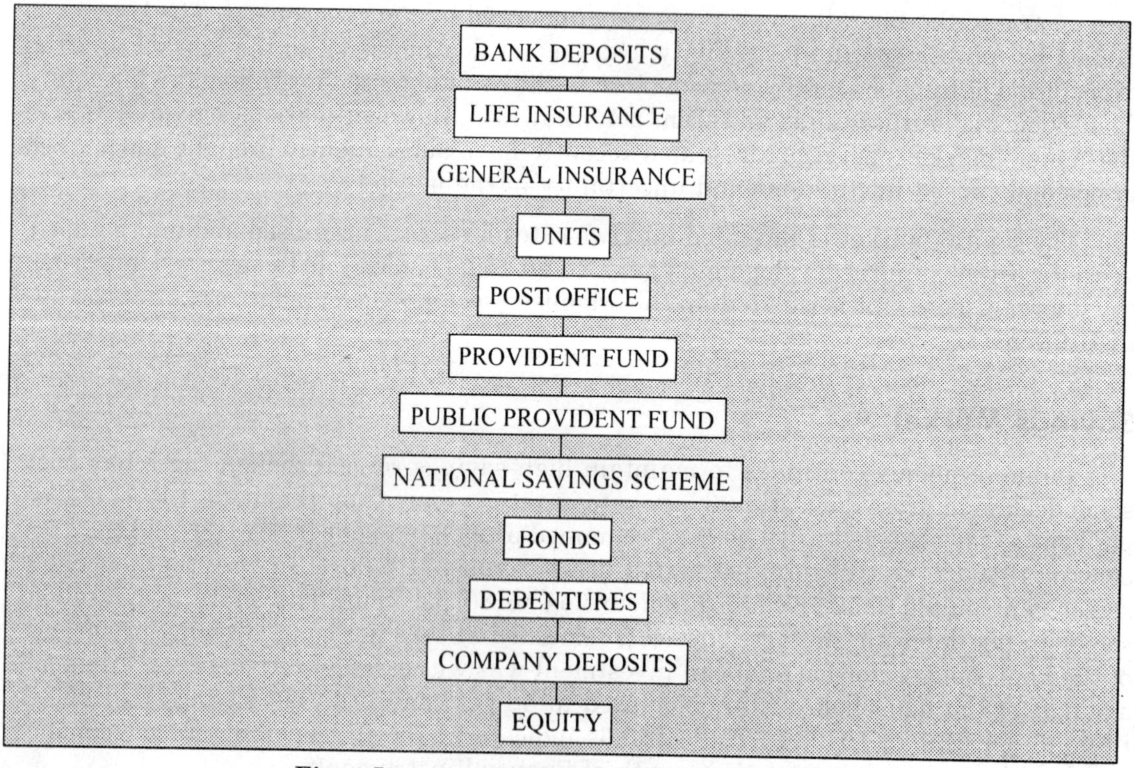


**Fig. 1 Instruments of the Savings Market**

## DEVELOPMENT AND INVESTMENT INSTITUTIONS

Functionally, there are two types of financial institutions in the Indian capital market, namely, developmental institutions and investment institutions. In the former category, there are institutions of all-India stature, namely, IDBI, IFCI, ICICI and IRBI, and State-level stature, namely, State Finance and Development Corporations. In the category of investment institutions, there are all-India bodies like UTI, LIC, GIC, etc., and State-level bodies like the State Industrial Development Corporations (SIDCs) and State Industrial Investment Corporations (SIICs) and State Infrastructural Development Corporations. The all-India bodies provide finance, entrepreneurial guidance, training and technical guidance, etc., to the all-India projects and regional projects of medium and large size. They lend at concessional terms for the development of no-industry districts and backward regions. Among the all-India bodies, IDBI is the leader of financial institutions. But in 1988, SEBI was set up as the developmental and regulatory body for the securities industry in India.

The state-level bodies provide finance and entrepreneurial guidance to state-level small and medium entrepreneurs and undertake developmental and investment activities to promote infrastructure and industrial growth in the respective states. Some of them have set up industrial estates and undertaking joint ventures with the private sector and promoting industries in their respective states.

These are the main players in the market, either in the primary market or in the secondary market. Besides giving loans and advances to industrial units, they invest in their debentures and equity shares, provide the seed capital for new and small entrepreneurs, underwrite stocks, shares, debentures and various other instruments in the capital market or subscribe to near issues or buy or sell these instruments in the secondary market, etc. A number of mutual funds have also become players in the market since 1987.

**SEGMENTS OF CAPITAL MARKET**

| APEX BODY | INSTITUTIONS | | OPERATING MARKETS | |
|---|---|---|---|---|
| IDBI | IFCI | LIC | NEW ISSUE MARKET | INITIAL ISSUES |
| | ICICI | UTI | SECURITIES MARKET | FURTHER TRADING |
| | BANKS | GIC | DIRECT BORROWINGS | |
| | SFCs | FINANCE COMPANIES | – FROM BANKS | |
| | DEVELOPMENT AGENCIES | INVESTMENT COMPANIES | – FROM PUBLIC DEPOSITS | |
| | PFs | BROKERS | – OTHERS | |

**Fig. 2**

The SEBI as the regulatory authority deserves our first attention as this book is concerned with the security markets. A brief discussion on SEBI is given first, followed by the UTI.

Of the major players in the market, namely, the investment institutions like LIC, GIC and UTI, the bulk of the activity is generated by the UTI by its mobilisation of savings from the public through its various schemes, referred to as below. It has today investible funds to the tune of about ₹ 30,000 crore and it actively participates in trading in the market and in subscribing to new issues of share, debentures, etc.

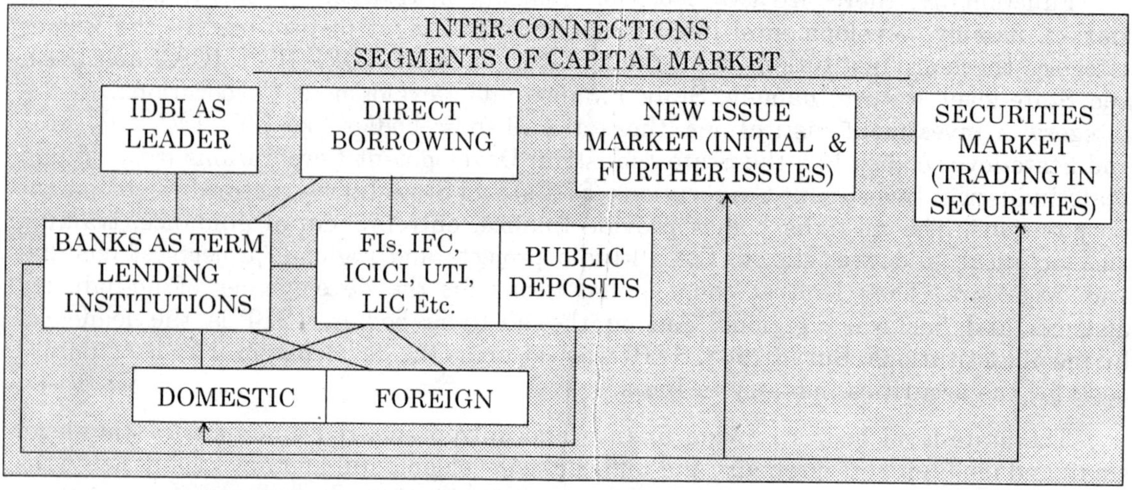


**Fig. 3 Capital Market Segmentation (Inter-connections)**

## FACTORS AFFECTING MARKETS

The liberalisation of the Industrial Policy since the initiation of the Seventh Five-Year Plan (1985) and the introduction of a number of new instruments like convertible debentures and cumulative convertible preference shares have facilitated the expansion of the capital market of the order referred to above. Resources raised through debentures rose by 118% in 1989-90. Of the total debenture issues, convertible issues constituted 91%. The 1980s have seen a quantum jump in the new issues and the cult of equity has begun to grow, aided by many tax benefits and the operations of mutual funds in the economy. A number of venture capital funds were set up by financial institutions to help new and risky ventures. Many public sector banks also came, LIC and GIC also came out with their mutual funds recently, which have helped the new issues market as well as the secondary market. In addition to the UTI, the mutual funds started mobilising funds for investment in the capital market since 1987.

The tax benefits include the exemption of dividend income up to ₹ 3,000 from income tax, raising of the exemption limit for deduction of income at source from ₹ 1,000 to ₹ 2,500 per annum as interest in debentures and tax exemption for investment in new equity issues of new companies up to a limit and fiscal concessions for venture capital funds, etc. Reduction of holding period for shares from 3 years to 1 year for computation of long-term capital gains is another tax concession. Besides, financial restructuring and deregulations have also helped the market sentiment.

Some of the policy measures have in particular, aided the capital market boom. Firstly, the ceiling on inter-corporate investment and loans was raised to 25% of the share capital of investing companies as against the earlier 10% ceiling. Secondly, the norms relating to foreign investment were relaxed in 1988 to allow foreign equity participation not only in new companies but also in existing companies up to a limit of 40% in a more or less automatic fashion. Thirdly, three new instruments for raising resources have been launched, namely, partly convertible debentures of 5 years with buyback facility, non-repatriable NRI bonds issued by the SBI and Offshore Funds by UTI and SBI.

## SPECIAL FEATURES OF THE INDIAN CAPITAL MARKET

The capital market in India has exhibited some special feasibility features in the recent years which are worthnoting here:

(1) Greater reliance on debt instruments as against equity and in particular, borrowing from financial institutions.

(2) Issue of debentures, particularly convertible debentures with automatic or compulsory conversion into equity without the normal option given to investors.

(3) Floatations of mega issues for the purpose of takeover, amalgamation, etc., and avoidance of borrowing from amalgamation, and financial institutions for the fear of their market discipline and conversion clause by the bigger companies.

(4) Avoidance of underwriting by some companies to reduce the costs and avoid scrutiny by the FIs.

(5) Fast growth of mutual funds and subsidiaries of banks for financial services, leading to larger mobilisation of savings from the capital market.

There are a number of other features of the capital market which are relatively more unhealthy and are brought out in the author's study on *"Ownership and Distribution Pattern of Shareholdings of Companies',* published in the Stock Exchange Review of March 1990. The share of small shareholders up to ₹ 10,000 has declined proportionately as compared to five years ago, while the relative share of large shareholders increased. This pattern of allotment is, therefore, regressive in nature. The results of the study also showed that the share of the corporate units increased while that of individuals declined, which is again unhealthy due to the fact that the real net savings emanate in India only from individuals and households and not from companies. The so-called boom in the capital market in 1989 was thus only a bubble built on the excess liquidity in the economy, caused by the RBI's creation of currency and expansion of money supply beyond the normal requirements of productive activity. The fact that the contribution of NRIs has declined is another disquieting feature in the capital market.

## OUTLOOK FOR CAPITAL MARKET

The capital market has taken a quantum jump in the last few years. A more liberal economic environment resulting in refreshing changes in licensing policy, improved performance by corporate leaders, introduction of new instruments and aggressive marketing of new issues set the tone for the new market trends. Never has the century old stock market in this country seen such frenzied activity in a short span of six years (1981-86) judged by the dramatic increase in investor population, the quantum of capital raised by the private corporate sector and the turnover of scrips in the secondary market.

As a consequence of the surge in the quantum of mobilisation of resources, the avowed aim of the government that the large private sector companies should meet the bulk of their long-term funds requirements from the capital market and thus reduce the strain on the financial institutions and banks was being fulfilled. In fact, even public sector enterprises have been increasingly resorting to the market to fund their investment needs with reduced dependence on the budgetary resources of the government. While increasing the number of individual investors have taken interest in new issues, the institutional purchases and support for non-convertible debentures and public sector bonds have also been substantial. The scheduled commercial banks have been permitted to hold in their portfolio shares and debentures of private corporate sector devolving on them through their underwriting or merchant banking commitment. The Reserve Bank of India recently allowed this investment by the commercial banks to the extent of 1.5 per cent of incremental deposits of the previous financial year. The banks were also permitted to invest in public sector bonds to the extent of another 1.5 per cent of their incremental deposits in the earlier year. Institutional support to the new issues market has, therefore, shown an increase.

The current and following years are expected to witness a marked transformation of the Indian industry. As a result of the modernisation of the existing plants, expansion of capacities to more economic levels, broadbanding, establishment of new units and upgrading of technology combined with far more liberal imports of raw materials, intermediates and components, there has been a very perceptible change. A much wider range of goods of better quality are visible in the marketplace and what is more significant readily available. The long waiting lists for several consumer durable items and premia have almost disappeared. The availability of essential intermediates like steel and cement has improved considerably. Infrastructure has been performing much better. The end result has been that, following the removal of production constraints in a large measure, we see keen competition in most sectors of a kind not witnessed in the last two decades. As an upshot, the corporate sector has been compelled to perform at higher levels of efficiency and emerge more cost-effective to be able to compete in the domestic and the competitive world markets.

The unfolding scenario in which market forces are gaining dominance will have a lasting impact on the industry. While it is producing strains for the weak below-par performers, it is creating abundant opportunities for the growth and expansion for the initiated and dynamic corporate managements. Obviously, there is a price to be paid for bringing about this transformation. However, what is reassuring is that companies with good brand image and aggressive marketing strategies are reaching out into new vistas, which is reflected in their larger sales and earnings. The increased supply of good quality of products at affordable prices backed by effective marketing and distribution will help open up the hitherto virtually untapped huge markets in the rural and semi-urban areas for a vast array of industrial products.

The recent developments in the corporate sector have had a marked impact on the stock markets. Even during the phase of downward correction, the good performers, especially those with a good product image, have held their own, while those with impressive track records, have seen a sharper fall in their share prices. This is, reflection of the greater awareness among the shareholders now in making investment decisions.

One of the weaknesses of the Indian stock exchange is the highly skewed activity. Out of about 3,500 companies listed on the stock exchanges, equity shares of only 200 to 250 companies are traded daily and actively. This causes wide fluctuations in the price of scrips and seriously impairs the marketability and liquidity of a large number of scrips of small and medium sized companies. Further, rapid growth in the turnover of stock exchanges has brought into focus their infrastructural limitations, calling for urgent improvement in systems and procedures and the need for effective regulation. The cumbersome and time-consuming transfer procedures on stock exchanges are accentuated by delays on part of companies to effect transfers and issues certificates. Inordinate delay in the issue of certificates by companies restricts the growth of floating stock in the market.

To redress these problems, several initiatives have been taken in order to improve the functioning of stock markets in this direction.

To promote instant dissemination of information of share prices, Press Trust of India (PTI) introduced a stockscan service, electronically linking stock exchanges of Mumbai, Ahmedabad, New Delhi and Kolkata. The stockscan service provides computerised network furnishing instantaneous information about price in their offices on computer screens. This service has been established to facilitate quick investment decisions, smoother flow of transactions and contribute towards the development of a healthy national securities market. It would also narrow down the price differentials in any scrip prevailing in different centres, tone up the functioning of the market and further help in the process of modernising stock exchanges in India.

Lengthy transfer and registration procedures have been serious impediments in the smooth flow of purchase and sale transactions. This has resulted in poor liquidity and inadequate growth in the floating stock in the market. The Stock Holding Corporation of India formed by the financial institutions in order to provide clearing house facilities to promote speedier transfer of securities will help alleviate the situation to some extent. This Corporation will act as a central clearing agency for registering of the transfers of securities and considerably reduce the time lag in effecting transfers. Credit Rating Information Services of India Ltd., (CRISIL) has been promoted by ICICI, UTI and other financial institutions to assess the credit standing of companies coming to the capital market and gives ratings to their debt instruments. The rating agency will enable the investors to make a more rational judgement of the risks involved.

The government has recently permitted the financial institutions and companies also to become members of the stock exchanges. This should bring about the needed upgrading of the quality of broking services to investors.

Further the government has also announced the formation of National Securities Board (NSE) on the lines of Securities Exchange Commission of USA. Other steps taken to protect the interest of investors include amendment of the Companies Act, which would extend the validity of transfer forms — currently two months to one year — creation of debenture redemption reserves by companies, publishing of six monthly reports of performance and the compulsory redemption of irredeemable preference shares.

Meeting the Seventh Plan targets of investment underscores identification of new avenues for additional resource mobilisation. The functioning of the capital market hence assumes a new dimension and the growing significance in financing development plans. With a view to examine the current trend in the capital market and suggest measures for its orderly growth, government appointed a Working Group on "Development of Capital Markets" under the chairmanship of Shri Abid Hussain, Member of Planning Commission. The Group's modus operandi involves examining the factors affecting the growth of the capital market, investment pattern and preferences, growth of different financial instruments and their roles, performance of new issues and suggest policies for strengthening and broadbasing the development of the market as also new instruments and institutional arrangements for channelising the greater flow of funds to the capital market. The recommendations of the Working Group would play a crucial role in initiating fresh policy measures to accelerate this process.

For further widening and deepening the capital market, it may be necessary to introduce new instruments for which the market offers considerable scope. The Vaghul Committee on money market recently recommended new instruments such as the commercial paper facility to be issued by the corporate sector for raising resources. Promotion of new debt instruments would be further facilitated by credit rating services offered by CRISIL.

Yet another development of considerable import is the permission given by the government to SBI Capital Markets, Canbank, LIC and GIC to float mutual funds. Unit Trust of India's schemes of India/Fund and Mastershares have already paved the way for more such funds. Creation of further institutional channels by way of mutual funds will attract a still larger number of investors into the capital market fold. It would give further support to the new issues and secondary markets, particularly of companies whose scrips are not actively traded. The UTI has played a significant catalytic role in garnering the savings of the community by continuously introducing new schemes with attractions to different investor segments. The schemes effectively marketed throughout the country have produced rewarding results.

The consolidation which the market has undergone is a healthy development, since it reflects investors becoming more choosy and cautious in managing their investment portfolio. This is a welcome development as it indicates greater investor maturity.

The impact of below normal performance of the agricultural sector and the decline in the overall economic growth rate would influence the flow of savings as well as moderate the growth of the capital market in the current year. Nevertheless, the transitory factors like drought should not cloud the immense potential of growth of the Indian capital market. In assessing the medium and long-term trend we cannot ignore the considerable strength the Indian economy has acquired over the years, both on the agricultural and industrial fronts. The capital market in the present decade has magnificently responded to meet the ever growing capital needs of both the private and public sectors. Despite the ten-fold increase in the total capital raised from the market in the short span of seven years by the private sector alone, the total mobilisation was only 5 per cent of the net household savings. There is no reason why the share of the household savings flowing into the capital market should not increase substantially in the coming years. The other factor which must be kept in view is that yield and earnings on equities in India are far higher than in most other countries where stock exchanges are fairly developed. Given the improvement in the general economic environment and better corporate results which are likely to follow in the wake of the massive investments in plant and technology that has taken place in the last five years, interest in corporate securities is likely to widen substantially.

The capital market has changed substantially with the scale and scope of its activities having been diversified in a multi-directional way. With the establishment of new institutions, the edifice of the capital market has strengthened and become broad-based. With the significant increase in savings, many investment avenues have opened up in recent years. The review shows that the capital market in India has grown on its own impetus. The changes brought about in it since independence have strengthened it. The potential of the Indian capital market is immense. It can help a great deal in establishing a welfare state in India by tapping public savings.

Financial innovation has brought undoubted benefits to the customer of financial services. The markets have shown that they can adapt quickly and flexibly to changing circumstances; they will probably continue to do so. Achieving the objective of bringing immediate benefits to individual firms requires continued alertness to ensure that risks are adequately assessed and controlled and are priced appropriately. The technology which has nurtured these innovations is also available to help in controlling them, for efficient markets require not only the absence of distorting restrictions but also good information on which to base decisions and allocate resources for good monetary returns. Experience has proved that no amount of fiscal and financial incentives alone, or even easy availability of finance, can bring success in industrialisation efforts, unless other inputs like resourceful entrepreneurship, latest and efficient technology/know-how, professionalised management, well-motivated and skilled manpower coupled with project counselling facilities and extension services are available at every stage during the life cycle of a project. In its promotional and developmental role, it has been, and continues to be, the endeavour of development banks or provide these non-financial inputs to the best possible extent, consistent with their resources and capability. This apart, the development banks will continue to play a significant role in widening the savings market and capital market and at the same time providing equal opportunities to employ the savings productively thereby increasing employment, raising the level of income, reducing poverty and improving the standard of living of the people.

In South Asia, ours is the only capital market which is capable of growing into an international centre. It has an inherent strength which very few markets possess. Both Singapore and Hong Kong are highly developed, but they do not possess inherent strength. With the centre of financial gravity shifting to the Middle East, the Indian Capital Market, is sure to command increasing interest. But, this can happen only if we are able to re-design our complex structure of regulations affecting the flow of capital. This would call for a new vision and a new strategy. We would have to emerge out of the maze we have built for ourselves. A step towards this is that we have opened up our closed economy on selective basis. We have to cast our sight to a new global horizon. Let us hope that we will be able to see the new vision and endeavour to achieve it in coming years.

## FINANCE HOUSE AND CAPITAL MARKET

The setting up of an institution in the nature of discount houses operating in UK has been engaging the attention of several committees over the last 15 years or so. The Banking Commission felt that at that point of the time, i.e., in 1972, there was no need for specialised acceptance and discount houses. However, the Commission recommended that after the bill market was sufficiently developed, such institutions might be formed as a joint stock company, which would offer the services of acceptance credit and discounting function as well as an intermediary to even out the demand for and supply of short-term finance in the market. Subsequently, the Chore Committee also considered this question and came to the conclusion that discount houses on the UK pattern for the purpose of giving purely rediscounting facilities for bills to commercial banks may not be *desideratum* in India. They recommended a discount house whose aim would be to even out liquidity imbalances in the banking system.

### Objective and Functions of Finance House

The Working Group on the Money Market (Vaghul Committee) has recommended that an autonomous public limited company, called the Finance House of India (FHI) be set up to deal in short-term money market instruments with the primary objective of imparting improved liquidity to these instruments. The institution would try to facilitate the smoothening of short-term liquidity imbalances and also to achieve integration of the short-term money market by functioning as a major money-market intermediary. It has been proposed that the FHI would be entrusted with the following functions:

*(a)* To Rediscount Commercial *Bills; (b)* Buy and sell short-term commercial *paper; (c)* Rediscount 182 days' *Treasury Bills* and actively participate in the development of a *secondary* market for treasury bills; *(d)* Undertake short-term *buyback arrangements* in government and other *approved securities; (e)* Provide *brokerage services* for the inter-bank *call money* market; *(f)* Provide services in any *other short-term* money market instrument which may be evolved.

### Capital and Resource Base of Finance House

The authorised capital of the FHI would be ₹ 100 crore of which ₹ 50 crore should be initially paid-up and the broad shares suggested are: RBI (40 per cent), public sector banks (40 per cent) and financial institutions (20 per cent). Also, it has been envisaged that for providing the required service, the Finance House, at times, may be under pressure. Accordingly, it should be provided a back-up line of credit from public sector banks of ₹ 100 crore at a fixed rate of 12 per cent. It has also been recommended that in order to impart sufficient liquidity to the FHI, Reserve Bank should provide adequate refinance facilities and the quantum of refinance as well as the rate of interest could be varied. As a matter of fact, through such variations, RBI is expected to provide necessary signals to the short-term money market.

## BILL REDISCOUNTING

One of the important functions of the FHI would be rediscounting of commercial bills. Wider use of bill finance for meeting working capital requirements has been advocated on more than one occasion. The Dahejia Committee in 1968 had suggested that commercial banks, industry and trade should try to initiate and develop the practice of issue of usance bills and their acceptance for the purpose of trade credit and for securing discounting facilities against them. The Narasimham Study Group observed in 1970 that the progressive use of the bill as an instrument of credit would be advantageous not only from the point of view of imposing financial discipline on borrowers, but also on lenders and it would be possible to meet the short-term liquidity requirements of banks by rediscounting these bills. Chore Committee while recognising the advantages of the existing systems of extending credit by a combination of the three types of lending, namely, cash credit, loans and bills, desired that wherever possible the use of cash credit should be supplemented by loans and bills. Chore Committee also recommended enforcing the use of drawee bills by making it compulsory for banks to extend at least 50 per cent of the cash credit limit against raw materials by way of drawee bills. Subsequently, Chakravarty Committee also discussed at length the defects of the cash credit system, and the task of cash management is passed on by the borrower to the Bank. Another aspect is the considerable benefit derived by borrowers akin to interest income on their temporarily surplus funds. The Chakravarty Committee also noted that the cash credit system has slowed down the development of the bill market despite its well-known advantages to leaders and borrowers and also despite the official policy aimed at promoting the use of bill finances.

The bill, being a self-liquidating short-term asset, is an eminently suitable financial instrument for banks. As the date of repayment is definite under the bill system, it facilitates the credit planning by banks. Despite these merits, the inland bills purchased and discounted as percentage of net bank credit has come down from 10.54 in March 1978 to 5.87 in September 1986. Only about 25 per cent of total inland bills purchased and discounted are being rediscounted.

Here it should be noted that several procedural problems have hindered the use of bill finance. These are the levy of stamp duty at varying levels by different State Governments, non-availability of stamp paper in required denominations as and when required, and the need to affix stamps on each bill. Apart from these procedural difficulties, there is some reluctance to undertake the additional paperwork involved in handling documents or titles of deeds.

The cost of administering the bill system by banks is also somewhat high on account of detailed bookkeeping. The principal obstacle to the growth of the bill market is, however, the reluctance of the large buyers in the public and the private sectors to accept the payment discipline involved in bill finance. Even the public sector units and government departments have been found to be adverse to accept the bills drawn on them. Another obstacle in the spread of bill culture is the absence of Acceptance Houses in India which could vouch for the bills of the lesser known finance firms.

Thus, to encourage the growth of the bill market, the procedural problems mentioned above will have to be removed promptly and the large buyers in the public and the private sectors will have to accept the payment discipline involved in bill finance. Already the Reserve Bank of India has taken certain steps for promotion of bill finance. These include a reduction in the proportion of receivable finance under the cash credit facilities, discretion to banks to sanction *ad hoc* bill limits, stipulation on big parties to attain a ratio of bill acceptances to credit purchases of 25 per cent by April 1, 1988, etc. However, the Vaghul Committee's recommendation of imposing a penal rate at 2 percentage points above the maximum lending rate for failure to pay the bill on the due date has not yet been implemented. This recommendation, we feel is worth implementing. It should not be for the banks alone to enforce the use of bills for credit purchases. The government/bureau of public enterprises should issue strict guidelines to departmental undertakings and public sector organisations that payments for all credit purchases should be made only in the form of bills and the bills accepted in this regard should be strictly honoured on due dates. Once such a directive is issued, the public sector organisations would be forced to take this factor into account while planning their operations and cash flow.

At present, apart from commercial banks, the institutions which are permitted to rediscount bills are: LIC, UTI, GIC, ICICI, IRBI and ECGC. The Working Group has envisaged that the number of participants may be increased, so that there is adequate flow of resources to the bill market. Initially it may not be proper to allow a large number of companies/trusts to participate in the bill rediscounting market, as this may divert short-term deposits with banks to the money market which would raise the cost of funds to the banks. The banking system performs a very useful role in socio-economic development which calls for a substantial accretion to the bank's resources at a moderate cost. For this, it is necessary to ensure that there is no substantial diversion of resources from the banking system to the money market. We, however, agree with the recommendation of the Working Group that further rediscount by the institutions should be freely permitted amongst the participants in the market. This would impart greater liquidity to the market and an active secondary market would emerge. In order to enable this multiple rediscounting, the procedural simplifications for bill rediscounting (such as rediscounting on the basis of certificates instead of physically endorsing and lodging each bill), as suggested by the Working Group will need to be implemented. Also, the participants in the market will have to provide rediscount facility at major centres and not at Mumbai alone as at present.

## BUYING AND SELLING OF SHORT-TERM COMMERCIAL PAPERS

It has been recommended by the Working Group that 'A' class companies could float commercial papers in order to meet their short-term liquidity requirements. These commercial papers could be subscribed by all the participants in the commercial paper market which would include 'A' rated companies, financial institutions, banks and other holders of short-term funds.

Though the Working Group has tried to allay the fears of banks that their interest may suffer through the introduction of commercial papers by 'A' rated companies, we feel that there is genuine reason for the banks to be concerned about this move. This particular measure (and several other measures adopted in the past) would lead to further disintermediation. The dependence of first class companies on banks would be reduced and banks will be gradually saddled with only second class borrowal accounts and sick units. The interest spread available to banks in lending to the 'A' class companies is much higher than the small commission the banks can hope to earn by acting as issuers of the commercial papers. Thus, the issue of commercial papers would definitely have an adverse effect on the viability and profitability of the banks which is already under severe strain. Also, such resources raised by the companies directly from the market would be outside the purview of credit control measures of the Reserve Bank.

## REDISCOUNTING 182 DAYS' TREASURY BILLS

The scheme of 182 days' Treasury Bills does not appear to have taken off. The amount of Treasury Bills auctioned has been negligible at around ₹ 15 to ₹ 20 crore, only per month. One reason for this may be the relatively low return fixed by the Reserve Bank of India on such Treasury Bills which is somewhat out of alignment with the market rates. Though RBI has announced the facility of refinance to the extent of 50 per cent of the holding of the Treasury Bills, it appears that unless the discount rate of these Treasury Bills becomes more aligned with that for other instruments, this may prove to be very attractive and in that case, the role of the Finance House in developing the secondary market will not be very significant. Of course, the situation may change over a period of time. If a secondary market develops, that itself may popularise Treasury Bills.

## DEALING IN GOVERNMENT AND OTHER APPROVED DATED SECURITIES

It has been proposed that the Finance House would undertake short-term buyback arrangements in government and other approved dated securities to impart short-term liquidity to these securities. This may be a desirable feature as at present, there is hardly any secondary market for the dated securities. However, it is rather difficult to comment upon this function without the details of the terms and conditions of the negotiations between the Finance House and the buyer/sellers of Government securities.

## CALL MONEY MARKET

It has been suggested by the Working Group that the proposed Finance House may provide brokerage services for the inter-bank call money market. In another section of the report, the Working Group has said that there is no need for brokers to be reintroduced into the call money market. Such services may be felt necessary after freeing the call money rate. As the ceiling on the call money rate is still applicable, it is felt that the proposed Finance House is unlikely to have any major role to play in this regard.

It is interesting to note here that the Working Group has recommended that barring LIC and UTI, the call money market would be strictly an inter-bank market, the justification being that otherwise, the cost of funds to the banking system would increase. However, the same argument holds good for the bill rediscounting market also, for which the Working Group has envisaged a large number of participants including companies.

## MARKET DETERMINED INTEREST RATES

In order to achieve efficient money market operations, the Working Group has recommended freeing the interest rates in several segments of the short-term money market. However, far the present both the call money rate and the bill rediscounting rate are subject to same ceilings. The Working Group has rightly observed that the needs of the economy dictate that a framework of an overall administered structure will have to be continued with a significant element of cross-subsidisation. In the context of the highly regulated monetary and the banking system, any attempt to rapidly deregulate only one segment may create adverse repercussions on other areas of regulation. In view of this, adequate safeguards need to be taken while gradually moving away from administered interest rates to market determined interest rates. It may be recalled here that the move for introducing flexibility in the determination of short-term deposit rates of banks in 1985 did not really work.

## NEW INITIATIVES

Though the capital markets in India have evolved over a long period, they gathered considerable momentum only after various initiatives undertaken by the Government securities and Exchange Board of India (SEBI) beginning the early 1990s. The activity in the market picked up from 2003-04 significantly reflecting effectiveness of the measures initiated to develop the market and restore investor confidence.

Various reforms initiated in the financial markets since the early 1990s have focussed on:

(i) removing the restrictions on pricing of assets;

(ii) building of institutional and technological infrastructure;

(iii) strengthening the risk management practices;

(iv) fine-tuning of the market microstructure;

(v) changes in the legal framework to remove structural rigidities; and

(vi) widening and deepening of the market with new participants and instruments.

Overseen by SEBI, the Indian capital market dealt in scrips of a large number of listed companies with a wide geographical outreach, providing a world-class trading and settlement system, a wide range of product availability with a fast growing derivatives market and well laid down corporate governance and investor protection. The reforms in the capital market are aimed at enhancing the efficiency safety, integrity and transparency of the market. The key reform measures for the capital market are given below:

## CAPITAL MARKET REFORM MEASURES

- With the repeal of the Capital Issues (Control) Act, 1947, companies were given freedom to price their issues. The book-building process in the new issue of capital was introduced with a view to further strengthen the price discovery process.

- In the secondary market, the floor-based open outcry trading system was replaced by electronic trading system in all the stock exchanges.
- The account period settlement system was replaced by rolling settlement, thus, reducing the scope for speculation. The rolling settlement cycle was shortened from T+5 to T+3 with effect from April 1, 2002. This process was enabled by a shift to electronic book entry transfer system through depository mechanism.
- The risk management system was made more comprehensive with trading members being subject to margins based on trading volumes and some other parameters and exposure norms based on the capital deposited with the exchange. The mark-to-market margins based on 99 per cent value at risk were introduced to capture the risk profile of trading members.
- The Indian companies were allowed to raise funds from abroad, through American/Global Depository Receipts (ADRs/GDRs), foreign currency convertible bonds (FCCBs) and external commercial borrowings (ECBs). The Reserve Bank allowed two-way fungibility of ADRs/GDRs in February 2002.
- Foreign Institutional Investors (FIIs) were allowed to participate in the capital market.
- For strengthening the process of information flows from the listed companies, several measures were introduced: (i) while sufficient disclosures are mandatory for the companies at the stage of public issue, the listed companies are also required under the listing agreement to make disclosures on a continuing basis; (ii) for ensuring quick flow of information to the publilc, the decision pertaining to dividend, bonus and right announcements or any material event are now required to be disclosed to the public within 15 minutes of the conclusion of the board meeting in which the decisions are taken; (iii) the accounting practices were streamlined with norms introduced for segment reporting, related party transactions and consolidated balance sheets.
- Insider trading was made a criminal offence. The regulations governing substantial acquisition of shares and takeovers of companies were also introduced aimed at protecting the interests of minority shareholders by making the takeover process more transparent.
- For providing market participants instruments for hedging and risk management, several types of derivative products on equities were introduced. Non-transparent products like 'badla' were banned.
- Measures to expand the market for corporate bonds: Exchange-traded currency and interest rate futures are to be launched and a transparent credit derivatives market is to be developed with appropriate safeguards;
- Tradability of domestic convertible bonds is to be enhanced through the mechanism of enabling investors to separate the embedded equity option from the convertible bond, and trade it separately;
- Development of a market-based system for classifying financial instruments based on their complexity and implicit risks is to be encouraged.

- Permanent Account Number (PAN): Requirement of PAN has been extended to all transactions in the financial market, subject to suitable threshold exemption limits.
- National market for securities: Empowered Committee of State Finance Ministers to be requested to work with the Central Government to create a pan-Indian market for securities that will expand the market base and enhance the revenues of the State Governments.

The impact of various reform measures could be seen in the primary as well as secondary segments of the capital market.

The reform in the Indian capital market would gain added significance in the context of a measure of internationalization of Indian capital markets. For the Indian system of derive the full benefits and avert risks involved in the process, a structured and sequenced integration would be needed. The greater interaction of Indian and international markets would necessarily involve further improving our procedures and practices. Foreign investors are used to open trading systems within the framework of prudential regulation. Their markets are also characterized by adequate disclosure and research based information and severe penalties for insider trading. Our markets would need, both for their own development and to promote fruitful linkages with foreign capital market, to conform to these principles.

## FINANCIAL STABILITY

From a financial stability perspective, it is necessary to have a balanced financial system whereby both financial markets and financial institutions play an important role. Notwithstanding a long history, the capital market in India remained on the periphery of the financial system. However, a series of reforms introduced since the early 1990s has brought about a structural transformation of the capital market.

Free pricing in the primary capital market has allowed corporates to price their issues based on their fundamentals and conditions in the market. In the secondary market, the move to an electronic trading system has resulted in transparency in trades, better price discovery and lower transaction costs. The efficiency of the market has improved through faster execution of trades. The operational efficiency of the stock market has also been strengthened through improvements in the clearing and settlement practices and the risk management process. Almost the entire delivery of securities now takes place in dematerialized form. During the last ten years or so, there has been no instance of postponement or clubbing of settlements at two major stock exchanges (BSE and NSE), despite defaults by brokers. The cases of bad deliveries have become almost nil. The setting up of trade/settlement guarantee funds has considerably reduced the settlement risk. The integrity and transparency of the market has improved with the wider availability of information regarding the corporates' performance at quarterly intervals, which has improved the price discovery process. The trading and settlement framework in the Indian stock exchanges now compares favourably with the international best frameworks.

Chart 1: 10-year Government Security Yield

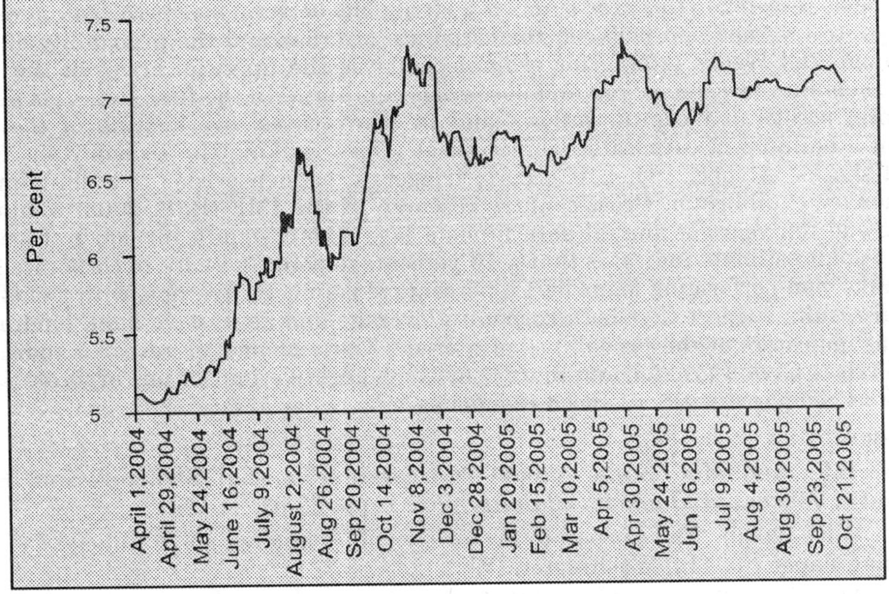


## CORPORATE LEVERAGE AND FINANCIAL STABILITY — BOX : 1

It is widely acknowledged that the quality of loan portfolios of financial institutions is directly dependent upon the financial health and profitability of their borrowers, particularly the non-financial enterprise sector. The key role played by the corporate sector in exacerbating financial distress in Korea during the Asian crisis is well documented. Following from this episode, there has been a renewed interest as to whether and how the corporate sector can engender financial stability.

Recent theoretical and empirical work on the corporate sector and financial distress has examined how firms respond to macroeconomic shocks and whether this response, in turn, impacts the financing and investment decisions of the corporate sector and through these decisions, the macroeconomy. A major part of this literature has focused on two aspects that are key to ensuring the repayment of corporate obligations: corporate net worth and cash flows, and marketable collateral. The first approach, the "financial accelerator" approach emphasizes the role of microeconomic rigidities that occur due to informational asymmetries, where corporate net worth plays the role of collateral and helps to overcome incentive problems in lending. In these studies, macroeconomic shocks affect the real sector through corporate balance sheet effects. The alternate approach, known as the "collateral" approach, stresses macroeconomic rigidities in the form of underdeveloped domestic financial markets and paucity of internationally acceptable collateral. In these studies, crisis susceptibility is driven by shortfall in collateral need to obtain domestic and foreign financing.

Through these two channels of corporate balance sheets and collateral, the corporate sector becomes susceptible to shocks. Levels of corporate leverage influence the ability of firms to withstand these shocks. The more leveraged and less liquid the corporate sector, the greater the vulnerability to shocks.

Prolonged distress in the corporate sector negatively affects firms' repayment capacity and creditworthiness and results in a worsening of bank asset quality, and ultimately, results in higher non-performing loans (NPLs). A macroeconomic shock reduces corporate equity and increases non-performing loans, with the size of the increase depending on the composition of corporate debt, (i.e., importance of non-bank financed debt).

Available research in this area points to a strong link between macroeconomic developments and corporate leverage and between the corporate leverage and the probability of financial crises. Stone and Weeks (2001), for example, analyse the financial crises of the 1990s by dividing them into two stages: pre and post-crisis equilibria. In the first stage, poor corporate governance, accelerated capital inflows and in many cases, overheating of the economy results in a build-up of corporate balance sheet stress, making the economy susceptible to financial shocks. A shock, when it occurs, triggers a sudden crisis, or a shift into a new contractionary equilibrium. Cross-country research at the IMF (IMF, 2003) comprising 47 countries and ten years of annual data funds a lagged, but significant effect of leverage on NPL. The point estimate indicates that a 10 percentage point increase in corporate leverage, raises banks' non-performing loans by 1.6 percentage points, on average, with a one-year lag. Empirical results suggest that both corporate leverage and aggressive bank lending can be significant indicators of the probability of a crisis. The econometric research indicates that financial crises have a greater and more consistent negative impact on corporate sectors in emerging as compared with advanced economies.

**References:**

Davis, E.P., and M.R. Stone, (2004), 'Corporate Financial Structure and Financial Stability', *Journal of Financial Stability*, Vol. 1, pp. 65-91.

Stone, M.R., (2000), 'The Corporate Sector Dynamics of Systemic Financial Crises', IMF Working Paper No. 114, Washington DC.

Stone, M.R., and Weeks, M., (2001), 'Systemic Financial Crises, Balance Sheets and Model Uncertainty', IMF Working Paper No. 162, Washington DC.

## CONCLUSION

Capital markets play a vital role in providing liquidity and investment instruments. A liquid corporate bond market can play a critical role in supporting economic development as it supplements the banking system to meet the requirements of the corporate sector for long-term capital investment and asset creation. The domestic capital market can help financial stability by reducing currency mismatches and lengthening the duration of debt. The private corporate debt market, which is an important segment of the capital market, plays a crucial role in promoting financial stability by providing an alternative means of long-term resources. Such markets also improve economic efficiency by generating market-determined interest rates that reflect the opportunity costs of funds at different maturities. In economies lacking well-developed capital debt markets, long-term interest rates may not be competitively determined and thus may not reflect the true cost of funds. This, in turn, will make it difficult for banks to price long-term lending, and borrowers will lack a market reference with which to judge borrowing costs. In cases where the market for long-term debt contracts in the local currency is not developed, beginning of the early 1990s. The activity in the market, which remained subdued between 1997-98 and 2003-04, has picked up significantly reflecting effectiveness of the measures initiated to develop the market and restore investor confidence. The strong macroeconomic fundamentals and higher growth rate trajectory embarked upon by the Indian economy have also contributed to the strong upturn in resource mobilization from the primary capital market.

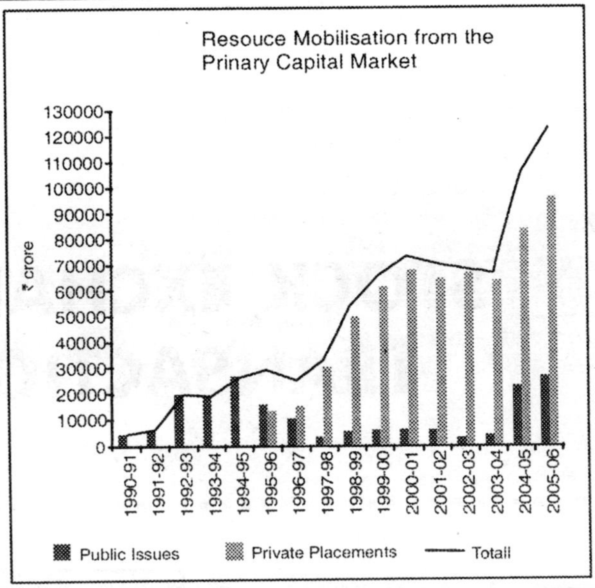


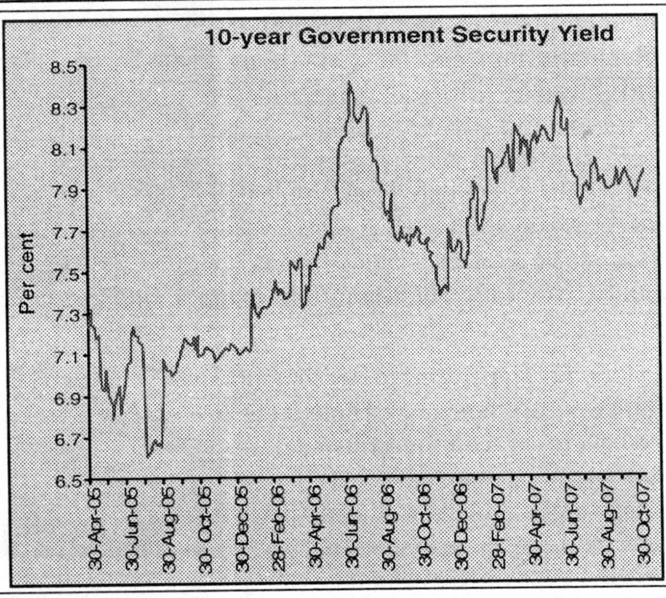


Beginning of the second half of the 1990s, the pattern of financing of investments by the Indian corporate sector has undergone a significant change. Corporates now rely heavily on internal source of funds, which constituted 60.7 per cent of total funds during 2004-05 and 2010-11 as against 29.9 per cent during 1990-91 and 1994-95. As a result, the debt-equity ratio declined sharply during the same period. Owing to increased investment activity and corporate reliance on external sources, both debt and equity, increased. The Indian capital market has put the worst behind and moved towards strong growth. The camulatiue amount mobilised as on November 30, 2010 through 1 POs, FPOs and private placement stood at Rs. 2,30,233 crore as compared to Rs. 2,87,240 crore in 2009-10. The capital Markets is riding on the strong health of the Indian cooporate sector.

❖❖❖

CHAPTER 12

# STOCK EXCHANGE TRANSACTION

## INTRODUCTION

A growing body of empirial research shows that stock market development matters for growth as access to external capital allows financially constrained firms to expand. It is argued that countries with better developed financial systems, especially those with liquid stock exhanges, tend to grow faster. Recent studies shows that both the banking sector and the stock market promote growth in the Indian economy and that they compliment each other.

Securities markets in India comprise equity, debt, foreign exchange and derivatives markets, including futures markets in commodities. These markets are key components of the financial sector because of their transparency in disseminating price information. Markets help in discovery of the price of assets and the price of risk in the economy. They help to shape the behaviour of firms, and the behaviour of owners of capital in making decisions about which firms and industries to allocate scarce capital too. A study of stock exchange transactions assumes greater importance in the context of the unique role of securities markets to the Indian economy.

Stock exchanges are the most perfect type of market for securities whether of government and semi-government bodies or other public bodies as also for shares and debentures issued by the joint-stock companies. In the stock market, purchases and sales of shares are made in conditions of free competition. Government securities are traded outside the trading ring in the form of over-the-counter sales or purchases. The bargains that are struck in the trading ring by the members of *the* stock exchanges are at the fairest prices determined by the basic laws of supply and demand.

## FUNCTIONS OF STOCK EXCHANGES

Stock exchanges provide liquidity to the listed companies. By giving quotations to the listed companies, they help trading and raise funds from the market. Savings of investors flow into public loans and to joint-stock enterprises because of this ready marketability and unequalled facility for transfer of ownership of stocks, shares and securities provided by the recognised stock exchanges. As a result, over the hundred years during which the stock exchanges have existed in this country and through their medium, the Central and State Governments have raised crore of rupees by floating public loans; Municipal Corporations, Improvement Trusts, Local Bodies and State Finance Corporations have obtained from the public their financial requirements, and industry, trade and commerce — the backbone of the country's economy — have secured capital of crore of rupees through the issue of stocks, shares and debentures for financing their day-to-day activities, organising new ventures and completing projects of expansion, diversification and modernisation. By obtaining the listing and trading facilities, public investment is increased and companies were able to raise more funds. The quoted companies with wide public interest have enjoyed some tax benefits and asset valuation has become easier for tax and other purposes.

**BSE: SCALING NEW HEIGHTS MARKET** **BOX : 1**

India's biggest bourse, in terms of listed companies and market capitalization, the Bombay Stock Exchange (BSE) has played a pioneering role in the Indian Securities Market – one of the oldest in the world. Much before actual legislations were enacted, the BSE had formulated a comprehensive set of rules and regulations for the Indian Capital Markets. It also laid down best practices adopted by the Indian Capital Markets after India gained its Independence.

With 932 registered trading members and 12,500 trading terminals, the BSE network stretches across 397 cities in India. Today, the BSE trading platform offers liquidity to the securities of 4,833 companies the largest number of companies listed. Despite intense competition, BSE has a sizeable market share and is one of the top two stock exchanges of the country. Registering almost 2.1 million transactions per day the average daily turnover of the BSE is about ₹ 47 billion as recorded in the month of May 2007. While thousands of investors seek BSE for a wide range of investment opportunities in equity, derivatives and debt. Over 500 foreign institutions also invest funds through it. Responding to the growing demand, BSE offers easy access to the securities market through its internet trading facility $WEB_X$.

**Achievements**

The biggest achievement of BSE as a brand is that it is synonymous with capital markets in India. The BSE SENSEX is the benchmark equity index that reflects the robustness of the economy and finance. A par with international standards, BSE has been a pioneer in several areas and is the first stock exchange in Asia and second stock exchange in the world to get ISO 9001:2000 certification for the entire surveillance function. Today, all departments of BSE are ISO 9001: 2000 certified. It is also the first in India to introduce Equity Derivatives, the first in India to launch a Free Float Index, the first in India to launch dollar-linked version of BSE 200, the first in India to launch an Exchange Enabled Internet Trading Platform WEBx 2001, and the first to have an exclusive facility for financial training. It is also the only exchange to offer Weekly Options in four stocks.

The real time surveillance system of BSE monitors the markets online and throws alerts on slightest indications of market irregularities. These alerts are then examined by way of strict procedures, after which necessary action is initiated. In fact, there was no default reported on 17$^{th}$ of May, 2004, the day the market crashed to a record low with no member being declared a defaulter.

This reflects the robust and efficient 'risk management system' at BSE. There are several other achievements to BSE's credit. The Annual Report of 2005-06 won the Institute of Chartered Accountants of India (ICAI) Award for Excellence in Financial Reporting in the 'Service Sector' category III of the ICAI Awards. BSE's social responsibility efforts all over Maharashtra and Gujarat was awarded the Golden Peacock Global Award for Corporate Social Responsibility.

**History**

The oldest exchange in Asia and the first exchange in the country to be granted permanent recognition under the Securities Contract Regulations Act, 1956, the BSE has had an interesting rise to prominence over the past 130 years.

While the BSE is now synonymous with Dalal Street, it wasn't always so. In fact, the first venues of the earliest stock broker meetings in the 1850s were amidst rather natural environs-under banyan trees – in front of the Town Hall where Horniman Circle is now situated. A decade later the brokers moved their venue to another set of foliage, this time under banyan trees at the junction of Meadows Street and Mahatma Gandhi Road, growing in numbers, the men eventually found a permanent place in 1874 and one that they could quite literally call their own. The new place was aptly called Dalal Street.

Subsequently the 'Native Share and Stock Brokers Association' a precursor to today's BSE was born in1875 and formally constituted in 1887. In 2002, the name The Stock Exchange Bombay was changed to BSE. The BSE which had introduced securities trading in India replaced its open outcry system of trading in 1995, when the totally automated trading through the BSE Online Trading (BOLT) system was put into practice. The BOLT network was expanded, nationwide in 1997.

## ROLE OF THE STOCK MARKET IN FINANCIAL ECONOMIC GROWTH

A growing body of empirical research shows that stock market development matters for growth as access to external capital allows financially constrained firms to expand. It is argued that countries with better-developed financial systems, especially those with liquid stock exchanges, tend to grow faster. On the other hand, Singh (1997) argues that stock market expansion is not a necessary natural progression of a country's financial development and stock market development may not help in achieving quicker industrialization and faster long-term economic growth in most of the developing countries because of several reasons. First, because of inherent volatility and arbitrariness of the stock market, the resulting pricing process is a poor guide to efficient investment allocation. Second, in the wake of unfavourable economic shocks, the interactions between the stock and currency markets may exacerbate macroeconomic instability and reduce long-term economic growth. Third, stock market development is likely to undermine the role of existing banking systems in developing countries, which have not been without merit in several countries, not least in highly successful East Asian economies.

A study on financial development and economic growth suggests that stock markets and financial intermediaries have grown hand-in-hand in the emerging market economies, which is popularly attributed to 'complementarity hypothesis'. Some other studies also find that the levels of banking development and stock market liquidity exert a positive influence on economic growth. Levine and Zervos (1998) provide information on the independent impact of stock markets and banks on economic growth, capital accumulation and productivity in their cross-country study. They find that the initial level of stock market liquidity and the initial level of banking development are both positively and significantly correlated with future rates of economic growth, capital accumulation and productivity growth even after controlling for a few initial social, economic and political factors. These results do not lend much support to models that emphasise the tensions between bank-based and market-based systems as they suggest that stock markets provide different financial functions from those provided by banks. However, Levine and Zervos do not find that stock market size, measured by market capitalization divided by GDP, is robustly correlated with growth. This implies that simply listing on a stock exchange does not necessarily foster resources allocation. Instead, it is the ability to trade ownership of the economy's productive technologies that influences resources allocation and growth (Levine, 2003). Similar results were obtained by Beck and Levine (2003) by using panel techniques. Industry level studies have also found a positive relationship between financial development and growth (Rajan and Zingales, 1998), but an increase in financial development disproportionately boosts the growth of those companies that are naturally heavy users of external finance. Using firm-level data, Demirguc-Kunt and Maksimovic (1998) show that the proportion of firms that grow at rates exceeding the rate at which each firm can grow with only retained earnings and short-term borrowing is positively associated with stock market liquidity (and banking system size). Thus, there is ample literature supporting the role of financial development and the stock market in economic growth by easing external financing constraints.

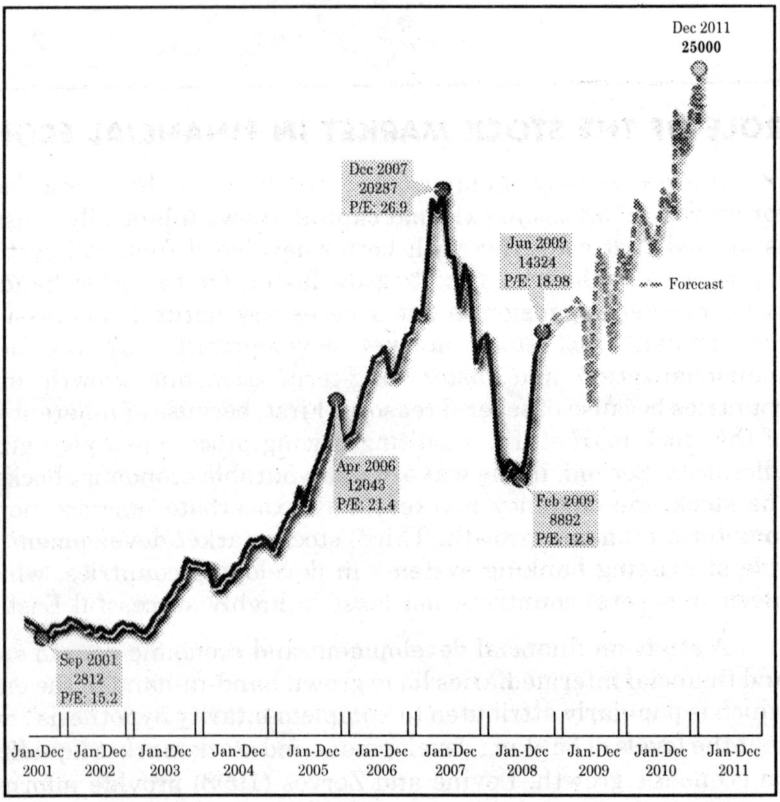


In tune with the growth in the new issues market during the eighties, the secondary market also expanded fast during this period. The number of stock exchanges has increased from 8 in 1980 to a total of 21 in early 1992. The membership of the stock exchanges has also increased substantially to around 3,000 by end 1992 from about 1,200 a decade ago. The listed companies of all stock exchanges stood at above 6,500 in 1992. The market capitalisation has also shown a substantial increase in the eighties. The volume of daily turnover of trade has also increased more than tenfold over the decade to ₹ 250 crore in 1992.

**GLOSSARY** **BOX : 2**

**Share:** The smallest unit representing the ownership in a company. A shareholder has voting rights equivalent to the percentage of his shareholding in the company.

**Stock exchange:** The organised market where shares are traded.

**Stock index:** A basket of stocks of companies, usually chosen from different sectors representing the economy; each stock is allocated a weightage according to its market capitalisation. An average of the gains on each of these stocks is considered on a daily basis and the broad stock market movement is assessed.

**Initial public offering:** The sale of shares/bonds for the first time to the public is known as the initial public offering (IPO). After such a sale, the share-issuing company is said to have gone public. The shares are listed on the stock exchanges with whom listing agreements are entered into at the time of the IPO.

**Primary market:** Where new securities are offered to the general public.

**Secondary market:** Where stocks offered earlier in the primary market are traded. Investors, traders and speculators trade in the listed securities in this segment. The daily price and volume statistics reported in the papers pertain to the secondary market.

**Broker:** An intermediary between the investor and the stock exchange. A broker has a membership of the stock exchange that authorises him to transact the exchange on behalf of his clients, and he charges a percentage of the trade value as a fee for services rendered called brokerage.

**Depository:** A company that maintains a record of investors' dematerialised/shareholdings in individual accounts, which are known as demat accounts. This is akin to maintaining a bank account — credited when shares are bought and debited on purchase.

**SEBI:** The regulatory body that lays down the framewok of policies and guidelines for all participants in the capital market.

The stock exchanges also act as the interface for companies looking to raise capital from investors by selling a part of the ownership rights (shares/stocks). Companies looking to offer their shares to companies looking to on their shares in investors need to seek approval from the stock market regulator — the Securities and Exchange Board of India (SEBI) — and the stock exchanges.

They further need to enter into listing agreements with the stock exchanges, which require them to adhere to certain guidelines to protect investors' interests.

**DOES STOCK MARKET PROMOTE ECONOMIC GROWTH IN INDIA?** **BOX : 3**

In order to establish the relationship of various components of the financial sector, *viz.*, banking sector and stock market, with economic growth in India, regression technique has been used. As the monthly GDP series is not available, seasonally adjusted monthly index of industrial production (IIP) was used as a proxy for economic activity. Before carrying out the regression analysis using ordinary least square (OLS), the monthly data were adjusted for seasonality and then the variables were log transformed. As an indicator of the capital market development, market capitalisation (MCAP) as a percentage of GDP, which measures the size of the market, and value traded ratio (VTR), which reflects the liquidity of the market, have been used. For the banking sector, bank credit (BCR) as a percentage of GDP has been taken as a measure of banking sector development. The period of the analysis was from April 1995 to June 2006.

It is found that both the stock market and the banking sector abet the level of economic activity in the country (equation 1). However, the relationship between stock market and economic activity is not strong as the coefficients of stock market activity, *viz.*, MCAP and VTR, though significant, are very small. On the other hand, bank credit plays a very significant role. This confirms the bank-dominated financial system in India.

$$\underset{(16.9)}{LIIP = 1.27} + \underset{(2.2)}{0.02\ LMCAP} + 0.02\ LVTR + \underset{(5.0)}{} \underset{(34.4)}{0.43\ LBCR} + \underset{(6.0)}{0.47\ AR(1)} \quad \text{– (Equation 1)}$$

Adjusted $R^2 = 0.99$; F-statistics - 3240.7; DW Statistics = 2.24

(Figures in parentheses represent t-statistics.)

It is also found that both the banking sector and the economic growth promote stock market activity in India (equation 2).

$$LMCAP = \underset{(-3.2)}{-\ 9.01} + \underset{(2.7)}{1.25\ LIIP} + \underset{(4.7)}{1.32\ LBCR} + \underset{(25.9)}{0.89\ AR(1)} \quad \text{– (Equation 2)}$$

Adjusted $R^2 - 0.97$; F-statistics = 904.6; DW Statistics = 2.28

(Figures in parentheses represent t-statistics.)

**References:**

Shah, A., and Susan Thomas, 1997: "Securities Markets: Towards Greater Efficiency." *India Development Report*, Oxford University Press.

Nagaishi, M., 1999: "Stock Market Development and Economic Growth: Dubious Relationship." *Economic and Political Weekly*, July 17.

## PRIMARY AND SECONDARY

The stock market can be subdivided into two segments — the primary market and the secondary market. The primary market is the segment that offers subscriptions to new issues. Companies that need to raise capital to run their businesses offer investors a fresh stake in their companies.

These offers are commonly referred to as public issues or initial public offerings (IPOs) — when shares are offered to the public for the fist time — and the offered stock is listed for trading on the stock exchange. Once they are listed, they are bought and sold between existing and new investors in the secondary market.

Once the shares are listed, investors who either skipped the opportunity to participate in the IPO or those who consider the stock to be undervalued at the prevailing price can buy the shares from the secondary market by placing an order through a broker. The broker then sends the order to the stock exchange where it is matched.

The flow of an order is as follows: You place a purchase order with your broker for 100 shares of ABC & Co., at ₹ 50 per share. The broker sends your order to the stock exchange via his terminal, which is then matched with a sell order at the same price. This implies that at the exchange, your order will be matched against a sale order for ABC & Co.'s shares at a price of ₹ 50 per share. Once the order finds its match, the trade is executed. After the trade is executed, the broker should send you an immediate order confirmation, followed by a contract note within 24 hours of the trade being executed.

## INDEX FUNDS

The average opinion of the stock market is expressed through a stock market index. This has given rise to an investment approach known as indexing. While following an indexing strategy, the idea is to try and earn similar returns as given by a stock market index.

The first way to execute this strategy is by investing in the constituents of a stock market index in the same proportion as the proportion in the index. But this is a complicated strategy for individual investors as weightages keep changing and the investors will have to keep adjusting investment all the times.

A better way is to let someone else do it for you. An index fund is the way to go. Index fund is a mutual fund that collects money from investors and invest in stocks that make up a stock market index in the same proportion as their proportion in the index.

It's very difficult for an investor to keep beating the market (or an index, which is a representation of the market). In the last two decades, more than 85% of the fund managers in the United States have underperformed the S&P 500, one of the most broadbased indexes there.

So many mutual fund managers started buying stocks that constituted the various indices in the same proportion. And this became known as closet indexation, from which index funds evolved. John Boggle was the first to launch an index fund. It was called the Vanguard 500 and it was an index fund based on the S&P 500.

Another reason that makes index funds attractive is their lesser expense ratio, which represents the expenses of the mutual fund expressed as a percentage of the total fund assets.

Index funds do not require the services of high price fund managers or any sort of research. This typically keeps the expense ratios low.

Index funds run the risk of not doing well when the markets are not doing well.

## STOCK MARKET INDICES

Every index created and maintained by a stock exchange represents a certain section of the stock market or offers an indication of the movement of the overall market.

The indices tracks the movement and pulse of listed stocks.

## THE BSE SENSEX

The sensex, or the Bombay Stock Exchange's sensitive index, from which it derives its abbreviated form is regarded in popular lore as the barometer of Indian Stock Exchanges. It is however, only one of several indices used to measure the performance of stock markets. Introduced in1986, it tracks the movement of 30 constitutent stocks representing sample companies from various sectors. The size of the companies as well as how actively their stock is traded are crucial determinants of whether a particular scrip figures in the sensex. As these factors keep changing, the constituent scrips of the sensex also are changed periodically. Since frequent changes would make comparisons overtime problematic, the Index Committee seeks a balance between the need to keep the sensex a representative index and the need for continuity. There have been a total of 44 changes in the constituents of the index since it was first compiled. The index has 1978-79 as its base year and the base value is 100, as on calculation of the Sensex. First for each share its price on that day is multiplied by the total number of shares of that company which gives the full market capitalization and then by a free-float factor, to get the free-float market capitalisation for that scrip. The 30 numbers thus obtained are then totalled and the total is divided by the index divisor, which reflects the corresponding value in the base period.

**Indices On 21-08-2008**

| | Close | Change |
|---|---|---|
| Sensex | 14243.73 | – 434.5 |
| S&P CNX Nifty | 4283.85 | – 131.9 |
| BSE 100 | 7454.53 | – 223.91 |
| BSE 500 | 5527.11 | – 155.47 |
| BSE Midcap | 5707.46 | – 118.91 |
| BSE Smallcap | 6937.02 | – 129.21 |
| S&P CNX 500 | 3434 | – 102.9 |
| CNX Midcap | 5640.4 | – 123.65 |
| **SECTORAL** | | |
| BSE Auto | 3800.18 | – 58.09 |
| BSE C Goods | 3756.15 | – 38.62 |
| BSE C Durables | 11907.73 | – 361.79 |
| BSE FMCG | 2140.3 | – 21.41 |
| BSE Health Care | 4271.14 | – 65.62 |
| BSE IT | 3822.46 | – 80.76 |
| BSE Metals | 12166.91 | – 308.74 |
| BSE Oil & Gas | 9838.12 | – 194.35 |
| BSE PSU | 6717.09 | – 258.57 |
| BSE Bankex | 6577.91 | – 357.87 |
| BSE Teck | 2978.53 | – 69.66 |
| CNX IT | 3817.35 | – 95.3 |

***Source:*** *ET* 22-08-2008.

## FREE FLOAT MARKET CAPITALISATION

The market capitalization of a company is the total value of all the shares of that company at a given price per share. This was used to calculate the sensex till about four years ago. But, from September 1, 2003, the sensex was shifted to a free-float methodology. The principle underlying this was that since the stock exchange index must measure what's happening in the markets, shares that are not available for public trading should not be included in its calculation. A free-float index therefore, is a more accurate reflection of what's happening to shares actually being actively traded. Also, it tends to prevent the dominance of a few firms. Most stock market indices globally, including the DOW, FTSE, DAX, Nikkei and MSCI, work on a free-float basis. For the sensex, the free-float adjustment factor varies from 0 to 1, with lower numbers indicating that few of the relevant company's shares are available for trading and a high number meaning the opposite. For instance, the adjustment factor for ICICI Bank currently is 1, which means that between 95% and 100% of its stock is publicly traded, while it is 0.20 for Wipro, suggesting only 15-20% of Wipro shares are available to the public.

## OTHER STOCK INDICES

As it comprises only the 30 largest and most actively traded stocks, which accounts for around one-fifth of the market capitalization of the BSE, the sensex cannot be a full indicator of all that's happening to stocks in BSE. Hence, there are broader-based indices like the BSE 100, which includes 100 scrips, and BSE 200, which is based on 200. There are also smallcap and mid-cap indices to reflect the fortunes of firms with small or medium-sized market capitalization, besides sector specific indices. Which index one uses depends on what one wants to analyse. There is no one index that can be regarded as the best for all purposes.

Each index has enumerated detailed parameters on which stocks can be included in the index. For instance, the BSE Sensex, which is made up of 30 stocks, is representative of stocks of large companies with high trading and liquidity. The scrip that is eligible to form part of the BSE Sensex should figure among the top 100 companies on the basis of market capitlization, it should have been traded on each and every trading day in the last 6 months, the company should be a leader in its sector, etc. Similarly, the S&P Nifty index is made up of 50 stocks. The stocks forming the index represent 25 sectors of the economy. The stocks eligible for inclusion in the Nifty are those that have a 6 monthly average market capitalization of a minimum of ₹ 500 crore during the last 6 months, they should have at least 12 per cent floating stock (i.e., stock not held by promoters and associates), etc.

## NSE NATIONAL STOCK EXCHANGE OF INDIA LIMITED

NSE is the unchallenged market leader since Oct. 1995. Approximately 90% of capital market volumes in India were routed through NSE in 2006-07. NSE has around 50,000 terminals across 1,500 plus locations in India. NSE is the world's fourth largest Stock Exchange in terms of number of trades in equity shares. NSE is the world's largest Stock Exchange in terms of Single Stock Futures.

## THE NIFTY INDEX

The Nifty Index is composed of the top 50 stocks listed on the National Stock Exchange (NSE). It is a simplified tool, which helps investors and ordinary people alike, understand what happens in the stock market and by extension, the economy. If the index performs well, it is a signal that companies in India are performing well and consequently that the country is doing well.

The Nifty Index is based upon solid economic research and is internationally respected and recognized as a pioneering effort in providing simpler understanding of market complexities.

The Nifty Index is computed and disseminated by NSE, the 4th largest stock exchange in the world in terms of trades in the capital markets.

An upbeat economy is usually reflected in a strong performance of the Nifty Index. A rising index is also indicative that the investors are gung-ho about the future. Ups and downs on a short-term basis are inherent in stock markets. Over the long-term however, the index will be reflective of the economic trend.

The introduction of futures and options provided more opportunities to participate in the stock market. The vibrancy provided by NSE encouraged more and more companies to list on the NSE – thus giving investors a larger canvas of the India dream. India is moving, India is booming.

**Uses of the Nifty Index**

(1) The NSE index – Nifty 50 is universally considered the barometer of the Indian economy.
(2) Nifty index can be used by individuals to track market movements and compare performance of individual companies *vis-à-vis* market performance.
(3) Shareholders' evaluation of management decisions – performance of a company *vis-à-vis* the market generally reflects the perception of the investor.
(4) Assist traders and market intermediaries to evaluate performance and sentiments across the market.
(5) Index funds can replace Nifty indices to earn market returns.
(6) Derivatives trading – investors can use Nifty indices for hedging their exposures in the equity markets.
(7) Benchmarking NAV performances – Nifty is the benchmark for performance of open ended and close ended funds.

## PLAYERS IN THE MARKET

The stock market today is no longer the domain of only a few large brokers. Since the start of the current bull-run (i.e., since April 2003), the types of players in the market have undergone a change.

### The Players

Besides the long-term retail investors such as you and me, the market also boasts of Foreign Institutional Investors (FIIs), domestic mutual funds, brokers and day traders.

### The Role Played by Each

**Retail Investor:** This category of investors is scattered and deal in much smaller quantities as compared to the other market players. As a result, they seldom influence market movement.

## FIIs and Domestic Mutual Funds

These institutional investors are the real 'Market-makers'. The large amount of money that they are able to garner and invest help to improve market depth. While FII money could be for both, the long-term as well as the short-term, domestic mutual funds generally remain invested for a longer periond of time.

**Brokers:** The stock broker is the key financial intermediary that helps it disseminate economic, corporate and market information and intelligence to general investors. The research reports churned out by large brokerage houses and the tips doled out by brokers influence the investment decision (buy, hold or sell) of not only investors like you and me but also, at times of the institutional investors.

**Day traders:** Since the investment tenure for this investor category is very brief, they help to create liquidity in the overall market. The amount of risk that their investment decisions involve is very high.

## FIIs Rule the Roost

Indian equities have managed to attract more than their share of foreign funds. This is because as compared to other emerging economies, India is yet very attractive. However, at the same time, since FIIs have become dominant players, if they undertake large withdrawals, the markets instantly drop. An immediate example that comes to mind is the 300-point correction that took place two weeks back during which the FIIs pulled out funds to the tune of $95 million.

**Net Mutual Fund Investment in the Stock Market**

| Period | Net Investment in Equities (₹) |
|---|---|
| April 2000 – March 2001 | – 2,767 crore |
| April 2001 – March 2002 | – 3,796 crore |
| April 2002 – March 2003 | – 2,067 crore |
| April 2003 – March 2004 | 1,308 crore |
| April 2004 – March 2005 | 448 crore |
| April 2005 – March 2006 | 14,306 crore |

***Source:*** SEBI
As on: 18-April-06.

## Domestic Mutual Fund Not That Far Behind

True, the current stock market buoyancy is mainly on account of FII money. However, mutual funds have also supported this stock market rally. This is clearly reflected in their net investment figures *(See: Net Mutual Fund Investment in the Stock Market).*

## Preferable Investment Route

Retail investors seldom call the shots in the stock market. With domestic mutual funds soon becoming a force to reckon with, it is advisable to take an exposure in the capital markets through them. Mutual fund investing is the ideal answer to investing in the current market scenario, which is spiked with uncertainty and volatility.

## TRADING

**For trading in physical securities,** the sub-brokers collect the trade orders from their clients and place these orders with the main broker for execution in the market. The main broker enters the details of each trade against each sub-broker in a separate account kept for each sub-broker.

After execution of the trade, the main broker issues the contract note. Mostly the contract note is issued in the name of the sub-broker who in turn issues separate purchase/sale note to his clients. In this case, in the books kept by the main broker, all trades are shown against the sub-broker and the main broker does not track details of each individual client. However, there are some cases where brokers issue contract notes, directly in the name of the client.

Based on the commercial understanding between the broker and the sub-broker, the sub-broker may decide on when to deliver, to the main broker, securities against sale orders and funds against purchase orders. Very often, these are handed over by the sub-broker to the broker just before the pay-in.

**Even in case of trading in demat securities** the same system can be followed. However, in this case, as there is no fear of bad deliveries unlike in the case of physical securities, the brokers can directly issue the contract note in the name of the client. This is in addition to facilitating a cost-effective settlement (as can be seen from the section below) with a clean audit trail, may provide further confidence to the clients.

In this case the sub-brokers need to provide the details of the clients to the main broker for issuing the contract notes.

## E-TRADING AND DEMAT SERVICES

Gone are the days when you left orders with your broker, received confirmations on the price and quantity of the shares at the end of the day and the payment made upfront or received after delays. Your securities settlement took days to reflect in your account. Internet has changed the way you do trading. The entire process is speedy with limited to zero paperwork. As per Mr. Dipankar Mookerjee, AGM, Bank of Baroda "E-Trading has saved time, money and energy as it helps me access the market from anywhere at any time".

**The process:** Logon to the brokers site of your choice where you get live real time quotes, place a buy or sell order on the spot, and direct the site to debit the requisite amount. In sometime you get your confirmation and after the trade settlement your bank and depository accounts will reflect the changes which you can view anywhere anytime. Online trading has become seamless. All that you need is a PC, a modem, subscription to an Internet Service Provider (ISP), a saving and a depository account with any bank providing online trading facility. Along with stocks one can trade in Mutual Funds and investment instruments. The advantage with online trading is that you can operate in both BSE and NSE depending on the broking firm.

NSE introduced for the first time in India, fully automated screen based trading. It uses a modern, fully computerised trading system designed to offer investors across the length and breadth of the country a safe and easy way to invest. The NSE trading system called 'National Exchange for Automated Trading' (NEAT) is a fully automated screen based trading system, which adopts the principle of an order driven market.

## To Trade online using e-broking facility

- Register yourself with the online trading portals listed on the site.
- You must be a registered iConnect user.
- On placing an order for buy/sell of securities through the listed online trading portal, click on "Pay Through" — Bank listed on the online portal which will direct you to a login screen of your account.
- Once the details of your Login ID and Password are entered.
- You are required to verify the transaction details and confirm the transaction by entering your Transaction ID and Password. An e-mail confirmation will follow regarding the status of your transaction once your order is executed.
- Your account status will be updated on a real time basis.
- Your securities status can be viewed online after the day of settlement.

Contrary to common perceptions, trading through internet does not require either any expertise in working on the computer, or any special financial skills.

The safety of transactions on the internet depends on the encryption system used. The better this transaction system, the more difficult it is for any person to hack the site. Secondly, you too can ensure the safety of the transactions online. You normally get a secured user id and password, the secrecy of which is to be maintained entirely by you. Thirdly, if the transaction system requires no manual intervention, you further improve the safety in the transactions. Which means orders are directly sent to the exchange ensuring that you get the best and right price.

## Demat

Demat is the process of converting your physical (paper) shares into electronic form. Rapidly most share transactions are taking place in Demat form.

One has to open a separate account for dematerialisation. If you already have a Demat account elsewhere, you could also transfer the balance by requesting for a transfer.

To buy and sell your shares, you have to simply instruct your bank and your broker. The transaction will then reflect in your Demat account after successful completion of the same.

With Demat services, you won't have to worry about bad deliveries, forgery and duplicate or stolen share certificates. Apart from safety, you can also save on transaction costs settlement.

The bank will provide you a quarterly statement which shows the current portfolio of your shares and also a transaction statement on a monthly basis, if you have transacted in the preceding month. This helps you keep a record of your shares and further ensures their safety.

You can get overdraft facility against select Demat scrips. Interest rates for loans against Demat shares are lower than the rates for loans against scrips.

You no longer have to pay any stamp duty when you transfer your shares. What's more, it takes just 3-4 weeks to dematerialise your shares. And when you buy shares deliveries are immediate.

You don't have to worry at all as the online broker will update you on IPOs, Rights and Bonus Issues in Demat form.

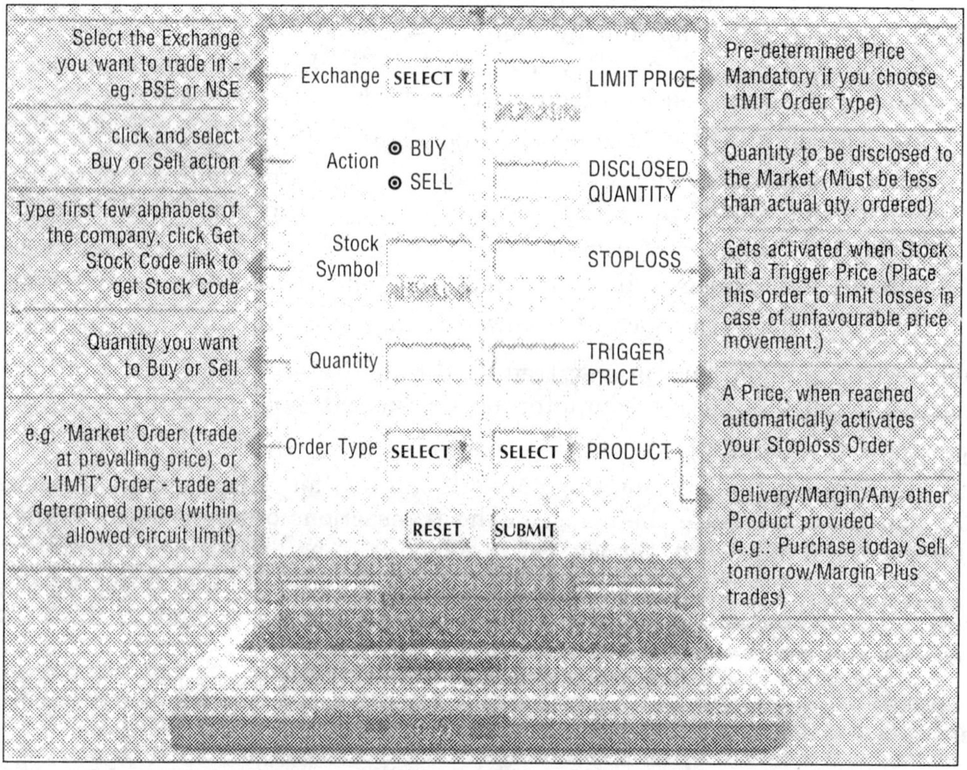


**With the Demat a/c you get –**

- Faster delivery and settlement cycles
- Waiver of stamp duty on transfer of securities
- Low transaction cost for purchase and sale of securities
- Allotment of IPO, bonus and rights shares in electronic form
- No loss of share certificates
- No risk of fake certificates.

## DAY TRADING AND THE BUSINESS MEDIA

Investors who trade daily, or daily traders as they are popularly called, have to time the market. And in order to successfully time the market, they are always on the lookout for predictions and rumours that keep appearing almost daily in various sections of the business media.

Everyday, they have to have an opinion on where the stocks are headed towards the end of the day. Now, doing this successfully day-in and day-out is next to impossible.

This search for information is abetted by the business news channels and media who try and answer questions like "Why have the markets fallen today?" or "Why have the markets risen today?" In fact, huge number of people now make a living trying to answer this question.

Nassim Nicholas Taleb in his book *Fooled by Randomness* says, "In that sense the description coming from journalism is certainly not just an unrealistic representation of the world but rather the one that can fool you the most by grabbing your attention via your emotional apparatus – the cheapest to deliver sensation".

News on the stock market fluctuations fulfils these criteria. And as far as journalists are concerned, Taleb again has the last word: "people do not realize that the media is paid to get your attention. For a journalist, silence rarely surpasses any word."

Also, investors, analysts and the business media at times go overboard with their focus on quarterly earnings.

At times, when companies miss the earnings estimates by a small target, investors tend to react as if the company has almost gone bankrupt and sell the stock which drives down its price. And the business media is certainly to be blamed for some amount of overreaction.

As John Allen Paulous points out in his book *A Mathematician Plays the Stock Market,* "Overreactions are abetted by the all-crisis-all-the-time business media". And this is really uncalled for.

Paulous further points out, "Just as beauty and academic quality don't change as rapidly as *ad hoc* lists and magazine rankings do so, it seems, the fundamentals of companies don't change as quickly as our mercurial reactions to news about them do".

But then day traders are addicted to trading and need to trade come what may. This desire for trading all the times is what leads to losses at times. Having suffered a loss, the tendency is to blame the market for it and stay away from it thereon.

Benjamin Graham, the guru of Warren Buffet, had some advice for such people "Mr Market has another endearing characteristic: He doesn't mind being ignored. If his quotation is uninteresting to you today, he will be back with a new one tomorrow. Transactions are strictly at your option."

Graham further said, "Mr Market is there to serve you, not to guide you. It is his pocketbook, not his wisdom that you will find useful. If he shows up someday in a particularly foolish mood, you are free to either ignore him or to take advantage of him, but it will be disastrous if you fall under his influence. Indeed, if you aren't certain that you understand and can value your business far better than Mr Market, you don't belong in the game." So, the point being made here is that trying to figure out where the market is headed today in a day-out is a losing proposition all the way.

## Hassle Free Investing

Trading with ICICIdirect.com is a fast, easy, transparent and hassle-free way to trade in shares. ICICIdirect.com offers you a wide choice of products for investing in the stock market such as:

- Trade in Equity and Derivatives,
- Invest in 16 open ended Mutual funds,
- Apply for IPOs and other financial products.

ICICIdirect.com offers a unique 3-in-l account integrating your banking, broking and demat accounts. When you place a buy or sell order with ICICIdirect.com, the system checks the funds and shares available in your bank and the demat accounts respectively and executes the trade on the exchange, online. This enables you to trade in shares without going through the hassles of tracking settlement cycles, chasing your broker and writing cheques and transfer instructions.

ICICIdirect.com uses the most advanced commercially available 128-bit encryption technology enabled Secure Socket Layer (SSL), which has been universally accepted on the World Wide Web for authenticated and encrypted communication between clients and servers.

ICICIdirect.com equips its customers with latest information and decision-making tools to make an investment. The website is an investor's delight with a database of over 5,000 companies. It's 'My Research' is step-by-step guide to research. You can virtually analyse a company's entire balance sheet on the website.

ICICIdirect.com builds relationship with its customer by conducting educative customer sessions, which covers basic and advanced techniques of derivatives and equity markets. In this endeavour, ICICIdirect.com has trained more than 2,50,000 customers on various products across all the major towns in the country.

ICICIdirect.com has printed an easy to understand book *'Introduction to the Stock Analysis'*. The comic format of the book makes it an interesting reading.

ICICIdirect.com makes the investing process a fast, simple, secure and hassle-free experience for the retail investor.

## Settlement

Currently, the stock exchanges follow a T+2 settlement cycle, which implies that if your order was executed on Monday, it must be settled by Wednesday.

You must ensure that you have given your broker an adequate sum to pay for your purchase within 24 hours of the trade, while the seller must ensure that he has issued a debit instruction to his depository participant to release the shares to his own broker within the same time. The respective brokers at their end must ensure that they pay in the funds and the securities to the exchange on day T+2 to settle the transaction. Once your broker receives the 100 shares of ABC & Co., he is required to transfer these to your demat account, where the depository will credit the shares against your name. On the other hand, the seller should receive a cheque, net of the brokerage, from his broker.

## Safeguards

Besides providing a fair ground for trading and investing in shares, it is also the stock exchange's function to arbitrate between its trading members, i.e., brokers, and between brokers and their clients. To account for the possibility of default by brokers, stock exchanges maintain an investor protection fund (IPF). The fund is used to settle claims of investors whose trading member has been declared a defaulter. The maximum claim payable from the IPF to an investor is ₹ 10 lakh.

SEBI performs the role of a market watchdog — all listed companies, stock exchanges and intermediaries are bound by its guidelines. Investors also have the option of appealing to SEBI against violation of their rights, though stock exchanges should be their first stop.

**EQUITY CULT RELYING ON PUBLIC** **BOX : 4**

**Market value of all listed shares — 1980: ₹ 6,750 crore; 2003: ₹ 7 lakh crore**

**Stock in Trade: Dhirubhai Ambani addressing shareholders**

**1985:** In the parched primary market of today, not many will recall February 11,1986. On that day, 110 companies came out with public issues. The seeds of such exuberance were sown through the late 1970s and early 1980s when scores of multinational companies offered their equity shares to the Indian public — mostly under directions from the government. But the prime mover of the equity cult creation in the 1980s was Reliance Industries, which through its three issues between 1977 and 1985, raised an army of 12 million shareholders. Reliance created wealth for the masses — and democratised stock markets — much before the Infotech companies entered the markets. That was reflected in the value of the BSE Sensex which rose from an insipid 148 points in 1980 to 1,048 points in 1990 — over seven times in 10 years. But in the absence of a watchful regulator, scamsters like Harshad Mehta and Ketan Parekh rigged the markets, wiping out the wealth and confidence of small investors. A series of clean-up steps in the past five years and the spread of mutual funds are likely to create a safer and lasting equity culture.

**Small investors at the BSE**

## PRIMARY AND SECONDARY — BOX : 5

**Primary Market**

This is the market in which you are allotted the securities by the issuer of securities in the public/rights issue.

- *For Fixed-price issues:* you are required to submit the amount payable on making the application along with your application form to the collecting bank.
- *For Book-built issues:* you can make a bid by submitting a completed Bid-cum-Application Form and the Bid amount at any of the Bid Collection Centres of the syndicate members.

**Secondary Market**

This is the market where you buy or sell securities in exchanges through brokers/sub-brokers.

- Settlement guarantee is ensured for transactions on stock exchanges.
- If you do not get money/securities for whatsoever reason, then there is an institutional arrangement to settle your claims in the exchange.
- If the broker defaults, investors can seek protection from the Investor Protection Fund of the Exchanges.

## INVESTMENT CHOICES IN THE SECURITIES MARKET — BOX : 6

Equity Shares — investment through Primary Market

Equity Shares — investment through Secondary Market

Bonds and debentures — investment through Primary Market

Bonds and debentures — investment through Secondary Market

Mutual Fund Schemes

*Debt-oriented mutual funds*

*Equity-oriented mutual funds*

Derivatives

*Options — on stocks and index*
*Futures — on stocks and index*

**Equity Shares**

- Equity shares are primarily volatile instruments
- Equity shares yield returns in terms of dividends and capital appreciation
- Liquidity of investment in equity shares depends upon the trading volumes of the share
- Company performance should be monitored close to track the investment performance
- It is possible to buy even a single share dematerialised mode.

**Bonds**

A bond is a loan given by the buyer to the issuer of the instrument. These are debt instruments. Over and above the scheduled interest payments as and when applicable, the holder of a bond is entitled to receive the par value/face value of the instrument at the specified maturity date.

**Debentures**

Debentures are also debt instruments

- Debt instruments are required to be rated by credit rating agencies
- Investors should track the ratings of the same.

**Mutual Funds**

- Professionally managed
- Provides diversification of portfolio
- Liquidity
- Transparency
- Choice of schemes
- Regulated by SEBI.

**Mutual Funds**

- Close-ended Mutual Fund Schemes
  listed on stock exchanges and traded at listed prices
- Open-ended Mutual Fund Schemes
  do not have a fixed maturity
- Innovative schemes like index funds, sector funds, money market funds, gilt funds, etc.
  Net Asset Value of a scheme is:
  Market value of the assets of the scheme less liabilities
  *divided by*
  Number of units outstanding.

**Derivatives**

- Derives its value from prices or index of prices of securities
- Clearing corporation is the legal counterparty to all trades executed on the exchange and guarantees settlement
- Elaborate and comprehensive nature of the exchange ensures market stability and integrity.

## TRANSACTING IN THE SECURITIES MARKET

You should take into account the following factors before investing in securities:

*(i)* whether there is a regulatory framework in place in respect of the security and you are protected in case of any eventuality;

(ii) whether the offer of the security is in compliance with the due process of law;

(iii) whether the transaction has any counter-party risk

(iv) whether the security can be liquidated to cash easily

(v) whether the security will generate returns compatible with its risk;

(vi) whether the security fits into your investment portfolio and meets your investment goals.

**Rights**

- to receive documents regarding your investment
- to demand certificate of registration of concerned intermediary
- to receive the securities on allotment/transfer on time
- to receive corporate benefits, i.e., dividends, rights, bonus interest/redemption etc.
- to participate and vote in general meetings
- to receive Annual Reports, etc.
- to apply for winding up of a company, if need be, etc.

**Responsibilities**

- to remain vigilant about the company/intermediary
- to pay/deliver securities as and when called upon to do so
- to exercise the rights conferred on you.

## SLBS: THE WIN-WIN SITUATION

The Securities Lending and Borrowing Scheme offers several advantages to all participants. While it helps traders gain from arbitrage opportunities, the lenders can earn money from the shares that are lying idle

**MARKET**

- Enhances liquidity and helps in the price discovery process, that is, in judging the fair value of the stock
- Makes the cash market settlement process more stringent
- Enables informed investors to take a balanced view of the market
- Leads to efficient futures prices

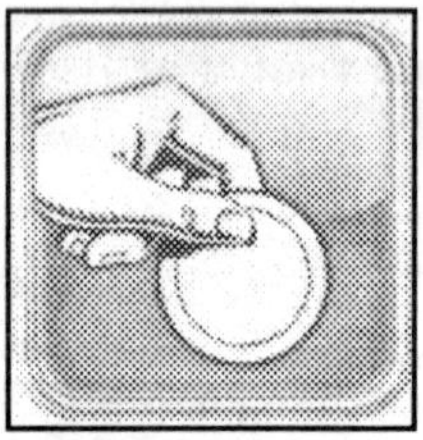

**LENDERS**

- Enables long-term investors to earn money from their idle shares
- Provides opportunities to earn money in bear markets, that is, when prices are going down.
- Lenders are rewarded adequately as the lending fee is determined on the basis of demand and supply

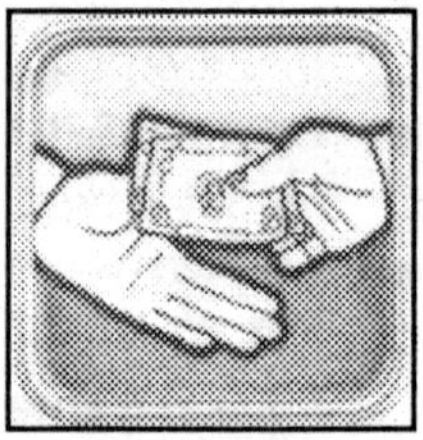

**BORROWERS**

- Promotes the practice of covered short selling, which reduces risk
- Helps investors to adopt alternative investment strategies, such as arbitrage
- Promotes disciplined trading practices by penalising the defaulting traders.

## Pros and Cons

SLBS helps in exploiting arbitrage opportunities between the cash and derivatives markets. When the futures are trading at a discount to the cash market, one can short sell the shares by borrowing them through SLBS while simultaneously buying the futures contract. Let's assume the stock of ABC is trading at ₹ 200 in the cash market and at ₹ 180 in the futures market. The market lot is 100 shares, while the market-determined cost of borrowing the shares through SLBS is ₹ 5 per share. If we borrow shares in the cash market and sell them, and simultaneously buy the futures contract, it will entail a profit of ₹ 2,000 [100 x (200 – 180)]. Even after paying ₹ 500 as borrowing cost, we will generate ₹ 1,500 as riskless profit.

Though SLBS seems beneficial, investors have ignored it and all efforts to garner their interest have failed. Between June 2009 and June 2010, there have only been 106 trades, amounting to a meagre ₹ 6.42 lakh. The majority of the participants prefer the derivatives segment for short selling. According to experts, the reason for the lack of interest is the high cost associated with SLBS. According to Santanu Syam, Executive Director of Operations at Angel Broking: "A borrower needs to pay the full amount upfront, besides additional margins. The sum of all margins works out to as high as 100 per cent or sometimes even more". Also, SLBS is applicable only to stocks that are traded in the F&O segment.

The system forces investors to shell out more than they need to pay in the derivatives segment. For example, if an investor wants to borrow 125 shares of Infosys at a price of ₹ 2,600, it would involve a payment of ₹ 3.25 lakh, plus the cost of borrowing. Also, margins such as cash margins are as high as 25 per cent of the lending price. So, a short seller will need to pay ₹ 4.06 lakh. In the derivatives segment, the investor will pay about 40 per cent margin (all inclusive). Therefore, the same could be short sold with a margin of ₹ 1.3 lakh.

Short selling is beneficial when the markets are overvalued or when stocks are trading at unwarranted premiums over their fair values. Also, it enhances liquidity and provides stability to the stock markets. "To make the scheme more useful, the regulator should revise the margin requirement and introduce scrips other than those listed in the F&O segment", says Syam. Hopefully, the recent approval by SEBI to allow physical settlement in the derivatives segment will be the impetus that revives SLBS.

## BOOK BUILDING

In the last few years, a large majority of public offers, both initial public offers and follow-on public offers included, have used the book-building process to raise money from the stock market.

Book-building is a process of price discovery used in public offers. The issuer sets a base price and a band within which the investor is allowed to bid for shares. The investors has to bid for a number of shares he wishes to subscribe to within this band. Further, an order book, in which investors can state the number of shares they are willing to buy at a price within the band, is built. Hence, the term 'book-building'.

Once the issue period is over and the book has been built, the book running lead manager (a merchant banker who manages the issue) along with the issuer arrives at a cut-off price. The cut-off price is the price discovered by the market. It is the price at which the shares are issued to the investors. Investors bidding at a price below the cut-off price are ignored.

But, how exactly is the cut-off price fixed? The cut-off price is arrived at by the method of Dutch auction. In a Dutch auction, the price of an item is lowered, until it gets its first bid and then the item is sold at that price.

Let's say a company wants to issue one million shares. The floor price for one share of face value ₹ 10 is ₹ 58 and band is between ₹ 58 and ₹ 65.

At ₹ 65 on the basis of the bids received, investors are ready to buy 2,00,000 shares. So, the cut-off price cannot be set at ₹ 65 as only 2,00,000 shares will be sold. In the next step, the price is lowered to ₹ 64, at which investors are ready to buy 4,00,000 shares. So, if the cut-off price is set at ₹ 64, around 6,00,000 shares will be sold. This still leaves 4,00,000 shares. The price is now lowered to ₹ 63 at which investors are ready to buy 4,00,000 shares. Now, if the cut-off price is set at ₹ 63, all one million shares will be sold.

Investors who had applied for shares at ₹ 65 and ₹ 64 will also be issued shares at ₹ 63. The extra money paid by them while applying will be returned to them.

## INVESTMENT GUIDELINES

- Equities have an inherent ability to beat inflation.
- The only way you can evaluate the market is through its valuation and not sensex levels. If you are looking at sensex levels, you are messing big time.
- From valuation point of view, the market is fairly valued at the point in time and not cheap.
- It took 14 innings for Sachin Tendulkar to make the 34th century. In the meantime, everybody said that he does not enjoy his game and that he has lost touch. But, he bounced back and proved it. The sensex is like Sachin Tendulkar's 34th century. Every time the sensex reaches 6,000 levels, people say *thak gaya hai* and start to book profits.
- The biggest concern is that Indians don't own enough stocks. It's the reverse colonization of India. If Infosys declares good numbers, the celebration happens in Hong Kong, Singapore, US and other markets, not in India.
- The world market capitalization to world GDP is skewed towards the developed countries. In the developed market, the market capitalization to GDP is 2-3 times, sometimes even higher. In emerging markets, including India, it is 0.1-1. Thus, the share of emerging market to world market is very low. This has to and will move up.
- There is a preponement of consumption in India because of quick loans available, which is resulting in growth. At present, we have 5% debt to GDP, we can only go up from here to perhaps 30% debt as seen in Asian markets or as high as 80% like the US markets. The other critical element that India has is human capital. Both these factors coupled will ensure growth in India.

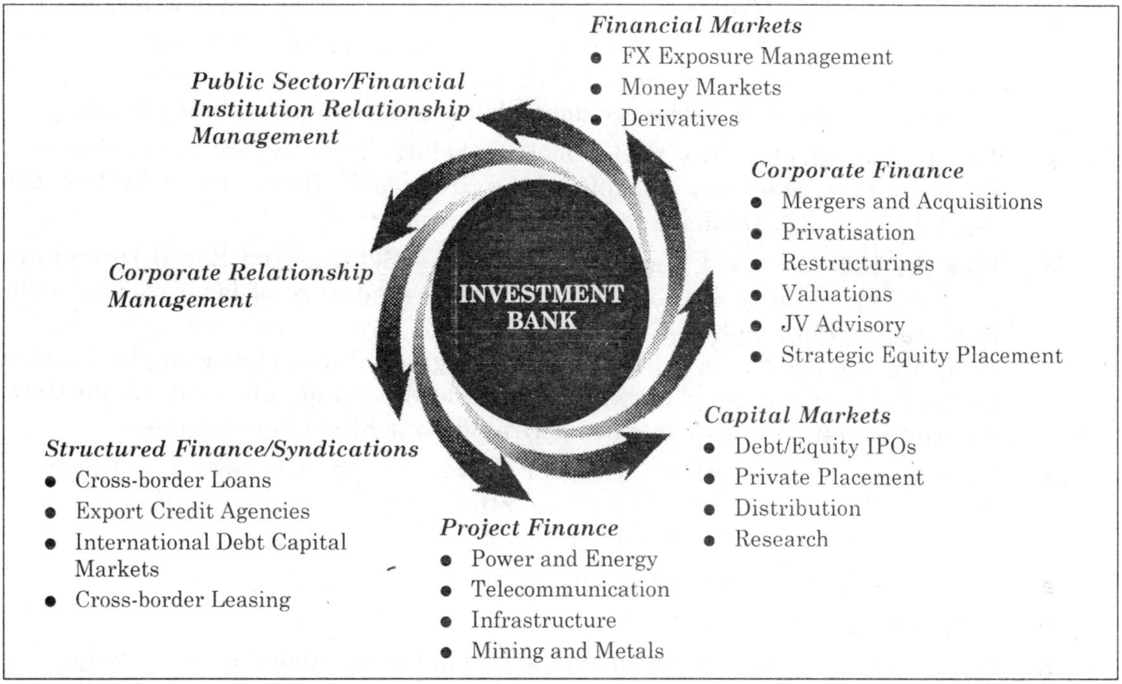


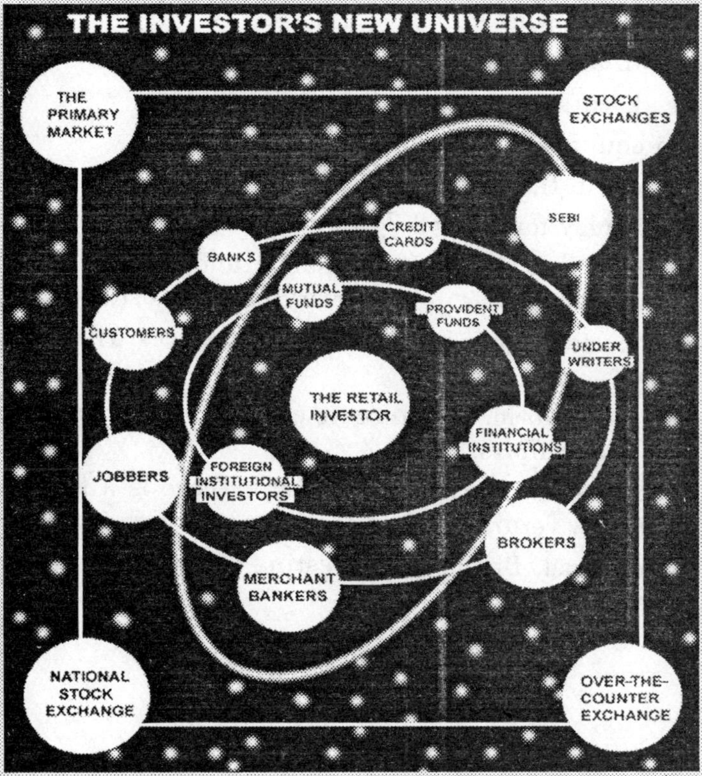


* The retail investor will still be the centre of the institutionalised universe. But his portfolio decisions will be taken by the institutions through which he will be forced to channelise his investments.
* Spinning on twin axes–huge sums of money and research — the foreign institutional investors, the mutual funds, the public provident funds, and the financial institutions will become the major players in the markets.
* The need for capital and research will force the intermediaries in the markets like the merchant bankers, the stock brokers, the jobbers, and the underwriters to enter the orbit of corporation.
* Online trading in equity, a market for debt instruments, and a bourse for small companies will force the markets — the stock exchanges, the NSE, the OTCEI, and the primary markets — into a new trajectory.
* Like a roving satellite, SEBI will patrol the frontiers of the brave new universe, keeping a vigilant eye on the players, their transactions, and catalysing the institutionalisation of the stock-markets.

**Fig. 12.1**

- The long-term growth story for India remains intact. This does not mean the future will be all rosy and markets will only keep going up. Minor hurdles and risks will always be there in the short-term, leading to some correction or selling. Investment strategy depends on different individual's needs.
- Two important elements that I look at before investing in a company are: whether that company is generating free cash flows and whether the promoter is ready to share his wealth with me.
- Like the Indian cricket team where Virender Sehwag and Rahul Dravid are equally important, your portfolio must have a mixture of low-risk and high-risk stocks. Both Sehwag, who will hit and Dravid, who will stand like a wall, are required in a portfolio. On any given day, Sehwag might make a century or get out on a duck, but Dravid will stand tall most of the time. Sehwag is your mid-cap stock and Dravid your blue chip company.
- In every day-to-day activity, you look forward for the advice of a professional. So, even investments should be done after professional advice. MFs offer you a ready platform with professional help.
- You are safer off investing in mutual funds.
- MFs don't sell by choice.
- Net Asset Value is only an indicator of what your money is doing today.
- Please don't time the market. Invest regularly. Systematic Investment Plan is the best way to enter into equities.
- Don't panic. Equities are all about taking risks.
- Don't make wrong asset allocations.
- Don't borrow to invest in equities.
- Don't ever leverage to invest in the stock markets.
- When you play the market, play for limited downside and maximum upside.
- Everything in life is a cycle and there are economic and country cycles. Currently we are in a secular bull cycle, where everything is positive.
- In spite of overall market performance, individual performances will always be rewarded.
- This is the best business in the world. You allocate capital to a company and then enjoy the benefits of their efforts.
- Good stocks are always expensive. For a small investor there is a trade-off between good company and low returns or bad company and high returns.
- Mid-caps are not necessarily bad. But before investing think this way. You want to eat well or sleep well.

**Flow Chart — Investing right in shares**

Choose a conveniently located broker/sub-broker

↓

Make sure the broker/sub-broker has authorised access to the NSE

↓

Sign a properly drafted broker client agreement. You are now ready to buy or sell shares on the NSE through the broker

↓

Whenever you want to buy or sell shares given written instructions to your broker

↓

Insist on getting an order confirmation slip the day your order is placed on the NSE

↓

Insist on getting a trade confirmation slip the day the trade on your order takes place

↓

Obtain a contract note for the deal which correctly specifies the price and the brokerage charged

↓

Deliver shares or money as the case may be well within the specified timeframe

↓

Insist on collecting your shares or your money, as the case may be well within the specified timeframe

↓

Contact your nearest Investor Service Centre in case you need clarification or you have a grievance

## RIGHTS AND OBLIGATIONS OF AN INVESTOR

| Rights | Obligations |
|---|---|
| **The right to access** | **The obligation to be systematic** |
| The best price, | To sign a proper agreement with your broker |
| The speediest service, | Have every deal recorded on an enforceable contract note |
| The safest form of trading like dematerialised shares | **The obligations to be correct** |
| **The right to get** | Keep your shares in good condition |
| Proof of price/Proof of brokerage charged | Keep your signature verification records up to date |
| Your money on time | **The obligation to be timely** |
| Your shares on time | Make sure you pay on time when you buy |
| Auction where delivery in normal/rectified bad/ objection-bad delivery not received | Make sure you deliver shares in time when you sell |
| | Make sure you pay your broker his brokerage charges in time |

| | |
|---|---|
| Square up where delivery not received in auction<br>Shares that are genuine<br>**The right for redress**<br>Against fraudulent price<br>Against unfair brokerage<br>Against delays of money or shares<br>Against investor unfriendly companies | Make sure to send securities for transfer in your name in time<br>Make sure not to keep blank documents for over 21 days after the last pay-in day stamp affixed on the backside of the transfer deed.<br>Make sure to deliver the documents with all the papers forwarded by the company upon getting them from the company under company objection<br>Make sure to extend cooperation where fresh T.D. is to be signed against original T.D. becoming invalid. |

**Summary of Settlement Cycle for Regular Sub-Segment**

| Day | Particulars | Activity |
|---|---|---|
| 1-7 | Wednesday-Tuesday | Trading period. |
| 8 | Wednesday | Custodians report trades which they will not settle. Such trades will be added to the member obligation. |
| 13 | Monday | Pay-in of securities; delivery of documents by the delivering members at the Clearing House. |
| 14 | Tuesday | Pay-in of funds by members through the Clearing Bank. |
| | | Shortage identification at Clearing House. |
| 15 | Wednesday | Pay-out day for securities and funds Auction for shortages. |
| 17 | Friday | Auction pay-in day for securities and funds. Bad delivery reporting by the receiving member to the clearing house and intimation to the delivering member. |
| 18 | Saturday | Auction pay-out Pickup of bad deliveries for rectification. |
| 20 | Monday | Bad delivery rectification/replacement by the delivering member. |
| 22 | Wednesday | Auction for bad delivery not rectified replaced. |
| 24 | Friday | Bad delivery auction pay-in. |
| 25 | Saturday | Bad delivery auction pay-out. |

**Summary of Settlement Cycle for account period settlement in Book Entry Sub-Segment**

| Day | Particulars | Activity |
|---|---|---|
| 1-7 | Wednesday-Tuesday | Trading period |
| 8 | Wednesday | Custodians report trades which they will not settle. Such trades will be added to the member obligation. |
| | | Pay-in of securities; delivery of documents by the delivering members at the Clearing House. |
| 14 | Tuesday | Pay-in of securities through the depository and shortages identified by the Depository.<br>Pay-in of funds by members through the Clearing banks.<br>Pay-out day for securities through the Depository and funds through the Clearing Banks. |
| 15 | Wednesday | Auction for shortages. |
| 17 | Friday | Auction pay-in and pay-out for securities and funds. |

## BENEFITS OF SCRIPLESS TRADING AND SETTLEMENT

In the depository system, the ownership and transfer of securities takes place by means of electronic book entries. At the outset, this system rids the Capital Market of the dangers related to handling of paper. That is not all. The depository provides numerous other direct and indirect benefits like:

- option to deliver dematerialised securities in the dematerialised or physical segment with effect from April 6,1998 on both NSE and BSE. But physical securities not allowed to be delivered in dematerialised segment, making dematerialised stocks held with investor more-liquid than physical stocks;
- elimination of bad deliveries and all risks associated with physical certificates, such as loss, theft, mutilation, etc.;
- reduction in handling of huge volumes of paper;
- no stamp duty for transfer of equity instruments and units of mutual funds in the depository (In case of physical shares, stamp duty of 0.5% is payable on transfer of shares);
- immediate transfer and registration of securities, increasing liquidity of stocks with the investor;
- pay-in and pay-out of securities and funds is on the same day for scripless trades;
- faster settlement cycle;
- faster disbursement of Corporate benefits like Rights, Bonus, etc.;
- reduction in rate of interest on loans granted against pledge of dematerialised securities by many banks;
- reduction in brokerage by many brokers for trading in dematerialised securities;
- periodic status reports to investors on their holdings and transactions, leading to better controls.

## PATEL COMMITTEE

A high-powered committee under the chairmanship of Shri G. S. Patel, former Chairman of the Unit Trust of India, was set up by the Union Government in May 1984 to make a comprehensive review of the functioning of the stock exchanges and make recommendations.

The terms of reference of the committee included *inter alia,* the following:

- to examine the general functioning of the stock exchanges as an integral part of the financial system;
- to suggest measures to improve the overall service to investors by the members of stock exchanges and to encourage small investors particularly in semi-urban and rural areas to invest in industrial securities;
- to look into the existing system of organisation and management of stock exchanges with a view to broadbase it so as to make it representative of all concerned interests and to suggest a uniform model of organisation, etc.

After deliberations which lasted more than a year, the committee submitted its report to the Union Finance Ministry in December 1985. In the light of the recommendations made by the committee in their interim report, the government issued several guidelines and directives to the stock exchanges relating to matters such as bringing down the cost of public issue of securities, listing of securities on the stock exchange, creation of a Customers' Protection Fund and insurance cover for members of stock exchanges, etc.

The Sensex has fallen more than a thousand points over the last few days. With the benefit of hindsight, one can safely say that the bubble has been pricked and what stock market experts had initially termed as a correction has all the makings of a crash.

When it comes to the stock markets, one is never really sure.

As James Surrowiecki points out in his book *"The Wisdom of Crowds*". The problem with the stock market is that there is never a point at which you can say that it's over, never a point at which you will definitely be proved right or wrong.

A crash is an exact opposite of a bubble. In a crash, investors become convinced that the stock prices will simply keep going down and hence they keep selling and drive down prices. Stock market history tells us that most major crashes have been out of proportion with their immediate causes.

The question to be asked here is, "why do crashes happen when they do?"

As Suroiweciki points out, "Perhaps the best analogy is that offered by the biologist Per Bak, who compares a market crash to the collapse of sand pile. As you add grains of sand of a pile, it will keep its shape as it grows bigger. But at some point, one grain of sand too many will send the pile tumbling."

Given their obviousness in retrospect, why do bubbles happen in the first place? The simple answer to this is that bubbles are caused by excess cash coming into a particular investment theme, in this particular case, stocks. But that still leaves the bigger question unanswered, "Why does excess cash flow into a particular investment theme?"

In his book *Irrational Exuberance*, Robert Shiller introduces the concept of naturally occurring Ponzi schemes. The stock market, he says, is a very good example of a naturally occurring Ponzi scheme.

A Ponzi scheme is a financial fraud, designed in a way wherein the initial lot of investors are promised very high returns. As the news about the high returns spreads, more investors want to invest in the scheme. The money brought in by these new investors is used to service the returns of the initial investors. And so this scheme keeps running as long as the money coming into the scheme is greater than the money leaving the scheme.

On the other hand, a naturally occurring Ponzi scheme occurs without the contrivance of a fraudulent manager. As stock prices go up attracting success for some investors, this attracts public attention and the news spreads. Stories about stock markets going up, spread very fast. Investors, in an optimistic mood, want to buy stock and take the stock price further up. This leads to more investors entering the market fuelling an even greater price rise and the cycle gets repeated over and over.

## Regulation on Trading

One of the important management functions is regulation of trading. The computer records the data on prices and volume of trade on a daily basis. These data are fed memberwise and scripwise. The changes in prices and trade volumes thus recorded are used for the management decision on trade and regulation. The control measures are as follows:

(a) margins on daily purchases and sales, scripwise at a rate varying up to 50% of the value of deals to be deposited with the exchange as non-interest bearing deposit; as also the margins on the outstanding position of brokers.

(b) margins on carry forward deals at the time of settlement to be deposited by members until these deals are squared up.

(c) *ad hoc* margins on members, if their turnover increases over a permitted level.

(d) price band fixation if there is high volatility in price of any scrip or stoppage of trade in any scrip, if its price change is beyond a limit with the help of circuit breakers (at say 10% or 20%).

The management has to keep a watch on the price and volume trends scripwise and memberwise as trading takes place during the day and to help impose margins on members/scrips and to regulate trading in an orderly manner.

## MANAGEMENT PERSPECTIVES

The new era of management of stock exchanges is to be started by more systematic reforms by SEBI. The era of management by lapses (mismanagement) has ostensibly ended and a new concept of management by rules has started. The basic objectives of management are reconstituted to place investor interests on the top of the broker interests. The functions of stock exchanges are therefore to be performed more scientifically by vigorous enforcement of rules without any bias or partiality and giving transparency to their operations. For this purpose, all stock exchanges have to strengthen their manpower expertise through appointment of executive director and other expert personnel and for proper computerisation and automation. Management decision-making is streamlined to enforce a code of conduct on members and discipline them to promote the public image of stock exchanges. A new management information system is to be built up for better enforcement of rules against listed companies and against member brokers in their activity and in their reporting system. The management of stock exchanges is thus in a stage of transformation into scientific and professional management in the years to come. Management audit and performance accounting have thus become more relevant than cost accounting or reporting accounting in the stock exchanges.

The attached chart shows the organisational set up for management and administration of stock exchanges in India. The decisions made by the governing board are implemented by the executive director and secretary through various departments which perform the functions of listing, regulation of trading, provision of settlement and clearance, etc. The decisions are sometimes taken by the committees appointed by the governing board for specific purposes.

The various departments are seen in the chart.

These departments are functionally based, keeping the services to be rendered to the members and the public in mind. These departments are all interlinked and coordination on a daily basis is the responsibility of the secretary.

**Stock Exchange Authority**

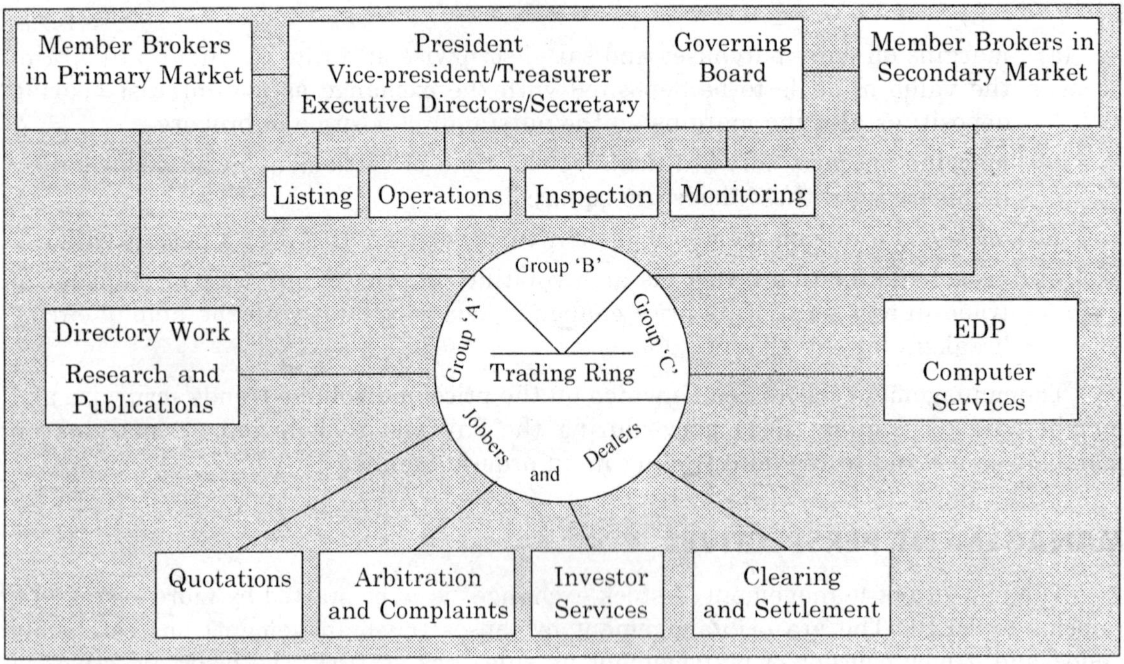


## NEW MARKET STRUCTURE

The Pherwani Committee recommended the national market system based on the new stock exchange to be set up at Navi Mumbai. To make the national market system effective, the Committee recommended several support agencies to provide high quality trading, settlement and depository services. In this context, it has recommended that there should be three tiers namely stock exchanges at Mumbai, Kolkata, etc.; regional stock exchanges like those in major state capitals and additional trading floors sponsored or managed by principal or regional stock exchanges. But the Committee has missed the basic issue of an efficient market structure for securities trading. This structure should be on a multi-tier basis, depending on the asset size and trading volume of companies and asset preferences of investors but not on the classification of existing stock exchanges as trading houses. The structure of securities markets should be on the following lines:

(1) Regular stock markets which are 21 in number at present.

(2) National market system with a separate set of licensed brokers all over the country mostly banks and corporate units with a high paid-up capital of over ₹ 1 crore.

(3) Retail broking through a series of registered sub-brokers attached to the regular stock markets or to NMS.

(4) Trading floors licensed for trading in unlisted companies.

(5) OTCEI for risky and venturesome companies and companies which cannot satisfy the listing requirements of regular stock exchanges. The structured markets in securities should be based on common law but with separate rules and regulations for each in respect of listing and trading, etc.

The emerging role of stock exchanges would also depend on the extent of the openness of these markets to foreigners. Assuming the open entry to foreign funds which has already been mooted, Indian markets have to fall in line with the structure and practices of foreign markets. The structure of markets to be set up would be as follows:

**Market Structure**

| **Regular Stock Exchanges (21)** | **OTCEI (1)** | **National Market System (NMS) (1)** | **Trading Floors for Non-listed Companies** |
|---|---|---|---|
| Attached trading Floors for Sub-brokers to deal | Licensed Dealers and Sub-brokers | Licensed Dealers all over the country | Licensed Brokers |

The prerequisites for modem trading system under the above structure are as follows:

(1) Interlinking of stock exchanges electronically.

(2) Automatic computer trading for OTCEI and NMS.

(3) Specialised agencies for information dissemination.

(4) Selected corporations for processing and dissemination of market data.

(5) Efficient telecommunications network and other methods of communications to be entrusted to a separate corporation.

The Pherwani Committee Report emphasised the need for development of support services of the following types:

(1) Securities facilities support corporation for giving the needed space, electronic network and telecommunications systems for stock exchanges, member brokers and other supporting agencies.

(2) National clearing and settlement corporation for arranging payment and delivery as between the exchanges at the national level.

(3) Central depository trust to immobilise the physical certificates and their transfers to be replaced by book entries. For extension of the service to investors and public, changes in law, practices of companies and a high level of computerisation programme are all necessary.

## INITIAL PUBLIC OFFERING (IPO) SCAM

One individual is all it took to blatantly sabotage the Initial Public Offering (IPO) system and bring out all the loopholes that exist therein. Everyone, from the depository participant to the lending bank and from National Securities Depository Ltd., (NSDL) to SEBI were somewhere in the picture either because of incorrect action or inaction. The net result was that the people who stuck to the rulebook (read: retail investors) as in most cases were short-changed.

### How it happened:

As per SEBI's 'Disclosure and Investor Protection Guidelines', 35 per cent of the shares offered in any public issue must be offered to retail investors. As each individual in this category cannot apply for shares worth more than ₹ 1 lakh, the window is open to a large number of investors to ensure large retail participation.

It is precisely this well-intended mechanism that has been used as a window of opportunity. Multiple fake names, each holding different demat accounts were used, all bearing the same communication address. Each of these accounts was used to separately apply for shares of YES Bank during its IPO. Each of these applications amounted to less than ₹ 1 lakh, so that all the applications qualified for the retail segment. As a result, there was an over-application of shares in this segment and many law-abiding retail investors were allotted fewer shares or none at all. Whether by pro rata allotment or by the lottery system, a large number of shares were cornered by a single investor at the cost of the retail investors.

**IN BRIEF**

- Multiple fake names, each holding different demat accounts were used, all bearing the same communication address, to apply for shares of YES Bank during its IPO.
- As a result, many law-abiding retail investors were allotted fewer shares or none at all.
- Unscrupulous brokers may be using the IPO route as a mechanism to convert their client's black money into white.
- A lack of action against the culprits could dent investors' confidence in the stock market yet once again.

### The Players

(1) Roopalben Panchal (Ahmedabad) subscribed to YES Bank's IPO through 6,315 demat accounts and was allotted a total of 9,47,000 shares. Similarly, Sugandh Estates & Investment Pvt. Ltd., (Ahmedabad) was allotted a total of 1,97,000 shares by operating 1,315 demat accounts.

(2) The depository participant for all the demat accounts in the above two cases was Karvy Stock Broking Limited (Karvy).

(3) The lead managers for the issue were DSP Merrill Lynch Limited and Enam Financial Consultants Private Limited.

(4) All the bank accounts were maintained with Bharat Overseas Bank and Vijaya Bank.

## The Danger

Unscrupulous brokers may be using the IPO route as a mechanism to convert their client's 'black' money into 'white'. High Net worth Individuals (HNIs) with idle cash, approach such market intermediaries who take a flat charge (say 5 per cent) on the total amount invested. Through an already existing network of benami accounts, the broker applies for IPOs on behalf of the HNI. Each application is for shares worth less than ₹ 1 lakh, so as to ensure allotment in the retail investor category; through the vast number of demat accounts, a substantial number of shares are cornered.

With a buoyant secondary market, within days of listing, the allotted shares are disposed of. Apart from the Securities Transaction Tax (STT) on the transaction value and short-term capital gains on the profit made (at the rate of 10 per cent) the investor incurs no substantial loss and walks away with the additional benefit of having his idle cash converted into white 'income'.

Apart from obviously inviting unwanted speculators and scamsters, it conveys the message that the Indian IPO system is fundamentally flawed.

## CHANGES IN IPO NORMS

SEBI has put an end to the system of discretionary allotments to institutional buyers in public issues. This will give retail investors a fair deal.

There was an interesting phenomenon associated with IPOs. Issues were oversubscribed many times over within minutes of opening. In most cases, it was merely a means of luring retail investors. So, to ensure fair play, the stock market regulator, SEBI, has plugged certain loopholes related to allotment of shares to Qualified Institutional Buyers (QIBs).

### Luring Retail Investors

Earlier QIBs, particularly FIIs, used to bid for huge quantities at the upper end of the price band in the book building processes. As a result, the issue would be oversubscribed on the first day itself. This was possible as QIBs were allowed to bid without any upfront monetary commitment, unlike retail and high net worth investors who had to pay-up 100 per cent of the bid value at the time of application. Further, merchant bankers used to allot shares on a discretionary basis to select 'long-term' investors.

### Revised Provisions

The revised norms in respect of QIBs' participation in book built issues cover two broad aspects — monetary commitment and basis of allotment. The new provisions provide that QIBs shall put in a margin of at least 10 per cent while submitting their bids.

Further, SEBI has ended the regime of preferential treatment to select institutional investors. Proportionate allotment would be applicable in the same way as it is to retail investors, i.e., pro rata allotment (applicants are allotted shares in the ratio of their subscriptions to total applications received).

The new rules also dictate that out of the existing 50 per cent available for QIBs, 5 per cent would be specifically for mutual funds registered with SEBI. In addition, these mutual funds would also be eligible for allotment from the remaining 45 per cent apportioned to QIBs.

## Going Forward

SEBI's changes in IPO norms are laudable and would certainly give a moral boost to retail investors. The diktat would end discretionary allotment to QIBs and promises to ensure fair play towards small investors. Proportionate allotment is necessary to increase the depth of the market by increasing participation from all quarters of investors, including retail. Though discretionary allotment is an international norm, regulators in developed markets may learn a few lessons from their Indian counterpart too.

Mutual funds and retail investors have welcomed SEBI's move. In fact, it was necessary as retail investors are the true essence of the stock market and a large base of retail investors provides stability to the market. Hence, small investors should be protected and encouraged to invest in equities by making the system transparent and just.

## SEBI AT WORK

The Securities and Exchange Board of India (SEBI), our country's financial markets' regulator, seems to have learnt its lessons from the past hiccups to prove that it is truly regulating the markets, SEBI has initiated a two-way action — first, control and second, improvement. Control measures taken are:

## Redefining Insiders

SEBI has taken an important step to curb insider trading by redefining the term 'insiders' to include fund managers, FIIs, banks, brokers and large stakeholders. SEBI has taken this measure as a result of a specific case where a fund manager took a large stake in a company and used price-sensitive information obtained from promoters and company representatives to make a significant gain on sale of the shares. SEBI has banned him from accessing the securities markets for the next five years.

Insider regulations, promulgated by SEBI, require companies to frame a model code of internal procedures and a code of conduct and implement it. A key requirement to ensure conformity of these procedures is to institute a mechanism of monitoring the compliance of such regulations, which needs to be fulfilled. This could include a process of obtaining periodic certification of compliance from independent designated persons.

Further, the current insider regulation allows four working days for disclosure of information of any trading in securities of a company by 'insiders' to company and then five days for the company to disclose the information to the stock exchanges. This duration is too long and needs to be condensed considerably as such time lag can potentially keep investors uninformed of any large purchase or sale of securities by 'insiders', an event which can influence their investment decisions for as long as nine days and could therefore be prejudicial to their interest.

SEBI has also come out with a consultative paper on introduction of 'short swing profit' regulations aimed at restricting any purchase and sale of securities by 'designated insiders' within a span of six months. These regulations are based on objective criteria. Since the intent of the designated insider is immaterial, there is no scope for interpretation, and accordingly, the enforcement of such regulations can be done promptly. The accuracy of expected gains from the transactions in equity securities has a negative correlation with time. A longer period of holding of investment increases the risks associated with the investment owing to exposure to market volatility. Hence, a higher period of holding would act as a disincentive to the insiders to indulge in insider trading.

Such regulation would be limited in application to only cover a specific set of insiders, primarily senior management personnel and beneficial owners of the company with 10% or more holding. It would restrict only short-term booking of profits using price sensitive information not available publicly.

Internationally, a combination of criminal, civil and administrative measures is adopted for enforcement of insider trading regulations.

SEBI has generally been adopting administrative measures in most of these cases comprising suspension of certificate of registrations of brokers/sub-brokers for a specified period, restrictions on access to capital markets for a specified period and/or prohibition from buying, selling or dealing in securities for a specified period. In contrast, SEC enforces civil actions by way of imposition of penalties and affecting disgorgements of profits on the defaulters.

The legislative framework of India has evolved over the period and currently it provides a strong platform to check insider trading though there exists a scope for further reinforcement. These reforms need to be backed by higher degree of regulatory enforcement. A concentrated and pre-emptive approach is required to be followed for optimum use of all relevant measures namely, administrative, civil and criminal proceedings depending on the facts and circumstances of each case. This entails a wider use of enforcement tools for which clear criteria on 'required action' should be laid down.

## Corporate Governance

SEBI has taken up the issue of Corporate Governance by deciding to go ahead with certain important amendments without waiting for the Companies Act to be revised. The amendments include strengthening responsibilities of audit committees, improving the quality of financial disclosures including those of related party transactions, improving disclosures related to compensation paid to non-executive directors, etc.

## Primary Market Strict Disclosure Norms

In spite of the IPO boom, SEBI has shown that it has its feet firm on the ground. The regulator denied Data Access a go ahead for its IPO even though the company had reached the stage of final launch (even the application forms had been distributed). The reason for stopping the IPO was for want of clarifications to fulfil disclosure requirements. It came to light that Data Access owed ₹ 84 crore to BSNL as of December 2003 and that the company had violated FERA guidelines in certain cases.

## Cap on Brokerage

It has come to SEBI's notice that some larger fund houses are paying exorbitant amounts of brokerage to distributors to sell their products. The result is that distributors are misselling products. To tackle this problem, SEBI is now considering a cap on brokerages for mutual fund distributors.

## Late Trading

Taking the cue of late-trading malpractices in the US, SEBI has issued guidelines that ensure strict cut-off timing on redemptions is followed by the mutual fund industry. Late trading is a practice used by large investors such as institutions and banks where such investors twist mutual funds to accept redemptions at current day's NAV even after cut-off time, if they expect the markets to fall the next day. For instance, if the mutual fund has a cut-off time of 3 p.m. after which redemptions submitted will be at next day's NAV, a large investor expecting markets to slide the next day, will submit a redemption to be at current day's NAV. SEBI regulations clearly state that for valid applications received up to 3 p.m. on a business day by the mutual fund along with a local cheque or a demand draft payable at par at the place where the application is received, the closing NAV of the day on which application is received shall be applicable. In respect of valid applications received after 3 p.m. on a business day by the mutual fund along with a local cheque or a DD payable at par at the place where the application is received, the closing NAV of the next business day shall be applicable. This puts retail investors at par on fair play in mutual fund investing.

**THE NORMS** **BOX : 7**

**SEBI (Insider Trading) REGULATIONS, 1992**

**Section 2 (e):** "Insider" means any person who is or was connected with the company, or is deemed to have been connected with the company, and who is reasonably expected to have access, by virtue of such connection, to unpublished price-sensitive information in respect of securities of the company or who has received or has had access to such unpublished price-sensitive information.

**Section 2 (h)(i)a:** A "person is deemed to be connected person" if such a person is in a company under the same management, or group or any subsidiary company thereof, within the meaning of Section 1(b) of Section 370, or Sub-section (11) of Section 372, of the Companies Act, 1956, or Sub-clause (g) of Section 2 of the MRTP Act, 1969 (54 of 1969) as the case may be.

> **Section 2(k)(v):** "Unpublished price-sensitive information means any information" means any information which relates to the following matters (amalgamation, mergers and takeovers) or is of concern to a company and is not generally known or published by such company for general information, but which if published or known, is likely to materially affect the price of securities of that company.
>
> **Section 4:** Any insider who deals in securities or communicates any information or counsels any person dealing in securities in contravention of the provision of Regulation 3 shall be guilty of insider trading.

## Measures taken to improve the market are:

### Margin Trading

To improve liquidity in the stock markets, Securities and Exchange Board of India (SEBI) in March 2004, introduced margin trading in the cash segment of the markets, i.e., allowing an investor to borrow funds from a broker to purchase stocks. With this facility, an investor can take a higher exposure in the markets with a lower amount of own funds. To be eligible to offer margin trading to their clients, brokers should have a net worth of at least ₹ 3 crore. To ensure that this facility is not mis-utilised, SEBI has stipulated that the total exposure a broker can have towards margin trading should not exceed the borrowed funds and 50% of the broker's net worth. Also, the exposure to a single client should not exceed 10% of the total exposure of the broker. Presently, the margin trading facility is available only for 150 stocks that come under the Group-I of the SEBI risk management system.

## Operational Aspects of Margin Trading

To begin margin trading, you need to sign an agreement with your broker. The model agreement is provided by SEBI that includes key conditions governing margin trading. Further, at any point in time you cannot avail this facility from more than one broker.

Broadly speaking, margin trading is trading in the securities market with borrowed resources — funds or securities. As margin trading is providing a facility to investors to trade in the market with margin money, it essentially is a leveraged mechanism. As the client trades on the borrowed securities by paying margin, this may be treated as margin trading on the sell side. Globally, in all the major markets, the facility of margin trading and securities lending is available to investors.

Under the new margin trading system, a broker can borrow funds from banks and NBFCs and on lend these funds to clients up to five times his net worth. He can lend from his own sources also, but will not be allowed to use client's money or money from individual investors for margin trading — unlike *badla,* where retail clients and corporate bodies could lend money. SEBI has allowed margin trading only for corporate brokers with a minimum net worth of ₹ 3 crore. Only Group I securities (highly-liquid securities), numbering about 150, are included, where the impact cost is less than I per cent. It is the cost of executing a particular lot of transactions on the stock exchange. Initially the client will have to finance his purchases up to 50 per cent, with the balance being financed by the broker. The margin will not be allowed to go below 40 per cent, with maintenance margin set at 40 per cent. If margin calls are not met on a T+l basis, or if the balance is below 30 per cent, the broker can liquidate the security.

The main reason for the introduction of this system by SEBI in March 2004 is to achieve its twofold objective attaining international standards as other markets also have this product, and the other as a precursor to the physical settlement in the derivatives markets. (Physical settlement in derivatives requires the availability of the funds and the securities for the smooth settlement of trade.)

In March 2005, SEBI introduced certain amendments to attract retail investors. In addition to margin trading being allowed on selected Group 1 scrips, margin trading will also be allowed on new scrips that are listed after Initial Public Offerings (IPOs) provided they meet the conditions for inclusion in the derivatives segment. Secondly, earlier you needed to pay cash towards margin money. The new amendments stipulate that bank fixed deposits and bank guarantees would also be treated as cash equivalents and would be accepted as margin money.

Margin trading is surely going to increase the retail participation in the cash equity markets of the country. It enables a customer to leverage his cash and securities and helps broaden the market beyond cash rich individuals or corporates.

## Badla *vs.* Margin Trading

Badla or carry forward system which was in vogue for several decades in the Indian markets also involved funding of share purchase by financiers and lending of securities for short sales. The average margin on badla varied from scrip to scrip averaging between 1-2 per cent per month.

Margin trading, as proposed by SEBI, also anticipates part-financing by brokers for the client's positions as well as stock lending for meeting the obligations of short sellers in the market. The initial margin has been kept at 50 per cent, which is similar to that prevailing in the US markets. The principal benefits are:

- Margin trading helps the investor build a larger position in equities.
- It offers the possibility of superior returns compared to pure cash transactions in case of surge in stock prices.
- It is a high-risk-high-return investment strategy. The potential losses could be more than initial investment.
- The broker can off-load your investment without your consent if you don't pay up the margin requirement.

Avoid over-exposure and excessive speculation.

## FUTURES CONTRACT VERSUS FORWARD CONTRACT

A futures contract is an agreement between two parties to buy or sell a specified and standardised quantity and quality of an asset or a security on a certain date at a certain price agreed at the time of entering into the contract on the futures exchanges.

A forward contract is an agreement entered between two parties to buy or sell an asset at a future date for an agreed price while entering into a forward agreement. The terms and conditions of forward contracts are customised based on negotiations between the counterparties. A forward contract is not traded on an exchange.

A futures contract is highly standardised in terms of the quantity and quality of an asset as specified by the exchange. The size of the forward contract is customised as per the negotiated terms of agreement between a buyer and seller.

The contract price of a futures contract is transparent given the availability of a trading screen that provides both bidding and asking prices at any given time. The contract prices of forward agreements are not transparent given the bilateral nature of the agreement and non-disclosure of prices in public domain.

## MARKET SENTIMENT

Market sentiment is the mood of the investors and other players in the capital market. A lot of the price movements are linked to the market sentiment because it determines the manner in which an investor will behave when it comes to investing.

### Positive Outlook

The presence of several favourable factors helps in improving market sentiment and this leads to optimism that often pushes share prices higher. Once the market sentiment is good then other favourable news and factors leads to sharp gains as investors are ready to invest more, expecting better times.

### Negative Outlook

If there are losses suffered by the investors then their sentiment is likely to be depressed leading to a tendency to hold back from making further investments. This leads to a situation where even if there are any news then the market will see the negative aspect leading to a fall in share values.

### Decision-making Process

Stability in the markets and expectation about a good performance in the future leads to improvement in sentiment as far as investors are concerned. This will lead to better decision-making so that investors make a careful analysis of the actual situation.

## Creating Liquidity in Illiquid Stocks

A large number of listed stocks suffer from illiquidity. Investors in such stocks are stuck with shares with no exit route. To offer such investors an exit option SEBI has worked out a method of reviving trading in over 4,000 such illiquid stocks. A separate segment called the 'call auction market' will be set up for trading in these stocks. The order book in this segment will remain open for a longer period for buyers and sellers to give their quotes, in order to match demand and supply for these illiquid stocks. The settlements also will be done over a longer period, instead of the regular three days or T+3. In this market, buy and sell prices will be determined via consensus as against automatic matching in the exchange trading system.

Globally, it is believed that the facility of the securities and funds borrowing is important to support the rolling settlement and the physical settlement of derivatives. It is also important from the perspective of the better price discovery, efficiency of the system, hedging and arbitrage.

Reporting requirements, stipulation and monitoring of limits, and standardised duration of borrowing, etc., require more clarification, say market sources. Minimum net worth criteria, the limits on borrowing and several other measures like disclosure norms make the scheme quite transparent and with adequate risk management measures.

With India's economy and financial markets integrating at a global level, investors are faced with increasingly complex financial scenarios and options. This is truly the time for good regulation to support an investor to make sound investment decisions.

## 16 REASONS TO CHEER

(1) US Federal Reserve has cut interest rate and more cuts are likely.

(2) Interest rates in India too expected to fall.

(3) Strong gross domestic product (GDP) growth in India.

(4) Inflation seems to be on the decline.

(5) Rupee is unlikely to appreciate significantly in the near term on Central Bank intervention.

(6) Indian companies expected to report steady earnings growth.

(7) Sustained government spending seen for infrastructure and rural development.

(8) Expansion plans of Indian companies seem to be on course.

(9) Valuation of Indian equities seen sustainable.

(10) Sustained inflow of money from foreign institutions.

(11) Rising participation by domestic mutual funds and insurance.

(12) Belief that Indian economy is largely immune to crisis in the business.

(13) Indian banks negligible exposure to the US sub-prime market.

(14) Healthy foreign exchange.

(15) Improvement in fiscal deficit, thanks to higher tax collections.

(16) Oil prices are expected to fall on likely US slow down.

**Wrong 'Un...**

- Latest IIP numbers have been disappointing.
- No end seen in sub-prime crisis.
- Left parties objection to nuclear deal has created political uncertainty.

***Source:*** ET, 20th Sept. 07

## CONCLUSION

The Indian stock markets have evolved dramatically since 1991-92 to become, not only reasonably transparent, but also effectively well regulated. The paperless trading environment has reduced manipulations to a large extent and the financial markets have started rewarding companies with higher P/E ratios who have treated the minority fairly. With all trades guaranteed by the stock exchanges, and with settlement cycles of "T+2", the stock exchanges themselves have gained in stature and are now viewed more respectably. Even the government at the Centre has grudgingly accepted the stock-markets to be a barometer of economic well-being.

That corporate India has restructured successfully over the last 15 years and that reforms will deepen as we go forward is acknowledged worldwide. Further, there is a growing realisation that the country (India) will have one of the youngest populations — over 50 per cent of the country's one billion people will be under the age of 25, in the next 10 years, i.e., by 2015. This single demographic fact will drive economics in the years to come.

All this and more have increasingly made Indian stock markets the preferred destination for asset managers. But what is more interesting is that the understanding of Indian markets has deepened significantly. It is not only the mutual funds which are looking at India, but also "family offices and endowments" which have vast pools of money to invest directly in the market. In the face of such far-sighted investment strategies, a lot of pressure will be put on the analyst community to evolve beyond the myopic, price-driven analysis and spread the research net wider and deeper before arriving at any conclusions. And as the number of astute investors will escalate, cheap stocks and dark horses will be harder to locate and preserve. To remain ahead of the index and the peer group alike, investors will need to keep up a constant search to segregate the performers from the outperformers.

All this augurs well for challenging and interesting times ahead, which will throw up huge opportunities over the next decade.

Given below are the Do's and Don'ts in general for investors who are dealing in the stock markets.

## DO'S

(1) Always deal with the market intermediaries registered with SEBI/Exchanges.

(2) Give clear and unambiguous instructions to your broker/agent/depository participant.

(3) Always insist on contract notes from your broker. In case of doubt of the transactions, verify the genuineness of the same on the exchange website.

(4) Always settle the dues through the normal banking channels with the market intermediaries.

(5) Before placing an order with the market intermediaries please check about the credentials of the companies, its management, its fundamentals and recent announcements made by them and various other disclosures made under various regulations. The sources of information are the websites of the exchanges and companies, databases of data vendor, business magazines, etc.

(6) Adopt trading/investment strategies commensurate with your risk-bearing capacity as all investments carry risk, the degree of which varies according to the investment strategy adopted.

(7) Please carry out due-diligence before registering as client with any intermediary. Further, the investors are requested to carefully read and understand the contents stated in the Risk Disclosure Document, which forms part of the investor registration requirement for dealing through brokers in stock market.

(8) Be cautious about stocks, which show a sudden spurt in price or trading activity, especially low price stocks.

(9) Please be informed that there are no guaranteed returns on investment in stock markets.

## DON'TS

(1) Don't deal with unregistered brokers/sub-brokers, intermediaries.

(2) Don't deal based on rumours generally called 'tips'.

(3) Don't fall prey to promises of guaranteed returns.

(4) Don't get misled by companies showing approvals/registrations from government agencies as the approvals could be for certain other purposes and not for the securities you are buying.

(5) Don't leave the custody of your demat transaction slip book in the hands of any intermediary.

(6) Don't get carried away with onslaught of advertisements about the financial performance of companies in print and electronic media.

(7) Don't blindly follow media reports on corporate developments, as they could be misleading.

(8) Don't blindly imitate investment decisions of others who may have profited from their investment decisions.

## TERMS COMMONLY USED IN THE SHARE MARKET

**At Best**

Instructions from client to broker authorizing him to use his discretion and execute an order at best possible price. Also see limiting orders.

**Badla**

Carrying forward payment from one settlement period to another without affecting delivery or payment. Also see ulta badla.

**Bear**

An individual who expects the prices to go down.

**Bear Market**

A weak or falling market characterized by absence of buyers. Also see Bull market.

**Blue Chip**

Shares of well established profitable companies enjoying high investments status.

**Book Closure**

Dates between which a company keeps its register of members closed updation, prior to payment of dividends or issue new shares.

**Bull Market**

A rising market with abundance of buyers and few sellers. Also see Bear market.

**Cum**

Means 'inclusive'. A cum price includes the right to any recently delivered dividend (cd) or right share (cr) or bonus share (cb). Also see Ex.

**Clearing House**

A central agency for effecting delivery and settlement of contracts between all members.

**Ex.**

Means 'without'. An Ex price excludes recently declared dividend (xd) or right share (xr) or bonus share (xb). Also see cum.

**Floating Stock**

The fraction of the paid-up equity capital of the company which normally participates in the day-to-day trading. It rarely exceeds 15-20% of its equity capital.

**Kerb Dealings**

Transactions done between members after official close of trading hours.

**Limit Orders**

Instructions to the broker limiting him to buy at a stated maximum price or selling at a stated minimum price. Also see At best.

**Moorat**

Auspicious trading on Diwali and Budget day during specified hours.

**Pari Passu**

Terms used to describe new issues of securities which have some right as similar issues already in existence.

**Stamp Duty**

The *ad valorem* duty of ½% payable by buyer for transfer of shares in his name.

**Ulta Badla**

Payment made by a seller to the buyer for loan of securities which the seller wishes to defer deliveries. Also see Badla.

## STOCK STORY IS STILL ALIVE

The country's stock exchanges may be in a weak phase, but the long-term story is intact for India, whose stock market is set to emerge as big as that of the US by 2050, says a report by accounting firm Grant Thornton International. China and India are expected to jointly emerge as powerhouses for capital flows in the 21st Century.

**BRIC vs G7**

- BRIC (Brazil, Russia, India, China) as a group is forecast to surpass the G7 group of US, UK, Canada, Japan, France, Germany and Italy by 2032.

**Asian Drama**

- Deregulation and market reforms will power an entrepreneurial surge across Asia. India will be aided by an emerging workforce.
- At the end of 2007, the market capitalisation of both India and China exceeded their respective GDP value.

**Busy, busy BSE**

- The market capitalisation of the Bomaby Stock Exchange (BSE), which has more listed companies than any other exchange in the region, crossed $1 trillion (₹ 42 lakh crore) in 2007 – the first time it did so.
- The BSE's market cap increased from $ 819 billion in 2006 to $ 1,819 billion at the end of 2007.

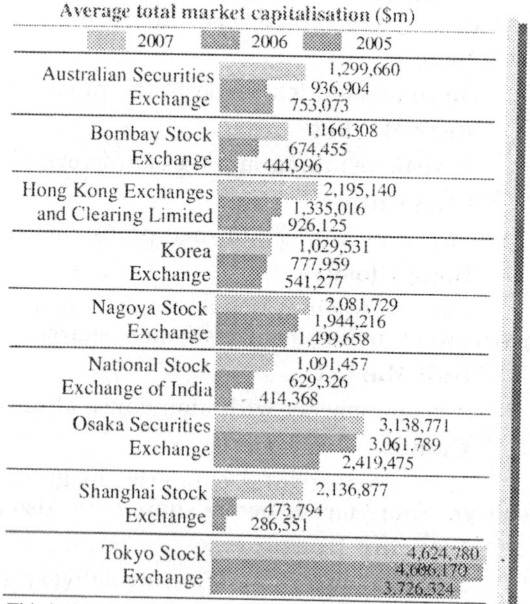


This is the sum of the total market capitalisation at the end of each month in a given year, divided by 12. Information was not available for all markets for all years.

Graphic: PRANAB, **Source:** Grant Thornton International

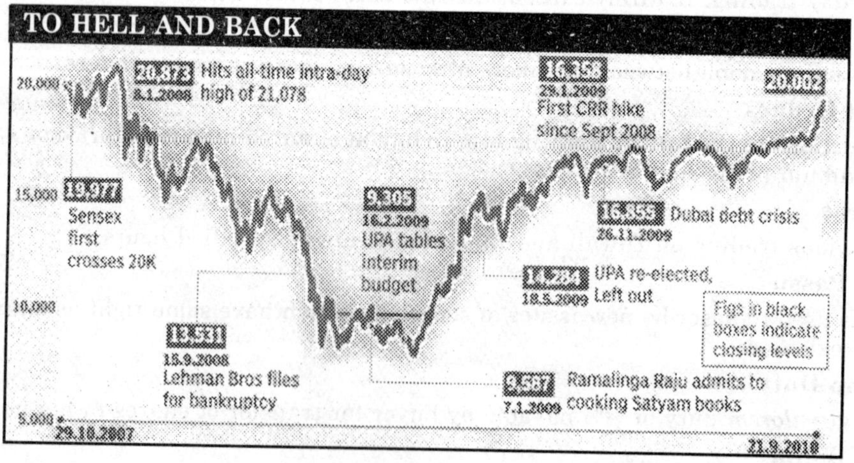


❖❖❖

CHAPTER 13

# THE NEW ISSUE MARKET

## INTRODUCTION

The industrial securities market is divided into two parts, namely, New Issue Market and Stock Market. The new issue market derives its name from the fact that it makes available a new block of securities for public subscription. The new issue market provides additional funds for starting a new enterprise or for either expansion or diversification of the existing one. Money is raised through equity shares, preference shares, debentures, rights, bonus shares, etc. Financial institutions like development corporations, investment corporations, investment banks and merchant banks play a key role in the new issue market.

The need for developed and well-integrated new issues market assumes importance as the Indian economy maintain its momentum with growth accelerating to double digit during 2009-10, propelled by strong growth in manufacturing. Against this back doop, this chapter takes a look at the new issues market in a new perspective.

## THE CONCEPT

The new issue market deals with the raising of fresh capital for cash or consideration other than cash by corporate sector, government and semi-government bodies, PSUs, etc., and encompasses all institutions dealing in the issue of fresh claims. All the financial institutions are part of the new issue market.

The main function of new issue market is to facilitate the transfer of resources from savers to entrepreneurs to establish new enterprises through a complex of financial institutions.

New issues are classified in various ways:

| | | |
|---|---|---|
| (1) | Issues by new companies | Issues by old companies |
| (2) | New money issues | New non-money issues |

From the operational stand point of view, the general function of the new issue market is split into three distinct services:

(1) Organisation

(2) Underwriting

(3) Distribution

This calls for the presence of specialist agencies in the market.

## DISTINCTIVE FEATURES OF THE NEW ISSUE MARKET

- The new issue market deals with securities, which are issued for the first time for public subscription.
- The new issue market enjoys neither any tangible form nor any administrative organisational set up nor is subject to any centralised control and administration for the execution of the business. It renders service to the lenders and borrowers of funds at the time of any particular operations.

**FINANCIAL SYSTEM — GOVERNMENT SECTOR**

| | | | |
|---|---|---|---|
| RBI | CREATION OF MONEY — | AD HOC TBS | MONEY MARKET |
| | LENDING | TBS (91 DAYS) | LENDING AND INVESTMENT (FOR PUBLIC SECTOR UNDERTAKING) |
| | | TBS (182 DAYS) | |
| BANKS FIs. | LENDING AND INVEST-MENT | SHORT-TERM ADVANCES | |
| RBI BANKS FIs CORPORATE SECTOR PFs., ETC. | INVESTMENT IN GOVT. AND SEMI-GOVT. SECURITIES | SHORT-TERM MEDIUM-TERM LONG-TERM (OLD AND NEW SECURITIES) | STOCK AND CAPITAL MARKETS |

**Fig. 1**

- The new issue market provides the issuing company with funds for starting a new enterprise (equity) or for either expansion or diversification of an existing unit. So, the contribution of the new issue market is direct.

However, the new issue market is economically an integral part of a single market, i.e., industrial securities market.

## OBJECTIVES OF THE NEW ISSUE MARKET

There has been a better understanding of the role of the new issue market in advanced countries through endogenous growth theory. The key to growth in this model is continuous productivity advances that take place through technology advancement. This makes productivity the main engine of growth. The new issues market provides the core platform for new enterprises to grow and provide the much needed impetus to the growth of industrial, technological and service sector with the assistance of innovative technology.

The basic objective of the new issue market must be to aid industrial growth and thereby economic growth and development.

The primary role is to intermediate resources from savers to investors and allocate them in an efficient manner among competing and up-coming enterprise, thereby contributing to growth.

The other objective is to accelerate the process of industrialisation.

The growth of the new issue market provided the much needed impetus to the robust performance of the secondary markets as well.

## FUNCTIONS OF THE NEW ISSUE MARKET

The main functions of a new issue market is to facilitate transfer of resources from savers to the users. The savers are individuals, commercial banks, insurance companies, etc. The users are public limited companies and the government. The new issue market plays an important role of mobilizing the funds from the savers and transfer them to borrowers for production purposes, an important requisite of economic growth. It is not only a platform for raising finance to establish new enterprises but also for expansion/diversification/modernizations of existing units. On this basis, that new issue market can be classified as:

(1) Market where firms go to the public for the first time through initial public offering (IPO).

(2) Market where firms which are already trading raise additional capital through seasoned equity offering (SEO).

The government and the corporate sector are the main borrowers from the capital market and are the issuers of securities. The methods of raising funds in the cases of corporate sector are retained earnings out of profits and external borrowings. These borrowings may take any of the following forms, which are in addition to the original issue of share capital in the form of equity and preference shares (including CCPs).

The new issue market provides three services of great significance.

**(1) Origination:** Before an issue is actually floated in the market, the company undertake a thorough investigation, collect relevant data, analyse and process it of the project proposal. This is called origination. It is done for a merchant bank or any other financial institution.

**(2) Underwriting:** Underwriting is an agreement whereby the underwriter promises to subscribe to a specified number of shares or debentures or specific amount of stock in the event or public not subscribing to the issue.

In India, underwriters are classified into two categories – Institutional and Non-institutional (Brokers).

**(3) Distribution:** Distribution is the function of sale of securities to investors. This service is performed by brokers and agents.

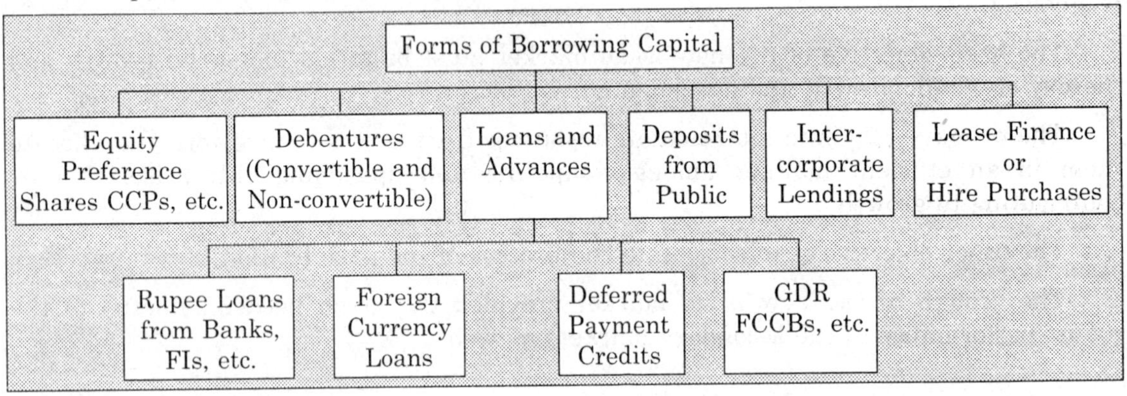


**Fig. 2**

The objectives for which funds are raised may be for setting up new projects, expansion, diversification, modernisation of existing projects, mergers and takeovers, etc. The proportion in which funds are raised in various forms as own capital (equity) and debt capital (borrowings and debentures, etc.), indicate the capital structure of the company and measures the leverage in the forms of ratio of borrowed funds to owned capital and the servicing commitments of the company on borrowed funds.

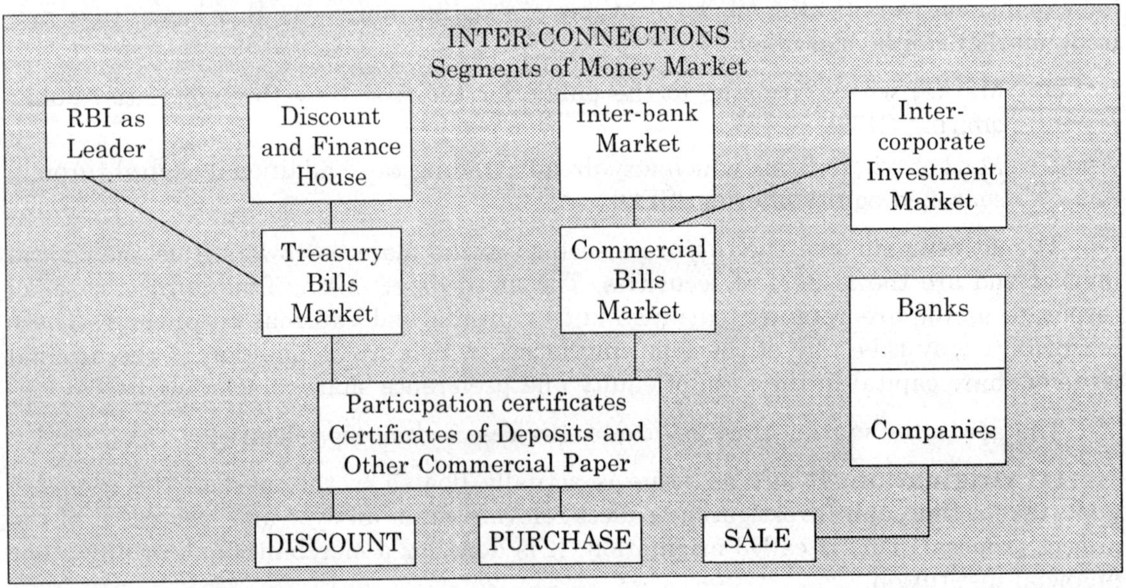


**Fig. 3 Inter-connections of Money Market Segment**

## Principal Steps of a Public Issue

The new shares/debentures may be offered either directly to the public through a prospectus or indirectly through an offer for sale involving financial intermediaries or issuing houses.

The main steps involved in public issue are:

(1) Draft prospectus
(2) Fulfilment of Entry Norms (EN)
(3) Appointment of underwriters
(4) Appointments of bankers
(5) Initiating allotment procedure
(6) Brokers to the issue
(7) Filing documents
(8) Printing of prospectus and application forms
(9) Listing the issue
(10) Publication in newspapers
(11) Allotment of shares
(12) Underwriters' liability
(13) Operational listing

## Central Listing Authority (CLA)

A central listing authority has been set up and its functions have been detailed under Regulation 8 of SEBI (CLA) Regulations, 2003.

The main functions of CLA are;

- processing application for letter precedent to listing from applicants.
- making recommendations to the SEBI on issues pertaining to the protection of the interest of investors in securities.
- making suggestions for the development and regulation of the securities market including listing agreements, listing conditions and disclosures to be made in offer documents.
- Undertaking any other functions as many be delegated to in by the SEBI.

## Methods of Floatation

Initial issues (IPO) are those floated by new companies/start-ups for the first time.

Further issues are floated by the existing enterprises.

The issues are classified as those given for cash for exchange of technical know-how, exchange of shares of another company or exchange for any other services rendered by the agencies or promoters.

## Offer Through Prospectus

The placement of the issues may be through prospectus, offer of sale, private placement and right issue.

Public issue with prospectus is the most popular method of raising funds by the public limited companies. This involves inviting subscription from the public through issue of prospectus.

For the first time in five years, Indian businesses have to share their domination in the optimism league table. India now shares the top spot on the optimism league table with the Philippines, where a similar proportion of the respondents are as optimistic on the outlook of their country's economy over the ensuing 12 months.

Businesses around the world remain resilient in the face of global financial turmoil, according to the Grant Thorton International Business Report (IBR). The annual survey of private businesses shows that despite concerns over the global financial crisis, 42 per cent of businesses across the globe are still feeling optimistic.

India's optimism relating to exports in 2008 has increased significantly by 16 per cent (second highest increase after the Philippines).

**Powering Ahead**

**Some bare facts about Reliance Power's initial public offer**

| Category | Shares reserved | Application money per share | No. of times over-subscribed | Amount collected (in ₹ crore) | Total bid amount (₹ crore) |
|---|---|---|---|---|---|
| QIB* | 13.68 cr | Rs.45 | 82.5 | 50,787 | 5,07,870 |
| HNI* | 2.28 cr | Rs.115 | 190.5 | 49,949.1 | 1,95,453 |
| Retail | 6.84 cr | Rs. 115 | 14.4 | 11,327.04 | 42,353.28 |
| Total | | | | **1,12,063.14** | **7,45,676.28** |

| 50 lakh | ₹ 7,45,676.28 cr. | 72.9 times |
|---|---|---|
| No. of applications | Total bid amount | Oversubscribed |

- Although the call rate in the money market is currently hovering around 8 per cent, even at the rate of 6 per cent, bankers would make ₹ 18.4 crore per day on the money garnered but intended to be refunded without interest payment. And on an average basis this money lies with banks for around 10 days before they start giving refund to the investors. This, in turn, translates into a floating income of around ₹ 184 crore for the bankers as a whole.
- There are seven private sector banks, ICICI Bank, ABN-Amro, HSBC, Standard Chartered, HDFC Bank, Kotak Mahindra and AXIS Bank, involved in this IPO.
- Market regulation bans promoters from using the application money till the time of allotment. As a result the application money is parked in an escrow amount. Once the allotment is made, the actual amount is transferred to the promoters.

* QIB refers to qualified institutional bidders

* HNI refers to high net worth individuals.

## Offer of Sale

The method of "offer of sale" consists of outright sale by the company instead of offering shares to the public or through intermediaries such as issuing houses or share brokers. In this case, the company sells shares *en bloc* at an agreed price to brokers or merchant bankers who in turn resell them to the investing public. The issuing houses may act as agents of the company in such cases. Offer of sale of shares takes place in the case of existing shareholders purchasing *en bloc* and then reselling them to the public. Similarly, foreign collaborators or promoters may sell their shares to the Indian public through offer of sale which may be either through brokers or through prospectus.

## Private Placement

The third method of issue of shares is private placement which is defined as sale by the issuing house or broker to his own clients of securities previously purchased by him. Under this method the issuing houses or financial intermediaries buy them outright with the intention of placing them with their clients afterwards. Here the brokers act as almost wholesalers selling them in retail to the public. These brokers would make their profit in the process of reselling to the public. This method of private placement is used to a limited extent in India but is very popular abroad. Before the issues are placed in the market by the promoters, they sell to their own friends and well-wishers as the government guidelines require a minimum contribution from the promoters and their friends. Private placement is also made by bargaining with the financial institutions for their share of contribution. The newly-established OTCEI (Over the Counter Exchange of India) has adopted this method for the companies to be listed on it.

**Table 1**

**Resource Mobilization through Primary Market** **(₹ crore)**

| Mode | Calendar Year | | | |
|---|---|---|---|---|
| | 2004 | 2005 | 2006 | 2007 |
| 1. Debt | 2,383 | 66 | 389 | 594 |
| 2. Equity | 33,475 | 30,325 | 32,672 | 58,722 |
| *Of which, IPOs* | 12,402 | 9,918 | 24,779 | 33,912 |
| *Number of IPOs* | 26 | 55 | 75 | 100 |
| *Mean IPO size* | 477 | 180 | 330 | 339 |
| 3. Private Placement | 93,506 | 83,812 | 1,17,407 | 1,11,838[a] |
| 4. Euro Issues (ADR/GDR) | 2,029 | 9,788 | 11,301 | 41,567 |
| **Total (1 to 4)** | **1,31,393** | **1,23,991** | **1,61,769** | **2,12,721** |

***Source:*** SEBI and RBI (for Euro Issues)

[a] Till November 2007.

## THE LEADING COUNTRIES

Chinese companies led the world in mobilising money from investors in 2007; India Inc. Came in at a distant #9.

| | PROCEEDS* | SHARE** | NUMBER OF ISSUES |
|---|---|---|---|
| China | 58,095.9 | 18.8 | 216 |
| US | 39,726.5 | 12.8 | 184 |
| Brazil | 30,627.5 | 9.9 | 63 |
| Russian Federation | 20,061.7 | 6.5 | 22 |
| United Kingdom | 16,582.0 | 5.4 | 101 |
| Spain | 15,682.8 | 5.1 | 11 |
| Germany | 10,099.3 | 3.3 | 40 |
| Hong Kong | 9,150.9 | 3.0 | 46 |
| India | 8,291.7 | 2.7 | 91 |
| Australia | 5,885.4 | 1.9 | 134 |

* in $ million ** in per cent

Total amount raised through IPOs (75 countries): 309,748.6

Number of issues (global): 1,578

## THE WORLD IS THEIR OYSTER

Chinese and Spanish companies dominated the list of the world's largest IPOs, but a Russian company topped the charts.

| WHEN | ISSUER | NATION | PROCEEDS* | OVERSUBSCRIPTION** |
|---|---|---|---|---|
| May | OAO VTB Bank | Russian Federation | 7,988.10 | 3 |
| December | Iberdrola Renovables | Spain | 6,565.30 | 3 |
| April | China Citic Bank | China | 5,945.60 | 230 |
| November | China Railway Engg Group | China | 5876.60 | 39 |
| October | Criteria Caixa Corpn. | Spain | 5,429.40 | NA |

NA: Not available *in $ million ** Number of times

## THE LEADING INDIAN COMPANIES

Domestic companies raised large amounts from the primary market.

| WHEN | ISSUER | PROCEEDS* | OVERSUBSCRIPTION** |
|---|---|---|---|
| June | DLF | 2,267.8 (Rs 9,187.5 crore) | 3.3 |
| September | Power Grid Crop of India | 738.9 (Rs 2,984.45 crore) | 64.5 |
| February | Idea Cellular | 555.1 (Rs 2,125 crore) | 49.56 |
| November | Mundra Port and Special Eco Zone | 451.2 (Rs 1,771 crore) | 115.32 |
| July | HDIL | 367.6 (Rs 1,485 crore) | 5.58 |

* in $ million **Number of times

Source: Thomson Financial & Capital Market

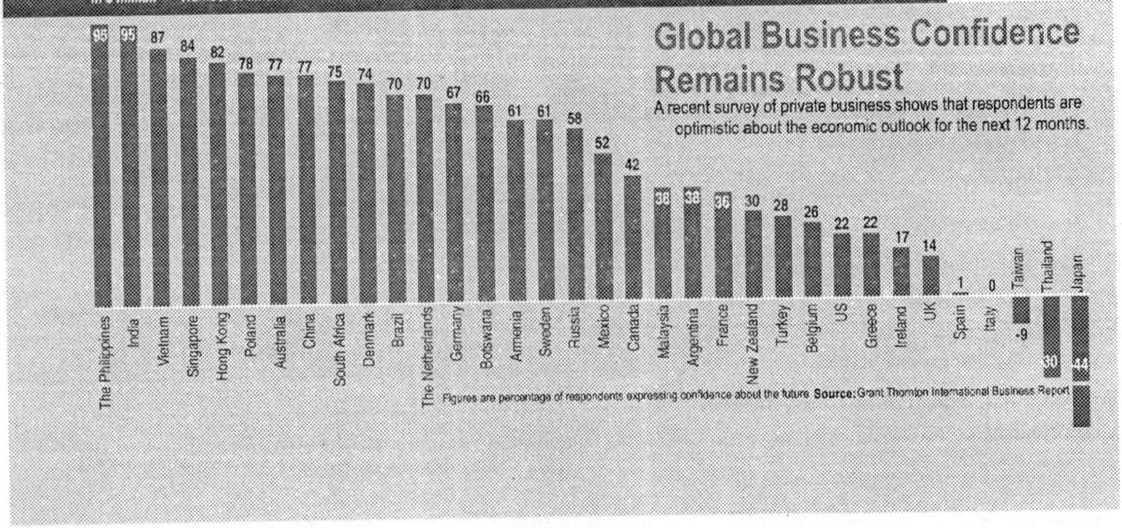


Figures are percentage of respondents expressing confidence about the future **Source:** Grant Thornton International Business Report

## Rights Issue

Another important method of placing shares to the public is the rights issue which is next in importance to the placing of shares through prospectus. The rights issue is an offer with a preemption right to the shareholder of existing companies to contribute to the share capital or its debt capital in the form of debentures. An existing company can issue rights to augment its equity base, if necessary. These are offered to the existing shareholders in a particular proportion to their existing shareownership. The ratio in which the new shares or debentures are offered to the existing shareholders of the company would depend on their requirements of capital. The rights are themselves transferable and saleable in the market. No new company can issue rights shares. Under the Companies Act, where a company increases its subscribed capital by the issue of new shares either after two years of its formation or after one year of the first issue of shares whichever is earlier, these have to be first offered to the existing shareholders with the right to reserve them in favour of a nominee.

## Players in the New Issue Market

There are many players in the new issue market. The important of them are the following:

(1) Merchant bankers
(2) Registrars
(3) Collecting and co-ordinating bankers
(4) Underwriters and brokers
(5) Printers, advertising agencies and mailing agencies.
(6) Investment bankers
(7) Venture capitalists
(8) Foreign Financial Institutions (FIIs).
(9) SEBI

## SEGMENT OF SECURITIES MARKETS

The major activity of the securities market is the mobilisation of funds from savings and their channelisation into investment. The principal instruments are equity shares, preference shares, debentures and bonds. The major characteristics of securities are their transferability and marketability. It comprises two markets, namely, new issues market for primary market and stock market or secondary market.

Segments of the Markets

| New Issues Market (Primary Market) | Stock Market (Secondary Market) |
|---|---|
| (a) New Issues by new companies | (a) Trading in existing securities |
| (b) Further issues by existing companies (issues are securities like equity shares, preference shares, debentures, bonds, Govt. securities, etc.) | (b) Listing of new issues for investment and disinvestment by savers/investors |
| | (c) Imparting liquidity or encashability to stocks and shares |

**Fig. 4 Market Segmentations**

The investors in the primary issues or new issues would be only buying in the primary market but cannot sell there. Their activity is limited to major operations of buying and selling in the secondary market only. Investors or institutions and buyers and sellers would deal in the secondary market through the intermediaries or brokers. The issuers of securities are the corporate units, government and semi-government bodies and public sector undertakings. The public, savers, investors and institutions, etc., can invest in both the primary and secondary markets. Their investments would be the sources of funds for the issuers of securities.

The primary market is called new issue market or the capital market while the secondary market is called the stock market. In the primary market, the government and the public sector undertakings as well as corporate units borrow funds or issue capital in the form of securities, shares, bonds, etc. The activity here refers to raising capital of ownership or debt nature. In this market, the primary savers or investors can keep their funds for a return. In the secondary market, they can both buy and sell existing securities, invest and disinvest or rechannel funds from one company into another or one type of security into another.

The secondary market is thus an important adjunct of the primary market. The activity in these two markets is interlinked and the indicators are also related, although separate in themselves.

The new issues, which are floated in the primary market, are permitted to be issued to the public by the Controller of Capital Issues at a price which is at par (face value) in the case of new companies or at a premium or par in the case of existing companies. The Capital Issues Controller is the authority to regulate the entry of issuers of securities into the capital market. But in the secondary market, the Union Ministry of Finance, Stock Exchange Division controls and regulates the stock markets and the stock exchange authorities. The stock markets are directly regulated by their own board of directors, namely, the stock exchange authorities, with the consent and approval of the government. The stock exchanges are recognised bodies to trade and deal in securities through their members who are brokers. The stock exchange authorities are self-regulatory bodies under the overall supervision of the stock exchange division of the government.

In the primary market, the brokers act as underwriters, managers, registrars and even merchant bankers to the new issues. In the secondary market, the claims of a long-term nature of one year and above are traded both on the spot for forward trading basis. This trading imparts liquidity to investments and thus promotes savings and substantial investment. These claims can be converted into money at any time although at a loss of capital in various degrees. The linkage between the RBI and banks is through cash or claims on money. Similarly, there are linkages as between banks, financial institutions and brokers. The financial institutions can only change the velocity of circulation of money (cash and credit) while dealing in the primary and secondary markets, but the banks can influence both creation of money and its velocity.

**Financial System — Business Sector**

| Sector | Nature of Assets | | Markets |
|---|---|---|---|
| BANKS and FIs | | BORROWINGS<br>Equity Shares<br>Preference Shares<br>Cumulative Debentures —<br>Secured and Unsecured<br>Convertible and<br>Non-convertible | STOCK MARKET<br>(Trading in<br>Old Securities) |
| Govt. Sector | | | |
| Foreign Sector | | Public Deposits<br>New Issues<br>Further Issues<br>Purchase of Old Securities | Capital Market<br>(Borrowing,<br>Deposits, Issue of<br>New Securities) |
| Household Sector | | | |

Basically, the functions of these markets are:

(1) Provision for securitisation of the debt or capital issued, which promotes savings mobilisation through new capital issues.

(2) Extending facilities for trading (buying and selling) in these securities so as to impart liquidity to these instruments so that investors can disinvest while new savers can invest and enter the market. This will facilitate the reallocation of funds as between securities or companies.

(3) Making a quotation for a share available to the investors and companies so that their net asset values (NAVs) are known and they can be used for tax purposes.

(4) This market also enables the companies to raise more capital from the capital market than is possible without these facilities for disinvestment, trading and liquidity.

(5) For the economy as a whole, these markets help mobilisation of savings for financing of corporate and government investment in order that economic growth and rise in incomes of the people can take place on a continuing basis.

**SEGMENTS OF MONEY MARKET**

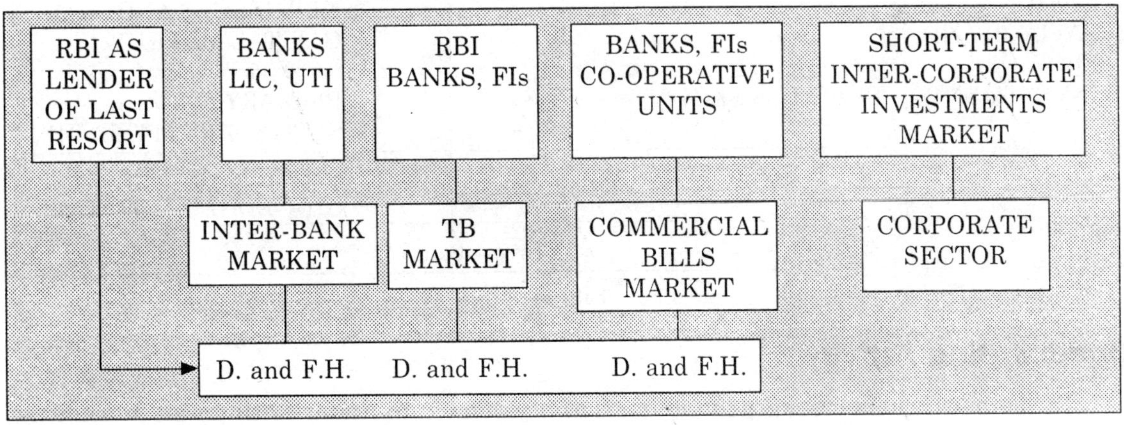

These markets have thus a vital role to play for investors at the micro-level and for the economy at the macro-level. For investors, it provides a venue for use of their savings for earning an income, capital appreciation and returns. For the economy, it facilitates savings mobilisation for capital formation which is necessary for substantial economic growth.

The constituents of the markets are:

(1) issuers of securities like companies and government;

(2) investors or traders who buy and sell securities; and

(3) intermediaries like brokers, merchant bankers, etc., who mediate between issuers and investors and as between buyers and sellers.

The new issues of companies are in the form of shares — equity and preference shares — debentures, etc. The securities issued by the companies and government are listed on the stock markets after they are floated and issued to the public. So far as the Government and the Semi-government securities are concerned, they are automatically listed for trading without any conditions or fees but in the case of corporate securities, the companies have to approach the respective stock exchanges where their registered office is located for the purpose of listing. A listing agreement is entered into, containing all the rules and regulations governing the conduct of the companies in respect of shares listed and the relations between the stock exchange and listed companies. The listed shares can be bought and sold and traded, which will lead to price formation for shares. The resultant price may be at par or face value or at a premium or discount of the face value depending upon the demand for and supply of these shares. These demand and supply forces may in turn depend on the physical and financial performance of the companies in question and their future prospects, etc.

**MOBILISATION OF SAVINGS AND PROMOTION OF INVESTMENT**

| | | | |
|---|---|---|---|
| NATIONAL SAVINGS AND FLOW OF INVESTMENT | SECTORS | S/I | MARKETS |
| | HOUSEHOLD SECTOR | S > I | PRIMARY MARKETS |
| | FOREIGN SECTOR | S > S | ALL MARKETS — NEW ISSUES AND CAPITAL MARKET |
| | BUSINESS SECTOR | I > S | PRIMARY AND SECONDARY MARKETS |
| | GOVT. SECTOR | I > S | STOCK MARKETS — GILT-EDGED MARKETS |
| | S: Savings | 1 : Investment | |

**Fig. 5**

## Underwriting Activity

In the new issues market, the major activity relates to underwriting and marketing of new issues. In India all financial institutions and brokers undertake this business.

Banks have entered this market in a big way by starting their own divisions of merchant banking or their subsidiaries. Insurance and investment companies are also an important category of underwriters. While banks and financial institutions account for the bulk of underwriting, UTI, insurance and consultancy companies and brokers account for the rest.

Underwriters and financial institutions subscribed more for preference shares and debentures than for equity shares as the latter are more attractive to the investing public and thus devolve less on the underwriters. The amount subscribed by them is higher in debentures as part of their policy of investment in corporate sector in high yielding and fixed income securities.

Brokers help in the floatation of new issues not only through underwriting or as managing brokers but also as financial consultants, advising on the proper capital structure, methods of raising capital and requirements of the Companies Act and the Securities Contracts (Regulation) Act, and listing requirements, etc.

## PROBLEMS OF THE NEW ISSUE MARKET

It will be pertinent to summarise briefly the main problems of the new issue market here. Firstly, the new issue market could not mobilise adequate savings from the public as less than 10% financial savings of the household sector are mobilised for investment in shares and debentures. A large portion of the capital requirements of companies is placed on the market privately or with financial institutions.

Secondly, the new issue market suffers from functional and institutional gaps, particularly in terms of the new instruments to appeal to the investing public. Thus, a wholesale market for new issues is yet to develop in India and merchant banking is in its infancy. The merchant banks are presently not playing a developmental role. In technical, managerial and entrepreneurial aspects, particulars in project preparation and technical aspects, adequate attention has not been given so far. This would be the responsibility of merchant banks and is not at present performed by them with the result that small investors are duped by the companies. Merchant bankers are now asked by the SEBI to do this. Thirdly, with a risk aversion in the new issue market, funds are diverted from the risk market to less risky debentures as well as deposits with the companies. Companies have themselves shifted away in the eighties from equity financing to debt financing and to larger reliance on debentures of convertible nature in more recent years. The costs of floatation have also been found to be abnormally high, particularly for new and small-sized companies. There is much scope for rationalising and economising the administrative costs of floatation of new issues in which banks can play an important role through merchant banking divisions.

In semi-urban and rural areas if the investor has to send application forms to centres where banks are authorised to accept them, he has to spend on securing a bank draft, postal charges for sending, and suffer loss of interest and collection charges for refund orders. There are inordinate delays in allotment of shares, refunding of application money, posting of share certificates and effecting transfer of shares, etc. These are to be despatched by registered post, or by certificate of posting in some cases, which is not done by many companies at present and they do not pay any interest for the delayed period as required by law.

All these problems would amount to considerable hardship to the small investors in the countryside. Similarly, dividend warrants, refund orders, interest payment not being encashable at par in all centres; the investors again lose. As the time taken for allotment is often two to three months or even more, there is considerable loss of interest on money to investors. The time limit for allotment was reduced to 30 days in 1996. These hardships are more in rural and semi-urban areas and do great injustice to them *vis-a-vis* those in metropolitan centres.

Another feature of the market is that existing companies with a good track record received good response for new issues as compared with new companies. The underwriting support and devolution on underwriters was more in the case of new companies due to the cautious response of investors to these companies. There was also evidence to show that investors do prefer debentures to equities and more so, if they are convertible debentures. Recently, new regulations are imposed by SEBI on merchant banks, which may improve the climate of investment in the new issue market. The merchant banks have to give due diligence certificate: they have to certify the bona fides of the information contained in the prospectus, justify the price fixed for the share and take the full responsibility for vetting and scrutiny in the case of rights issues. Their code of conduct is enforced by their own Association (AMB).

## Primary Market — Problems

The experiment in free pricing, being new in India created some problems of undue over pricing initially by some companies. Soon within a few months, investors became more discrete in making investments in new issues with hefty premiums. Many new issues have become flops in raising subscriptions, if their premiums are unreasonably high. It is now obvious that the experiment of free pricing will survive the criticism of the public particularly due to stricter norms by SEBI for better disclosures and more rational justification of the premium fixed by merchant bankers.

Accompanying the demand for control on premium is the pressure of the public to regulate the timing of the entry of companies in the new issue market and on the quantum of their issue. These steps being retrograde steps for the ongoing reforms, it is left to merchant bankers and the companies to decide on the basis of their experience and expertise. The demand for such controls emerged due to unrestricted entry of companies and the bunching of new issues at the same time and high premiums confusing the investors as to what to contribute with their limited funds.

The problem of timing and bunching of new issues will also lead to investor problems in the form of scramble for limited resources and inadequate appraisal of the projects. This may result in poor response to some new issues.

**PRIMARY CONCERNS** **BOX : 1**

**The New Issue Market could see more Realistic Pricing**

Investor, rattled the market meltdown, are unlikely to commit their savings to new issues in a hurry. Stories of panicky investors rushing to banks to stop payment of their cheques to Reliance Power on the day the market crashed are well-known. Reports about premium in the grey markets whittling down considerably in the aftermath of the crash inspired many retail investors to try to stop payment in places like Ahmedabad and Mumbai.

Edgy investors were quoting the case of Tata Steel, which completed the allotment of the country's biggest rights issue of over ₹ 9,650 crore and dispatched the refund cheques within a month. The Tata Steel cumulative convertible preference shares which listed on 24 January, 2009 barely managed to quote at a premium of 4 per cent above their face value of Rs. 100. Six of these preference shares will be converted into one share of Tata Steel on September 2009.

J. Kumar Infra projects, which closed its ₹ 140 crore IPO on 23 January, 2009 was over-subscribed by just two times, thanks to the participation of qualified institutional buyers. In a normal market, a company in the engineering and construction company in the infrastructure segment would have seen massive over-subscription.

A few analysts expect sanity to be restored at last. Issues being oversubscribed 50 times and 100 times works against investors as crowding inevitably elbows out genuine long-term investors. Promoters were also becoming greedy and went in for aggressive pricing on the advice of investment bankers, who promised to sell anything and everything at a fancy price. "There will be a lull and aggressive pricing will certainly come down", says Amitabh Chakraborty, CEO, Religare Securities. "On the flip side, pricing will be more realistic, issues won't be over-subscribed as much and bunching will take a back seat", says Nilesh Shah, CEO, Ambit Capital.

Some brokers reveal that a major finance company, which was offering to part fund the IPO's application money, played truant in the Reliance Power case, failing to put in the applications, despite cashing in the brokers margin cheques. While these are stray cases limited to one or two companies, all the finance companies' shares have seen a sharp drop in their share prices. This was on the reckoning that margin-funding both in the primary markets and secondary markets, one of their major sources of profit, would fall sharply. India Infoline was the most badly hit with the shares, losing 31 per cent from 31 December, 2009 levels. Geojit Financial was amongst the few which actually saw a rise in its share price during the carnage period.

The magnitude of discontent amongst the investors will be put to test in the first week of February, when many issues are expected to hit the market. Response to Emaar MGF, one of the largest realty firms after DLF, will be more muted and the company is expected to raise around ₹ 7,000 crore, accounting for a little over 10 per cent of its post-issue capital.

Some issues may also be deferred. There are several mega-issues like SBI Rights, Jindal Power, Rural Electrification and National Hydro, which were planning to tap the markets before the end of the current financial year. "The exuberance will go as will the hype being built around the primary issues. Quality issues will have no problem", says K.N. Vaidyanathan, CEO, Alchemy Capital, a portfolio management and fund advisory firm. Vaidyanathan adds that realistic pricing of issues will be seen in the immediate future, which will mean good news for investors.

## EXISTING MALPRACTICES

At present, there are many malpractices in both the primary and secondary markets. In the primary market, for example, there are many self-styled merchant bankers and investment consultants without sufficient expertise and infrastructure for proper service. Many issues and manipulation of prices are done on paper even before listing. There are other malpractices resorted to by bankers and registrars to the new issues. Allotments with or without premium are given to the favoured persons. There are delays in finalising the allotments and despatch to allotment letters and refund orders before the due dates. The provisions of the Companies Act and other relevant Acts are not adhered to and no punitive action is taken against them. Many companies have violated the rules of stock exchanges and listing requirements and no punishment is meted out to them as it is not possible under their rules and regulations. All these malpractices have resulted in increasing grievances of investors and a loss of confidence in the markets.

There is a wide variety of malpractices in the secondary market also despite its regulation by the stock exchange authorities. The intermediaries or member brokers do not render proper service to the customers, do not show the brokerage charged and do not pass contract notes regularly and in time. Trading in the market is devoid of transparency and fair practices. There is a large element of rigging of shares, manipulation of prices of shares, insider trading and a large spread between the bid and offer prices of jobbers. There are other unfair practices also in the market such as delay in delivery of shares and in making payments for sales by the brokers to their customers, in addition to the problems of odd lots and poor liquidity of a number of shares in the secondary market. More recently, because it can operate only if it is recognised by the government under the Securities Contracts (Regulations) Act, 1956 gross violations of the guidelines and lack of system has resulted in a scam of the century. The only way to rebuild investors' confidence in the market is to improve the system and reorient the system that it is efficient and prompt. Brokers are disciplined and accountable. The recognition is granted under Section 3 of the Act by the Central Government, Union Ministry of Finance.

The powers of the Central Government under that Act are far-reaching and include the following in particular:

(1) Grant and withdrawal of recognition, approval or change of bye-laws.
(2) Call for periodical returns from the Stock Exchange.
(3) Direct enquiries on the members or on the Stock Exchange.
(4) Liability of the Exchange to submit annual reports.
(5) Directing the Stock Exchange to make certain rules.
(6) Supersede the governing board of the Exchange.
(7) Suspend the governing board of the Exchange.
(8) Impose any other conditions or regulations for trading.

## Objectives

The important objectives of the Act are the following:

(i) to empower the Central Government to control the stock exchanges in India,

(ii) to provide reasonable uniformity in respect of the rules and bye-laws of the different stock exchanges in the country,

(iii) to ensure orderly and healthy development of the stock exchanges,

(iv) to protect the interest of the investors,

(v) to prevent unhealthy speculations and undesirable activities like the 1992 scam on the stock exchanges.

## BYE-LAWS

Besides the above Act, the Securities Contracts (Regulation) Rules were also made in 1957 to regulate certain matters of trading on the stock exchanges. There are also bye-laws of the exchanges, which are concerned with the following subjects:

Opening/Closing of the stock exchanges, timing of trading, regulation of bank transfers, regulation of badla or carry over business, control of the settlement and other activities of the stock exchange, fixation of margins, fixation of market prices or making up prices (Havala rates), regulation of taravani business (jobbing), etc., regulation of brokers' trading brokerage charges, trading rules on the exchange, arbitration and settlement of disputes, settlement and clearing of the trading, etc., are other matters needing regulation to a certain extent.

## RECENT TRENDS IN NEW ISSUE MARKET

In primary capital market grew in 2006 and 2007 after the satback of 2005. The amount funds raised from the primary market was only ₹ 910 crore in 1983-84. After a boom during 1992 to 1997, the primary market bounced back from 2003-04. Table 13.2 shows the number of issues made and the amount raised from 1990-91 to 2006-07.

## IPO OUTLOOK 2008

The bearish trend in the stock market in 2008 so far has taken a toll on the initial public offering (IPOs). However, the amount raised in the first five months of 2008 has jumped to ₹ 16,258.50 crore as against ₹ 8,926.48 crore in the same period last year, mainly because of Reliance Power, which raised around ₹ 13,000 crore via an IPO. Without Reliance Power, funds mobilized till May 2008 would have been lower than that in the same period last year. The number of companies raised money so far has also declined from 44 in 2007 to 19 this year 2008.

The Assocham study 'IPO Outlook 2008', said as companies have been shying away from the primary market, the number of new offering dropped to mere one in April and May each. A large number of companies are planning to postpone their investment plans or opting for external borrowing. This is primarily because of tough economic scenario – high commodity prices, reduced capital inflows, higher interest cost and global recessionary expectations.

**Table 13.2**

**THE IPO MARKET**

| Year April - March | No. of Issues | Amount (₹ in Crore) |
|---|---|---|
| 1990-91 | 141 | 1,704.35 |
| 1991-92 | 196 | 1,711.36 |
| 1992-93 | 528 | 6,060.82 |
| 1993-94 | 770 | 12,544.04 |
| 1994-95 | 1343 | 13,311.60 |
| 1995-96 | 1428 | 10,981.72 |
| 1996-97 | 753 | 11,648.00 |
| 1997-98 | 58 | 1,132.00 |
| 1998-99 | 22 | 509.00 |
| 1999-2000 | 56 | 2,975.00 |
| 2000-01 | 115 | 2,479.00 |
| 2001-02 | 26 | 1,032.00 |
| 2002-03 | 26 | 1,039.00 |
| 2003-04 | 23 | 19,200.00 |
| 2004-05 | 55 | 30,325.00 |
| 2005-06 | 73 | 19,852.46 |
| 2006-07 | 100 | 34,179.11 |
| 2007-08 | 22 | 52,254.00 |

## IMPENDING IPO BOOM

In the next two quarters of 2011, India Inc is expected to raise over ₹ 80,000 crore through the IPO route alone (debt and equity) of which almost 50 per cent is to be raised by the public sector enterprises. In the last few weeks, the secondary market has witnessed high octane volatility as the Sensex gyrated between 21,000 and 19,000. With so many public offerings lined up, either in the form of maiden issues or follow-up offerings, and the secondary market behaving the way it is, won't it impact the primary market?

Indian companies are gearing up to access capital markets in a big way in the next six months. In a way, this would bode well to mop up the liquidity entering the country, as India is clearly being recognised as one of the growth havens by overseas funds. With the US not expected to grow in the coming year and beyond, with European countries like Spain, Portugal and Italy continuing to exhibit fiscal weakness and with UK tightening its fiscal policy and bracing for austerity in the next couple of years, growth will have to come from emerging markets, and within that space, India will stand out, given its domestic consumption story. "Continued fund flows into India would have normally resulted in market imbalances and made the markets very volatile. If more companies access the capital markets, the overall market capitalisation gets spread across a larger set of companies and reduces the risk. This would keep a check on price/ earnings multiples running out of hand. Debt funds also will attract overseas money given the high rates prevailing in our markets."

**Returns from IPO in the past two years – 2009-2010**

| Company | Opening date | Issue amount (₹ in crore) | Offer price (₹) | Close price on listing (₹) | Mkt price as on 23.11.10 (₹) |
|---|---|---|---|---|---|
| Edserv Softsystems | 05.02.09 | 23.84 | 60.00 | 137.55 | 205.35 |
| **Mahindra Holidays** | **23.06.09** | **277.96** | **300.00** | **317.10** | **363.70** |
| Excel Infoways | 14.07.09 | 48.17 | 85.00 | 95.65 | 45.55 |
| **Raj Oil Mills** | **20.07.09** | **114.00** | **120.00** | **119.30** | **52.25** |
| Adani Power | 28.07.09 | 3016.52 | 100.00 | 100.05 | 138.75 |
| **NHPC** | **07.08.09** | **6038.55** | **36.00** | **36.70** | **28.85** |
| Jindal Cotex | 27.08.09 | 84.38 | 75.00 | 87.25 | 139.20 |
| **Globus Spirits** | **31.08.09** | **75.00** | **100.00** | **90.75** | **177.10** |
| Oil India | 07.09.09 | 2777.25 | 1050.00 | 1140.55 | 1377.70 |
| **Pipavav Shipyard** | **16.09.09** | **498.67** | **58.00** | **56.80** | **84.05** |
| Thinksoft Global Services | 22.09.09 | 45.58 | 125.00 | 164.30 | 92.70 |
| **Euro Multivision** | **22.09.09** | **66.00** | **75.00** | **53.20** | **26.90** |
| Indiabulls Power | 12.10.09 | 1758.15 | 45.00 | 39.25 | 27.10 |
| **Den Networks** | **28.10.09** | **392.40** | **195.00** | **163.10** | **215.10** |
| Astec Lifesciences | 29.10.09 | 61.50 | 82.00 | 83.90 | 68.00 |
| **COX & KINGS** | **18.11.09** | **610.39** | **330.00** | **426.05** | **519.95** |
| MBL Infrastructures | 27.11.09 | 102.60 | 180.00 | 205.75 | 196.45 |
| **JSW Energy** | **07.12.09** | **2700.00** | **100.00** | **100.75** | **111.05** |
| Godraj Properties | 09.12.09 | 468.85 | 490.00 | 534.55 | 651.30 |
| **D.B. Corp.** | **11.12.09** | **384.22** | **212.00** | **265.90** | **263.20** |
| Infinite Computer Solutions | 11.01.10 | 189.80 | 165.00 | 191.60 | 163.80 |
| **Jubilant Foodworks** | **18.01.10** | **328.72** | **145.00** | **229.00** | **585.00** |
| Aqua Logistics | 25.01.10 | 150.00 | 220.00 | 244.30 | 51.00 |
| **Thangamayil Jewellery** | **27.01.10** | **28.75** | **75.00** | **71.10** | **173.55** |
| Syncom Healthcare | 27.01.10 | 56.25 | 75.00 | 87.85 | 47.00 |
| **Vascon Engineers** | **27.01.10** | **178.20** | **165.00** | **147.20** | **134.10** |
| D B Realty | 29.01.10 | 1500.00 | 468.00 | 455.40 | 312.00 |

| | | | | | |
|---|---|---|---|---|---|
| **Emmbi Polyarns** | **01.02.10** | **43.08** | **45.00** | **28.65** | **18.15** |
| Arss Infrastructure Projects | 08.02.10 | 103.00 | 450.00 | 736.30 | 1026.85 |
| **Hathway Cable & Datacom** | **09.02.10** | **666.00** | **240.00** | **207.80** | **178.20** |
| Texmo Pipes & Products | 16.02.10 | 45.00 | 90.00 | 137.25 | 52.35 |
| **Man Infraconstruction** | **18.02.10** | **141.75** | **252.00** | **348.25** | **312.75** |
| United Bank of India | 23.02.10 | 325.15 | 66.00 | 68.80 | 117.35 |
| **DQ Entertainment (INTL)** | **08.03.10** | **128.16** | **80.00** | **108.55** | **109.65** |
| Pradip Overseas | 11.03.10 | 116.60 | 110.00 | 107.15 | 87.90 |
| **IL & FS Transportation Networks** | **11.03.10** | **700.00** | **258.00** | **273.75** | **295.85** |
| Persistent Systems | 17.03.10 | 168.01 | 310.00 | 408.00 | 389.85 |
| **Shree Ganesh Jewellery House** | **19.03.10** | **371.02** | **260.00** | **163.25** | **204.45** |
| Intrasoft Technologies | 23.03.10 | 53.65 | 145.00 | 159.35 | 99.35 |
| **Goenka Diamond & Jewels** | **23.03.10** | **135.00** | **135.00** | **127.85** | **72.95** |
| Talwalkars Better Value Fitness | 21.04.10 | 77.44 | 128.00 | 162.60 | 271.60 |
| **Nitesh Estates** | **23.04.10** | **405.00** | **54.0** | **50.95** | **36.60** |
| Tarapur Transformers | 26.04.10 | 63.75 | 75.00 | 56.90 | 34.65 |
| **Mandhana Industries** | **27.04.10** | **107.90** | **130.00** | **133.65** | **265.20** |
| SJVN | 29.04.10 | 1062.74 | 26.00 | 25.05 | 23.90 |
| **Jaypee Infratech** | **29.04.10** | **2262.00** | **102.00** | **91.30** | **79.35** |
| Parabolic Drugs | 14.06.10 | 200.00 | 75.00 | 64.80 | 63.60 |
| **Aster Silicates** | **24.06.10** | **53.10** | **118.00** | **199.10** | **40.25** |
| Technofab Engineering | 29.06.10 | 71.66 | 240.00 | 295.96 | 199.10 |
| **Hindustan Media Ventures** | **05.07.10** | **270.00** | **166.00** | **189.20** | **169.80** |
| Midfield Industries | 19.07.10 | 59.85 | 133.00 | 163.05 | 419.20 |
| **SKS Microfinance** | **28.07.10** | **1628.78** | **985.00** | **1088.58** | **712.80** |
| Bajaj Corp | 02.08.10 | 297.00 | 660.00 | 758.25 | 583.45 |
| **Prakash Steelage** | **05.08.10** | **68.75** | **110.00** | **187.95** | **159.05** |
| Gujarat Pipavav Port | 23.08.10 | 553.85 | 46.00 | 54.05 | 58.10 |
| **Indosolar** | **13.09.10** | **357.00** | **29.00** | **23.70** | **25.60** |
| Career Point Infosystems | 16.09.10 | 115.00 | 310.00 | 632.35 | 421.95 |
| **Eros International Media** | **17.09.10** | **350.00** | **175.00** | **190.05** | **187.50** |
| Mocrosec Financial Services | 17.09.10 | 147.50 | 118.00 | 110.90 | 70.10 |
| **Orient Green Power Co.** | **21.09.10** | **900.00** | **47.00** | **44.90** | **32.80** |
| Ramky Infrastructure | 21.09.10 | 530.00 | 450.00 | 387.35 | 355.60 |
| **Electrosteel Steels** | **21.09.10** | **285.28** | **11.00** | **11.25** | **10.56** |
| VA Tech Wabag | 22.09.10 | 472.59 | 1310.00 | 1709.40 | 1649.30 |

| | | | | | |
|---|---|---|---|---|---|
| **Gallant Ispat** | **22.09.10** | **33.50** | **50.00** | **81.60** | **54.40** |
| Cantabil Retail India | 22.09.10 | 105.00 | 135.00 | 104.75 | 73.35 |
| **Tecpro Systems** | **23.09.10** | **267.69** | **355.00** | **407.85** | **394.90** |
| Ashoka Buildcon | 24.09.10 | 225.00 | 324.00 | 333.35 | 302.45 |
| **Sea TV Network** | **27.09.10** | **50.20** | **100.00** | **106.00** | **83.80** |
| Bedmutha Industries | 28.09.10 | 91.80 | 102.00 | 180.80 | 86.10 |
| **Commercial Engineers** | **30.09.10** | **172.41** | **127.00** | **112.25** | **101.70** |
| BS Transcomm | 06.10.10 | 190.45 | 248.00 | 378.50 | 192.45 |
| **Oberoi Realty** | **06.10.10** | **1028.61** | **260.00** | **282.95** | **270.45** |
| Prestige Estates Projects | 12.10.10 | 1200.00 | 183.00 | 192.55 | 165.90 |
| **Gyscoal Alloys** | **13.10.10** | **54.67** | **71.00** | **81.55** | **53.65** |
| Coal India | 18.10.10 | 15199.44 | 245.00 | 342.35 | 320.00 |
| **Gravita India** | **01.11.10** | **45.00** | **125.00** | **210.40** | **260.25** |
| R.P.P. Infra Projects | 18.11.10 | 44.20 | 68.00 | Not Yet Listed | |

***Source:*** Prime Database

## Upcoming IPOs

| List of Clients | ₹ crore |
|---|---|
| Abhijeet Power | 1,500 |
| **Emaar MGF Land** | **1,600** |
| Embassy Realty | 2,000 |
| **Endurance Technologies** | **1,000** |
| Future Ventures | 1,000 |
| **Great Offshore** | **750** |
| Indian Oil | 18,000 |
| **Indigo Airlines** | **2,500** |
| Intas Pharmaceuticals | 800 |
| **IOT Infra & Energy Serv.** | **750** |
| Jindal Power | 7,000 |
| **Jindal Thermal Power** | **1,500** |

| List of Clients | ₹ crore |
|---|---|
| Joyalukkas | 1,500 |
| **Lavasa** | **2,000** |
| Lokmat Newspaper | 500 |
| **Micromox** | **500** |
| Muthoot Finance | 2,000 |
| **ONGC** | **12,000** |
| Raheja Universal | 1,000 |
| **Sahara Prime** | **3,000** |
| SAIL | 8,000 |
| **Shree Renuka Infra Projects** | **1,500** |
| Sterlite Energy | 3,000 |
| **Super Religare** | **500** |

However, the key concerns are the timing of the public offerings and the fair price. Investors are looking for the correct price of public offers. If the pricing is right, the issuer will be successful — as in the case of Coal India compared to NHPC or SJUN, where the returns were not so encouraging.

Investors are always hungry for good stocks. Flagship PSUs in India have a high net worth, good profit potential and monopoly in the product market. Investors usually give higher weight to these companies' shares compared to other shares in the market, and consider these shares more reliable since the government also brings out the public issue on the basis of a conservative price formula.

Therefore, retail investors are bound to show great interest in buying these shares as these PSUs are more likely to perform better after the listing due to increased liquidity and better governance practices and a more professional approach as they get exposed to greater scrutiny by the retail and other investors as per the terms of listing provisions.

Apart from PSUs making a beeline for the capital market, a number of large private sector companies from various sectors, like Emaar MGF and Embassy Realty from the real estate, Indigo Airlines from aviation, Abhijeet Power, Jindal Power and Sterlite Energy from the power and energy sector, have also drawn up capital raising plans.

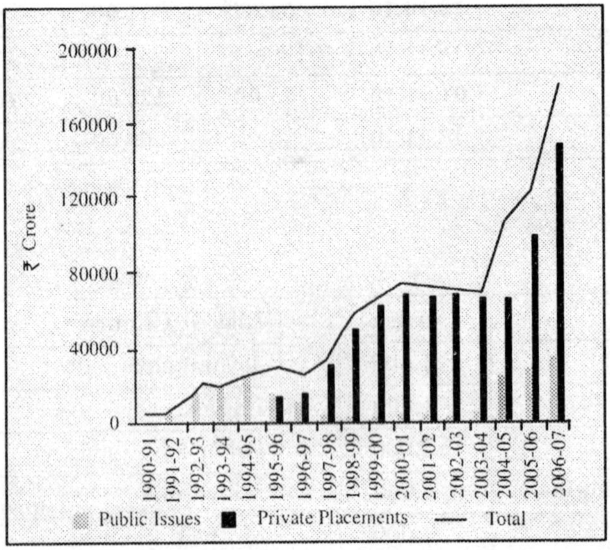


**Chart 1 : Resource Mobilisation from the Primary Capital Market**

Since 1997-98, however, the private placement segment started gaining prominence. Private placement rose from ₹ 59,215 crore in 2003 to ₹ 1,11,838 crore till November, 2007. It accounted for over 75 per cent of resources mobilized from the primary capital market. Although this segment lacked transparency, it provided an alternative mechanism for raising resources by the corporates in a cost-effective and time saving manner. As the unbridled growth of the private placement segment, to which several banks also had significant exposure, posed some systemic risk, the SEBI brought this segment under its regulatory purview to ensure its orderly growth.

The success of the IPOs (Initial Public Offer) rests on sound fundamentals, attractive valuations and focused IPO promotion strategies. In addition, robust support from both institutional and retail investors help the companies to sail through the IPO market comfortably.

## Recent Developments in the Indian Equity Market

The Indian equity market has witnessed a series of reforms since the early 1990s. The reform measures were aimed at:

(i) creating growth enabling institutions;

(ii) boosting competitive conditions in the equity market through improved price discovery mechanism;

(iii) putting in place an appropriate regulatory framework;

(iv) reducing the transaction costs; and

(v) reducing information asymmetry, thereby boosting.

Other reform measures are as follows:

- The most significant reform in respect of the primary capital market was the introduction of free pricing.
- The issuers of securities were allowed to raise capital from the market without requiring any consent from any authority for either making the issue or pricing it. All companies are now able to price issues based on market conditions.
- Restrictions on rights and bonus issues were also removed.
- The improvement in disclosure standards has enhanced transparency, thereby improving the level of investor protection.
- Issuers also have the option of raising resources through fixed price mechanism or the book-building process.

## CONCLUSION

The Indian New Issues (equity) market has witnessed a significant improvement since the reform process began in the early 1990s. There has been a visible improvement in efficiency and levels of transparency. Though the size of the public issues has remained small as corporates have tended to prefer the international capital market and the private placement market, apart from relying on the internal resources and bank credit.

The transaction cost has declined and volatility has also been contained. Nevertheless, the role of the Indian capital market, equity as well as debt, in domestic economic activity continues to be relatively less significant. Savings of the household sector in the form of shares and debentures and units of mutual funds remain at relatively low levels, reflecting households' preference for safe and contractual instruments as opposed to capital market based instruments.

The organisation of the New Issue Market (NIM) comprises the institutional structure of the market, namely, origination, underwriting and distribution. NIM in India suffers from a serious institutional lacuna, the absence of specialist issue house services, weakness of the underwriting system and lack of genuine investment demand for new issues.

Financial sector reforms have been successful in bringing significant improvements in various market segments by effecting regulatory and legal changes, building up of institutional infrastructure, constant fine tuning in market microstructure and substantial upgradation of technological infrastructure. Efficient, stable and healthy financial markets constitute the bedrock for successful conduct of monetary policy; hence, improving the effectiveness of the transmission channel of monetary policy necessitated significant reforms in the money and government securities markets. Facilitating integration of domestic financial market was the other major objective of financial market reforms.

The major objective of reforms in the Government securities market was to impart liquidity and depth to the market by broadening the investor base and by ensuring market-clearing interest rate mechanism. Keeping this in view, a number of reform measures were initiated in this segment which had a positive impact on both the primary and the secondary markets.

Financial market reforms have helped in improving the price discovery in the primary market, while the secondary markets have attained greater depth and liquidity. The number of instruments and participants has also increased. The capital markets has become a safer place for investors as various risks involved at various stages of trading and settlement have been either completely eliminated or reduced considerably. Liquidity in the stock market has improved considerably. The Government securities market has witnessed a transformation from a captive bank-dominated market to an active debt market operating at market related/determined interest rates. Among the financial market segments, the linkages among the money, Government securities and foreign exchange markets have been established and are growing. The presence of foreign institutional investors has strengthened the integration between the domestic and international capital markets.

❖❖❖

CHAPTER 14

# GOVERNMENT SECURITIES MARKET

## INTRODUCTION

The Government securities market is at the core of financial markets in most countries. It deals with tradable debt instruments issued by the government for meeting its financal requirements. The development of the primary segment of this market enables the managers of public debt to raise resources from the market in a cost-effective manner with due recognition to associated risks. A vibrant secondary segment of the Government securities market helps in the effective operation of monetary policy through application of indirect instruments such as open market operation, for which Government securities act as collateral. The Government securities market is also regarded as the backbone of fixed income securities markets as it provides the benchmark yield and impacts liquidity to other financial markets. The existence of an efficient Government securities market is seen as an essential precursor in particular, for development of the corporate debt market. Furthermore, the Government securities market acts as a channel for integration of various segments of the domestic financial market and helps in establishing inter-linkages between the domestic and external financial markets.

## TRADING IN GOVERNMENT SECURITIES

Trading in Government securities is referred to as the gilt-edged market. This is mostly over the counter market and trading is confined to banks, financial institutions and PFs. The role of brokers is to intermediate as between the above institutions through their contacts with the money managers in the banks. The government sector is a major borrower in India and Government securities represent government debt to the other sectors of the economy. The government sector includes the Central and State Governments, local and municipal bodies and semi-government bodies, whose securities are guaranteed by the Central or State Governments. These agencies or bodies borrow every year from the capital market in the form of new loans and bonds floated. Besides, their old securities are also traded in the stock market.

Government securities are held by the RBI, and the working of two major techniques — Open market operations and Statutory Liquidity Ratio (SLR) are closely connected with the dynamics of the market for this instrument. Commercial banks are required to maintain their secondary reserve requirements in the form of these securities. These securities constitute more than 70 per cent of investment portfolio of Central Bank of India (RBI). Commercial banks can obtain accommodation from the RBI against the collateral of these securities. Government securities constitute the ultimate source of liquidity in the economy. As government security is a claim on the government, it is an absolutely secured financial instrument which guarantees the certainty of both income and capital. It is, therefore, called a 'gilt-edged' security or stock.

The object of this chapter is to set out briefly the development of Government securities market in India since the early 1990s, in order to identify the key issues that need to be addressed to meet the emerging challenges. The Government securities market has been steadily rising and has become a matter of concern in recent years. In this backdrop, the mechanics of its management by the apex bank are discussed. If the country is really caught in the debt trap, what then are the policy alternatives to extricate itself from the fiscal crisis.

## THE EVOLUTION OF THE GOVERNMENT SECURITIES MARKET

The evolution of the Government securities market in India has been in line with the developments in other countries. Slow development of the market in 1970s and 1980s was shaped by the need to meet the growing financing requirements of the government. This essentially resulted in financial repression as progressively higher statutory requirements were stipulated, mandating banks to invest in Government securities at administered interest rates. Although this captive financing provided low cost resources to the government, it impeded the development of the market and distorted the interest rate structure. Furthermore, such arrangements along with automatic monetisation of government deficits hampered the conduct of monetary policy.

Recognising the need for a well developed Government securities market, the Reserve Bank, in co-ordination with the government, initiated a series of measures from the early 1990s to deregulate the market of administered price and quality controls. Consequently, the Government securities market has witnessed significant transformation in various dimensions, *viz.*, market-based price discovery, widening of investor base, introduction of new instruments, establishment of primary dealers, and electronic trading and settlement infrastructure. This in turn, has enabled the Reserve Bank to perform its functions in tandem with the evolving economic and financial conditions.

Government securities market with the fresh issuance of Government of India (GoI) dated securities amounting to ₹ 1,62,000 crore in 2007, the market capitalization of GoI securities increased to ₹ 13,18,419 crore. The zero-coupon rate on one-year bonds edged up to 6.78 to 8.07 per cent. Similarly, the range of zero-coupon rate on 10 year bonds moved in the range of 7.5 to 8.37 per cent in 2007.

## ROLE OF THE GOVERNMENT SECURITIES MARKET

The supply of Government securities is generally exogenous to the market, determined mainly by the fiscal policy of the government. The demand for the Government securities may be fragmented into several components implying that the demand curve is not uniformly downward sloping, but is rather kinked (Commonwealth of Australia, 2002). For instance, the demand by investors such as insurance companies and superannuation funds is in the nature of 'buy and hold' as the revenue streams from Government securities generally match with their liability payment stream. These investors may have very few substitutes and, hence, their demand is less price sensitive. Mandated investments in Government securities by banks and other institutions would also fall into the category of 'buy and hold'. The demand from other investors in Government securities is more for active trading and portfolio management. These investors may have many substitutes for Government securities and, hence, their demand is generally more price elastic. The overall demand is, therefore, determined by the balance between these two groups of investors. Greater the share of active investors higher is the demand elasticity or price sensitivity of Government securities. Increased volume of Government securities may increase concerns of a default by the government which may affect the risk characteristics of the instrument. This may result in a fall in prices as yields steepen. At the other end of the spectrum, very limited supply of Government securities may generate concerns over liquidity. Illiquidity premium can then drive down the prices, although there could be some resistance to the downward bias, if 'buy and hold' investors dominate the market. Thus, very high volumes as well as very low volumes of Government securities may result in a fall in prices of Government securities.

Activity in the Government securities market affects overall investment in the economy in two ways.

First, it may adversely affect private investment by directly competing for the limited resources.

Second, the Government securities market can also have a positive influence on private investment by enabling the development of private bond market by putting in place a basic financial infrastructure, including laws, institutions, products, services, repo and derivatives markets and by playing a role as an informational benchmark. And, more importantly, the yield curve, also known as term structure of interest rates, of Government securities serves as a public good in financial markets.

Third, by offering a risk-free benchmark, the Government securities market also facilitates the development of other financial markets and serves as a channel of integration of various segments of the financial market. The Government securities market, which is often the predominant segment of the overall debt market in many economies, also plays a crucial role in the monetary policy transmission mechanism 10. Thus, the Government securities market facilitates efficiency in the price discovery mechanism across other segments of the financial market, which is an important condition for financial stability.

Fourth for the central bank, a developed Government securities market allows greater application of indirect or market-based instruments of monetary policy such as open market (including repo) operations. A greater recourse to the market by the government for meeting its funding requirements expands the eligible set of collaterals, thereby enabling the central bank to conduct monetary policy through indirect instruments. The expanding quantum of eligible collaterals has provided flexibility to central banks in many developing economies in their conduct of monetary policy, especially in sterilising capital flows.

Fifth, since the Government securities market plays a crucial role in the conduct of monetary policy operations, central banks take a keen interest in developing a deep, liquid and vibrant Government securities market. In India, the Reserve Bank has taken several initiatives towards widening the investor base; enhancing transparency in primary issuances; expanding choice of instruments; benchmarking and consolidation of securities across key maturities; and putting in place appropriate safeguard and sound trading and settlement infrastructure.

Finally, the development of the Government securities market is essential for establishing the risk-free benchmarks in financial markets and ensuring their functioning in an efficient manner.

## SIGNIFICANCE OF THE GOVERNMENT SECURITIES MARKET

The need to develop the Government securities market emerges from the three roles it seeks to play, i.e., for the financial markets, for the government and for the central bank. As alluded to earlier, the Government securities market serves as the backbone of fixed income markets through the creation of risk-free benchmarks of a sovereign borrower. *Ipso facto*, it acts as a channel of integration of various segments of the financial market. The Government securities market constitutes a key segment of the financial market, offering virtually credit risk-free highly liquid financial instruments, which market participants are more willing to transact and take positions. The willingness of market participants to transact in Government securities, in turn, imparts liquidity to these instruments, which benefits all segments of the financial market. Consequently, Government securities are used by dealers as a major hedging tool for interest rate risk and as underlying assets and collateral for related markets, such as repo, futures and options. Furthermore, large borrowings by the government also provide an impetus to the development of the bond market.

Additionally,

(1) For the government (issuer), a deep and liquid Government securities market facilitates its borrowings from the market at reasonable cost.

(2) A developed Government securities market provides flexibility to the manager of public debt to optimise maturity and cost of even a lumpy government borrowing.

(3) For the Central Bank (RBI), a developed Government securities market allows greater application of indirect or market-based instruments – open market (including repo) operations.

(4) It also plays a crucial role in the monetary policy transmission mechanism.

## Principal Functions

The Government securities market performs three valuable functions: *(i)* it provides resources, both short- and long-term, to the government, *(ii)* it acts as a benchmark for pricing corporate papers for varying maturities, and *(iii)* a healthy government securities market facilitates the conduct of open market operations (OMO), an indirect monetary policy instrument of paramount importance for managing overall liquidity in the system.

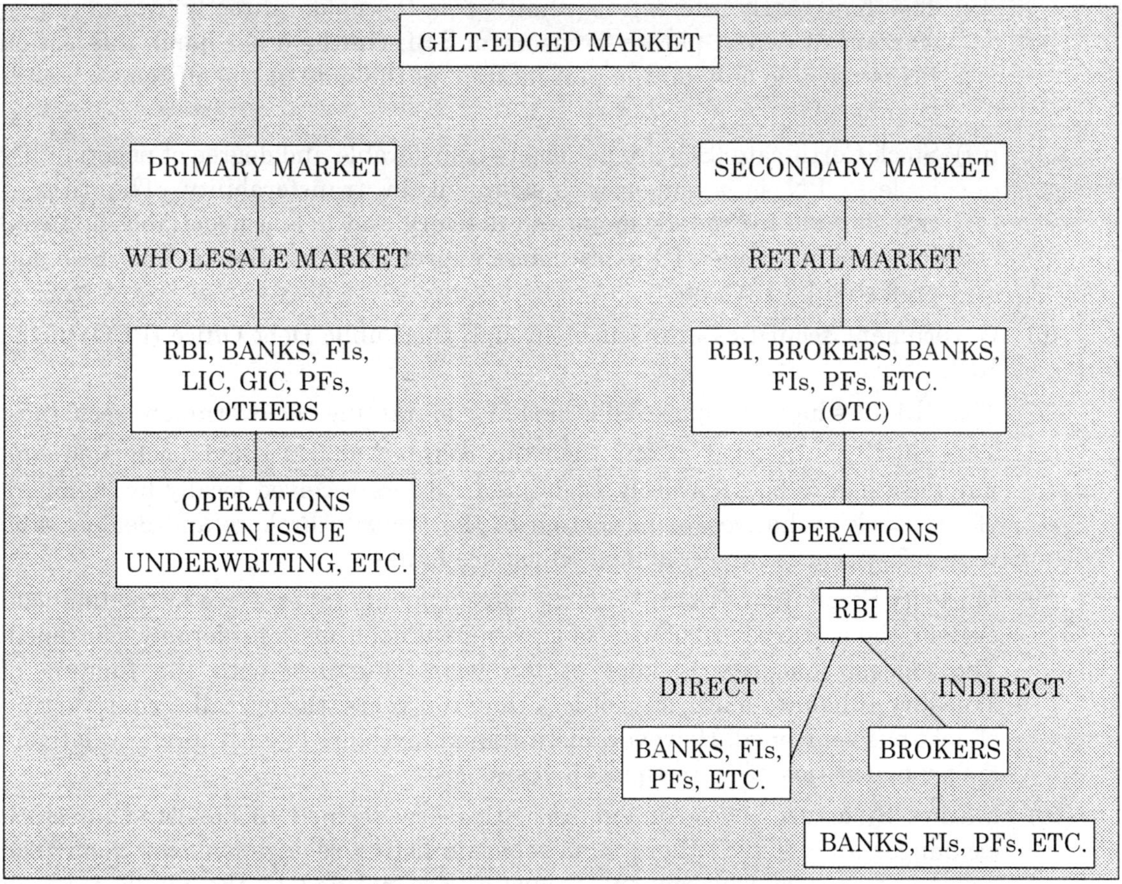


**Fig. 1 Gilt-Edged Market Segmentation**

### Salient Features of Government Securities:

(1) These securities are normally issued in denomination of ₹ 1,000.

(2) The interest on Government securities is payable half-yearly. Interest in respect of Central and State Government securities exempt from income tax subject to certain limits.

(3) Central Government securities are more liquid than State Government and Semi-government securities. The market activity in respect of Semi-government securities is very less.

(4) There are three forms of Central and State Government securities, (i) Inscribed stock or Stock Certificate (SC) (ii) Promissory Note (PN), and (iii) Bearer Bond.

However, at present most Government securities are in the form of promissory note (PN). Promissory note of any loan can be converted into stock certificates of any other loan or *vice versa*.

(5) The specific features of stock certificates (SC) are:

(*i*) They are safer than PN as the name of the holder is registered in the books of the Public Debt Office (PDO).

(*ii*) The half-yearly interest is remitted to the holder directly by an interest warrant drawn at par on Treasury or SBI. On the other hand, interest on PN is payable only on the presentation of the note at the office at which it is enfaced.

(*iii*) Stock Certificate (SC) are not easily transferable and degree of negotiability is less. PN is a superior instrument in transferability. The title is transferable by endorsement and delivery and it is a negotiable financial instrument. Thus, PNs are mostly preferred by Banks and SCs are preferred by LIC, etc.

(6) Government securities are issued through the Public Debt Office (PDO) of the RBI.

(7) The RBI does have its approved brokers for marketing of Government securities.

(8) The gilt-edged market is an 'over-the counter' market and each sale and purchase has to be separately negotiated. Orders received locally by members of the stock exchange are passed on to the security brokers and dealers who then try various sources, among which are banks.

(9) Maturity Structure of Debt: With the developments taken place in the financial system, the maturity structure of government debt has considerably shortened. The longest maturity is kept at ten years. Further, with the funding of Treasury Bills into maturities of less than ten years, the overall term structure of debt has shortened. However, institutional investors like LIC prefer relatively longer maturities of more than 15 years.

(10) Market Structure: Government securities are deemed to be listed on stock exchanges and as such there is no separate listing requirement for them. The primary issues of Government securities are notified to the public through issue of government notification and press communication. SEBI has also been granted 'No objection' to these issues without insisting on vetting of offer document.

The RBI has advised the banks that, securities transactions should be undertaken directly between banks and no bank should engage the services of any brokers. In such transactions banks may however undertake securities transactions among themselves or with non-bank clients through members of the NSE, wherein transactions are transparent.

(11) Tax Deduction at Source (TDS) interest on Government securities is subject to tax deducted at source. This has led to the unhealthy practice of voucher trading around interest payments dates purely to gain tax advantage. The Union Budget

of 1997 has removed TDS on interest income of Government securities. This helps in improving the secondary market for Government securities.

## Principal Forms of Government Securities

There are three forms in which Government securities are held: (i) Stock or Book Debt, (ii) Promissory Notes, and (iii) Bearer Bonds.

**(i) Stock Certificates:** When the debt is held in the form of stock, the owner is given a certificate to the effect that the owner is the holder of a stock (loan or loans) registered in the books of PDO of RBI, as to its rate of interest, dates when interest is payable and its maturity. This stock certificate is not transferable by mere endorsement as the execution of a transfer deed is necessary for its transfer. Stocks can be held jointly by more than one person but these will have to be transferred by all the surviving joint holders. Stock certificates need not be presented for interest payment but interest warrants are sent by the PDO to the holders on the due dates. These certificates are the only form of Government security which can be held by Trustees of specified Trusts or holders of offices other than public offices. The officials holding the office can negotiate and sign for their respective offices in respect of these certificates. These stocks can also be held in the form of Subsidiary General Ledger accounts (SGL) with the PDO of the RBI. This form of holding in SGL is restricted to institutions, agencies, banks and those with a corporate status having regular dealings with the RBI.

**(ii) Promissory Notes:** This is a promise by the government, Central/State, to a person named therein, to pay a specified amount at a specified date and to pay interest at a fixed rate at periodical intervals at a particular office of the RBI. It is a negotiable instrument payable to the order of a specified person and transferable by endorsement.

**(iii) Bearer Bonds:** A bearer bond certificate that the bearer is entitled to a certain sum specified in rupees on the date indicated in accordance with the terms of a particular loan to which the bond relates. Printed coupons for interest payable to bearer are attached to the bond. The interest is paid to the holder of the coupon and the bond is discharged on the due date of the loan to which it relates by physical presentation of the bearer. A change of ownership is effected by simple delivery of bonds by the transferor to the transferee. Examples are prize bonds and premium prize bonds. More recently, this form of loan issue was stopped by the government.

The stock certificates are the best of the three forms of holdings from the point of view of security and convenience of big holders of government debt. As between promissory notes and bearer bonds, the former are more secure but the latter are more easy to transfer, and get interest and repayment with the least difficulty. Thus, a promissory note stands in between stock certificates and bearer bonds, from the point of view of security, on the one hand, and the ease and convenience for transfer, on the other. Transactions in the stock exchange take place mainly in the form of these promissory notes as these can be transferred by endorsement and are a good delivery against contracts under the stock exchange rules.

## SEGMENT OF GOVERNMENT SECURITIES

Existence of a well-developed government securities market is essential for the pursuit of a market-based monetary policy. Well-developed government securities market is also required to develop a domestic rupee yield curve, which could provide a credible benchmark for pricing of securities in other markets.

In the securities market, an important segment is the gilt-edged market of which comprises, the Central and State Government securities, bonds of local bodies and semi-government organisations. The Reserve Bank arranges for the issue of these securities through banks and financial institutions and acts as the manager and underwriter of the issues, particularly with respect to Central Government securities. As a part of its functions, the apex bank acts as a banker to the Central and State Governments and as manager of the public debt of the Central Government. In this context, it arranges for the accepting of subscriptions to the Central loans, issue of securities, servicing of these securities and, repayment of loans, etc. As a part of the RBI credit control policy, the banks have to invest 38.5% of their aggregate deposits in the Central and State Government securities and other approved securities. Besides financial institutions, LIC, GIC, etc., have also to invest a part of their funds in Government securities. It is thus necessary for banks and financial institutions to invest in Government securities as a statutory obligation. But in view of the lower interest rates on these securities than those on other instruments of the corporate sector, the public and individuals are not much interested in these securities. Thus, the market in Government securities is a captive one and of a limited nature. The secondary market in these securities is also limited to transactions as between the banks and the RBI and among banks and financial institutions.

The market in these securities is Over The Counter (OTC), through telephones, personal contact, telex, etc., and hence the data on prices and yields, etc., are not properly reported to the stock exchange where they are quoted. But as the manager of the public debt of the government and through the operations undertaken in the open market (called open market operations), the RBI collects some information on prices and compiles data on yields. The prices and yields on Government securities are thus compiled and published by the RBI, regularly in their monthly and annual publications. Fig. 1 presents a picture of sections within the gilt-edged market, namely, primary and secondary sections, representing the issue of Government securities, wholesale and trading in retail respectively. The players in the market are the RBI, Banks, FIs and brokers. The RBI is the main lead manager and underwriter with respect to Central Government securities and a major holder of these securities. The banks and financial institutions, PFs and companies deal in these securities with or without the help of brokers. The RBI conducts open market operations of purchase and sale directly with banks and financial institutions or with the help of brokers.

### Operations in Government Securities Market

**Switch Operations:** These are purchase of one Government security against the sale of another, for an equivalent face value. Switch operations seems to be useful to banks and FIs to improve their yields on their investments in Government securities. Sometimes, there are triangular switch transactions in which one investor's sale or purchase in matured by the purchase or sale transactions of another investor, the RBI fixes annual quota, based on the size of the bank for switch transactions. RBI maintains separate list of securities for purchase and sale transactions. Different scrips are included in the two lists having regard to the stock of securities and dates of their maturities.

**Grooming:** It can be defined as acquiring securities nearing maturity to facilitate redemption and making available on tap a variety of loans to broaden the gilt-edged market.

## PRIMARY MARKET

After the switchover to auction-based system for issuing securities, the amount of market-based primary issuance of Government securities increased by more than ten-fold from about ₹ 12,000 crore in 1991-92 to about ₹ 1,40,000 crore in 2001-02. This was accompanied by a sharp decline in primary subscription by the Reserve Bank from 45.9 per cent in 1992-93 to 1.45 per cent in 1993-94 and to mere 0.74 per cent in 1994-95. However, in the recent years, devolvement/private placement on the Reserve Bank was higher at around 30 per cent in 1999-2000 and 25 per cent in 2001-02, essentially reflecting the liquidity management operations undertaken by the Reserve Bank. These securities are, however, off-loaded in the market to contain the monetary impact.

The switchover to the system of borrowing at market-related rates provided the flexibility to modulate the maturity structure according to the needs. In the initial years of reforms, the maturity structure was shortened to reduce the cost, apart from making the Government securities attractive to investors in terms of their tenor. Consequently, the weighted average maturity, which was around 16 years in 1990-91, was reduced to 6.59 years in 1997-98. This, in turn, resulted in significant hunching of redemptions. Consequently, it was considered desirable to elongate the maturity profile of the Government debt.

The secondary market for Government securities provides a platform for original investors to trade their holdings before maturity. Traditionally, the trading platform was over-the-counter (OTC) before introduction of trading in stock exchanges in various countries. For instance, in China, trading in treasury bonds was banned till 1980. Subsequently, an OTC trading was initiated. Trading at the Shanghai Stock Exchange commenced in 1992. Banks trade in the inter-bank market, which is largely a repo and 'buy and hold' market. Since 1997, banks in China have been prohibited from trading stock exchanges to avoid speculation. In Thailand, the Thai Bond Market Association began trading in government bonds in centralized data base on Malaysia debt securities i.e., Bond informations and Dissemination System (BIDS), which facilitates OTC trading of government bonds in 1998. The central bank of Malaysia operates in Malaysia (Box 1).

**POLICY DEVELOPMENTS IN PRIMARY MARKET** **BOX : 1**

In the Primary Market the following policy initiatives were undertaken during 2006-07:

- SEBI notified the disclosures and other related requirements for companies desirous of issuing Indian Depository Receipts in India. It was mandated that the issuer must be listed in its home country, must not have been barred by any regulatory body, and should have a good track record of compliance of securities market regulations. SEBI stipulated the requirements of issue size, subscription to the issue and disclosures to be made in the prospectus of the issue such as general information, disclaimer clause, offering details, risk factors and financial information among other requirements.
- As a condition of continuous listing, listed companies have to maintain a minimum level of public shareholding at 25 per cent of the total shares issued. The exemptions include companies which are required to maintain more than 10 per cent, but less than 25 per cent in accordance with the Rule 19 2(b) of the Securities Contracts (Regulation) Rules, 1957 and the companies, that have two crore or more of listed shares and ₹ 1,000 crore or more of market capitalisation. SEBI has also provided a transparent mechanism to graduate to compliance of the continuous listing requirements for companies which are currently non-compliant or companies which might become non-compliant in future.
- SEBI has specified that shareholding pattern will be indicated by listed companies under three categories, *viz.*, shares held by promoter and promoter group., shares held by public "and shares held by custodians and against which Depository Receipts have been issued".
- In accordance with the guidelines issued by SEBI, the issuers are required to state on the cover page of the offer document whether they have opted for an IPO grading from the rating agencies. In case the issuers opt for a grading, they are required to disclose the grades including the unaccepted grades in the prospectus and abridged prospectus.
- SEBI facilitated a quick and cost-effective method of raising funds termed as Qualified Institutional Placement (QIP) from the Indian securities market by way of the private placement of securities or convertible bonds (but not warrants) with the Qualified Institutional buyers. Listed companies having equity shares of same class listed on a stock exchange having nationwide trading terminals and complying with the minimum public shareholding under continuous listing requirement are eligible to raise funds through the QIP route.
- SEBI stipulated that the benefit of 'no lock-in' on the pre-issue shares of an unlisted company making an IPO, currently available to the shares held by Venture Capital Funds (VCFs)/Foreign Venture Capital Investors (FVCls), shall be limited to: (a) the shares held by VCFs or FVCls registered with SEBI for a period of at least one year as on the date of filing draft prospectus with SEBI, and (b) the shares issued to SEBI registered VCFs/FVCls upon conversion of convertible instruments during the period of one year prior to the date of filing draft prospectus with SEBI provided that the period of holding such convertible instruments as fully paid-up, together with the period of holding shares resulting from conversion by the VCFs and FVCls is at least one year as on the date of filing the draft prospectus with SEBI.
- In order to regulate pre-issue publicity by companies which are planning to make an issue of securities, SEBI amended the Disclosure and Investor Protection

Guidelines to introduce "Restrictions on Pre-issue Publicity" from the time the issuer company's Board approves the issue till the actual allotment of shares of the issue. The restrictions, *inter alia,* require an issuer company to ensure that its publicity is consistent with its past practices, does not contain projections or estimates or any information extraneous to the offer document filed with SEBI.

## SECONDARY MARKET

The secondary market for Government securities provides a platform for original investors to trade their holdings before maturity.

As a result of a series of structural and institutional reforms, a deep, wide and vibrant gilt market has emerged. The secondary market turnover of Government securities in India has been rising steadily, reflecting increased liquidity in the market and increased trading activity by market participants. Over the 11-year period ended March 2007, turnover increased 18-fold. This sharp increase in turnover, particularly in the last 2 to 3 years, in part, was due to a sustained rally in the Government securities market.

The major objective of reforms in the Government securities market was to impart liquidity and depth to the market by broadening the investor base and by ensuring market-clearing interest rate mechanism. Keeping this in view, a number of reform measures were initiated in this segment which had a positive impact on both the primary and the secondary markets. (Box 2).

### MEASURES UNDERTAKEN IN THE AREA OF SECONDARY MARKET — BOX : 2

- In continuation of the comprehensive risk management system put in place since May 13, 2005 in T+1 rolling settlement scenario for the cash market, the stock exchanges were advised to update the applicable Value at Risk (VaR) margin at least five times in a day by taking the closing price of the previous day at the start of trading and the prices at 11:00 a.m., 12:30 p.m., 2:00 p.m. and at the end of the trading session. This has been done to align the risk management framework across the cash and derivative markets.
- In order to strengthen the 'Know Your Client' norms and to have sound audit trail of the transactions in the securities market, PAN has been made mandatory with effect from January 1, 2007 for operating a Beneficiary Owner account and for trading in the cash segment similar to transactions in the futures and options segment of the stock exchanges.
- In order to implement the Union Budget proposal on creation of a unified platform for trading of corporate bonds, SEBI stipulated that the BSE Limited would set up and maintain the corporate bond reporting platform. The reporting shall be made for all trades in listed debt securities issued by all institutions such as banks, public sector undertakings, municipal corporations, corporate bodies and companies. Also, SEBI and RBI have set up an internal Working Group to implement the Budget 2006-07 announcement of creating a single, unified exchange-traded market for corporate bonds.
- In line with the Government of India's policy on foreign investments in infrastructure companies in the Indian securities market, the limits for foreign investment in stock

exchanges, depositories and clearing corporations, have been specified as follows: (a) Foreign investment up to 49 per cent will be allowed in these companies with a separate Foreign Direct Investment (FDI) cap of 26 per cent and cap of 23 per cent on FII investment; (b) FDI will be allowed with specific prior approval of FIPB; (c) FII will be allowed only through purchases in the secondary market; (d) FII shall not seek and will not get representation on the Board of Directors; and (e) No foreign investor, including persons acting in concert, will hold more than 5 per cent of the equity in these companies.

- The application process of FII investment was simplified and new categories of investment (insurance and re-insurance companies, foreign central banks, investment managers, international organizations) were included under FII.
- GoI raised the cumulative debt investment limits from US$1.75 billion to US$2 billion and US$0.5 billion to US$1.5 billion for FII/sub-account investments in Government securities and corporate debt, respectively. RBI, in its mid-term review of monetary policy, further enhanced the limit of FII investment on Central and State Government Securities to US$2.6 billion by December 31, 2006 and further to US$3.2 billion by March 31, 2007.
- Initial Issue Expenses and Dividend Distribution Procedure for Mutual Funds were rationalised.
- In compliance with the proposal made in the Budget 2005-06, Mutual Funds were permitted to introduce Gold Exchange Traded Funds.
- Pursuant to the Union Budget 2006-07, the aggregate ceiling for the mutual fund industry to invest in ADRs/GDRs issued by Indian companies, equity of overseas companies listed on recognised stock exchanges overseas and rated debt securities was raised from US$1 billion to US$3 billion.
- In the Government securities market, the RBI ceased to participate in primary issues of Central Government securities from April 1, 2006 in line with the provisions of FRBM Act. Intra-day short sale in Government securities was also permitted with effect from February 28, 2006. 'When Issued' transactions in Government securities have been allowed with effect from August 1, 2006.
- Demutualisation of BSE, the oldest stock exchange in Asia, is well under way in accordance with the provisions of SEBI scheme for demutualisation. The exchange ceased to be an Association of Persons and became a company under the Companies Act in August 2005. A public issue in the first half of 2007 will ensure that at least 51 per cent of equity is held by public other than trading members. The change in the ownership structure is in keeping with the evolution of BSE as a modern, professionally managed, transparent, competitive and efficient stock exchange.
- Foreign institutional investors have been allowed to invest in security receipts.
- The report submitted by the Committee on Fuller Capital Account Convertibility (Chairman, Shri S.S.Tarapore) while considering fuller capital account convertibility, incidentally observed that though the overall regime had undergone a significant degree of liberalisation, in practice, some regulations relating to an earlier period of tight controls continued to remain, giving rise to a disconnect between the regulatory intent and the procedure in use. As a follow-up action of the Committee's recommendations, a RBI task force has been set up to identify the anomalies in the present regulatory framework for current and capital accounts and that rectification should be undertaken within a period of three months.

The turnover in the secondary market for Government securities manifested asymmetric response to the interest rate cycle, i.e., the market turned liquid and active during downward movement in interest rates but turned lacklustre when interest rates rise, as a result. The turnover as percentage of GDP which had increased sharply between 2001-02 and 2004-05 when interest rates softened declined sharply thereafter when interest rates hardened.

**Table 1**

**Secondary Market Transactions in Central Government Securities**

*(Amount in ₹ crore)*

| Year | Outright | Repo | Total | Col.4 as per cent of GDP | Yield* (in per cent) |
|---|---|---|---|---|---|
| 1 | 2 | 3 | 4 | 5 | 6 |
| 1999-2000 | 4,56,493 | 82,739 | 5,39,232 | 27.6 | 11.70 |
| 2000-01 | 5,72,145 | 1,25,976 | 6,98,121 | 33.2 | 10.95 |
| 2001-02 | 12,11,941 | 3,61,932 | 15,73,873 | 69.0 | 9.44 |
| 2002-03 | 13,78,160 | 5,63,515 | 19,41,675 | 79.0 | 7.34 |
| 2003-04 | 16,83,711 | 9,55,533 | 26,39,244 | 95.4 | 5.71 |
| 2004-05 | 11,60,632 | 15,62,990 | 27,23,622 | 87.3 | 6.11 |
| 2005-06 | 8,81,632 | 16,98,770 | 25,80,401 | 72.3 | 7.34 |
| 2006-07 | 3,34,901 | 11,31,461 | 14,66,362 | 35.5 | 7.89 |
| 2007-08 (Apr-Oct) | 7,23,717 | 19,38,492 | 26,62,209 | 57.5 | 8.19 |

* : Weighted average yield on Central Government primary securities.

**Note:** The figures relate to Central Government securities excluding T-Bills.

***Source:*** Trend and progress 2006-07.

The investor preference for short-term securities and prevailing macroeconomic conditions and consequent issuance of relatively short-term securities prevented the emergence of yield curve over a longer horizon during the 1990s. With the moderation in inflationary conditions, the government increased the maturity pattern of primary issuances. As a result, the yield curve for Government securities has emerged for a horizon of 30 years since 2002-03. The response of short-term rates to changes in the policy rates has been quicker and more pronounced than long-term rates. Reflecting the ripple impact of policy changes.

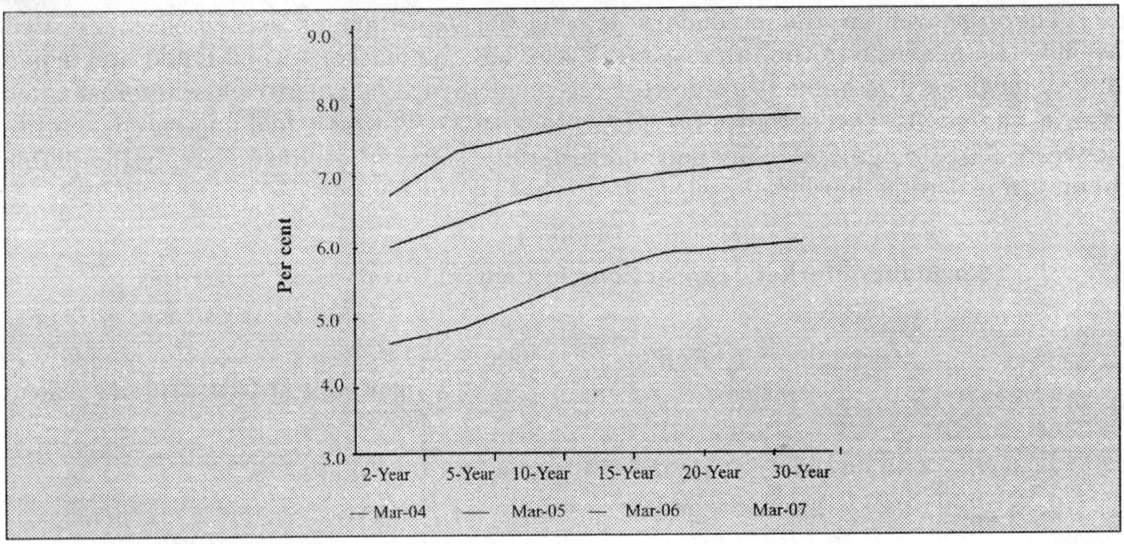


**Fig. 2 : Yield Curves for Government Securities**

## RESERVE BANK AND THE GOVERNMENT SECURITIES MARKET – LEGAL FRAMEWORK

Reserve Bank's operations in the Government securities market are governed by Sections 20, 21 and 21A of the Reserve Bank of India Act, 1934. Under these provisions, the Reserve Bank is entrusted with the function of management of public debt and issue of new loans of the Union Government and the State Governments. The legal framework for Reserve Bank's conduct of open market operations is provided under Section 17(8) of the Reserve Bank of India Act, 1934 under which the reserve bank is authorised to purchase and sell securities of the Union Government or a State Government of any maturity and the security of a local authority specified by the Central Government on the recommendations of the Central Board of the Reserve Bank. Central Government securities are used by the Reserve Bank for its open market operations and liquidity adjustment facility (LAF). Effective April 3, 2007, the State Development Loans were also permitted as eligible securities for LAF operations. The new Chapter III-D of the Reserve Bank of India (Amendment) Act, 2006 has empowered the Reserve Bank to determine policy relating to interest rates products and regulate the agencies dealing *inter alia,* in securities.

The Reserve Bank derives its regulatory power over the Government securities market from Section 16 of the Securities Contract (Regulation) Act (SCRA), 1956, amended in March 2000, under which the government has delegated the powers exercisable by it to the Reserve Bank. The Reserve Bank, is thus, authorized to regulate dealings in Government securities, money market securities, gold related securities and securities derived from these securities as also ready forward contracts in debt securities.

The Government Securities Act, which seeks to replace the Public Debt Act, 1944, was passed in August, 2006. This Act envisages the consolidation and amendment of the law relating to issue and management of Government securities by the Reserve Bank.

The Act includes the provisions of the erstwhile Public Debt Act relating to issuance of new loans, payment of half-yearly interest; retirement of rupee loans, and all matters pertaining to debt certificates and registration of debt holdings,. Besides, the new Act gives flexibility for holding Government securities in depositories, while at the same time specifically excluding Government securities from the purview of the Depositories Act, 1996. The Act enables lien marking and pledging of securities for raising loans against Government securities, recognizes electronic form of record maintenance, enlarges dematerialization facility through Bond Ledger Account and liberalises norms relating to nomination and legal representation. The Act also provides the Reserve Bank with substantive powers to design and introduce an instrument of transfer suited to the computer environment. It also allows the Reserve Bank to issue duplicate securities, new securities on conversion, consolidate with others like Government securities, sub-divide the securities and renew, strip (separately for interest and principal) or reconstitute the securities. The Act, however, is yet to come into force, pending notification of Rules under it.

## MANDATED INVESTMENTS IN GOVERNMENT SECURITIES

Banks are the largest investors in Government securities. In terms of the SLR provisions of the Banking Regulation Act, 1949, banks are required to maintain a minimum of 25 per cent of their Net Demand and Time Liabilities (NDTL) in liquid assets such as cash, gold and unencumbered Government securities or other approved securities as Statutory Liquidity Ratio (SLR). The minimum SLR stipulation for scheduled urban co-operative banks (UCBs) is the same as for scheduled commercial banks (SCBs) from April 1, 2003. However, for non-scheduled (UCBs), the minimum SLR requirement is 15 per cent for banks with NDTL of over ₹ 25 crore and 10 per cent for the remaining non-scheduled UCBs. The minimum SLR stipulation for regional rural banks (RRBs) is the same as for SCBs. From April 1, 2003 the coverage under the SLR has also been made akin to SCBs. All deposits with sponsor banks, which were earlier considered as part of the SLR, were to be converted into approved securities on maturity in order to be reckoned for the SLR purpose. Recently, the Banking Regulation Amendments Act, 2007 has removed the floor limit of 25 per cent for SLR for scheduled banks.

The second largest category of investors in the Government securities market is the insurance companies. According to the stipulations of the Insurance Regulation and Development Authority of India (IRDA), all companies carrying out the business of life insurance should invest a minimum of 25 per cent of their controlled funds in Government securities. Similarly, companies carrying on general insurance business are required to invest 30 per cent of their total assets in Government securities and other guaranteed securities, of which not less than 20 per cent should be in Central Government securities. For pension and general annuity business, the IRDA stipulates that 20 per cent of their assets should be invested in Government securities.

The non-government provident funds, superannuation funds and gratuity funds are required by the Central Government from January 24, 2005 to invest 40 per cent of their incremental accretions in Central and State Government securities and Exchange Board of India (SEBI) and any other negotiable securities fully and unconditionally guaranteed by the Central/State Governments. The exposure of a trust to any individual gilt fund, however, should not exceed five per cent of its total portfolio at any point of time.

Non-banking financial companies (NBFCs) accepting public deposits are required to maintain 15 per cent of such outstanding deposits in liquid assets, of which not less than 10 per cent should be maintained in approved securities, including Government securities and government guaranteed bonds. Investment in Government securities should be in dematerialized form which can be maintained in Constituents Subsidiary General Ledger (CSGL) Account of a SCB/Stock Holding Corporation of India Limited (SHCIL). In order to increase the security and liquidity of their deposits, residuary non-banking companies (RNBCs), are required to invest not less than 95 per cent of their aggregate liability to depositors (ALD) as outstanding on December 31, 2005 and entire incremental deposits over this level in directed investments, which include Government securities, rated and listed securities and debt-oriented mutual funds. From April 1, 2007, the entire ALD is required to be invested in directed investments only.

## NEW INNOVATIONS

The Government securities markets have gained importance in most countries in the overall financial system in recent years. Initiatives have been taken to make them more vibrant and active by improving liquidity and depth; enhancing transparency of primary issuances; widening investor base; fine-tuning auction procedures; benchmarking and consolidating across key maturities; developing new instruments; and putting in place appropriate safeguards and sound trading and settlement infrastructure. Furthermore, managers of public debt across countries are paying greater attention to minimising the cost of borrowings in the medium to long-term, while striking a balance between the cost and the risks in the short run.

The Government securities market in India has evolved over the years. Several measures have been initiated since the early 1990s to develop a deep and liquid Government securities market for reducing the cost of government market borrowings, providing appropriate benchmarks for pricing other financial instruments and conducting monetary policy in a flexible manner. While significant progress has been made in this direction, the evolving economic conditions and the move towards fuller capital account convertibility necessitate further fine-tuning of the operating framework so as to ensure smooth debt management operations.

The switchover to auction based system of issuance of Government securities in the early 1990s was a major step towards development of the Government securities market. The investor base has become more voluntary and diversified with the participation by non-banking entities. Taking into account market preferences, new instruments with innovative features have been introduced from time-to-time. Technological developments have enabled the introduction of screen-based anonymous trading and reporting platform. This has facilitated dissemination of trading with a minimum time lag, besides enabling electronic bidding in primary auctions and facilitating efficient order matching. Furthermore, the operationalisation of the CCIL has ensured guaranteed settlement of trades and has, therefore, imparted considerable stability to the Government securities market. The strategy of consolidation of Government securities mainly through re-issuances has resulted in critical mass in key maturities, facilitating the emergence of market benchmarks. The operation of a system of market intermediaries in the form of PDs has facilitated the Reserve Bank's smooth withdrawal from the primary market from April 1, 2006 as provided in the FRBM Act. *(Box 3)*

**CASE STUDY — THE CLEARING CORPORATION OF INDIA LTD., (CCIL) | BOX : 3**

India embarked on an important innovation, by world standards, when the idea of *novation* at the clearning corporation was applied to trades on the OTC market. Traditionally, there was a divide around the world between exchange ecosystems — that had transparent trading coupled with risk management at the clearing corporation as opposed to the OTC market which had neither.

In India, it was felt that even if the problem of transparency in trading could not be addressed, it was possible to make progress by introducing risk management at the clearing corporation. The clearing corporation would interpose itself into transactions, becoming the legal counterparty to both sides of the trade, and thus eliminate counterparty credit risk.

As argued above, a key feature of a sound financial sector is having a framework supportive of exit by firms. A clearing corporation is the institutional mechanism through which the externalities of firm failure are controlled. Even if a firm fails, counterparties on the OTC market are not affected by that failure because the clearing corporation is the counterparty. The introduction of a clearing corporation into the system makes it possible to lower entry barriers, by bringing in firms into the OTC market that have weak credit. It also makes it possible to have financial sector policy framework where more firm failure and exit of weak firms takes place in a smooth manner.

These ideas led to the creation of the Clearing Corporation of India Ltd., (CCIL). CCIL has undoubtedly been a valuable institution which has given a more modern, more stable financial system. However, the policy framework in which CCIL has operated has flaws on competition policy at two levels:

**(1) Competitive conditions on the bond market and currency market**

The *raison d'etre* of a clearing corporation is to lower entry barriers. Once the clearing corporation handles firm failure, there are no difficulties in opening up entry to a large number of firms that might otherwise be considered weak credits. However, even though CCIL was created, bond market participation and currecny market participation has remained restricted to the small club of financial firms that existed before CCIL. The key economic benefit of building a clearing corporation — lowered entry barriers — has not been obtained.

**(2) Competitive conditions for critical securities industry infrastructure**

CCIL has monopoly status in performing clearing services for fixed income and currency markets. It is the only clearing corporation with access to clearing in central bank funds and connectivity into RBI settlement systems. The other clearing corporation in India — the National Securities Clearing Corporation Ltd., (NSSCL) — is prohibited from performing these functions. This reflects the segmentation of the Indian securities industry into three parts, regulated by RBI, FMC and SEBI. Such segmentation, and the consequent loss of competition, is suboptimal. Particularly, when dealing with the OTC market, it is easy to have competition between the two clearing corporation.

In a competitive policy framework, every palyer on the OTC market for currencies of fixed income would be free to choose between multiple clearing corporations based on price and services. Using cross-margining arrangements between clearing corporations, it would be possible to obtain seamless functioning when the two counterparties to a trade are customers of two different clearing corporations. Such a competitive framework would drive both NSCCL and CCIL to higher levels of cost efficiency, quality of service and customer responsiveness, which would improve India's ability to export financial services.

The CCIL case is thus an ironic blend of intellectual success and opportunity lost. On one hand, India's ability to conceive of an institution like CCIL, and swiftly translate the broad idea into a smoothly functioning institution, has been the envy of the world. But at the same time, the larger policy problems of segmentation and faulty competition policy have induced a lost opportunity, whereby India has benefited less from the creation of CCIL than could have been the case.

## THE ROLE OF THE RESERVE BANK

The Reserve Bank has actively pursued the development of the Government securities market since the early 1990s for a variety of reasons. First, with the Reserve Bank acting as the debt manager to the government, a well-developed and liquid Government securities market is essential to ensure the smooth passage of government's market borrowings to finance its deficit. Second, the development of the Government securities market is also necessary to facilitate the emergence of a risk-free rupee yield curve to serve as a benchmark for pricing other debt instruments. Finally, the Government securities market plays a key role in the effective transmission of monetary policy impulses in a deregulated environment.

In order to foster the development of the Government securities market, primacy was accorded to migrate from a regime of administered interest rates to a market-oriented system. Accordingly, in the early 1990s the Reserve Bank initiated several measures. First, it introduced the auction system for issuance of Government securities. While initially only yield based multiple price auctions were conducted, uniform price based auctions were also employed during uncertain market conditions and while issuing new instruments. Second, as the captive investor base was viewed as constraining the development of the market, the statutory prescription for banks investment in government and other approved securities was scaled down from the peak level in February 1992 to the statutory minimum level of 25 per cent by April 1997. As a result, the focus shifted towards the widening of the investor base. A network of intermediaries in the form of primary dealers was developed for this purpose. Retail participation has been promoted in the primary market (through a system of non-competitive bidding in the auctions) as well as in the secondary market (by allowing retail trading in stock exchanges). Simultaneously, the Reserve Bank also introduced new instruments with innovative features to cater to diverse market preferences, although the success in this regard has been limited.

Third, with the discontinuance of the process of unconstrained recourse by the government from the Reserve Bank through automatic monetization of deficit and conversion of non-marketable securities to marketable securities, the Reserve Bank gained more operational freedom. Fourth, in an effort to increase liquidity, the Reserve Bank has since the late 1990s, pursued a strategy of passive consolidation of debt by raising progressively higher share of market borrowings through re-issuances. This has resulted in critical mass in key maturities, and is facilitating the emergence of market benchmarks. Finally, the Reserve Bank is also undertaking measures to strengthen the technological infrastructure for trading and settlement. A screen-based anonymous trading and reporting platform has been introduced in the form of NDS-OM, which enables electronic bidding in primary auctions and disseminates trading information with a minimum time lag. Furthermore, with the setting up of CCIL, an efficient settlement mechanism has also been institutionalized, which has imparted considerable stability to the Government securities market.

## NEW CHALLENGES

The Government securities market has witnessed significant transformation across countries over the years in terms of system of issuance, instruments, investors, and trading and settlement infrastructure. It has grown internationally in tune with the financing requirements of governments. The fiscal discipline exercised by many countries in recent years has restricted the size of the market. Accordingly, countries have focussed on improving trading liquidity of the market through various measures. Many countries in the recent past have pursued a strategy of managing the cost of government borrowing in the medium to long-term so as to reduce the rollover risk and other market risks in the debt stock, although this may entail higher debt service costs in the short run. Historically, in most countries, the central banks as managers of public debt have played a key role in developing the Government securities markets.

The evolving economic conditions and move towards fuller capital account convertibility, however, necessitated further fine-tuning of the operating framework so as to ensure smooth debt management operations. There are certain issues which need to be addressed for making the Government securities market more vibrant and also to meet the debt management objectives in an efficient manner. In the absence of instruments to allow market participants to take a forward looking view on interest rates, turnover in the secondary market has been observed to rise during the falling interest rate cycle, but decline during the rising interest rate cycle. In this context, introduction of intra-day 'short selling', followed by the permission for short selling up to five trading days are steps in the right direction. Liquidity could be improved further through active consolidation of existing securities, phased increase in marked-to-market portfolio of banks and early introduction of STRIPS. In view of the restriction on the Reserve Bank's subscription to Central Government securities in the primary market under the FRBM Act, it is crucial to diversify the investor base further. The investor base also needs to be widened in view of the possibility of reduction in the captive investor base resulting from any scaling down of the SLR from the present level; the floor of SLR has been removed by the Banking Regulation (Amendment) Act, 2007 which is deemed to have come into force on January 23, 2007. Any decision in this regard will of course depend on overall macroeconomic and monetary conditions. State Government securities are relatively illiquid, which affects the cost of borrowing for the State Government. Some of the measures taken for improving liquidity of Central Government securities may need to be considered for State Government securities as well.

## REFORM MEASURES

The Reserve Bank initiated various reform measures to strengthen the Government securities market. With the aligning of coupons with the market interest rate, the gilt-edged market has gradually widened with the participation of several non-bank players. Presently apart from banks and insurance companies investor base includes the private corporate sector, mutual funds, finance companies as also individuals. Introduction of order Matching segment on NOS (NOS-OM) gave a further impetus to the development of the Government securities market. Currently, 134 members operate on NOS-OM. In order to increase the number of participants in NDS-OM, access has been allowed to insurance companies, mutual funds and pension and provident funds. Further, extending indirect access to all "gilt accountholders" to NOS-OM through constituent subsidiary general ledger (CSGL) option is under active consideration.

There is now a wide range of securities available to market participants for investment and hedging of financial risk. These include 364-day, 182-day and 91-day Treasury bills through auctions. In the long-term segment the *vanilla* or the fixed coupon bonds are the most commonly used instruments, although floating rate bonds (FRBs) were introduced in September 1995 but not followed up until 2002 due to lack of interest, from market participants. The Reserve Bank is also actively pursuing the creation and development of the Separate Trading of Registered Interest and Principal of Securities (STRIPS) market. The enabling legal provisions for STRIPS will come into effect with the finalization of regulations relating to the Government Securities Act, 2006 and STRIPS can then be introduced once the appropriate system development is complete.

- New auction-based instruments were introduced with varying maturities such as 364-day, 182-day, 91-day and 14-day Treasury bills and the zero coupon bond. The auction system was also introduced for Government of India dated securities. An innovative features of 'part payment' was added to the auction of Government of India dated securities.
- In the long-term segment, Floating Rate Bonds (FRBs) benchmarked to the 364-day Treasury bill yields and a 10-year loan with embedded call and put options exercisable on or after 5 years from the date of issue were introduced.
- A system of Primary Dealers (PDs) was made operational in March 1996.
- Foreign Institutional Investors (FIIs) were allowed to set up 100 per cent debt funds to invest in Government (Central and State) dated securities in both primary and secondary markets.
- The system of automatic magnetization of budget deficit through *ad hoc* Treasury bills which hampered the development of the market was phased out over a period of three years from 1993-94 to 1996-97 and was replied by the system of Ways and Means Advances (WMA) with effect from April 1, 1997.
- The Delivery-versus-Payment System (DvP) was introduced in 1995 for the settlement of transactions in Government securities, A screen-based trade reporting system with the use 01 VSAT communication network complemented

by a centralized Subsidiary General Ledger (SGL) accounting system was put in place.

- Since timely flow of information is a critical factor in evolving the efficient price discovery mechanism, improvements were brought in transparency of operations and data dissemination.
- Retail trading in Government securities at select stock exchanges commenced in January 2003.

The switchover to auction based system of issuance of Government securities in the early 1990s was a major step towards the development of the Government securities market. The investor base has become more voluntary and diversified with the participation by non-banking entities such as insurance companies, mutual funds, co-operative banks and other non-banking financial companies. The development of primary dealer system is an important step in the evolution of the Government securities market. Taking into account market preferences, new instruments with innovative features have been introduced which include zero coupon bonds and floating rate bonds. Technological developments have enabled the introduction of screen-based anonymous trading and reporting platform – NOS-OM. Furthermore, the operationalisation of the CCIL has ensured guaranteed settlement of trades and has, therefore, imparted considerable stability to the Government securities market. The strategy of consolidation of Government securities mainly through re-issuances has resulted in critical mass in key maturities, facilitating the emergence of market benchmarks.

The FRBM Act prohibits the Reserve Bank from participating in the primary auctions of Government securities from April 1, 2006. Although this is a positive development, it could have some adverse impact on the market in the short-run. The Reserve Bank, therefore, took several structural and developmental measures for the Government securities market. These included: (i) phased introduction of short sale to increase turnover and improve liquidity in the secondary market; (ii) phased introduction of trading in 'When Issued' market in respect of Central Government dated securities for better price discovery in the primary market; (iii) revised scheme for underwriting of Central Government securities auctions requiring 100 per cent underwriting by PDs accompanied by performance based liquidity support to PDs; (iv) allowing standalone PDs to diversify their business to mitigate risk arising from concentration of business in one activity; and (v) allowing banks to conduct PD business departmentally by merging their respective PD subsidiaries that would serve to mitigate the business risks of stand-alone PDs. These measures would make the Government securities market more vibrant and thereby help in strengthening financial stability.

DFHI is allowed to participate in the Government securities market. And, the Securities Trading Corporation of India (STCI), commenced its operation in June 1994. Further, a system of satellite dealers (SDs), as a second tier of dealer system in trading and distribution from December, 1996 to broaden the market and impart momentum to the secondary market activity. However, SD system was discontinued from May 31, 2002, as it did not yield the desired results.

## CONCLUSION

The Government securities market in India has evolved and gained importance over the years. Several measures have been initiated since the early 1990s to develop a deep and liquid Government securities market for reducing the cost of government market borrowings, providing appropriate benchmarks for pricing other financial instruments and conducting monetary policy in a flexible manner.

The switchover to auction based system of issuance of Government securities technological developments have facilitated the growth of the market. Furthermore, the operationalisation of the Clearing Corporation of India Limited (CCIL) has ensured guaranteed settlement of trades and imparted considerable stability to the Government securities market.

The functioning of the Government securities market since the mid-1990s indicates consistent increase in the size of the market in tandem with the growth in market borrowings of both the Central and the State Governments. The weighted average cost of market borrowings declined consistently up to 2003-04, which enabled elongation of weighted average maturity of primary issuances. The government has been raising progressively higher share of market borrowings through re-issuances under the strategy of passive consolidation of debt reflecting the effectiveness of various measures initiated to develop the market, turnover in the secondary market has increased manifold over the years, before declining in 2004-05 and 2005-06. The holding pattern of government debt shows some increase in the relative share of non-banks, reflecting a progressive diversification of the investor base. The Government securities market has increasingly displayed co-movements with the money market and has also responded to the changes in international interest rate from time-to-time.

With the implementation of the Fiscal Responsibility and Budget Management (FRBM) Act, 2003, Government securities market has assumed vital importance. The Government securities Act, 2006 empowered the Reserve Bank to continue with efforts to broaden and deepen the market in terms of participants, instruments and processes.

Notwithstanding the substantial progress in the Government securities market, certain issues need to be addressed for its further development. Under the FRBM regime, the Reserve Bank cannot participate in the primary market. PDs, as underwriters, are, therefore, required to absorb the unsubscribed securities in the auctions. Any consequent escalation in the cost of government borrowing can be mitigated by greater diversification of the investor base. It also needs to be widened to counter the possible reduction in the captive investor base. Increase in trading volumes in the secondary market would largely hinge on the improvement in trading liquidity in key maturities across the yield curve. This would require active consolidation of Government securities, in addition to the present system of passive consolidation. The development of critical mass in the key securities and the matching of coupon payment dates would also pave the way for the introduction of the system for separate trading for registered interest and principal of securities (STRIPS). Illiquidity in State Government securities affects the cost of borrowing for the State Governments. Therefore, there is a need to extend measures taken for enhancing liquidity in Central Government securities to State Government securities as well.

## ANNEXURE I

### REVISED GUIDELINE FOR PRIMARY DEALERS

The Reserve Bank no longer participates in primary issues of Government securities from April 1, 2006, in accordance with the provisions of FRBM Act, 2003. An Internal Technical Group on Central Government securities market, which was constituted in December 2004 to examine the implications of the Reserve Bank's withdrawal from the primary market on its debt management function and to address the emerging needs, submitted its report in July 2005. In line with the recommendations of the group and after discussions with the market participants, a revised scheme of underwriting commitment for PDs was formulated in April 2006, which replaced the earlier requirements of bidding commitment and voluntary underwriting by PDs.

As per the revised scheme, the underwriting commitment is divided into two parts, *viz.*: *(i)* minimum underwriting commitment (MUC), and *(ii)* additional competitive underwriting (ACU). The MUC of each PD is computed to ensure that at least 50 per cent of each issue is mandatory covered by the aggregate amount of MUC of PDs. The MUC is uniform for all PDs, irrespective of their capital or balance sheet size. Given that there are 17 PDs at present, each PD is required to underwrite about 3 percent of the notified amount of each auction as MUC. The remaining portion of the notified amount is open to competitive underwriting through underwriting auctions. Each PD is required to bid in the ACU for a minimum of 3.0 per cent and not more that 30 per cent of the notified amount. All successful bidders in the ACU get commission as per the auction rules.

Besides the changes in underwriting for PDs, the permitted structure of PD business has been expanded to include banks, subject to certain minimum eligibility criteria. Banks which do not have a partly or wholly-owned subsidiary, are eligible to apply for the PD licence if they fulfil the following criteria: *(a)* minimum net owned funds (NOF) of ₹ 1,000 crore; *(b)* minimum CRAR of nine percent; and *(c)* net NPAs of less than three per cent and a profit making record for the last three years. Indian banks and foreign banks in India which are undertaking PD business through partly/wholly-owned subsidiaries and through group companies, respectively, are also allowed to undertake PD business departmentally by merging/taking over PD business from their subsidiaries/group companies, subject to fulfilling the above mentioned criteria. The bank-PDs are subject to all obligations applicable to standalone PDs and as may be prescribed from time-to-time. Bank-PDs are required to maintain separate books of accounts for transactions relating to PD business (distinct from the normal banking business) with necessary audit trails. They are required to ensure that, at any point of time, there is a minimum balance of ₹ 100 crore of Government securities earmarked for PD business. Bank-PDs are also required to adhere to the following norms:

- No separate capital adequacy is prescribed for PD business, and the capital adequacy requirement for a bank will also apply to its PD business.
- The Government dated securities and Treasury bills under PD business are reckoned for the SLR purpose.
- The investment valuation guidelines as applicable to banks with regard to 'held for trading' portfolio are also applicable to the portfolio of Government dated securities and Treasury bills earmarked for PD business.
- The Reserve Bank's instructions to PDs are also applicable to bank-PDs to the extent applicable.

Following the revised scheme of underwriting commitment and the discontinuance of bidding commitment, the methodology for calculating limits for PDs under the Reserve

Bank's Liquidity Support Scheme has also been revised. Of the total liquidity support, 50 per cent of the amount is divided equally among all the standalone PDs. The remaining half is divided amongst the PDs, based on their performance in the primary and the secondary markets, giving due weightage to their turnover in Treasury bills and dated Government securities. The PD-wise quantum of liquidity support is revised every half-year (April-September and October-March) based on the market performance of PDs in the preceding six months.

## ANNEXURE II

### REFORMS IN THE GOVERNMENT SECURITIES MARKET

| Year | Reform Initiated | Objective | Outcome |
|---|---|---|---|
| 1 | 2 | 3 | 4 |
| June 1992 | Introduction of auction method for issue of Central Government securities. | To make yields on Government securities market determined. | Price discovery has improved over a period of time. |
| January 1994 | Zero Coupon Bond was issued for the first time. Securities Trading Corporation of India (STCI) commenced operations. | To add new instruments and intermediaries. | STCI and other PDs have become important intermediaries in the Government securities market. |
| August 1994 | Agreement between the Reserve Bank and Government of India on limiting issue of *ad hoc* Treasury bills. | To do away with automatic monetization. | Cash management of government has improved. |
| March 1995 | Primary Dealer system introduced. | To strengthen the market intermediation and support primary issue. | PD system has evolved as an important segment of Government securities market. |
| July 1995 | Delivery *versus* Payment (DvP) system in Government securities was introduced. | To reduce settlement risk. | Transition from DvP-I method (funds and securities settlement on gross basis) to DvP-III method (funds and securities settlement on net basis) has been made. |
| September 1995 | Floating Rate Bonds (FRBs) introduced. | To add more instruments. | FRBs were discontinued after the first issuance due to lack of market enthusiasm. FRBs were reintroduced in November 2001 but were again discountinued in October 2004. |

| 1 | 2 | 3 | 4 |
|---|---|---|---|
| January 1997 | Technical Advisory Committee (TAC) was constituted. | To advise Reserve Bank on developing Government securities, money and forex markets. | Plays a pivotal role in implementing the Reserve Bank's reform agenda based on a consultative approach. |
| March 1997 | Introduction WMA system for Centre. | Discontinuation of automatic monetization. | Transparency and pricing has improved. Has imparted greater autonomy in monetary policy-making. |
| April 1997 | FIMMDA was established. | Introduction of self-regulation and development of market practices and ethics. | Market practices have improved. |
| July 1997 | Foreign Institutional Investors (FIIs) were permitted to invest in Government securities. | To broaden the market. | FIIs have become important players in the market, particularly in the Treasury bill segment. |
| December 1997 | Capital Indexed Bonds were issued. | To help investors hedge inflation risk. | Efforts are being made to revitalize this product. |
| April 2000 | Sale of securities allotted in primary issues on the same day. | To improve secondary market. | This has also helped in managing the overnight risk. |
| February 2002 | Clearing Corporation of India Limited (CCIL) was established. | To act as a clearing agency for transactions in Government securities. | Stability in market has improved, greatly mitigating the settlement risk. |
| June 2002 | PDs were brought under the jurisdiction of Board for Financial Supervision (BFS). | For integrated supervision of market. | The position is being reported periodically to BFS. |
| October 2002 | Trade data of NDS made available on Reserve Bank website. | To improve transparency. | The measure is helping the small investors as well. |
| January 2003 | Retail trading of Government securities permitted on stock exchanges. | To facilitate easier access and wider participation. | This has not taken off very well. Efforts are being made to improve the position. |
| February 2003 | Regulated constituents permitted participation in repo markets. | To widen the market. | Activity in the repo market has improved. |
| June 2003 | Interest Rate Futures were introduced. | To facilitate hedging of interest rate risk. | These futures have not taken off. |
| July 2003 | Government debt buy-back scheme was implemented. | To reduce interest burden of government and help banks offload illiquid securities. | Other measures for active consolidation being considered. |

| 1 | 2 | 3 | 4 |
|---|---|---|---|
| March 2004 | Introduction of DvP III | To obtain netting efficiency and to enable rollover of repos. | Running successfully. |
| April 2004 | Introduction of RTGS. | To provide real time, online, large value inter-bank payment and settlements. | Running successfully. |
| August 2005 | The Negotiated Dealing System-Order Matching (NDS-OM), an anonymous order matching system which allows straight-through processing (STP) was established. | To provide the NDS members with a more efficient trading platform. | Over 60 per cent of transactions in Government securities are done through NDS-OM. |
| February 2006 | Intra-day selling permitted. This was later extended to five trading days, effective January 31, 2007. | To improve liquidity in market, particularly in the rising interest rates phase. | Is in a nascent stage of development. |
| August 2006 | Commencement of 'When Issued' trading. | Efficient price discovery and distribution of auctioned stock. | Is in a nascent stage of development. |
| August 2006 | Government Securities Act, 2006 passed by the Parliament. | To facilitate wider participation in Government securities market and create the enabling provisions for issue of Separately Traded Registered. | Awaiting notification of the Rules. |

***Source:*** RBI.

❖❖❖

CHAPTER 15

# INVESTOR'S PROTECTION

## INTRODUCTION

A regime of financial liberalisation makes it imperative to have strong measures for investor protection in order to ensure that the benefits of liberalisation are not largely cornered by some small sections of the society, mainly company promoters and market intermediaries. Without strict regulation, strong cornering tendencies of the above kind will have no check. This was actually witnessed in India a year ago in the virulent form of 'preferential allotments' of shares to promoters and foreign collaborators at heavily discounted prices. Interestingly, this loot went on despite opposition by Indian public financial institutions. Unfortunately, free markets have no self-correcting devices against such abuses.

The Securities and Exchange Board of India (SEBI) is the apex regulatory and development agency of the capital market and stock exchanges in India. In this Chapter, the working of SEBI, its operations and an analysis has been dealt with precisely.

## INTEGRATION AND GROWTH

It was in the 1980s that India witnessed a phenomenal growth and development of the securities market. For the first time it showed a potential not only to mobilise the savings of the household sector, but also to allocate it with some degree of efficiency for industrial development.

Many factors have contributed to this growth. The dilution of the holding of the multinational companies at affordable prices in the latter part of the 1970s had generated considerable interest in the securities market among lay savers — an interest which was carried well into the next decade.

Several companies came in the early part of 1980s and raised large resources from the market especially through debt instruments, which further sustained investor interest. During that phase, India was entering into the period of liberalisation and decontrol which was to accelerate and gather momentum in the 1990s. These are some of the factors which spurred the growth of the market.

The securities market in India came to be firmly integrated with the financial system of the country. The corporate sector was relying on the securities market for meeting their long-term requirement of funds, the securities market competed on equal terms with the development of financial institutions which were the traditional purveyors of long-term capital. The emergence of the securities market was one of the major economic processes of the 1980s.

These changes in the capital structure of the companies gave birth to new intermediaries and institutions in the securities market thereby creating a new awareness and interest in investment opportunities. However, in spite of these developments, its quality continued to lag behind and there was an absence of adequate professionalism and competition among the various players in the market.

In order to sustain the growth of the market and form the growing awareness into a committed and discerning group of investors, it was necessary to remove the trading malpractices and inadequacies prevailing in the market. It was also found to be necessary to provide the investors with an organised and well-regulated marketplace.

## PAST MODELS

To quote J.K. Galbraith, "*recurrent speculative insanity* and the *associated financial deprivation and devastation are, I am persuaded, inherent in the system*". These features of the financial markets create a greater necessity for a regulatory system.

The past models of regulation appear, albeit in hindsight (but no less relevant for that) to have suffered from the following deficiencies:

- Lack of clarity of objectives or tendency to burden the regulatory functions with many objectives.
- The regulatory regimen, instead of 'managing by objectives' tended to control operational details.
- The regulations, while wearing the garb of generally applicable rules, tended to be discretionary in their application.
- Regulatory functions were fragmented and carried out as they were by a multiplicity of government departments.
- The regulation did not work towards maintaining health, efficiency and healthy growth of regulated organisations, but tended to restrict entry and competition.
- The regulators tended to build empires and the cost of regulation became very high in relation to the benefits.
- Finally, the approach to regulation was not dynamic, in the sense it did not allow for modifications in keeping with the technological and market changes.

As seen earlier, the liberalised *milieu* does require regulation, but of a different kind. Many of the regulatory concepts and mechanisms of the past have now been given up or substantially modified not only because they do not fit into the mode of liberalisation, but they have been proved to be inadequate and often counter-productive. The practice of regulation of banking and the capital market have taken an entirely new look. Obviously, the new models have to draw some lessons from the weaknesses of the past. To my mind, these lessons are:

- The regulatory function should have a sharp objective of fostering fair competition and correcting market deficiencies and irregularities with a view to bringing about healthy growth of the sector and the protection of participants.
- The regulatory body should be autonomous and fragmentation of regulating agencies and laws should be avoided.
- While enactments empowering a regulatory body are important, the practices of regulations as well as the organisation of the regulatory body are much more so.
- No amount of regulation can be a substitute for efficient and honest management of the regulated entities and for an internal system of checks and balances. It's important to take a look at the entire gamut of changes that are taking place in the securities market regulation in India against this background.

The need for setting up an independent government agency to regulate and develop the stock and capital market in India was recognised when the Sixth Plan was launched in 1985.

## THE RIGHT OF AN INVESTOR

As a shareholder/debentureholder of a company, an investor enjoys certain rights, which can be briefly stated as follows:

(*i*) To receive the share/debenture certificate(s) on allotment/transfer, as the case may be, in due time. However, after dematerialisation of securities, the investors generally do not hold scrips in physical forms: thus, such an investor has the right to have his Demat account credited.

(*ii*) To receive copies of the abridged Annual Report; the Balance Sheet and the Profit and Loss Account; and the Auditors' Report (this is applicable for only shareholders). A debentureholder has the right to receive a copy of the trust deed on request.

(*iii*) To participate and vote in the Annual General Meeting either through proxies or personally (this is also applicable for only shareholders).

(*iv*) To receive dividends/interests/principals in due time.

(*v*) To receive corporate benefits like rights, bonus, etc., if approved.

(*vi*) To apply to the National Company Law Tribunal (NCLT)[1] to call or direct the Annual General Meeting (this is also applicable only for shareholders).

1. The Company Law Board is now dissolved, and its powers are now mostly vested in National Company Law Tribunal.

(*vii*) To inspect the minutes book of the General Meetings and to receive copies thereof (this is also relevant in respect only of shareholders).

(*viii*) To proceed against the company by way of civil or criminal proceedings.

(*ix*) To apply for the winding-up of the company.

(*x*) To receive the residual proceeds.

Besides the above rights which one enjoys as an individual investor a shareholder has the following rights as a group:

(*i*) To requisition an Extraordinary General Meeting.

(*ii*) To demand a poll on any resolution.

(*iii*) To apply to the NCLT to investigate the affairs of the company.

(*iv*) To apply to the NCLT for relief in cases of oppression and/or mismanagement.

It should be noted that all the above-mentioned rights may not necessarily be absolute. For example, the transfer of a security may be refused by the company as per statutory provisions. In the pre-dematerialisation days, the securities had to be sent along with a valid and stamped transfer deed duly signed by or on behalf of the transferor (seller) and the transferee (buyer). Thus, if the transfer deed were outdated (invalid), torn, mutilated, overwritten, defaced, or if there were mistakes in writing the folio/certificate/distinctive numbers, etc., the transfer might have been refused.

The investor has the right to sell the securities he holds at a price and time of his choice. He can do so personally with another person or through a recognised stock exchange. Similarly, one has the right to buy securities from any one or through a recognised stock exchange at a mutually acceptable price and time. At present, however, almost all transactions are carried out on-screen, and therefore, the chances of not getting the proper price-time priority is eliminated (see trading mechanism discussed in detail in Chapter 3). Moreover, the trading system generates and maintains an audit trail of the orders entered on the system by assigning a unique order number to all the orders. The investor has the right to ask the broker/trading member for his unique order number. Further, as soon as his order is executed, a trade-confirmation slip is generated which displays the trade number, trade time, quantity and price at which his order was executed. The trading member is obliged to give his clients a trade confirmation slip the moment a trade takes place. At the end of the day, the investor should receive a *Contract Note.*

A contract note is a confirmation of trade(s) done on a particular day for and on behalf of a client. A contract note establishes a legally enforceable relationship between the trading member and client in respect of settlement of trades executed in the exchange. These notes are made in duplicate, and the member and client should keep one copy each.

If the deal is routed through a registered sub-broker of a trading member the investor has the right to receive a *purchase/sale note* within 24 hours of the trade being executed. The trading member (TM) with whom the sub-broker is associated will issue the sub-broker back-to-back contract notes giving details of all the transactions done by the sub-broker through the TM's terminal.

The investor should check the following points in the *contract note*:

(*i*) It should be in the prescribed proforma.

(*ii*) Name and address of the TM.

(*iii*) The SEBI registration number of the TM.

(*iv*) Details of trade, *viz.,* order number, trade number, trade time, security name, quantity, rate, brokerage, settlement number, details of other levies.

(*v*) The trade-price has been shown separately from the brokerage charged.

(*vi*) Signature of authorized signatory.

In respect of sales/purchase note, the investors should check the following:

(*i*) It should be in the prescribed proforma.

(*ii*) Name, address and SEBI registration number of the registered sub-broker.

(*iii*) Name, address and SEBI registration number of the relevant trading member.

(*iv*) Details of trade, *viz.,* order number, trade number, trade time, security name, quantity, rate, brokerage, settlement number, details of other levies.

(*v*) The trade price has been shown separately from the brokerage charged.

(*vi*) Signature of the authorised signatory.

As stipulated by SEBI, the maximum brokerage that can be charged is 2.5% of the trade-value. This maximum brokerage is inclusive of the brokerage charged by the sub-broker (sub-brokerage cannot be more than 1.5% of the trade-value).

In addition, the TM can charge:

(*a*) Service tax @5% of the brokerage.

(*b*) Transaction charges levied by the stock exchange.

(*c*) Penalties that arise on behalf of client.

## INVESTORS' GRIEVANCE AND REDRESSAL FORA

There will be occasions when the investors will have a grievance against the company/TM/sub-broker. We present below a schematic representation of the nature of the grievances (which are commonly harboured by an investor) and the appropriate authority with whom such grievance may be taken up.

| Nature of grievances | Can be taken up with |
|---|---|
| In case of any public issue, non-receipt of<br>• Refund order<br>• Interest on delayed refund<br>• Allotment advice<br>• Duplicates for all of the above and revalidations | <br>— SEBI<br>— Dept. of Company Affairs<br>— Stock Exchange<br>— Registrars to the issue |
| In case of a listed security, non-receipt of the certificates after:<br>• Transfer<br>• Transmission | <br><br>— SEBI<br>— DCA |

| | |
|---|---|
| • Conversion<br>• Endorsement<br>• Consolidation<br>• Splitting<br>• Duplicates of securities | — Stock Exchange<br>– do –<br>– do –<br>– do –<br>– do – |
| Regarding listed Debentures, non-receipt of Interest due<br>• Redemption proceeds<br>• Interest on delayed payment | — SEBI<br>— The Debenture Trustees<br>— Stock Exchange |
| Regarding bad delivery of shares | Bad delivery cell of the relevant Stock Exchange |
| Regarding shares or debentures in unlisted companies | Dept. of Company Affairs |
| Deposits in collective investment schemes like plantations, etc. | SEBI |
| Units of Mutual Fund | SEBI |
| Fixed Deposits in Banks and Finance Companies | Reserve Bank of India |
| Fixed Deposits in manufacturing companies | Dept. of Company Affairs |

Investor Information Centres and Grievance Cells have been set up in every recognised stock exchange, which, in addition to the complaints in respect of securities traded/listed with them, take up all other complaints regarding the trades effected in the exchange and the relevant member of the exchange.

As clear from the above table, SEBI, the stock exchanges, Department of Company Affairs, the Debenture Trustees, the RBI — all can have a complaint referred to them. SEBI has prescribed a list of penalties for administrative lapses. They are as follows:

**Penalties prescribed under Securities and Exchange Board of India Act, 1992**

| Section | Default | Maximum Penalty (₹) | Penalties Liable |
|---|---|---|---|
| 15A(*a*) | Failure to furnish any document return or report to SEBI when required under the Act, rules or regulations. | ₹ 1,00,000 per day of default or ₹ 1 crore, whichever is less. | Whoever commits the failure. |
| 15A(*b*) | Failure to file any return or furnish any information, books, etc., under the regulations. | ₹ 1,00,000 per day of default or ₹ 1 crore, whichever is less. | Whoever commits the failure. |
| 15A(*c*) | Failure to maintain books of account or record. | ₹ 1,00,000 per day of default or ₹ 1 crore, whichever is less. | Whoever commits the failure. |
| 15B | Failure by an intermediary to enter into any agreement with his client | ₹ 1,00,000 per day of default or ₹ 1 crore, whichever is less. | This intermediary who is required under the Act, rules or regulations to enter into such agreement but who fails to do so. |

| | | | |
|---|---|---|---|
| 15C | Failure by listed company or an intermediary to redress grievances of the investors. | ₹ 1,00,000 per day of default or ₹ 1 crore, whichever is less. | The listed company or intermediary who is required by the Board to redress the grievances, but who fails to do so. |
| 15D(a) | Failure to obtain from SEBI a certificate of registration for sponsoring or carrying on any collective investment scheme including mutual fund. | ₹ 1,00,000 per day of default or ₹ 1 crore, whichever is less. | Whoever commits the default. |
| 15D(*b*) | Failure to comply with the terms and conditions of registration for collective investment scheme, including mutual fund. | ₹ 1,00,000 per day of default or ₹ 1 crore, whichever is less. | Any registered collective investment scheme, including mutual fund for sponsoring or carrying on any investment scheme committing the default. |
| 15D(*c*) | Failure to make an application for listing of a collective investment scheme as provided for in the concerned regulations. | ₹ 1,00,000 per day of default or ₹ 1 crore, whichever is less. | Any registered collective investment scheme including mutual fund committing the default. |
| 15D(*d*) | Failure to despatch unit certificates to the holders of the units under any collective investment scheme, including mutual fund in he manner provided for in concerned regulations. | ₹ 1,00,000 per day of default or ₹ 1 crore, whichever is less. | Any registered collective investment scheme committing the failure. |
| 15D(*e*) | Failure to refund application money to the investors within the prescribed period. | ₹ 1,00,000 per day of default or ₹ 1 crore, whichever is less. | The company committing the default. |
| 15D(*f*) | Failure to invest money collected in the manner or within the period prescribed by the concerned regulations. | ₹ 1,00,000 per day of default or ₹ 1 crore, whichever is less. | Any registered collective investment scheme, including mutual fund committing the default. |
| 15E | Failure by an asset management company of a mutual fund, to comply with any regulations governing its activities. | ₹ 1,00,000 per day of default or ₹ 1 crore, whichever is less. | The asset management company committing the default. |
| 15F(a) | Failure by a registered stock broker to issue contract notes in the form and manner specified by the stock exchange. | Five times the amount for which the contract note was required to be issued. | The stock broker committing the default. |

| | | | |
|---|---|---|---|
| 15F(*b*) | Failure by registered stock broker to deliver to the investor any security or make payment of the amount due to him. | ₹ 1,00,000 per day of default or ₹ 1 crore, whichever is less. | The stock broker committing the default. |
| 15F(*c*) | Charging by any registered stock broker, brokerage in excess of the rate prescribed by the regulations. | ₹ 1,00,000 or 5 times of the excess brokerage charged, whichever is higher. | The stock broker committing the default. |
| 15G(*i*)* | Dealing by an insider either on his own behalf or on behalf of any other person in securities of a body corporate on any stock exchange on the basis of any unpublished information. | Up to ₹ 25 crore or 3 times the amount of profits made, whichever is higher. | The concerned insider. |
| 15G(*ii*)* | Communicating by an insider, any unpublished price-sensitive information to any person with or without his request except as required in the ordinary course of business or as required by law. | Up to ₹ 25 crore or 3 times the amount of profits made, whichever is higher. | The concerned insider. |
| 15G(*iii*)* | Counselling, by an insider, of any other person to deal in securities of any body corporate on the basis of any unpublished price-sensitive information. | Up to ₹ 25 crore or 3 times the amount of profits made, whichever is higher. | The concerned insider. |
| 15H(*i*)# | Failure to disclosure the aggregate of shareholding in a body corporate before he acquires any shares in the body corporate. | Up to ₹ 25 crore or 3 times the amount of profits made, whichever is higher. | The person who is required under the Act, rules or regulations to make such disclosure. |
| 15H(*ii*)# | Failure to make a public announcement to acquire shares at a minimum price. | Up to ₹ 25 crore or 3 times the amount of profits made, whichever is higher. | The person who is required under the Act, rules or regulations to make a public announcement. |
| 15H(*iii*)# | Failure to make a public offer by sending to shareholders of the concerned company letters of offer. | Up to ₹ 25 crore or 3 times the amount of profits made, whichever is higher. | The person who is required under the Act, rules or regulations to make a public offer. |
| 15H(*iv*)# | Failure to make payment of consideration to the shareholders who sold their shares pursuant to letter of offer. | Up to ₹ 25 crore or 3 times the amount of profits made, whichever is higher. | The person who is required under the Act, rules or regulations to make payment of consideration to shareholders who sold their shares. |

| | | | |
|---|---|---|---|
| 15HA | Indulging in fraudulent and unfair trade practices. | Up to ₹ 25 crore or 3 times the amount of profits made, whichever is higher. | Any person who indulges in fraudulent and unfair trade practices. |
| 15HB | Failure to comply with any provisions of Act, Rules, Regulations or Directions where no separate penalty is provided. | Up to ₹ 1 crore. | Any person contravening. |

* The penalty leviable under Sections 15G(*i*), (*ii*), and (*iii*) pertains to defaults under the SEBI (Insider Trading) Regulations, 1992.

# The penalty leviable under Sections 15H(*i*) to (*iv*) pertains to defaults under the SEBI (Substantial Acquisition of Shares and Takeovers) Regulations, 1994.

## INVESTOR PROTECTION AT THE NATIONAL STOCK EXCHANGE

For investor protection, two funds have been set up for the NSE — Settlement Guarantee Fund and Investor Protection Fund.

The National Securities Clearing Corporation Ltd., has set up the Settlement Guarantee Fund (SGF) which is intended primarily to guarantee completion of settlement up to the normal payout for trades executed in the regular market. However, it will not act as guaranteer in case of objections against a company.

The SGF therefore ensures that the settlement is not held up on account of failure of TMs to meet their obligations and all market participants (trading members, custodians, investors, etc.), who have completed their part of the obligations are not affected in any manner whatsoever.

The Investor Protection Fund (IPF) is maintained by the exchange to take care of investor claims, which may arise out of non-settlement of obligations by the TMs for trades executed on the exchange. The IPF is used to settle claims of such investors whose trading member has been declared a defaulter.

## SECURITIES AND EXCHANGE BOARD OF INDIA (SEBI)

Keeping in mind these necessities, the government felt the need for setting up of an apex body wholly for the protection of the investors' potential, existing and prospective. This body would also be crucial for the promotion of orderly and healthy growth of the securities market. And thus was born the Securities and Exchange Board of India (SEBI) on April 12, 1988, through an administrative resolution as an interim body under the overall administrative control of the Union Ministry of Finance, as a precursor to the statutory board.

With the establishment of SEBI and the SEBI Act, there have been several changes in the regulatory framework for the securities market in India.

However, subsequent to the enactment of the SEBI Act, 1992 and the repeal of the Capital Issues (Control) Act, 1947 by the Capital Issues (Control) Act, 1992, the present framework for the securities market is provided by various Acts.

The SEBI Act of 1992, which is administered by SEBI, lays down the objectives of SEBI and its powers and functions. Subsequent to the repeal of the Capital Issues (Control) Act, 1947, SEBI separately issued Disclosure and Investor Protection Guidelines in 1992 which laid down the framework for issue of capital by certain categories of companies.

The Companies Act, 1956, is administered fully by the department of company affairs, and the company law board, ministry of law, justice and company affairs, Government of India.

The Securities Contracts (Regulation) Act, 1956, is administered by the Union Ministry of Finance, Department of Economic Affairs, Government of India. However, through the SEBI Act and subsequent notifications issued by the Central Government, certain critical sections of the Act can now be administered also by the regulatory body.

The objective of the SEBI Act is "*... to protect the interests of investors in securities and to promote the development of and regulate the securities market and also for matters connected therewith or incidental thereto*".

The Board of members of SEBI consists of a Chairman, two members from the officials of the ministries of the Central Government dealing with finance and law, one member from amongst the officials of the Reserve Bank of India, two other members appointed by Central Government, who would be professionals with adequate knowledge of the securities market.

The Board ensures that the interest of the investors is protected and the development of the securities market is well promoted. Its regulating job is to the business in stock exchanges and any other securities market, registering and regulating the working of stock brokers, sub-brokers, share transfer agents, bankers to an issue, merchant bankers, underwriters, etc., and regulating the working of collective investment schemes including mutual funds. It also promotes self-regulatory organisations, prohibits fraudulent and unfair trade practices in the securities market and promoting investors' education. Its other functions extend to regulate substantial acquisition of shares and takeovers, calling for information, undertaking inspection, conducting enquiries and audits of the stock exchanges and intermediaries, etc.

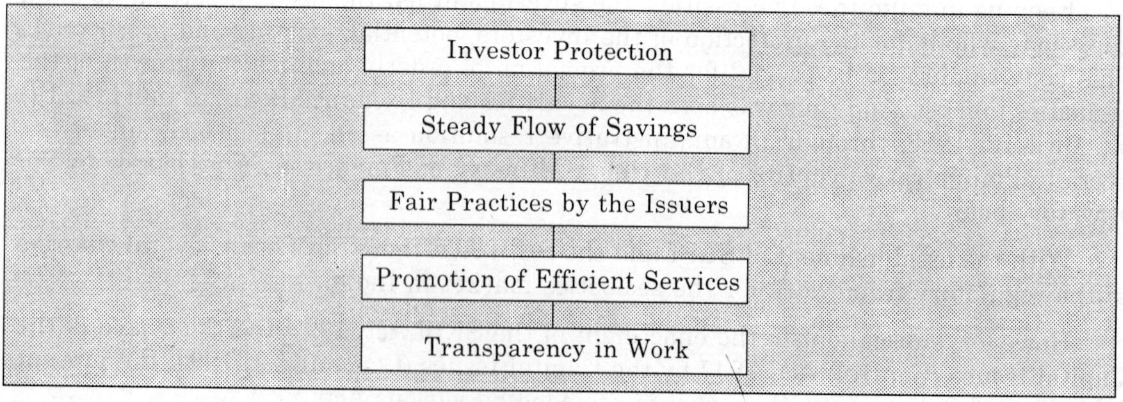


**Fig. 1 Objectives of SEBI**

The Act specifies the functions as follows:

| Regulatory | Developmental |
|---|---|
| (*a*) Registration of brokers and sub-brokers and other players in the market. | (*a*) Investor education. |
| (*b*) Registration of collective Investment Schemes and Mutual Funds. | (*b*) Training of Intermediaries. |
| (*c*) Regulation of stock exchanges and other SROs, merchant banks, Portfolio Managers, etc. | (*c*) Promotion of fair practices and a code of conduct for all SROs. |
| (*d*) Prohibition of all fraudulent and unfair trade practices. | (*d*) Conducting Research and Publishing information useful to all market participants. |
| (*e*) Controlling Insider Trading and takeover bids and imposing penalties for such practices. | |

The role of a regulatory body for securities market in a country is determined by the stage of development of the securities market in the country. In the Indian context, with regard to the emerging nature of the market, the regulatory body must necessarily have the twin role of development and regulation. Regulatory and developmental functions are strongly interlinked and have the same objectives in the long-run. Very often, the outcome of such well-regulated structures are rapid and are a healthy development. The twin role of SEBI has accordingly been enshrined in the preamble of the SEBI Act, 1992. The regulatory measures taken by SEBI, therefore, would always be subservient to the needs of market development and enough to enforce the required degree of discipline and foster high standards of fairness and integrity of the market and thereby protect the interest of the investors.

**SEBI's UNIVERSE**

| | |
|---|---|
| Stock exchanges | 26 |
| Subsidiaries | 12 |
| Broking terminals | 450 |
| Stock brokers | 9,658 |
| Sub-brokers | 13,195 |
| Listed companies | 10,000 |
| Depositories | 2 |
| Depository participants | 377 |
| Accounts (million) | 3.9 |
| Companies under compulsory demat | 3,441 |
| Portfolio managers | 46 |
| Bond trustees | 39 |
| Registrars and transfer agents | 126 |
| Bankers to issue | 81 |
| Credit rating agencies | 4 |

| | |
|---|---|
| Foreign venture capital funds | 6 |
| Domestic venture capital funds | 39 |
| Mutual funds | 39 |
| Schemes | 417 |
| Foreign institutional investors (FIIs) | 488 |
| Sub-accounts of FIIs | 1,336 |

SEBI's efforts has always been to create an effective surveillance mechanism for the securities market, and encourage responsible and accountable autonomy on the part of all players in the market, who should discipline themselves and observe the rules of the game.

The Board also endeavours to provide a regulatory framework which would facilitate an efficient mobilisation and allocation of resources through the securities market. This would also ensure that the necessary services are provided to industry and commerce and private investors in the most efficient and economical manner, stimulate competition, encourage innovation and be responsive to international developments. The SEBI has also formed a framework which is flexible and at the same time cost-effective, thereby providing it with the clarity to guide and not cramp the changes. It also serves the purpose of inspiring confidence on the part of the investors and other users of the market by ensuring that the marketplace is, competitive in positive manner to do business and allied transactions.

## JOB ENTRUSTED TO SEBI

(1) SEBI shall create a proper and conducive atmosphere required for raising money from the capital market. The atmosphere includes the rules, regulations, trade practices, customs and relations among institutions, brokers, investors and companies. It shall endeavour to restore the trust of investors and particularly to safeguard the interest of the small investors. This can be achieved by meeting the needs of the persons connected with the security market and establishing proper coordination among the three main groups directly connected with its operations, namely, (*a*) Investors, (*b*) Corporate Sectors, and (*c*) Intermediaries.

(2) SEBI shall educate investors and make them aware of their rights in clear and specific terms. It shall provide investors with information and see that the market maintains liquidity, safety and profitability of the securities which are crucial for any investments.

(3) SEBI shall create a proper investment climate and enable the corporate sector to raise industrial securities easily, efficiently and at affordable minimum cost.

(4) SEBI shall develop a proper infrastructure so that the market automatically facilitates expansion and growth of business to middlemen like brokers, jobbers, commercial banks, merchant bankers, mutual funds, etc. Thus, it will ensure that they provide efficient service to their constituents, namely, investors and the corporate sector at a competitive price.

(5) SEBI shall make more effective the law in the existing status as far as they relate to the industrial securities, mutual funds, investments in units, LIC savings plan, Chit-fund companies and securities issued by housing/industrial societies and corporations with the purpose of making investment in housing/ industrial projects.

(6) SEBI shall create the framework for more open, orderly, and unprejudiced conduct in relation to takeovers and mergers in the corporate sector to ensure fair and equal treatment to all the security holders, and to facilitate such takeovers and mergers in the interest of efficiency by prescribing a mechanism for more orderly conduct.

## APPROACH OF SEBI

To achieve its objectives, the Board shall play a dual role by working as a controlling authority and a development institution. Briefly its role is described below:

(1) It shall devise laws with a unified set of objectives, single administrative authority and an integrated framework to deal with all the aspects of the securities market.

(2) It shall also play an active role in interaction with the Institute of Chartered Accountants of India in upgrading and making more effective the accounting and auditing standards. It shall try to bring in discipline in management in financial reporting and act firmly with cases where window dressing and accounting tricks are employed to the detriment of the interest of users of such financial statements.

(3) It shall introduce a system of two-stage disclosure at the time of initial issue and make compulsory for the companies to provide detailed information to all the stock exchanges, journalists and investors on demand.

(4) It will examine the feasibility of introducing a dealers' network by which securities can be bought or sold over the counter as in a retail shop. This will smoothen liquidity and investment opportunities.

(5) It shall work as an authoritative institution to see that the intermediaries are financially sound and equipped with professional and competent manpower.

(6) It shall make law-making and observance flexible enough to suit the prevailing market conditions and circumstances. It will ensure that the rules are versatile and non-rigid to provide automatic and self-regulatory growth.

## FUNCTIONS OF THE BOARD

Subject to the provisions of this Act, it shall be the duty of the Board to protect the interest of investors in securities and to promote the development of, and to regulate the securities market by such measures as it thinks fit.

## (A) Regulatory

(1) regulating the business in stock exchanges and any other securities markets;

(2) registering and regulating the working of stock brokers, sub-brokers, share transfer agents, bankers to an issue, trustees of trust deeds, registrars to an issue, merchant bankers, underwriters, portfolio managers, investment advisors and such other intermediaries who may be associated with securities markets in any manner;

(3) registering and regulating the working of collective investment schemes including mutual funds;

(4) regulating self-regulatory organisations;

(5) prohibiting fraudulent and unfair trade practices relating to securities markets;

(6) prohibiting inside trading in securities;

(7) regulating substantial acquisition of shares and takeover of companies;

(8) calling for formation from undertaking inspection, conducting inquiries and audits of the stock exchanges and intermediaries and self-regulatory organisations in the securities market;

(9) levying fees or other charges for carrying out the purposes of this section.

## (B) Developmental

(1) promoting investors' education;

(2) promoting self-regulating organisations;

(3) training of intermediaries of securities markets;

(6) promotion of fair practices and code of conduct for all SROs;

(7) conducting research and publishing information useful to all market participants.

## REFORMS IN PRIMARY MARKET

Merchant Bankers are one of the key intermediaries in the primary market. Before SEBI was set up as a statutory body, the Union Ministry of Finance had issued guidelines for merchant bankers, which gave SEBI the power to authorise merchant bankers. These guidelines specified that any person or body proposing to engage in merchant banking activities would need to be authorised by SEBI on the basis of the authorisation criteria laid down in the guidelines.

With the view to encourage small merchant bankers to participate in certain types of issue management activities and allow more lead managers in issues, SEBI had classified merchant bankers into three categories, each with different responsibilities and capital requirements.

The portfolio managers are now regulated by the Securities and Exchange Board of India (portfolio managers) Rules and Regulations, 1993. These rules prescribe the conditions for grant or renewal of a certificate to portfolio managers, and no person can now act as a portfolio manager without registration with SEBI.

The registrars to issues and share transfer agents play a significant role in the securities market. These two intermediaries are now regulated by the SEBI Rules and Regulations, 1993. Here too, similar to the other managers, certain conditions, criteria and procedures for grant of registration, code of conduct, capital adequacy requirements, general obligations and responsibilities, procedures for inspection and liability for action in case of default which includes suspension or cancellation of registration exist.

SEBI has been constantly trying to look into methods of investor protection. However, it has been receiving investor complaints directly since its inception. To handle the ever increasing complaints, the SEBI has introduced an automated complaints handling system. To create an awareness among the issuers and intermediaries of the need to redress investor grievances quickly, SEBI has been issuing fortnightly press releases publishing the names of the companies against whom maximum number of complaints have been received.

A major drawback of the SEBI Act of 1992 is that it does not provide it with the powers to take action against these erring companies. It has therefore been taking up these complaints with the Department of Company Affairs (DCA) who has the power vested under it by the Companies Act for redressal of the grievances.

SEBI is constantly reviewing its policies and exploring the scope for further reforms in the primary market. It is also carrying out significant and wide ranging reforms in the financial disclosures, issue procedures and allotment process and has also issued a consultative paper proposing these reforms to seek the views of market participants.

Although reforms have been carried out in a number of areas, SEBI is aware of the scope and need for further reforms in the secondary market. The exchanges are yet to be fully automated and they have to go a long way to introduce screen-based trading. There is also a need to link the 21 stock exchanges across the country. Moreover, the stock exchanges have to be brought close to the investors and access to the stock exchanges made easy. The settlement cycles would have to be further shortened for ensuring efficient and faster settlement of trade transactions. SEBI is moving in the direction of setting up the systems for derivative trading.

## SEBI REFORMS ON STOCK EXCHANGES

The SEBI regulation of stock exchange and their members had started as early as February 1992 and the reforms later introduced have been on a continuous basis. It was started with the licensing and registration of brokers and sub-brokers in the recognized stock exchanges. This was later extended to underwriters, portfolio managers and other categories of players in the stock market including foreign securities firms, FFIs, Debenture Trustees, Collecting bankers, etc.

The other reforms are briefly summarized below:

(1) Compulsory audit and inspection of stock exchanges and their member brokers and their accounts.

(2) Transparency in the prices and brokerage charged by brokers by showing them in their contract notes.

(3) Broker accounts and client accounts are to be kept separate and clients' money are to be separately maintained in bank's accounts and the same to be reported to the stock exchanges.

(4) Board of Directors of stock exchanges has to be reconstituted so as to include non-brokers, public representatives, and government representatives to the extent of 50% of the total number of members.

(5) Capital adequacy norms have been laid down for members of various stock exchanges separately and depending on their turnover of trade and other factors.

(6) Guidelines have been laid down for dealings of FFIs and foreign broker firms in the Indian stock exchanges through Indian brokers.

(7) Badla and carry forward business which was banned on major exchanges early in 1995 was reintroduced in October 1996 and renewal business was also subject to close scrutiny, for cash shares.

(8) New guidelines for corporate members have been laid down with limited liability of directors and opening up of their membership to more than one stock exchange without the limiting requirement of experience of five years in one exchange, as imposed earlier.

## SEBI'S GOALS FOR THIS YEAR 2011

The Securities and Exchange Board of India, under its new chief UK Sinha, has its job cut out for the current financial year. While increasing investor awareness and surveillance remain its top priority, it also proposes to step up focus on investigation. The proposed initiatives were discussed at the Sebi board meeting.

**UK SINHA**
Chairman, Sebi

**Increases Investor Awareness**

**Financial education** programmes for school children

**International seminar** with Organization for Economic Cooperation and Development on investor education

**A toll-free** helpline to handle investor queries in different languages

**Centralised web-based** investor grievances tracking system

**Electronic campaign** to demystify the securities market

**Workshops across** the country to spread financial literacy

**Upgrade Surveillance Mechanism**

**To create** a forensic accounting cell to improve quality of financial information disclosed and to assist in detection of financial irregularities so as to serve as an effective early warning mechanism

**To set up** a unified filling and dissemination platform to make available information filed with Sebi in user-friendly and analysable form to the investors and various stakeholders

**Implementing data** warehousing and business intelligence System to enhance the capability of investigation in terms of computation and speed of data analysis

**Initiatives for Market Infrastructure Institutions**

**Review and** standardisation of business continuity plan and disaster recovery of stock exchanges and depositories

**Guidelines in** respect of co-location and high frequency trading

**Regulatory framework** and inter-operability of clearing corporation

**Exit policy** on stock exchanges, which are derecognised/have sought voluntary derecognition

**Extension of** call auction mechanism to IPO and illiquid scrips

**Risk assessment** on trading system

**Beef up Investigation Techniques**

**Setting up** of investigation laboratory to be used as an incubation room for innovation

**Use of** latest technology software tools

**Utillising the** services of professional firms

**Regulate investment Advisors Through a self regulatory Organisation**

**Formulate Regulations for Alternative investment funds**

**Derivatives and new products segment**

**To introduce** derivatives for hedging interest rate risk

**To put** in place risk management and risk containment measures for derivatives on volatility

**Enhance Compliance Level among the Market Intermediaries**

**Standardisation of** rating symbols and definitions

**Disclosing track** records of the merchant bankers

**Maintenance of** records of due diligence by merchant bankers

**Streamlining capital** adequacy standards for market intermediaries

**Measures to** deal with unauthorised trading

## GUIDELINES TO INVESTORS

(1) Deal with a registered members of the stock exchange. If you are dealing with a sub-broker, make sure that all bills and contracts are made in the name of a registered broker.

(2) Insist that all your deals are done in the trading ring.

(3) Give specific orders to buy or sell within the fixed price limits and/or time periods within which orders have to be executed.

(4) Insist on contract notes to be passed on to you on the dates, when the orders are executed.

(5) Make sure that your deal is registered with the stock exchange in a Souda Block Book. In case of a dispute, this will help trace the details of the deal easily.

(6) Collect a settlement table from the stock exchange mentioning the pay-in and pay-out days. Each stock exchange has its own trading periods which are called settlements. All transactions done within this period are settled at the end of it. All payments for shares bought and their deliveries take place on the pay-in day. An awareness of pay-in and pay-out days is useful when a broker tries to make excuses.

(7) Keep separate records of dealings in specified shares (Group A) and non-specified share (Group B). The settlement for each is on different days.

(8) Execute periodic settlements of dues and delivery of shares to avoid accumulation of transactions.

(9) Insist on delivery. If the company returns your papers and shares with objections, contact your broker immediately.

(10) Ensure that shares bought are transferred in your name before the company's book closure date. This is necessary to make sure that you receive benefits like dividend, interest and bonus shares. All companies have a book closure date on which the list of shareholders in the company is finalised.

(11) Complain if the broker does not deliver the shares bought in your name. Proceed to contact another broker with the bill/contract given to you by the earlier broker, and the exchange authorities and the latter will purchase the shares on your behalf. In such an event, the first broker will have to pay the difference in price.

(12) Do not sell shares that are not transferred in your name after the book closure as these are not valid in the market.

(13) Do not sell/deal in shares where any one of the holders has passed away. In cases where the holder has died, a succession certificate is necessary. In case where one of the joint shareholders passes away, the surviving holder should send the shares along with the death certificate to the company. Only after the name of the deceased has been deleted from the shares, can they be transferred.

(14) Do not expect the money for shares to come immediately. It will take at least a fortnight or a month from the date of transaction.

(15) Unless you have a special arrangement with the broker, do not expect the adjustment of purchases and sales against one another. One pays first and receives later.

(16) Do not take delays or harassment lying down. You have to complain to the Grievance Cell of the stock exchange or the Securities and Exchange Board of India (SEBI) in case of delay or harassment.

## THE GOVERNMENT INITIATIVE FOR INVESTOR PROTECTION

The Government of India set up a Committee under the Chairmanship of Dr. N. L. Mitra to look into different aspects of investor protection in 2001. The Committee's principal recommendations are as follows:

- There is a need for a specific Act for protecting investor's interest. The Act should codify, amend and consolidate laws and practice for the purpose of protecting investors' interest in corporate investments.
- A judicial forum is needed for the redressal of investors' grievance.

- The provisions relating to investor education and protection fund should be removed from the Companies Act, 1956 and included in the SEBI Act, 1992, and the fund should be administered by SEBI.
- SEBI should have the power and function of a regulator but it should not have the powers to award compensation, which is the job of a justice-delivery system. According to the principles of natural justice, no organisation can be a regulator, investigator and judge at the same time.
- The SEBI Act, 1992 should be amended to provide for statutory standing committees on investor protection and market operation.
- The forum of consumer courts should be activated and used effectively, particularly for grievance redressal of small investors.

## ROLE OF THE CONSUMER FORUM

An aggrieved investor has the right to approach the consumer forum for deficient service. Section 2 (1) (o) of the Consumer Protection (Amendment) Act, 1993 includes provisions of facilities in connection with banking, financing and insurance under 'services'. Section 2 (1) (d) of the same Act defines a consumer 'as any person who buys any goods or hires or avails of any services for a consideration......' An aggrieved investor, insofar as he qualifies as a consumer, can approach the District Consumer Disputes Redressal Forum. The procedure for filing a complaint is quite simple and no court fee is involved. If he is dissatisfied with the ruling of the District Forum, he can appeal to the State Consumer Disputes Redressal Commission. Finally, he can approach the National Consumer Disputes Redressal Commission.

Apart from consumer courts, the investor may take conventional legal action against companies/brokers, etc., as already indicated above. In this context, it may also be noted that the *press* has also a significant role to play in mitigating the problem of the investors. Highlighting irregularities by companies/brokers, the media can put indirect pressure on the violating parties. For example, a company will find it difficult to successfully mobilise funds from the market if its reputation is spoiled by adverse press coverage. Also, the appropriate authorities would be constrained to act swiftly and initiate penal measures against persistent violators in the face of a sustained onslaught from the press/media.

## LEGISLATIVE PROTECTION TO INVESTORS

The Companies Act and the Listing Agreement of the Stock Exchanges provide certain safeguards to investors. The normal complaints against companies and the protection available are listed below:

| Complaints | Legislative Provision | Relief Provided |
|---|---|---|
| 1. Delay in refund of excess application money or allotment letters | Section 73 of the Companies Act as amended by amendment Act of 1988 | Payment of interest for the delayed period beyond 30 days from the closure of subscription list at the rate of 15%. |
| 2. Delay in transfer of shares | Section 111 of the Companies Act | A time limit of two months provided in the Act for effecting transfer. As |

| | | |
|---|---|---|
| | | per the Listing Agreement, the time limit is only one month from the lodgement of shares. |
| 3. Refusal to transfer of shares | Section 22(A) of SC(R) Act. This Section lists the reasons for which transfer of shares can be refused | Transfer can be refused only for specific and valid reasons given in the Act and not otherwise. |
| 4. Problem of odd lots | Listing Agreement provides for issue of certificates in marketable lots and avoidance of odd lots | Need for consolidation of odd lots and ensuring the issue of shares only in marketable lots through conversion of debentures or rights issue, provision of an odd lot trading session and listing out brokers willing to trade in odd lots. |
| 5. Takeover bids | New Clauses of 40(A) and 40(B) of Listing Agreement SEBI Rules on takeover Bids | Purchases or acquisition of shares beyond 5 to be notified to the stock exchange. Acquisition beyond 10% puts an obligation on the transferor and transferee and intermediary to notify the Stock Exchange and the public and offer to the other shareholders of the company to buy at their price or the highest market price during the preceding six months. |
| 6. Insider trading, rigging and other malpractices | SEBI (Insider Trading) Regulation, 1992 | The investors have to guard themselves regarding the price and their investment. |
| 7. Delay and non-payment of interest/fixed deposits by companies | Section 58(A) of the Companies Act | Complain to the Company Law Board. |
| 8. Delay and non-payment of dues or non-delivery of shares, etc., by brokers | Rules, bye-laws, etc., of the Stock Exchange | Complain to the Grievance Cell of the concerned Stock Exchange and to SEBI. |

***Note:*** The SEBI has also been receiving investor complaints and besides taking up the matters with companies, merchant bankers, etc., they are publicizing such complaints in the newspapers for the public to know and isolate the concerned companies. The Dept. of company affairs is also receiving complaints against companies and the matter is also pursued by them.

## EVALUATION OF THE WORKING OF SEBI

Notwithstanding the fact that SEBI's functioning has come under severe criticism, it is able to make a dent into the jungle of stock market. In spite of the hesitant attitude of the government in tackling the situation, SEBI started its activity on a firm note. The constituents, which enjoyed the degree of freedom more than permitted levels, would normally be unwilling to curtail their activities. Even the stock exchanges have come into conflict with SEBI regarding the exercise of powers relating to calling for periodical returns, prescribing maintenance of certain documents, approving bye-laws and licensing of dealers in securities in certain areas. As a matter of fact, the Central Government has the authority to exercise these powers under the Securities Contracts Regulation Act, 1956. These are now sought to be transferred to SEBI through the new legislation.

If one realises the fact that the regulation of stock market activity is challenging, the going turns out to be always tough. Even in its limited span of existence of just five years, it was able to make its presence felt by every constituent of the capital market. It is true that SEBI has had tussle with almost every participating institutions in the capital market in respect of one or the other issue. The going should have been little softer. Instead of taking up the entire work with such a great speed, it should have implemented its policies in a sequential manner, allowing the participant institutions to learn the art of compliance. More so, SEBI should have taken at least public financial institutions and governing boards of stock exchanges into confidence, while formulating the guidelines for different issues, instead of throwing the responsibility on them unilaterally.

While creating the SEBI, the government seems to have been influenced by the legislative developments in USA. The parallel to SEBI in USA is Securities and Exchange Commission (SEC), created under Securities Exchange Act, 1934. Unlike SEBI, the SEC was given wide ranging powers for the purpose of protecting the investors' interests. Significant among them include the following:

(1) to monitor the working of stock exchanges;

(2) to insist on the companies for the supply of extensive information on a regular basis;

(3) to penalise members of stock exchanges who were found to violate securities laws;

(4) to debar the wrong-doers from any activity in the stock market and impose on them civil penalties and initiate criminal proceedings;

(5) to make rules about the manipulative practices;

(6) to move court for checking insider trading; and

(7) to prosecute the company and its directors on its own, even without receiving complaints by an aggrieved investor in respect of supplying inadequate, incomplete and incorrect information.

## LIMITATIONS

The principal drawbacks in the functioning of SEBI are as follows:

(1) Limited transparency;

(2) Bureaucratic administration;

(3) Lack of professionalism;

(4) Long and complex procedures;

(5) Lack of serious approach to investors' needs;

(6) Fraudulent activities;

(7) Counter-productive regulations;

(8) Lack of adequate powers;

(9) Weak legislation;

(10) Too mechanical procedures;

(11) Minimum accountability; and

(12) Lack of confidence of all players in the capital market including investors, especially small.

Investor confidence is at the heart of capital market development. A *sine qua non* for orderly market activity and investor protection is an effective but not overly intrusive regulatory framework. The Securities and Exchange Board of India is now the authority vested with this regulatory responsibility. The role model for SEBI when it was conceived was the Securities and Exchange Commission of the US but SEBI's power and authority are circumscribed by the government in ways in which its US counterpart is not.

## MORE POWERS OF SEBI

Despite this limitation, SEBI has been establishing itself as a professional and autonomous body and is steadily learning the nuances, intricacies and technicalities of the market. Nor has it been adverse to cracking the regulatory whip for perceived breaches of the law such as insider trading. To be able to discharge its functions effectively, however, SEBI should be vested, like the SEC of the US with adequate power and have full operational autonomy. I do not see, for instance, the logic in having an appellate authority in government to oversee SEBI's decisions. If any of its decisions were to be contested, the appropriate place to do so would be a court of law rather than

### PERILS OF LACK OF INDEPENDENCE — BOX : 1

Before the Asian crisis began in 1997, Korea's specialized banks and non-bank financial institutions were under the authority of the ministry of finance and economy. The ministry's supervision of non-bank was generally recognized as weak, encouraging regulatory arbitrage and excessive risk taking. As in many other Asian crisis countries, politically motivated forbearance was widespread. The most glaring examples of political interference in financial sector supervision were the government's decisions to intervene in certain banks or to provide them with government funds for recapitalization.

In ***Japan***, the lack of independence of the financial supervision function within the ministry of finance is also widely believed to have contributed to financial sector weaknesses. Although there was probably little direct political pressure on the ministry of finance to exercise forbearance, the system lacked transparency and was known for widespread implicit government guarantees of banking sector liabilities. Following a decline in the ministry's reputation as a supervisor in the late 1990s, the Japanese government created a new, integrated Financial Supervisory Agency, which was more independent and transparent than its predecessor had been. However, the agency, which reports to the prime minister's office rather than to the finance ministry, has achieved disappointing results to date.

Ineffective regulation, weak and dispersed supervision, and political interference in ***Venezuela*** were among the main factors in the weakening of banks in the run-up to the 1994 banking crisis. Former central bank president Ruth de Krivoy has emphasized that one of the main lessons of this crisis was that there was a need for more independence for financial sector regulators and supervisors and political support for their work.

another governmental agency. For SEBI to be effective, it should obviously have regulatory discipline. As early as in 1991, the Committee on the Financial System had suggested uniform legislation and equality of treatment between the UTI and other mutual funds. The recent events have only reinforced the validity of this recommendation. It is essential — if only to sustain investor confidence — for a large national institution like the Unit Trust to have full transparency in all its operations and there is no reason why any set of its transactions should be shrouded in secrecy or be outside the regulatory discipline of SEBI.

Ever since the SEBI Act (1992) was enacted, Merchant Bankers, Stock Brokers, Sub-brokers, Portfolio Managers, Share Transfer Agents, Registrars to an issue and all collective investment schemes including mutual funds are now governed by the rules and regulations notified by the SEBI.

To make SEBI perform and act like SEC of USA, the government should extend powers to penalise and debar the wrong-doers. Further, the government should also consider granting powers for the *suo moto* action on any matter connected with the capital market. SEBI could not prevent or at least unearth the scam, primarily because it had no authority to go into the matter on its own and could do no more than urging the government to take suitable action to curb the speculative bursts in stock prices. Thus, if the SEBI is to be successful in its role as a market regulator, it needs to have more powers to prosecute the errant members of the system. If every announcement could be taken to court and eventually changed, there is no case for setting up of a separate regulatory body like SEBI.

SEBI, in the short period of its existence, has brought out guidelines for disclosure and investor protection and it has certainly made the disclosure levels in the prospectuses much more wide and meaningful, without interfering with the pricing of issues or trying to raise any other barriers for those attempting to access the market. It has put in place regulations and codes of conduct for intermediaries like merchant bankers, brokers, registrars and mutual funds. It has encouraged investors' associations and self-regulatory organisations of merchant bankers. It has issued series of educational advertisements for investor protection guidance. It has persuaded stock exchanges to have broad-based boards and to go for prudential norms of capital adequacy for brokers and norms for broker-client relationships and has undertaken inspection of stock exchanges. It is attempting to develop a strong cash market for the benefit of investors and trying to encourage transparency and fairness in market transactions. It has issued regulations concerning insider trading and would soon come out with a code for takeovers.

SEBI, as any regulator should do, constantly keep in mind that regulation should not stifle enterprise, creativity and innovativeness. SEBI should pursue its regulatory function for investor protection with vigour and visibility, but should also bend its energies to the development of the securities market on healthy lines. After all, the goal of regulation in the ultimate analysis is to encourage development to take place in an enterprising fair manner.

**THE STOCK EXCHANGE REGULATOR OF THE FUTURE** **BOX : 2**

Can SEBI transform itself into a supper-regulator capable of overseeing fairness and transparency in a stock market that will boast a myriad innovative trading instruments and increased trading volumes?

The surprising answer to that question is that it can. Only it can no longer rely on self-regulatory organizations (SROs) such as stock exchanges to regulate the markets. After all, the track record of the stock markets in India shows that SROs haven't really been effective. SEBI even had to take the extreme step of dismissing the entire board of directors of BSE in March 2001, when allegations were raised over office-bearers using their positions to access sensitive information.

The solution could lie in moving towards the UK model of financial regulation. In 1997, the United Kingdom scrapped its regulatory structure — this was instituted in the wake of the Big Bang of 1986 — which essentially took the form of a string of SROs under the aegis of the Securities and Investment Board (SIB). Today, the country boasts a Financial Services Authority (FSA) that regulates not just the securities market, but also the banking and insurance sector.

A regulator like the UK's could make sense in the future Indian context where financial services companies will operate across securities trading, banking, and insurance. Only a super-regulator, like the FSA, overseeing all sectors can ensure fairness and transparency. But even if India were to follow the American or French model — separate regulators for each of these sectors — the regulator will need to possess formidable investigatory powers, much like the SEC, and be able to levy substantial fines for infringements. The catch with multiple regulators? The story of the run on Madhavpura Mercantile Cooperative Bank in 2001 — cooperative banks have dotted-line regulatory relationships with the Reserve Bank of India and the State Registrar of Cooperatives — holds the answer.

## GRIEVANCES

| Grievance related to | Whom to contact |
|---|---|
| Issue/Company | Compliance officer of the issuer company/Lead Manager/Stock Exchange |
| Trading/Broker/Sub-broker | Investor Grievance Cell of concerned Exchange |
| Mutual Fund | Compliance Office of Mutual Fund |
| Depository Services | Investor Relation Cell of Concerned Depository |
| Corporate Action | Concerned Company/Exchange |
| Intermediary | Compliance officer of the intermediary/Affiliated industry association/SRO |

If your grievances still remain unredressed after your taking up of the same with the concerned entity/company you may write to the Office of the Investor Assistance and Education located at:

*Office of Investor Assistance and Education*

Securities and Exchange Board of India,
4th Floor, Exchange Plaza,
G Block, Bandra-Kurla Complex,
Bandra (E), Mumbai-400 051.

The Office of Investor Assistance and Education

*Takes up Grievances Against the Following:*

- Bankers to Issue
- Brokers
- Clearing and Settlement Organisations
- Credit Rating Agencies
- Custodians
- Debenture Trustees
- Depositories
- Depository Participants
- Derivative Exchanges and Related Organisations

*also against*

- Foreign Institutional Investors
- Foreign Venture Capital Investors
- Merchant Bankers
- Mutual Funds
- Portfolio Managers
- Registrars and Transfer Agents
- Securities Exchanges
- Securities Lending Intermediaries
- Sub-brokers
- Underwriters
- Venture Capital Funds

The Office of Investor Assistance and Education

*Takes up Grievances Relating to the Following:*

- Buyback of Securities
- Collective Investment Schemes
- Compliance with Listing Conditions
- Corporate Governance
- Corporate Restructuring
- Debentures
- Delisting of Securities
- Issue of Securities
- Non-receipt of Dividend
- Substantial Acquisition and Takeovers
- Transfer of Securities

## MORE WORK IS NEEDED

Despite the importance of regulatory independence as a component of good regulatory governance, current practice in many countries falls short of the ideal. Much work remains to be done to strengthen the independence of regulatory agencies around the world and, by the same token, improve the quality of regulatory governance.

In the interest of financial stability, as much attention should be given to ensuring the independence of the supervisory agencies as has been given to ensuring central bank independence. The current trend toward the unification of supervisory agencies provides an opportunity not only to harmonize independence arrangements among sector supervisors but also to raise them to a higher level.

Effective independence cannot be achieved without support from the broader political environment, however. Vested political interests in the financial system remain strong in many parts of the world, and the cost of overriding regulators is often low. Nevertheless, the need to pursue the goal of independent and accountable regulators and supervisors in the interest of long-term financial stability is as great as ever. Politicians must be convinced of this view.

Ensuring investor protection, having a transparent system of trade, settlement and payment, enforcing adequate disclosure of information, upholding the right to obtain truthful and sufficient information, etc., are essential prerequisites of an efficient capital market. In recent times, some progress have been made in that direction in India. However, cases of price-rigging are still a common feature of the Indian Stock Markets. Thus, we still have a long way to go before we can approach perfection in this regard.

## CONCLUSION

The smooth operations of the securities market and its healthy growth and development, depends to a large extent on the quality and integrity of the market. Unfair practices like insider trading, market manipulation and other securities related fraud affect the integrity, fairness and efficiency of the securities market, thereby reducing the confidence of the investors. Despite the growth in the securities market, there was no regulation in the country to prevent insider trading. Today, however, insider trading is a criminal offence punishable in accordance with the provisions of the SEBI Act, 1992.

SEBI became statutory towards the end of its fourth year of operations. However, it was proactive in its twin role of investor protection through regulation and market development even when it was a non-statutory body. It managed to do so by responding to the requirements of a growing market itself and to a wide range of issues concerning investor protection.

❖❖❖

CHAPTER 16

# FINANCIAL SERVICES

## INTRODUCTION

Access to safe, easy and affordable credit and other financial services is recognised as a precondition for accelerating growth and reducing income disparities and poverty. Access to a well-functioning financial system, by creating equal opportunities enables to integrate better into the economy and accelerate economic development. In this process the process of spread of financial services in paramount to economic growth and the health of the developing economy and society.

Financial services are an integral part of the financial system. The importance of developing appropriate financial institutions, financial markets and financial services in promoting economic growth can be hardly overemphasized. Financial services are broadly of two groups, products and services tools. The services of the financial institutions have emerged as the key parameters of defining performance. Globalisation has brought about a massive change in the attitude and performance of the financial institutions. Increasing competition has improved the product range, enhanced delivery channels and quality of services, lowered costs and kept pressure on the financial institutions to adopt state-of the art technology.

Financial system plays a very important role in our economy; in fact, it is difficult to imagine how our economic system could function efficiently without many of their services. The financial systems are the heart of our economic structure, since they have the ability, in cooperation with the Reserve Bank of India, to cater and add to the money supply of the nation and thus create additional purchasing power.

In this Chapter, focus is on the functions of the financial system.

## FINANCE FUNCTION

Finance is the lifeblood of an economy. It is rightly termed as *the science of money*. We need finance for the production of goods and services as well as their distribution. The efficiency of production and marketing operations is directly influenced by the manner in which the finance function of the enterprise is performed by the finance personnel. Finance function assumes an important role in the business system and it should be given equal importance, as with production and marketing functions. Under the systems approach we have an integration and coordination of these three vital sub-systems of business going hand-in-hand and offering both ways and means to accomplish the common goals of the enterprise, *viz.*, productivity and satisfaction.

*"Finance is that administrative area or set of administrative functions in an organisation which relate with the arrangement of cash and credit, so-that the organisation may have the means of to carry-out its objectives as satisfactory as possible."*

The major objectives of finance function are:

(1) Mobilisation of resources for the economy;

(2) Channelising the money in productive activities;

(3) Generating income or profit;

(4) Creating assets for the use of masses;

(5) Contributing to the activities of promotion of the economy; and

(6) Equitable development of the economy. In the process, finance transforms the economy.

### Financial Intermediaries

Financial intermediaries are the institutions which collect savings from others, issuing in return claims against themselves, and use the funds thus acquired to purchase ownership or debt claims. They are interposed between ultimate borrowers and lenders to acquire the primary securities of borrowers and provide other securities for the portfolios of lenders. Their outstanding feature is that they issue to savers claims whose characteristics are quite different from those that they buy and hold. They do not merely intermediate, but in the process they also create higher degree of safety and liquidity. Their basic function is to satisfy simultaneously the portfolio preferences of lenders and borrowers.

The increasing differentiation of financial assets tends to promote the development of financial structure. New types of financial assets are created to suit the needs of different spending units and a variegated structure of financial intermediaries emerges out in a rapidly developing economy. Markets for goods and markets for securities are simultaneously the media through which spending units seek optimal adjustment between income and spending, net worth and wealth.

Financial intermediaries play a very important role in the saving-investment process by raising the level of saving and investment and allocating more efficiently scarce savings among most productive investments. Commercial banks, which are one of the oldest financial intermediaries, often fall short of the diversified requirements of ultimate savers and investors. This creates a favourable climate for the emergence and growth of NFI. The new specialised types of financial assets are created to suit the demand structure and an array of new types of financial intermediaries are established to meet the demand for increasing specialisation.

A satisfactory classification of financial intermediaries will vary from place-to-place and time-to-time. Generally, they are grouped under five different categories as follows:

(1) The banking system (Central Bank, Commercial Banks, Cooperative Banks, Savings Banks, etc.)

(2) Other depository organisations (mutual funds, savings and loan associations, credit unions, etc.)

(3) Insurance organisations (Life Insurance, General Insurance, Postal Insurance, Pension Funds, Provident Funds, etc.)

(4) Development banks

(5) Non-banking finance companies

(6) Financial markets, and

(7) Other financial intermediaries.

The financial services sector has been dominated by bank intermediation. It is only the growth of the equity markets since the mid1980s and financial liberalisation since the early 1990s that has led to the development of alternatives in the form of financial markets and products. Nevertheless bank intermediation is still predominant.

Efficient and well-functioning financial markets are characterised by liquidity and high turnovers providing investors an opportunity to enter/exit at minimal costs. The creation of a market microstructure and proper regulation are a prerequisite for ensuring this. There is also a need for efficient self-regulatory organisations. However, ultimately, financial stability is contingent on effective control systems and the quality of governance within the participating financial institutions and agencies.

The other aspects that have a bearing on financial stability is market-design, the extent of integration of the markets and contagion risk, structural rigidities that could lead to a concentration of an adverse event on a single market or a few institutions and last but not the least, the risk management abilities of participants. In view of this, the approach to market development in India has been measured and calibrated, comprising the gradual opening up of various segments of the financial markets rather than following a big-bang approach.

Schematic Presentation of Function of the Financial System

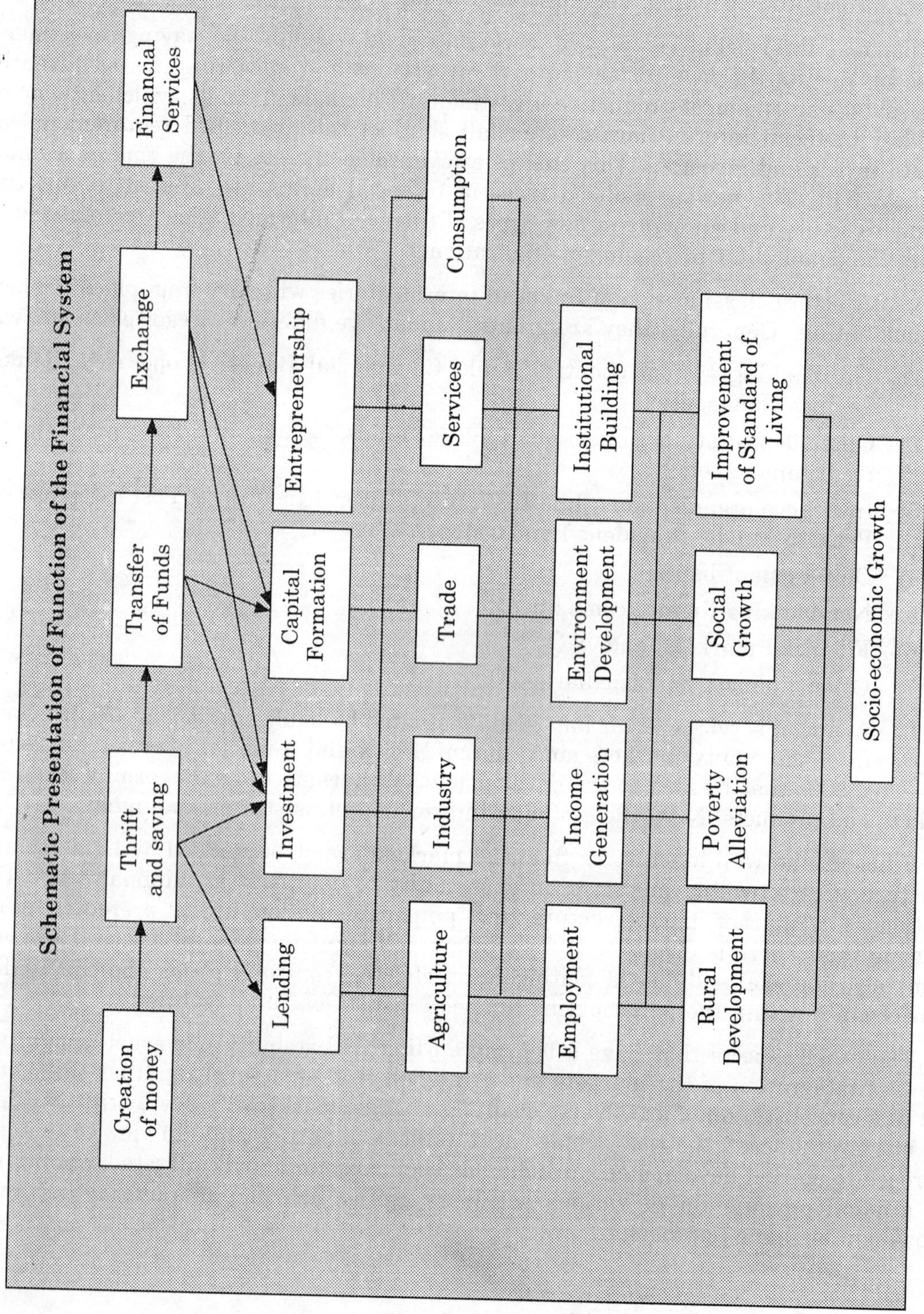

The Indian financial market can be categorised for analytical purposes into the money market, the foreign exchange market, the Government securities market, the equity market, the corporate bond market and the credit market.

The foreign exchange, money and Government securities markets are within the regulatory ambit of the Reserve Bank. The corporate bond market and the equity market are regulated by SEBI. With its overall regulatory and supervisory powers overall credit institutions, credit markets come under the Reserve Bank regulation.

The Reserve Bank has been regulating the money, foreign exchange and Government securities markets through its regulatory and supervisory powers. Under Section 16 of the Securities (Contract) Regulation Act, 1956 (SCRA), in 2000 the government notified that contracts for sale and purchase of Government securities, gold related securities, money market securities and securities derived from these securities and ready forward contracts in debt securities would come under the regulatory purview of the Reserve Bank. In addition to SCRA, the power of the Reserve Bank to regulate these markets is derived from the Banking Regulation Act, 1949 and the Foreign Exchange Management Act, 1999. The regulatory power of the Reserve Bank has further been formalised through amendment of the RBI Act in 2006 where a new Chapter III D has been inserted defining and clarifying its role in the regulation of transactions in derivatives, the money market and the securities market. This Chapter has also defined the terms 'derivatives', 'repo' and 'reverse repo', 'money market instruments' and 'securities' in a clear and unambiguous manner.

## FINANCIAL SERVICES

If we are to achieve a consistent growth rate of over 6 per cent every year for the next decade, the demand for capital is going to be enormous. This demand for capital cannot be met through domestic savings. The demand also exists in competition to other emerging markets. Capital account convertibility of the rupee, therefore, is inevitable. The financial sector not only has to overcome its domestic vulnerability but also has to prepare to face foreign competition in the domestic market and compete in the international market by taking their Indian clients abroad. They will have to diversify their asset base for distributing risks and protecting capital which is already under threat.

Financial services are beginning to acquire a new meaning. The old stereotypes are giving way to a totally new set of paradigms. As the reforms programme gathers momentum, the dinosaurs will become extinct and only those species – big or small – who respond to the changes in the environment and suitably modify their structure, organization and processes will survive.

The Indian financial system was tailored to meet the requirements of the specific model of mixed economy which we tried to implement for the first forty odd years the old ways are apparently unsuitable for India. The global and domestic context has dramatically changed during the last decade. It is in this context that we should look at the status and future of financial services in India.

The provider of the financial service is necessarily only an intermediary. The nature of intermediation is different for different service providers which can be mainly classified into five groups: financial institutions, commercial banks, merchant (investment) banks, brokerage houses and advisors. The process of intermediation reshapes the risks associated with a transaction.

## Meaning of Financial Services

In general, all types of activities which are of a financial nature could be brought under the term 'financial services'. The term "financial services" in a broad sense means "mobilizing and allocating savings". Thus, it includes all activities involved in the transformation of savings into investment.

The 'financial services' can also be called 'financial intermediation'. Financial intermediation is a process by which funds are mobilized from a large number of savers and make them available to all those who are in need of it and particularly to corporate customers. Thus, financial services sector is a key area and it is very vital for industrial developments. A well developed financial service industry is absolutely necessary to mobilize the savings and to allocate them to various investible channels and thereby to promote industrial development in a country.

The financial intermediaries offer a multimedia of financial services to savers, investors, industries, traders, agriculturists, governments, etc., Financial services is a process by which funds are mobilized from a large number of savers and make them available to all those who are in need of it. The financial services has undergone a metamorphosis since 1990. The importance of financial services is gaining momentum all over the world.

The financial service the worldover has undergone a profound transformation since the early 1990s. The changed operating environment for the financial intermediaries, underpinned by globalization, deregulation, advances in information technology, introduction of innovative instruments and management practices has resulted in intense competitive pressures to provide financial services. This has exposed the financial system/financial intermediaries to newer risks and posed serious regulatory and supervisory challenges.

Five cities – Mumbai, Delhi, Bengaluru, Kolkata and Channai, cornered the bulk of financial services. According to RBI, they accounted for 44.5 per cent of bank deposits and 53.6 per cent of bank lending at the end of March 2008. Likewise, the share of these five cities is more in respect of equity, mutual funds and insurance. It follows that all the innovative financial services are at use in these centres.

Financial services are beginning to acquire a new meaning. The old stereotypes are giving way to a totally new set of paradigms. As the reforms programme gathers momentum, the dinosaurs will become extinct and only those species – big or small – who respond to the changes in the environment and suitably modify their structure, organization and processes will survive.

The Indian financial system was tailored to meet the requirements of the specific model of mixed economy which we tried to implement for the first forty odd years, the old ways are apparently unsuitable for India. The global and domestic contexts have dramatically changed during the last decade. It is in this context that we should look at the status and future of financial services in India.

The provider of the financial service is necessarily only an intermediary. The nature of intermediation is different for different service providers which can be mainly classified in five groups: financial institutions, commercial banks, merchant (investment) banks, brokerage houses and advisors. The process of intermediation reshapes the risks associated with a transaction.

### Users of Financial Services

Financial institutions sell their services to households, businesses and government.

The household sector includes small mainly unregulated firms and individuals. Their main financial needs are for payment of services, saving and small credit. They seek convenience, liquidity and security.

Businesses have more complicated financial needs. It needs short-term credit to finance inventories and long-term funds to finance capital expansion.

All governments use payment services. In most developing countries, governments, like businesses, are net borrowers, and they use the financial system as a source of funding for current and capital spending. In industrial countries, government deficits are financed by borrowing from banks. Governments have also used the financial system to serve development or other goals.

## PROVIDERS OF FINANCIAL SERVICES

Different financial institutions provide services that are both complementary to and competitive with each other. Deposit institutions offer payment and liquid deposit facilities, and contractual savings opportunities that cater to the longer-term needs of customers. Collective investment institutions offer small inverstors the benefits of professional management and low-cost risk diversification, encouraging them to diversify their savings into marketable securities. On the lending side, commercial banks have traditionally provided working capital and trade finance, but longer-term lending is gaining with the spread of universal banking. Factoring companies provide long-term investment finance.

Money and capital markets provide investment instruments appropriate for contractual savings and collective investment institutions, whose services to the saving public are thereby improved. The efficient functioning of financial markets also depends on institutions that lend and borrow little on their own account: investment banks, securities brokers, and credit rating agencies. Commercial banks also improve the working of financial markets by providing credit and payment facilities to market-markers and other market participants.

Different financial institutions and markets compete for a limited pool of savings by offering different instruments. Money and capital markets increase competition between suppliers. Money markets give merchant banks, or commercial banks with limited branch networks, greater access to funds. Because such banks specilized in lending to larger corporations, the corporate loan market may be highly competitive, even though few large domestic banks may continue to dominate the retail deposit market.

Money markets also provide large corporations and non-bank financial institutions with efficient short-term instruments for investing their liquid funds and thus compete directly with commercial banks' traditional deposit facilities. They also enable large corporation to issue short-term securities in the form of commercial paper and thus further reduce the market enable contractual savings and collective investment institutions to play a more active role in the financial system.

The complementary and competitive interaction of financial institutions has policy implications. To promote an efficient financial system there must be competition, but the system must also offer an array of services. Rather than restrict the growth and diversification of the main banking groups, governments in the greater competition by encouraging money and capital markets, specialized credit institutions (such as leasing and factoring companies), and contractual savings and collective investment institutions. Economies too small to support such specialized institutions can spur competition by allowing economic agents to buy.

## Classification of Financial Services

The financial intermediaries in India can be traditionally classified into two:

(1) Capital market intermediaries and

(2) Money market intermediaries.

The capital market intermediaries consist of term lending institutions and investing institutions which mainly provide long term funds. On the other hand, money market consists of commercial banks, co-operative banks and other agencies which supply only short term funds. Hence, the term 'financial services industry' included all kinds of organizations which intermediate and facilitate financial transactions of both individuals and corporate customers.

## SCOPE OF FINANCIAL SERVICES

Financial services cover a wide range of activities. They can be broadly classified into two namely:

(1) Traditional activities, and

(2) Modern activities.

## Some Key Financial Services

In India, non-banking financial institutions have been in the forefront in providing specialized financial services to industry, traders, individuals and communities.

- Mutual funds in the public and private sector have been garnering savings for investment in the primary, secondary and debt market. The Indian mutual fund industry has mobilized over ₹ 5,50,000 crore as on June 2008 and has tremendous potential to manage on aggregate amount in the range of ₹ 14,70,000 to ₹ 18,50,000 crore by 2012 as compared to ₹ 5,64,599.28 crore at the end June 2008 or ₹ 6,00,266.32 crore in May 2008.

- Shelter is a basic human need. Housing finance raises the welfare of the households that live in it. Housing finance is translating many a dream into a reality.
- Smaller and less well-established enterprises find leasing and attractive source of long-term finance.
- Venture capital is a temporary start-up financing in the form of equity capital or loans, with returns linked to profits and managerial control.
- Factoring finances inventories and receivables. It brings all services together in one package.
- Forfaiting is an alternative source of trade finance mainly for exporters. The delay in receiving payments from importers acts as a hurdle for exporters in expanding their business. Forfaiting is an option available to the exporters for financing exports.
- Depositories is a bank for securities, which are maintained in electronic data form instead of physical paper certificates.
- The money market/mutual funds invest in money market instruments of very high quality and of very short maturities.
- Insurance is a financial service for collecting the savings of the public and providing them with a risk coverage.
- A merchant banker is a financial intermediary who helps to transfer capital from those who possess it to those who need it.
- Custodial services provide agency services like safe keeping of shares and debentures, collection of interest and dividend and reporting of matters on corporate development and corporate securities to foreign investors.
- Securitisation is a technique whereby a financial company converts its ill-liquid, non-negotiable and high value financial assets into securities of small value which are made tradable and transferable.
- Financial intermediaries have set up corporate advisory services to customer. As new avenues of finance like Euro, loans, GDRs, etc., are available to corporate, this service is of immense help to the customers.

## Traditional activities

Traditionally, the financial intermediaries have been rendering a wide range of services encompassing both capital and money market activities. They can be grouped under two heads *viz;*

(1) Fund-based activities, and

(2) Non-fund-based activities.

## Fund-based activities

The traditional services which come under fund-based activities are the following:

(1) Underwriting of or investment in shares, debentures, bonds, etc., of new issues (primary market activities).

(2) Dealing in secondary market activities.

(3) Participating in money market instruments like commercial papers, certificate of deposits, Treasury bills, discounting of bills, etc.

(4) Involving in equipment leasing, hire purchase, venture capital, seed capital, etc.

(5) Dealing in foreign exchange market activities.

## Non-fund-based activities

Financial intermediaries provide services on the basis of non-fund activities also. This can also be called "fee-based' activity. Today, customers whether individual or corporate are not satisfied with mere provision of finance. They expect more from financial service companies. Hence, a wide variety of services, are being provided under this head. They include the following:

(1) Managing the capital issues, i.e., management of pre-issue and post-issues activities relating to the capital issue in accordance with the SEBI guidelines and thus enabling their promoters to market their issues.

(2) Making arrangements for the placement of capital and debt instruments with investment institutions.

(3) Arrangement of funds from financial institutions for the client's project cost or his working capital requirements.

(4) Assisting in the process of getting all government and other clearances.

## Modern Activities

Besides the above traditional services, the financial intermediaries render innumerable services in recent times. Most of them are in the nature of non-fund based activity. In view of the importance, these activities have been discussed in brief under the head 'New financial products and services'. However, some of the modern services provided by them are given in brief hereunder:

(1) Rendering project advisory services right from the preparation of the project report till the raising of funds for starting the project with necessary government approval.

(2) Planning for mergers and acquisitions and assisting for their smooth carry-out.

(3) Guiding corporate customers in capital restructuring.

(4) Acting as trustees to the debentureholders.

(5) Recommending suitable changes in the management structure and management style with a view to achieving better results.

(6) Structuring the financial collaboration/joint ventures by identifying suitable joint venture partner and preparing joint venture agreement.

(7) Rehabilitating and reconstructing sick companies through appropriate scheme of reconstruction and facilitating the implementation of the scheme.

(8) Hedging of risks due to exchange rate risk, interest rate risk, economic risk and political risk by using swaps and other derivative products.

(9) Managing the portfolio of large public sector corporations.

(10) Undertaking risk management services like insurance services, buyback options, etc.

(11) Advising the clients on the question of selecting the best source of funds taking into consideration the quantum of funds required, their cost, lending period, etc.

(12) Guiding the clients in the minimization of the cost of debt and in the determination of the optimum debt-equity mix.

(13) Undertaking services relating to the capital market such as:

(a) Clearing services,

(b) Registration and transfers,

(c) Safe-custody of securities,

(d) Collection of income on securities.

(14) Promoting credit rating agencies for the purpose of rating companies which want to go public by the issue of debt instruments.

Financial intermediaries have to perform the task of financial innovation to meet the dynamically changing needs of the economy and to help the investors cope with an increasingly volatile and uncertain marketplace. There is a dire necessity for the financial intermediaries to go for innovation due to the following reasons:

**(i) Low Profitability:** The profitability of the major financial intermediary, namely the banks has been very much affected in recent times. There is a decline in the profitability of traditional banking products. So, they have been compelled to seek out new products which may fetch high returns.

**(ii) Keen Competition:** The entry of many financial intermediaries in the financial sector market has led to severe competition among themselves. This keen competition has paved the way for the entry of varied nature of innovative financial products so as to meet the varied requirements of the investors.

**(iii) Economic Liberalisation:** Reform of the financial sector constitutes the most important component of India's programmer towards economic liberalisation. The recent economic liberalisation measures have opened the door to foreign competitors to enter into our domestic market. Deregulation in the form of elimination of exchange controls and interest rate ceilings have made the market more competitive. Innovation has become a must for survival.

(iv) **Improved Communication Technology:** The communication technology has become so advanced that even the world's issuers can be linked with the investors in the global financial market without any difficulty by means of offering so many options and opportunities. Hence, innovative products are brought into the domestic market in no time.

(v) **Customer Services:** Now a days, the customer's expectations are very great. They want newer products at lower cost or at lower credit risk to place, the existing ones. To meet this increased customer sophistication, to invent a new product which may suit to the requirement of the investing public. Innovations thus help them in soliciting new business.

(vi) **Global Impact:** Many of the providers and users of capital have changed their roles all over the world. Financial intermediaries have come out of their traditional approach and they are ready to assume more credit risks. As a consequence, many innovations have taken place in the global financial sector which has its own impact on the domestic sector also.

(vii) **Investor Awareness:** With a growing awareness amongst the investing public, there has been a distinct shift from investing the savings in physical assets like gold, silver, land, etc., to financial assets, they go from 'risk-free' bank deposits to risky investments in shares. To meet the growing awareness of the public, innovation has become the need of the hour.

## FINANCIAL ENGINEERING

Thus, the growing need for innovation has assumed immense importance, in recent times. This process is being referred to as financial engineering. Financial engineering is the lifeblood of any financial ability. "Financial engineering is the design, the development and the implementation of innovative financial instruments and processes and the formulation of creative solutions to problems in finance".

## INNOVATIVE FINANCIAL SERVICES

The eighties have been years of exciting and progressive change in the banking business emerging from disintermediation process that has set in and consequential diversification being resorted to by banks in India in a big way. Pursuant to this, certain new non-conventional and sophisticated services, based on customer conveniences and preferences, have been added to the banking arena. Significant among those are housing finance, hire-purchase, leasing, factoring, merchant banking, mutual funds, consumer loans and venture capital finance, being provided by banks on their own or through subsidiaries set up exclusively to look after and manage these new areas of business. Some of these activities were there earlier too, but they have got a major fillip with more entrants into the business due to increased opportunities perceived or with certain liberalisation measures in these lines of activities.

Apart from the above, we are experiencing computer revolution and many other important innovations such as introduction of new financial instruments like certificates of deposits, commercial paper, participation certificates and cheques and credit cards, to cope with the emergent competitive environment. Besides, investment management including investment counselling and tax services are also evolving innovative packages to meet consumer demands.

Further, in view of the growing equity culture in the economy, banks may have to become active in distributing stock and shares, debentures and bonds even their own depositors. We also find corporate sector companies branching out as finance companies, undertaking a vast array of financial services.

Several banks have expanded their overseas operations and have undertaken financing the import-export business of their clients in a professional manner, many times competing with large international banks. The international banking scene has undergone drastic changes, with the introduction of computer and telecommunication technology, which have led to geographical and financial integration of international financial market in recent years. International banks have diversified their business into capital market operations since new profit opportunities have been noticed in this field. Responding to these changes in the international environment, commercial banks in India have also been trying to diversify in such areas as consumer credit, credit cards, travellers' cheques, etc. It is, however felt that we should not aim at something which is not in our competence and that overseas bank offices should be used more as centres for information for exports.

## FINANCIAL SERVICES AND TRADE IN FINANCIAL SERVICES

The financial services sector is not only the largest sub-sector of the services sector; it is also the fastest growing sub-sector in both developed and developing economies. In addition to contributing to output, it also contributes significantly to employment generation.

The Financial Service Agreement (FSA) under the aegis of the General Agreement on Trade in Services (GATS) provides the multilateral legal framework for 95% of world trade in financial services. Over the last decade, international trade in financial services has increased at a more rapid pace than growth.

Among the 19 countries in the Asia-Pacific region for which the liberalisation indices are available, India ranks 12th in deposit taking and 15th in lending (arranged in descending order). The indices were much below the regional averages as also world averages.

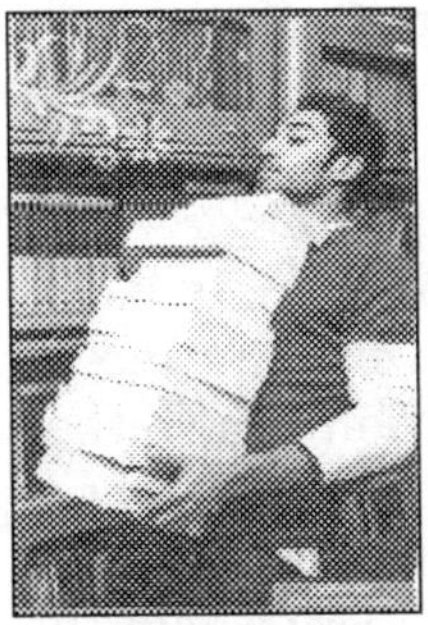

Nevertheless, India's move to sign the FSA could be said as strategic and timely, as by 1997 India had already implemented several reform measures in the financial sector in general and the banking sector in particular.

### Mode 1

India is unbound in Mode I, i.e., cross-border supply. Mode 1 is mostly applicable to the non-residents. In order to attract inflow of foreign exchange various facilities, both deposit-taking and lending, have been made available in India to persons of Indian nationality or

Indian origin settled abroad and overseas corporate bodies predominantly owned by such persons, to open and maintain various kinds of bank accounts.

## Internet Banking

Internet banking has just taken roots in India, with a few banks offering banking services on the Internet. Internet banking has the potential for banks to lower the transaction cost, offer increasing number of products and services in a timeless manner, thereby maximizing customer satisfaction, enhancing geographical reach and enabling entry into new markets. Within the country, Internet banking has hitherto not made much headway due to several psychological, technological and socio-economic reasons. However, so far as the non-residents are concerned, Internet banking possesses a lot of potential, as many of these factors would not be relevant for non-residents.

## Mode 2: Consumption Abroad

A foreign tourist visiting India can open a current/savings banks account with fund remitted from abroad in a specified manner or by selling his 'brought in' foreign exchange in India. In such a case, the balance in the account can be converted into foreign currency at the time of departure of the tourist from India provided certain conditions are satisfied.

## Mode 3: Commercial Presence

Commercial presence of foreign banks (FBs) in India is allowed in two ways: (a) through opening of offices in India, and (b) through foreign investment in domestic banks.

In commercial presence, foreign banks operating in India are doing their business quite efficiently. Based on the assessment of performance of the FBs, State Bank Group, nationalized banks, and private banks over the period 1990-91 to 2001-02 it was observed that the FBs had shown higher RoA than the domestic banks, put emphasis on non-interest income and cost control, had higher capital adequacy ratios and low NPA ratios, and were more productive in terms of labour productivity. Domestic banks were facing competition from these banks. In fact, a lot of 'consumerism' that emerged in Indian banking sphere could be attributed to the foreign banks operating in India. A similar conclusion could be made about technological development. However, in recent years, many FBs, which had entered into India in the post-liberalization era, either closed down or restructured their operations. Many factors contributed to this. These included, *inter alia,* poor foreign trade environment as against an optimistic assessment at the time of entry by these banks, competition from domestic banks, particularly in the retail banking segment, and convergence in the regulatory and supervisory environment of domestic and foreign banks. There is also a debate as to whether foreign banks can be allowed to operate also through subsidiaries. In future, India's commitments under the FSA may also increase.

In the domestic financial sector, the markets have deepened and widened significantly with the introduction of more players and more instruments. Although the developed countries continue to dominate the scene of trade in financial services the developing countries are increasingly integrating themselves, introducing more of innovations and becoming technologically more capable.

## Four Modes

Trade in services is defined in terms of four modes of supply asunder:

- **Mode I:** *Cross-border supply of services* in which the service is supplied from the territory of one member into the territory of another member (e.g., taking a loan or the purchase of insurance cover by a consumer from a financial institution located abroad).
- **Mode 2:** *Consumption abroad* or cross-border consumption of services in which the service is supplied in the territory of one member to a service consumer coming from another member (e.g., the purchase of financial services by consumers while travelling abroad).
- **Mode 3:** *Commercial presence* in which the services is supplied by setting up a business or professional establishment, such as, a subsidiary corporation or a branch or representative office in the territory of one member by a service supplier of another member (e.g., a foreign bank or other financial institution opening a branch office or subsidiary in India). This is sometimes referred to as the investment mode, and the trade covered under this mode is known as establishment trade.
- **Mode 4:** *Movement of natural persons* which involves a "natural person" — a human being — from one member country going to the territory of another member to provide a service there for short-term, non-immigrant business-related purposes. Natural persons may either be employees of service suppliers (e.g., a US bank sending a manager to a branch office in India to manage its operations for three years) or independent services suppliers in their own right (e.g., an IT professional from India hired by a US firm to work in the US for five years).

## Internationalization of Financial Services

Internationalization of financial services is defined as: (a) eliminating discrimination in the treatment between foreign and domestic financial services providers, and (b) removing barriers to the cross-border provisions of financial services. The FSA, under the auspices of the GATS (MEN, National Treatment and Market Access), does exactly both, and hence, a country by signing into the FSA consciously promotes internationalization of its financial service sector.

## Financial Sector Assessment (FSA): India's Commitments

In insurance, India's entry limitations are accompanied by restrictions on foreign equity also. India is, in fact, the only participant in direct insurance, which has left the commercial presence mode completely unbound. It, therefore, retains the discretion to impose any Article XVI restriction, including on entry and foreign equity.

As in insurance, in banking, entry limitations are accompanied by restrictions on foreign equity also. Since India allows entry only through branches (restricted to 12 per annum), this amounts to a prohibition on foreign equity participation. Interestingly, India is the only country, which allows entry only in the form of branches of foreign banks licensed and supervised as banks in the home country. This may reflect the desire to shift the regulatory and supervisory burden to the home country.

As regards pre-commitment to future liberalization, India will allow an increased number of branches rather to a change in regime. In banking, the pre-commitment is 12 branch licences per year both for new entrants and existing banks, subject to 15% maximum share of foreign assets to the total assets of the banking system.

## Factors Affecting Access to Financial Services

A number of factors affecting access to financial services have been identified. These are:

(1) Gender issues
(2) Age factor
(3) Legal identity
(4) Limited literacy
(5) Place of living
(6) Psychological barriers
(7) Cultural barriers
(8) Social barriers
(9) Social security payments
(10) Level of income
(11) Bank charges
(12) Terms and conditions
(13) Types of occupations
(14) Caste and religion
(15) Attractiveness of the product
(16) Cumbersome procedure
(17) Bias of financial institutions
(18) Pride and prejudices of the white collar
(19) Wrongful assessment
(20) Willingness to spread services
(21) Employment barriers

(22) Lack of opportunities
(23) Owning assets
(24) Difficulty in smoothening income to cope with shocks
(25) Exclusion from mainstream society.

## GATS and Indian Banking Sector

India's commitments in banking under the FSA are relatively at a lower side, reflecting its gradual and cautious approach, which was any way visible during the process of negotiation. The liberalization index of India and a few countries in the Asia-Pacific region constructed on the basis of their commitments in the FSA in respect of banking are presented in the Appendix.

**New Products in Forex Market:** New products have also emerged in the forex markets of developed countries. Some of these products are yet to make full entry in Indian markets. Among them, the following are the important ones:

**(a) Forward Contracts:** A forward transaction is one where the delivery of a foreign currency takes place at a specified future date for a specified price. It may have a fixed maturity, e.g., 31$^{st}$ May or a flexible maturity, e.g., 1$^{st}$ to 31$^{st}$ May. There is an obligation to honour this contract at any cost, failing which, there will be some penalty. Forward contracts are permitted only for genuine business transactions. It can be extended to other transactions like interest payments.

**(b) Options:** As the very name implies, it is a contract wherein the buyer of the option has a right to buy or sell a fixed amount of currency against another currency at a fixed rate on a future date according to his option. There is no obligation to buy or sell, but it is completely left to his option. Options may be of two types namely call options and put options. Under call options, the customer has an option to buy and it is the option to sell under put options. Options trading would lead to speculation and hence there are much restrictions in India.

**(c) Futures:** It is a contract wherein there is an agreement to buy or sell a stated quantity of foreign currency at a future date at a price agreed to between the parties on the stated exchange. Unlike options, there is an obligation to buy or sell foreign exchange on a future date at a specified rate. It can be dealt only in a stock exchange.

**(d) Swaps:** A swap refers to a transaction wherein a financial intermediary buys and sells a specified foreign currency simultaneously for different maturity dates – say, for instance, purchase of spot and sale of forward or *vice versa* with different maturities. Thus, swaps would result in simultaneous buying and selling of the same foreign currency of the same value for different maturities to eliminate exposure risk. It can also be used as a tool to enter arbitrage operations, if any, between two countries. It can also be used in the interest rate market also. It is explained in detail under the Chapter Derivatives.

**Salient Featurs of Small Savings Schemes**

| *Scheme* | *Interest Payable, Rates, Periodicity, etc.* | *Denominations and Investment Limits* | *Salient Features Including Tax Rebate* |
|---|---|---|---|
| **Post Office Savings Account** | 3.50% p.a. on Individual/Joint and Pension Account, PF, SF, Gratuity Fund account and Sanchayika Account, 3% p.a. on Public Account, Security Deposit Account — for purchase of motor vehicle or tractor. 2% p.a. on official capacity and other accounts. | Minimum ₹ 50/-. Maximum ₹ 1,00,000/- for an individul account. ₹ 2,00,000/- for joint account.<br>No limit on group, institutional or official capacity accounts. | Cheque facility available. Cheques are also accepted by scheduled banks.<br>Interest is totally exempted from income tax as per prevailing IT Act.<br>Deposits completely exempt from wealth tax. |
| **5-year Post Office Recurring Deposit Account** | ₹ 100/- account fetches ₹ 7,289.00 on maturity. Account can be continued for another 5 years on year-to-year basis. | Minimum ₹ 10/- per month or any amount in multiples of ₹ 5/-. No maximum limit. | Any number of accounts can be opened. One withdrawal up to 50% of the balance allowed after one year. Ful maturity value allowed on R.D. Account up to ₹ 50 denomination in case of death of depositor as per rules. 6 and 12 months advance deposits earn rebate.<br>If there are more than 4 defaults in monthly deposits, the account shall be treated as discontinued. Revival of the account is permitted only within a period of 2 months from the month of fifth default. The account in which defaulted instalments are deposited along with default fee, is not treated as discontinued.<br>Account can be prematurely closed after 3 years from the date of opening of account and on such premature closure of the account, interest at the rate applicable from time-to-time on Post Office Savings Account shall be payable. However, to premature closure of account is permissible until the period for which the advance deposits made, is over. Interest earned is deductible under Sec. 80L of IT Act. Deposits exempt from wealth tax. |

| *Scheme* | *Interest Payable, Rates, Periodicity, etc.* | *Denominations and Investment Limits* | *Salient Features Including Tax Rebate* |
|---|---|---|---|
| **Post Office Time Deposit Account** | Interest payable annually but calculated quarterly<br>*Period Rates Effective Rate*<br>1-Year Account 6.25% 6.40<br>2-Year Account 6.50% 6.66%<br>3-Year Account 7.25% 7.45%<br>5-Year Account 7.50% 7.71% | Minimum ₹ 50.<br>No maximum limit | Account can be opened by individual, Trust Regimental fund and welfare fund 2, 3 and 5 year accounts can be closed after one year at a discount. Account can be closed after six months but before one year without interest. Interest deductible under Section 80L of IT Act Deposits exempt from wealth tax.<br>Maturity period is 6 years. |
| **Post Office Monthly Income Scheme** | 8% per annum payable monthly i.e., ₹ 80/- will be paid every month on a deposit of ₹ 12,000/- in addition 10% bonus also payable on maturity i.e., ₹ 1,200/- will be paid as bonus after 6 years for deposit of ₹ 12,000/-. The depositor may not opt for a payment of interest through post-dated cheques. | Minimum ₹ 1,000/-<br>Maximum ₹ 3 lakh in single account, ₹ 6 lakh in joint account. Total investment of an individual in his/her single accounts together with his/her share in joint accounts should not exceed ₹ 3 lakh. | Can be prematurely encashed after one year at 5% discount. However, no such deduction shall be made if the account is closed after three years from the date of opening of such account. Interest and Bonus deductible under Sec. 80L of IT Act.<br>Deposits exempt from wealth tax. |
| **6-year National Savings Certificate (VIII Issue)** | 8.16% p.a. (8% interest compounded six monthly) payable at maturity.<br>₹ 1,000/- grows to ₹ 1,601<br>₹ 5,000/- grows to ₹ 8,005<br>₹ 10,000/- grows to ₹ 16,010 | Minimum ₹ 100/-<br>No maximum limit.<br>Available in denominations of ₹ 100/-, 500/-,<br>₹ 1,000/-, ₹ 5,000/- and ₹ 10,000/-. | A certificate can be purchased by:<br>(i) An adult for himself or on behalf of a minor or to a minor.<br>(ii) Two adults jointly (iii) Trust (iv) HUF<br>Deposits qualify for tax rebate under Sec. 88 of IT Act. The interest accruing annually and deemed to be reinvested will also qualify for tax rebate under Sec. 88 of IT Act. Such interest wil be entitled to deduction under Sec. 80L of the IT Act. Can be encashed after 6 years.<br>Deposits exempt from wealth tax. |

| *Scheme* | *Interest Payable, Rates, Periodicity, etc.* | *Denominations & Investment Limits* | *Salient Features Including Tax Rebate* |
|---|---|---|---|
| **15-year Public Provident Fund Account** | 8% per annum compounded yearly. | Minimum ₹ 500/-.<br>Maximum ₹ 70,000/- in a financial year.<br>Deposits can be made in lump sum or in 12 instalments. | PPF account can be opened by an individual in his/her name or on behalf of a minor or whom he/she is the guardian, and also on behalf of HUF as Karta. Non-Resident Indians are not eligible to open an account under the Public Provident Scheme, w.e.f., 25th July, 2003 vide GSR 585 (E). Provided that if a resider who subsequently becomes NRI during currency of maturity period prescribed under PPF scheme may continue to subscribe to the fund till its maturity on a non-repatriation basis. Deposits qualify for Income Tax rebate under Sec. 88 of IT Act. Deposits completely exempt from Wealth Tax. **Interest credited to the fund is totally exempted from income tax as per prevailing IT Act.** Withdrawal is permissible every year from 7th financial year. Loan facility available from the 3rd financial year. No attachment under court decree facility to extend account beyond 15 years for further one or more block period of 5 years without any loss of benefits. |
| **Kisan Vikas Patrika** | Money doubles in 8 years and 7 months. Facility of premature encashment is also available as per the table given below for the certificates of denomination of ₹ 1,000 and at proportionate rates for other denominations<br>After 2½ years ₹ 1170.51 — After 6 years ₹ 1543.30<br>After 3 years - ₹ 1207.95 — After 6½ years ₹ 1649.13<br>After 3½ years ₹ 1267.19 — After 7 years ₹ 1713.82<br>After 4 years ₹ 1310.80 — After 7½ years ₹ 1781.06<br>After 4½ years ₹ 1,355.90 — After 8 years but less than 8 years 7 months ₹ 1850.93<br>After 5 years ₹ 1435.63<br>After 5½ years ₹ 1488.49 | No limit on investment Available in denominations of ₹ 100/- Rs. 500/-, ₹ 1000, Rs. 5,000/-, ₹ 10,000, in all Post Offices, and ₹ 50,000/- in all Head Post Offices. | A certificate can be purchased by:<br>(*i*) An adult for himself or on behalf of a minor or to a minor.<br>(*ii*) Jointly by Two adults.<br>(*iii*) Trust<br>Amount of interest accrued every year can be shown for income tax purposes. |

LIMITED AVENUES FOR RETIREES

| | *6.5% bonds* | *8% bonds* | *Fixed deposit** | *Post Office monthly income scheme* | *Post Office time deposit* | *LIC Varishtha* | *MIP-MFs*** |
|---|---|---|---|---|---|---|---|
| Tenure (yrs.) | 5 | 6 | 3 | 6 | 5 | For life | No fixed tenure |
| Minimum invst.<br>Maximum invst. | 1,000<br>No limit | 1,000<br>No limit | 20,000<br>No limit | 1,000<br>3,00,000 individual/ 6,00,000 jointly | 50<br>No limit | 33,335*<br>2,66,665* | 5,000<br>No limit |
| Safety/Rating | Highest | Highest | AAA | Highest | Highest | Highest | Moderate risk |
| Interest rates (%) | 6.50 | 8.,00 | 6.50 | 8.00 | 7.50❖ | 9.00 | 7.00-9.00 |
| Frequency of interest | Half-yearly | Half-yearly | Monthly | Monthly | Annually | Monthly | Monthly |
| Tax benefits (income) | Tax free | Sec. 80L | Sec. 80L | Sec. 80L | Sec. 80L | Taxable | Tax free |
| On maturity | Principal | Principal | Principal | Principal + 10% bonus on maturity | Principal | No maturity period but exit option available after 15 years | Principal |
| Collateral | No | No | Loan facility available | No | Yes | Loan facility available | Yes |
| Amount invested | 1,00,000 | 1,00,000 | 1,00,000 | 1,00,000 | 1,00,000 | 1,00,000 | 1,00,000 |
| Amount interest | 6,500 | 8,000 | 6,500 | 8,000 | 7,714 | 9,000-9,381 | 7,000-9,000 |

* Maximum and minimum amounts for monthly option.
** Monthly Income Plan from Mutual Fund with under 15% equally exposure
❖ Compounded quarterly.
*Source:* www.personalfn.com.

## FOREIGN EXCHANGE SERVICES AVAILABLE

(1) Buy and sale of Foreign Currency Notes, Foreign Travellers' Cheques, Drafts and Foreign Remittances.

(2) Foreign Exchange for Business Trips, Medical Treatment Abroad, Higher Studies, Tourism, Employment or Immigration.

(3) Foreign Bank Guarantee, Letter of Credit, Imports and Export Finance, Pre-shipment/Post-shipment Credit Facility.

(4) Foreign Currency – Non-resident A/c. (NRE, NRO, FCNR) Facilities, Exchange Earner Foreign Currency A/c. (EEFC), Resident Foreign Currency A/c. (RFC), Resident Foreign Currency (Domestic) A/c. (RFC Domestic).

## INSTITUTIONS AND MARKETS

Commercial banks are likely to remain the dominant institutions for some time. Banks can be made more efficient by improving their management systems and increasing the competition they face. Better management requires new lending policies, better loan recovery procedures, more sophisticated information systems, and better-trained staff. The entry of new banks, domestic or foreign, can stimulate competition.

Countries also need to develop other financial institutions, whose services compete with and complement those of commercial banks. Non-bank financial intermediaries, such as development finance institutions, insurance companies, and pension funds, are potentially important sources of long-term finance. Most of the existing development banks are insolvent, however. Where they are to be restructured, rather than closed or merged with commercial banks, thought must be given to their future role and viability. Any diversification should build on the experience of their staffs and on their existing client relationships. As more of the population becomes able to and desires to make provision for retirement, contractual savings institutions will grow in size. Permitting pension funds and insurance companies to invest in financial instruments other than low-interest government bonds can greatly increase the supply of long-term finance to the private sector.

Many developing countries have benefited from the creation of money and capital markets. Money markets can provide competition for banks, a flexible means for managing liquidity, a benchmark for market-based interest rates, and an instrument of monetary policy. Capital markets can be a source of long-term finance — both debt and equity — and can help to foster sounder corporate capital structures.

Most developing countries have a long-established informal financial sector that provides services to the noncorporate sector — households, small farmers, and small businesses. Although family and friends are usually the most important source of credit, pawnbrokers provide a substantial amount of credit to those with marketable collateral, and moneylenders to those without. Merchants provide financing to their customers, and purchasing agents advance funds to their suppliers. Rotating savings and credit associations are ubiquitous in the developing world.

Financial institutions have often been weakened by being forced to channel credit to small-scale borrowers. Because such borrowers do not maintain financial accounts, formal lenders find it difficult to predict who is likely to repay. Moreover, if the borrower is in a group favoured by government, formal intermediaries may find it difficult to collect. The informal sector, in contrast, has been able to serve such borrowers. Informal lending has severe drawbacks, however. The scale of lending is small, the range of services is limited, markets are fragmented, and interest rates are sometimes usurious. Nevertheless, these institutions help clients that formal institutions often find too costly or risky to serve. Some countries have recognized this and have established programmes to link informal markets more closely with formal markets. The most successful formal programmes for the non-corporate sector utilize rather than suppress indigenous systems, take deposits as well as lend, and levy charges that cover costs.

## COMMERCIAL BANKS

Commercial banks are the heart of our financial system. They hold the deposits of millions of persons, governments and business units. They make funds available through their lending and investing activities to borrowers — individuals, business firms, and governments. In doing so, they facilitate both the flow of goods and services from producers to consumers and the financial activities of governments. They provide a large portion of our medium of exchange and they are the media through which monetary policy is effected. These facts obviously add up to the conclusion that the commercial banking system of the nation is important to the functioning of its economy.

Commercial banks play a very important role in our economy; in fact, it is difficult to imagine how our economic system could function efficiently without many of their services. They are the heart of our financial structure, since they have the ability, in cooperation with the Reserve Bank of India, to add to the money supply of the nation and create additional purchasing power. Banks' lendings, investments and related activities facilitate the economic processes of production, distribution and consumption.

The major task of banks and other financial institutions is to act as intermediaries, channeling savings into investment and consumption: through them, the investment requirements of savers are reconciled with the credit needs of investors and consumers.

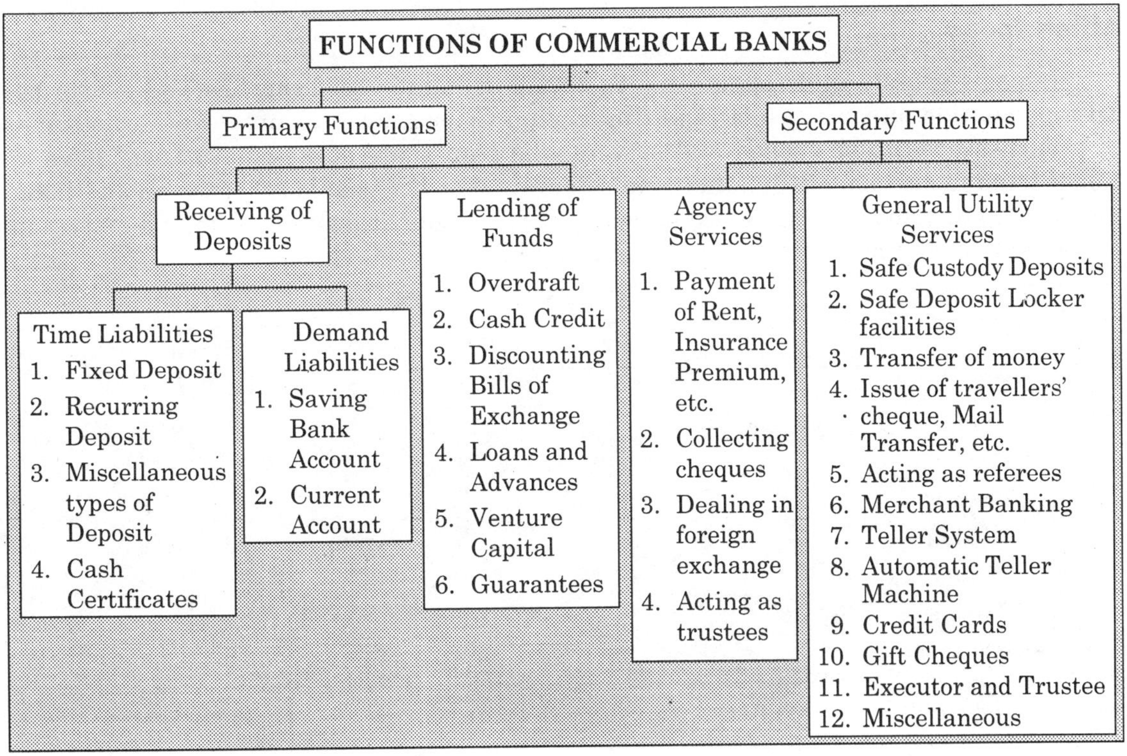

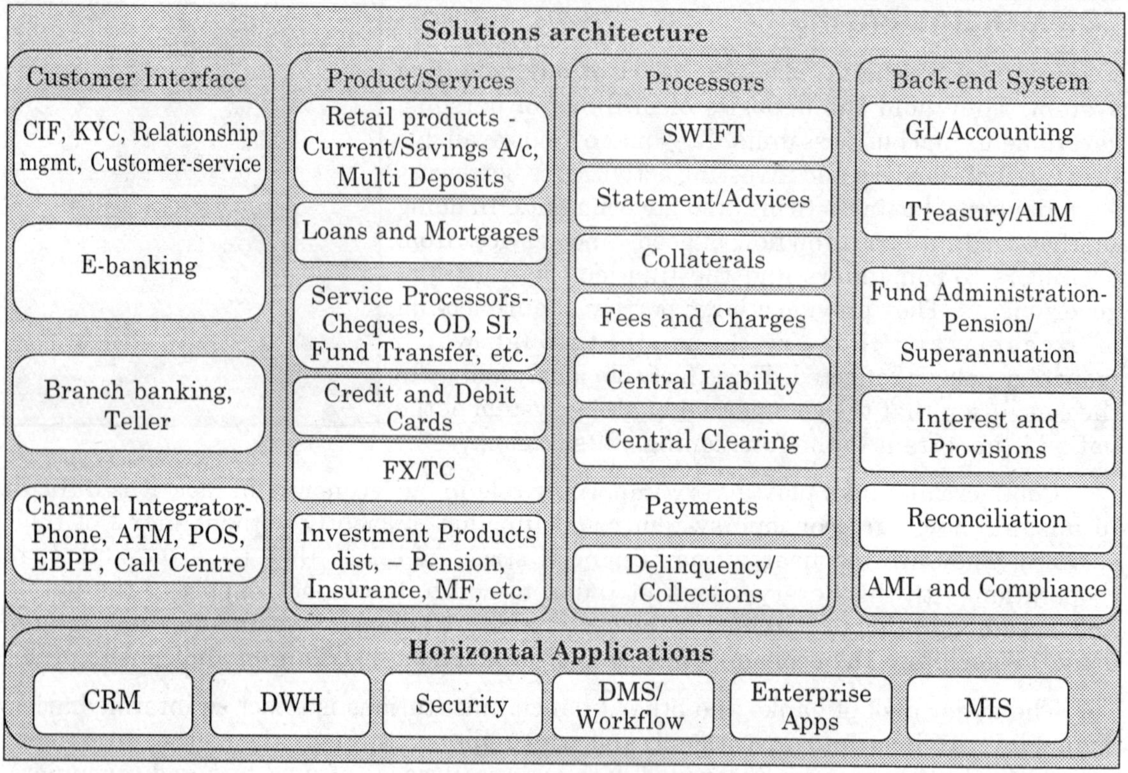


## Miles to go

India is grossly underpenetrated in terms of number of branches and ATMs per lakh population, according to a report by Boston Consultancy Group. Several thousands of branches need to be opened and players who gain share of distribution will have an upper hand in customer acquisition and retention. For PSU banks, there is an additional elements of distribution excellence network optimization, branch redesign and mastering the alternate channels internet, call centre and ATMs, the report said.

**BANKING PENETRATION**

| | ATMs | Branches |
|---|---|---|
| US | 130 | 30 |
| Spain | 126.6 | 95.9 |
| UK | 47 | 21 |
| Mexico | 20 | 8 |
| Thailand | 17.1 | 7.2 |
| Philippines | 6 | 7.7 |
| China | 5.5 | 1.5 |
| Indonesia | 4.8 | 8.4 |
| India | 3.4 | 6.0 |

*(No. per lakh of population)*

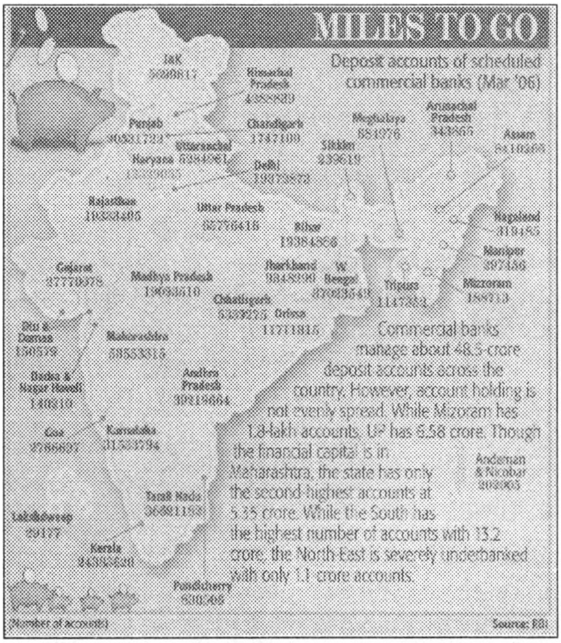
MILES TO GO
Deposit accounts of scheduled commercial banks (Mar '06)
Commercial banks manage about 48.5-crore deposit accounts across the country. However, account holding is not evenly spread. While Mizoram has 1.8-lakh accounts, UP has 6.58 crore. Though the financial capital is in Maharashtra, the state has only the second-highest accounts at 5.35 crore. While the South has the highest number of accounts with 13.2 crore, the North-East is severely underbanked with only 1.1-crore accounts.
(Number of accounts)
Source: RBI

The technology that keeps you in touch...

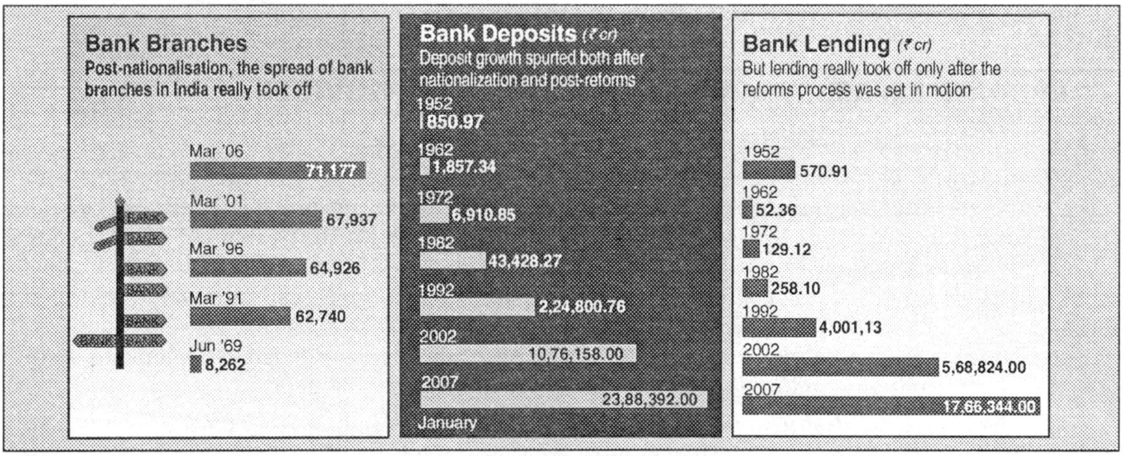
Bank Branches
Post-nationalisation, the spread of bank branches in India really took off
Mar '06 71,177
Mar '01 67,937
Mar '96 64,926
Mar '91 62,740
Jun '69 8,262
BANK
Bank Deposits (₹ cr)
Deposit growth spurted both after nationalization and post-reforms
1952 850.97
1962 1,857.34
1972 6,910.85
1982 43,428.27
1992 2,24,800.76
2002 10,76,158.00
2007 23,88,392.00
January
Bank Lending (₹ cr)
But lending really took off only after the reforms process was set in motion
1952 570.91
1962 52.36
1972 129.12
1982 258.10
1992 4,001,13
2002 5,68,824.00
2007 17,66,344.00

If this process of transference is to be carried out efficiently, it is absolutely essential that the banks are involved. Indeed, in performing their tasks, they realise important economies of scale: the savings placed at their disposal are employed in numerous and large transactions adapted to the specific needs of borrowers. In this way, they are able to make substantial cost savings for both savers and borrowers, who would otherwise have to make individual transactions with each other. However, there is more to these economies of scale than just the cost aspect.

Commercial banks have been referred to as '*department stores* of *finance*' as they provide a wide variety of financial services. In addition to the acceptance of deposits, lending and investing, they provide a multitude of services, including transfer of funds, collection, foreign exchange, safe custody, safe deposit locker, travellers' cheque, merchant banking services, credit cards, gift cheques, etc. They also play an important role in entrepreneurship development. The functions of commercial banks touches all economic activities from agriculture, industry, trade, exports and consumption.

Similarly, cooperative banks offer many of these services in rural areas.

The complexion of the Indian banking scene is all set to see a remarkable change. With the entry of new private banks on a large scale, the expansion of foreign bank branches made easier, the number of non-banking financial institutions and their business growing fast, the banks are in the middle of a tough competitive arena.

## CORPORATE TREASURY MANAGEMENT SERVICE PROVIDED BY BANKS

**BOX : 1**

***Depository services:*** These include: cash vault services to provide protection and processing capabilities; electronic cash letters to enable scanning and transmitting cheque images and data for deposit into accounts; pre-encoded deposits that provide faster cheque clearance; returned items solutions to help manage returned items with detailed images; activity reporting to improve efficiency and increase collection rates; zero balance sweep accounts that concentrate funds into one centralized account to use cash resources productively while retaining a centralized disbursing authority and remote deposit solutions to scan cheque at the company end and electronically send the images for deposit.

***Collection and disbursement services:*** This involves helping setting up systems to collect funds from customers or other sundry debtors (payers). It also includes flexibility in payment options for international transactions such as cash in advance, open account, letter of credit, or payment on a collection basis. Cheque image deposit solutions are designed to make cheque deposits electronically into the business deposit accounts, with both speed and accuracy directly from the company's office; lockbox imaging to view, retrieve and store remittance documents information, automated clearing house to deliver debits and credits on an electronic and automated basis and wire transfers that offer same-day availability.

***CTM service provides*** also enable disbursement of funds to vendors, employees, investors, or other payees. They provide account analysis, itemized information on accounts and balances, account reconcilement with detailed checking account information, outsourcing the printing and distribution of payable and payroll cheques, controlled disbursement accounts that provide precise dollar totals cheques that will clear daily so that the business can make accurate funding and investment decisions, disbursement imaging viewing to retrieve and manage cheque images online, cheque matching services that protect businesses against cheque fraud by matching issued cheques with those presented for payments on a daily basis.

***Liquidity and cash management services:*** This include liquid reserve accounts with flexibility to earn a competitive return on investing excess daily cash balances while providing daily investment confirmations and automated repurchases that ensures that bills are paid on time and the excess funds put to good use. Help is provided to link business checking accounts with money market mutual funds, allowing firms to minimize idle cash balances in their checking accounts and maximize the return earned on excess funds invested.

***Export and import related services:*** Exporters are assisted by providing a range of related services that help in hastening the delivery of goods in order to expedite receipt of payment, manage liquidity by ensuring that payment is received within the agreed time period, ensure that the payment is correct and settlement is directed to the bank where a depository account is maintained. Export licences vary from country-to-country and stringent conditions usually apply to products related to natural resources, national security, safety or health. Export services help in adapting products for exports to meet such conditions, provide assistance with freight forwarding and insurance against loss, damage and delay in transit since international shipment coverage is significantly different from domestic coverage.

## PRIVATE BANKING SERVICES

The private banks are offering the best advice on a whole range of assets classes. They are offering specialized products and customized services for their clients. As such, private banking is attracting more individuals as the booming economy spawns new millionaires.

- Private banking is personal.
- It is purely relationship driven
- Private banking focuses on wealth management
- Offers a variety of services that go beyond investment advisory
- Clients also get doorstep banking services
- Offers holistic services covering all asset classes
- Manages multiple assets in different countries
- Helps in acquiring companies

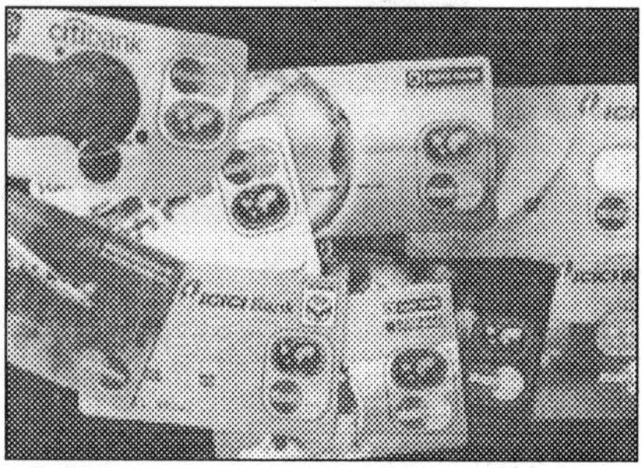

### What else Can You Get with Private Banking?

**Complete tax planning:** Private bankers advise on all aspects of tax planning and even help compute tax from all sources like business income, house property and capital gains. Also suggest tax reduction strategies.

**Succession planning:** Succession planning is often overlooked by most investors. A private bank helps with a proper succession planning, ensuring that your wealth goes to your legal heirs. This protects your wealth and ensures that the transition is smooth.

**Art advisory:** This is a new area private banks have got into. With art, fast emerging as an investment class in India, bankers help in understanding art and distinguish the various artists. They also help in identifying and allocating funds to various artists.

**Trust services:** The banks are now providing trust services to support activities like education, poverty alleviation, or trust that is solely to benefit a family or young ones. The bank advises on transferring assets to a trust and plans how best the trust can manage its assets.

**Estate planning:** Distribution of your wealth and real estate as per your wishes can sometimes be a chore. Private bankers ensure that your wealth, even house items, is distributed among your legal heirs in accordance with your wishes.

**Aircraft financing:** There's a complete advisory on which aircraft to buy (for personal use or for office services), including how you can pay for the same and also get the best interest rate.

**Co-investment opportunities:** Private bankers also advise on co-investment opportunities in the areas of real estate, unlisted companies, or other asset classes where both the bank and the client can invest jointly.

**M-Banking Services at Your Fingertips**

| | |
|---|---|
| **Account Services** | Check Balance<br>Check last 3 transactions<br>Transfer funds to other accounts of same as well as other banks<br>Request for cheque book<br>Request to stop cheque payment<br>Check the status of cheque |
| **Credit Card Services** | Check Balance<br>Details of last payment<br>Payment due date |
| **Demat Account Services** | Enquiry about account, bill, ISIN, etc.<br>Check transaction status |
| **Loan Account Services** | Amortization Schedule<br>Income tax certificate provisional and final<br>Reschedulement Letter<br>Reset Letter<br>Interest Certificate<br>Loan Agreement Copy<br>Welcome Letter |
| **Bill Services** | Pay bills<br>Bill presentment |

| | |
|---|---|
| **Other Services** | Locate a branch, ATM or Customer care centre<br>Recharge pre-paid mobile phones<br>Check payments made towards mobile phones<br>Apply for a new bank account, demat account, credit card loan |

A CHRONOLOGY OF CARD PAYMENTS IN INDIA

## PLAY YOUR CARDS RIGHT

Very soon, you will be able to swipe your debit card to withdraw cash from any point of sale, thanks to a directive from the RBI. But it was not always so easy to spend or pile on debt.

**1950: The Pioneers:** Diners Club issues the world's first credit card allowing members to charge meals at 27 New York restaurants.

**1982: First Plastic:** Andhra Bank launches India's first credit card. Five-star hotels start accepting credit cards for room charges.

**1990: Who's Using Cards:** Usage of credit cards still restricted to under 1,00,000 users, mostly in metros.

**1997-98: Follow the Leader:** SBI, India's largest bank, launches its credit card. Still, less than a million Indians use plastic.

**1998: Masterstroke:** Mastercard introduces India's first pin-based point-of-sale debit card for convenient access to bank accounts at merchants and ATM.

**1999: New Era:** 'Plastic' becomes a fashion statement. HDFC Bank launches India's first signature-based VISA debit card.

**2002: Red vs. Blue:** It's a plastic world. ICICI Bank introduces debit cards. Not to be outdone, HDFC Bank launches credit cards.

**2005: It's Free:** Competition peaks as ICICI takes the radical step of waiving joining and annual fees. Over 12 million card users celebrate.

**July 2009: Back to the Future:** RBI says debit cards may be used to withdraw cash from any point of sale. Is cash returning as the mode of payment again?

## Electronic Clearing Service

Electronic Clearing Service (ECS) is a mechanism of electronic funds transfer for transactions that entail an outgo of specified amounts at regular intervals. It is used by corporates to make various payments to their employees or investors; banks for accepting EMIs (equated monthly instalments) and utilities to collect payments for various bills.

Out of the two variants of the facility, that is, ECS credit and ECS debit, it is the latter that primarily concerns an individual user — termed beneficiary in this context. Individuals intending to make payments to these utilities or discharge their EMIs have to sign up with these entities to participate. From the individual's point of view, ECS mandate is in the nature of issuing standing instructions to his/her bank for making payments on a predecided date. You can also use the facility to make your insurance premium and EMI payments as well as mutual fund investments through systematic investment plan (SIP) route.

To avail of this service, you have to give the organisation—for instance, the telephone utility you pay bills to every month or the fund house in whose scheme you invest SIP — a mandate that represents your consent to avail of the facility and authorisation to your bank to honour the payment when due. It contains details such as your name, bank account number, branch, etc, along with the date on which your accounts is to be debited. The mandate forms can be obtained either from the entities' websites or their designated centres.

**METHODS USED TO CHEK BANK BALANCE**

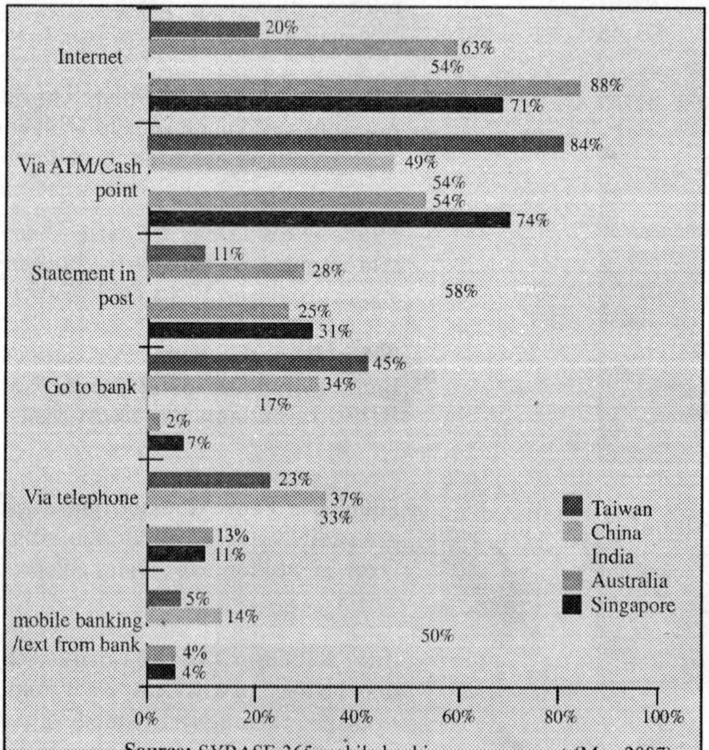


**Source:** SYBASE 365 mobile banking survey report (May 2007)

## Transacting with Your Mobile

In Mobile Banking, the bank customer can actually see his/her banking transactions on his/her mobile phone screen as opposed to hearing a message through the phone in Phone Banking.

Mobile Banking, which is offered by different banks with different branding, is a new age concept, when the mobile technology platform becomes the facilitator of communication and transactions between the customer and the bank. It brings in one major advantage - the customer need not physically go to the branch. Nor are banking hours a restriction mobile banking can happen anytime, across 24 hours.

With more and more banks putting it in use, Mobile Banking is a reality today. A few years back the usage of mobile was restricted to making and receiving calls. Now, science and technology make it possible to transact through the mobile phone.

Mobile banking is the state of the art process that has been introduced in the banks to make sure that the customers are better equipped with all the systems and process. This helps to carry out the transaction quickly and the account holders can check their account balance and the newly available schemes from the mobile web itself. As the advertisement of a leading bank says, it brings the bank branch inside your pocket.

Two prominent transactions, which enable mobile payments, are based on either SMS or the Internet. The former is perceived to be more user-friendly. In the latter, you will need to install an application on your mobile phone.

## Doorstep Banking Services

Doorstep banking, a convenient banking option for pick-up from and delivery to your place of business. You don't have to risk carrying cash to or from the bank. Deposit/ withdraw cash, deliver/collect trade documents and deposit cheques at the safety of your office, with ICICI Bank's Doorstep Banking Services for Current Account customers.

## Key Benefits of Doorstep Banking

- It's convenient. You get service at your doorstep. So, no travelling to the branch.
- It's secure. Cash-in-transit insurance, multiple verification and reconciliation procedures make the facility fool-proof.
- It's flexible. You can choose between daily services or services on call.
- It's hassle-free. Experienced agencies help you with your transactions.

## How Doorstep Banking Works?

At a time specified by you, a designated agent will visit your business premise. All you need to do is confirm the agent's identity, match the unique transaction ID and handover the cash/cheques/documents in an evelope.

Doorstep Banking Service is especially designed for entities having large number of branch transactions everyday. It helps you focus on your core business activity without spending time and efforts on visiting the branch for banking transactions.

## Imagine Your Bank Being So Close, Right At Your Doorstep

To enroll, contact your Relationship Manager today or any ICICI Bank branch. For further details, SMS 'Doorstep <city name>' to 5676766 or call your local corporate care numbers.

## THE BANKING OMBUDSMAN SCHEME:

Focused attention is given to the customer service dimension of the banking sector by sensitising banks to render good and efficient customer service, and encourage involvement of Boards of banks in evolving policies keeping in view the needs and aspirations of customers. The Reserve Bank has set up a full-fledged Customer Service Department with a view to making the banks more customer-friendly. The Reserve Bank has taken a number of steps to disseminate instrumentations/guidelines relating to customer-service and grievance redressal by banks through the multi-lingual website by placing all customer related notifications and press releases in a specific page titled 'For Common Person'. Customers of commercial banks can also approach the Reserve Bank with their grievances and queries through 'Contact Us' mode of the website. A complaint form for lodging complaints with the Banking ombudsman has also been made functional.

The Banking Ombudsman Scheme was first notified by the Reserve Bank on June 14, 1995 under Section 35A of the Banking Regulation Act, 1949 to provide for a system of redressal of grievances against banks. The scheme sought to establish a system of expeditious and inexpensive resolution of customer complaints.

The complaints against banks are handled at two levels in the Reserve Bank. Fifteen Banking Ombudsman Offices handle the complaints maintainable in terms of the provisions of the Banking Ombudsman Scheme. Regulatory departments in the Reserve Bank handle complaints that are not maintainable under the provisions of the Banking Ombudsman Scheme. The complaints have been categorised into deposit accounts, loans and advances, credit cards, activities of direct selling agents, harassment in recovery of loans and general/others.

## A LITANY OF COMPLAINTS

You can approach the Banking Ombusdman for any grievance that falls under the following categories. But before you shoot off your complaint, take note of these do's and don'ts.

**Category-wise Receipt of Complaints**

| Nature of Complaints | Complaints Received During | | | % To Aggregate Complaints | |
|---|---|---|---|---|---|
| | 2007-08 | 2008-09 | 2009-10 | 2008-09 | 2009-10 |
| Deposit Accounts | 5,612 | 6,706 | 3,681 | 9.7 | 4.7 |
| Remittances | 5,213 | 5,335 | 5,708 | 7.7 | 7.2 |
| Credit Cards | 10,129 | 17,648 | 18,810 | 25.5 | 23.7 |
| Loans and Advances | 6,054 | 8,174 | 6,612 | 11.8 | 8.3 |
| Charges Without Notice | 3,740 | 4,794 | 4,764 | 6.9 | 6 |
| Pension | 1,582 | 2,916 | 4,831 | 4.2 | 6.1 |
| Failure to Meet Commitments | 6,388 | 11,824 | 11,569 | 17.2 | 14.6 |
| DSAs and Recovery Agents | 3,128 | 3,018 | 1,609 | 4.4 | 2 |
| Notes and Coins | 141 | 113 | 158 | 0.2 | 0.2 |
| Others | 5,900 | 8,589 | 18,840 | 12.4 | 23.8 |
| Out of Subject | – | – | 2,684 | – | 3.4 |
| Total | 47,887 | 69,117 | 79,266 | 100 | 100 |

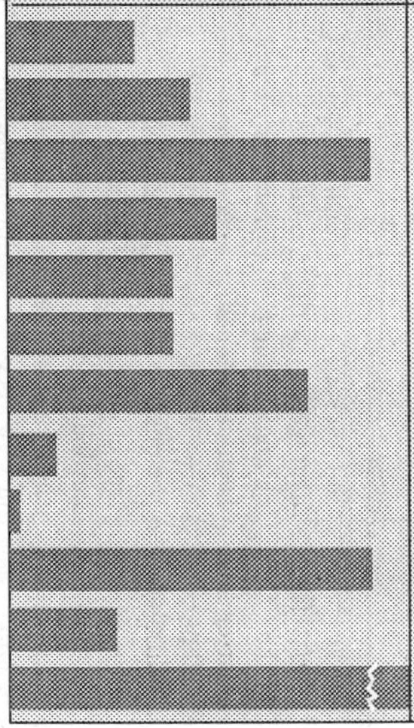

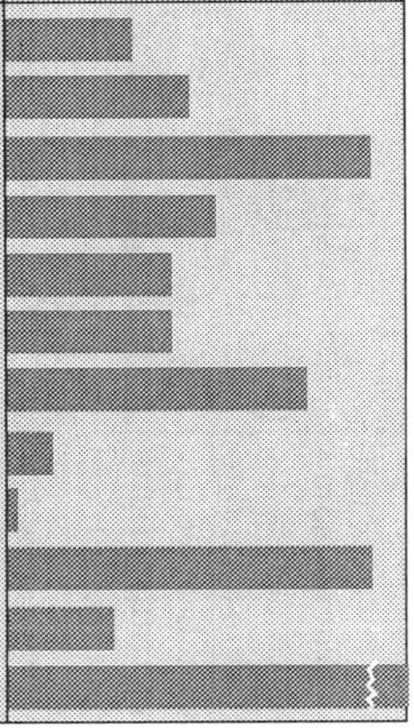

*Source:* RBI

**When to File Your Complaint with the Ombudsman ?**

**You can lodge a** complaint only after exhausting the option of approaching the concerned bank officials

**The complaint** must fall under the Ombudsman's purview. Else, it will be rejected

**Any complaint related** to deficiency in service or failure to adhere to the code of commitment will be admitted

**The Ombudsman** will not take up your complaint if you have already approached other forums or courts

**You must file your** complaint within a year of receiving a reply from the bank or within 13 months of complaining to the bank

**You can visit the website** the RBI or mail it to the concerned Ombudsman's office. You can also send your complaint by regular post

## BANK SERVICES COME AT A PRICE

The schedule of service charges and fees put up on your bank's website could provide some answers. While carrying out various transactions, accountholders seldom make an effort to take note of the charges applicable. Here's an indicative list of charges various banks levy on transactions executed by a regular savings accountholder

| | SBI | ICICI | HDFC | AXIS | Kotak Mahindra | HSBC |
|---|---|---|---|---|---|---|
| Non-maintenance of Average Quarterly Balance (AQB) | ₹ 225 per quarter | ₹ 750 per quarter | ₹ 750 per quarter | ₹ 750 per quarter** | If AQB more than 50% but less than required AQB: ₹ 750; AQB less than 50% ₹ 1,000 ^^ | If AQB < ₹ 10,000: ₹ 1,000 per quarter; if AQBI> ₹ 10,000 and < ₹ 25,000; ₹ 750 per quarter |
| Branch transactions/ cash transactions | ₹ 5 per debit entry, if the total number of entries exceeds 30 in a 6-month period. Applicable to channels other than alternative channels | At the base branch-Nil for the first 12 transactions of a qtr; Thereafter in the quarter, ₹ 50 per transaction | 3 free transactions in the quarter and ₹ 60 per additional transaction on non-maintenance of min balance (cash deposit/ withdrawal) 5 cash transactions at branch allowed free per month. Every additional transaction charged @ ₹ 100 per transaction | In case the average quarterly balance has not been maintained, three transactions per quarter are free of charge, beyond which there is a charge of ₹ 100 per transaction. In case the balance is maintained, there is no restriction on the number of transactions per quarter | Cash deposit at non-home branches - ₹ 2.5 per 1,000 (minimum 50 maximum 10,000); Cash withdrawal at non-home branches: free up to ₹ 50,000 per day ^^ | 12 transactions free per quarter, post which ₹ 50 per transaction will be charged |
| Cheque book charges | 25 leafs free in a year (other than multi-city cheque book); ₹ 2 per cheque leaf thereafter | Nil for 30 payable-at-par cheque leaves in a quarter; ₹ 30 for every additional | 25 cheque leafs free per calendar quarter; Additional cheque book of 25 leafs will be charged at ₹ | One cheque book per quarter free; ₹ 50 per cheque book thereafter if the AQB is maintained. In case of non-maintenance of AQB, all | 25 at par cheques issued free of cost; ₹ 1.5 per cheque leaf thereafter ^^ | 12 transactions free per quarter, post which ₹ 50 per transaction |

| | | | | | | |
|---|---|---|---|---|---|---|
| | | cheque book of 15 leaves | 50 per cheque book; ₹ 5 per leaf on non-maintenance of minimum balance | cheque books issued to the customer are charged at ₹ 5 per cheque leaf | | |
| **Stop payment** | ₹ 50-200 | ₹ 50-100 (free through phone banking) | ₹ 50-100 (free through phone banking) | ₹ 100 per instrument; ₹ 200 for a series of instruents (beyond three cheques) | ₹ 100; Free over net banking | ₹ 100 per instrument |
| **ATM/Debit Card annual maintenance charges** | ₹ 100 (for international ATM-cum-Debit Card) | ₹ 99 | ₹ 100 | ₹ 100 ^ | ₹ 100 for classic debit card | ₹ 150 |

• The list is not exhaustive • The charges are applicable to a regular savings account and do not include service tax • In case of RTGS transactions, banks levy a charge of ₹ 25 per remittance between ₹ 1-5 lakh and ₹ 50 for remittance of over ₹ 5 lakh; NEFT charge is ₹ 5 per remittance up to ₹ 1 lakh • Use of third party ATMs (over and above the five free transactions in a month) will attract a fee of ₹ 20 in the case of most banks for collection of outstation cheques, most banks charge ₹ 50 per instrument for cheque amount of up to ₹ 10,000, ₹ 100 per instrument for cheque amount between ₹ 10,000-1,00,000 and ₹ 150 for cheques with value of more than ₹ 1,00,001 • ^ For Visa/Mastercard International Card • **For Easy/Access Savings Account requiring AQB of ₹ 5,000 • ^^ For Edge Savings Account

*Source:* Bank websites

## CLICK AND SAVE

### Virtual reality

**Chances of mis-selling** are higher in the physical world than in the online world

**Going online involves** paperwork only once. After that, it's paperiess; transactions can be done from anywhere in the world

**In the current** environment, it is tough for distributors to physically service retail investors, unless they charge a fee

**Transactions through stock** exchange are yet to pick up

**Stock brokers are** in the volumes business, which is short-term in nature, while mutual funds are more of long-term investments

**Portfolio tracking and** advice is best offered through the online route rather than physical route

**The Net Result**

| Parameter | Physical | Online |
|---|---|---|
| **Paperwork** | Everytime you invest you have to fill forms, write cheques, provide proof of KYC compliance and send it to the registrar | Form filling is done just once when the account is opened. After that, investments can be done with a click from anywhere in the world |
| **Statement of transaction** | For each and every investment, you get a statement | You can watch your statement online |
| **Portfolio valuation** | You have to sit and calculate - a tedious process | Updated on a daily basis automatically |
| **Systematic Investment Plan (SIP)** | Need to give physical instruction | Can prepone/postpone SIPs online |
| **Research** | You need hard copies, which come for a cost and may not be up to date | It is available online at most portals |

## NON-BANKING FINANCE COMPANIES

The Non-Banking Finance Companies (NBFCs) when compared to commercial and cooperative banks are a heterogenous group of finance companies. These companies also intermediate between the savers and the investors. The NBFCs, in advanced countries have grown phenomenally and are now coming up in a massive way in the developing countries like Brazil, India, Jordan, Korea and Malaysia. The different categories, of the NBFCs include loan companies, investment companies, hire-purchase finance companies, equipment leasing companies, mutual benefit finance companies, miscellaneous finance companies, miscellaneous non-banking companies, residuary non-banking companies and housing finance companies. A wide variety of companies and markets are operating in an environment of macroeconomic stability.

### Types of Non-bank Financial Services

(1) Merchant Banking and New Issue Marketing.
(2) Underwriting and Loan Syndication.
(3) Bill Discounting and Money Market Operations.
(4) Housing Finance.
(5) Lease and Hire Purchase Financing.
(6) Venture Capital Funds.
(7) Investment Financing.

(8) Investment Consultancy and Advice.
(9) Mergers, Acquisitions, Amalgamations.
(10) Capital Restructuring, Revaluations and Designing Capital Structure.
(11) Portfolio Management Services.
(12) Corporate Asset Management Services.
(13) Technical Consultancy and Project Preparation.
(14) Mutual Funds.
(15) New Issue House Services.
(16) Depositories.

## ROLE OF NBFCs

Non-Banking Finance Companies (NBFCs) are an integral part of India's financial system. They play an important role in financial intermediation by acting as a link between savers and investors, and have been able to mobilise deposits on a substantial scale in recent years. As estimated by the RBI, regulated deposits of NBFCs at the end of March 1997 formed 12.5 per cent of the aggregate deposits of scheduled commercial banks. Besides, during 1981-1996 non-banking deposits with households increased from 0.5% of GDP to 1.3%, while bank deposits held by households increased from 3.6% of GDP to 4.4% of GDP in the same period.

There are various categories of NBFCs including loan companies, investment companies, hire-purchase finance companies, equipment leasing companies, mutual benefit finance companies, chit funds and housing finance companies. Historically, NBFCs were no regulated till the mid-sixties, but after several unhealthy practices came to light, the RBI Act was amended and regulation extended to the non-banks.

While housing finance companies are regulated by the National Housing Bank, other NBFCs are regulated by the Reserve Bank of India, under the provisions of Chapter III B of the RBI Act and the respective directions issued to the different categories of NBFCs. Regulation covers their deposit-taking activity including period of acceptance of deposits, quantum, interest rate, etc. Ceilings stipulated on acceptance of deposits are related to net owned funds (NOF)[1+] and are different for different types of companies.

### Competitive Edge of NBFCs

NBFCs supplement the activities of banks in deposit taking and lending and play a dynamic role in the economy. By providing more options to savers and investors; they have helped broaden the market. Because they accept a large volume of small deposits, they reach depositors in all segments, particularly the small savers. Another advantage enjoyed by NBFCs lies in their reach to cater to the specialised credit requirements of certain categories of borrowers not served by the organised banking system. The growth of NBFCs and their edge over banks in certain respects are explained by the fact that there was greater regulation over banks, while NBFCs were relatively free and would offer marginally higher rates of interest on deposits. Their simple procedures and greater customer orientation, and ability to offer higher returns on investment and extend credit to those who are not eligible to receive loans from commercial banks also helped the sector grow.

**Chart 1**

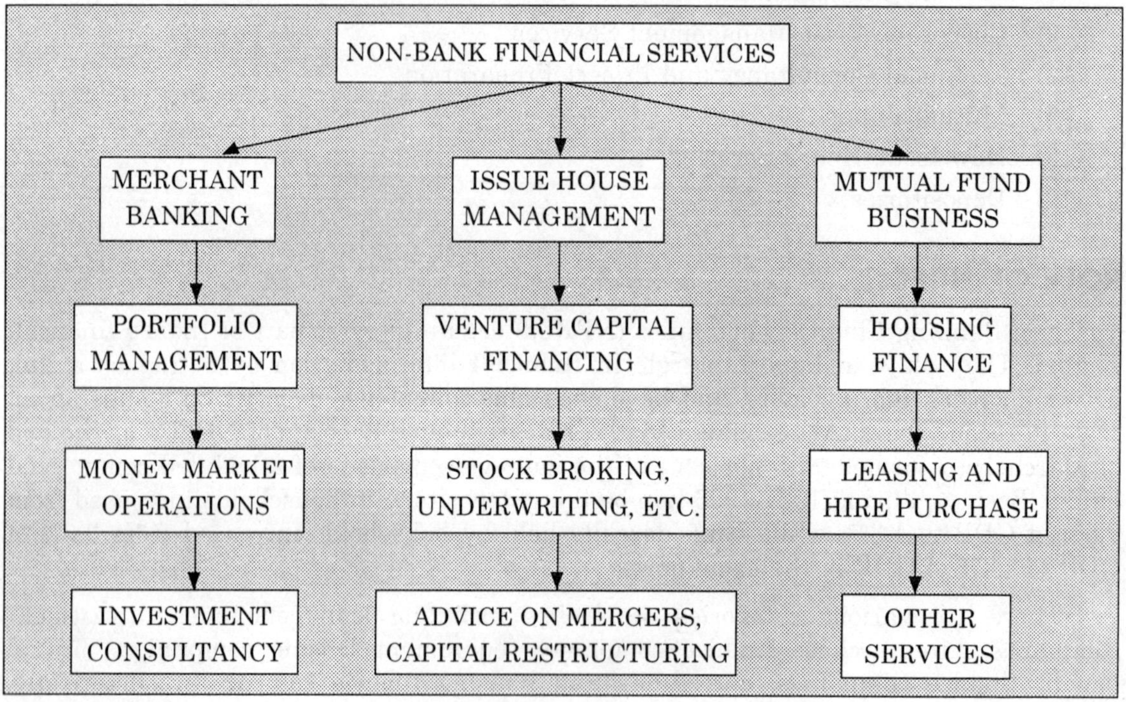


## MUTUAL FUNDS

A mutual fund is basically a risk reduction tool. Risk reduction is achieved by *diversification* of the portfolio. Diversification means that a mutual fund invests in a large number of shares and instruments which lowers the risk. Further, the fund managers' investment decisions are based on the basis of intensive research and are backed by informed judgement and experience. A mutual fund collects money from investors and invests it for them. The entire income/profits are distributed to the investors in proportion to their investments. The pooling of funds from a large number of investors ensures that the total corpus of a mutual fund is very large. Due to the large funds, mutual funds are normally able to buy cheaper and sell dearer than individual investors. This is because of better market rates and lower rates of brokerage.

Secondly, optimum diversification is possible because of large funds. Whereas, an individual investor cannot hold more than a few companies' shares because of limited funds, a mutual fund invests in a large number of shares to reduce risk. In simple terms, a mutual fund follows the saying "*Don't put all your eggs in one basket*". This reduces the risk for the investor.

Unit Trust of India, the first mutual fund, was established in 1964. There are over 30 mutual funds operating in the country. Together, they have mobilised over ₹ 4,50,000 crore and employed the funds in equity and income securities of companies.

**SERVICES PROVIDED BY GLOBAL M AND A ADVISORS** **BOX : 2**

***Takeovers and acquisitions:*** Global M&A advisor collaborate actively to create attractive acquisition opportunities, by carrying out an exclusive search, to a brief agreed with the client, for relevant 'best-fit' targets in designated territories. Through dedicated research and extensive local and international contacts, they produce a recommended list of attractive businesses. Once the client agrees upon the target companies, the advisors initiate discussions with prospective vendors. They also provide assistance in obtaining additional information, value the target and then recommend the most suitable way to structure a deal. Then, in conjunction with the client, they negotiate terms, draft the letter of intent and manage the transaction safely to legal completion.

***Fund raising, venture capital and restructuring:*** For clients wishing to raise development or venture capital, or refinance or restructure the balance sheet of an existing business, global M&A advisors assist in raising and negotiating the necessary mix of funding. This could cover the areas of equity, mezzanine, senior debt, working capital facilities and asset financing. The clients business is presented in the most favourable light to an agreed list of senior decision-makers, within relevant financial institutions, drawn from the advisors extensive list of contacts. By obtaining competing offers, the most attractive terms are sought to be made available. They also assist over-leveraged companies in working out new financing arrangements with their creditors including the raising of new capital and/or the sale of assets.

***IPOs, stock market flotations and 'take-privates':*** For unlisted companies with an established trading record, a flotation on a suitable stock market may be sensible strategic step forward. The global mergers and acquisitions advisors evaluate the suitability of the business for a stock market flotation or initial public offering (IPO) and recommend a programme of preparatory work, before approaching an agreed short list of potential sponsors or investors directly. They then help the company to select the most relevant brokers, lawyers and other members of the advisory team to make the floatation a success. In case it is felt that the continued growth of a public company is best ensured by taking the company off the stock market into private hands, the advisors seek out the best financing partner and assist in all aspects of the public to private transaction.

***MBOS, MBIS, private equity transactions:*** M&A advisors assist companies to raise private equity funding on the best available terms for a management buyout (MBO) or buy-in (MBI). MBOs and MBIs are technically complicated, time-consuming and often risky for management teams. These advisors help protect management from risk and introduce them to relevant financial institutions to raise the finance required. They work with the management team to produce a business plan, which sells the investment opportunity and guides them through the minefield of issues which they will inevitably face. They also negotiate with financial institutions to achieve the best possible equity deal for the management team and negotiate the purchase of the business on the most favourable terms available. Partners of these firms have regular personal contact with the leading private equity investors and providers of debt finance.

## INSURANCE COMPANIES

Life Insurance Corporation of India (LIC) guarantees full protection against risk of death of the saver. The main functions of Life Insurance Corporation are:

(*i*) Mobilise people's savings through insurance-linked savings schemes;
(*ii*) Encourage thrift;
(*iii*) Invest the funds productively; and
(*iv*) Spread life insurance and provide life insurance protection at a reasonable cost.

**Insurance Services**

- Financial
  - Policy Servicing
  - Policy Loans
  - Settlement of Claims
    - (i) Death
    - (ii) Non-early Death
    - (iii) Maturity
  - Covering Risks
  - Rate Fixation
  - Investment
  - Market Player
  - Acturial Services
    - (i) Fixing Premium Rates
    - (ii) Studying the Risks
  - Pension Services
    - (i) Selling Annuity Schemes
    - (ii) Paying Regular Specified Intervals
  - Selling Products
  - Treasury Services
  - Alternative Premium Payment Channels
- Non-financial
  - Insurance Awareness
  - Selling Insurance Products
  - Medical Examination
  - Minimizing Risks
  - Registration
  - Promoting Efficiency
  - Regulating Investments
  - Adjudication
  - Supervising
  - Rural Sector obligations
  - Social Sector obligations

Accretions to the fund for the year 1994-95 have been estimated at ₹ 8,500 crore and the yield on investments made during 1993-94 is expected to improve further. The Corporation will, within the statutory framework, continue to strive to provide better and better returns to the policyholders, whose money it holds in trust. For, in the ultimate analysis, the responsibility of ensuring that *"peoples' money is used for peoples' welfare"* will be the prime motivating factor in planning investments.

The General Insurance Corporation of India (GIC) established since the nationalisation of general insurance companies in the country in 1973 and its four subsidiaries, *viz.*, National Insurance Co. Ltd., New India Assurance Co. Ltd., Oriental

Fire & General Insurance Co. Ltd., and United India Insurance Co. Ltd., operates a number of insurance schemes to cater to the diverse needs of various sections of society. In accordance with the guidelines issued by the Government of India from time-to-time and in terms of the provisions of the Insurance Act, 1938, 70% of annual accretions to investible funds to the general insurance industry are required to be channelised into socially-oriented sectors of the economy. GIC's market operations (sale and purchase of corporate securities) have a stabilising effect of the stock market. GIC has been providing financial assistance to the industrial sector by participating with other AIFIs in consortium financing of the industrial sector projects since 1976, by extending term loans and underwriting of equity shares/preference shares/debentures of both existing and new industrial undertakings. The four subsidiaries were delinked from GIC in December 2000 and insurance was thrown open to private sectors.

The measures go a long way in rebuilding confidence (financial and human) mobilising savings, giving boost to trade, especially export, boost to financial health and protection to property and lives. In turn, industry sets an impetus for growth.

The insurance sector serves as an important financial intermediary providing insurance cover, both on life and other risks. It is also an important source of funds for the corporate sector as also the government to direct investment into socially desired sectors.

Likewise, postal insurance, provident funds and, pension funds provide financial security to savers as well as provide funds for development activities of the governments. Similarly, small savings too mobilise savings and encourage thrift (that is economising).

## DEVELOPMENT BANKS

Development banks are those banks engaged in the promotion, development of industry, agriculture and other key sectors. These banks differ from commercial banks in the sense that they do not mobilise savings of the people but invest the resources in a productive manner. Additionally, these banks provide all the developmental services, so as to accelerate the growth of the economy.

In one sense, the operations of this institution are no different from others, being characterised by either lending or investment or both. However, in another sense, the development financing institution is created to fulfil a vitally different need. Its *raison d'etre* is to further the cause of development. The nature of its banking activity has to be such as would assist that process. It is a chosen instrument for facilitating and stimulating economic growth. The traditional commercial banks, on the other hand, were guided more or less by commercial considerations, though the character of commercial banking has changed a great deal in recent years towards a developmental role.

The task of a development finance institution is complex and the course of its journey, tortuous. However, glorious the ideal of development, those charged with its realisation need to be imbued with vision as they steer along their path, facing many impediments.

A development bank has the opportunity to promote enterprises, that is, to conceive investment proposals and to stimulate others to pursue them or itself to carry them through from conception to realization. In principle, a development bank is well suited to assume this kind of role. Yet enterprise creation is fraught with costs and risks which a development bank cannot neglect. Development banks can prudently undertake them only when they have the requisite financial strength, technical expertise and the managerial skill to deal with them effectively.

## VENTURE CAPITAL

### The Genesis

VC funding is not a new concept. In the US, the thousands of companies over the last couple of decades have been funded through VCFs. Companies such as Digital Equipment, Sun Microsystems, Apple, Federal Express, Compaq, Intel, Microsoft and Genetech are famous examples of companies that received VC funding early in their development. Today all these companies are star performers in their own fields. VCFs have now exited from most of these companies after making their pile of cash. But what is important is that it were the VCFs who came to the aid of these companies when they had acute requirement of funds. So VCFs have played a major role in their success.

VCFs are also not new to India. VC funding in India was started at the initiative of the government, when IDBI established its first VCF in 1987. What really obstructed VCF growth in the country was the lack of quality proposals from Indian entrepreneurs. Before liberalisation, most of the focus of entrepreneurs was in building empires — large size companies, with little or no competence in terms of technology.

Things have changed in the past couple of years. A large herd of entrepreneurs have entered knowledge and technology intensive and IT-related industries. They have all been bitten by a deep desire to succeed. They don't mind giving up their cosy jobs and skyrocketing salaries to try their hands at new ventures.

They have become bolder and quicker and have shown the wherewithal to perform and show results. It has been this mix of boldness and competence, which has helped in catapulting VC funding in the country. Moreover, these new economy entrepreneurs are now looking at market capitalisation as a measure of their success and are not averse to bringing in new partners and even selling off their companies for better valuations.

The success of Indians in US has also played a part in motivating the entrepreneurial spirit in India, leading to a boom in start-ups. Traditional financiers, who insist on profitability record or collateral, would have been a bad idea for these companies. IPOs were also ruled out by the mandatory regulation of three-year profitability track record. This is where the VCFs entered. Already enthused by their experiences in the US and confident of the skills of Indian entrepreneurs, these VCFs started committing funds to the Indian IT sector. These VCFs looked at Indian companies as attractive funding options, not only as the platform to serve the rest of the globe, but also their ability to create intrinsic value based on successfully established US internet models.

Returns in the UD market could have been decreasing due to the overcrowding or the internet business. So most of these funds started looking at other investment options. India, with its second largest English speaking population and the requisite technological skills and software knowledge, became the obvious choice.

Over the years, venture capital has given birth to what are today mega corporations. Venture capital in most cases came in at the idea stage. Examples are many — Tandem Computers (non-stop computers), Gentech (bio-medical products), Apple Computers, Qume Corporation (computer printers).

**The Paradigm Shift in Venture Capital**

| | The Old | The New |
|---|---|---|
| See And Start-up Capital | • Conditional Loans<br>• Equity Support From Financial Institutions<br>• Social Development Funds<br>• Informal Sources | • Conditional Loans<br>• Equity Support From Financial Institutions<br>• Social Development Funds<br>• Informal Sources<br>• Venture Leasing |
| Expansion | • Term Loans | • Equity Support From Financial Institutions<br>• Private Equity<br>• Convertible Debentures<br>• Cumulative Preference Shares |
| Bridge Financing | | • Bank Loans<br>• Special Purpose Vehicles |

## Vision of Venture Capital

The vision of venture capital is focussed on new projects, seed capital, technology and innovation.

**Venture Capital Aims at:**

- Fuels ambitions and dreams
- Breathes life into promising business ventures
- Charts the course of incisive business ideas
- Provides foresight with a free sense of direction
- Helps in building enterprise vision
- Smoothly glide over rough passages
- Partners enterprises on to script thrilling success
- Complements acumen and enterprise with a steady flow of resources
- Inspires enterprises to script thrilling success
- Venture capital finances are plotted on a firm life cycle curve.

## Salient Features of Venture Capital

(a) It is a high risk venture. The success rate in developed economies like USA is around 60%, whereas in a developing country like ours, the success rate is expected to be around 20%-30%.

(*b*) It finances high-tech projects.

(*c*) The gestation period is long. The benefit or profit from the venture capital investment will start accruing only after an average period of 4 to 5 years.

(*d*) Venture capitalist also makes available to the assisted units the managerial and marketing assistance.

(*e*) When the assisted company has reached a certain stage of profitability, the venture capitalist sells his shares in the stock market at a hefty premium. He thus makes good profit as well as gets his locked up funds released for redeployment in some other ventures.

(*f*) Provision to have conditional loans which unlike the conventional loans, don't carry interest charge. Instead, it carries a royalty linked to sales generated by the company after commercialization. The rate of royalty is fixed depending on the profitability of the business and the fund's requirement of a reasonable return. The conditional loan is essentially a quasi-equity instrument which does not place a servicing burden on the company in the initial periods and seeks a return commensurate with the success of the ventures.

(*g*) It is an equity or quasi-equity form of investment.

(*h*) It is a long-term investment and the returns are in the forms of capital gains.

(*i*) It is an active form of investment with a higher degree of involvement in the management of a venture.

## Forms of Venture Capital

Based on the four stages of development of a business, the venture capital financing may be classified as seed finance, start-up finance, beginner's finance and establishment finance. During the first stage of starting a business, i.e., at the formulation of an idea stage, the risk associated is very high. Here an idea needs to be translated into a business proposition. So the finance required at this stage is the seed finance from the venture capital fund. The second stage being the implementation phase, start-up finance from Venture Capital is required for the purpose of implementing the appropriate production processes. In the third stage, commercial production is to be started and beginners finance is required to develop the marketing and other infrastructures. In the fourth and the last stage, when the business is fully established, it requires finance for its growth and expansion so as to reap the economies of the scale. Here establishment finance is sought from the venture capital fund. The degree of risk associated with a business gradually diminishes in every subsequent stage of business development. A comprehensive venture capital financing may take all of the above forms.

**Venture Capital: Stages of Financing**

**Seed Money Stage:** Small amount of financing needed to prove a concept or develop a product. Marketing is not included in this stage.

→ **Start-up:** Financing for a firm that started up in the past one year. Funds are likely to pay for marketing and product development.

↓ **First-round Financing:** Additional money to begin sales and manufacturing after a firm has spent its start-up capital.

← **Second-round Financing:** Funds earmarked for working capital for a firm that is selling its product, but is still losing money.

↓ **Third-round Financing:** Financing for a firm that is breaking even and is contemplating an expansion project.

→ **Fourth-round Financing:** Money provided for firms that are likely to go public soon. Also known as bridge financing.

## Functions of Venture Capital

Venture capital plays the crucial role in fostering industrial development by exploring vast and untapped potentialities. The key functions of venture capital are:

(*i*) Venture capital provides finance as well as skills to new enterprises and new ventures of existing ones based on high technology innovations. It provides seed capital funds to finance innovations even in the prestart stage. In the development stage that follows, the conceptual stage venture capitalist develops a business plan (in partnership with the entrepreneur) which will detail the market opportunity, the product, the development and financial needs. In this crucial stage, the venture capitalist has to assess the intrinsic merits of the technological innovation, ensure that the innovation is directed at a clearly defined market opportunity and satisfies himself that the management team at the helm of affairs is competent enough to achieve the targets of the business plan. Therefore, venture capitalist helps the firm to move to the exploitation state, i.e., launching of the innovation. While launching the innovation the venture capitalist will seek to establish a timeframe for achieving the predetermined development marketing, sales and profit targets. In each investment, as the venture capitalist assumes absolute risk, his role is not restricted to that of a mere supplier of funds but that of an active partner with total investment in the assisted project. Thus, the venture capitalist is expected to perform not only the role of a financier but also a skilled and multi-faceted intermediary supplying a broad spectrum of specialist services — technical, commercial, managerial, financial and entrepreneurial.

(*ii*) Venture capitalist fills the gap in the owner's funds in relation to the quantum of equity required to support the successful launching of a new business or the optimum scale of operations of an existing business. It acts as a trigger in launching new business and as a catalyst in stimulating existing firms to achieve optimum performance.

(*iii*) Venture capitalist's duty extends even as far as to see that the firm has proper and adequate commercial banking and receivable financing.

**The Venture Capital Guide**

| | IDBI | TDICI | RCTC | SBI Caps | Grindlays | Canfina |
|---|---|---|---|---|---|---|
| Size of funds (₹ crore) | NA | (*a*) ₹ 20<br>(*b*) ₹ 100 | NA | NA | 12 | NA |
| Assistance per project (₹ crore) | ₹ 2.50 | ₹ 2 | Need-based depending on merits of each case | up to | — | — |
| Nature of assistance | Conditional Loan/ Equity | Conditional Loan/Equity | Loan/Equity | Equity | Equity | Equity/ Conditional loan |
| Promoter's contribution | | (*i*) 10% of project cost if it is < 50<br>(*ii*) 15% cost of it is < 50 lakh | To be decided on likely risk, technology and resource capability | — | — | NA |
| Terms of assistance | (*a*) Initially @ 6% during development period and thereafter 17% pa. Royalty on sales in some cases<br>(*b*) Equity subscription in exceptional cases | (*a*) If equity subscribed when disinvestment made, option given to promoters to buy back at negotiated price<br>(*b*) No int; only a change on commercial implementation of the project | Initially @ 6% pa during development period and on commercialisation @ 14% royalty in some cases. Repayment within 10/12 years. In case of equity participation buy-back facility | Disinvestment after commercialisation of the project | | |
| NA | NA | | | | | |
| No. of projects assisted | 41 | 46 | 168 (Dec. 1988) | 21 | 16 | 2 |
| Amount sanctioned (₹ crore) | 31.44 | 23.17 | 2 | 10 | 9.6 | 0.34 |
| Key industries | | Medical applied research, polio vaccines, electronic equipment for defence applications, autocomponents, chemicals | Foodfeed tech, chemicals tech, chemicals and application software, biotech, diagnostics and vaccines, drug and plasma | Watches, seamless metal, ceramics, cement | MEG, colour picture tubes, drydock | NA |

***Note:*** Credit Capital Venture Fund, the other private sector fund, is not operational yet.

(*iv*) Venture capitalist assists the entrepreneurs in locating, interviewing and employing outstanding corporate achievers to professionalise the firm.

Venture capital assistance provided by the financial institution is in the form of project loans, equity, conditional loan (quasi-equity), a comprehensive techno-managerial support and guidance service including technology information service.

The essential objective of Venture Capital is to achieve high returns on its investment. This makes 'cashing out' (i.e., withdrawing from the investments) imperative, unless further extraordinary returns are expected.

The role the Venture Capital need not be restricted to manufacturing industries. Some of the ventures funded in UK by Venture Capital funds included sale of antique remodelled jewellery, publishing of specialist books, the baby and health care market, retirement homes, distribution of indoor plants and plant arrangements to the major retail shops, and even small houses. In India, Venture Capital activity would play a catalytic role in encouraging the entrepreneurial process in the Indian industrial scene. In encouraging a new class of promoters, viz., investors, innovators, professional executives and technocrats, it would lead to greater dispersion of economic power.

**HOW DO VENTURE CAPITAL FUNDS INVEST?** **BOX : 1**

Typically VCFs enter a company at a very early stage (see graph). Angel investors are the highest risk takers as they enter the company at the concept or the seed stage. The VCFs enter at the early growth stage, when the company management has identified the business prototype and customer base. The VCFs thus lead the company through its expansion, helping with backend systems, sales and market share growth.

When considering an investment, venture capitalists carefully screen the technical and business merits of the proposed company. Given the nature of risks associated with the funding at such an early stage, most VCFs lay a lot of importance to the management quality. "A VCF manager does not take more than five minutes to decide if the management quality is not okay", explains an industry expert. The two key points that a VCF manager sees are whether the entrepreneur has a vision and whether the management team is cohesive. Here he looks out for various questions like:

- How do entrepreneurs work together?
- How compatiable is the VCF with the team?
- How complete is the management expertise in the area of business? This means, do the team have members with expertise in various aspects of business?
- How is the chemistry between the various members of team?

They also check on the softer issues like temperament of team-members, past records and overall management competence. Thus, behind the financial and business analysis of the proposed business plan, it is these soft issues which finally lead to the VC funding in a company.

## Venture Capital Funds

The guidelines on 'venture capital' issued by the Reserve Bank of India towards the end of 1988, were a recognition of their role in the Indian conditions. As the situation stood at the end of 1989, venture capital funds still had a long way to go. The Technology

Development and Investment Corporation of India, a subsidiary of ICICI, Technology Development Fund set up by Industrial Development Bank of India (IDBI), the Equity Development Scheme set up by SBI Capital Markets Limited and Canfina, which have been joined by India Investment Fund promoted by Grindlays Bank, are some of the venture capital institutions set up in India. The Credicapital Venture Fund is the first private sector venture capital company to go public. More companies are expected to enter the field soon, with the International Finance Corporation, Washington, and the World Bank both planning venture capital joint ventures in India. These ventures are successful to a large extent.

## Working of Venture Capital

A promoter comes forward either with a new but as yet an untried product or process. He needs a financial backer to help him to set up his plans or buyout a part or the whole of an existing enterprise. He may not be able to go to the regular bank or conventional financial institutions for one of the two reasons: the product may be untried and there may be teething problem to overcome in its design and marketing. Alternatively, their promoter may have no previous track record as investor. In such cases, the financier (a venture capitalist) may come forward and lend him the money on the understanding that, if the enterprise proves successful, it will 'go public', i.e., it will make an initial public offer (IPO) of its share. The more successful the venture has been, the higher will be the profit made by both the promoter and financier through sale of shares.

## The difference between Seed Capital and Venture Capital

The seed capital schemes as these are understood in India are not the same as venture capital. The primary purpose of the former is to help the technocrat entrepreneurs setting up manufacturing activities to meet the promoter's contribution and thus takes the form of 'gap-filling', whereas in case of venture capital, the primary return sought by the venture capitalist is the eventual capital gain by investing in companies having attractive growth and earning potential rather than a steady interest or dividend yield.

## The difference between Venture Capital and Term Financing

The difference between venture capital and term financing lies in the preferred investment instrument, in the type of collateral accepted and in the magnitude of the risk involved. In the case of venture capital, the collateral often takes the form of intangible assets such as research results, innovative marketing ideas or managerial and technical skills. The cash flows of venture capital client mostly start with a long period of negative results.

## Schemes in Operation

It is intended that the venture capital assistance should go mainly to the schemes with the following objectives:

(*a*) to encourage the indigenous technology and its commercial application.

(*b*) to adopt and modify the applications of imported technology in such a manner that it will be appropriate to the Indian environment.

The assistance is generally being provided for the purpose of:

(*i*) Setting up of pilot projects

(*ii*) For technological innovations and modernisation

(*iii*) For developing appropriate technology

(*iv*) For meeting the cost of marketing surveys and market promotion programmes. Of course, venture capital excludes financing of enterprises engaged in trading, broking, investment or financial services, agencies or liaison work.

Venture capital in India is available mainly in three forms, equity, conditional loans and income notes. Income note is a novel way of financing, made by venture capital in India. It is a hybrid security combining the feature of conventional and conditional loans, where the entrepreneur has to pay the interest as well as the royalty. Some private sector venture capital companies have started region specific and industry specific venture funds. For example, Credit Capital Venture Fund (CCVF) of the Credit Capital group has started a region specific fund known as South Asian Regional Apex (SARA) fund to be invested in 10 specified states of the country. Similarly, it has also started an industry specific fund, such as Information Technology Fund and the Auto Ancillary Fund, its modus operandi to focus on financing promising ventures in these industries. A novel security like 'participating debenture' has been introduced by the Twentieth Century Finance Corporation.

## Advantages of Venture Capital

Venture capital has made significant contributions to technological innovations and promotion of entrepreneurism. Many of the pathbreaking technologies worldover in the fields of bio-technology, microelectronics, computers (e.g., Apple, Micro, Lotus, Intel Microsoft, etc.), have emerged from small businesses set up by people with ideas (but no financial resources) and supported by venture capital.

(1) *Economy-oriented*

(*a*) Helps in the industrialization of the country.

(*b*) Helps in the technological development of the country.

(*c*) Generates employment.

(*d*) Helps in developing entrepreneurial skills.

(2) *Investor-oriented*

(*a*) Benefit to the investors is that they are invited to invest only after the company starts earning profit, so the risk is less and the healthy growth of capital market is entrusted.

(*b*) Profit to Venture Capital Companies/Venture Capital Funds.

(3) *Entrepreneur-oriented*

(*a*) Helps small and medium first generation entrepreneurs to translate their ideas into a reality.

(*b*) Promotes and fosters entrepreneurship in the country.

## MERCHANT BANKING SERVICES

Till early 1960s, there was no merchant banking in the Indian Banking system. It was the Grindlays Bank which started merchant banking services as far back as 1967. After Grindlays Bank, other foreign banks like Citibank and Chartered Bank, started these services in India. Till 1970s, the main services rendered were management of share issues and sub-aspects of financial consultancies. In mid-1970s, there was a boom in the capital market with the introduction of "Foreign Exchange Regulation Act, (FERA) (1973)." This created an awareness in the investing public about the capital market. This also encouraged a few commercial banks and financial institutions to set up merchant banking divisions. In addition, private financial brokers also started private merchant banking organisations. Today, the Merchant Banking set up in the country is broadly divided into the following groups:

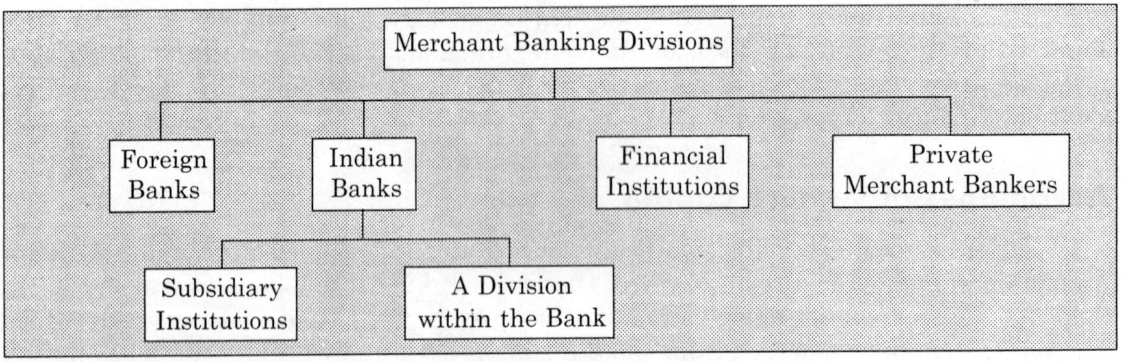


**Fig. 1 Set-up of Merchant Banking in India**

(1) *Foreign Banks*: Along with Grindlays Bank, Citibank, Chartered Bank and Hong Kong Bank are also active in merchant banking.

(2) *Indian Banks*: State Bank of India took the lead among Indian banks and is at present well established in the merchant banking field. The other banks that followed suit are Bank of India, Central Bank of India, Bank of Baroda, Punjab National Bank, UCO Bank and Canara Bank which have established similar divisions at their respective head offices and other important centres.

(3) *Private Merchant Bankers:* Leading private broker firms were already doing consultancy for Portfolio Investment. They took advantage of the situation and started 'Merchant Banking and Consultancy' services in a big way. Today, firms like J. M. Financial Consultants, Champaklal Investments and Financial Consultancy, V. B. Desai Consultants, etc., are some of the leading private merchant bankers in our country.

*Financial Institutions:* Industrial Credit and Investment Corporation of India (ICICI) has a well established merchant banking office. Recently, Industrial Reconstruction Corporation of India (IRCI) has also started its merchant banking operations though its main concentration and attention is on mergers, amalgamations and takeovers.

In the early stages, the role of merchant banking in India was largely confined to the management of public issues of equity capital. This was due to the fact that several public issues (which came to be popularly known as FERA issues) came to the market at that time and there was, at that stage, an almost total absence of competent issue management services in the country. Today, the scope of merchant banking has gone much beyond just issue management. Banks' merchant banking divisions are now engaged in providing a wide spectrum of financial and related services to their customers.

## Role of Merchant Banks

To promote the new issue market there is need for a qualitative improvement in the offer of new issues both in terms of time taken and the cost of floatation. At present the time taken for organising a new issue is between 12 to 18 months and the cost of raising new capital varies from 3% to 8% and sometimes even 20%. This can be brought down relatively by specialized merchant banking institutions by catering to the requirements of both large and small industrial units. Cost of floatation of equity and preference capital is higher for new companies than for existing companies, indicating thereby the difficulties experienced by new companies in making a new issue. Merchant banks can help saving in the cost of new companies.

The new issue market has not succeeded fully in mobilising savings partly due to the preference of the public to company deposits and partly due to low yield on equities as compared to those on fixed interest securities. There has been a decline in the proportion of share capital in the total capital employed due to the steep rise in the cost of new issues. There are certain minimum costs to be incurred in respect of fees to brokers, promoters' expenses, underwriting commission, etc., irrespective of the size of the project. While bigger companies are able to manage this, small industrialists find it extremely difficult to meet this minimum cost with uncertain prospects of public response. The existing big companies have been relying more on their own internal resource in order to avoid the high cost of making public issues.

## Merchant Banking Services

Let us first see how merchant banking services are understood and what is the nature of the services that are offered at present in India. Merchant banking services are activities, i.e., counselling corporate clients, who are in need of capital, on capital structure, form of capital to be raised, the terms and conditions of issue, underwriting of the issue, timing of the issue and preparation of the prospectus and publicity for grooming the issue for the market. They may also relate to the private placement of capital and the raising of long-term loans, either in foreign exchange or in rupee currency, from the national/state financial institutions, and short-term working capital from commercial banks. These activities are mainly stock-exchange-oriented, relating as they do to the issue of fresh capital for a new company setting up an enterprise, or for the existing ones which want to finance the expansion and diversification of other businesses. A few proposals of mergers and amalgamations have also been handled. In essence, therefore, in India, merchant banking services have been looked upon mainly as those consisting of issue house functions connected with the raising of capital from financial institutions and the market and sometimes shaping the proposals for mergers and amalgamations of existing companies into integrated corporate enterprises. It may be recalled that, in the old days, many of these functions were discharged by prominent firms of brokers and that some of them have recently set up consultancy organisations which function as managers to the issue of capital in the market. In addition, proposals for the dilution of equity capital of foreign majority companies and the issue of capital by branches of foreign companies are now sponsored by merchant banks.

**Chart : 1**

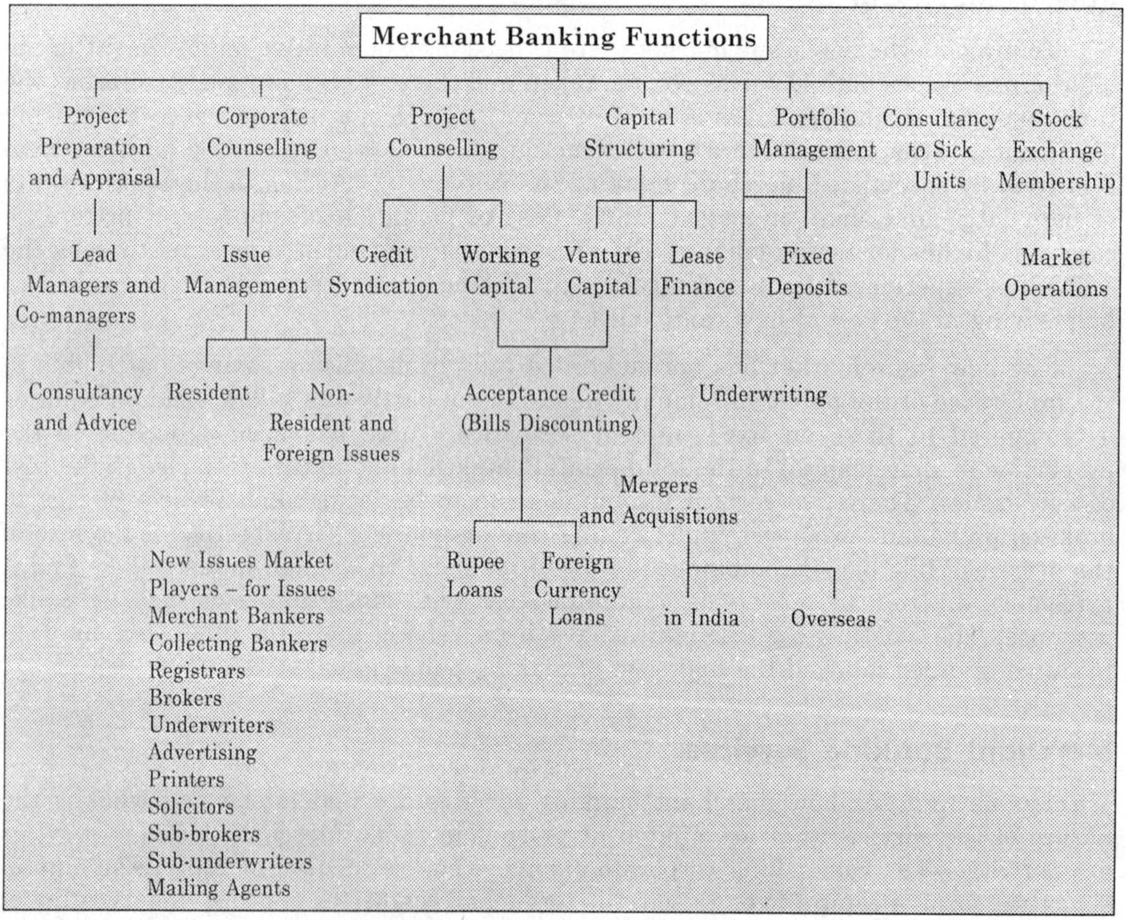


While there is no doubt that one of the important functions of merchant banking relates to issue house activities, there are others which are equally important. It would, therefore, be most useful to study first the functions which the merchant banks in the United Kingdom and investment banks in the United States generally perform, and then attempt to analyse which of them are essentially relevant in Indian conditions. It would then be possible to find out in what way these functions may be adapted to our requirements within the framework of the government's industrial policy and the programme of industrial development under the Five-Year Plans.

## Project Finance

Once a client has decided upon the specific project he wishes to set up, the Merchant Banking Division provides a comprehensive package of services for financial structuring and funding. The division works in close collaboration with the customer and the technical consultants for the preparation of a complete financial dossier; negotiates on behalf of the client with financial institutions and banks for the term finance, and assists him in the preparation of the complex loan documentation.

A project finance assignment fully tests the creativity of the merchant banker; and, quite often, the entire gamut of merchant banking services, including loan syndication, issue management, euro-currency financing and supplier or buyer credits are brought to bear on a single large assignment.

## Corporate Finance

The pioneering role and expertise of the Merchant Banking Division in the sphere of public issue management is well-known. This product has been important in the banks' portfolio of services; and its continuing importance seems assured in the foreseeable future in the context of the recent and welcome growth witnessed in the capital markets in India.

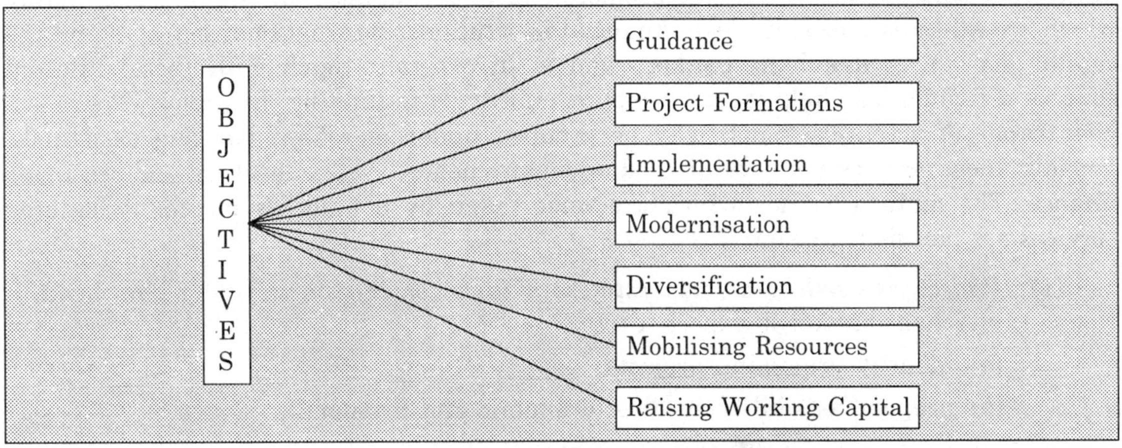


**Fig. 2 Objectives of Merchant Banking**

The involvement of the Merchant Banking Division with a public issue, be it of equity, convertible debentures or non-convertible debentures, includes the structuring of the issue, obtaining all approvals (including the consent of the Controller of Capital Issues), appointment of underwriters, brokers and bankers to the issue, preparation of the prospectus, and coordination of all the agencies concerned with clock-work precision.

The merchant banker's presence in all the major financial centres as well his long established relationships with the underwriter and broker fraternities, makes possible the high degree of synchronisation required to ensure the success of an issue.

## Entrepreneur Starting a New Project

An entrepreneur who is the promoter of a new project first obtains a Letter of Indent (LoI) from the Government of India and then gets it converted into an Industrial Licence for setting up the proposed project. Generally speaking, the project report is ready and the company is incorporated, by the time the promoter approaches the merchant banker. Though, technically speaking, the promoter can take the help of the merchant banker for projects of any size, it is generally the projects costing over ₹ 1 crore which are taken by the promoters to the merchant bankers.

## Existing Units

Companies planning modernisation, expansion or diversification for their existing units need the help of merchant bankers. Amalgamation, absorption and reconstruction are some of the additional activities for which merchant banking assistance is availed of.

## What Comprises Merchant Banking (MB) Assistance

For small size projects, a promoter can raise the required funds by recourse to the traditional source of finance, viz., bank finance. However, for medium and large size projects, the promoters cannot exclusively depend on banks who normally do not give large term loans. In such cases, the promoters have to find alternative sources of finance which are all-India and state level financial institutions, international markets and the capital market. A merchant banker, who is in constant touch with these different sources of finance, can help these promoters effectively in funding the project. There is a wide range of activities which may be grouped under merchant banking assistance. Broadly, these activities may be divided under two heads, viz., counselling and procuring finance. The main activities which are undertaken by a bank as merchant banking services are mentioned below:

(1) *Project counselling or reinvestment studies for investors*: Under this head, a merchant banker is expected to:
   (*a*) identify promising projects,
   (*b*) prepare feasibility studies (economic and financial),
   (*c*) prepare indepth project reports,
   (*d*) assist investors in obtaining licences,
   (*e*) do precise capital structuring,
   (*f*) arrange and negotiate foreign collaborations, and
   (*g*) give guidance on amalgamations, mergers and takeovers.

(2) *Syndication of loans and project finance:* Once the project is identified and clearance is obtained from the government departments, the undermentioned steps are to be taken:

(*a*) Aid in applying to financial institutions, banks and other sources of finance.

(*b*) Expert advice on government policies, demand-supply gaps, raw material availability, product-mix, plan capacity utilisation, requirements of plant and machinery and the like.

(*c*) Consultation about alternative sources of finance, debt-equity ratios, 'over-run' finance.

(*d*) Liaison with government departments, financial institutions, banks, etc.

(*e*) Advice and assistance for modernisation, expansion and diversification.

(3) *Issue Management (including equity dilution):* Management of the public issue of shares/debentures (or even an offer for sales) has been the traditional service rendered by merchant bankers in India. Actually, with this service, the merchant banker was introduced in the Indian financial world. Following are the services rendered by the merchant banker under this head:

(*a*) deciding on the size and timing of a public issue in the light of the market condition,

(*b*) preparing the base of successful issue marketing from the initial documentation, liaison with the Controller of Capital Issues for clearances, etc., to the preparation of the actual launch of the proposed issue,

(*c*) optimum underwriting support,

(*d*) appointment of bankers and brokers as well as issue houses,

(*e*) issue management,

(*f*) professional liaison with share market functionaries like brokers, portfolio managers and financial press for pre-selling and media coverage,

(*g*) preparation of draft prospectus and other documents,

(*h*) wide coverage throughout the country for collection of applications, and

(*i*) preparation of advertising and promotional material.

(4) *Provision of working capital*: Since merchant banking is a part of the banking system, the client has to be assisted in arranging for working capital finance especially for the new ventures. If the requirement of the client is substantially large, then it is desirable to arrange for the syndication on behalf of the promoters. There has been a recent change in arrangement for the working capital finance by issue of debentures on 'Rights' basis. Merchant bankers play a great role in helping the clients in the preparation of the necessary forms for the financial institutions such as LIC, GIC, UTI, who are the major supporters for such issue. He arranges for the trustees for the debentures and also ensures that the balance portion is tied up with the other bankers.

(5) *Foreign Currency Loans*: The merchant banker also arranges for export credit for various countries. He also arranges for foreign currency loan like Eurodollar, IFCI loans, etc.

(6) *Portfolio management for non-residents*: The merchant banker assists in this area by identifying suitable arrangements of investment suitable to each Non-resident Indian. In short, these include:

(*a*) guidance on purchase and sale of securities

(*b*) handling of such transactions

(*c*) advice on market conditions

(*d*) safe custody of documents

(*e*) collection of earnings (dividend, interest, etc.)

(*f*) service as a link between non-residents and Reserve Bank of India for obtaining necessary permission.

Besides this, leasing business is also being talked about in the banking as well as the financial sector. This is a new dimension in which the merchant bankers have been working on, and in fact, a few banks have already ventured into this field.

Moreover, marketing is also a very important function which the merchant banker has to take into account since he has to create the business for himself. He also has to have a close association with his own clients, understand their future expansion/modernisation programmes and advise them the way in which these programmes are to be carried out. His imagination and expertise plays a great role in this area.

He is also expected to be very active in finding out the new ventures opening up in the country. This information can be gathered from the Controller of Capital Issues, Registrar of Companies and State and Central Financial Institutions.

## Project Counselling

If it consists of mere technical appraisal, the department makes use of the services of the Technical and Industrial Consultancy Division. Once convinced of the technical feasibility and commercial viability of the project, the merchant banker's next job is to prepare a *structure of finance*. To determine the structure of finance on the basis of different available sources, the department keeps in view:

(*i*) The norms laid down by term-lending institutions regarding the debt-equity ratio and the promoter's minimum contribution to the total cost of the project;

(*ii*) The availability of various backward area subsidies; and

(*iii*) In case of equity issue, the norms laid down by the stock exchanges for the listing of shares.

The structuring of finance also covers advice on setting up units in the 'joint sector', where state level financial institutions contribute 26% of the equity share capital, while the private promoter contributes 25% and the balance of 49% of the shares are made available to the public. On the other hand, in a 'state assisted unit', state financial institutions contribute 11%, the promoters 40% and the public 49% of the equity share capital. For listing purposes, stock exchanges require that the minimum 60% of the equity share capital should be offered to the public in case of units promoted by private promoters and 49% in the case of a joint sector or state assisted project.

## Syndication of Term Loans

This involves the preparation and submission of applications to All-India Financial Institutions, such as:

| | | |
|---|---|---|
| IDBI | — | Industrial Development Bank of India |
| ICICI | — | Industrial Credit & Investment Corporation of India Limited |
| IFCI | — | Industrial Finance Corporation of India or to state level institutions, such as mentioned below: |
| SIICOM | — | State Industrial Investment Corporation of Maharashtra |
| GIIC | — | Gujarat Industrial Investment Corporation |
| MPAVN | — | Madhya Pradesh Audyogik Vikas Nigam Ltd., |
| PICUP | — | Pradeshiya Industrial Investment Corporation of Uttar Pradesh. |

In case the above institutions do not tie-up the entire term loan requirement and leave some gap in the term loan, to fill such a gap the merchant banker turns to commercial banks. To finalise the cost of the project, he scrutinises the various items under capital cost and requires the following:

(*i*) Estimates of the cost of land and building;

(*ii*) The latest quotations for plant and machinery;

(*iii*) The estimates of preliminary and pre-operative expense;

(*iv*) The rate of interest on term loans during the construction period;

(*v*) Public issue expense;

(*vi*) Margin money for working capital, etc.

Once the total cost of the project is determined, a finance model is worked out, keeping in mind the norms of financial institutions regarding the debt-equity ratio (generally 2:1), the promoters' contribution (generally 17.5% to 20% of the project cost), etc. The syndication of the term loans not only covers rupee term loans but takes into account foreign currency loans for the import of capital goods, if any, under the line of credit available with the term-lending institutions. The assistance for raising foreign currency loans in the Euro dollar market is also given when the licence granted specifically permits the raising of such finances.

## Management of Public Issue

This comprises assistance in:

(*i*) Obtaining the acknowledgement or consent of Controller of Capital Issues (CCI);

(*ii*) The tying up of underwriting of the issue as per requirement;

(*iii*) The preparation of the prospectus;

(*iv*) Grooming the issue to ensure full subscription;

(*v*) Obtaining compliance of the listing requirements of stock exchanges;

(*vi*) Appointing registrars to the issue, advertisers and printers, etc.

A strong liaison with stock broking firms is absolutely necessary for the successful management of public issues.

## The Future

For the merchant banking division, the development of new services to meet the changing market conditions is an ongoing process. Today, the entire merchant banking industry in India is faced with the challenge of attracting Non-resident Indian (NRI) investment into India, particularly under the scheme for portfolio investments through stock exchanges. Despite the several policy liberalisations which have been announced by the government in the past year, the response from NRIs, to date, is far below expectations. One important reason for the poor response to the portfolio investment scheme is quite clearly the lack of information with the non-resident investors perturbed regarding the changing conditions in the Indian stock markets. The merchant banking division is now in the process of introducing a comprehensive portfolio advisory service which will try to fill up this information gap, offer expert counselling on investment opportunities, undertake to buy/sell orders, periodically evaluate the portfolio, and look after all the administrative formalities, such as attending to tax returns, collections and remittances of dividend, etc., in compliance with the Reserve Bank of India's and Securities and Exchange Board of India (SEBI) guidelines.

Merchant banking essentially involves selling an issue for a company and handling related work. In the wake of liberalisation of the financial sector, we are seeing certain merchant banking prospects emerging — be it an Indian company or foreign or a multinational, playing in the primary and secondary markets competitively. They are the *prima donnas* of the primary stage. There are about 1,200 merchant bankers in the country of which, the SEBI has granted registration to 790 merchant bankers in four different categories. SEBI also granted registration to 36 underwriters and 8 portfolio managers on the basis of its Rules and Regulations, 1993, up to the end of March 1995. They compete on an average for about 1,000 issues for about ₹ 15,000 crore every year. They act as lead managers, co-managers, issue managers, financial advisers, etc. The domination of the public sector continues, with seven of the top ten managers coming from its ranks. The mushroom growth of merchant banks has given rise to unethical means to sell shares. For a healthy growth of the market operation, the SEBI should enforce strict control on merchant banks and remove the weeds of manipulation and corruption in the market. Stipulation of proper checks and regulation will raise the confidence of investing public in the dynamic and vibrant market mechanism which will be in the larger interests of the society as well as of the economy.

# FACTORING SERVICES

Selling goods on favourable terms is an important key to achieve growth in the volume of business. With the increase in the volume of production and sales, timely collection and efficient management of receivables has assumed greater importance. In particular, small-scale industries have been facing innumerable problems when timely collection is not received. This blocks the very fund flow system and affects industries. Thus, factoring provides a new avenue of finance. As an innovative financial system, factoring is of immense benefit to industries.

Factoring companies specialise in financing inventories and receivables. The unique feature of factoring is that a factor brings all the services together in one package.

Factoring thus offers a clear solution to the problems created by working capital setting locked up in trade debts. This Chapter deals with this important financial system.

## Debt-collection Service

Factoring is a debt-collection service where the factor — usually a financial institution — buys out a client's (supplier's) book debts (accounts receivables). At present, only a part of the receivables are financed by banks and other financial institutions through bill discounting. Full service factoring also involves the factor taking over the administration of client's sales ledger, chasing debtors and evaluating credit risks.

Factoring is a financial service designed to help firms in better management of their receivables. Called a para-banking practice, it is widely used in the developed world. It has taken roots in India only recently. The Reserve Bank of India set up a study group to suggest a format for promotion of factoring services. Some guidelines have been announced.

In old-line factoring or full-factoring, the factor:

(*a*) runs the sales ledger for clients,

(*b*) takes the responsibility for debt collection,

(*c*) provides cover against debt default, and

(*d*) makes available funds against debts assigned to it.

Factoring service is a continuing arrangement under which a financing institution takes on the credit and collection responsibilities of its client, purchases and recovers his trade dues. A factor smoothens the payment and mechanism for supplies. It involves an outright sale of the receivables of a firm to a financial institution, called the *factor*, specialising in management of trade credit. The factor collects the accounts on the due dates, makes payments to the firm and assumes the risks associated with the collection of accounts. The fee charged is usually a percentage of the value of the receivables factored.

## Meaning

Factoring basically means purchase of book-debts of clients. If working capital funds could be recycled with greater velocity through better management of credit extended to buyers and collection of their dues, industrial units can improve their profitability considerably. It is this factor which can help factoring services to emerge as a new financial service. In order to be an economically viable proposition, a factoring agency has to build-up a suitable infrastructure so as to ensure optimum efficiency in the working of credit and collection departments so that the fixed costs are absorbed at low unit costs.

Profile of a good factoring candidate:

- Rapid growth in its present start-up phase, with a good sales niche and satisfied customers;
- Product permits mark-ups to cover factoring costs and does not require substantial after-sales service or involve long-term progress payments;

- Inventory (such as imports) must be purchased well before sales;
- Accounts receivables are reliable and unencumbered;
- The company may also be one that's in its mature stage in the business cycle, using factoring to supplement other forms of longer-term financing.

**Mechanics of Factoring**

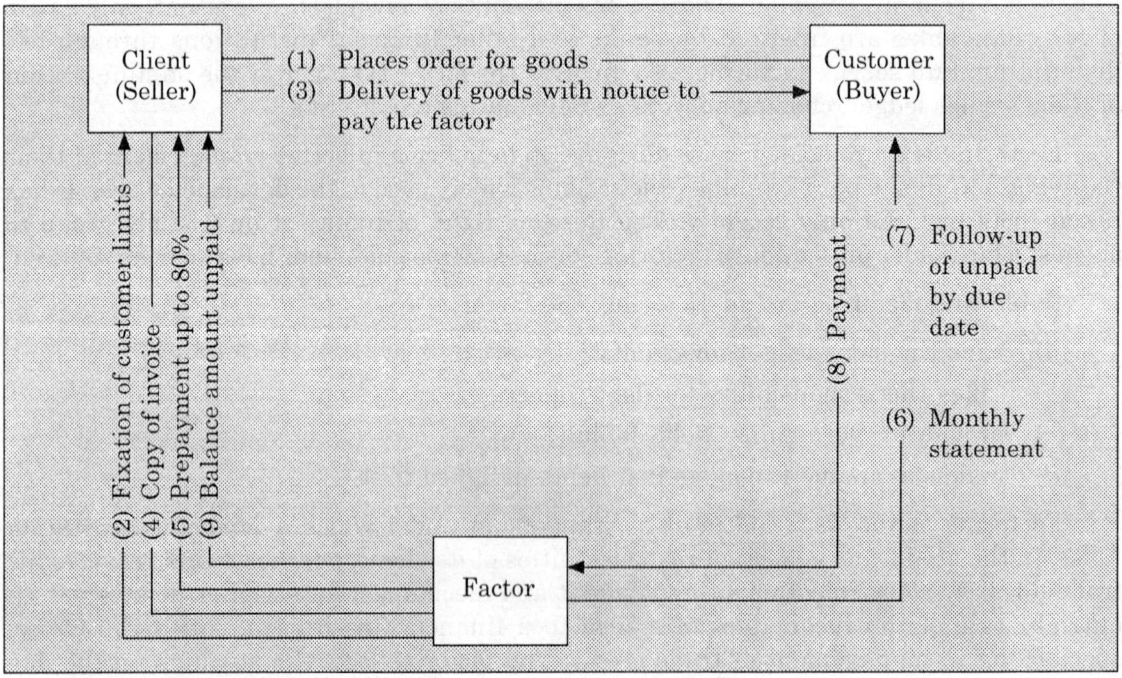


**Fig. 13.1**

The steps involved in factoring are enumerated below:

Step I: The customer places an order with the seller (the client).

Step II: The factor and the seller enter into a factoring agreement about the various terms of factoring.

Step III: Sale contract is entered into with the buyer and the goods are delivered. The invoice with the notice to pay the factor is sent along with.

Step IV: The copy of invoice covering the above sale is to the factor, who maintains the sale ledger.

Step V: The factor prepays 80% of the invoice value.

Step VI and VII: Monthly statements are sent by the factor to the buyer. If there are any unpaid invoices, follow-up action is initiated.

Step VIII: The buyer settles the invoices on expiry of credit period allowed.

Step IX: The balance 20% less the cost of factoring is paid by the factor to the client.

## How it Works?

A factor purchases the receivables of a client, maintains a separate sales ledger and attends to the client's bookkeeping work relating to the accounts receivable. The mechanisms are simple: The seller of a product negotiates with the factor to set up a factoring relationship. The latter does a credit check on the buyer and, if he is found creditworthy, gives its approval and sets a credit limit and period for the latter. The client then sells the goods to the buyer and sends the invoices to the factor. The factor, in turn, hands over the invoices to the buyer and pays the seller after retaining a margin. The retained amount is paid to the seller after the factor recovers the dues from the buyer.

Factoring helps the seller by putting hard cash in his hands faster. The main problem sellers face relates to delay in payments, particularly when the buyers are public sector giants like the Railways, State Electricity Boards and the PWDs. Faced with this tight-fisted lot and many large private sector companies which cause hardship to suppliers by delaying payments, it is not surprising that the RBI study group has identified the numerous small and medium-scale units as the potential users of factoring services.

**HEALTHY CASH FLOW**

**How Does Factoring Work**

**A** sells goods to **B** on credit ▶ This sales is account receivable for **A** ▶ Factoring cos purchase invoice at a discount from **A**

They will payback balance to **A** after deducting a fee ◀ Factoring cos will collect invoice amount from **B**

Fee will depend on biz volume, credit history of **B** and time taken for invoice payment ▶ Rate will be higher in a non-recourse arrangement in which if **B** fails to pay then factoring cos have to bear the loss

**How Does It Help**

- **It** is most beneficial to new companies that cannot access credit
- **Factoring** cos are not concerned with credit-worthiness of the seller
- **They are** more interested in the entity responsible for invoice payment

## Export Factoring

Many export businesses are likely to benefit by factoring services — those developing new products, those exploring new markets and those growing rapidly. Exporters of certain goods/services such as leather, tobacco, machine tools and other engineering items, ready-made garments, electronic and electrical goods and computer software, who are small and many in number, may find export factoring services attractive.

## Types of Service

Factoring agreements can be classified into two: recourse factoring and non-recourse factoring. Based on the nature of finance offered by the factor, arrangements can also be classified into advance and maturity factoring. There are again special types of arrangements such as bank participation, supplier guarantee, confidential and international factoring.

Thus, the various services fall under one of the following six main types: full factoring (also called old-line factoring), recourse factoring, maturity factoring, advance factoring, undisclosed factoring (also called confidential factoring) and invoice discounting.

In non-recourse service, the factor has no recourse to the firm in the event of a customer defaulting on payments. Thus, it assumes the risk of bad debts. Even under this arrangement, the factor retains the right recourse, if the customer falls to pay for any reason other than financial distress. In recourse factoring, the firm bears the credit risk inherent in the receivables assigned to the factor.

(*a*) Where the *factor* provides an advance against the uncontrolled and '*not due*' receivables of a firm, it is known as advance factoring arrangement.

(*b*) Mature factoring is where assistance is provided against collections and possible insurance against bad debts.

(*c*) Under bank participation factoring, the firm creates a floating charge on the factor reserves in favour of commercial banks and borrows against these reserves.

(*d*) Under supplier guarantee factoring, the arrangement is designed to help a firm which acts as an intermediary between the supplier and the customer. Under this arrangement, the factor provides a guarantee to the supplier against the invoices raised by him on the firm. The firm raises the bills on the ultimate customers and assigns them to the factor. This arrangement is advantageous to both because the factor takes care of collection of bills for both the parties. The intermediary is also able to earn a gross profit with no financial commitment on its part.

(*e*) International factoring generally refers to the factoring of export sale. In addition, an international factoring house also undertakes completion of all legal and procedural formalities connected with the export sale.

Factoring has many similarities with bill discounting. Both make available to the supplier finance against invoices. Both discount (purchase at a price lower than the face value) invoices which the buyer would have otherwise paid to the supplier at the end of the credit period. It is here, however that the similarities end.

The discounted bills may be rediscounted several times before they mature for payment. The last holder of the bill receives the full amount of the bill. Debt purchased under factoring cannot be rediscounted, as least as of now. It can only be refinanced.

**TYPES OF FACTORING** **BOX : 2**

**(i) Notified factoring**

Here, the customer is intimated about the assignment of debt to a factor and also directed to make payments to the factor instead of to the firm. This is invariably done by a legend on the invoice which states that the receivables arising out from the invoice has been assigned to or sold to the factor.

**(ii) Non-notified or confidential factoring**

Under this facility, the supplier/factor arrangement is not declared to the customer unless or until there is a breach of the agreement on the part of the client, or exceptionally, where the factor considers himself to be at risk.

**(iii) With recourse/without recourse factoring**

Under a '*with recourse*' arrangement, the client will carry the credit risk in respect of debts sold to the factor. In '*without recourse*' factoring, the bad debts are borne by the factor.

**(iv) Bank participation factoring**

The client creates a floating charge on the factoring reserves in favour of banks and borrows against these reserves.

**(v) Export factoring**

There is usually the presence of 2 factors: an export factor and an import factor. The former buys the invoices of a (local) client exporter and assumes the risk in case of default by the overseas customer. Because of distance, different conditions or lack of information, the export factor usually farms out to an agent (or affiliate company), known as the import factor, the administrative job of servicing the debts owed to its exporting client.

The factor buys the book debt of the client at a discount, normally 20 per cent, giving 80 per cent of the invoice value to the client. The factor pays back the discounted 20 per cent to the client when the latter's customer makes payment.

The commission and fees received in the course of providing his service is what the factor earns. These earnings are higher than the earnings from bill discounting. With the discounting rate at a minimum of 16.5 per cent (bank rate), the minimum cost of factoring works out to about 19 per cent. The responsibility for collecting debts rests with the factor who must ensure that customers pay on time, unlike in bills finance.

### Linkages between Banks and Factors

Financial services can be obtained by the suppliers from the banks and factoring organisations. Thus, a proper linkage between the two assumes importance. Banks and factors must furnish information to each other about those parties who approach more than one agency. The debt may be assigned to the factors by the suppliers and the factor may borrow from the banks. The supplier may as an alternative, borrow from the banks and avail of all other services from a factor.

## FORFAITING SERVICES

Forfaiting is a "financial tool" to exporters enabling them to convert their "credit sales" into "cash sales" by discounting their receivables with an agency called a **Forfaiter**. It is not only a "Financing Tool" but also an important "Risk Management" tool to exporters, because by selling the export receivables to the forfaitor, the exporter is relieved of the inherent political and commercial risks involved in international trade.

## The Concepts

The word *forfaiting* is derived from the French word 'forfait' which means surrender of rights. In the export financing context, forfaiting is an arrangement by which the exporter surrenders export receivables to the forfaiting agency and receives the full value of the export before realisation.

In consideration of parting with the funds in advance, the forfaiting agency deducts a discount fee, which is the London Inter Bank Offered Rate (LIBOR), plus a premium which varies according to the risk of the country to which the export is made. A commitment fee, ranging between 0.5 per cent and 1.5 per cent and a documentation fee, where the transaction involves extensive documentation, are also charged by the agency. In India, there are no forfaiting agencies. However, the Export Import Bank of India (Exim Bank) is facilitating this right with an overseas forfaiting agency for which they charge 0.25 per cent commission.

Forfaiting is a source of finance which enables exporters to get funds from the institution called *forfaiter* on transferring the right to recover the debts from the importer. It is a technique deployed for financing goods on medium-term, deferred basis. The term "a forfait" is a French word which means "to give something" or "give up one's right". In the case of forfaiting, the exporter surrenders his right to receive payments in future for immediate cash payments. The exporter gets the money from the forfaiter. The responsibility of recovering the amount on the due date and also shouldering any risk rests with the forfaiter. Forfaiting is the non-recourse purchase by a financial institution of receivables arising from export of goods and services.

## What is Forfaiting?

Forfaiting is a mechanism of financing exports:

- by discounting export receivables
- evidenced by bills of exchange or promissory notes
- without recourse to the seller (viz., exporter)
- carrying medium to long-term maturities
- on a fixed rate basis (discount)
- up to 100 per cent of the contract value.

Simply put, forfaiting is the non-recourse discounting of export receivables. In a forfaiting transaction, the exporter surrenders, without recourse to him, his rights to claim for payment on goods delivered to an importer, in return for immediate cash payment from a forfaiter. As a result, an exporter in India can convert a credit sale into a cash sale, with no recourse to the exporter or his banker.

## The Difference between Factoring and Forfaiting

International factoring is a method whereby the factor undertakes to collect the debts assigned by exporters. International forfaiting is a method whereby the exporter sells the export bills to the forfaiter for cash. Forfaiting is resorted to for export of capital goods on medium and long-term credit. Factoring is mainly short-term trade finance. In forfaiting, the importer's banker normally needs to provide a guarantee. In factoring, such a guarantee is usually not stipulated. The factor acts as an agent of exporters to whom the accounts receivables are assigned by the exporters. Forfaiters, after having made payment to exporters become the sole owners to collect the debts. The factor does not undertake the risk which lies with the exporter while the forfaiters after buying the exporter's debts assume all risks involved.

## The Advantages of Forfaiting

The most oputstanding benefit of *forfaiting* is its flexibility. The institutions engaged in *forfaiting* provide the service in a manner which best meets the needs of the exporter and the importer. The bank guarantee provided by the importer obviates the need to make a thorough check on the creditworthiness of the importer. Only the guarantor bank's standing needs to be checked out besides the general economic scenario of the importing country.

The benefits accruing to the exporter are numerous. First, the exporter only needs to fulfil his commercial obligations under the contract and submit the correct documents. The finance is provided without recourse. This means that the fluctuations in the interest rates during the credit period do not matter for the exporter. Fluctuations in interest rates also do not matter during the commitment period if the bank has agreed for a fixed discount rate. Fluctuations in exchange rates after discounting have no effect on the amount realised by the exporter. The exporter has an assurance of receiving payment notwithstanding the risks regarding the buyer, the buyer's bank and the buyer's country. The exporter's botherations regarding administering the sales ledger and collection of payment are taken over by the *forfaiter*. Many large companies retain export receivables on their accounts if they already have large, idle cash balances or if they have alternate cheaper sources of financing. However, they can always *forfait* these receivables at a later stage when there is a cash crunch or when interest rates fall or if the balance sheet date is at hand.

It is generally assumed that *forfaiting* is suitable for capital goods only. This has also been the case in general in the past. However, the situation today has changed considerably for the worse with many countries having to face cash flow problems. And so it is quite common for *forfaiters* now to finance even commodity exporters for periods up to 180 to 360 days. It is estimated that about 15 to 20 per cent of the *forfaiting* market today is represented by transactions involving commodity exports up to 180 to 360 days.

## The Growth of Forfaiting Business

With the increased volume of trade between the developed and developing countries, exporters in developed countries were in search of some alternative mode of trade finance as the buyers of the developing countries required credit that could not be offered through the traditional means of finance. Forfaiting originated in West Germany and Switzerland in 1960s and extended to all countries later. London soon became the most vibrant market. Some of the international operators are Chase Manhattan, Security Pacific and Citibank.

### The Problem Areas in Forfaiting Services

Primarily, the absence of a legal framework for settling disputes between the exporter, importer and forfaiter are major hindrances to these services. Lack of an accurate database on importers and their status in their countries is another problem. The risks — commercial, political and sovereign — may sometimes be high. Raising finance for the forfaiter to meet the demand of its clients may act as a problem in times of tight money market conditions. Absence of a developed secondary market may also pose difficulties for the success of these services.

The Indian exporters can be attracted towards forfaiting if: (i) the minimum value of the forfaiting transaction is brought down to a reasonable level to suit the Indian context, (ii) a forfaiting agency is established in India, and (iii) proper education about the advantages of forfaiting is imparted to the exporters extensively. A move in this direction has to be initiated by the Reserve Bank of India, EXIM Bank and the commercial banks so as to attract more exporters to enjoy the benefits of forfaiting.

*Forfaiting* has been increasing in popularity because of the limitations of the traditional sources of export finance. Finance is a critical part of any export package and quite often winning or losing an export contract hinges on the kind of financial package being offered. Finance for exports needs to be fast, cheap and flexible and on all these counts, *forfaiting* meets the bill.

With the decline in the attractiveness of the traditional modes of export financing, the benefits of *forfaiting* become quite self-evident. With a view to increase exports, financial institutions and banks could indeed take a hard look at *forfaiting* at least to put the Indian exporter on par with his competitors from other countries. Over a period of time, *forfaiting* is likely to emerge as an alternate source of trade finance especially for deferred exports.

## TECHNOLOGY BEHIND NSE

NEAT is a state-of-the-art client server based application. At the server end, all trading information is stored in an in-memory database to achieve minimum response time and maximum system availability for users. The trading server software runs on a fault tolerant STRATUS main frame computer while the client software runs under Windows on PCs.

The telecommunications network uses X.25 protocol and is the backbone of the automated trading system. Each trading member trades on the NSE with other members through a PC located in the trading member's own office, anywhere in India. The trading members on the Wholesale Debt market segment are linked to the Central computer at the NSE through dedicated high speed (64 Kbps) lines and VSAT terminals.

These leased lines are multiplexed using dedicated 2 Mbps, optical fibre links. The WDM participants connect to the trading system through dial-up links.

The Exchange uses powerful RISC-based UNIX servers, procured from Digital and HP for the back office processing. The latest software platforms like ORACLE 7 RDBMS, GUPTA-SQL/ORACLE FORMS 4.5 Front-Ends, etc., have been used for the exchange applications. This exchange currently manages its data centre operations, system and database administration, design and development of in-house systems and design and implementation of telecommunication solutions.

## Future Plans

The exchange endeavours to continuously upgrade its systems so that it remains on the cutting edge of technology and the best practices. The exchange constantly attempts to address user needs. In this process it has adopted a participative and open approach whereby suggestions and inputs from members are constantly obtained and implemented wherever necessary and feasible. The immediate expansion plans of the exchange consist of spreading to more locations in India so as to enable investors in every part of the country to get easy access to the NSE.

As part of its strategy to introduce new trading segments, NSE, is in the process of introducing derivatives trading. This will be done as soon as regulatory approvals are obtained and derivatives trading is permitted in the country.

The NSE plans to launch its derivatives segment with trading in index futures based on the NSE-50. This will be followed by index options and subsequently option on select securities. The NSCCL that guarantees cash settlements on the NSE will do the same for NSE's derivative market.

The exchange plans to start a retail debt segment to cater to the growing demands of the investors in the debt segment. This segment would deal essentially in corporate debentures and bonds. The Wholesale Debt Market (WDM) segment which provides trading facilities in whole range of debt instruments caters to large trades for institutional investors like Banks, Primary Dealers, Mutual Funds, Provident Funds and Corporates. In order to encourage members to develop retail investor base and draw specific focus to this category of investors, it is proposed to create a separate retail debt segment. The segment will initially focus on corporate bonds and debentures and trades in this segment will be in the market lot similarly equities. A separate market to trade in debentures may give a specific centre to debt players. Consequently, trading members can develop expertise to deal in debt instruments. The segment to commence operation soon will be provided as an additional screen to all members.

## The National Securities Depository Ltd.,

The Indian Capital Market took a further step in its rapid modernisation when the National Securities Depository Limited (NSDL) was set-up as the first depository in India. NSDL, which commenced operations in November 1996, has been promoted by the Industrial Development Bank of India (largest development financial institution in India), the Unit Trust of India (largest mutual fund in India) and the National Stock Exchange of India Limited (largest stock exchange in India). Subsequently, State Bank of India (largest bank in India) also became a shareholder by taking 4.76% stake in NSDL.

NSDL interacts with investors and clearing members through market intermediaries called Depository Participants (DPs). NSDL performs a wide range of securities related functions through the DPs:

- Maintenance of individual investors' beneficial holdings in an electronic form.
- Dematerialisation and rematerialisation of securities.
- Account transfer for settlement of trades in electronic shares.
- Allotments in the electronic form in case of initial public offerings.
- Distribution of non-cash corporate actions.
- Facility for Freezing/Locking of investor accounts.
- Facility for pledge and hypothecation of securities.

A DP could be a public financial institution, bank, custodian or a stockbroker. As on January 5, 1998, 40 participants offering depository services at more than 140 different locations were operational.

Besides DPs, the other business partners of NSDL are issuing companies/their share transfer agents (SHR), clearing corporations/houses (CC/CH) and clearing members (CM). As on January 5, 1998, 162 companies had entered into agreements with NSDL. Amongst these, dematerialisation facilities were available for shares of 128 companies and trading facilities were available for 115 securities.

NSDL facilitates settlement of trades carried out in the book-entry (BE) segment of stock exchanges. The actual settlement function is performed by the CC/CH of the stock exchange. Trading in dematerialised securities commenced on December 26, 1996 in the National Stock Exchange (NSE). As on January 5, 1998, 730 out of 1,010 active member brokers of NSE had opened accounts with NSDL to be able to trade in the BE segment. Trading facilities have also been made available on the dematerialised segment (DEMAT) of the Stock Exchange, Mumbai (BSE) from December 29, 1997.

## Payment and Settlement Systems

The payment and settlement systems are at the core of financial system infrastructure in a country. A well-functioning payment and settlement system is crucial for the successful implementation of monetary policy and maintaining the financial stability. Central banks have therefore, always maintained a keen interest in the development of a payment and settlement system as part of their responsibilities for monetary and financial stability. In India, the development of a safe, secure and sound payment and settlement system has been the key policy objective. In this direction, the Reserve Bank, apart from performing the regulatory and supervisory functions, has also been making efforts to promote functionality and modernisation of the payment and settlement systems on an ongoing basis.

The RBI has developed robust payment and settlements, both retail and large value. The services in operation are:

(i) Real Time Gross Settlement (RTGS)
(ii) National Electronic Fund Transfer (NEFT)
(iii) Electronic clearing service credit and debit (ECS)
(iv) Card based payments
(v) e-payment
  (a) Internet
  (b) Mobile
(vi) National Financial Switch (NFS)
(vii) MICR Clearing
(viii) e-purse
(ix) Automated Teller Machine (ATM)
(x) Electronic Fund Transfer (EFT)

In addition the Clearing Corporation of India Ltd., (CCIL) set up by banks and financial institutions (FIS) clears and settles interbank trades in government securities and foreign exchange is well as money market product, i.e., collateralised borrowing and lending obligations (CBLO). It also deals in repo transactions. The CCIL also provides continuous linked settlement services for banks in India by availing the third party services of a settlement bank.

## Banking and Technology

Information Technology (IT) has made steady inroads into the financial sector. In fact, IT has brought about a significant change in many aspects relating to financial stability. Banks, customers and the regulators have benefited alike from the increasing use of information technology by the banking sector. Computerisation of transaction processing at banks has enabled the availability of audit trails which could be used for analysis. The greatest beneficiary of use of IT in the banking sector is the payments and settlement systems. With the migration of traditional paper-based funds movement to quick and more efficient electronic modes, funds transfers have become easy and efficient to perform. More importantly, these systems have ensured settlement finality being achieved within timeframes which are much smaller than was possible under the manual system. Quicker funds settlement has a direct impact on availability of money, which has a positive impact on liquidity management.

IT has provided for better asset-liability management, which was a relatively difficult task in a manual based system spanning a large number of branches of banks, geographically spread across the country. This has helped banks in better funds management, thereby improving profitability for banks. IT has also improved information availability as also their timeliness. Concepts such as core banking systems, internet banking, anytime banking and anywhere banking have all been made possible with the help of IT. All these have made banking transactions to be performed in a manner, which is beneficial not only for the customer and his banker but for the economy as a whole.

## RTGS Operations – Impact on the Financial Sector

The RTGS system has brought about some significant benefits to the Indian financial system. Apart from enhancing the stability of the financial system, it has improved the efficiency of the system on terms of efficient cash management by banks, immediate transfer to the customer's account and reduction in transaction cost. In the pre-RTGS regime, banks settled their interbanks obligations by issue of paper based instruments which used to be cleared in net clearing system called 'interbank clearing'. Efficiency of the inter-bank clearing was highly dependent on efficient transportation of paper instrument and use of a good number of staff either to collect or to handover the instruments. Fragmented interbank clearing settlement taking place at different centres in the country also interfered with efficient cash management systems in banks and placed an additional burden of pooling of funds at a centralized account. The RTGS system ensures settlement finality in the books of the Reserve Bank on a real time basis, thereby providing a confidence to the sending bank as well as the receiving bank that the payment transaction has been completed and the receiving bank can make use of the funds so received immediately. The RTGS also altered the scenario by providing a platform of settling all interbank transactions at Mumbai. The time window for settling interbank transactions has also been widened from the earlier position of 'within the banking hours' to the RTGS operating hours of '9.00 a.m. to 5.00 p.m on week days and 9.00 a.m. 2.30 p.m. on Saturday'.

The RTGS system is also used for customer transactions. No minimum or maximum limit has been fixed on such transactions so far. Technically, time critical transactions of smaller value can also be routed through the RTGS. In terms of RTGS operating guidelines, the receiving banks are required to apply credit to the customers account as quickly as possible or return the transaction within two hours, if the credit cannot be applied for some reason. Thus, banks are supposed to credit the beneficiary's account within two hours. Utilising this RTGS infrastructure, a good number of banks have developed payment products for their customers. Customers of internet enabled banks making requests for funds transfer through internet within the RTGS hours can find the beneficiary's account credited within a few minutes if the receiving banks have also built straight-through-processing engines at their end. One bank has developed a product which facilitates remittance of funds from Gulf countries in a straight-through-processing mode from end-to-end facilitating credit to customers' accounts within two hours.

## Credit Counselling

In several countries, the system of credit counselling organisations is already in operation. The first well-known credit counselling agency was created in 1951 in the United States to promote financial literacy and help consumers to avoid bankruptcy. Subsequently, several other countries established such organizations. For instance, the Banking Code in the UK provides that member banks shall discuss financial problems with customers and together evolve a plan for resolving these problems. Canada established a non-profit counselling organization in 2000 called Credit Counselling Canada (CCC), which seeks to enhance the quality and availability of not-for-profit credit counselling for all its citizens. The Bank Negara Malaysia has established a Credit Counselling and Debt Management (CCDM) agency to provide advice to individuals on credit counselling and loan restructuring.

The arrangement is expected to be a prompt and cost-effective means of debt settlement based on the repayment plan between the creditor and the debtor without intervention of courts. In view of rising personal bankruptcies, primarily on unsecured debt, Credit counselling of Singapore (CCS) was established in 2003 to assist financially distressed consumers. In India, the working group constituted by the Reserve Bank to examine procedures and processes for agricultural loans (Chairman: Shri C. P. Swarankar) recommended that banks should actively consider opening of counselling centres, either individually or with pooled resources for credit and technical counselling with a view to giving special thrust to the relatively underdeveloped regions.

## FINANCIAL SERVICES AND MANAGEMENT

In the capitalist method of production, the role of capital and finance in the economic activity cannot be over emphasised. Over the years, countries in the communist and socialist folds, have also shifted to capitalistic method of production and established and developed the stock and capital markets in their countries. Increasing role of private sector, market-oriented economies, competition and efficiency have become the key words of economic activity. Thus, many communist countries like Poland, China, Russia, etc., have set up stock exchanges and shifted emphasis to privatisation of the means of production, distribution and/or capital. Even the so-called socialistic countries like UK, France, etc., have privatised a number of public enterprises and shifted emphasis to the role of private sector.

## MAKING CUSTOMER CENTRICITY PAY IN GOOD TIMES AND BAD :

**Lessons from Ten Leading Companies**

In these challenging financial times many companies may be tempted to drop customer-centric business models that have become popular over the last decade. However, a recent Booz & Company study has found that companies that truly have a customer-centric business model have been able to reduce product development costs and increase customer retention and revenues — imperatives for all businesses, particularly when competition for scarce customer dollars is fiercer than ever.

### Operating Model Evolution to Support Consumer Centricity

| Inhabiting Customer Centricity | | Enabling Customer Centricity |
|---|---|---|
| External view is not valued | **Customer Listening** | Customer and suppliers in close collaboration with organisation |
| Unclear who is ultimate decision-maker — particularly when decisions span functions | **Decision Rights** | Clear decision rights and streamlined governance process speed time to market |
| One-size-fits-all approach to customers, with standard products, pricing, and services | **Customer Understanding** | Needs of customer groups and individual customers understood and used to develop compelling offers |

| | | |
|---|---|---|
| Metrics focused on product profitability (or revenue), average market share, and business unit-level cost control | **Metrics and Incentives** | Customer profitability central to financial metrics |
| No defined customer function within the organisation | **Organisational Structure** | Customer function has own mandate and is represented on executive team with customer P and L accountability |

***Source:*** Booz & Company

## Macroeconomic Management

In any area of activity, good management is the *sine qua non* of success through efficiency and cost effectiveness. The objectives of management may change in detail but basically all aim at efficiency, productivity and lowering of costs and raising of profits. If it is in the area of the services, the quality and cost-effectiveness would still count as important prerequisites for its success. It is in this background, that input availability and their efficient use for low cost output are necessary to promote competitive efficiency and economy. The main input resources that any economy needs are land, water, air, energy, etc., which nature endows and labour, technology, entreprise, etc., which man acquires by his efforts and applies in the productive process. Thus, man and nature whose endowments vary from country-to-country are the two blades of the same scissors and they join in the productive process. It is the ingenuity and expertise of management to combine them in the proper proportions, so as to reduce the costs to the minimum and raise the profits or quality of service to the maximum depending on the technology used.

The activity analysis of any economy, firm or company involves the technological relationship between inputs and outputs. It is the management function to see that this relation of inputs and outputs is most up to date, modern and cost-effective. This activity may be in the provision of services as in the case of financial services, trading or manufacturing, etc., where efficiency and competition are the landmarks of success, management has a role which is judged by the results in terms of cost of service quality, profits, etc.

**CAPITAL MARKET MANAGEMENT**

**Encompasses Organised Money and Capital Markets Involving Marketable Claims on Money**

| Cash Management | Credit Management | Asset Management |
|---|---|---|
| RBI,<br>Banks,<br>Financial Institutions,<br>Government,<br>Companies, etc.,<br>Economic Units,<br>Users of Cash and Public | Banks,<br>Financial Institutions,<br>Government,<br>Companies,<br>Productive Units,<br>Users of Credit,<br>Savers and Investors,<br>Public | Government,<br>Business,<br>Companies,<br>Productive Units,<br>Households,<br>Savers and Investors<br>Public |

## CHALLENGES FACING THE FINANCIAL SERVICES

The financial service sector is facing many challenges in its attempt to fulfil the ever-growing financial demands of the economy. Some of the important challenges are:

(1) Volatility of the market
(2) Lack of investor awareness
(3) Complex procedures
(4) Lack of transparancy
(5) Lack of awareness of financial services
(6) Increasing customer expectations
(7) Lack of technical knowledge
(8) Lack of specialisation
(9) Lack of efficient risk management system
(10) Lack of professionalisation
(11) Deficiencies in performance appraisals
(12) Concentration of wealth, on account of malpractices
(13) Lack of safety
(14) Deficiency in marketing process
(15) Prevailing high handedness and arrogance.

In the post-liberalisation era, the finance sector is witnessing a complete metamorphosis. Deregulation measures have included the freeing up of direct controls over ownership, liberalizing interest rates and credit allocation, degregulating foreign exchange trsaction controls, freeing up the entry of new firms, and expanding and broadanening the base of the banking system, both for nationals and international business ventures. At the same time, non-banking financial institutions, securities markets iand money markets have developed to mobilize and allocate savings. Experience suggests that financial liberalisation needs to be undertaken alongside macroeconomic reforms.

But it is becoming very clear that, if Indian financial intermediaries have to survive, they have grow. This is partly because, with increasing globalisation, we cannot limit the operations of foreign FI forever. As Indian companies go abroad, they will need a variety of banking services there. If Indian banks are not available to provide them, they will have to turn to foreign banks. Sooner or later, these banks will try to capture their accounts in India. It will make sense for the companies, as it is always more efficient to use a smaller number of service providers.

Financial intermediaries are now using mobile technology in order to provide new and innovative products and services to its customers. Importantly, managing and facilitating of mobile transactions falls cheaper for banks compared to other channels, thereby allowing them to pass on the additional savings onto the customer.

The financial services over the years has deepened and widened. The concept of financial services continues to improve and change to keep space with the rapid growth of the economy.

## CONCLUSION

The financial system in India comprises a large number of financial institutions and financial markets for catering to the financing requirements of various segments of society.

A stable financial system promotes efficient allocation of economic resources, geographically and overtime. The changing contours of finanaicl system have expanded the sources of finance and its utility. The developments relating to technological innovation, diversity of financial instruments and emergence of financial conglomerates have all spread the reach to the people. In fact, the soundness of the financial system is crucial for providing support to the strong macroeconomic dynamics.

The regulators like the Reserve Bank of India, the secutiries and Exchange Board of India, the Insurance Regulatory and Development Authority, the National Bank for Agriculture and Rural Development PERDA and others are striving to restore financial stability and order in the financial system. Financial stability does not require that all parts of the financial system operate in most efficient manner all the time. A stable financial system rather has the ability to resolve imbalances through self-corrective mechanism before they precipitate a crisis.

The financial intermediaries offer a multitude of financial services to savers, investors, industries, traders, agriculturists, governments, etc. Financial service is a process by which funds are mobilised from a large number of savers and make them available to all those who are in need of it. The financial services has undergone a metamorphosis since 1990. The importance of financial services is gaining momentum all over the world.

The financial service the worldover has undergone a profound transformation since the early 1990s. The changed operating environment for the financial intermediaries, underpinned by globalisation, deregulation, advances in information technology, introduction of innovative instruments and management practices has resulted in intense competitive pressures to provide financial services. This has exposed the financial system/financial intermediaries to newer risks and posed serious regulatory and supervisory challenges.

Without question, electronic money has helped the world's economy grow and prosper. This digitization has contributed to advances like ATMs, credit cards and online banking. The transformation happening underneath is far more profound. Unprecedented computing power and advanced analytics turn oceans of ones and zeros into insights, in real time. Which means we could have a safer, more transparent and intelligent financial system for a smarter planet.

We see many of these changes happening in India today. By embracing Information Technology, banks in India are today servicing customers better and making forays in previously untapped markets – like rural areas. Risk reduction, real time application of data and transparency are some of the benefits that the industry is enjoying today.

These changes are exciting, but more are needed. Because the benefits of smarter finance are clear – for regulators, bankers, investors, companies and communities, rich and poor around the world, all of whose prosperity depends on a money system that is stable, secure and accessible to all.

Deepening the financial system and widening its reach is crucial for both accelerating growth and for equitable distribution. The key to enhanced financial services is extension of institutional credit, reduction in transaction costs, financial counselling, promotion of financial literacy, availability of suitable finanical products and use of modern information technology.

"A customer is the most important visitor on our premises. He is not dependent on us. We are dependent on him. He is not an interruption to our work. He is the purpose of it. He is not an outsider to our business. He is part of it. We are not doing him a favour by serving him. He is doing us a favour by giving us the opportunity to-do-so."

Mahatma Gandhi

**The stock exchange building – Belgium**

❖❖❖

## ANNEXURE : 1

### BANKING CHALLENGES IN THE NEW MILLENNIUM

The changes affecting the banking sector in the wake of globalization and opening up of the economy in the early nineties has provoked much reflection on ways to strengthen the banking system. The Chief Executives of banks have identified a number of priorities to make the banking sector sound and vibrant to play a crucial role in the accelerated development of the economy. The banking sector reforms, implemented since 1991, have brought in a near-total metamorphosis of the sector and made the PSBs serious about the risk-return trade-off on the one hand and maximization of the shareholders' value, on the other. Maximizing the shareholders' value has, in fact, assumed paramount importance, particularly for the banks, which have gone public, because these banks are now accountable to millions of their shareholders rather than the Union Government as their single shareholder. This has propelled the PSBs to become conscious of their performance on a continuous basis and shift the focus from expansion (volume) to efficiency (margin).

**1. Technology:** The public sector banks have a challenging task ahead to remain competitive in an environment of ever advancing technology levels in banking. They will need new Banking Solutions to replace their existing Legacy Systems and to network their branches. Government and the Reserve Bank will need to facilitate this transition by determined actions within the next five years. In this connection, there is need to create an Apex Body with statutory powers to develop, disseminate and regulate technology for interbank networks, and payment systems so as to enable the banks to reach the global standards.

**2. Human Resource Management:** At present the human resource policies in banks are mainly guided by the concept of permanent employment and its necessary concomitants of creating career paths, terminal benefits, etc., for the employees. In this fast-changing world of worker mobility — both horizontally and vertically — and value systems, the public sector banks will need the freedom not only to hire the right talent at market related compensation but also to shed surplus manpower. Bank-centric wage negotiations should be allowed. All this calls for a close relook into the Statute Books as well as Management Practice of the banks.

**3. Risk Management and Regulatory Implications:** To reach the international standards of capital adequacy, risk management and accounting practices, the right talent at appropriate levels of management needs to be inducted laterally and the banks should have the necessary freedom to do so.

**4. Structural Issues:** Structure of a bank is generally business and technology driven. Therefore, whether or not the government reduces its holdings to $\frac{1}{3}$ rd levels, the initiative to decide on the best structure should be left to the individual banks themselves. Also, issues internal to the organizational structure should be left to the individual banks, while the government and the regulator could confine their role to providing a stable macroenvironment and supervision to protect the interests of the stakeholders and the shareholders.

**5. Corporate Governance:** Irrespective of the nature of the organization, corporate governance has to ensure transparency and efficiency in the running of the organization. Accordingly, the government's decision to reduce its equity holdings to $\frac{1}{3}$ levels should get reflected in corporate governance also. Therefore, all structural strengthening to exercise flexibility and autonomy should be ensured.

**6. Rural Banking:** Having committed 75 per cent of their branch network to serving rural and semi-urban population, public sector banks have to adopt a financial engineering approach to rural banking. The delivery systems have to be made cost-effective. Therefore, there is a need for redesigning the rural banking system to deliver new products and services and to make the priority sector more receptive and productive. In this connections, the regulatory constraint on banks' allocation of credit flows also needs a relook. Commercialized agriculture should be considered as a potential avenue for new business. There is need for a paradigm shift in rural finance and in both mobilization and allocation of resources through other intermediaries including NBFCs.

**7. Management of NPAs:** There are several impediments including statutory, legal and political in the recovery of bank loans and advances. Therefore, restructuring of borrowal accounts should be left to individual bank decision subject to full transparency. Then only the public sector banks can better function as business organizations in pursuit of excellence and sound financial performance.

## ANNEXURE : 2

### MERCHANT BANKING SERVICES

The banks offer package financial arrangement and assistance to small-scale industries in their promotional and expansion activities and act as banker to capital issues. The banks —

- study the economic viability and technical feasibility of the proposals and help in preparation of market survey reports with the assistance of technical consultants;
- provide assistance to entrepreneurs in obtaining various government consents required for industrial projects right from the time the application for letter of intent is made;
- assist the entrepreneur in raising rupee resources in the form of debentures, term loans, deferred payment guarantees from financial institutions;
- assist in raising foreign exchange resources required for import of plant and machinery, components, raw materials, etc., by arranging through the Bank's foreign correspondents, suppliers' credit, buyers' credit and foreign currency loans;
- determine capital structure, assist to obtain consent of SEBI finalisation of syndication of underwriting arrangements, handling of share applications and relative allotment in consultation with stock exchange;
- finance export of capital equipment on deferred payment terms.
- manages public issues for raising capital, helps establish liaison with government lending bodies for raising long-term development finance, assesses the strengths and weaknesses of the company through management audits and suggests tailor-made solutions to eliminate the weaknesses.
- provides practical training in the line, if necessary;
- provides assistance in obtaining government clearance, procurement of machinery and equipment and marketing of products;
- extends assistance and guidance in implementation of the project.

A novel feature of the scheme is that the bank will provide from a panel of industrialists a 'foster father' to guide and assist the budding entrepreneurs.

**Entrepreneurial Assistance by Banks**

Many of the scheduled commercial banks provide counselling to industry, mostly in the small-scale and a few of them provide merchant banking services to the corporate sector. Besides, providing working capital, banks play a key role in entrepreneurial assistance and development.

**New Entrepreneur Development Agency**

1. *Scope.* New Entrepreneur Development Agency is established to assist educated unemployed graduates to set up small-scale industrial units in urban and metropolitan areas.

2. *Identification and selection of entrepreneurs.* Sponsorship of government institutions and agencies like Small Industries Service Institute (SISI), University Employment Guidance Bureau, Directorate of Industries and Commerce (DICs) and such other agencies is essential. The candidates, thus identified, will be interviewed by a panel of experts for final selection.

3. *Selection of projects.* The selected candidates will be provided with identified project profiles and will be assisted in selecting the projects suitable to their aptitude and backgrounds.

4. *Training.* The candidates on identifying the projects will undergo training under the Entrepreneur Development Programme to be conducted by agencies like SISI, ITCOT, etc. Practical training will also be arranged in industries, wherever possible.

5. *Marketing tie-up.* The candidates will be assisted in getting marketing tie-up with user industries, wherever possible.

6. *Size of the project.* Projects with credit requirements up to ₹ 5 lakh are only eligible for finance under this scheme. 100% finance will be provided in the beginning and the margin will be built up to 20% over a period of time, depending on the profitability envisaged.

7. *Security.* Assets created with bank finance and personal guarantee of the parents wherever necessary.

8. *Repayment.* Repayment of term loans will be based on the profitability projection and within 7 years.

9. *Registration.* The units will have to be registered as small-scale industries with the DICs or the District Industries Centres as the case may be.

## ANNEXURE : 3

### THE THEORETICAL PARADIGM OF THE ROLE MODEL

The risk-return model splits the overall bank performance into two components: (i) return on equity (RoE), and (ii) risk. The second component, i.e., risk explains the variability in RoE. The RoE model can be divided into three stages asunder:

**Stage I**

The RoE measures bank accounting profits per rupee of book equity capital, and is defined as 'net income' divided by 'average equity'. Thus,

$$\text{RoE} = \frac{\text{Net Income}}{\text{Average Equity}^{*}} \quad \text{... (1)}$$

Dividing both the numerator and the denominator by 'average assets', equation 1 can be rewritten as:

RoE = (Net Income/Average Assets) × (Average Assets/Average Equity) or,
RoE = Return on Assets (RoA) × Equity Multiplier (EM) ... (2)

where, the RoA is defined as 'net income' divided by 'average total assets' and measures bank profits per rupee of assets, and the EM is defined as 'average assets' divided by 'average equity', and measures a bank's leverage or the rupee amount of assets pyramided on the bank's base of equity capital. The EM is nothing but the reciprocal of the capital/asset ratio.

A bank's EM compares assets with equity and large values indicate a large amount of debt financing related to equity. EM thus measures financial leverage and represents both a profit and a risk measurement. EM affects bank's profits because it has a multiplier impact on RoA to determine bank's RoE. It is also a risk measure because it reflects how many assets can go into default before a bank becomes insolvent.

**Stage II**

Stage II of the RoE decomposition analysis splits the RoA further into two components. From above,

$$RoA = \frac{\text{Net Income}}{\text{Average Assets}} \quad \dots (3)$$

Dividing both the numerator and the denominator by 'Total Income', equation 3 can be rewritten as:

RoA = (Net Income/Total Income) × (Total Income/Average Assets)

= Profit Margin (PM) × Asset Utilization (AU) ... (4)

Where, the PM is defined as 'net income' divided by 'total income' (both interest and non-interest income), and measures profits per rupee of total income, and the AU is defined as 'total income' divided by 'average total assets', and measures total income per rupee of assets. Thus, equation 2 can be rewritten asunder:

RoE = PM × AU × EM ... (5)

The advantage of this method is that one can pinpoint the basic variables that determine the RoE performance. The RoE model contains three alternative measures of profitability, i.e., RoE, RoA and PM, which have the same numerator, i.e., net income, but different denominators, i.e., average equity, average assets and total income, respectively, and thus provides different perspectives on profitability analysis.

**Stage III**

Stage III further decomposes both the PM and AU. Each component of Stage III is analyzed with respect to a bank's 'total income' or 'total assets'. For example, it is possible to look at wages and salaries per rupee of income or assets. The objective of Stage III analysis is to identify symptoms of good or bad performance by focussing on trends and significant peer-group differences. This facilitates identification of the proximate causes for poor performance as also formulation of appropriate remedial measures.

* Since net income, reported on annual basis, is a "flow" variable, and assets and equities, reported as at the financial year-end, are "stock" variables, to ensure stock-flow compatibility, the "stock" variables have been averaged out. A two-year moving average has been taken for the purpose.

*Sources:* Sinkey, Joseph F. (Jr.) (1999), 'Commercial Bank Management, 4th Edition. pp. 269-278. Taxman (1999), 'Practical Guide to Instructions of the Reserve Bank of India for Banks and Banking Operations', Volume 1, pp. 99.

**Efficiency Indicators of Top 25 Global Banks**

| Efficiency Indicator | Average (Median) | Range |
|---|---|---|
| Capital/Assets Ratio | 4.98 | 2.06-7.56 |
| Real Profit Growth | 25.7 | (–) 217.1-2070.8 |
| Profit on Average Capital | 13.45 | (–) 1.0-35.6 |
| Return on Assets | 0.52 | (–) 0.05-2.22 |
| Cost/Income Ratio | 68.33 | 54.04-98.03 |
| BIS Capital Ratio | 11.46 | 8.9-19.10 |
| Non-performing Loans to Total Loans | 2.4 | 0.3-14.86 |

***Source*:** The Banker, July 2000, p. 178.

***Notes*:** (1) For some of the banks, data relate to 31.12.1999 and for others data relate to 31.3.2000.
(2) There are conceptual differences between the indicators as exist in the case of global banks in India. Therefore, the above-mentioned data can at best be treated as approximations.

## ANNEXURE : 4

### CODE OF BANK'S COMMITMENT

This is a voluntary Code which sets minimum standards for Banking practices for banks to follow when they are dealing with individual customers. It provides protection to you and explains how banks are expected to deal with you for your day-to-day operations. In the Code, you denote the customer and 'we' the bank the customers deal with.

**Objectives of the Code**

The Code has been developed by the Banking Codes and Standard Board of India (BCSBI) to:

(a) Promote good and fair banking practices by setting minimum standards in dealing with you;

(b) Increase transparency so that you can have better understanding of what you can reasonably expect of the services;

(c) Encourage market forces to competition through competition, to achieve higher operating standards;

(d) Promote a fair and cordial relationship between you and your bank;

(e) Foster confidence in the banking system.

The standards of the Code are covered by the key commitments.

**Application of Code**

Unless it says otherwise, all parts of this Code applies to all the products and services listed below, whether they are provided by branches or subsidiaries across the counter, over the phone, by post, through interactive electronic devices, on the internet or by any other method. However, all products discussed here may or may not be offered by all banks.

(a) Current accounts, saving account, term deposits, recurring deposit, PPF accounts and all other deposit accounts.

(b) Payments services such as pensions, payment orders, remittances by way of Demand Draft and via., transfers.

(c) Banking services relating to government transactions.

(d) Demat accounts, equity, government bonds.

(e) Indian currency notes exchange facility

(f) Collection of cheques, safe custody services, safe deposit locker facility.

(g) Loans and overdrafts.

(h) Foreign exchange service including money changing.

(i) Third party insurance and investment products sold through our branches.

(j) Card products including credit cards, debit cards, ATM cards and services. (including credit cards offered by our subsidiaries/companies promoted by us).

**Key Commitments**

Our key commitments to you

To act fairly and reasonably in all our dealings with you by:

(a) Providing minimum banking facilities of receipt and payment of cash/cheques at the banks counter.

(b) Meeting the commitments and standards in this Code for the products and services, we offer, and in the procedures and practices our staff follow:

(c) Making sure our products and services meet relevant laws and regulations in letter and spirit.

(d) Ensuring that our dealings with you rest on ethical principles of integrity and transparency.

(e) Operating secure and reliable banking and payment systems.

**To help you to understand how our financial products and services work by:**

(a) Giving you information about them in any one or more of the following languages: Hindi, English or the appropriate local language.

(b) Ensuring that our advertising and promotional literature is clear and not misleading.

(c) Ensuring that you are given clear information about our products and services, the terms and conditions and the interest rates/service charges, which apply to them.

(d) Giving you information or what are the benefits to you, how you can avail of the benefits, what are their financial implications and whom you can contact for addressing your queries and how.

**To help you use your account or service by:**

(a) Providing you regular appropriate updates.

(b) Keeping you informed about changes in the interest rates, changes or terms and conditions.

**To deal quickly and sympathetically with things that go wrong by:**

(a) Correcting mistakes promptly and cancelling any bank charges that we apply due to our mistake.

(b) Handling you complaints promptly.

(c) Telling you how to take your complaint inward if you are still not satisfied (see para number 7).

(d) Providing suitable alternative avenues to alleviate problems arising out of technological failure.

**To treat all your personal information as private and confidential**

We will treat all your personal information as private and confidential subject to matters mentioned in para under 5 below.

**To publicise the Code we will**

(a) Provide you (existing customer) with a copy of the Code.

(b) Provide you (new customer) with a copy of the Code when you open your account.

(c) Make this Code available on request either over the counter or by electronic communication or mail.

(d) Make available this Code at every branch and/on website, and

(e) Ensure that our staff are trained to provide relevant information about the Code and to put the Code into practice.

**To adopt and practice a non-discrimination policy**

We will not discriminate on the basis of age, race, gender, marital status, religion or disability.

**Monitoring**

The Banking Code and Standards Board of India whose directors include members of the Governing Council monitor the Code. The contact details are as follows:

The Banking Codes and Standards Board of India

Reserve Bank of India Building, C-7, 4th floor, Bandra-Kurla Complex, Mumbai-400 061. Telephone: 26573716; Fax: 26573719

E-mail: ceo.bcsb@rbi.org.in; Website; www.bcsbi.org.in

**Getting Help**

If you have any enquiries about the Code, you should contact us at our designated telephone helpdesk or customer-service number or contact the Indian Banks' Association at the following address:

Indian Banks' Association, Stadium House, Block I & II, Veer Nariman Road, Mumbai-400 020. Tel. No. 022-22844999; Fax: 022-22835638

E-mail: ibastadium@vsnl Website: www.iba.org.net.in <http://www.iba.org.in>

Or contact the Banking Codes and Standards Board of India at the address above.

We will have notices in all our branches and on our website explaining that copies of the Code are available and how you can get one and that we will make a copy available to you on request.

**Review of the Code**

The Code will be reviewed within a period of three years. The review will be undertaken in a transparent manner.

CHAPTER 17

# CREDIT RATING IN INDIA

## INTRODUCTION

The role of financial markets in a market economy is that of an efficient intermediator, mediating between savers and investors, mobilizing capital on one hand and efficiently allocating them between competing uses on the other. Such an allocative role hinges crucially on the availability of reliable information. The doctrine of "efficient market allocation" in fact has as its bedrock, what economists label "perfect information". An investor in search of investment avenues has recourse to various sources of information-offer documents of the issuer(s), research reports of market intermediaries, media reports, etc. In addition to these sources, Credit Rating Agencies have come to occupy a pivotal role as information providers, particularly for credit related opinions in respect of debt instruments; a role that has been strengthened by the perception that their opinions are independent, objective, well researched and credible.

The factors leading to the growing importance of the credit rating system in many parts of the world over the last two decades are:

(1) the increasing role of capital and money markets consequent to disintermediation;

(2) increased securitisation of borrowing and lending consequent to disintermediation;

(3) globalisation of the credit market;

(4) the continuing growth of information technology;

(5) the growth of confidence in the efficiency of the market mechanism; and

(6) the withdrawal of government safety nets and the trend towards privatisation.

It was this growing demand on rating services that enable credit rating agencies to charge issuers for their services. This was much in variance with the mode of financing used hitherto — with no fees charged to the issuers, a credit rating agency used to provide rating information through the sale of their publication and other materials.

The concept of credit rating originated in America in the Southern Hemisphere in 1895.

Credit rating serves as a valuable input in the decision-making process of different participants in the capital market including the regulators. Although credit rating is relatively new in India, the level of awareness as well as its actual use are increasing steadily. With the liberalisation and consequent restructuring of the financial services sector, credit rating is becoming even more important. In this context, it is essential that the major players in the market, particularly the investors, understand the significance as well as the limitations of credit rating. This article attempts to answer some questions that are frequently asked about credit rating.

## WHAT IS CREDIT RATING?

Credit rating is a symbolic indicator of the current opinion of a rating agency and of the relative capability and willingness of an issuer of a debt programme to service the debt obligations as per the terms of the contract. This groups together a large number of similar (but not necessarily identical) debt instruments under different categories according to their credit quality as judged by their inherent protective factors.

## CREDIT RATING: THE CONCEPT

Ratings, usually expressed in alphabetical or alphanumeric symbols, are a simple and easily understood tool enabling the investor to differentiate between debt instruments on the basis of their underlying credit quality. The credit rating is thus *a symbolic indicator of the current opinion of the relative capability of the issuer to service its debt obligation in a timely fashion, with specific reference to the instrument being rated.* It is focussed on communicating to the investors, the relative ranking of the default loss probability for a given fixed income investment, in comparison with other rated instruments.

A *rating is specific* to a debt instrument and is intended as a grade, an analysis of the credit risk associated with the particular instrument. It is based upon the relative capability and willingness of the issuer of the instrument to service the debt obligations (both principal and interest) as per the terms of the contract. Thus, a rating is neither a general purpose evaluation of the issuer, nor an overall assessment of the credit risk likely to be involved in all the debts contracted or to be contracted by such entity.

The primary objective of rating is to provide *guidance* to investors/creditors in determining a credit risk associated with a debt instrument/credit obligation. It does not amount to a recommendation to buy, hold or sell an instrument as it does not take into consideration factors such as market prices, personal risk preferences and other considerations which may influence an investment decision. The rating process is itself based on certain 'givens'. The agency, for instance, does not perform an audit. Instead, it is required to rely on information provided by the issuer and collected by analysts from different sources, including interactions in person with various entities. Consequently, the agency does not guarantee the completeness or accuracy of the information on which the rating is based.

"In determining a rating, both quantitative and qualitative analysis are employed. The judgement is qualitative in nature and the role of the quantitative analysis is to help make the best possible overall qualitative judgement because, ultimately, a rating is an opinion."
*Standard & Poor's.*

## Credit Rating as Elucidated by the Leading Rating Agencies of the World

"A rating is an opinion on the future ability and legal obligation of the issuer to make timely payments for principal and interest on a specific fixed income security. The rating measures the probability that the issuer will default on the security over its life, which depending on the instrument may be a matter of days to 30 years or more. In addition, long-term ratings incorporate an assessment of the expected monetary loss should a default occur."
*Moody's*

"Credit ratings help investors by providing an easily recognizable, simple tool that couples a possibly unknown issuer with an informative and meaningful symbol of credit quality."
*Standard & Poor's*

## What Credit Rating is Not?

Credit rating is neither a general purpose evaluation of a corporate entity nor an overall assessment of the credit risk likely to be involved in all the debts contracted or to be contracted by such an issuer. A rating is specific to a debt instrument and is intended to grade different and specific debt instruments in terms of credit risks associated with the particular instruments. A rating does not amount to any recommendation to buy, hold or sell an instrument as it does not take into consideration factors such as – market prices, personal risk preferences of an investor and such other considerations, which may influence an investment decision.

The credit ratings assess the debt servicing capabilities and guide the investors as to the degree of certainty of timely payment of principal and interest on the debt instrument under consideration. These ratings are not recommendations but are carefully assessed opinions.

## TYPES OF CREDIT RATING

Credit ratings are of different types, depending upon the requirements of the rater and the rated. The following are the common types of rating:

(i) *Bond Rating:* Rating the bonds or debt securities issued by a company, government or quasi-government body is called bond rating. This occupies the major business of credit rating agencies.

(ii) *Equity Rating:* The rating of equity of capital market is called equity rating.

(iii) *Commercial Paper Rating:* It is mandatory on the part of a corporate body to obtain the ratings of an approved credit rating agency to issue commercial paper. In USA, 100% of commercial paper volume is rated. In India, P1 rating is prescribed for issue of commercial paper by corporate bodies.

(iv) *Sovereign Rating:* This includes rating a country as to its creditworthiness, probability to risk, etc.

## NEED FOR CREDIT RATING AGENCIES

Credit Rating Agencies (CRAs) are mainly commercial institutions which earn revenue for the publication and evaluation of the creditworthiness of their clients. They have been playing an important role in the management of financial market risk, particularly in global securities and banking markets: they issue creditworthiness opinions that help to overcome the information asymmetry that exists between those issuing debt instruments and those investing in these instruments. CRAs originated in the USA at the turn of the $20^{th}$ century and concentrated on rating of corporate bonds. Their activities subsequently increased in scope and scale. At present, no major type of security, issuer or geographic area is excluded. CRAs now define a truly global benchmark for credit risk. Since the Great Depression, the CRA's benchmark has also been used in the regulation of financial markets. For example, banks and certain other types of investors are only allowed to hold lower risk securities rated 'investment grade' as per the Basel norms. Over the past few decades these companies have engaged in providing ratings for a wide range of more complex financial instruments, known as structured finance products.

## ROLE OF CREDIT RATING AGENCIES

Credit rating agencies (CRAs), specialising in analysing and evaluating the credit-worthiness of cooperate and sovereign issues of debt securities, play a key role in financial markets by helping to reduce the information asymmetry between lenders and investors, on the one side, and issuers on the other, about the creditworthiness of companies or countries. The CRAs thus contribute in solving principal agent problems. The CRAs also offer ancillary business services. These include risk management and consulting services to help financial institutions and other firms manage credit and operational risks. CRAs role has increased with financial globalization and has received an additional boost from Basel II, which incorporates the ratings of CRAs into the rules for setting weights for credit risk so far (2008), four rating agencies have been granted accreditation on the basis of the six parameters, viz., objectivity, independence, internatioal access transparency/disclosure, credibility and resources.

## CREDIT RATING VS. FINANCIAL ANALYSIS

Credit rating is, essentially, business analysis, which has a much broader connotation than financial analysis. One significant factor which adds value to the analysis of a rating agency is that the rating is normally done at the request of and with the active cooperation of the issuer. So, the rating agency has access to unpublished information and the discussions with the senior management of issuers give meaningful insights into corporate plans and strategies. The rating agencies also make necessary adjustments to published accounts for the purpose of their analysis and juxtapose the issuer against the backdrop of the industry in question and the general economic environment. And, at the culmination of this detailed process, the rating emerges as the well-considered view of a dozen or more highly qualified and experienced professionals. The rating agencies zealously safeguard their independence and scrupulously avoid any conflict of interest with the various players in the capital market. If any analyst or group of analysts are able to ensure all these, we probably have another rating agency in the making. And this has happened with credit rating agencies analysing, assessing and rating the participants in the capital market.

## FACTORS CONTRIBUTING TO THE SUCCESS OF THE RATING SYSTEM

The driving force behind the rating industry is essentially the question of reputation for analytical credibility. Wilson (1994) sums it up succinctly. "Every time a rating is assigned, the agency's name, integrity and credibility are on line and subject to inspection by the whole community." This section focusses on the ingredients essential for the rating system to function effectively and serve the interests of all market participants and regulators.

### (a) Credible and Independent Structure and Procedures

To quote from Standard & Poor's:

"Ratings are of value only as long as they are credible. Credibility arises primarily from the rater being independent of the issuer's business. The investor is willing to accept the rater's judgement only where such credibility exists. When enough investors are willing to accept the judgement of a particular rater, that rater gains recognition as a rating agency."

According to Moody's:

"The rating agency must do all it can to preserve its credibility and integrity in the marketplace. As a primary ingredient of credibility, the agency must maintain independence from all interested market forces — including issuers, securities underwriters, or government."

A few other critical factors that serve to enhance the credibility of a rating agency are:

- objectivity and impartiality of opinions;
- analytical integrity and consistency;
- professionalism and relevant expertise across industry;
- strict rules of confidentiality relating to the sensitive and confidential information of the issuer;
- timeliness of rating review and announcement of changes;
- ability to reach a wide range of investors by means of press reports, print or electronic publications and more investor-friendly research services.

### (b) Reliance on the Market Mechanism

Reliance on the capital market for resource allocation generates a strong demand for investment related information. Rating agencies provide this information. An investor would be willing to look at rating as an important input for his investment decision only when there is a perceived default risk.

### (c) Corporate Disclosure and Credit Education

Rating agencies are not and should not assume the role of regulators. They are mostly carrying out an assignment on the mandate of an issuer and, in some countries, the issuer has the option of publishing or not publishing the rating assigned. This may result in investors not having all essential information required for his decision. The regulatory guidelines for mandatory disclosure of ratings could ensure that the information reaches the users. However, it is not sufficient for the information to reach the investor, he must be capable of arriving at meaningful conclusions by interpreting the assigned rating. He should also be aware of the limitations of credit rating and should not assume that the rating amounts to an insurance or guarantee against default risk.

### (d) Creation of Active Debt Market

The continued growth and evolution of the credit rating business would depend on the size and growth of the debt market. An active primary and secondary debt market is crucial for rating agencies to continue to provide their services.

## Benefits of Credit Rating

The benefits to various parties concerned with credit rating are listed below:

*Investors*

(*i*) It enables the investors to get superior information at low cost.

(*ii*) It enables the investors to take calculated risk in their investment decisions.

(*iii*) It encourages the common man to invest his savings in corporate securities and get high returns.

## Corporate Borrowers

(*i*) It facilitates companies with good rating to enter the capital market confidently and raise funds at comparatively cheaper rates.

(*ii*) It can be used as a marketing tool.

(*iii*) It facilitates foreign collaborations.

(*iv*) It encourages discipline among the corporate borrowers.

## Credit Rating Companies

The existence and development of credit rating companies largely depends upon their performance. Honest and impartial credit rating agencies would definitely thrive, as long as they sustain their credibility.

## Government

(*i*) Fair and good ratings motivate the public to invest their savings in good shares, deposits and debentures. Thus, the idle savings of the public are channelised for productive uses.

(*ii*) It facilitates the formulation of public policy guidelines on institutional investments.

(*iii*) Credit rating system plays a vital role in investor protection without casting burden for that responsibility on the government.

## RATING METHODOLOGY

The rating exercise commences at the request of a company. A rating applies to a particular debt obligation of the company and is not a general purpose evaluation of the company. The focus of the evaluation is on the ability and the willingness of the company to meet the financial obligations on the debt instrument in a timely manner.

In evaluation and monitoring ratings, both qualitative and quantitative criteria are employed. The methodology involves an analysis of the past performance of the company and an assessment of its future prospects, which involves judgement of the company's competitive position and evaluation of its management and strategies. In order to eliminate subjectivity, a multi-layered decision-making process is applied in assigning a rating, which ensures that no single individual decides on a rating.

The key factors considered are:

### Business Analysis

- Industry risk (nature and basis of competition; key success factors; demand-supply position; structure of industry; cyclical seasonal factors; government policies; etc.)
- Market position of the company within the industry (market share; competitive advantages; selling and distribution arrangements; product and customer diversity; etc.)
- Operating efficiency of the company (locational advantages; labour relationships; cost structure; technological advantages and manufacturing efficiency as compared to those of competitors; etc.)
- Legal position (terms of prospectus, trustees and their responsibilities; systems for timely payment and for protection against forgery/fraud; etc.)

### Financial Analysis

- Accounting quality (overstatement/understatement of profits; auditors' qualifications; method of income recognition, inventory valuation and depreciation policies; off-balance sheet liabilities; etc.)
- Earnings protection (sources of future earnings growth; profitability ratios; earnings in relation to fixed income charges; etc.)
- Adequacy of cash flows (in relation to debt and fixed and working capital needs; sustainability of cash flows; capital spending flexibility; working capital management; etc.)

**THE RATING PROCESS**

Review of the public information on the client
↓
Questionnaire
↓
Meeting with client
↓
Preparation of draft report
↓
Draft report sent to subject client for review as to factual accuracy
↓
Amended report (following client comments) sent to rating committee members
↓
Rating committee meeting/discussion and assignment of rating
↓
Client advised of rating
↓
Rating made public

- Financial flexibility (alternative financing plans in times of stress; ability to raise funds; asset redeployment potential; etc.)

## Management Evaluation

- Track record of the management; planning and control systems; depth of managerial talent; succession plans.
- Evaluation of capacity to overcome adverse situations.
- Goals, philosophy and strategies.

The above factors are considered for companies with manufacturing activities. The assessment of finance companies lays emphasis on the following factors in addition to the financial analysis and management evaluation as outlined above.

## Regulatory and Competitive Environment

- Structure and regulatory framework of the financial system.
- Trends in regulation/deregulation and their impact on the company.

## Fundamental Analysis

- Capital adequacy (assessment of true net worth of the company, its adequacy in relation to the volume of business and the risk profile of the assets).

- Asset quality (quality of the company's credit-risk management; systems for monitoring credit; sector risk; exposure to individual borrowers; management of problem credits; etc.)
- Liquidity management (capital structure; term matching of assets and liabilities; policy on liquid assets in relation to financing commitments and maturing deposits).
- Profitability and financial position (historic profits; spreads on fund deployment; revenues on non-fund based services; accretion to reserves; etc.)
- Interest and tax sensitivity (exposure to interest rate changes; tax law changes and hedge against interest rate, etc.)

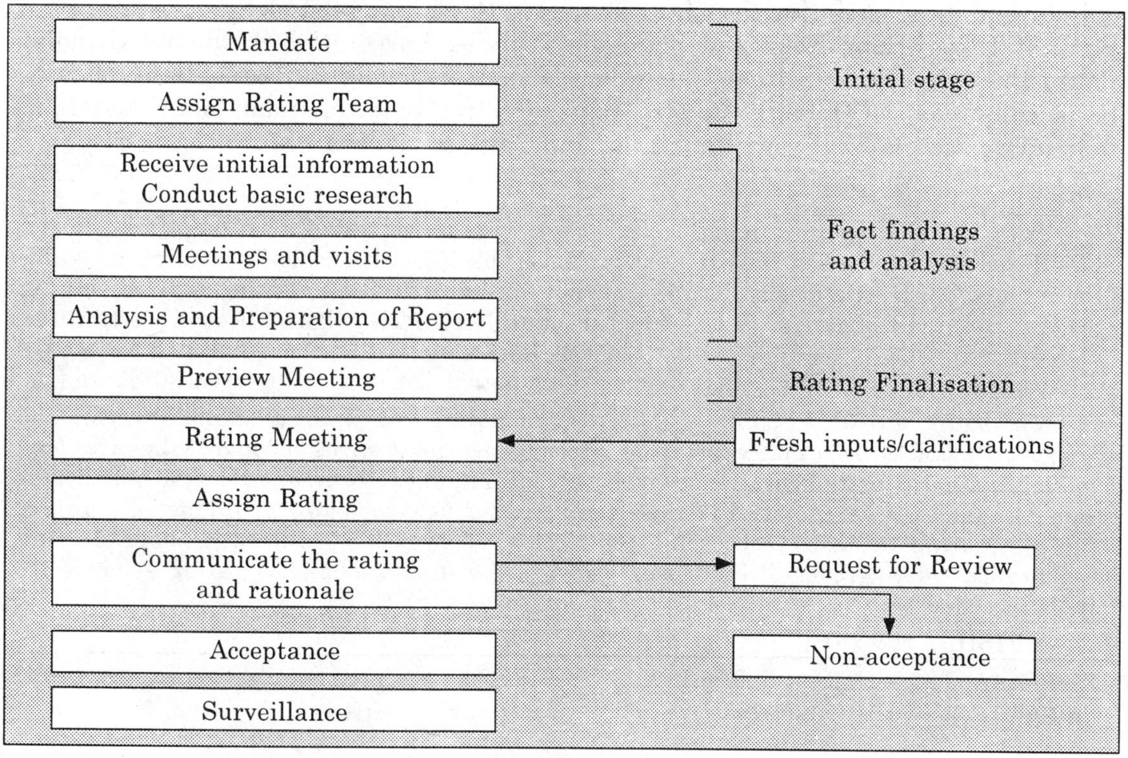

## CREDIT RATING AGENCIES IN INDIA

In India, the first rating agency CRISIL, Credit Rating Information Services of India Ltd., was promoted by ICICI in 1987 followed by ICRA (Investment Information and Credit Rating Agency) promoted by IFCI in 1991 and (CARE) Credit Analysis and Research promoted by IDBI. With economic liberalisation, industrial development and increasing trend of financial disintermediation, there is a genuine need for authentic investment information specifically designed to facilitate the decision-making process of investors and other participants of the financial services world.

### The Ratings

The ratings are symbolic presentation of the agency's opinion. The ratings can be classified according to the merit into four main categories: High Investment grade, Investment grade, Speculative grade and Poor grade. The symbols used by CRISIL, CARE and ICRA are different, but their thrust and interpretations are identical. These can be best summarised as follows:

**(a) Credit Rating Information Services of India Limited (CRISIL)**

The Credit Rating Information Services of India Limited (CRISIL), the first rating agency in India, was promoted in 1987 by the Industrial Credit and Investment Corporation of India Limited (ICICI) and Unit Trust of India (UTI). Other shareholders include Asian Development Bank, Life Insurance Corporation of India, State Bank of India, Housing Development Finance Corporation Limited, General Insurance Corporation of India and its subsidiaries, Standard Chartered Bank, Banque IndoSuez, Sakura Bank, Bank of Tokyo, Hong Kong and Shanghai Banking Corporation, Citibank, Grindlays Bank, Duetsche Bank, Societe Generale, Banque Nationale de Paris, Bank of India, Bank of Baroda, UCO Bank, Canara Bank, Central Bank of India, Allahabad Bank, Indian Overseas Bank, Vysya Bank Ltd., and Bank of Madura Ltd.,

**Notes:**

ICD = Inter Corporate Deposit, CD = Certificate of Deposit, CP = Commercial Paper, FD = Fixed Deposit, PCD/NCD/OCD = Parity Convertible/Non-convertible/Optionally Convertible Debentures, OFCD = Optionally Fully Convertible Debentures, FRD = Floating Rate Debentures, SO = Structured Obligation, FRN = Floating Rate Note, PTC = Pass Through Certificates, PCN = Partly Convertible Note, FRB = Floating Rate Bond, ARN = Auction Rated Note, RUF = Revolving Underwriting Facility, CCPS = Cumulative Convertible Preferential Share.

The suffix of a '+' (Plus) or '–' (Minus) sign reflects comparative standing within the category. 'F' is used as a prefix for Fixed Deposit Ratings. Prefixes "L" and "M" denote long and medium-term instruments, respectively. "P" suffixed in parentheses after symbol indicates that instrument is being issued to raise resources for new company for financing a project and the rating assumes successful completion of project. ↑ Indicates upgrade and ↓ indicates a downgrade. CRISIL uses prefix of "pf" to its long-term rating symbols for preference shares.

**CRISIL**

| | | | | |
|---|---|---|---|---|
| AAA/FAAA | = Highest Safety | P1 | = | Very Strong |
| AA/FAA | = High Safety | P2 | = | Strong |

| | | | | | |
|---|---|---|---|---|---|
| A/FA | = Adequate Safety | | P3 = | Adequate | |
| BBB | = Moderate Safety | | | | |
| BB/FB | = Inadequate Safety | | | | |
| **CARE** | | | | | |
| CP = Commercial Paper | | NCD/ PCD/ OCD | FD = Fixed Deposits | | |
| Symbol | Explanation | Symbol | Symbol | Explanation | |
| PR1 | Superior | CARE AAA | CARE AAA (FD) | Best Quality | High Investment grade |
| PR2 | Strong | CARE AA | CARE AA (FD) | High Quality | -do- |
| PR3 | Adequate | CARE A | CARE A (FD) | Adequate Safety | Investment Grade |
| PR4 | Risk Prone | CARE BBB | CARE BBB (FD) | Moderate Safety | -do- |
| PR5 | Default | CARE BB | CARE BB (FD) | Inadequate Safety | Speculative Grade |
| | | CARE B | CARE B (FD) | Risk Prone | -do- |
| | | CARE C | CARE C (FD) | High Risk | Poor Grade |
| | | CARE D | CARE D (FD) | Default | -do- |
| **ICRA** | | | | | |
| CP = Commercial *Paper* | | FCD/PCD/NCD = Fully/Partly *Non-convertible Debentures* | | CD/FD = Certificate of *Deposit/Fixed Deposit* | |
| A1 Highest Safety | | LAAA Highest Safety | | MAAA Highest Safety | |
| A2 High Safety | | LAA High Safety | | MAA High Safety | |
| A3 Adequate Safety | | LA Adequate Safety | | MA Adequate Safety | |
| A4 Risk Prone | | LBBB Moderate Safety | | MB Inadequate Safety | |
| | | LBB Inadequate Safety | | MC Risk Prone | |
| | | LB Risk Prone | | | |
| | | LC Substantial Risk | | | |
| | | LD Default | | | |

CRISIL's principal objective is to rate debt obligations of Indian companies. Its ratings provide a guide to the investors as to the degree of certainty of timely payment of interest and principal on a particular debt instrument. CRISIL rates debentures, fixed deposit programmes, short-term instruments like commercial paper, structured obligations and preference shares.

Since its inception in March 31, 1994, CRISIL has rated in all 926 debt instruments issued by 668 companies. CRISIL has introduced CRISIL Card, CRISIL View, CRISIL Ban Card and CRISIL Rating Digest Service.

## Investment Information and Credit Rating Agency of India Limited (ICRA)

ICRA Limited (formerly Investment Information and Credit Agency of India Limited) was established in 1991 by leading Indian financial/investment institutions, commercial banks, and financial services companies as an independent and professional Investment Information and Credit Rating Agency. In 1999, the US-based global rating agency Moody's Investors Service picked up an equity stake in ICRA through its subsidiary, Moody's Investment Company India (Private) Limited. Currently, Moody's is our single-largest shareholder. ICRA's Board of Directors is chaired by Mr. D. N. Ghosh, formerly, Chairman, State Bank of India, and includes leading professionals from industry, banking and academia. Today, ICRA and its subsidiaries together form the ICRA Group of Companies (Group ICRA).

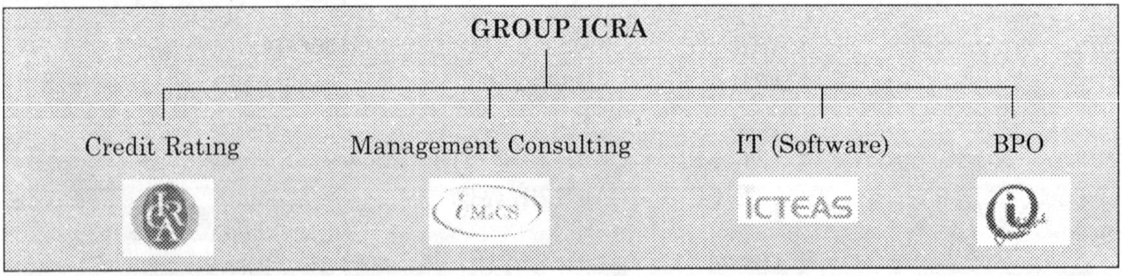


## EXPERTISE AND COVERAGE

Over the years, ICRA has built-up in-depth expertise in diverse sectors of the Indian economy. The key areas of specialisation include, among others are the following:

- Economic research
- Corporate sector: including automobiles, pharmaceuticals, cement and building materials, textiles, hotels, metals and mining, media and retail
- Public finance sector: including State Governments, and municipal and urban local bodies
- Financial sector: including banks, insurance companies, and financial services companies
- Infrastructure and utilities: including power, oil and gas, and transportation
- Structured finance sector

Each of the sectors that ICRA specialises in is headed by a Sector Head, who is supported by a team of dedicated analysts. ICRA's sectoral focus provides for a specialised approach, higher rating consistency, and faster turnaround.

ICRA credit rating provides an investor with a simple indicator expressing the underlying credit quality in a debt issue programme. ICRA credit ratings also establish a link between risk and return. They thus provide a yardstick against which to measure the risk inherent in an instrument. An investor uses the rating to assess the risk-level and compares the offered rate of return with his expected rate of return (for the given level of risk) to optimise his risk-return trade-off.

The relatively unknown issuer is also benefited by having access to a much wider investor base as credit rating minimises the role of 'name recognition' in an investment decision.

In addition, ICRA provides 'general assessment' report on different aspects of the company's operations and management.

## THE RATING PROCESS

ICRA's rating process is initiated on receipt of a formal request (or mandate) from the prospective issuer. A rating team, which usually consists of two analysts with the expertise and skills required to evaluate the business of the issuer, is involved with the rating assignment. An issuer is provided with a list of information requirements and the broad framework for discussions. These requirements are derived from ICRA's understanding of the issurer's business, and broadly cover all aspects that have a bearing on the rating.

ICRA also draws on secondary sources of information, including its own research. The rating involves assessment of a number of qualitative factors with a view to estimating the future debt-servicing capacity of the issuer. This requires extensive interaction with issuer's management, specifically on subjects relating to plans, outlook, competitive position, and funding policies.

Plant visits are made to gain a better understanding of the issuer's production process, make an assessment of the state of equipment and main facilities, evaluate the quality of technical personnel, and form an opinion on the key variables that influence the level, quality and cost of production. These visits also help in assessing the progress of projects under implementation.

After completing the analysis, a Rating Report is prepared, which is presented to ICRA's Rating Committee. A presentation on the issuer's business and management is also made by the Rating Team. the Rating Committee is the final authority for assigning ratings.

The assigned rating, along with the key issues, is communicated to the issuer's top management for acceptance.

If the issuer does not find the rating acceptable, it has a right to appeal for a review. Such reviews are usually taken up only if the issuer provides fresh inputs. During a review, the issuer's response is presented to the Rating Committee. If the inputs and/or fresh clarifications so warrant, the Rating Committee would revise the initial rating decision. Non-accepted ratings are not disclosed and complete confidentiality is maintained on them.

ICRA-asigned ratings once accepted are subject to regular periodic reviews. The assigned rating may be retained or revised (that is, upgraded or downgraded) following review.

## The Rating Methodology

ICRA considers all relevant factors that have a bearing on the future cash generation and debt-servicing ability of the issuer. These factors include: industry characteristics, regulations, competitive position of the issuer, operational efficiency, management quality, commitment to new projects and other associate companies, and funding policies of the issuer. A detailed analysis of past financial statements is made to assess performance under "real world" business dynamics. Estimates of future earnings over the next 3-5 years under various sensitivity scenarios are drawn up and evaluated against the claims and obligations that require servicing. Primarily, it is the relative comfort on the level and quality of the issuer's cash flows to service obligations that determines its rating.

## The Rating Scale

Long-term Rating Scale: For Bonds, NCDs, and other Debt Instruments (Excluding Public Deposits) with original maturity exceeding one year.

| | |
|---|---|
| LAAA | The highest-credit-quality rating assigned by ICRA. The rated instrument carries the lowest credit risk. |
| LAA | The high-credit-quality rating assigned by ICRA. The rated instrument carries low credit risk. |
| LA | The adequate-credit-quality rating assigned by ICRA. The rated instrument carries average credit risk. |
| LBBB | The moderate-credit-quality rating assigned by ICRA. The rated instrument carries higher than average credit risk. |
| LBB | The inadequate-credit-quality rating assigned by ICRA. The rated instrument carries high credit risk. |
| LB | The risk-prone-credit-quality rating assigned by ICRA. The rated instrument carries very high credit risk. |
| LC | The poor-credit-quality rating assigned by ICRA. The rated instrument has limited prospect of recovery. |
| LD | The lowest-credit-quality rating assigned by ICRA. The rated instrument has very low prospect of recovery. |

## Medium-term Rating Scale: For Public Deposit Programmes

| | |
|---|---|
| MAAA | The highest-credit-quality rating assigned by ICRA. The rated deposits programme carries the lowest credit risk. |
| MAA | The high-credit-quality rating assigned by ICRA. The rated deposits programme carries low credit risk. |
| MA | The adequate-credit-quality rating assigned by ICRA. The rated deposits programme carries average credit risk. |

MB The inadequate-credit-quality rating assigned by ICRA. The rated deposits programme carries high credit risk.

MC The risk-prone-credit-quality rating assigned by ICRA. The rated deposits programme carries very high credit risk.

MD The lowest-credit-quality rating assigned by ICRA. The rated instrument has very low prospect of recovery.

Short-term Rating Scale: for instruments with original maturity within one year.

A1 The highest-credit-quality rating assigned by ICRA to short-term debt instruments. Instruments rated in this category carry the lowest credit risk in the short-term. Within this category, certain instruments are assigned the rating of A1 + to reflect their relatively stronger credit quality.

A2 The above-average-credit-quality rating assigned by ICRA to short-term debt instruments. However, instruments rated in this category carry higher credit risk than instruments rated A1.

A3 The moderate-credit-quality rating assigned by ICRA to short-term debt instruments. However, instruments rated in this category carry higher credit risk than instruments rated A2 and A1.

A4 The risk-prone-credit-quality rating assigned by ICRA to short-term debt instruments. Instruments rated in this category carry high credit risk.

A5 The lowest-credit-quality rating assigned by ICRA to short-term debt instruments. Instruments rated in this category have very low prospect of recovery.

Note: For the rating categories LAA through to LC the sign of + (plus) or – (minus) may be appended to the rating symbols to indicate their relative position within the rating categories concerned. Thus, the rating of LAA + is one notch higher than LAA, while LAA – is one notch lower than LAA.

For the short-term ratings of A1 through to A4, the sign of + (plus) may be appended to the rating symbols to indicate their relatively stronger position within the rating categories concerned. Thus, the rating of A2+ is one notch higher than A2.

(SO): The letters SO in parentheses suffixed to a rating symbol stand for Structured Obligation. An SO rating is specific to the rated issue, its terms, and its structure. So, ratings do not represent ICRA's opinion on the general credit quality of the issuers concerned.

### (c) Credit Analysis and Research Limited (CARE)

The Industrial Development Bank of India (IDBI) jointly with Canara Bank, UTI, private sector banks and financial services companies promoted the Credit Analysis and Research institution to offer credit rating information and equity research services to the Indian industry and business institutions. CARE, incorporated on April 21, 1993, commenced its operations in October 1993.

CARE undertakes rating of all types of debt instruments like commercial paper, fixed deposits, bonds, debentures and structural obligations, involving an independent and professional assessment of debt servicing capabilities of companies.

### (d) Duff and Phelps Credit Rating India Private Ltd., (DCR)

The Duff and Phelps is a leading international credit rating agency. Duff and Phelps with J. M. Financial and Alliance group set up DCR in India. DCR rates the companys', debt instruments since 1996. It has provided effective competition to the existing agencies. The popular symbol employed by DCR is $D_1$, $D_2$, $D_3$, etc., depending upon the credit satus.

### (e) Fitch Ratings (India) Ltd., (FRIL)

Fitch Ratings (India) Ltd., is a 100% owned subsidiary of a foreign company. It is recognised by the SEBI for its operations in India.

### (f) Onida Individual Credit Rating Agency Ltd., (ONICRA)

ONICRA sponsored by Onida Finance Ltd., has taken up the task of credit rating individual borrowers.

### (g) SME Rating Agency (SMERA)

SMERA operational from September, 2005, is a third-party credit rating agency for MSMES. It provides ratings that are comprehensive, transparent and reliable and which would enable the rated units to borrow funds at competitive rates of interest. As on March 31, 2009, SMREA had completed 3,438 cumulative ratings for MSMES Risk profiling studies in repsect of 13 MSME clusters have also been completed.

## Credit Rating Mandatory in India

Credit rating is mandatory in India for the issuance of certain debt instruments of the following nature:

- Public issue of debentures/bonds with conversion/redemption period exceeding 18 months.
- Commercial paper can be issued in India, *inter alia*, if the programme has a rating not below 'A2' from ICRA (or its equivalent from the other rating agencies), and
- Fixed deposit programmes of all non-banking finance companies with net owned funds above ₹ 200 lakh need to be compulsorily rated by March 31, 1995, as per the recent Reserve Bank of India guidelines. The non-banking finance companies with net owned funds between ₹ 50 lakh and ₹ 200 lakh should also get their fixed deposit programmes rated within March 31, 1996.

Having regard to the fact that fixed deposits are unsecured debts and are subscribed by the unorganised sector, i.e., the common people, who are most vulnerable, the government is considering an amendment in the Companies Act, to provide for mandatory credit rating of fixed deposits.

## Use of Rating by Regulators in India

The RBI prescribes a number of regulatory uses of ratings. The RBI requires that a NBFC must have minimum investment grade credit rating if it intends to accept public deposits. Furthermore, unrated or underrated NBFCs in the category of equipment leasing and hire purchase finance companies are required to disclose the fact of their being unrated, to the public, if they intend raising deposits. Finally, as per money market regulations of RBI, a corporate must get an issue of CP rated and can issue such paper subject to a minimum rating.

In the area of investments, SEBI stipulated that ratings are compulsory on all public issues of debentures with maturity exceeding 18 months. SEBI has also made ratings mandatory for acceptance of public deposits by Collective Investment Schemes. If the size of the issue is larger than ₹ 100 crore, two ratings are required.

Pension funds can only invest in debt-securities that have two ratings, as per the stipulations of Government of India.

## Risks of Use of Ratings by Regulators

Of particular interest to policymakers and of course to market participants is implications of use of ratings by regulators.

First, reputed rating agencies feel that when regulators rely on ratings, there is a potential of laxity. It tends to create demand for easy and accommodating raters. In other words, it stimulates 'rating shopping', i.e., issuers will be inclined to seek the cheapest and least demanding credit rating agency.

Second, and following from the earlier point, it creates a continuous revenue source for rating agencies.

Third, the ratings induced by regulatory requirement could induce ritualism and even enhance risk. Thus, issuers will get rated because they are required to do so and investors will tend to use it as a proxy for internal analysis. It is argued that in such situations, ratings may actually end up increasing the risk.

Fourth, regulatory use of ratings tends to provide official sanction for rating agencies' assumptions and their ratings, thus increasing the risk of moral hazard. Sometimes, it is argued that while assessing creditworthiness of government owned banks or public sector units, ratings may be higher than justified, though there is no evidence to support this argument.

Fifth, the more profuse use of ratings would increase the demand for ratings and, therefore, indirectly also increase the influence of CRA on financial markets. Thus, there is a potential challenge to the financial stability by CRA.

Sixth, it is held that when regulators tend to rely on ratings, often it seems to be under an assumption of uniform/standard ratings and rating criteria by different rating agencies, an assumption that is not necessarily valid at all times.

Seventh, there is an expectation, especially among some developing countries that ratings by themselves can be used as a stimulus to developing financial markets without realizing that the requirement of mandatory ratings on domestic debt instruments, etc., are no substitutes to a strong regulatory framework, transparency, accounting and disclosure standards. There is indeed the bigger issue of institutional factors relevant to debt and ratings at best is one aspect.

Finally, it is clear that there are many dilemmas for regulators in using the ratings. Prescription of eligibility criteria based on reputation of the rating agency, length of service, acceptability by market participants, and actual track record would only entrench the oligopolistic nature of the market. On the other hand, easy eligibility criteria would increase the laxity and moral hazard. There have been suggestions to develop official substitutes for regulatory induced rating, and this idea is not favoured by many since there is a fear of possible political influence on official bodies.

Another suggestion to increase accountability of CRAs whose ratings are used by regulators is prescription of codes of conduct for rating agencies to enhance market discipline. CRAs could be encouraged to disclose relevant aspects of their organization, including among others, their ownership, staff, etc. They could be asked to disclose a record of their assessments and results. They may also be asked to publicise more explicitly their methodologies. The entire process of ratings could be codified by developing modalities for consultation, sharing of preliminary ratings, detailed explanations, etc.

**Use of ratings in regulation:** As ratings have gained greater acceptance in the marketplace, regulators of financial markets and institutions have increasingly used ratings to simplify the task of prudential oversight. Today, we have regulations governing new issuance and purchase of securities by investors and financial institutions, and ratings for securities issuance or investment purposes.

Selectively applied, regulations may also help to foster the development of the rating system. It should be remembered, however, that regulations alone cannot force market participants to utilise the rating agency's service, particularly if they serve to limit the range of securities issued. Credibility cannot come from regulations. The rating agencies in such a scenario have to prove their credibility.

## Regulation of Credit Rating Agencies

The question of regulation of credit rating agencies evokes mixed response. While a section of people believe that ratings, being opinions, should not be regulated, others feel that given the critical role rating agencies are supposed to play in the market, there must be a regulator overseeing their functioning. But probably, the ideal solution would be to have guidelines for the formation of credit rating agencies ensuring that people who do the rating are independent and the method followed is transparent. For example, rating agencies may be required to be registered with the regulator, say SEBI.

Such 'registrations' as a nationally recognised organisation would lend additional credibility in the eyes of the investors and other users of the ratings, provided of course, the criterion for registration are transparent and based on sound logic.

## THE RATING CHALLENGE

Borrowers, be it an individual or a corporate entity, are rated for their creditworthiness. And why not? The banks themselves are now entering the capital market to raise funds. It has become all the more important in the context of the new code of greater transparency and prudential norms. While ratings act as a guide to the average investor, it also enhances the credibility of the rated organisation.

Presently, credit rating is mandatory in India for debt instruments with conversion/redemption exceeding 18 months for fixed deposit programmes of all non-banking finance companies. It is optional for PSU Bonds and privately placed non-convertible debentures. Rating of equity has been left out. However, with the deepening of the capital market and globalisation, equity must also be brought into the purview.

Are the Indian rating agencies able to meet evaluation standards and eliminate influence of vested interests? For this, it is imperative that they are independent. In the Indian case, the existing three rating agencies, *viz.,* CRISIL, ICRA and CARE are promoted by financial institutions. They may well serve as inhouse rating agents to assess credit risk of their customers. But what would be the yardsticks and whether they would remain impartial when their promoters themselves would be the clients? We may think of other independent rating agencies in the field but there is every likelihood that industrial groups may start their own rating agencies, on the patterns of their own financial agencies. In such an eventuality, there is every danger of such agencies becoming an inhouse sort of entity thereby compromising on objectivity in rating standards. Multiple agencies may increase competition in rating but it may also land up in indifferent rating standards and there is also the risk of succumbing to pressures for attracting business.

There have been three criticisms of Indian credit rating agencies. First, that they assign ratings which are not comparable against international standards; secondly, the rating symbols they assign are internally inconsistent, and thirdly, agencies are not kept at arm's length from their sponsors.

The first is accepted even by the rating industry itself, but it is hard for the Indian agencies to match international ratings. That is since both Moody's and Standard & Poor's had, for a long time, put India's sovereign rating in the speculative grade. Meanwhile, no corporate can get ratings exceeding the sovereign rating. That way, not even the best Indian corporates could get ratings higher than 'BB'.

Unless agencies have a long-term view and keep off short-term profitability considerations, the industry will not mature. If one of the agencies thinks that a corporate has walked off with a higher rating just because it could arm-twist the rating agency, could not the other agencies publish their own ratings and let the market decide which rating they would use? Internationally, it is accepted that corporates are rated by more than one agency and the lower of the ratings are usually used.

## FUTURE SCENARIO

As our economy opens up and is exposed to competitive climate of international finance and as investment decisions will involve more and more complex considerations, the rating system will gain strong foothold. Very soon, the ratings will become an accepted and inevitable norm in the market. In a deregulated system, such an objective and credible system has an important role to play. The ratings have gained good acceptability with various investors and this trend is expected to consolidate itself.

With the emergence of debt markets and the imminent introduction of security instruments for mortgaged debts, the work of rating agencies is bound to multiply. The credit rating agencies will have to develop their own support systems to evaluate debts. Additional skill will need to be developed for an access to overseas debt markets. Moody's has set up an establishment in India and Standard & Poor's is said to have decided to do so in the near future.

Other areas of new developments include Equity Research and Credit Analysis Ratings of various companies. The rating agencies will provide opinions about prospects of a company, estimates about EPS and P/E ratio, future projections, etc. With the available expertise and data banks, the rating agencies are eminently suited to undertake such an exercise.

The IOSCO (International Organisation of Securities Commission) in its consultation paper of March 2008 laid down some important recommendations on the functioning of the CRAs. These include:

- A CRA should take steps to ensure that the decision-making process for reviewing and potentially downgrading the current rating of a structured finance product is conducted in an objective manner.
- CRAs should establish an independent function responsible for periodically reviewing both the methodologies and models and the changes to the methodologies and models used in the rating process.
- CRAs should adopt reasonable measures to ensure that the information they use is of sufficient quality to support a credible rating.
- Where a CRA rates a structured finance product, it should provide investors and/or subscribers (depending on the CRA's business model) with sufficient information about its loss and cash flow analysis so that an investor allowed to invest in the product can understand the basis for the CRA's rating.

Studies have also suggested moving towards a system where credit ratings are paid for by investors, and where arrangers and servicers disclose for free the complete data on the individual loans underlying the structured finance products. As a second-best policy, the current practice of issuers paying the CRAs may be continued. The payment, however, has to be made upfront (the so-called "Cuomo Plan"), irrespective of the rating issued, and credit shopping (and paid advice by rating agencies to issuers) should be banned (Pagano, *et al,* 2009). The need to enhance transparency by determining the information that issuers and rating agencies must disseminate to the investing public has also been emphasised.

## CONCLUSION

The growth of the financial system, in particular, the financial markets and financial intermediaries necessitate to assess the quality, capabality and dependability by the investor. In this background, credit rating assumes a great importance.

The primary benefit of credit rating has been to enable the investor to identify the risks associated with various debt obligations. The other benefits, include decreasing the potential conflict between the underwriters and the investors, providing greater liquidity in secondary markets, encouraging increased disclosure on the part of companies, better accounting standards and improved financial information for the promotion of individual and institutional investor protection.

Nevertheless, the analysis has highlighted the fact that, at present, ratings are not widely used by individual investors. With the eruption of new financial instruments and the realisation on the part of the investor of the invaluable service that credit rating agencies provide, credit rating is bound to find its niche in the investment decision-making process and act as a positive step in the direction of increasing investor protection. Thus, credit rating has firmly docked itself on the shores of the Indian capital market and is definitely here to stay. The credit rating agencies have ample opportunities to play a unique role in strengthening the capital market and building investors' confidence in the Indian financial system.

The global financial turmoil brought into sharp focus the role of credit rating agencies in better risk assessment and measurement. During 2008-09, the RBI has granted accreditation on the basis of six parameters, viz., objectivity, independence, international access, transparency, disclosure credibility and resources to CARE, CRISIL, Fitch India and ICRA. Banks have to use the chosen CRAS and their ratings consistently for each type of claim, for both risk weighting and risk management purposes. The CRAS, thus, play a crucial role in strengthening the financial system and accelerate sustainable growth.

From the above, it is clear that, here in India there are many systemic constraints on the development or rating services, e.g., low disclosure levels, poor audit quality and long time lags in the availability of data. There is also a need to educate the investors to have the right expectations. All this has led to ratings being reduced from being an evaluation tool to a mere certification tool, thereby at times defeating the very purpose of existence of rating agencies.

# APPENDIX - 1

## Genesis and the Nature of the Crisis

The world economy experienced a sustained period of growth with only moderate fluctuations coupled with low inflation, a phenomenon popularly termed as the 'Great Moderation' till the precipitation of the recent global crisis. This prolonged period of macroeconomic stability was essentially attributed to efficiently functioning markets and the benefits of globalisation. However, what remained hidden within these overall signs of prosperity were the immensely complex financial systems and the systemic risks they entailed due to the policy of 'benign neglect' followed by authorities. In addition, some structural imbalances had also developed in the world economy in terms of mismatches between savings and investments and production and consumption across nations that manifested in the widening current account imbalances in some part mirrored with surpluses in others, misalignment in exchange rates and booming asset prices. These developments had to unwind at some point of time and when the unwinding began, they manifested themselves in the form of the worst ever global financial crisis since the 'Great Depression' of the 1930s.

The speed and intensity with which the US sub-prime crisis that appeared in mid-2007 transformed itself into a global financial crisis and then into a global economic crisis has attracted the attention of all. In the post-mortem analysis, a number of micro and macroeconomic factors have been listed in the literature as the proximate causes of the crisis – role of easy money, financial innovations and global imbalances on the one hand to regulatory loopholes both at the national and global level on the other. At the fulcrum of the crisis was too much of leverage. Easy credit combined with underpricing of risks both by the households as well as financial intermediaries created bubbles real estate, energy and other sectors that had to face a disorderly unwinding. The recent crisis has necessitated the need to revisit the global regulatory and supervisory structures and perimeters against the backdrop of rapid financial innovations. The analysis of the various causes of the crisis has evolved a whole new debate on the relevance of various economic tenets and has challenged the economic doctrine that assumed the self-correcting mechanism of the markets. There is also a view which holds responsible the policy frameworks and growth strategies pursued by economies in the various regions.

A comparison of the recent crisis with the various episodes of crises in the past reveals that some semblance can be found amongst them with regard to the underlying causes. As in the past, the main causes of the recent crisis are linked to systemic fragilities and imbalances that contributed to the inadequate functioning of the global economy. Leading up to the crisis, these factors became more pronounced due to major weaknesses in financial regulation, supervision and monitoring of the financial sector and inadequate surveillance and early warning. These, together with over-reliance on market self-regulation, overall lack of transparency with distorted incentive structure led to excessive risk-taking, unsustainable high asset prices, irresponsible leveraging and high levels of consumption which were fuelled by easy credit and inflated asset prices. In terms of impact, however, the recent crisis seems to be more widespread than many other previous episodes and is considered to be closest to the Great Depression of the 1930s. The estimates of output loss place this crisis above most of the episodes in the past with majority of the advanced and emerging market economies facing the downturn as a result of the rapid transmission of the crisis from the epicentre to the periphery. In fact, the same forces of globalisation and international finance that had led to developments in poorer countries over the past decades also carried with them the seeds of contagion, which resulted in the international transmission of shocks.

As a result, the so-called 'decoupling theory' which was in full force just before the recent crisis, came under question in an increasingly interdependent world. The crisis that emerged in the US spread to other advanced economies quickly and at a later stage spread to emerging and developing economies through various channels – financial, trade and confidence – despite their relatively sound macroeconomic fundamentals and policy frameworks. Thus, the established views on the efficiency of markets and the role of public policy both came under severe criticism, which posed new challenges for the discipline of economics. More fundamentally, the old debate on the 'role of finance in economic growth' has again come to the centre stage, while the potential costs and benefits of financial globalisation have become the focus of policy discussions in international fora. At the same time, the adequacy and efficacy of the current international financial architecture to prevent and manage global crises has resurfaced again.

**Manifestation of the Crisis:**

Almost all segments of the global financial markets experienced tremours of the financial crisis, though at variant degrees. Interbank markets in advanced economies were the first to be affected with severe liquidity crisis as banks became reluctant to lend to each other on fear of counterparty risks. Subsequently, the crisis spread to the money markets as manifested in abnormal level of spreads, shortening of maturities, and contraction, or even closure, of some market segments. In the wake of credit and money markets witnessing a squeeze and equity prices plummeting, banks and other financial institutions experienced erosion in their access to funding and capital base, owing to accumulating mark-to-market losses. Stock markets in EMEs, on the other hand, bore much of the heat of the crisis as equity markets all over the world witnessed high volatility, and suffered sharp decline in prices and turnover. Commodity prices, which reached record highs during the initial stages of the crisis witnessed a sharp reversal in trend since the collapse of Lehman Brothers in September 2008. The depth and spread of the crisis can be gauged from the successive revisions in the estimates of write-downs, decline in trade and finally the contraction in economic activity.

In the backdrop of large scale disruptions in international financial markets and deteriorating macroeconomic conditions, financial institutions also suffered significantly. Commercial banks suffered from decline in profitability and large mark to market losses. The crisis almost sidelined the investment banking industry, while the financial performance of the monoline insurers and hedge fund were impacted severely. The banking systems of emerging market economies, on the contrary, showed relative resilience during the crisis on account of their limited exposure to the toxic assets and the regulatory and supervisory measures taken to strengthen their balance sheets in the aftermath of the East Asian crisis.

The increasing globalisation and trade integration have brought enormous economic and financial benefits to the EMEs, but have also widened channels through which a slow down in economic activity in advanced economies could spread to the EMEs. Initially, it appeared that EMEs were better positioned to weather the storm created by the global financial meltdown on the back of substantial foreign exchange reserve cushion, improved policy frameworks and generally robust banking sector and corporate balance sheets. However, any hope about EMEs escaping unscathed could not sustain much after the failure of Lehman Brothers in September 2008 and ensuing rise in the global risk aversion; EMEs were also adversely affected by the spillover effects of the macroeconomic turbulences created by global financial meltdown. The EMEs were affected through contraction in world trade especially during the second half of 2008. Net private capital flows to EMEs also reversed reflecting global deleveraging and risk aversion on the part of investors, which led to tightening of external financing conditions. Finally, their growth was also impacted.

***Source:*** RBI, 2008-09

## APPENDIX - 2

### Impact of the Global Crisis on Asia

The current global economic slow down has had a significant impact on the Asian economy through its external sector linkages. The Asian economics were witnessing high growth led by an export-driven growth model. During the 1990s, world trade rose by around 7 per cent on average, providing impetus to Asian economies growth performance. The Asian region is highly dependent on exports particularly on US consumption, which is responsible for about one-fourth of Asia's export value added. In the midst of the global financial crisis, the demand for Asian exports dropped significantly, resulting in overall contraction in trade. In the last quarter of 2008, real exports fell by 6.5 per cent in the United States, 6.7 per cent in the euro area, 13.8 per cent in Japan and an estimated 10 per cent in China. Industrial production in the Asian economies decelerated significantly in line with the sharp deceleration in demand from the advanced economies (Chart). The Asian economies rely heavily on the export sectors, the contribution of final external demand to total value added.

As the crisis struck the world economy, trade and financial flows, which used to act as powerful drivers of globalisation, abated at the end of 2008, further transmitting the effect of the crisis across borders. The crisis has resulted in significant weakening of consumer and investor confidence. Despite efforts of rebalancing growth through domestic sectors, the poor consumer and investor confidence prolonged the recovery from the crisis. The most interesting fact which emerged from the crisis is that there was a synchronised fall in confidence which heightened the uncertainty. The weakening of economic activity and wealth effects due to corrections in asset prices resulted in a huge fall in consumption and investment activity.

In the period of weakening of demand both domestically and externally, discretionary fiscal measures were undertaken in Asian economies. As a result, the strong fiscal response played an important role in stabilising Asian economies during the first half of 2009. As per the IMF, simulations using the IMF's Global Integrated Monetary and Fiscal (GIMF) model estimated that fiscal stimulus accounted for, on average, about $1\frac{3}{4}$ percentage points of GDP growth in the first half of 2009 in Asia.

**Chart : Impact of the Global Crisis on Trade in Asian Economics**

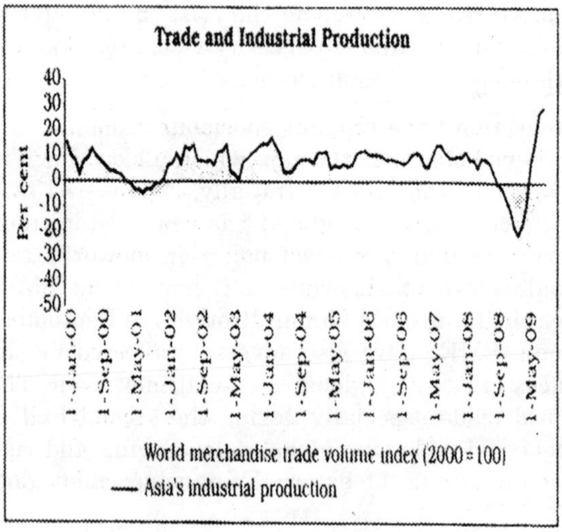


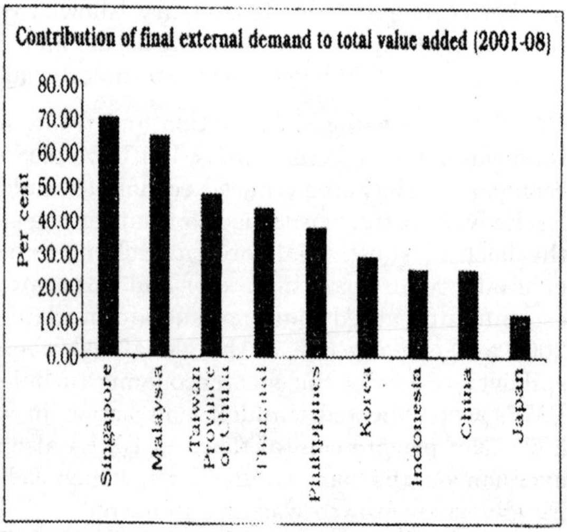

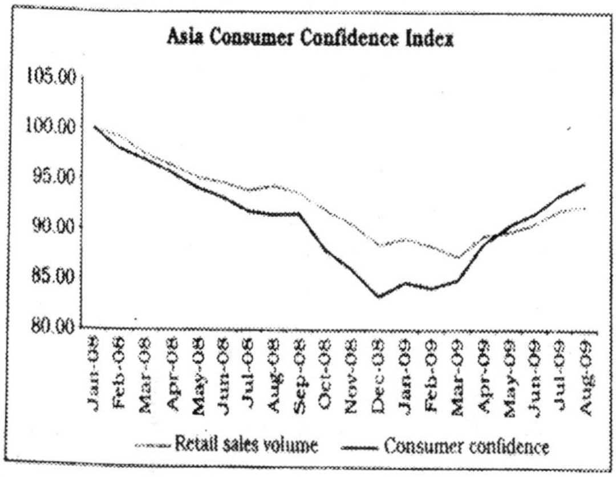


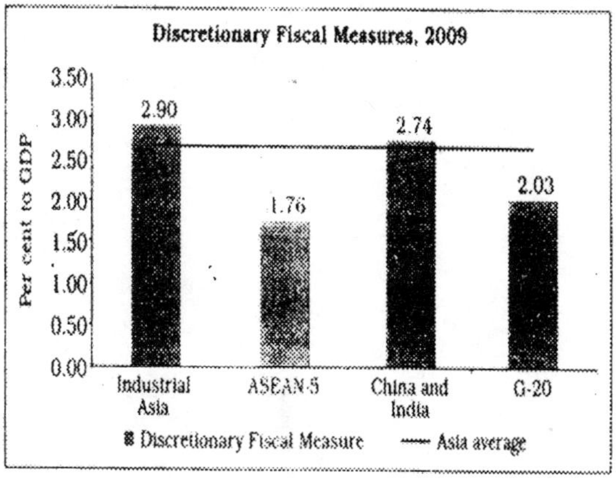


## References

(1) Adams, C. 2006. "Global Current Account Imbalances". Lee Kuan Yew School and Public Policy. National University of Singapore.

(2) Jongwanich, J. 2007. "Determinants of Export Performance in East and Southeast Asia." ERD Working Paper No. 106.

Economics and Research Department, Asian Development Bank, Manila.

(3) Asian Development Bank, 2009. Asian Development Outlook, 2009. Manila, Philippines.